The 9 Competencies and 31 Component Behaviors (EPAS, 2022)	Chapter(s) Where Referenced
Competency 6: Engage with Individuals, Families, Groups, Organizations, and Communities	**1, 3, 5, 6, 7, 11, 13, 14, 15, 16, 18**
a. Apply knowledge of human behavior and person-in-environment, and other multidisciplinary theoretical frameworks to engage with clients and constituencies	**1, 5, 6, 11, 13, 14, 15, 16, 18**
b. Use empathy, reflection, and interpersonal skills to effectively engage diverse clients and constituencies	**1, 3, 5, 6, 7, 11, 15, 16, 18**
Competency 7: Assess Individuals, Families, Groups, Organizations, and Communities	**1, 3, 5, 6, 7, 8, 9, 10, 11, 12, 13, 14, 16, 18**
a. Apply knowledge of human behavior and person-in-environment and other culturally responsive multidisciplinary theoretical frameworks when assessing clients and constituencies	**1, 3, 5, 6, 8, 9, 10, 11, 12, 13, 14, 16, 18**
b. Demonstrate respect for client self-determination during the assessment process collaborating with clients and constituencies in developing mutually agreed-on goals	**1, 3, 5, 7, 8, 9, 10, 11, 12, 13, 16**
Competency 8: Intervene with Individuals, Families, Groups, Organizations, and Communities	**1, 3, 11, 13, 14, 15, 16, 17, 18, 19**
a. Engage with clients and constituencies to critically choose and implement culturally responsive, evidenced-based interventions to achieve mutually agreed-on practice goals and enhance capacities of clients and constituencies	**1, 3, 11, 13, 14, 15, 16, 17, 18, 19**
b. Incorporate culturally responsive methods to negotiate, mediate, and advocate, with and on behalf of clients and constituencies	**1, 3, 11, 16, 17**
Competency 9: Evaluate Practice with Individuals, Families, Groups, Organizations, and Communities	**1, 3, 7, 12, 13, 14, 17, 19**
a. Select and use appropriate methods for evaluation of outcome	**1, 7, 12, 13, 14, 17, 19**
b. Critically analyze outcomes and apply evaluation findings to improve practice effectiveness with individuals, families, groups, organizations, and communities	**1, 3, 12, 13, 14, 17, 19**

Eleventh Edition

Direct Social Work
Practice: Theory and Skills

Dean H. Hepworth   MSW, PhD
Professor Emeritus, University of Utah and Arizona State University

Pa Der Vang   MSW, PhD
St. Catherine University

Joan Marie Blakey   MSW, PhD
Tulane University

Craig Schwalbe   MSW, PhD
Columbia University

Caroline B. R. Evans   MSW, PhD
University of North Carolina at Chapel Hill–SUPER Project

Ronald H. Rooney   MSSA, PhD
Professor Emeritus, University of Minnesota

Glenda Dewberry Rooney   MSW, PhD
Professor Emeritus, Augsburg University

Kimberly Strom   MSW, PhD
University of North Carolina at Chapel Hill

CENGAGE

Australia • Brazil • Canada • Mexico • Singapore • United Kingdom • United States

Direct Social Work Practice: *Theory and Skills*, Eleventh Edition

Dean H. Hepworth, Pa Der Vang, Joan Marie Blakey, Craig Schwalbe, Caroline B. R. Evans, Ronald H. Rooney, Glenda Dewberry Rooney, and Kimberly Strom

SVP, Higher Education Product Management: Erin Joyner

VP, Product Management, Learning Experiences: Thais Alencar

Product Director: Jason Fremder

Product Manager: Ali Balchunas

Product Assistant: Martina Grant

Content Manager: Neha Chawla, MPS Limited

Digital Delivery Quality Partner: Andy Baker

VP, Product Marketing: Jason Sakos

IP Analyst: Deanna Ettinger

IP Project Manager: Anjali Kambli, Lumina Datamatics Ltd.

Production Service: MPS Limited

Designer: Erin Griffin

Cover Image Source: Edwin Tan/Getty Images Artur Debat/Getty Images

For product information and technology assistance, contact us at
**Cengage Customer & Sales Support, 1-800-354-9706
or support.cengage.com.**

For permission to use material from this text or product, submit all requests online at **www.copyright.com.**

Library of Congress Control Number: 2021915033

ISBN: 978-0-357-63059-4

Cengage
200 Pier 4 Boulevard
Boston, MA 02210
USA

Cengage is a leading provider of customized learning solutions with employees residing in nearly 40 different countries and sales in more than 125 countries around the world. Find your local representative at **www.cengage.com**.

To learn more about Cengage platforms and services, register or access your online learning solution, or purchase materials for your course, visit **www.cengage.com**.

Notice to the Reader

Publisher does not warrant or guarantee any of the products described herein or perform any independent analysis in connection with any of the product information contained herein. Publisher does not assume, and expressly disclaims, any obligation to obtain and include information other than that provided to it by the manufacturer. The reader is expressly warned to consider and adopt all safety precautions that might be indicated by the activities described herein and to avoid all potential hazards. By following the instructions contained herein, the reader willingly assumes all risks in connection with such instructions. The publisher makes no representations or warranties of any kind, including but not limited to, the warranties of fitness for particular purpose or merchantability, nor are any such representations implied with respect to the material set forth herein, and the publisher takes no responsibility with respect to such material. The publisher shall not be liable for any special, consequential, or exemplary damages resulting, in whole or part, from the readers' use of, or reliance upon, this material.

Printed at CLDPC, USA, 11-22

Brief Contents

Part 4   The Termination Phase   431

Contents

Part 1   Introduction   1

Part 2   Exploring, Assessing, and Planning   75

Chapter 11   Understanding Social Work Groups   216

Chapter 12   Developing Goals and Formulating a Contract   238

Part 3   The Change-Oriented Phase   271

Chapter 14   Balancing Micro and Macro Social Work Practice: Roles, Theories, and Intervention Strategies   317

Chapter 15   Enhancing Family Functioning and Relationships   339

Part 4   The Termination Phase   431

Preface

When we, your authors, teach BSW and MSW students, we are often confronted with the question "what should I do if ...?" The easy (and usually correct) answer is "it depends." How social workers respond in any given situation *depends* on a variety of factors: the setting in which they work, the client, the nature of the helping relationship that has developed, the advantages and disadvantages of any given action or choice, and so on.

We wrote this book to help answer the "it depends"—to equip you with the knowledge and critical thinking to weigh factors involved in decisions throughout the helping process, both as a student social worker and as a professional. At first, that process can seem cumbersome. It can be difficult to internalize important perspectives, digest all this new information, and then employ these perspectives and this information as needed during client interactions. All learning is a process. Learning social work practice involves becoming acquainted with the concepts in this book, understanding the pros and cons of various choices, becoming familiar with the different variables that affect practice, and using this knowledge and these skills in supervision, in work with colleagues and classmates, and in practice with clients.

As social workers ourselves, we have the utmost respect for the complexity of the work, the power that professionals hold, and the grave situations in which we are entrusted to help others. In this text, we have tried to provide you with a foundation to practice with excellence and integrity in this vital profession. We write this in a context in which many marginalized persons are fearful about the values and the motives of dominant social structures and the professionals who work in them, including social workers. The text acknowledges tensions and realities in contemporary practice, and it reinforces the importance of listening effectively, acting compassionately, thinking incisively, and pursuing social justice across an array of settings and client systems. As in previous editions, the design and the content clearly link the text to skill development and core competencies specified by Council on Social Work Education (CSWE) and Educational Policy and Accreditation Standards (EPAS) (2022), and the text reflects updates in the NASW Code of Ethics as well as the salient literature. Where previous

editions referenced videos, this version converts those into written case studies so that readers can apply the examples without the necessity of video access.

The Structure of The Text

The book has four parts. Part 1 introduces the reader to the social work profession and direct practice and provides an overview of the helping process, including core competencies, the role of evidence-based practice, the domains and roles of social work, and the elements of ethical practice.

Part 2 presents the beginning phase of the helping process. It addresses strategies and skills for building relationships, providing direction and focus in interviews, avoiding common communication errors, and substituting better options. Subsequent chapters in this section address problem and strengths exploration, theories and techniques for individual, family, and group assessment, and the processes involved in goal setting.

Part 3 presents the middle, or goal attainment, phase of the helping process. It describes change-oriented strategies, including updated material on interventions common to social work practice. Readers learn to incorporate the orienting perspectives into all aspects of the change process.

Part 4 deals with the final phase of the helping process, incorporating material on evaluating and terminating social work relationships in an array of circumstances.

Alternative Chapter Order

This book is structured around phases of practice at systems levels ranging from individual to family to group to macro practice. Some instructors prefer to teach all content about a particular mode of practice in one block. Those instructors whose courses emphasize individual contacts may choose to present chapters in a different order than we have organized them (see Table P-1). They may teach content in Chapters 5 through 9, skip ahead to Chapters 12 and 13, and then delve into Chapters 17 and 18. Similarly, family content can be grouped by using Chapters 10 and 15 together, and group content by using Chapters 11 and 16 together. We have presented the chapters in the book in the current order because we think that presentation of intervention by phases fits a systems perspective better than beginning with a choice of intervention mode.

Table P-1 Organization of Chapters by Mode of Practice

Mode of Practice
Across levels Chapters 1–4 and 19
Individual Chapters 5–9, 12, 13, 17, and 18
Family Chapters 10 and 15
Group Chapters 11 and 16
Macro Chapter 14

The Empowerment Series: Relationship with the Educational Policy Statement and Accreditation Standards (EPAS), and Professional Competencies

This book is part of the Cengage Learning Empowerment Series and addresses accreditation standards established by the CSWE. Our intent is to facilitate programs' ability to link content provided in this textbook with expectations for student learning and accomplishment. As is true in almost all learning, students must acquire knowledge before they are expected to apply it to practice situations.

CSWE has identified nine core competencies that are critical for professional practice (CSWE, 2022). For clarity, we 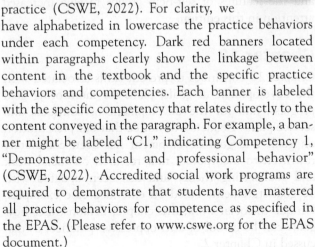 have alphabetized in lowercase the practice behaviors under each competency. Dark red banners located within paragraphs clearly show the linkage between content in the textbook and the specific practice behaviors and competencies. Each banner is labeled with the specific competency that relates directly to the content conveyed in the paragraph. For example, a banner might be labeled "C1," indicating Competency 1, "Demonstrate ethical and professional behavior" (CSWE, 2022). Accredited social work programs are required to demonstrate that students have mastered all practice behaviors for competence as specified in the EPAS. (Please refer to www.cswe.org for the EPAS document.)

Corresponding to each banner, "Competency Notes" at the end of each chapter explain the relationship between chapter content and CSWE's competencies. A summary chart of the icon locations in all chapters and their respective competency or practice behavior is placed in the front matter of the book.

New Features and Resources for the 11th Edition

The 11th edition substantially confronts the social upheaval occasioned by the COVID-19 pandemic and the resurgent attention in the United States to civil rights and social justice. Social workers are agents of change as well as representatives of entrenched, often biased, power structures. The conflicting roles and obligations that result can lead to confusion for students and eventual distress and burnout. The revised text addresses these tensions forthrightly, introducing six orienting perspectives that align to create a client-centered practice philosophy. The first three chapters have been reorganized to introduce readers to the current context of direct practice, the direct practice philosophy that shapes the text, and the arc of the helping relationship, from engagement to termination. Throughout the text, readers will find integration of the orienting perspectives that make up our practice philosophy, updated case examples reflective of a variety of client populations and service settings, and sound, supported guidance for thinking and acting in various social work roles. The following highlights changes chapter by chapter.

Chapter 1

Chapter 1 introduces you to the social work profession and explains its context, mission, features, and values. We included an updated presentation of evidence-based practice, reframed the presentation of social work challenges to opportunities, revised the values and social work roles sections, and presented the case study more quickly in the chapter. We added a description of environmental justice and contemporary issues facing social work practice. Finally, references to the NASW Code of Ethics have been revised to reflect the new 2021 Code of Ethics.

Chapter 2

Chapter 2 introduces our "orienting frameworks" for social work practice. These are the major theories and philosophies that ground social work practice in its mission for social justice and human welfare. The six orienting frameworks include: the ecosystems perspective, the strengths perspective, cultural humility, anti-oppressive practice, trauma-informed practice, and evidence-informed practice. Contemporary manifestations of these frameworks are referenced throughout the text.

Chapter 3

Physical conditions of interviews now include adaptations to remote interviews frequent during the pandemic. Intake forms include suggestions for nonbinary gender identification.

Chapter 4

This chapter includes NASW Code of Ethics changes made in 2021 and a discussion of codes from other nations. It features extra attention to ethical considerations in the electronic delivery of services and introduces the concepts of moral distress and moral courage as key components of ethical action in challenging times.

Chapter 5

This chapter has been substantially streamlined from previous editions. It retains its focus on the beginning phases of the helping relationship, including an extended discussion of role preparation, empathic listening, and authenticity in relationships. Based on emerging research on empathy and our collective experience in the classroom, we have reduced the framework for empathy from six levels to three, simplifying your learning. Moreover, we have created direct ties between the processes of role preparation, empathic listening, and authenticity with the orienting frameworks introduced in Chapter 2.

Chapter 6

Like Chapter 5, Chapter 6 has been substantially streamlined compared to earlier editions. At the same time, the chapter retains its focus on developing concrete communication skills using new dialogue and updated case examples, and it shows how the purposeful and contingent use of communication skills can help you to position your practice within the social justice mission of the profession.

Chapter 7

The list of problematic social worker verbal behavior now includes making a declaration rather than inviting a discussion about options. Inappropriate interviewing technique barriers now includes vague effusive positivity and failing to be aware of implicit and cognitive biases.

Chapter 8

Chapter 8 has been updated to include information on telesocial work, trauma assessment, adverse childhood experiences, neurobiological theory, and assessment with immigrants and refugees. The section on the use of tools and assessments has been updated, and new information on ICD-11 has been integrated.

Chapter 9

Chapter 9 now has a section on implicit bias, additional information on evidenced-base practices, and content on the American Society of Addiction Medicine criteria for targeted assessment.

Chapter 10

Chapter 10 has been reorganized and adds new content that can help social work students integrate family systems assessments into their practice. It includes expanded attention to self-awareness and cultural humility in social work practice with diverse families and a detailed articulation of a family systems framework for assessment of family strengths and adaptive capacity. The chapter ends with a description of three assessment strategies, including the use of circular questions, genograms, and standardized assessment scales.

Chapter 11

The chapter has been revised to acquaint readers with the concepts for understanding groups whether or not they are tasked with starting a new group. The purpose and the features of self-help groups receive increased attention in this edition.

Chapter 12

Chapter 12 continues to present skills associated with the development of goals, plans for monitoring goal progress, and for the development of contracts and service plans. Readers will notice that our presentation on goals and goal development has been completely rewritten to incorporate new research on social work and goal-setting theory and has been updated with 30 goal statements based on extended case examples. Unique to social work, this chapter demonstrates how goals can be a tool of anti-oppressive practice, as discussed in Chapter 2.

Chapter 13

Chapter 13 outlines eight therapeutic approaches for working with individuals, families, and groups. Students will receive comprehensive knowledge and skills to choose and implement interventions to facilitate change and match the strategy to the problem by utilizing a person-in-situation and person-in-environment framework.

Chapter 14

Chapter 14 provides a condensed foundation for understanding macro practice. In this chapter, you will become familiar with assessing macro-level problems and utilizing change efforts directed toward systems that benefit individuals as members of groups and communities, demonstrating the similarities between micro and macro practice and the helping process as it appears at the macro practice level. Readers will learn assessment questions and other available sources of data to guide intervention decisions and evaluate macro practice activities.

Chapter 15

Chapter 15 was revised to conceptualize social work with families in the diverse settings in which social workers routinely encounter families, in addition to traditional family therapy settings and programs. Moreover, the chapter presents intervention skills that are at the heart of most contemporary evidence-based approaches to social work with families. Interventions are organized into first- and second-order change strategies, and new content was included to support skill-training interventions, as well as to emphasize the continuity between intervention strategies presented in earlier chapters and their application to social work with families.

Chapter 16

This chapter has been streamlined to build on Chapter 11. It discusses the roles that treatment and task groups play in solidarity and social action. It describes innovative and culturally adept group interventions such as photovoice.

Chapter 17

This chapter links to earlier coverage of empathy and includes a review of new research on empathy. It adds cultural bias as a barrier to interpretation. Many examples have been revised and adapted, including new skill development examples. The decision about when interpretation is appropriate has been clarified.

Chapter 18

Chapter 18 addresses cross-racial and cross-cultural experience barriers and describes skills to address them, such as broaching. Case examples identify and resolve relational dynamics between the social worker and clients. The discussion of transference reactions now includes assessment of possible influences of trauma.

Chapter 19

Revisions to this chapter build on goal setting content in Chapter 12 and emphasized the ways in which evaluations and endings are influenced by assumptions and values.

Instructor Ancillaries

Additional instructor resources for this product are available online. Instructor assets include an instructor's manual, Microsoft PowerPoint® slides, and a test bank powered by Cognero®. Sign up or sign in at **www.cengage.com** to search for and access this product and its online resources.

Online Instructor's Manual

The instructor's manual (IM) contains a variety of resources to aid instructors in preparing and presenting text material in a manner that meets their personal preferences and course needs. It presents chapter-by-chapter suggestions and resources to enhance and facilitate learning.

Online Test Bank

For assessment support, the updated test bank powered by Cognero® includes true/false, multiple-choice, matching, short answer, and essay questions for each chapter.

Online PowerPoint

These vibrant PowerPoint lecture slides for each chapter assist you with your lecture by providing concept coverage using images, figures, and tables directly from the textbook.

Acknowledgments

We want to express our thanks and admiration for Dean Hepworth, a social work educator and the first author of this text, for his inspiration and example in developing a text that would help students become more effective practitioners.

In addition, we want to thank the following colleagues for their help in providing useful comments and suggestions. We have been supported by colleagues who contributed expertise from their areas of scholarship, including Marilyn Ghezzi and Rachel Goode. Research assistants Melissa McGovern and Jonathan Bell conducted comprehensive literature reviews, tracked bibliographic changes, and reviewed drafts with keen eyes. Finally, we are grateful to our students—the users of this text— and social workers in the field for their suggestions, case examples, and encouragement.

This edition could not have been completed without the support, inspiration, and challenge of our colleagues, friends, and families, including: George Gottfried, Alexi Tao, Lola Dewberry, Louis Evans, Alia Evans, and Alena Evans.

Finally, we want to express special appreciation to Neha Chawla and the rest of the team from Cengage for their responsiveness, support, expertise, and patience.

About the Authors

Dean H. Hepworth, MSW, PhD, is Professor Emeritus at the School of Social Work, Arizona State University, Tempe Arizona, and the University of Utah. Dean has extensive practice experience in individual psychotherapy and marriage and family therapy. Dean was the lead author and active in the production of the first four editions, and he is the coauthor of *Improving Therapeutic Communication*. He is now retired and lives in Phoenix, Arizona.

Pa Der Vang, MSW, PhD, is an Associate Professor in the St. Catherine University Social Work Department in St. Paul, Minnesota. She earned her master's and PhD in Social Work from the University of Minnesota–Twin Cities. Her publications and focus center on Hmong and the immigrant experience. Her area of teaching is primarily direct practice with individuals, families, and groups. She cofounded the Minnesota Hmong Social Workers' Coalition located in St. Paul, Minnesota, and currently serves on the Minnesota Board of Social Work.

Joan Marie Blakey, MSW, PhD, is a tenured Associate Professor in the Tulane School of Social Work. She received her doctorate from the University of Chicago's School of Social Administration (Crowne Family School of Social Work, Policy, and Practice). She also attended the University of Minnesota–Twin Cities, where she received both her Bachelor of Science degree in African American Studies, Sociology, and Youth Studies and her Master of Social Work degree. Dr. Blakey's current research agenda and consulting work with universities/colleges, public school systems, for-profit and nonprofit organizations focuses on diversity, equity, inclusion, and belonging. She promotes antiracist and anti-oppressive practice within the social work profession. Dr. Blakey's work consistently has been about transforming systems to recognize and embrace peoples' full humanity with the goal of creating and fostering equity-centered, trauma-informed policies and practices that lead to collective well-being and social justice.

Craig Schwalbe, MSW, PhD, is a Professor at the Columbia University School of Social Work. Dr. Schwalbe began his career with more than 10 years of direct practice in child welfare and mental health agency settings. His current scholarship focuses on the development of evidence-based strategies on behalf of court-involved youths. He was the recipient of the William T. Grant Scholars Award in 2009, which funded a study of success and failure on probation, and co-led a UNICEF-funded international development effort to design and implement juvenile diversion programs for delinquent youths in Jordan.

Caroline B. R. Evans, MSW, PhD, is the lead evaluator for the Substance Use Prevention, Education, and Research (SUPER) project at the University of North Carolina at Chapel Hill. Her practice experience and passion include extensive work with the Latinx population in a hospital setting and in various outpatient community mental health settings. Her research interests include youth violence, bullying, adolescent substance use, racial/ethnic healthcare disparities, and social justice. Dr. Evans is coauthor of *Bullying and Victimization Across the Lifespan: Playground Politics and Power.*

Ronald H. Rooney, MSSA, PhD, is a Professor Emeritus at the School of Social Work, University of Minnesota. Dr. Rooney is also the author of *Strategies for Work with Involuntary Clients.* His experience includes practice, consultation, and training in child welfare and working with involuntary clients. He has made international presentations in Canada, Great Britain, Holland, South Korea, Taiwan, and Australia.

Glenda Dewberry Rooney, MSW, PhD, is Professor Emeritus, Department of Social Work, Augsburg University, Minneapolis, Minnesota. She taught undergraduate and graduate direct practice courses, ethics, research, and organization and administration. Her practice experience includes child welfare, mental health, and work with families and children. In addition to her practice experience, she has been involved with agencies concerned with children, youth, and families as a trainer and as clinical, program, and management consultant in community-based research projects. Active in retirement, Dr. Rooney continues as an advocate for child welfare policies and practices that strengthen and support children and families.

Kimberly Strom, MSW, PhD, is the Smith P. Theimann Jr. Distinguished Professor of Ethics and Professional Practice at the UNC–Chapel Hill School of Social Work and Director of the UNC Office of Ethics and Policy. Her scholarly interests involve ethics, moral courage, and academic leadership. Dr. Strom is active internationally in consultation, training, and research on ethics. She is the author of *Straight Talk about Professional Ethics, The Ethics of Practice with Minors,* and is coauthor of the texts *Best of Boards* and *Teaching Social Work Values and Ethics: A Curriculum Resource.*

Introduction

1 The Challenges and Opportunities of Social Work
2 Orienting Frameworks for Social Work Practice
3 Overview of the Helping Process
4 Operationalizing Social Work Values and Ethics

Part 1 of this book provides you with a background on the factors that shape direct social work practice: the historic and contemporary contexts and the perspectives, processes and ethical foundations that will prepare you to learn the specific direct practice skills described in Part 2.

Chapter 1 introduces you to the social work profession and explains its context, mission, features, and values.

Chapter 2 outlines six orienting perspectives that provide a framework for direct social work practice.

Chapter 3 offers an overview of the helping process, including exploration, implementation, and termination.

Finally, **Chapter 4** introduces the values and ethics that guide direct social work practice.

The Challenges and Opportunities of Social Work

Chapter Overview

This chapter presents a context and philosophy for social work practice, definitions of direct and clinical practice, and descriptions of the varied roles played by direct social work practitioners.

After completing this chapter, you will be able to:

- Understand the historic and contemporary factors influencing direct social work practice.

- Understand the mission, purposes, roles, and opportunities of direct social work services.

- Identify the value perspectives that guide social workers.

- Describe the nine CSWE EPAS competencies that inform and evaluate social work practice.

- Delineate the roles performed by direct-practice social workers.

- Describe some contemporary issues that you may encounter or experience in social work practice.

The EPAS Competencies in Chapter 1

The Council on Social Work Education (CSWE) accredits social work programs. CSWE's Educational Policy and Accreditation Standards (EPAS) describe the processes and criteria for accreditation, including setting nine multidimensional competencies that programs must use in educating students and evaluating their performance (CSWE, 2015). These competencies are discussed later in this chapter. Each chapter in this book begins with a list of the competencies linked to the chapter, and throughout the book, icons [**C**] indicate the specific competencies addressed in that section. Because it is an overview of the profession, Chapter 1 prepares you to demonstrate all nine of the EPAS competencies:

- Competency 1: Demonstrate Ethical and Professional Behavior

- Competency 2: Engage Anti-Racism, Diversity, Equity, and Inclusion in Practice

- Competency 3: Advance Human Rights, and Social, Racial, Economic, and Environmental Justice

- Competency 4: Engage in Practice-Informed Research and Research-Informed Practice

- Competency 5: Engage in Policy Practice

- Competency 6: Engage with Individuals, Families, Groups, Organizations, and Communities

- Competency 7: Assess Individuals, Families, Groups, Organizations, and Communities

- Competency 8: Intervene with Individuals, Families, Groups, Organizations, and Communities

- Competency 9: Evaluate Practice with Individuals, Families, Groups, Organizations, and Communities

The Mission of Social Work

The mission of social work is to enhance human functioning by promoting and ensuring client access to resources such as health, safety, education, and income. Through the framework of social justice, social workers strive to support and empower vulnerable populations (CSWE, 2021; NASW, 2021a). Vulnerable populations include those who are economically, socially, and environmentally oppressed and marginalized due to their group identification, such as people of color, the elderly, women, youth, immigrants and refugees, and those with disabilities. The International Federation of Social Workers (IFSW) defines social work as a practice-based profession and an academic discipline that promotes social change and development, social cohesion, and the empowerment and liberation of people (IFSW, 2019). Principles of social justice, human rights, collective responsibility, and respect for diversity are central to social work. Social work engages individuals, groups, and societal structures (e.g., organizations, communities, and policy) to address life challenges and enhance well-being (IFSW, 2019). The mission of social work in the United States and the international definition of social work both emphasize the importance of empowerment of marginalized peoples and structural, societal change. Although social workers work across different settings using different methodologies, the commitment to social justice is central to the profession. This commitment distinguishes and unifies the profession and encourages social workers to look beyond narrow perspectives that are limited to particular roles or settings.

The concept of **social justice** maintains that all people should have equal rights to resources offered by a society, regardless of their circumstances or group identity. The pursuit of social justice includes creating social institutions that support the welfare of individuals and groups, removing barriers to accessing resources, and leveraging institutional and social power to advocate for resources for clients. **Economic justice** refers to those aspects of social justice that relate to economic well-being, such as access to employment, a livable wage, pay equity, nondiscrimination in employment, and access to sources of income such as social security and Temporary Assistance to Needy Families (TANF). **Environmental justice** promotes the notion that no group or community should bear a disproportionate share of environmental hazards or risks. This term also refers to the fair treatment and meaningful involvement of all people, regardless of race, color, national origin, ability, or income with respect to the development, implementation, and enforcement of environmental laws, regulations, and policies.

Direct Social Work Practice

The term *direct social work practice* refers to the face-to-face contact that social workers have with their clients, including interactions with individuals, couples, families, groups, and clients in the community. Direct social work practice takes many forms in a wide array of settings, encompasses a variety of roles, and employs an ever-evolving body of knowledge and skills. It builds on a rich history of social work practice, beginning with the progressive movement, and takes place amid dynamic and sometimes challenging contemporary conditions. This section introduces you to the context of direct social work practice and encourages you to think critically about the intersection between social work and the practice environment. It also briefly describes macro social work roles for the purpose of clarifying and distinguishing between direct practice roles and macro practice roles. Direct practice may at times involve macro roles, depending on the needs of the client and issue.

Social work practice generally focusses on client systems at three levels, sometimes described as micro-, mezzo-, and macro-levels. **Micro-level practice** serves individuals, couples, and families. Practice at the micro level is designated as **direct practice** because practitioners' change efforts are focused primarily on small client systems through face-to-face or electronic contact. Examples of micro-level practice roles include (1) therapist, (2) case manager, (3) advocate, (4) educator, and (5) mediator. More roles are described in Table 1-1.

Mezzo-level practice is defined as direct social work practice with groups or organizations (Garthwait, 2012). Mezzo intervention is designed to change the systems that directly affect clients, such as the family, peer group, or classroom. Activities of practitioners at the mezzo level include (1) administrator, (2) facilitator, and (3) program developer (Garthwait, 2012). **Macro-level practice** involves the processes of social work practice focused on social planning and community organization. At this level, social workers serve as professional change agents who collaborate with community action systems composed of individuals, groups, or organizations to deal with social problems at a community and/or policy level, or macro-level social workers may be involved in community or organizational development either locally, regionally, or globally. For example, social workers may work with citizen groups or with private, public, or governmental organizations to create institutional or community change. Examples of social work practice roles at the macro level include

Table 1-1   Social Work Roles and Functions

Social Work Role and Function	Description
Advocate	Proponent for needed resources, such as services or policy, on behalf of individual clients and client groups.
Broker	Intermediary who connects clients with resources and is responsible for identifying, locating, and linking client systems to needed resources.
Case manager/coordinator	Responsible for assessing the needs of a client and arranging and coordinating the timely delivery of essential goods and services provided by other resources.
Clinician	Uses relational skills with psychotherapeutic theories and evidence-based models in diagnoses, assessment, and intervention for people who experience mental health, emotional, behavioral, or interpersonal problems.
Consultant/consultee	Provides advice to clients or other professionals and receives advice from experts.
Counselor	Provides emotional support and guidance to clients as they resolve personal, interpersonal, emotional, and behavioral difficulties.
Facilitator/expediter	Ensures that the delivery of a service is the best it can be. This role is typically involved in planning the service and its implementation.
Integrated electronic technology provider	Develops and oversees the functionality of technology used in the delivery of electronics-based social services, record keeping, biofeedback, and client systems.
Mediator/arbitrator	Provides a neutral forum in which clients and service providers can come to a satisfactory resolution if a service is denied to a client.
Organizational analyst	Pinpoints factors in the structure, policies, and procedures of an organization that have an impact on service delivery.
Planner	Plans and develops programs and structure to respond to unmet and emerging client needs. May be involved in policy development, grant writing, and establishing contracts with other providers.
Policy and procedure developer	Develops policies and procedures to ensure that clients' needs and interests are efficiently met.
Program developer	Develops services in response to the emerging needs of clients and new client populations by seeking to fill a gap in a service or services.
Researcher/research consumer	Uses research in any form to ensure the conduct of evidence-based practice.
System maintenance and enhancement	Ensures the ongoing functioning of structures, policies, and functional relationships within the institutional and systems environment that have an impact on the effectiveness of service delivery. This role may include monitoring and evaluation.
Supervisor	Supports and ensures that quality social work practice is performed by supervisees; guides supervisees on the use of theory in practice to ensure effective service delivery.

Table 1-2   Macro Social Work Practice Realms and Roles

Social Work Role and Function	Description
Community organizer	Actively works with community members, neighborhoods, organizations, and institutions to create social change within the community.
Evaluator	Use the skills of evaluation, such as quantitative and qualitative research and analysis, to ensure that clients receive interventions that have been shown to be successful.
Grant writer/fundraiser	Engages in activities to raise funds to support new or current programs and organizations.
Lobbyist	Advocates for legislation.
Planning specialist	Manages the grant-giving process to establish new programming, writes new policy for new programs, and actively participates in the design and establishment of new programs.
Policy analyst	Engages in policy-related functions, such as researching and advocating for and/or writing policies.
Researcher	Searches for and gathers information to inform programs, organizations, and practice.

(1) community developer, (2) community organizer, (3) policy analyst/developer, (4) researcher, and (5) planner (Garthwait, 2012).

Regardless of the level at which they practice, social workers share a foundation of knowledge, skills, and values. Sometimes referred to as generalist practice, in the United States, these abilities form the structure of Bachelor of Social Work (BSW) education and the beginning content of Master of Social Work (MSW) programs. These fundamental competencies are described later in this chapter. MSW education builds on the generalist foundation with specialized content added, organized in various ways based on the structure and goals of the particular MSW program. Foundational generalist social work education prepares all social workers to practice social work in many roles, directed at enhancing the client's relationship with the various resources.

Direct social work practice involves the micro and mezzo levels of social work practice. Direct social work practitioners perform many roles in addition to delivering face-to-face services; they collaborate with other professionals, organizations, and institutions, and they act as advocates with providers, agency administrators, policy-making boards, and legislatures, among others. Direct social work practice takes place in a variety of settings, including public agencies, such as schools, military settings, and child welfare organizations; nonprofit or nongovernmental organizations (NGOs), such as rape crisis centers, domestic violence agencies, refugee resettlement agencies, and faith-based organizations; and for-profit settings, such as private health-care clinics, residential recovery or eldercare settings, and corporate employee

assistance programs. Services may be organized by the life-cycle stage of clients (e.g., children, adolescents and young adults, older adults), by problem area (e.g., child welfare, domestic violence, health and mental health, substance abuse, antipoverty issues, work programs), by mode of intervention (e.g., individual case management, group-work, counseling), and by agency setting (e.g., school social work, hospital social work, county-based services).

Roles

Social workers perform several roles. The underlying purpose of each role is to enhance the client's connection with resources and to promote client functioning. Humans need essential resources for optimal functioning, including but not limited to food, health care, shelter, and income. Other resources that all humans should have a right to include education, safety, dignity, autonomy, community, and relationships in the multitude of systems that serve to enhance functioning. The roles listed here are neither mutually exclusive nor exhaustive, and a social worker may play multiple roles simultaneously. For example, case managers may also assume the roles of broker, client advocate, and counselor as they seek to connect clients to resources. Or planners may also assume the roles of systems maintenance, facilitating, and developing. Roles may be listed in job titles, but they are not necessarily job titles; they are duties completed by social workers. For example, foster care workers may find themselves advocating, facilitating, and mediating on behalf of clients.

Social Work Values

Six social work values provide a framework for practice and this book. They are drawn from the NASW Code of Ethics and are introduced briefly here and discussed at length in Chapter 4. These values are:

- Service
- Social justice
- Dignity and worth of the person
- Importance of human relationships
- Integrity
- Competence

What do these values mean for direct social work practice? Considered individually, they are not exclusive to social work. Their unique combination, however, differentiates social work from other professions. Considered in their entirety, the values make it clear

Figure 1-1 Clinical Social Work

Clinical social work practice is a type of direct practice. It includes the resolution and prevention of psychosocial problems experienced by individuals, families, and groups using accepted therapeutic practices and modalities (Asakura et al., 2020). This definition includes mental health treatment, but it extends more broadly to other emotional, behavioral, and relational difficulties as well. Specht and Courtney (1994) articulated concerns regarding the movement of social work toward psychotherapy and billable services and the abandonment of its primary mission of ensuring social justice and equal access to resources for clients. With this recognition, we encourage an intent on the part of clinical social workers to integrate social justice concepts into the practice of psychotherapy.

Figure 1-2 Social Work Values

The National Association of Social Workers (NASW) was established in 1955 through the consolidation of the following organizations:

- American Association of Social Workers
- American Association of Psychiatric Social Workers
- American Association of Group Workers
- Association for the Study of Community Organization
- American Association of Medical Social Workers
- American Association of Medical Social Workers
- National Association of School Social Workers

It is the largest membership organization of professional social workers in the world. The NASW works to enhance the professional growth and development of its members, to create and maintain professional standards, and to advance sound social policies. https://www.socialworkers.org/About.

The NASW published the first version of its Code of Ethics in 1960. Since then, the NASW Code of Ethics has emerged as the standard-bearer for defining the values and principles that guide social workers' conduct in all practice areas. The latest version of the Code of Ethics was published in 2017 (https://www.socialworkers.org/About/Ethics/Code-of-Ethics).

Social workers and social work students are encouraged to regularly check the NASW website, as well as their local chapter, for updates to the Code of Ethics, continuing education opportunities, and discussions of current issues.

Figure 1-3 CSWE EPAS

Founded in 1952, the Council on Social Work Education (CSWE) is the national association representing social work education in the United States. Through its many initiatives, activities, and centers, CSWE supports quality social work education and provides opportunities for leadership and professional development so that social workers play a central role in achieving the profession's goals of social and economic justice. CSWE's Commission on Accreditation is recognized by the Council for Higher Education Accreditation as the sole accrediting agency for social work education in the United States and its territories. The CSWE uses the EPAS to accredit BSW and MSW programs. The nine EPAS competencies support academic excellence by establishing thresholds for professional competence. They permit programs to use traditional and emerging models and methods of curriculum design by balancing requirements that promote comparable outcomes across programs with a level of flexibility that encourages programs to differentiate. For more information, please visit https://www.cswe.org/Home.aspx.

that social work's identity derives from its connection with the institution of social welfare. According to Gilbert (1977), social welfare represents a special mechanism devised to aid those who suffer from the variety of ills found in industrial society: "Whenever other major institutions, be they familial, religious, economic, or educational in nature, fall short in their helping and resource providing functions, social welfare spans the gap" (p. 402).

Social Work Competencies

What does it mean to be a competent social worker? Many entities that regulate the practice of social work set forth standards of competent practice. These entities include state licensing boards, professional associations, and accrediting agencies, as well as legislative bodies. Earlier, we introduced the nine EPAS competencies from the CSWE, which form the essential proficiencies for BSW and MSW students. Social work educators use these competencies to measure the performance of their programs and the abilities of their students. We present and describe them here in order to familiarize you with the multidimensional knowledge, skills, and values that make up the practice of social work.

EPAS Competency 1—Demonstrate Ethical and Professional Behavior

Competency 1 requires that social workers understand the value base and ethical **C1** standards of the profession, the NASW Code of Ethics, as well as relevant laws and regulations that may affect social work practice at various levels. Social workers must understand the frameworks of ethical decision making and how to apply principles of critical thinking to those frameworks in practice, research, and policy. Social workers must also recognize their own personal values, the distinction between personal and professional values, and how their personal experiences and reactions influence their professional judgment and behavior. This competency also asks that social workers demonstrate professionalism in written and verbal communication.

It is understood that ethical social work practice entails lifelong learning, whereby social workers commit to updating their skills continually to ensure that they are relevant and effective. According to this competency, social workers also must understand emerging forms of technology and the ethical use of technology in social work practice. Hence, social workers must use technology mindfully and responsibly, in ways that protect client confidentiality.

EPAS Competency 2—Engage Anti-Racism, Diversity, Equity, and Inclusion in Practice

Social workers are guided in Competency 2 to understand how diversity and difference C2 characterize and shape the human experience and are critical to the formation of identity. They understand the dimensions of diversity as the intersection of multiple factors, including, but not limited to, age, class, color, ability, culture, ethnicity, gender, gender identity and expression, immigration status, marital status, physical and mental ability, political ideology, race, religion/spirituality, sex, sexual orientation, and tribal sovereign status. This competency guides social workers to understand that as a consequence of difference, a person's life experiences may include oppression, poverty, marginalization, and alienation, as well as privilege, power, and acclaim. Social workers also understand the forms and mechanisms of oppression and discrimination and recognize the extent to which a culture's structures and values (e.g., social, economic, political, and cultural exclusions) may oppress, marginalize, alienate, or create privilege and power for certain groups. Social workers should be mindful of privilege and strive to embody cultural humility (discussed further in Chapter 2). Social workers play a large role in providing equitable services, advocating for change, and creating new policies and practices to meet the needs of those who have been oppressed.

To do this, social workers need to engage in continual education about differences in the cultures, histories, and experiences of different groups as well as of their own group. This also means that social workers must approach each client as an individual whose experience is unique. Social workers must learn as much as they can about the cultural frames that are significant for their clients before they can be open to learning the uniqueness of those clients (Dean, 2001; Johnson & Munch, 2009). Hence, when we report some cultural characteristics as

being commonly represented in some groups, it is shared in the sense of background information that must be further assessed with each individual.

EPAS Competency 3—Advance Human Rights, and Social, Racial, Economic, and Environmental Justice

Competency 3 requires that social workers advance human rights and social justice and C3 asserts that each person in society has basic human rights, such as freedom, safety, privacy, an adequate standard of living, health care, and education. This competency is also reflected in the value of social justice and the ethical principle that social workers are to challenge social justice in the NASW Code of Ethics (NASW, 2021a).

To meet this competency, social workers should be aware of the global implications of oppression, be knowledgeable about theories of justice and strategies to promote human and civil rights, and strive to incorporate social justice practices into direct service, policy and practices, organizations, institutions, and society. Social workers should also understand the mechanisms of oppression and discrimination in society and advocate for and engage in practices that advance human rights and social and economic justice. This competency clearly specifies that advocating for human rights and social and economic justice is a professional expectation.

EPAS Competency 4—Engage in Practice-Informed Research and Research-Informed Practice

Competency 4 states that social workers must recognize the mutual nature of C4 research and social work practice. Social workers understand different forms of research, such as quantitative and qualitative research methods, as well as the social worker's role in advancing social work as a science. Social workers also incorporate evaluation into their practice. Social workers utilize practice methods that are informed by culturally informed and ethical approaches that are derived from multidisciplinary sources and multiple ways of knowing. They also understand the processes for translating research findings into effective practice. Social workers use practice experience and theory to inform scientific inquiry and research, apply critical thinking to engage in the utilization of research methods and analysis of research findings, and use and translate research evidence to inform and improve practice, policy, and service delivery.

EPAS Competency 5—Engage in Policy Practice

Competency 5 requires that social workers engage in critical analysis and the development of policy that aligns with social justice values. Social workers advocate for new policy to advance social and economic well-being and to deliver effective social work services. One of the distinguishing features of social work as a helping profession is the understanding that all direct practice occurs in a policy context. Hence, social workers need to know about the history of and current structures for policies and services.

In pursuit of this competency, social workers analyze, formulate, and advocate for policies that advance the social well-being of their clients. They also collaborate with colleagues and clients for effective policy action. While some social workers provide direct services to clients, others act to influence the environments that support their clients, thereby developing and maintaining the social infrastructure that assists clients in meeting their needs.

EPAS Competency 6—Engage with Individuals, Families, Groups, Organizations, and Communities

Competency 6 identifies the first stage of the helping process: engagement. It focuses on engagement with an array of client systems, including individuals, families, groups, organizations, and communities. During the engagement phase, social workers apply their knowledge of human behavior in the social environment, communication skills, and interpersonal skills to build trust and rapport with clients as they begin the helping process.

Engagement is also utilized in macro-practice. While this book focuses on micro- and mezzo-interventions, direct practitioners are necessarily involved to some degree in macro-practices as well, such as administrative activities, or they may interface with the community as a part of their direct practice work. Knowledge of macro-practice is vital for the foundation of social work practice. Even social workers in direct practice roles may find themselves working in concert with concerned citizens and community leaders in planning and developing resources to prevent or combat social problems. These activities require the ability to engage with communities and to build trust and rapport with communities and organizations.

EPAS Competency 7—Assess Individuals, Families, Groups, Organizations, and Communities

Competency 7 discusses the second phase of the helping process: assessment. Assessment encompasses the knowledge, skills, and values needed to gather comprehensive and accurate information about various client systems and the problems they identify, and to come to conclusions about goals and next steps, in concert with the client's self-determination. Besides understanding the helping process (engagement, assessment, intervention, evaluation, termination), additional foundational knowledge needed in the assessment phase includes intrapersonal, interpersonal, and environmental factors. Social workers must understand the interactions among the biological, psychological, social, cultural, and spiritual aspects of human development and the impact on human functioning. Foundational knowledge also includes an understanding of the micro-, mezzo-, and macro-factors and the use of assessments that recognize the strengths and assets of clients. Foundational social work skills include interpersonal assessments such as interactions, both verbal and nonverbal, involving individuals, couples, families, and/or groups. Assessment of groups, families, communities and organizations may require social workers to apply systems theory in the assessments of relationships among different parties within and between systems. Systems theory refers to concepts such as the roles, rules, norms, boundaries within and between different systems. Social workers may also wish to conduct a strengths, weaknesses, opportunities, and threats (SWOT) analysis of communities and organizations as a part of their assessments.

EPAS Competency 8—Intervene with Individuals, Families, Groups, Organizations, and Communities

Competency 8 describes the criteria for the third phase in the helping process: intervention. *Intervention* refers to actions taken by the social worker to directly support the client's goals or to remove barriers to allow the client to achieve a particular goal. Interventions can range from referrals to another service to direct application of a treatment in order to alleviate or remove the problem identified by the client. Some social work roles serve an intervention capacity, such as a counselor who may serve as an intervention to a problem identified by the referral source. As with the first two competencies, we will consider interventions across the full spectrum of clients, including individuals, groups, and communities. Social workers must possess knowledge of theoretical frameworks from which to choose appropriate interventions. Interventions must be based on a thorough assessment of the problem and be conducted in collaboration with the client, and be directed toward achieving a specified goal. Social workers should possess a wide foundation of knowledge, including how to conduct interventions at the micro-, mezzo-, and macro-levels.

EPAS Competency 9—Evaluate Practice with Individuals, Families, Groups, Organizations, and Communities

Competency 9, the last of the competencies stipulated by CSWE, focuses on evaluation and the knowledge, skills, and values necessary to effectively monitor and gauge client progress and satisfaction and goal attainment, and to determine and measure outcomes. Evaluation can include evaluation of worker or service effectiveness, cost and efficiency, or the level of need for the service. Evaluation allows social workers to gather valuable data needed to provide a method for analyzing the service and can be used to demonstrate the need and effectiveness of the services, to support funding for the services, and to provide needed feedback to improve or adjust the service. Evaluation can be conducted with all levels of client systems, including individual clients, families, groups, communities, and institutions.

The final phase of the helping process includes termination, which includes skills such as helping the client to review what was learned and plan for the future, find closure with the helping relationship, and model healthy endings to relationships. Evaluation may also occur during the termination phase if social workers choose to informally or formally gather client feedback or measure client outcomes in the form of surveys, questionnaires, or discussion. We will discuss termination in Chapter 19, which covers the final phases of the helping process.

Contemporary Influences on Direct Practice

Like other professions and social institutions, changes in the environment in which social work is embedded present both opportunities and challenges for direct social work practice. There is a plethora of societal issues that require the attention of social workers. Only a few of them are named here; however, social workers are encouraged to consider the context in which they practice social work and to develop awareness about current social issues that affect client functioning. Next, we discuss only a few of the issues that have gained global attention due to their widespread nature and the record number of communities impacted.

Self-Care

Concerns about social worker burnout, compassion fatigue, and social workers leaving the field due to high stress has been a topic of discourse for decades. Recently, the NASW Code of Ethics (Barsky, 2021) adopted language to encourage social workers to engage in self-care to ensure commitment to the core features of the profession. Social workers are asked to take measures to care for themselves both professionally and personally. Social workers are faced with difficult cases, immediate and urgent human needs, high caseloads amid lack of resources, and trauma and crisis situations. These stressful situations require that social workers and social service systems engage in change at the macro-, mezzo-, and micro-levels to encourage not only that social workers recognize signs of stress and burnout in themselves and act to engage in self-care, but also for organizations and systems to implement policies and practices that promote balanced work environments. The inclusion of self-care in the code of ethics creates space for social workers themselves to advocate for and act on their own behalf to promote work-life balance, increased support, and sustainable work environments.

Pandemics

In 2020 and into 2021, the world grappled with twin pandemics—the coronavirus (COVID-19) pandemic and an ongoing pandemic of violence against Black and Brown people by law enforcement. Both absorbed the attention of the media, policy makers, and the public at large, and both have had significant impacts on social work practice and are ongoing.

The first few months following the announcement of the 2020 coronavirus pandemic revealed the challenges of initiating widespread testing, hospitalization, and emergency room visits when most insurance for health care in the United States is based on employment status, even with the advent of the Affordable Care Act (Cooper, 2020). Shortages in personal protection equipment, a lack of pandemic protocols within many provider agencies, and a social distancing requirement of 6 feet between two people posed challenges for the clients and providers of face-to-face services. The COVID-19 pandemic called on many health services, including social work, to transition to telehealth service models, which have required third-party payers to revise what could be considered billable. Telehealth and virtual meeting spaces made it possible for providers, clients, colleagues, family, and friends to interact despite geographic borders; many hope that this practice will continue even after the pandemic, as it filled a gap in access to social services.

The COVID-19 pandemic exacerbated racial disparities in employment, food, education, and health care, magnifying the need for social workers to address social inequalities in their practice. In addition, hate crimes and violence targeting Asian Americans skyrocketed following news reports that the virus originated in the city of Wuhan, China, as well as racist rhetoric from the White House and other sources labeling the virus as the "kung flu" or the "China virus." The pandemic gave Asian Americans a global platform to speak about the ongoing, continued, violence against Asians in America.

The notorious killings of George Floyd (in Minneapolis, Minnesota), Breonna Taylor (in Louisville, Kentucky), and Rasheed Brooks (in Atlanta, Georgia) by law enforcement in that same period rejuvenated a movement to reimagine policing in the United States, as well as raising awareness in the popular media about the continued oppression and marginalization of Black and Brown communities by those in power. In myriad ways, Black people, Indigenous people, and people of color continue to suffer repeated and chronic exposure to traumas, both contemporary and historical.

In response to the widespread attention given to these killings, social workers have been called on to advocate for policies to reduce police violence, as well as to examine the role of racism in their own service delivery settings. As key players in health care and mental health-care systems, educational systems, social welfare systems, and criminal and juvenile justice systems, among others, social workers have a history of participating in actions and policies that have oppressed and disempowered minoritized populations in the United States and elsewhere.

Social work must continue to be prepared to respond to environmental changes and events such as the COVID-19 pandemic and police violence against Black and Brown people. Moreover, social workers and social work agencies must go further to identify and change practices that disempower and oppress people of color. Throughout our history, social workers have adjusted quickly in response to current events and environmental and societal changes such as mass shootings, natural disasters, wartime, and immigration. Social workers must continue to engage in lifelong learning about social issues and take action in their own spheres of influence in response to current issues and social movements such as Black Lives Matter, Deferred Action for Childhood Arrivals (DACA), gay marriage, and the #MeToo movement, just to name a few.

Funding for Services

Social work is funded in many ways. Federal block grants provide funds to states and counties to administer needed social services to its residents. Social services also rely on public or private grants from foundations or private donors. Certain types of social services are billable and must rely on third-party payers or state-funded medical assistance programs for revenue.

Targeted funding places limitations on the types of services that social workers may provide and the length and frequency of these services. For example, insurance companies may be willing to reimburse only for particular diagnoses, limit services to a specific number of sessions, and refuse to pay for certain interventions, such as prevention, home-based care, psychoeducational groups, case management, crisis stabilization, or conjoint and family therapy. When funding follows a medical model of diagnosis-treatment-outcome, practitioners may feel pressured to diagnose patients solely for billing purposes.

The emphasis on demonstrable outcomes carries implications for treating complex or long-standing problems where relapse is common or change is incremental. Some aspects of successful direct practice, such as building a trusting relationship, helping clients to complete paperwork for peripheral services, securing transportation and safe housing, advocating for client needs, and coordinating complex systems, may not be captured in short-term measures, therapeutic benchmarks, or symptom scores.

The growth in third-party reimbursement has been accompanied by an erosion in block grant funding and safety net systems, creating further vulnerability for potential clients and fewer referral resources. Since 2000, each of the 13 federal block-grant-funded programs in the United States has endured significant funding decreases. For example, TANF has decreased by almost 33% since its creation in 1996 (Reich et al. 2017). Many populations (such as undocumented immigrants or families near the poverty level) and needs (such as dental care) do not qualify for funding. The results of such cuts overwhelm underfunded safety-net services and create dangerous delays for those seeking care. Cuts to safety-net services limit the variety and adequacy of resources available to clients in need.

Funding decreases can lead to staffing issues that leave social workers overworked, underpaid, and at an increased risk of burnout. The pressure for increased worker productivity to meet revenue targets reduces the amount of time available for clinical supervision, professional development, and self-care. The emphasis placed on billable services may affect access to services for clients who are unreliable in appearing for appointments or whose needs clearly exceed the care allocated (Horton, 2006).

Technological Advances

Like other disciplines, social work practice has been transformed by technological change. With advancements in technology and electronic communications and recordkeeping, social workers must possess specialized knowledge and skills in these areas. Leading social work associations in the United States, such as the CWSE, the NASW, the Association of Social Work Board (ASWB), and the Clinical Social Work Association (CSWA), have formulated standards for competency in the use of technology in social work practice. *Technology in Social Work Practice* (NASW, 2021b) demonstrates the widespread impact on routine functions such as informed consent, confidentiality, record keeping, supervision, electronic delivery of services, and professional education.

Powerful and accessible tools such as cell phones affect the process and content of service delivery. For example, information and communication technologies (ICT) can automate interventions and the monitoring of progress using apps to remind users to take medications, exercise, meditate, or make a journal entry. Apps can be used to check breathing and heart rates, as well as logging symptoms. ICT can facilitate instantaneous responses to people experiencing acute episodes of suicidal ideation, substance abuse, depression, and anxiety (Perron et al., 2010).

Websites deliver information for providers and service users on social issues, diagnoses and diseases, and efficacious practices, as well as current events and recent findings. Social media platforms and chat rooms allow people in need the ability to access information, support, and mutual aid (NASWMA, n.d.). In addition, social workers can deliver services electronically through text, phone, or video-based sessions. Such technological innovations allow timely, efficient, and accessible interventions (Bee et al., 2008). Some research even suggests that mental health outcomes are better for clients who choose online therapy over in-person approaches (Sanger & Sage, 2015).

The use of electronic devices in social work comes with serious risks and ethical considerations. In the same way that commercial transactions have given rise to surveillance capitalism (Naughton, 2019), online tools embedded into websites now have the capability to collect, store, and analyze data about users. Text messages, Internet searches, and posts on Instagram or Twitter trigger individually targeted advertising to best suit the interests of users. Geofencing technology tracks key words from public platforms; terms that are associated with risks of violence will trigger further investigation into the data profile of the person involved. There is a clear difference between posting "I'm going to bomb that job interview" and "I'm going to bomb that office," but both may attract the attention of a site monitor. These tools are used to protect the safety of individuals and the public, but it is easy to envision the ways that they can be used against the interests of the powerless, vulnerable, or disenfranchised. Technological surveillance arises in services and products from transportation to health care by way of personalized assistants and smart products (Naughton, 2019). Tracking devices and electronic communications can not only assist social workers who deliver services outside the office setting, but they also provide administrative data on the length of visits, the stops made, or other people in attendance. Data can not only make social work practice more efficient, safe, and accountable, but they can also create unanticipated exposure for clients and workers alike.

Globalization

The ascendance of technology brings a rapidly changing world into local context. Immigration, domestic migration, and relocation of refugees fleeing war, poverty, and violence challenge cultural, economic, and political status quos. These changes affect the regions where immigrants relocate, as well as those they leave behind. In 2018, India led the world in the rate of emigration at the same time that the United States led in immigration (Migration Policy Institute, 2018). Social workers practice at the center of these changes, helping new arrivals access basic resources and helping communities adapt to changing demographics caused by population losses, as well as additions (Miller et al., 2018). Against the backdrop of cultural dislocation and significant needs, immigrants are often faced with political and social backlash. In the past decade, European Union (EU) governments have wrestled with responsibility for accepting asylum seekers, with some countries refusing or delaying the disembarkation of new arrivals (Human Rights Watch, 2019). In the United States, policies restricting immigration from predominantly Muslim countries and across the southern U.S. border have resulted in humanitarian crises (Gladstone, 2018).

Social workers are engaged in the growing global humanitarian industries, requiring them to interact with a diverse clientele, as well as diverse colleagues. In some settings, such as the U.S. military, the clientele will predominantly be American, even when the service is in a foreign country. In other settings, international social workers will serve local populations. This requires cultural and regional knowledge, as well as language fluency that is specialized for work in clinical and health-care settings. Transnational work means reconciling the professional's educational preparation with the needs and regulations for the host country and setting. For example, practitioners trained outside the United States may lack the required coursework, and thus must return to school to be credentialed to practice in this country (CSWE, n.d.). NASW has also worked to ensure that U.S.-educated social workers have the ability to work internationally through creating memorandums of understanding with foreign councils of social work to ensure that social workers have the capability to practice across border lines (NASW Foundation, n.d.).

Social work is a global profession, and yet the roots of the profession vary across the world. In the United States and other countries, it advanced among the pillars of a developing civil society, whereas in others, it was intentionally created by governments to meet specific social welfare needs (Healy, 2013). The attention to globalization and the ease of access to global information provides opportunities for learning, as we can study how direct practice is formulated elsewhere and adapt practices accordingly. The growing international perspective adds another dimension to the demand for social workers to be culturally respectful, inquisitive, and informed.

Scientific Changes

Advances in scientific knowledge shape our understanding of the causes of problems and the efficacy of treatments. Breakthroughs in genetic, pharmacologic, and biologic knowledge challenge practitioner competence as professionals strive to stay abreast of new findings and consider their ethical and clinical implications for their work. For example, commercially available genetic testing can help in the early detection (and sometimes treatment) of diseases, but the results may be used to exclude people from employment and insurance. Historically, vulnerable groups such as lesbian/gay/bisexual/transgender/queer/questioning (LGBTQ+) persons, immigrants, and individuals with intellectual and developmental disabilities may be further marginalized and imperiled when genetic testing is conducted without true informed consent, or when important results are kept from the affected individuals and communities (Alvarez, 2019; Szubiak, 2017; Ganna et al. 2019).

New understanding about the connection of body and brain functioning will significantly affect the assessment and treatment of conditions ranging from diabetes to depression. For example, studies on immune or inflammatory causes of disease suggest that adversities such as racism, stress, and obesity may be related to low-grade inflammation, which can give rise to other health and mental health conditions (Brewer & Cooper, 2014; Bullmore, 2020). As such, immunological medicines for arthritis, cancer, and multiple sclerosis may thus have efficacy for treating depression, dementia, psychosis, or other brain disorders.

Studies on adverse childhood experiences (ACEs) have advanced our understanding of the singular and cumulative effects of events such as family separation, racial segregation, community violence, and food insecurity as causes of toxic stress. Extended or prolonged exposure to such stresses can alter brain development, affecting decision-making, attention, and learning, as well as the risks for an array of mental health, social, and physical problems (CDC, 2019). Recent research suggests that the effects of trauma can be passed down throughout families and communities via secondary and historical trauma (Beckerman & Sarracco, 2019). Social workers are well positioned to prevent ACEs through improved financial support for families, early childhood education, family-friendly work policies, antiviolence, anti–corporal punishment initiatives, and other systemic prevention and intervention efforts. These might seem like unconventional techniques for reducing health disparities, depression, heart disease, or sex trafficking, but clearly, new knowledge is changing direct practice, and it demands competence in evidence-based practices (CDC, 2019; Maguire-Jack al., 2019).

The embrace of medical-assisted treatment (MAT), or the use of medications in combination with counseling and behavioral therapies, has changed the approach to the treatment of addictions, as pharmacologic innovations such as Suboxone are used in the treatment of opiate overdoses or addictions (Szubiak, 2017). Along with MAT, harm reduction programs, which embrace a philosophy and intervention that seeks to reduce the harms associated with drug use and ineffective drug policies such as abstinence only, have significantly changed the prevention and treatment approaches for an array of issues, such as addiction and HIV. Effective direct practice will require dedication to understanding scientific developments and the ways that these complement or replace traditional methods. Further, as medical advancements increase our understanding of the connection between the mind and the body, interdisciplinary, team-provided services will increase to include professionals from an array of disciplines in order to serve clients' needs, such as medical, mental health, and social services (Zerden et al., 2020).

Sociopolitical Environment

Social work practice takes place within a local and global social and political context. Social and political cultures change over time, with influences on social and political views and climate. Often, sociopolitical movements occur when a large enough social or political mass confronts issues or concerns that surface as a result of the social or political climate. Depending on the social or political climate, certain groups may be at more risk for oppressive practices such as lack of power, violence, marginalization, impact on human rights, and barriers to basic rights and resources such as voting rights, health care, education, marriage, and income (Fisher, 2019). Social workers must be able to respond to the political and social climate in their practice, as well as to develop sensitivity to the way that current events may affect the well-being and functioning of clients and communities.

Social workers might also respond to social and political issues through advocacy, lobbying, demonstrating, and community awareness-raising. They may engage in these activities through direct, face-to-face contact with their clients, communities, and institutions. Some examples may include education and community awareness efforts through social media, community forums, meeting with legislators and policy-makers, and community campaigns. When the impact of the social and political climate results in negative impacts on the functioning of certain groups, social movements may arise in response. Some examples include Black Lives Matter, the #MeToo movement, community organization efforts centered on immigration and voting rights, the Stop Asian Hate movement, LGBTQ+ social movements, and marriage rights movements.

During these times, social workers must remain client centered and focused on promoting and advocating for social justice (Holosko, 2015; Stark, 2018). The domestic and global context of social work is shaped by controversial ideological transformations, contesting values about individual rights versus collective interests, technological advances, and restructuring of service and economic systems (Mänttäri-van der Kuip, 2020). Social workers must remain nimble and use continuing education to remain current on social and political issues that may affect clients' lives. In the next section, we ask the reader to apply the knowledge learned in this chapter to the Ramirez case.

Applying the Concepts to the Ramirez Case

The Ramirez case provides students with an opportunity to apply the many concepts discussed in this chapter. When reading the Ramirez case, keep in mind concepts such as social worker roles, social work values, social justice issues related to the plight of many immigrants, the client's strengths, and power dynamics in the helping relationship. Review Case Example 1 before continuing.

C2, 3, 6, 7, and 8

After looking at the Ramirez case, the social worker comes to understand that Tobias, like many social workers, practices in a setting where he performs dual roles, protecting both the community at large and vulnerable individuals, in addition to other supportive roles (Trotter, 2006). No matter where they are employed, social workers are influenced by the social work value of self-determination for their clients. For this reason, in addition to exploring school attendance issues with Mrs. Ramirez and her children, Tobias addressed Mrs. Ramirez's other concerns, such as her own physical and mental health (i.e., depression, anxiety, her physical injury) and her children's health.

Of course, social workers are not the only helping professionals who provide direct services to clients in need. However, they have a special interest in helping empower members of oppressed groups. Indeed, as a profession, social workers are committed to the pursuit of social justice for poor, disadvantaged, disenfranchised, and oppressed people (Watts & Hodgson, 2019). In this case, in addition to seeing his client, Mrs. Ramirez, as a parent struggling with school attendance issues, Tobias saw her as someone experiencing challenges possibly related to issues in the United States surrounding undocumented immigrants (Cleveland, 2010; Padilla et al., 2008). Nationalism and unfounded fears of declining resources for citizens have paved the way for increasing anti-immigrant sentiments among Americans. Threats of deportation and detention are fears experienced by undocumented immigrants in the United States. According to the NASW Immigration Toolkit (NASW, 2006, p. 4), "the plight of refugees and immigrants must be considered on the basis of human values and needs rather than on the basis of an ideological struggle related to foreign policy." The contrast between these two positions suggests that social workers grapple with issues of social justice in their everyday practice. As a social worker, Tobias obviously could not personally resolve the uncertain situation of undocumented immigrants. However, he could work with

Case Example 1: The Ramirez Case

Marta Ramirez was referred to child welfare services because her two elementary school-age children had more than seven days of unexcused absences from school during the semester, the standard for educational neglect in her state. When Tobias, a child welfare social worker, met with Mrs. Ramirez, he found that the children had missed a similar amount of time when they had previously lived in another state, as well as earlier, before they had emigrated without documents from Mexico. There had not been any earlier investigations, however, as the legal standard for educational neglect was different in the previous state. Mrs. Ramirez noted that her children had been frequently ill with "flu and asthma." She said that the children did not feel comfortable at the school. They felt that the teachers were mean to them because they were Hispanic. In addition,

Mrs. Ramirez had sustained a back injury on her job that limited her ability to get out of bed some mornings. As an immigrant without documents, Mrs. Ramirez was ineligible for the surgery that she needed to alleviate her condition. She also expressed fears related to her undocumented immigrant status. Finally, she acknowledged experiencing depression and anxiety.

Tobias shared with Mrs. Ramirez the reason for the referral under statute and asked for her perspective on school attendance. He explained that child welfare workers are called on to assist families in having their children educated. He also asked about how things were going for Mrs. Ramirez and her family in their community. In so doing, Tobias explained his dual roles of responding to the law violation and helping families address issues of concern to them.

Mrs. Ramirez and local health institutions to explore possible solutions.

Note that in this case example, Mrs. Ramirez did not seek assistance herself. Rather, she was referred by school staff because of her children's poor school attendance. Therefore, she would be referred to as a **legally mandated client**, who receives services under the threat of a court order. Those clients who apply for services themselves are referred to as **voluntary clients**. Many legally mandated clients, including those like Mrs. Ramirez, become more voluntary if their own concerns are explicitly addressed as part of the social work assessment. Many potential clients fall between the two extremes of legally mandated and voluntary clients, as they are neither legally coerced nor seeking a service themselves (Trotter, 2006). For example, clients who experience nonlegal pressures from family members, teachers, and referral sources are referred to as **nonvoluntary clients** (Rooney & Myrick, 2018).

Such assessments also seek to reveal strengths and potential resources. For example, Mrs. Ramirez's potential strengths and resources include her determination that her children have a better life than their parents, as well as other community and spiritual support systems, both locally and in her home country of Mexico. Those potential resources must be assessed in the context of both internal and external challenges, such as the lack of a health-care safety net for undocumented immigrants and Mrs. Ramirez's own medical and psychological concerns.

To best serve their clients, social workers must be willing to assume responsibilities and engage in actions that expand upon the functions of specific social agencies and their designated individual roles as staff members. For example, Tobias, the child welfare social worker who met with Mrs. Ramirez, assessed her issues and concerns and went beyond the child protection mission that he was originally given.

Because clients such as Mrs. Ramirez often know little about the available resources, social workers must act as brokers by referring people to resource systems such as public legal services, health-care agencies, child welfare divisions, mental health centers, centers for elderly persons, and family counseling agencies. Some individual clients or families may require goods and services from many different providers and may lack the language facility, physical or mental capacity, experience, or skills needed to take advantage of them. Social workers assume a variety of roles aimed at increasing access to resources for clients. For example, if Tobias had any personal values that might impede his work with Mrs. Ramirez and her children, he would ensure that his professional values supersede those personal values. He would try to understand Mrs. Ramirez from many perspectives, including her immigration status, gender, ethnicity, and other perspectives relevant to her situation.

This competency also includes the recommendation that social workers use reflection to manage their personal values. For example, early in his working with Mrs. Ramirez, Tobias wrote in his case notes that he suspected that her children were not attending school in part because she and other undocumented immigrants did not value education as much as their fellow students and families in their new community in the United States. Tobias's statement might be seen as a belief, a hypothesis, or a possible bias that could have profound implications for his work with Mrs. Ramirez and other immigrants. If he acted on his belief that her children were not attending primarily because she and other Mexican immigrants were not motivated to seek education, he might not explore other community- or school-based barriers to their attendance, such as their perception that they were not welcome. Holding members of oppressed groups personally responsible for all aspects of their condition is an unfortunate value predicated on the myth that all successful people lift themselves up by their own bootstraps. This competency therefore requires sensitivity to structures that may act to oppress clients.

Following this competency, Tobias would attempt to understand the issue of children's school attendance in a broader framework of understanding why Mrs. Ramirez and her children had moved to this locality. Awareness of the economic incentive of seeking a better income as an influence on immigration would be appropriate. For example, in addition to working directly with Mrs. Ramirez, Tobias or other social workers might approach the circumstance of undocumented immigrants in their community from the standpoint of community organization and advocacy, working to promote the interests of the group rather than solely those of the individual.

While this book focuses primarily on direct social work intervention, other courses and texts provide additional sources of information for pursuing this goal. Tobias's interaction with Mrs. Ramirez must be considered in the context of policies related to school attendance and policies related to health-care access.

Summary

This chapter introduced social work as a profession, marked by a specific context, mission, and well-established values, which includes the demonstration of specific competencies. As social workers and their clients operate in many different kinds and levels of environments, ecological and systems concepts are useful metaphors for conceptualizing what social workers and clients must deal with. Direct social work practice is characterized by multiple roles; these roles are often performed at the same time and are carried out at several system levels depending on the concerns addressed. Knowledge and skills related to some of these roles are taught in segments of the curriculum that lie outside direct practice courses. To do justice in one volume to the knowledge and skills entailed in all these roles is impossible; consequently, we have limited our focus primarily to the roles involved in providing direct service.

Chapter 2 will delve more deeply into the theoretical concepts that ground our vision for direct practice.

Competency Notes

C1 Demonstrate Ethical and Professional Behavior

- Demonstrate professional demeanor in behavior, appearance, and oral, written, and electronic communication.

C2 Engage Anti-Racism, Diversity, Equity, and Inclusion in Practice

- Demonstrate anti-racist social work practice at the individual, family, group, organizational, community, research, and policy levels, informed by the theories and voices of those who have been marginalized.

- Demonstrate cultural humility applying critical reflexivity, self-awareness, and self-regulation to manage the influence of bias, power, privilege, and values in working with clients and constituencies acknowledging them as experts of their own lived experiences.

C3 Advance Human Rights, and Social, Racial, Economic, and Environmental Justice

- Advocate for human rights at the individual and system levels.

C4 Engage in Practice-Informed Research and Research-Informed Practice

- Apply research findings to inform and improve practice, policy, and programs.

C5 Engage in Policy Practice

- Assess how social welfare and economic policies affect the delivery of and access to social services.
- Apply critical thinking to analyze, formulate, and advocate for policies that advance human rights and social, racial, economic, and environmental justice.

C6 Engage with Individuals, Families, Groups, Organizations, and Communities

- Apply knowledge of human behavior and person-in-environment, and other multidisciplinary theoretical frameworks to engage with clients and constituencies.
- Use empathy, reflection, and interpersonal skills to engage diverse clients and constituencies effectively.

C7 Assess Individuals, Families, Groups, Organizations, and Communities

- Apply knowledge of human behavior and person-in-environment and other culturally responsive multidisciplinary theoretical frameworks when assessing clients and constituencies.
- Demonstrate respect for client self-determination during the assessment process collaborating with clients and constituencies in developing mutually agreed-on goals.

C8 Intervene with Individuals, Families, Groups, Organizations, and Communities

- Engage with clients and constituencies to critically choose and implement culturally responsive, evidenced-based interventions to achieve mutually agreed-on practice goals and enhance capacities of clients and constituencies.
- Incorporate culturally responsive methods to negotiate, mediate, and advocate, with and on behalf of clients and constituencies.

C9 Evaluate Practice with Individuals, Families, Groups, Organizations, and Communities

- Select and use appropriate methods for the evaluation of outcomes.
- Critically analyze outcomes and apply evaluation findings to improve practice effectiveness with individuals, families, groups, organizations, and communities.

Chapter

2

Orienting Frameworks for Social Work Practice

Chapter Overview

This chapter introduces our philosophy of social work practice. Practice philosophies define a set of beliefs and attitudes about how social workers approach clients, address client problems, and engage in the helping process. While you already possess a set of beliefs about how to help others, the practice philosophies outlined here will lead you to an increased self-awareness when implementing the techniques and interventions presented throughout this book.

As a result of reading this chapter, you will be able to:

- Describe the importance of a social work practice philosophy.

- Define and identify the assumptions of six orienting perspectives for social work practice: ecosystems perspective, strengths perspective, cultural humility, anti-oppressive practice, trauma-informed practice, and evidence-informed practice.

- Articulate a philosophy of practice based on three principles: people are embedded in transactions within larger systems, collaboration between the client and social worker is vital, and social worker self-awareness is paramount.

The EPAS Competencies in Chapter 2

- Competency 2: Engage Anti-Racism, Diversity, Equity, and Inclusion in Practice

- Competency 3: Advance Human Rights and Social, Economic and Environmental Justice

- Competency 4: Engage in Practice-Informed Research and Research-Informed Practice

Philosophies of Practice

All social workers have philosophies of practice. That is, we all carry a set of assumptions about people and their problems that inform our efforts to promote social and economic justice and to enhance client quality of life. Some of us enter the profession believing that emotional support, information, and advice are the critical ingredients in the helping process, whereas others believe that macro-level change is the proper focus of social work. Many in the general public assume that communities bear the major responsibility for problem solving, while others are convinced that we should provide help to individuals who are willing to help themselves. These assumptions are informed by culture, education, socialization, and keystone experiences from which we take life lessons, and each provides a rationale for different styles of helping.

One of the first steps you will take in the act of becoming a professional social worker is to examine how helping assumptions influence your interactions with clients. You will learn about your assumptions through your own reflection (e.g., journaling), by role modeling from senior colleagues, through supervision, and from client feedback. Understanding how your assumptions impact your work is vitally important. Social workers should use self-awareness to evaluate the quality of their relationships with clients and to make decisions about interventions to employ at any given moment. The helping assumptions that social workers adopt have a direct bearing on these relational processes.

The philosophy of practice undergirding this text is informed by six orienting perspectives. These orienting perspectives define how social workers should approach people and their problems, and consequently inform the approaches social workers adopt in their day-to-day work with clients. Our contention is that the practice philosophy derived from these perspectives will help your practice conform to the ideals and mission of the profession, to facilitate your engagement with clients, and to guide you to more effective helping strategies irrespective of the setting in which you work.

Orienting Perspectives

The orienting perspectives informing our practice philosophy are presented in Figure 2-1. The model presents six

Case Example 1

Isaiah is a 14-year-old African American adolescent boy who was court ordered to attend an anger management group. He was originally charged with assault of a police officer, a class C violent felony, but was eventually adjudicated delinquent for resisting arrest, a class A misdemeanor. The probation officer reported that Isaiah was at "medium risk" of rearrest based on the results of an actuarial risk assessment, with elevated risk scores in the areas of peer delinquency, anger control, and marijuana use. However, Isaiah has avoided gang affiliation, gets along well with several of his teachers, and his parents are supportive and have strong bonds to their community.

Isaiah disagrees with the court requirement for anger management classes. In fact, he had this to say at his intake interview with the social worker:

The idea of the group is bulls**t. I will attend the group so that people will leave me alone, but I don't need it. This all started one night at about 6 p.m. My friends and I were standing on the corner near my house just messing around.

The cops are always harassing people. Two cops came by and shined a light in our faces. One of my friends says something smart. I don't remember what he said, but the cops got out of the car with two dogs and demanded to see our ID and questioned why we were standing on the corner. I said, man, we don't have no ID. We are just talking. About this time, my 10-year-old brother comes running up to me, telling me that Mama said to come home and eat. One cop pushed my little brother against the wall and begins patting him down, putting his hands inside his pants and touching his private parts saying he is searching for drugs. My little brother is scared and crying, so scared that he wets himself, and the cops laughed and called him a name. I was scared too, but I got so mad that I pushed the cop. Then, the two cops pushed me to the ground, put handcuffs on me, and put me into the police car. They took me to juvie, and I could not get out until the next morning. The problem is the cops are always harassing us. I don't want to go to no group. I don't have an anger problem. I don't need a group.

Figure 2-1 Orienting Perspectives for Social Work Practice

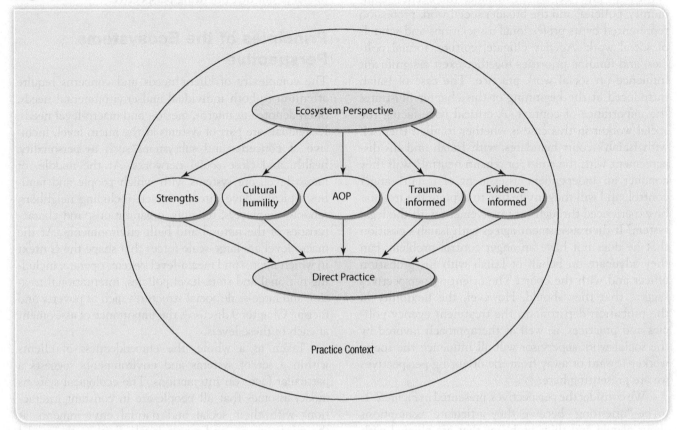

perspectives for practice that, together with Chapters 3 and 4, articulate our vision and values for direct social work practice.

Briefly, the model begins with the **ecological systems perspective** (Germain & Gitterman, 1996; Pincus & Minahan, 1973; Siporin, 1980). The ecological systems perspective, or ecosystems perspective, directs social workers to envision their clients within the context of their social and natural environments. Continuous interactions within client's social and natural environments shape and impact clients and their presenting problems. Social workers who adopt ecosystems thinking avoid reducing people and their problems to overly simplistic and reductionist explanations. All social work practice models, including the orienting perspectives to follow, assume the embeddedness of human beings within their social environments (e.g., family, work, school, peer group).

Next, the **strengths perspective** counters the tendency of helping professionals to pathologize people and their problems (Saleebey, 2013). Instead, social workers understand clients in terms of their competencies and assets and help clients leverage these strengths in order to effect change. **Cultural humility** counters a tendency of

helping systems to overvalue dominant cultural paradigms (Fisher-Borne et al., 2015). Instead, social workers strive to value, understand, and learn from the cultural lenses that shape their clients' values and preferences. **Antioppressive practice** counters a tendency for social workers to reenact oppression that is structured into social welfare systems and services (Morgaine & Capous-Desyllas, 2015). Instead, social workers conduct critical analyses of their own and their clients' positionality (i.e., location of individuals and groups in social hierarchies) and power and allow this analysis to shape social work activities and interventions in the direction of inclusion and empowerment. **Trauma-informed practice** counters a tendency to overlook common patterns created by traumatizing experiences, thereby retraumatizing clients (SAMHSA, 2014). Instead, social workers should assume that trauma is an inherent element of most client problems and strive to support client autonomy and safety in a trusting, collaborative relationship. Finally, **evidence-informed practice** provides strategies for integrating state-of-the-art science into decisions about interventions and programs (Gibbs, 2002). Evidence-informed practice is one element of a strategy to strengthen social work practice and to improve client outcomes.

Surrounding these orienting perspectives is the context of practice, which includes the agency, community, policies, and the broader social work profession represented by its professional associations and schools of social work. Agency climate, culture, formal policies, and funding priorities together exert a significant influence on social work practice. The case of Isaiah introduced at the beginning of this chapter illustrates the importance of context. A critical issue facing the social worker in this case is whether to align themselves with Isaiah's court mandates, with Isaiah and his disagreement with the court, or remain neutral? Will they conduct an independent assessment of Isaiah's anger control, and will they invite him to explore the traumas he experienced through his involvement with the legal system? If their assessment agrees with Isaiah's position that he does not have an anger control problem, can they advocate on behalf of Isaiah with his probation officer and with the court? The orienting perspectives suggest that they should. However, the flexibility of the probation department, the treatment agency policies and practices, as well as the approach favored by the social work supervisor will all influence the social worker toward or away from the orienting perspectives we are presenting here.

We consider the perspectives, presented in Figure 2-1, to be "orienting" because they articulate assumptions about people and their problems that are aligned with the social justice and welfare-enhancing missions of the profession and that are relevant to each phase of the helping process presented in this text (see Chapter 3). Next, we present each orienting perspective in greater detail, followed by a synthesis of these perspectives into a set of practice implications.

Ecosystems Perspective

Most of the clients you will see in your practice will have challenges and issues that cut across psychological and environmental needs. However, the temptation exists among social workers and all helping professionals to oversimplify our assessment of client challenges, especially focusing on internal psychological issues while giving limited attention to the social factors that contribute to the presenting problem(s). With the organization of the profession in the 1950s, social workers adopted a holistic point of view, where people and their problems were seen as embedded within interlocking social systems and within a complex social and physical ecology (Germain & Gitterman, 1996; Pincus & Minahan, 1973; Siporin, 1980).

Consequently, we have adopted the ecological systems model as our first orienting perspective.

Principles of the Ecosystems Perspective

The complexity of client needs and concerns require attention to both individual and environmental needs, often denoted as micro-, mezzo-, and macro-level needs. Individuals are part of systems at the micro level, inclusive of concerns and subsystems such as personality, health, and close social networks. At the middle, or mezzo level, are systems with which people and families typically have direct contact, including neighbors, schools, employers, religious organizations, and characteristics of the natural and built environments. At the macro level are large-scale forces that shape the context in which micro- and mezzo-level systems operate, including national and state-level policies, international treaties, and large-scale social structures such as poverty and racism. Chapter 9 discusses the importance of assessment at each of these levels.

Taken as a whole, the embeddedness of clients within a set of systems and environments suggests a particular focus on interactions. The ecological systems model assumes that all people are in constant interactions with their social and natural environments at the micro, mezzo, and macro levels. Further, the model assumes that the goodness-of-fit between individuals and their environments either supports their adaptive functioning or creates strain and exacerbates challenges (Ahmed et al., 2017).

The ecological systems model assumes that people are naturally inclined to achieve a maximum goodness-of-fit with their environment. This suggests, on the one hand, that most people spend considerable energy adapting themselves to the demands and expectations of their environments. They adopt preferences, behaviors, and attitudes to avoid conflict and maximize conformity to minimize strain and to pursue important goals, but the notion of interaction suggests that adaptation is not simply a one-way process. Indeed, people also effect change in their environments to strengthen their goodness-of-fit. This happens when people join social movements and, at a more micro-level, when people act intentionally to elicit favorable behaviors from others.

The ecological systems model makes two additional assumptions that are relevant to social workers across all settings and fields of practice (Mattaini, 2008). First, the principle of equifinality asserts that multiple pathways exist to achieve singular outcomes. For example, different childhood adversities (e.g., death of a parent, child abuse/neglect, parental divorce) can result in adolescent depression. Similarly, the principle of **multifinality** asserts that future outcomes are not determined given a particular starting point. Following the above example, although child abuse/neglect is a risk factor for later depression, not every child who is abused/neglected develops depression. Together, the principles of equifinality and multifinality have significant implications for social work practice. They support an individualized approach to practice that allows for creativity in the design of interventions and change efforts, recognizing that client preferences, values, and hope, are strong determinants of client efforts to enhance their goodness-of-fit.

The principles of equifinality and multifinality are supported by the burgeoning research on risk and resilience (Fraser, 2004). Risk factors are research-supported markers or predictors of negative developmental outcomes, while protective factors ameliorate the impact of risk factors and are associated with a decreased likelihood of developing negative outcomes. For example, Isaiah in our case example was assessed by his probation officer to associate with peers who were involved in delinquent behavior, including occasional marijuana use; two risk factors that predict future legal involvement. Nevertheless, not everyone who has risk factors such as these goes on to experience poor outcomes. Indeed, most adolescents like Isaiah "age out" of delinquent and rule-breaking behavior as they mature into adulthood. Moreover, people who have enough social support and who have adequate social problem-solving abilities are often shown to be resilient to poor outcomes even when facing adversity and risk. Thus, while it is crucial for social workers to understand research on the risk and protective factors that operate to increase the statistical likelihood of negative outcomes in their service population, social workers should practice with a sense of optimism and hope, recognizing that outcomes are not predetermined, and client systems have agency to influence their environments even as the social and natural environments may create strains that tax or challenge goodness-of-fit.

It is clear from the ecological systems perspective that the satisfaction of human needs and mastery of developmental tasks require adequate resources and positive transactions between people and their environments. For example, student learning is influenced by school quality, teacher competence, parental support, and self-efficacy, among other factors. Resource gaps and stressful transactions between individuals and environmental systems often conspire to block fulfillment of human needs and lead to impaired functioning.

Social work involves helping people meet their needs by linking them with essential resources, both in formal or institutional support systems and informally in the social networks that surround us all.

Critiques of the Ecosystems Perspective

While social workers have long embraced the ecological systems model, we recognize that the model is an incomplete guide for practice (Wakefield, 1996). The ecological systems model is descriptive rather than prescriptive. That is, it provides a set of metaphors to help us understand the interconnections among people and the various systems in which they interact, but the model does not provide a roadmap for practice. It does not illuminate the mechanisms through which people and their environments influence each other, nor about how to achieve an adequate goodness-of-fit. Additional theories are required to supplement the core assumptions of the ecological systems model. Furthermore, as a descriptive model or theory, the ecological systems model is inherently value neutral. The model does not suitably encompass many of the profession's values that social workers hold dear, including the value of fairness and of social justice.

Application of the Ecosystems Perspective

To adopt an ecological systems approach to social work practice, we recommend the following as a starting place:

1. Examine the embeddedness of your own life, recognizing how your own choices, opportunities, and aspirations are shaped by interactions in the micro-, mezzo-, and macro-levels of the ecosystems that create your context.

2. Be attentive to resource gaps and the ways in which additional resources might alter the goodness-of-fit of clients and their social and physical environments.

3. Look for opportunities to create change at multiple levels, recognizing that the adversity faced by clients need not translate into poor outcomes, and there are multiple pathways to achieve client goals.

Strengths Perspective

The context of social work often emphasizes the problems clients face and how adversities complicate problem solving.

C3

Despite ecological systems principles like multifinality and resilience, it can be easy for social workers to focus on client weaknesses and pathologies. However, an overemphasis on deficits and weaknesses can erode hope, an essential ingredient in the change process (See Collins, 2015 for a review). The strengths perspective emerged in social work as an alternative to the deficit-based approach (Kim & Whitehall Bolton, 2017). Rather than pathologizing individuals and using a deficits-based model (e.g., focusing on client weakness, system failures, and problems), the strengths perspective harnesses client strengths—resources, relationships, knowledge, life experience, and competencies—to promote growth and change. Further, the strengths perspective recognizes the importance of community support, encouraging all members in society to work toward self-determination and inclusion (Gray, 2011).

Principles of the Strengths Perspective

The strengths perspective assumes that all people have resources, relationships, knowledge, life experiences, and competencies that they can use to solve problems and to promote growth and change; it "… is a way of thinking … a distinctive lens for examining the world of practice" (Saleebey, 2002, p. 20). This perspective led to the development of specific intervention approaches that are decidedly strengths-based, for use with case management (Rapp, 1998; Rapp & Goscha, 2006), substance abuse (Siegal et al., 1995), domestic violence (Bell, 2003), elderly clients (Chapin & Cox, 2001), adolescent clients (Yip, 2006), and individual and family psychotherapy (de Shazer & Dolan, 2007; Freedman & Combs, 1996). Indeed, all interventions used within social work settings should take account of the resources, relationships, knowledge, life experiences, and competencies that clients bring to the problem-solving process. Thus, social workers should strive to incorporate the six principles of the strengths perspective shown in Figure 2-2 into all interactions with clients:

The strengths perspective is an orienting perspective because of its alignment with the deepest values of the profession, including social justice and the dignity and worth of all people. Social workers acting from a strengths perspective collaborate with clients to the greatest degree possible to support client self-determination in the resolution of their problems. Moreover, the strengths perspective guides social workers to mobilize client resources, relationships, knowledge,

Figure 2-2   Principles of the Strengths Perspective

1. Without exception, every individual, group, family, and community have resources, knowledge, life experiences, and competencies.

2. Trauma, abuse, illness, and adversity, while injurious, may provide sources of challenge and opportunity.

3. Assume that the upper limits of people's capacity to grow and change are unknown; take individual, group, and community aspirations seriously.

4. We best serve clients through collaboration.

5. Every environment is full of resources.

6. Care and caretaking are essential to human well-being.

(Saleebey, 2013, pp. 17–21)

life experiences, and competencies to achieve the goals that they value. Harnessing clients' strengths promotes their autonomy and independence and ensures successful functioning even after contact with the social worker has ended.

Critiques of the Strengths Perspective

At least three overarching critiques have been made of the strengths perspective. First, some view the strengths perspective as simply positive thinking, where client problems are either ignored or reframed into positive statements (Saleebey, 1996). Were this the case, we would not endorse the strengths perspective. Social workers should never invalidate or minimize the challenges and problems that clients report. To the contrary, the strengths perspective presents the hopeful view that all clients are capable of growth and change because all clients possess resources, relationships, knowledge, life experiences, and competencies that can be mobilized to resolve difficult problems. That is not to say that these sources of strength available to clients are always sufficient. The strengths perspective requires a realistic appraisal of problems and resource gaps as well as strengths.

Second, some assert that the strengths perspective is not a fully developed practice model with well-defined techniques and is not adequately supported by empirical evidence beyond descriptive case studies (Gray, 2011; Staudt et al., 2001). While several avowedly strengths-based models have been developed (e.g., brief solution focused therapy, narrative therapy, task

Case Example 2

The following dialogue occurred during the intake interview with Isaiah and the social worker from the anger management program. Notice how the social worker affirms strengths in Isaiah's social support network, demonstrating the application of the strengths perspective.

Social worker: It seems that you have a lot of respect for your mom.

Isaiah: What do you mean?

Social worker: You came here because she said you needed to come even though you wanted to be out with your friends.

Isaiah: Yeah, so?

Social worker: That says a lot to me about you. It says that you will listen to the people around you who care about you and your future.

Isaiah: I guess.

Social worker: It must have been important to your mom that you come to our appointment today.

Isaiah: She doesn't want me to get into any more trouble.

Social worker: What does she worry about?

Isaiah: That I won't be able to go to college.

Social worker: So, she wants you to go to college.

Isaiah: Yes. It's really important to her.

Social worker: Who else thinks about you and your future like that?

centered social work), we take the position that the strengths perspective is an orienting perspective that transcends all social work models of practice. The strengths perspective frames how social workers engage clients in a problem-solving process, whatever specific strategies are chosen.

Third, it has been argued that the strengths perspective fosters an individualistic approach to social work practice, precluding the structural analysis that points to macro-level forces that promote inequality, like racism, sexism, and classism (Gray, 2011; Smith, 2017). On the one hand, we agree with this critique. The strengths perspective is usually applied in direct practice settings with individuals, couples, or families or in community practice settings such as in community development organizations and advocacy agencies (Kretzmann & McKnight, 1993). Moreover, as with all orienting perspectives, we understand that none alone encompasses all aspects of a social work approach to practice. That the strengths perspective may not contribute to a structural analysis does not necessarily invalidate the utility of the strengths perspective for social work practice. On the other hand, the strengths perspective does not ignore the impact of discrimination and prejudice. Rather, it helps social workers and clients identify the ways in which client resources can be harnessed to counter the deficit-saturated labels and stigma that usually accompany macro-level oppression. Seen in this way, the strengths perspective is one element of resistance to oppression.

Application of the Strengths Perspective

The strengths perspective contributes to an empowering and liberating style of social work practice. Clients will benefit from a realistic appraisal of how their strengths (e.g., resources, relationships, knowledge, lived experience, competencies, and environments) can be activated to promote growth and change. This is not automatic, however. Many of the systems in which social workers encounter clients emphasize pathology, deficit, weaknesses, failures, and mistakes, both in their eligibility criteria as well as in their outlook toward clients. Therefore, we recommend the following to begin incorporating the strengths perspective in your work with clients:

1. To the greatest extent possible, focus your efforts with clients on goals that they defined in a collaborative process with you, supporting client self-determination and the exercise of meaningful choice.

2. Conduct a routine assessment of both personal and environmental strengths with all your clients.

3. Work collaboratively with clients, ensuring that clients are made to feel that they are the experts in their own lives.

Cultural Humility

Throughout your career, you will spend a considerable amount of time in organizations that work in cross-cultural contexts

C2

with populations that are different from you racially, culturally, and socioeconomically. Moreover, the assumptions that most social work agencies and service systems hold about people, their problems, and the helping process are rooted in the Western scientific tradition that reflects middle class white community standards for decorum and behavior that do not always match the standards and experiences of the populations they intend to serve. Clients who identify with nondominant cultural groups often report feeling marginalized and invalidated by social workers and service systems that lack an appreciation for diverse cultural points of view. While some assert that matching social workers to clients based on shared cultural backgrounds is the preferred solution to most cross-cultural challenges, this is neither always possible, equitable, nor effective (Cabral & Smith, 2011). Rather, research shows that social workers who convey self-awareness, humility, and comfort in cross-cultural encounters are more likely to facilitate client growth and empowerment (Hook et al., 2017).

Principles of Cultural Humility

Cultural humility is an orienting perspective that facilitates cross-cultural social work practice (Fisher-Borne et al., 2015). Social workers who practice cultural humility accept cultural differences and affirm the value and importance of all cultures. They exhibit curiosity about cultural differences and reflect deeply about how their own cultural orientation informs their helping efforts. Cultural humility also draws attention to the power differences that are inherent in the social worker–client relationship. Social workers who practice from within this framework seek to hold themselves and their service system accountable for the ways that clients can be oppressed or marginalized during the helping process.

Wherever possible, social workers mitigate power imbalances by exploring and employing helping strategies that are congruent with clients' cultural frameworks. For example, cultural norms may favor the use of herbal remedies, shaman or folk healers, and religious health rituals, which may be used concurrently with interventions and treatments obtained through the formal service systems that dominate the U.S. landscape (Lopez, 2005; Rybak & Decker-Fitts, 2009; Woodward et al., 2009). Finally, the practice of cultural humility orients social workers to be observant for opportunities to talk with clients directly about how cultural differences, racism, sexism, xenophobia, classism, ableism, and other discriminatory systems affect clients and the helping process. Rather than avoid uncomfortable discussions about differences, social

workers who embrace cultural humility seek them out (Owen et al.,2016).

While cultural humility may appear commonsensical to social workers who hold egalitarian values, expressing cultural humility is more difficult than it sounds. Our culturally informed worldview assumptions are usually latent or implicit and hidden from conscious awareness. It takes effort for social workers to explore their worldviews about problems, helping, and inequality. Sometimes, the process of self-exploration reveals hidden biases in social workers that conflict with other cherished values (Staats et al., 2016). These can be painful experiences that reveal the need for even deeper exploration and call on social workers to give up privileges or power. Furthermore, it takes conscious effort and skill to explore worldviews directly with clients. For some, these are uncomfortable conversations. However, data increasingly shows that clients appreciate opportunities to discuss the oppressions that they experience related to the problems they seek to resolve in relationship with social workers. Thus, social workers need to develop comfort for conversations with clients about cultural differences.

Critiques of Cultural Humility

Cultural humility has its roots in critiques of cultural competence. Cultural competence was introduced into social work in the 1980s (Danso, 2018; Sue et al., 2016). It has evolved to encompass three aspects: self-awareness, knowledge about others' culture, and communication and intervention strategies that are congruent with a cross-cultural interaction. Cultural humility and cultural competence share much in common. Both assert that self-awareness is the foundation of effective cross-cultural encounters. Both value knowledge and appreciation of the cultural worldviews of clients, and both have distinct practice implications for how social workers engage with clients across cultural differences.

Nevertheless, cultural humility and cultural competence distinguish themselves one from another in several ways. For example, whereas the goal of cultural competence is skillful use of culturally congruent communication and engagement strategies, the goal of cultural humility is humility regarding one's own worldview, understanding the other's worldview, and empowerment of the other to express their worldview in the helping context. Whereas, both approaches value cultural knowledge, cultural competence leads social workers toward a search of ever-increasing expertise in cultures other than their own, while cultural humility leads social workers to treat clients as the preeminent experts in their own cultures and worldviews.

Application of Cultural Humility

Despite the critiques, we take the position that cultural humility and cultural competence are complementary in practice and together yield a more comprehensive direction for engaging clients across culture. We choose to adopt "cultural humility" to title this section because it conveys the collaborative, client-centered spirit that characterizes all aspects of our philosophy of practice. Toward this end, we recommend the following to get started:

1. Explore your own identities and cultural worldviews and learn how these are expressed in daily interactions with colleagues and clients.

2. Actively affirm the cultural heritage and experiences that clients value and ensure that your helping efforts are in alignment with their worldviews to the greatest extent possible.

3. Increase your comfort in conversations about cultural differences, discrimination, and prejudice by seeking opportunities to engage in challenging dialogues and conversations with people who represent diverse cultural worldviews.

4. Become observant to occasions where the mechanisms of racism and white supremacy, sexism, classism, xenophobia, ableism, and homophobia are experienced by clients during the helping process.

Anti-Oppressive Social Work

Social workers throughout the world serve in contexts in which inequality and disparities are rooted in socially constructed and marginalized identities. Examples include white supremacy and racism, patriarchy and sexism, heteronormativity and homophobia, xenophobia, classism, ableism, and religious intolerance, among others. In the case example of Isaiah accompanying this chapter, the problems encountered by Isaiah have strong roots in persistent disproportionate minority contact in the criminal justice system and a history of conflict between law enforcement and members of minority communities (Kahn & Martin, 2016). Oppressive ideologies, or systems of oppression, contribute to the difficulties and challenges that bring clients into contact with social work helping systems.

Principles of Anti-Oppressive Social Work

The anti-oppressive practice model (AOP) links the social justice mission of the profession with direct practice with individuals, families, and small groups (Morgaine & Capous-Desyllas, 2015). The goal of AOP is to foster the full participation of clients in society irrespective of oppressive ideologies that justify exclusion, discrimination, and violence. In doing so, AOP contributes to macro-level changes by incrementally replacing oppressive ideologies with alternatives based on equality and acceptance.

Figure 2-3 illustrates the central tenets of the AOP model. AOP starts with the recognition of our profession's social justice ideals and the mechanisms of social injustice that operate in society. In regard to social justice, social workers are especially attentive to distributive justice, which is the position that the resources and benefits of society should be allocated fairly among its members according to a balance of need and effort (Barsky, 2019), and procedural justice, which

Figure 2-3 Components of Anti-Oppressive Social Work Practice

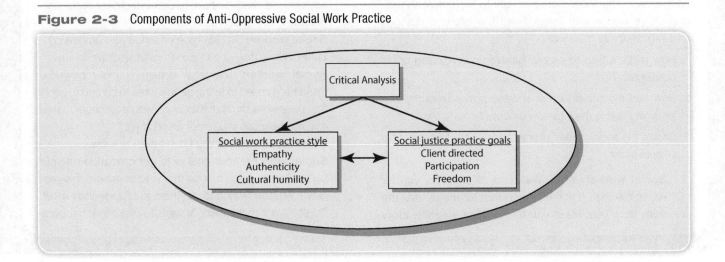

is the position that social processes, particularly the exercise of authority over others, should be fair rather than capricious or ad-hoc (Tyler, 2006), but it is not enough for social workers to believe in fairness. They also need to understand how oppressive hierarchies have been created and sustained and how the insidious effects of oppressive hierarchies may manifest in the lives of their clients. Social workers do this by educating themselves about the history of oppression and intergroup relations that is related to the experience of their clients and to see the manifestations of that history in client problems and strengths.

Motivated by our aspirations toward social justice and informed by our knowledge about mechanisms of injustice, AOP social workers utilize the discipline of **critical analysis** to understand how the power and positionality of our clients intersects with the power and positionality of social welfare helping systems, especially with the power and positionality of the social worker (Dominelli, 2018; Mattsson, 2014). **Power and positionality** refer to the relative location of individuals and groups in social hierarchies. Often, the understanding of ones' power and positionality is made more complex and rich by understanding the intersectionality of people's identity and experience, that people do not usually experience social life through the lens of a single social identity but rather through multiple social identities simultaneously (e.g., race, gender identity, socioeconomic status), creating a highly nuanced and individualized experience of power, privilege, and oppression.

This analysis informs how social workers implement helping efforts in practice, resulting in a *style* of social work directed toward goals and objectives that are motivated by a concern for social justice. Here, we define "style" to mean a loose constellation of social work behaviors and attributes that distinguish AOP practice from other traditional models of social work practice. For example, traditional social work practice fails to systematically address power and positionality in the social work relationship and has been subjected to criticisms of paternalism, of acting as though the social worker "knows best" (Reamer, 2013). Correcting this, AOP social workers talk about power and positionality with their clients, helping to create a mutual definition

Case Example 3

After assessing Isaiah's history of anger management and emotion regulation, the social worker concluded that Isaiah's angry outburst with the arresting police officer was an isolated occurrence provoked by the behavior of the police officers. While the anger management group offered by the program can teach useful skills in self-control, the social worker disagrees with probation about the urgency of an anger management program for Isaiah based on their assessment. The social worker sought to implement an anti-oppressive stance with Isaiah. Read the following dialogue and explore these questions:

1. How might it help to assess Isaiah's understanding of his positionality?

2. How can the social worker address power hierarchy and inequality during the interview process?

3. Should the social worker directly address the fairness of his original arrest?

Social worker: Wow. Well, first of all, thank you for telling me that. It is really important for me to hear the truth from you. Have you told anyone else this story about how the cops treated you and your brother that day?

Isaiah: My mom.

Social worker: And she said you had to come here today, and you still came. I imagine that you are feeling pretty powerless right now.

Isaiah: What?

Social worker: I mean, that you feel like you don't have any choices, that you have to do what other people say.

Isaiah: That's pretty much it.

Social worker: Do kids have influence with probation?

Isaiah: Naw, they don't listen to what we have to say.

Social worker: The legal system is really powerful. Probation is used to telling people what to do and expects that people will do what they say. Being a teenager makes it worse because you're not an adult yet.

Isaiah: Tell me something I don't already know.

Social worker: Your goal is to get probation off your back. One way you can do that is to complete this program. Another way is to get them to change their mind. Do you want to think about ways to make that happen?

of the macro-level forces (e.g., culture, policies, political climate) that affect the presenting problem and affect the client's experience of the helping process. AOP social workers use power explicitly and judiciously, exercising maximum restraint to elevate the power and autonomy of their clients, sharing power and decision-making whenever possible, and using their own power to advocate in those instances when formal power designated to the social worker provides clients with access to resources and influence that are otherwise closed to them.

AOP is a way of *doing social justice* that encompasses all aspects of social work practice (Finn, 2016). It is not a technique that is done to clients. Rather, it is an expression of the personal attributes and values of a social worker who is committed to the ideals of the profession. Therefore, AOP is intensely personal. AOP social workers strive to understand how systems of inequality and oppression are expressed in their own relationships with clients. As such, AOP is brave practice and sometimes painful practice, as social workers confront the realities of their own positionality.

Critiques of Anti-Oppressive Social Work

As a model for practice, AOP enjoys conceptual overlap with several other constructs and models associated with cross-cultural practice. AOP's focus on power and positionality is similar to the recognition of power differences and emphasis on accountability previously discussed in our treatment of cultural humility (Danso, 2018). Moreover, the "style" of practice associated with AOP in some ways encompasses a culturally humble approach. We have chosen to retain each as a distinct orienting perspective because both offer unique contributions to social work practice. While cultural humility focuses intently on the relational aspects of social work practice, AOP emphasizes the critical analysis of positionality, history, and the need for an explicitly liberatory objective for practice.

AOP also shares conceptual overlap with antiracist practice. Both emphasize a recognition of systems of oppression as the entry point for engaging clients in direct practice, and both emphasize the goals of client participation in decision-making and their liberation. Texts that emphasize AOP freely discuss racism among their focal concerns, and AOP and antiracism are often treated together without strong distinctions (Ramsundarsingh & Shier, 2017). On the other hand, advocates of an explicitly antiracist practice model point out that replacing racism with a more general emphasis on oppression makes it easier to default to a focus on

multiculturalism to avoid the critical analysis our definition of AOP calls for (Ladhani & Sitter, 2020). We agree with the spirit of this critique and caution you to remember that the critical analysis of positionality is central to client empowerment.

Application of Anti-Oppressive Social Work

A social worker's decision to adopt an AOP style depends on more than simply their personal convictions. It also depends on the values, mandates, and support embedded in the agencies that employ social workers. The ideals of AOP can conflict with the very same organizations tasked with serving and supporting vulnerable client populations. This conflict may be most acute for public social service agencies with social control mandates such as child welfare and criminal/juvenile justice and also large-scale public systems such as mental health and education. In these systems, the adoption of AOP may lead to a hybrid model where externally imposed practice mandates constrain social workers in their orientation to practice. Nevertheless, we believe that an AOP style of practice holds promise to strengthen social work in even those settings (Curry-Stevens & Nissen, 2011). Toward that end, we recommend the following steps to develop yourself as an AOP social worker:

1. Begin with systems of support. Locate colleagues and supervisors who support the ideals of AOP to serve as sources of advice, support, and accountability. Act to facilitate the development of policies of practice supportive of AOP.

2. Deepen your knowledge base about systems of oppression and learn about the specific history of intergroup relations that represent your client populations.

3. Conduct a critical analysis of your own positionality and that of your agency.

4. Have conversations about positionality and power with your clients. In these conversations, you should adopt an AOP style as described previously.

5. Finally, negotiate intervention goals with clients that are framed by social justice themes and perspectives.

Trauma-Informed Social Work

Trauma exposure is ubiquitous across all service systems. Ample research indicates that exposure to identifiable traumas can

C4

affect as many as 90% of clients served by social workers and other professionals (Ford & Blaustein, 2013; Ford et al., 2012; Hummer et al., 2010). Exposure to trauma can lead to multiple adverse outcomes, including poor mental health functioning (e.g., posttraumatic stress disorder [PTSD], depression, anxiety), difficulties with interpersonal relationships (e.g., social isolation, difficulty trusting others), substance use, physical (e.g., sleeplessness) and psychological (e.g., flashbacks) reactions, and other long-lasting effects.

Principles of Trauma-Informed Social Work

These insights have led to the emergence of trauma-informed practice. Trauma-informed practice is a strengths-based approach which guides social workers in how to work with individuals who have histories of trauma. It is a relational approach to social work that promotes a feeling of safety, collaboration, and empowerment and creates opportunities for individuals to rebuild, heal, and restore a sense of control and well-being (Substance Abuse and Mental Health Services Administration, 2014). Failure to adopt trauma-informed practices increases the likelihood that clients may suffer heightened distress associated with retraumatization, may not benefit from your work together, and may disengage from services (Harris & Fallot, 2001).

In a trauma-informed approach, the primary determinant of whether an experience is traumatic is based on the perspective of the people who are impacted. Isaiah, for example, described his encounter with law enforcement as traumatic in the case example. Moreover, there is often historical trauma in communities of color related to our country's history of slavery, ongoing racism and discrimination, and how the police treat people of color (Crosby, 2016). Therefore, our framework necessarily takes an expansive definition of trauma. Trauma can be an isolated event or an ongoing experience that can be physically and/or emotionally harmful or life threatening and causes individuals to feel distress, fear, helplessness, and hopelessness (SAMHSA, 2014). Common traumas include experiencing or witnessing physical or sexual assault; death of a loved one due to violence/accident/disaster; natural disaster (e.g., flood, hurricane), accident or fire; or repeated experiences of racism/discrimination. It includes exposure to events that are usually understood to present direct threats to people's physical and emotional integrity (e.g., combat, sexual and physical assault, serious accidents) and the experiences of terror and exclusion that accumulates for

members of a community over generations (e.g., hate crimes, genocide).

Figure 2-4 presents the principles of trauma-informed services for the fields of mental health and substance abuse treatment. There is substantial overlap between our presentation of a trauma-informed social work with Substance Abuse and Mental Health Services Administration (SAMHSA) principles, and indeed, our thinking has drawn heavily on these SAMHSA models. The adoption of a trauma-informed perspective requires that social workers engage deeply with their own sense of self-awareness, asking themselves how their approach to clients promotes a sense of safety and trustworthiness, whether their approach embeds clients more deeply with supportive communities or isolates them, and whether their approach is collaborative and maximizes the clients' autonomy.

Critiques of Trauma-Informed Social Work

Two concerns have been raised about the trauma-informed practice. First, some observers have pointed out that the principles of trauma-informed practice are not specific to service users who have been exposed to trauma, but, in fact, are principles of good practice for all clients (Berliner & Kolko, 2016; Mersky et al., 2019). That is, all social work services should be delivered in a manner that promotes a sense of safety, trust, and autonomy, for example. Second, notwithstanding systemwide evaluations that show how sustained initiatives can strengthen the trauma-awareness and trauma-informed practices among frontline workers (Connell et al., 2019), the imprecise definition of trauma-informed social work makes it difficult to evaluate in practice (Hanson & Lang, 2016). It is not clear that trauma-informed initiatives at either the system level nor the individual level of practice makes

---

Figure 2-4 SAMSHA Principles for Trauma Informed Practice

1. Safety
2. Trustworthiness
3. Peer support
4. Collaboration and mutuality
5. Empowerment, voice, or choice
6. Culture, history, gender

Source: Substance Abuse and Mental Health Services Administration. *SAMHSA's Concept of Trauma and Guidance for a Trauma-Informed Approach.* HHS Publication No. (SMA) 14-4884. Rockville, MD: Substance Abuse and Mental Health Services Administration, 2014.

a difference in client outcomes over and above those demonstrated in routine practice. Acknowledging these critiques, we nevertheless consider trauma-informed social work to be an orienting framework. The widespread exposure of social work clients to trauma makes it incumbent on all social workers to be sensitive and responsive to the presence and effects of trauma in their clients.

Application of Trauma-Informed Social Work

Trauma-informed social work can be challenging. The triggers of trauma reactions, or the conscious and unconscious reminders of prior trauma, are unavoidable, often unpredictable, and can be provoked by treatment systems that create toxic or stressful environments that constrain client control or choice or that invalidate client experiences, yet some social service systems like child welfare, mental health, and criminal or juvenile justice systems unavoidably constrain client choice and place significant strain on their clients. For these clients, too, receipt of trauma-informed practices is not a privilege for deserving clients but a prerequisite of effective social work practice for all.

For social workers who strive to adopt a trauma-informed perspective into their practice, we recommend the following:

1. Assess trauma as a part of routine practice, privileging client definitions of what experiences have been treated as traumatic.

2. Adopt a collaborative posture that supports client autonomy and choice wherever possible.

3. Strive to be trustworthy and transparent in your relationships with clients.

4. Create a sense of comfort, security, and safety in your agency.

5. Be aware of how your own experiences of trauma can be triggered in unexpected ways during your work with clients.

Evidence-Informed Social Work Practice

Social workers have a long history of integrating science into practice, stretching back to the founding of the profession in the settlement house movement. In social work's early history, social workers in settlement houses used community surveys to design programs and influence policy.

C4

Later, social workers adopted Freudian psychology, then empirical program evaluation, and finally the practitioner scientist model, all to bridge what became known as the practice-research gap (e.g., actions or practices supported by researcher are not necessarily easily integrated into social work practice). Despite these efforts, the explicit use of research by social workers has been a constant challenge because research is difficult to access, evaluate, and synthesize into practice. Responding to these challenges, evidence-informed social work practice has emerged in contemporary social work as a means of integrating research into practice, with the promise of improved client outcomes.

Evidence-informed social work practice is a deliberate effort to learn and integrate research into practice. Said most simply, evidence-informed social work practice enables social workers and their clients to be informed consumers of research. Social workers who adopt an evidence-informed approach discuss research findings with their clients to facilitate informed decision-making. Evidence-informed practice is an orienting perspective in part because it has been adopted as an ethical principle for the profession by the National Association of Social Workers (see Ethical Principal 5.02). Moreover, evidence-informed social work practice promises the benefit of effective outcomes to social workers and their clients and steers social workers away from ineffective practices.

Principles of Evidence-Informed Social Work

There are two central components of evidence-informed social work practice: evidence-informed decision-making and evidence-based practices. Evidence-informed decision-making is a strategy for integrating research evidence into practice and policy decisions. The goal of evidence-informed decision-making is to locate the best evidence available to answer important questions that arise from practice. "Evidence" in this context can mean the findings of research into the risk and protective factors associated with a presenting problem, empirically supported theory, and findings from qualitative studies and experimental research (Fraser, 2003). Importantly, evidence-informed decisions do not displace clients in the decision-making process. Rather, research evidence is considered by clients and social workers along with the practical experiences of social workers and the values and preferences held by clients. Strategies for quickly and efficiently searching for research evidence have been developed for social workers (Gibbs, 2002). Usually, this process entails a series of steps including: (1) formulating a specific question based on an important practice challenge, (2) conducting a search of the scientific literature to identify research studies that relate to the question (e.g., using Google Scholar or other search engines), (3) evaluating the relevance and quality of selected studies, (4) synthesizing study findings, and (5) formulating recommendations.

The process of evidence-informed decision-making often leads to the adoption of specific evidence-based practices (EBPs). EBPs are named interventions that have been tested in experimental research and found to consistently improve client outcomes (Drake et al., 2001). Over time, the fields of social work, psychology, psychiatry, and public health have developed such interventions as cognitive behavioral therapy (CBT) to treat affective disorders (Carpenter et al., 2018), trauma-focused CBT (TF-CBT) and eye movement desensitization and reprocessing (EMDR) to treat trauma (Cuijpers et al., 2018; Lewey et al., 2018), assertive community treatment (ACT) to support adults in the community with severe mental illnesses (DeLuca et al., 2018), and task-centered casework for a variety of case management applications (Reid, 1997). The development of evidence-informed practices entails a rigorous process of intervention development, pilot testing, and evaluation, often using random clinical trials (Fraser, 2003). Most EBPs have been developed to address a specific problem and have detailed manuals describing the underlying theory and intervention strategies to be employed. Specialized training for social workers is often necessary, which ensures greater client effectiveness and creates opportunities for professional advancement.

Critiques of Evidence-Informed Social Work

Despite the utility of evidence-informed practice, thoughtful observers have raised several concerns. First, some argue that the process of evidence-informed decision-making and the use of evidence-based practices take power and control from clients and social workers and places it in the hands of a distant researcher. Each of the orienting perspectives presented in this chapter rest on the strong assumption of collaboration and client control, of recognizing the expertise that clients bring to their encounters with social workers. Evidence-informed social work rests on the same foundation. Nearly all EBPs for social work assume a collaborative relationship between the social worker and the client. Neither evidence-based practices nor evidence-informed decision-making

necessarily diminish the power of clients. Instead, providing clients with relevant research information, including a discussion of its weaknesses and limitations, arms clients with information to enable greater choice, not less.

A second critique of evidence-informed social work practice concerns the generalizability of EBPs for diverse populations. Most EBPs have been developed and evaluated from a Western worldview, limiting their ecological validity for non-Western clients and populations. Ecological validity refers to the extent to which an intervention reflects clients' customs, values, and language and the degree to which the structure of an intervention matches clients' culturally informed needs and preferences, such as setting characteristics, racial/cultural match of social worker with client (Bernal et al., 1995; Soto et al., 2018). When social workers implement EBPs, it is crucial that they strengthen the ecological validity of the intervention by adapting the intervention's structure and characteristics to meet the cultural needs of the client (Barrio & Yamada, 2010). This entails a detailed analysis of the intervention's underlying theory of change, as well as its content, language, and methods. While undertaking the adaptation process, social workers should collaborate with key stakeholders and representatives of the target group (Cabassa & Baumann, 2013) and evaluate the acceptability and effectiveness of the adapted intervention in their practice (Fraser, 2003).

Third, research evidence for social work practice is derived from the Western scientific tradition that can conflict with indigenous knowledge and non-Western worldviews about problems and helping. Evidence-informed social work practice may lead to worldview conflicts when social workers fail to appreciate and understand client worldviews about problems and helping. The field of medical anthropology offers advice for learning about how indigenous or local knowledge about problems and helping shapes client worldviews. Social workers who adopt an evidence-informed practice model should routinely ask clients about their cultural beliefs related to the formation of problems and culturally sanctioned approaches for resolving problems (Kleinman & Benson, 2006). Often, the solution to worldview differences adopted by clients and social workers is to integrate complementary practices from both knowledge domains, as when social workers employ traditional healing methods (e.g., smudging, medicine wheel) alongside Western counseling practices in services with clients who identify with aboriginal peoples and nations (Oulanova & Moodley, 2017).

Application of Evidence-Informed Social Work

The adoption of an evidence-informed social work approach requires significant discipline on the part of social workers and support within their agencies. As asserted throughout this chapter, social workers need to exercise self-awareness about when and how their practice is informed by research evidence, practice wisdom, or unsupported opinion. Social workers have the responsibility to search for evidence and for training that will support an evidence-informed approach. Moreover, social workers should have explicit discussions with clients about the strengths and limitations of research evidence to foster collaborative relationships and support client decision-making to the greatest extent possible. Finally, most social workers should not take on the challenge of evidence-informed practice by themselves. This effort is most effective when it is supported by supervision, agency policy, and agency culture. The following will help you adopt an evidence-informed approach to practice:

1. Adopt an evidence-informed, critical mindset about practice. Develop the habit of asking critical questions that can be answered with data. For example, "What evidence-based practice is best suited to my client's presenting problem?"

2. Maintain flexibility in the adoption of evidence-based practices, taking care to match your intervention approaches with client preferences and with client presenting problems throughout the course of your work.

3. Seek specialized training and supervision in evidence-based practice models that are relevant to the context of your practice.

4. Collaborate with multiple stakeholders on the selection and translation of evidence-based practices for practice with diverse communities.

Principles for Practice

The philosophy of practice we endorse includes assumptions about people and the helping process derived from the six orienting perspectives. The considerable overlap among the perspectives leads us to highlight the following cross-cutting themes in social work's assumptions about people and the helping process.

First, consistent with the view of the ecological systems perspective, our philosophy of direct practice recognizes that people are embedded in interactions with their social and physical environments. The orienting perspectives share the assumption that people have strengths, defined as resources, relationships, knowledge, life experience, and competencies, that are used to facilitate the problem-solving process, as well as resource deficits that contribute to client problems. Among people's strengths are culturally informed worldviews that shape definitions about problems and strategies for overcoming them. Moreover, the problems and challenges people face are frequently influenced by a history of trauma, including the experiences of racism, sexism, xenophobia, and heterosexism, among other systems of oppression.

Second, the orienting perspectives all share the assumption of collaborative problem solving. Only through collaboration can social workers engage in a socially just practice that has as its goal more inclusive communities and a more just allocation of resources. Collaboration includes respect for client strengths, worldviews, self-determination, and autonomy. It means fairly representing expert social work knowledge, including scientific evidence, as a resource for problem solving, while keeping client decision-making prerogatives front and center in the helping relationship. Further, collaborative relationships built on trust and respect guard against the deleterious impact of trauma and retraumatization, as well as the effect of oppression and bias, that are present in many helping systems.

Third, the orienting perspectives all point to self-awareness as a cornerstone of effective, ethical practice. Self-awareness about the themes presented in these orienting perspectives will lead you to recognize how your role in the helping process can empower or disempower clients. For example, being mindful about the assumptions you make about people and their problems can help you see when you are focused too intently on perceived or assumed client deficits and pathology, blaming clients rather than a lack of resources or opportunities, ignoring the role of discrimination and marginalization based on group identity characteristics, and ignoring the role of trauma in the lives of clients. On the other hand, self-awareness can help you be deliberate in the use of skills and strategies presented in this text that affirm clients and fosters a sense of hope for change.

Summary

In this chapter, we have described six orienting perspectives for social work practice. These perspectives inform a comprehensive philosophy of practice that can promote social development, empower and liberate people, and enhance their well-being. Our philosophy, derived from multiple perspectives for practice, explains how a recognition of client embeddedness, collaboration, and self-awareness are critical components for social work practice. While it can appear that one or more of these perspectives may not always be relevant for specific situations or agency contexts, we believe that the utility of each will be demonstrated with practice and reflection within all practice settings and situations.

Competency Notes

C2   Engage Anti-Racism, Diversity, Equity, and Inclusion in Practice

- Demonstrate anti-racist social work practice at the individual, family, group, organizational, community, research, and policy levels, informed by the theories and voices of those who have been marginalized.
- Demonstrate cultural humility applying critical reflexivity, self-awareness, and self-regulation to manage the influence of bias, power, privilege, and values in working with clients and constituencies acknowledging them as experts of their own lived experiences.

C3   Advance Human Rights and Social, Economic, and Environmental Justice

- Advocate for human rights at the individual and system levels.

C4   Engage in Practice-Informed Research and Research-Informed Practice

- Apply research findings to inform and improve practice, policy, and programs.
- Identify strategies for use of quantitative and qualitative methods of research to advance the purposes of social work.

Overview of the Helping Process

Chapter Overview

This chapter provides an overview of the three phases of the helping process: (1) exploration, (2) implementation, and (3) termination. The helping process focuses on problem solving with social work clients in a variety of settings. Hence, the process is presented within the larger systems context as well as the themes of embeddedness, collaboration, and self-awareness presented in Chapter 2. This chapter begins to integrate orienting perspectives introduced in the second chapter. We will also present an overview of the structure and elements of client-centered interviews.

At the completion of your work on this chapter, you will be able to:

- Identify steps in the helping process from exploration through implementation and termination.

- Plan the structure and environment for effective, client-centered interviews.

The EPAS Competencies in Chapter 3

This chapter will give you the information needed to meet the following practice competencies:

- Competency 1: Demonstrate Ethical and Professional Behavior

- Competency 2: Engage Antiracism, Diversity, Equity, and Inclusion in Practice

- Competency 6: Engage with Individuals, Families, Groups, Organizations, and Communities

- Competency 7: Assess Individuals, Families, Groups, Organizations, and Communities

- Competency 8: Intervene with Individuals, Families, Groups, Organizations, and Communities

- Competency 9: Evaluate Practice with Individuals, Families, Groups, Organizations, and Communities

Whether motivated by internal or external forces, people seek social work services because current solutions are not working in their lives. How social services respond to people differs in the extent to which those services are problem versus goal focused. We take the position that social workers must respond to the problems compelling people to seek help or accept referral for services as well as to work creatively with them toward goal focused solutions that *improve* upon the initial problematic situation (McMillen et al., 2004). Whatever their approach to assisting clients, most direct social workers employ a process aimed at reducing client concerns. Next, the social worker and client jointly identify potential approaches to reduce those concerns and make decisions about which courses of action to pursue.

The first portion of this chapter provides an overview of the helping process and its three distinct phases. Subsequent parts of the book are organized to correspond to these phases and address them in greater depth. The latter part of this chapter focuses on the structure and processes involved in interviewing—a critical aspect of dealing with clients. Later chapters deal with the structure, processes, and skills involved in modifying the processes of families and groups.

The Helping Process

The helping process consists of three major phases (see Figure 3-1):

- Phase I: Exploration, engagement, assessment, and planning
- Phase II: Implementation and goal attainment
- Phase III: Evaluation and termination

Each of these phases has distinct objectives, and the helping process generally proceeds successively through them. The three phases, however, are not sharply demarcated by the activities and skills employed. Indeed, the techniques used in the three phases differ in terms of their frequency and intensity. For example, the processes of exploration and assessment are central during Phase I, but these techniques are used to a lesser degree during subsequent phases of the helping process. The phases, as we describe them, are consistent with the planned change process reflected in the Council on Social Work Education (CSWE) Educational Policy and Accreditation Standards (EPAS) including engagement, assessment, intervention,

Figure 3-1 Phases of the Helping Process and Constituent Activities and Processes

Phase I: Exploration, Engagement, Assessment, and Planning	Phase II: Implementation and Goal Attainment	Phase III: Evaluation and Termination
1. Exploring clients' problems by eliciting comprehensive data about the person(s), the problem, and environmental factors, including forces influencing the referral for contact.	1. Prioritize goals into general and specific tasks.	1. Assessing when client goals have been satisfactorily attained.
2. Establishing rapport and enhancing motivation.	2. Select and implement interventions influenced by best available evidence.	2. Helping the client develop strategies that maintain change and continue growth following the termination.
3. Formulating a multidimensional assessment of the problem, identifying systems that play a significant role in the difficulties, and identifying relevant resources that can be tapped or must be developed as strengths. This review should also include screens for trauma, cultural humility.	3. Plan task implementation, enhancing self-efficacy.	3. Successfully terminating the helping relationship.
4. Mutually negotiating goals to be accomplished in remedying or alleviating problems and formulating a contract.	4. Maintain focus within sessions.	
5. Making referrals.	5. Maintain continuity between sessions.	
	6. Monitor progress.	
	7. Identify and address barriers to change.	
	8. Employ appropriate self-disclosure and assertiveness to facilitate change.	

evaluation, and termination. The phases of assessment and evaluation are repeated throughout treatment, including plans for termination that are often formed at the beginning of service. Some forms of direct practice such as crisis intervention may proceed through all phases in a single session. In addition, a social worker may go back to previous phases during the helping process. For example, a social worker may reassess a problem or reevaluate an intervention and reestablish a contract during the helping process. Reengagement may occur as needed, or a social worker and client may stay in the engagement phase for an extended period before a thorough assessment can be made.

Physical Conditions

Before describing the steps in the initial phase of exploration, engagement, assessment, and planning, we will describe the physical conditions of contact between the social worker and client.

C6

Interviews sometimes occur in offices or other settings over which the social worker has some control. During the COVID-19 pandemic, many client interviews took place remotely through telephone or video conference. In such circumstances, the social worker must collaborate with clients in attempting to arrange for satisfactory interviewing circumstances. Interviews that take place in a client's home are subject to the client's preferences. The physical climate in which an interview is conducted partly determine how people feel about the interviews. That environment should be constructed to feel supportive and not intimidating to people. Indeed, the first conclusions clients draw about the values and competency of a setting are impacted by their first encounters with staff over the telephone or in person. If they are responded to promptly, courteously, and respectfully, this treatment may go a long way toward preparing for a successful interaction with the social worker. The following office or setting conditions are conducive to productive interviews:

1. Adequate ventilation and light.
2. Comfortable room temperature.
3. Ample space (to avoid a sense of being confined or crowded).
4. Attractive and clean furnishings and décor.
5. Chairs that adequately support the back.
6. Privacy appropriate to the cultural beliefs of the client.
7. Freedom from distraction.
8. Open space between clients.
9. Interior decorations that are sensitive to diverse client populations.
10. A door not fully closed if the client perceives danger from past trauma.

Remote interviews include arranging for adequate sound or visual contact. Clients may be multitasking with supervising a child's home education and monitoring smaller children. Privacy is important because people are likely to be guarded in revealing personal information and expressing feelings if other people can see or hear them. Likewise, interviewers sometimes have difficulty in concentrating or expressing themselves when others can hear them. Settings vary in the extent to which social workers can control these conditions. For example, in some in-person interviews or remote interviews, families may prefer to include trusted family members, friends, or spiritual leaders present to consider resolution of some issues (Burford & Hudson, 2009). In some settings, it may be impossible to ensure complete privacy. Even when interviewing a patient in a hospital bed, however, privacy can be maximized by closing doors, drawing curtains that separate beds, and requesting that nursing staff avoid nonessential interruptions. Privacy during home interviews may be even more difficult to arrange, but people will often take measures to reduce unnecessary intrusions or distractions if interviewers stress that privacy enhances the productivity of sessions (Allen & Tracy, 2009). Social workers in public social service settings often work in cubicle offices. To ensure privacy, they can conduct client interviews in special interview rooms.

11. Because interviews sometimes involve intense emotions by participants, freedom from distraction is desirable. Telephone calls, text messages, knocks on the door, and external noises can impair concentration and disrupt important dialogue. Moreover, clients are unlikely to feel important and valued if social workers permit avoidable intrusions. Other sources of distraction include crying, attention seeking, and restless behavior of clients' infants or children. Small children, of course, cannot be expected to sit quietly for more than short periods of time. For this reason, the social worker should encourage parents to make arrangements for the care of children during interviews, except when it is important to observe interaction between parents and their children. Because requiring such arrangements can create a barrier to service utilization, many social workers and agencies maintain a supply of toys for such occasions.

12. Having a desk between an interviewer and interviewee emphasizes the authority of the social worker. For clients from some cultural groups, emphasizing the authority or position of the social worker may be a useful way to indicate that they occupy a formal, appropriate position. With many others, a desk

between social worker and client creates a barrier that is not conducive to open communication. If the safety of the social worker is an issue, then a desk barrier can be useful, unless it prevents the social worker from leaving if necessary. In some instances, an interviewer may believe that maximizing the social worker's authority through a desk barrier will promote their service objectives. Those clients with trauma histories may prefer to sit close to the door or make sure they can see the door. If possible, give the client the option of where to sit. This will help them feel more relaxed.

13. In most circumstances, however, social workers strive to foster a sense of equality. Hence, they arrange their desks so that they can rotate their chairs to a position where there is open space between them and their clients. Others prefer to leave their desks entirely and use other chairs in the room when interviewing.

14. Social workers who interview children often find it useful to have available a small number of toys or items that children can manipulate with their hands as well as materials for drawing pictures. Such tools or devices seem to reduce tension for children in communicating with unfamiliar adults and assist them in telling their story (Krahenbuhl & Blades, 2006; Lamb & Brown, 2006; Lukas, 1993).

15. It should be noted that frequently social workers conduct interviews in less-than-ideal environments such as while transporting clients or in a restaurant. Sometimes such environments provide a level of comfort, such as not requiring face-to-face contact in a car, that can reduce stress for a client. The main point is to attempt to maximize the available conditions to support focus and privacy. .

Phase I: Exploration, Engagement, Assessment, and Planning

Phase I of the helping process lays the groundwork for subsequent implementation of interventions and strategies aimed at resolving clients' problems and promoting problem-solving skills. It represents a key step in all helping relationships regardless of duration or setting. Processes involved and tasks to be accomplished during Phase I include the following:

C6, 7, 8, and 9

1. Exploring clients' needs, wishes, and concerns by eliciting comprehensive data about their situation and relevant environmental factors, including forces influencing the referral for contact.

2. Establishing rapport and enhancing client motivation.

3. Formulating a multidimensional assessment of the problem, identifying systems that play a significant role in the difficulties, and identifying relevant resources that can be tapped or must be developed. Such assessment also includes an assessment of obstacles including sociostructural factors such as racism, discrimination, classism, and ableism along with attention to prior trauma history.

4. Mutually negotiating goals to be accomplished in remedying or alleviating problems and formulating a contract while emphasizing strengths and resources and being mindful of the ecological environment.

5. Making referrals as needed.

Problem Exploration

We introduce the process of problem exploration here and present it in more detail in Chapter 8. Contact begins with an initial exploration of the circumstances that led the person to meet with the social worker. Some people are anxious about the prospect of seeking help and lack knowledge about what to expect. Many are mandated to participate in services by authorities such as the courts, school officials, or parents, among others. The social worker often has information from an intake form or referral source about the circumstances that have brought the person into contact. The social worker also needs to examine what they might need to explore in prior to the first session to be familiar with the client's racial, ethnic, or cultural background such that they can proceed with cultural humility with some basic preparation. The first session should begin by asking questions such as:

C7

- "I have read your intake form. Can you tell me what brings you here, in your own words?"
- "How can I help you?"

Beginning questions should elicit an elaboration of the concern or pressures that bring the potential client into contact with the social worker. The social worker can begin to determine to what extent the motivation for contact was initiated by the potential client and to what extent the motivation represents a response to external forces. For example, adolescents are often referred by teachers who are concerned about their academic performance or classroom behavior. In such circumstances, the social worker should begin with a matter of fact, nonthreatening description of the circumstances that led to the referral. For example, the social worker might say the following:

- "You were referred by a teacher who was concerned about some changes in your behavior. That does not mean necessarily that there is a concern. I would like to check with you to see how things are going with you and whether I might be able to help."

The social worker should also give a clear, brief description of their view of the purpose of this first contact and encourage an exploration of how the social worker can be helpful, such as the following:

- "We are meeting both to explore your teacher's concerns and to hear from you about how things are going at school. My job is to find out those things you would like to see go better and to figure out ways that we might work together so that you get more out of school."

For example, a school social worker meeting with an adolescent explains how they came to be with them in their home. The parents were concerned about their daughter's sadness and potential for suicide. "Your parents were a little worried that you are anxious at school, more worried than you used to be. How does that sound to you?" This gives the adolescent an opportunity to present how they see the situation.

Skills in the exploratory process with individuals, couples, families, and groups are delineated later in this chapter and at length in subsequent chapters.

C6

When clients indicate that they are ready to discuss their problematic situations, it is appropriate to begin the process of exploring their concerns. Messages like the following are typically employed to initiate the exploration process:

- "Could you tell me about your situation?"
- "I would like to hear about what brought you here."
- "Tell me about what has been going on with you so that we can think together about what you can do about your concerns."
- "How are things going at school?"

The client will generally respond by beginning to relate their concerns. The social worker's role at this point is to draw out the client, to respond in ways that convey understanding, and to seek elaboration of information needed to gain a clear picture of factors involved in the client's difficulties.

Some clients spontaneously provide rich information with little prompting. Others, especially referred and involuntary clients, may hesitate, struggle with their emotions, or have difficulty finding the right words to express themselves.

Exploring Expectations

It is important to determine clients' expectations as a key antecedent to problem exploration. Such expectations vary considerably and are influenced by socioeconomic level, cultural background, level of sophistication, and previous

C6

experience with helping professionals. In fact, socialization that includes clarifying expectations about the roles of clients and social workers has been found to be associated with more successful outcomes, especially with involuntary clients (Rooney & Myrick, 2018).

In some instances, clients' expectations diverge markedly from what social workers can realistically provide. Unless social workers are aware of and deal successfully with such unrealistic expectations, clients may be keenly disappointed and disinclined to continue beyond the initial interview. In other instances, referred clients may have mistaken impressions about whether they can choose to work on concerns as they see them as opposed to the views of referral sources such as family members. By exploring these expectations, social workers create an opportunity to clarify the nature of the helping process and to work through clients' feelings of disappointment. Being aware of clients' expectations also helps social workers select their approaches and interventions based on their clients' needs and expectations.

Establishing Rapport and Enhancing Motivation

Effective communication in the helping relationship is crucial. Unless the social worker succeeds in engaging people, they may be reluctant to reveal vital information and feelings and, even worse, may not return after the initial session.

C6

Engaging clients successfully means establishing rapport such that the social worker conveys understanding of a person's thoughts and feelings, which reduces the level of threat and gains the trust of clients, who recognize that the social worker intends to be helpful. Consistent with orienting frameworks presented in Chapter 2, rapport is built on a trusting relationship that emphasizes client autonomy and empowerment. One condition of rapport is that clients perceive a social worker as understanding and genuinely interested in their well-being. For example, a social worker might begin building rapport with an adolescent client by discussing music, a topic that is important to many teenagers. To create such a positive perception amid individual differences (e.g., race or ethnicity, gender, sexual orientation, age), the social worker should model cultural humility by directly signaling their willingness, comfort, and interest in conversations about culture, race, and ethnicity. As presented in Chapter 2, the trauma-informed approach has major implications for developing rapport based on safety. Warmth, empathy, and authenticity described in Chapter 5 support cultural humility, anti-oppressive practice, trauma-informed practice, and evidence-based practice.

People may also draw conclusions about the openness of the agency to their concerns through the intake forms that they must complete. For example, agency forms asking about gender with only check boxes for male, female, or "other" may seem closed off to non-cisgender persons who may identify as transgender. The use of "other" as a selection for gender can marginalize transgender people; therefore, an open-ended text box may be preferred when asking for gender (Austin et al., 2016). Alternatively, a form could provide options, including: Woman; Man; Nonbinary; Prefer Not to Disclose; Prefer to Self-Describe (Spiel et al., 2019). Further, we recommend that social workers ask clients for their preferred gender pronouns to avoid using a pronoun that is incongruent with the client's gender identity (Ansara & Hegarty, 2014).

When people have been referred by others, they will need to be reassured that their wishes are important and that they do not necessarily have to work on the concerns noted by the referral source. Such people frequently have misgivings about the helping process or do not assume that it will be helpful. They do not perceive themselves as having a problem and often attribute the source of difficulties to another person, unfortunate circumstances, or procedures judged to be unfair or biased. These situations present social workers with several challenging tasks:

- Addressing and validating negative feelings.
- Attempting to help people understand problems identified by others as well as legal mandates and assessing the advantages and disadvantages of dealing with those concerns.

On the other hand, some clients freely acknowledge problems and have incentives for change yet assume a passive role, expecting others to work out the difficulties for them. Social workers must avoid taking on this impossible role and instead voice a belief in working collaboratively toward change. This involves mobilizing clients' abilities and energies in searching for remedial courses of action and implementing the tasks essential to successful problem resolution. In doing so, it is important to distinguish between the tasks and the goal.

It is easy to become overwhelmed with the steps needed for change even though the goal is desirable and mutually agreeable. Utilizing a **strengths-based perspective**, as introduced in Chapter 2, it is necessary to identify not just concerns but also what is going well in the client's life in order to highlight current coping mechanisms. One strategy is to acknowledge the person's problem(s) and explicitly recognize their motivation to actively work toward solutions. Phrasing the solution as a goal will help differentiate the goal from tasks. People do not lack motivation; rather, they sometimes lack motivation to work on the problems and goals perceived by others. In addition, motivation relates to past experience, which leads some people to expect either that they will be successful or that they will fail when they attempt to reach their goals. Hence, individuals with limited expectations for success often appear to lack motivation.

How to Establish Rapport

Establishing rapport begins by greeting the client(s) warmly and introducing yourself. Should the contact occur via telehealth or telesocial work through phone, Zoom, or other device, it is useful to check in with the client about how they feel about using this modality. The social worker should check on whether any adjustments need to be made, and the social worker may ask questions about how the interview is going. If the client system is a family, you should introduce yourself to each family member. In making introductions and addressing clients, it is important to extend the courtesy of asking clients how they prefer to be addressed; doing so conveys your respect and desire to use the title they prefer. Although some clients prefer the informality involved in using first names, social workers should be discreet in using first name introductions with all clients because of their diverse ethnic and social backgrounds.

With many clients, social workers must surmount formidable barriers before establishing rapport. Most people have had little or no prior experience with social work agencies and enter initial interviews or group sessions with uncertainty and apprehension. Many did not seek help initially. They may view having to seek assistance with their problems as evidence of failure. Moreover, revealing personal problems is embarrassing and even humiliating for some people, especially those who have difficulty confiding in others.

Establishing rapport and engagement with families includes efforts to join families by emphasizing the family unit. Such efforts with groups include acknowledging where each person is beginning in terms of motivations and goals about group participation.

Cultural factors and language differences are opportunities for rapport and also can be potential barriers to rapport even further. For example, some people have been conditioned by their norms and customs not to discuss personal or family problems with outsiders. For others, mistrust of helping professionals can be a healthy coping mechanism in coping with systems of power and oppression based on prior experiences or perceptions of social workers and other helping professionals. Social workers must know how to enter a community and engage community members in a culturally appropriate manner, which then builds trust and involves a high level of cultural discernment. Revealing problems to outsiders may be perceived as a reflection of personal inadequacy and as a stigma upon the entire family. Some people may also experience difficulty in developing rapport because of distrust that derives from a history of being exploited or discriminated against by other ethnic groups (Danso, 2018; Proctor & Davis, 1994).

Children may be unfamiliar with having conversational exchanges with unfamiliar adults (Lamb & Brown, 2006). For example, their exchanges with teachers may be primarily directive or a test of their knowledge. Asking them to describe events or family situations may be a new experience for them, and they may look for cues from the accompanying adult about how to proceed. Open-ended questions are advised to avoid providing leading questions.

Clients' difficulties in communicating openly tend to be exacerbated when their problems involve allegations of socially unacceptable behavior, such as child abuse, moral infractions, or criminal behavior. In groups, the pain is further compounded by having to expose one's difficulties to other group members, especially in early sessions when the reactions of other members represent the threat of the unknown.

One means of fostering rapport with clients is to employ a **warm-up period.** Social workers who neglect to engage in a warm-up period may encounter discomfort from some people whose natural style is not to begin with a business relationship without establishing a personal connection.

C6

Warm-up periods are also important in establishing rapport with adolescents, many of whom are in a stage of emancipating themselves from adults. Consequently, they may be wary of social workers. Connecting with an adolescent around their interest in music both develops rapport and provides clues into their concerns. The judgment of how much warm-up is necessary and how much is too much is a matter of art and experience with initially reluctant potential clients. With most people, a brief warm-up period is usually sufficient. When the preceding barriers do not apply, introductions and a brief discussion of a timely topic (unusual weather, a widely discussed local or national event, or a topic of known interest to the client) can adequately foster a climate conducive to exploring clients' concerns.

Many clients, in fact, expect to begin discussion of their problems directly, and their anxiety level may grow if social workers delay getting to the business at hand (Ivanoff et al., 1994). Tuning in to their feelings and explaining what they can expect in terms of their role and that of the social worker go a long way toward reducing these tensions. (We will discuss these topics in more depth in Chapter 5.)

Respect for clients is critical to establishing rapport, and we stress the importance of respecting clients' dignity and worth, uniqueness, capacities to solve problems, and other factors. An additional aspect of showing respect is demonstrating common courtesy. Being punctual, attending to the client's comfort, listening attentively,

remembering the client's name, and assisting a client who has limited mobility convey the message that the social worker values the client and esteems their dignity and worth. Courtesy should never be taken lightly.

Verbal and nonverbal messages from social workers that convey understanding and acceptance of clients' feelings and views also facilitate the development of rapport. This does not mean agreeing with or condoning clients' views or problems but rather apprehending and affirming clients' rights to have their own views, attitudes, and feelings.

Attentiveness to feelings and empathic responses to these feelings convey understanding that clients readily discern. Empathic responses clearly convey the message, "I am with you. I understand what you are saying and experiencing. Empathic responding is important not only in Phase I of the helping process but in subsequent phases as well. Mastery of this vital skill (discussed extensively in Chapter 5) requires consistent and sustained practice.

Authenticity, or genuineness, is another quality that facilitates rapport. Being authentic during the initial stages of the helping process means relating as a genuine person rather than assuming a contrived and sterile professional role. Authentic behavior by social workers also models openness, which encourages clients to reciprocate by lowering their defenses and relating more openly (Doster & Nesbitt, 1979).

Being authentic also permits the constructive use of humor, as elaborated in Chapter 7. Relating with a moderate level of authenticity, however, precludes a high level of self-disclosure. Rather, the focus is on the client, and the social worker reveals personal information or shares personal experiences judiciously. During the change-oriented phase of the helping process, however, social workers sometimes engage in self-disclosure when they believe that doing so may facilitate client growth.

Rapport is also enhanced by avoiding certain types of responses that block communication. To avoid hindering communication, social workers must be knowledgeable about such types of responses and must eliminate them from their communication repertoires. Toward this end, Chapter 7 identifies various types of responses and interviewing patterns that inhibit communication and describes strategies for eliminating them.

In this phase, it is important that social workers tap into client motivation by providing information about what to expect from the helping process. This socialization effort includes identifying the kinds of concerns with which the social worker and agency can help; client rights, including confidentiality and the circumstances in which it might be abridged; and information about what behaviors to expect from the social worker and what behaviors will be expected from the client (Trotter, 2015).

Structure of Interviews

Direct-practice social workers employ interviewing as the primary vehicle of influence, although administrators and social planners also rely heavily on interviewing skills to accomplish their objectives. With the increasing emphasis on evidence-informed practice, it becomes more important to develop core skills in interviewing that can be applied and revised according to varied situations. Skills in interviewing, active listening, discerning and confronting discrepancies, reframing, and reciprocal empathy are key ingredients in the generalist practice model (Adams et al., 2009). These nonspecific factors have a considerable impact on outcomes (Cameron & Keenan, 2010; Drisko, 2004).

Interviews in social work have a purpose and a structure. The purpose is to exchange information systematically with a view toward illuminating and solving problems, promoting growth, or planning strategies or actions aimed at improving people's quality of life. The structure of interviews varies somewhat from setting to setting, from client to client, and from one phase of the helping process to another. Indeed, skillful interviewers adapt flexibly both to different contexts and to the ebb and flow of each individual session.

Each interview is unique. Nevertheless, effective interviews conform to a general structure, share certain properties, and reflect the interviewer's use of certain basic skills. In considering these basic factors, we begin by focusing on the structure and processes involved in initial interviews.

Starting Where the Client Is

Social work researchers have suggested that motivational congruence—that is, the fit between client motivation and what the social worker attempts to provide—is a major factor in explaining more successful findings in studies of social work effectiveness (Reid & Hanrahan, 1982). Starting with client motivation aids social workers in establishing and sustaining rapport and in maintaining psychological contact with clients.

If, for example, a client appears to be in emotional distress at the beginning of the initial interview, the social worker might focus attention on the client's distress before proceeding to explore the client's problematic situation. An example of an appropriate focusing response would be, "It feels to me as if you are going through a difficult time. Could you tell me what this is like for you right now?" Discussion of the client's emotions and related factors tends to reduce the distress, which might otherwise impede the process of exploration. Moreover, responding sensitively to clients' emotions fosters rapport—clients begin to regard social workers as concerned, perceptive, and understanding persons.

Novice social workers sometimes have difficulty in starting where the client is because they worry that they will not present quickly and clearly the services of the agency, thus neglecting or delaying exploration of client concerns. Practice will allow them to relax and recognize that they can meet the expectations of their supervisors and others by focusing on client concerns while sharing content about the circumstances of referrals and their agency's services.

Starting where the client is has critical significance when social workers are working with involuntary clients. For example, social workers can often reduce negative feelings by clarifying the choices available to the involuntary client. If social workers fail to deal with their clients' negative feelings, they are likely to encounter persistent oppositional responses. These responses are frequently labeled as resistance, opposition to change, and lack of motivation. It is useful to reframe these responses by choosing not to interpret them with deficit labels but rather replacing them with expectations that these attitudes and behaviors are normal when something an individual values is threatened (Rooney & Myrick, 2018). As children and adolescents are often referred because adults are concerned about their behavior, they may be particularly oppositional, and the social worker can clarify that they want to hear how things are going from the child's or adolescent's viewpoint.

Language also poses a barrier with many clients learning English who experience monolingual settings focusing offering only English services. Where there are language differences, social workers must slow down the pace of communication and be especially sensitive to nonverbal indications that clients are confused. To avoid embarrassment, some clients who speak English as a second language sometimes indicate that they understand messages when, in fact, they do not.

Furthering Responses, Paraphrasing, and Feedback

To facilitate the process of exploration, social workers employ a multitude of skills, often blending two or more in a single response. One such skill, furthering responses, encourages clients to continue verbalizing their concerns. Furthering responses include actions such as repeating a word expressed by a client, nodding, or in other ways encouraging continued expression. It is done to convey attention, interest, and an expectation that the client will continue verbalizing. We discuss such responses in depth in Chapter 6.

Other responses facilitate communication (and rapport) by providing immediate feedback that assures clients that social workers have not only heard but also understood their messages. Simple reflections restate what

C6

clients have said using the same or similar language. When reflecting emotions, simple reflections stay at the same surface level as expressed by the client without adding to it and are the same as surface-level empathic response. **Complex reflections**, however, go beyond what the client has directly stated or implied, adding substantial meaning or emphasis to convey a more complex picture. When language barriers exist, social workers should be careful not to assume that they correctly understand the client or that the client understands the social worker.

If clients are hesitant about discussing personal or family problems with outsiders, social workers need to make special efforts to grasp their intended meanings. Many such clients are not accustomed to participating in interviews and tend not to state their concerns openly. Rather, they may send covert or hidden messages and expect social workers to discern their problems by reading between the lines. Social workers need to use feedback extensively to determine whether their perceptions of the clients' intended meanings are on target.

Using feedback to ascertain that the social worker has understood the client's intended meaning, and vice versa, can avoid unnecessary misunderstandings. In addition, clients generally appreciate a social worker's efforts to reach shared understanding, and they interpret patience and persistence in seeking to understand as evidence that the social worker respects and values

C1 and 2

them. Rather than make an inappropriate generalization based on assumptions about a client's cultural or ethnic identity, the cultural humility perspective would suggest that the social worker explore with the client the meaning of an issue from that client's perspective. For example, the social worker might ask, "Can you call on other family members for assistance?" without making an inappropriate cultural generalization that may or may not have relevance for a particular person or family.

Focusing in Depth

In addition to possessing discrete skills needed to elicit detailed information, social workers must be able to maintain the focus on problems until they have elicited comprehensive information. Adequate assessment of problems is not possible until a social worker possesses sufficient information concerning the various forces (involving individual, interpersonal, and environmental systems) that interact to produce the problems. Focusing skills (discussed at length in Chapter 6) blend the various skills identified so far with summarizing responses.

During exploration, social workers should elicit information relevant to numerous questions whose answers are crucial to understanding the factors, including ecological factors, that bear on the clients' problems. These questions serve as guideposts for social workers and provide direction to interviews.

Using Interpreters

Interpreters are often needed if there is a language difference between client and social worker, or the client is hearing impaired and requires a sign language interpreter. When clients are learning the English language, effective communication often requires the use of an interpreter, so that the social worker and client bridge both cultural value differences and language differences. To work effectively together, however, both the social worker and the interpreter must possess special skills. For their part, interpreters must be carefully selected and trained to understand the importance of the interview and their role in the process, as well as to interpret cultural nuances to the social worker. In this way, skilled interpreters assist social workers by translating far more than verbal content—they also convey nonverbal communication, cultural attitudes and beliefs, subtle expressions, emotional reactions, and expectations of clients.

The social worker should explain the interpreter's role to the client and ensure the client of neutrality and confidentiality on the part of both the social worker and the interpreter. Obviously, these factors should also be covered in the training process for interpreters. In addition, successful transcultural work through an interpreter requires that the social worker be acquainted with the client's history and culture and the interpreter's country of origin.

Social workers must also adapt to the slower pace of interviews when an interpreter is involved. When social workers and interpreters are skilled in collaborating in interviews, effective working relationships can evolve, and many clients experience the process as beneficial and therapeutic. As implied in this brief discussion, interviewing through an interpreter is a complex process requiring careful preparation of interviewers and interpreters.

Formulating a Multidimensional Assessment of the Problem, Identifying Systems, and Identifying Relevant Resources

Social workers must simultaneously establish rapport with their clients and explore their problems. These activities reinforce each other, as astute exploration yields both information and a sense of trust and confidence in the social worker.

C7

A social worker who demonstrates empathy can foster rapport and show the client that the social worker understands what they are expressing. This, in turn, encourages more openness on the client's part and expands their expression of feelings. The greater willingness to share deepens the social worker's understanding of the client's situation and the role that emotions play both in the client's difficulties and in their capabilities. Thus, the social worker's communication skills serve multiple functions: They not only establish rapport, but they facilitate relationship building and encourage information sharing as well.

Problem exploration is a critical process because the social worker must gather comprehensive information before they can understand the dimensions of a problem and their interaction. Exploration begins by attending to the emotional states and immediate concerns manifested by the client. Gradually, the social worker broadens the exploration to encompass relevant systems (e.g., individual, interpersonal, and environmental) and explores the most critical aspects of the problem in depth. During this discovery process, the social worker is also alert to and highlights client strengths in order to build on them throughout the helping process. Social workers can assist clients in identifying ways in which they are currently coping and exceptions when problems do occur (Green et al. 2005). For example, the school social worker working with a tardy and tired student can help identify days on which they are on time and rested for school and then trace back the environmental conditions at home that facilitated such an outcome.

Indeed, problem exploration skills are used during the entire assessment and helping process, beginning with the first contact with clients and continuing throughout the relationship. For example, during the engagement process, social workers listen for critical issues and challenges described by clients. Together, social workers and clients use this information to identify areas for greater focus. In addition to this ongoing process of assessment, social workers must formulate a working assessment from which flow the goals and contract upon which Phase II of the problem-solving process

is based. An adequate assessment includes analysis of the problem, the person(s), and the ecological context.

Because there are many possible areas that can be explored but limited time available to explore them, focusing on assessment is critical. Retaining such a focus is promoted by conducting the assessment in layers. At the first layer, social workers must focus their attention on issues of safety, legal mandates, and the client's wishes for service. The rationale for this threefold set of priorities is that client wishes should take precedence in circumstances in which legal mandates do not impinge on choices or in which no dangers to self or others exist. A second layer is then assessing for orienting perspectives. That is, the social worker will assess relevant systems, strengths, and resources, then review relevant factors related to anti-oppressive practice, cultural humility, and trauma.

The social worker next reviews factors that contribute to difficulties—for example, inadequate resources; decisions about a crucial aspect of one's life; difficulties in individual, interpersonal, or societal systems; or interactions between any of the preceding factors. Analysis of the problem also involves making judgments about the duration and severity of a problem as well as the extent to which the problem is susceptible to change, given the client's potential coping capacity. When considering the nature and severity of problems, social workers must weigh these factors against their own competencies and the types of services provided by the agency. If the problems call for services that are beyond the agency's function, such as prescribing medication or offering speech therapy, referral to another professional or agency may be indicated.

Analysis of the individual system includes assessment of the client's wants and needs, coping capacity, strengths and limitations, and motivation to work on the problem(s). In evaluating the first two dimensions, the social worker must assess such factors as flexibility, judgment, emotional characteristics, degree of responsibility, capacity to tolerate stress, ability to reason critically, cultural worldview, and interpersonal skills. These factors, which are critical in selecting appropriate and attainable goals, are discussed at length in Chapter 9.

Assessment of ecological factors entails consideration of the adequacy or deficiency, success or failure, and strengths or weaknesses of salient systems in the environment that bear on the client's problem. Influenced by the six orienting perspectives presented in Chapter 2, the social worker will include, for example, consideration of possible trauma. Such ecological assessment aims to identify systems that may be strengthened, mobilized, or developed to satisfy the client's unmet needs. Systems that often affect clients' needs include couple, family, and social support systems (e.g., kin, friends, neighbors, coworkers, peer groups, and ethnic reference groups); spiritual belief systems; child care, health care, and employment systems; various institutions (e.g., schools, employment); and the societal and physical environment. For example, in our earlier example, the social worker could work with the student and their parents to identify pertinent support systems, such as people who could provide transportation as well as conditions that foster a bedtime and morning routine that would help the student arrive at school on time and rested.

Cultural factors are also vital in ecological assessment because personal and social needs and the means of satisfying them vary widely from culture to culture. Moreover, the resources that can be tapped to meet clients' needs vary according to cultural contexts. Some cultures include indigenous helping persons, such as folk healers, religious leaders, and relatives from extended family units who have been invested with authority to assist members of that culture in times of crisis. These persons can often provide valuable assistance to social workers and their clients.

Assessment of the client's situational context also requires analyzing the circumstances as well as the actions and reactions of participants in the problematic interaction. Knowledge of the circumstances and specific behaviors of participants before, during, and after troubling events is crucial to understanding the forces that shape and maintain problematic behavior. Assessment, therefore, requires that social workers elicit detailed information about actual transactions between people.

Whether making assessments of individuals, per se, or assessments of individuals as subsets of couples, families, or groups, it is important to assess the functioning of these larger systems. These systems have unique properties, including power distribution, role definitions, rules, norms, channels of communication, and repetitive interactional patterns. Such systems also boast both strengths and problems that strongly shape the behavior of constituent members. It follows that individual difficulties tend to be related to systemic difficulties, so interventions must, therefore, be directed to both the system and the individual.

As information is gathered, social workers and clients collaborate in a synthesis. This conceptualization or assessment informs the goal setting activities that conclude Phase I of the helping process. Assessments of systems are based on a variety of data-gathering procedures. Finally, a working assessment involves synthesizing all relevant information gathered as part of the exploration process. To enhance the validity of such assessments, social workers should involve clients in the process by soliciting their perceptions and assisting them in gathering data about their perceived difficulties and hopes. Social workers can share their impressions with their clients, for example, and then invite affirmation or disconfirmation of those impressions. It is also beneficial to highlight their strengths and to identify other relevant resource systems that can be tapped or need to be developed to resolve the difficulties.

Eliciting Essential Information

During the exploration process, the social worker assesses the significance of information revealed as the client discusses problems and interacts with the social worker, group members, or significant others. Indeed, judgments about the meaning and significance of fragments of information guide social workers in deciding issues such as which aspects of a problem are salient and warrant further exploration, how ready a client is to explore certain facets of a problem more deeply, which patterned behaviors of the client or system interfere with effective functioning, and when and when not to draw out intense emotions.

The direction of problem exploration proceeds from general to specific. Clients' initial accounts of their problems are typically general in nature ("We fight over everything," "I don't seem to be able to make friends," "We just don't know how to cope with Scott. He won't do anything we ask," or "Child protection says I don't care for my children"). Clients' concerns typically have many facets, however, and accurate understanding requires careful assessment of each one. Although open-ended responses may be effective in launching problem explorations, other types of responses are used to probe for the detailed information needed to identify and unravel the various factors and systems that contribute to and maintain the problem. Responses that seek concreteness are employed to elicit such detailed information. These types of responses are considered **assessing emotional functioning.**

During the process of exploration, social workers must be keenly sensitive to clients' emotional reactions and to the part that emotional patterns play in their difficulties. Emotional reactions during the interview (e.g., crying, intense anxiety, anger, hurt feelings) often impede problem exploration and require detours aimed at helping clients regain their equanimity.

Emotional patterns that powerfully influence behavior in other contexts may also be problems in and of themselves that warrant careful exploration. Factors to be considered, instruments that assess emotional patterns such as depression and suicidal risk, and relevant skills are discussed in Chapter 9.

Exploring Cognitive Functioning

Because thought patterns, beliefs, and attitudes are powerful determinants of behavior, it is important to explore clients' opinions and interpretations of those circumstances and events deemed salient to their difficulties. Often, careful exploration reveals that misinformation, distorted meaning attributions, mistaken beliefs, and dysfunctional patterns of thought (such as rigid, dogmatic thinking) play major roles in clients' difficulties.

Messages commonly employed to explore clients' thinking include the following:

- "How did you come to that conclusion?"
- "What meaning do you make of ...?"

Assessment of cognitive functioning and other relevant assessment skills are discussed further in Chapter 9.

Exploring Suicidal Risk, Substance Abuse, Violence, and Sexual Abuse

Because of the prevalence and magnitude of problems associated with substance abuse (including alcohol), violence, and sexual abuse in our society, the possibility that these problems contribute to or represent the primary source of clients' difficulties should be routinely explored. Because of the significance of these problematic behaviors, we discuss them in detail in Chapters 8 and 9.

Mutually Negotiating Goals and Formulating a Contract

When social workers and their clients reach agreement about the nature of the problems involved, they are ready to enter the process of negotiating goals. We discuss the process of goal selection briefly in this chapter and at length in Chapter 13. This mutual process aims to identify what needs to be changed and what related actions need to be taken to resolve or ameliorate the problematic situation.

In general, goals should be aligned with the orienting frameworks we presented in Chapter 2. For example, an anti-oppressive practice approach suggests that goals should be framed as increases in client autonomy and empowerment; the ecosystems perspective considers goals at multiple levels (micro, mezzo, macro), recognizing that people are embedded within larger social structures that contribute to client problems and their maintenance. If agreement is not reached about the appropriateness of services, or if clients choose not to continue, then services may be terminated. In some situations, services are finished when the assessment is completed. In the case of involuntary clients, some may continue the social work contact under pressure even if agreement is not reached about the appropriateness of services or if problems are not acknowledged.

After goals have been negotiated, participants undertake the next task: formulating a contract. The contract, which is also mutually negotiated, consists of a formal agreement or understanding between the social worker and the client that specifies the goals to be accomplished, relevant strategies to be implemented, roles and responsibilities of participants, practical arrangements, and other factors. When the client system is a couple, family, or group, the contract also specifies group goals that tend to accelerate group movement and to facilitate accomplishment of group goals.

Mutually formulating a contract is a vital process because it demystifies the helping process and clarifies mutual expectations about what will be accomplished and how. Contracting with voluntary clients is relatively straightforward. The contract specifies what the client desires to accomplish through social work contact. Contracting with involuntary clients contains another layer of legally mandated problems or concerns in addition to the clients' expressed wishes.

Contracts need not focus only on reducing problems. They can also be focused on achieving goals that are not related to problem reduction. For example, a child referred for setting fires might work toward a goal of becoming safe, trustworthy, and reliable in striking matches under adult supervision. By focusing on goals as perceived by clients, an empowering momentum may be created that draws out hidden strengths and resources (De Jong & Berg, 2012). As introduced in Chapter 2, utilizing strengths and systems perspectives leads us to work with clients to discover and make best use of available resources. Sometimes, focusing on problems can be counterproductive. However, in funding and agency environments that are problem focused, both in terms of philosophy and funding streams, ignoring problem conceptions carries risk (McMillen et al., 2004).

When resolving the problematic situation requires satisfying more than one goal (the usual case), social workers should assist clients in assigning priorities to those goals so that the first efforts can be directed to the most burdensome aspects of the problem. Stimulating clients to elaborate goals enhances their commitment to participate actively in the problem-solving process by ensuring that goals are of maximal relevance to them. Techniques such as the miracle question from the solution-focused approach can be employed to engage clients in elaborating their vision of goals (De Jong & Berg, 2012). For example, a client might be asked to share a vision of how the situation would look if they were to awaken the next day and find that, by a miracle, the problem was gone. What would they notice as different?

These responses are useful in elaborating the elements of a goal. Essential elements of the goal selection process and the contracting process are discussed in depth in Chapter 12.

Making Referrals

Exploration of clients' problems often reveals that resources or services beyond those provided by the agency are needed to remedy or ameliorate presenting difficulties. This is especially true of clients who have multiple unmet needs. In such instances, referrals to other resources and service providers may be necessary. Unfortunately, clients may lack the knowledge or the skills needed to avail themselves of these badly needed resources. Social workers may assume the role of case manager in such instances (e.g., for persons with severe and persistent mental illness, individuals with developmental and physical disabilities, foster children, and infirm elderly clients). Linking clients to other resource systems requires careful handling if clients are to follow through in seeking and obtaining essential resources.

Phase II: Implementation and Goal Attainment

After mutually formulating a contract, the social worker and client(s) enter the heart of the problem-solving process: the implementation and goal attainment phase, also known as the action-oriented or change-oriented phase. Problem solving is a key part of the helping process, especially in the implementation phase of the intervention stage.

Phase II involves translating the plans formulated jointly by the social worker and individual clients, couples, families, or groups into actions. In short, the participants combine their efforts in working toward the goal assigned the highest priority. This process begins with dissecting the goal into general tasks that identify general strategies to be employed in pursuit of the goal. These general tasks are then subdivided into specific tasks that designate what the client and the social worker plan to do between one session and the next (Fortune et al., 2010).[1] Tasks may relate to the client's personal functioning or to their interaction with others, or they may involve interaction with other resource systems such as schools, hospitals, or law enforcement agencies. The processes of negotiating goals and tasks are discussed in detail in Chapter 12.

After formulating goals with clients, social workers select and implement interventions designed to assist clients in accomplishing those goals and subsidiary tasks. Interventions should relate directly to the problems that

were identified and the goals that were mutually negotiated with clients and derived from accurate assessment. Those interventions are based on the best available evidence of effectiveness. Helping efforts often fail when social workers employ global interventions without considering clients' views of their problems and ignore the uniqueness of each client's problems.

Interventions at other systems levels are generally consistent with this problem-solving process with some differences. For example, Chapter 14 focuses on developing resources and advocacy beyond individual problem solving. Chapter 15 focuses on enhancing family functioning, while Chapter 16 moves to enhancing group functioning.

Enhancing Self-Efficacy

Research findings (Maddux et al., 2013) have indicated that the helping process is greatly enhanced when clients experience an increased sense of self-efficacy as part of this process. Self-efficacy refers to an expectation or a belief that one can successfully accomplish tasks or perform behaviors associated with specified goals. Note that the concept overlaps with notions of individual empowerment.

The most powerful means for enhancing self-efficacy is to assist clients in practicing certain behaviors prerequisite to accomplishing their goals. Another potent technique is to make clients aware of their strengths and to recognize incremental progress of clients toward goal attainment.

Family and group members also represent potential resources for enhancing self-efficacy. Social workers can develop and tap these resources by assisting families and groups to accomplish tasks that involve perceiving and accrediting the strengths and progress of group and family members. We consider other sources of self-efficacy and relevant techniques in Chapter 13.

Monitoring Progress

As work toward goal attainment proceeds, it is important to monitor progress on a regular basis. The reasons for this are fourfold:

1. *To evaluate the effectiveness of change strategies and interventions.* Social workers are increasingly required to document the efficacy of services to satisfy third-party payers within a managed care system. In addition, social workers owe it to their clients to select interventions based on the best available evidence (Thyer, 2002). If an approach or intervention is not producing desired effects, social workers should determine the reasons for this failure or consider negotiating a different approach.

2. *To guide clients' efforts toward goal attainment.* Evaluating progress toward goals enhances continuity of focus and efforts and promotes efficient use of time (Corcoran & Vandiver, 1996).

3. *To keep abreast of clients' reactions to progress or lack of progress.* When they believe they are not progressing, clients tend to become discouraged and may lose confidence in the helping process. By evaluating progress periodically, social workers will be alerted to negative client reactions that might otherwise undermine the helping process.

4. *To concentrate on goal attainment and evaluate progress.* These efforts tend to sustain clients' motivation to work on their problems.

Methods of evaluating progress range from eliciting subjective opinions to using various types of measurement instruments. Chapters 12 and 19 include both quantitative and qualitative methods for monitoring progress and measuring change.

Barriers to Goal Accomplishment

As people strive to accomplish goals and related tasks, their progress is rarely smooth and uneventful. Instead, they typically encounter obstacles and experience anxiety, uncertainties, fears, and other undesirable reactions as they struggle to solve problems. Furthermore, family or group members or other significant persons may oppose such changes, may criticize the person for seeing a social worker, may make negative comments about the social worker, or by otherwise making change more difficult. For this reason, it is vital to involve significant others in the problem-solving process whenever feasible. Because of the challenges posed by these barriers to change, social workers must be mindful of their clients' struggles and be skillful in assisting them to surmount these obstacles. These barriers are presented in Chapter 7.

Barriers to goal accomplishment are frequently encountered in work with families and groups. Such barriers include behavior factors that limit participation of certain group members, problematic behaviors of group members, or processes within the group that impede progress. They also encompass impediments in the family's environment.

Still other barriers may involve organizational opposition to change within systems whose resources are essential to goal accomplishment. Denial of resources or services (e.g., health care, rehabilitation, or public assistance) by organizations or policies and procedures that unduly restrict clients' access to resources may require the social worker to assume the role of mediator or advocate.

Relational Reactions

As social workers and clients work together to solve problems, emotional reactions on the part of either party toward the other may impair the effectiveness of the working partnership and pose an obstacle to goal accomplishment. Clients, for example, may have unrealistic expectations about what can be accomplished with the social worker. They may experience disappointment, discouragement, hurt, anger, rejection, longing for closeness, or many other emotional reactions that may seriously impede progress toward goals.

Couple partners, parents, and group members may also experience relational reactions to other members of these larger client systems, resulting in problematic interactional patterns within these systems. We will review these referring to transference and countertransference in Chapters 17 and 18. Not uncommonly, these reactions reflect attitudes and beliefs learned from relationships with parents or significant others. In many other instances, however, the social worker or members of clients' systems may unknowingly behave in ways that trigger unfavorable relational reactions by individuals, family, or group members. In either event, it is critical to explore and resolve these harmful relational reactions. Otherwise, clients' efforts may be diverted from working toward goal accomplishment or—even worse—clients may prematurely withdraw from the helping process.

Social workers are susceptible to relational reactions as well. Social workers who relate in an authentic manner provide clients with experience that is transferable to the real world of the client's social environment. They communicate that they are human beings who are not immune to making blunders and experiencing emotions and desires as part of their relationships with clients. It is vital that social workers be aware of their reactions to clients and understand how to manage them. Otherwise, they may be working on their own problems rather than the client's issues, placing the helping process in severe jeopardy. For example, a social work student became aware that they were relating to a client who had difficulty in making and carrying out plans as if the client were a family member with whom the student had similar difficulties. Becoming aware of those associations through supervision made it possible to separate out the client before them from the family member. Chapter 18 offers advice to assist social workers in coping with potential relational reactions residing with the client(s), the social worker, or both.

Enhancing Clients' Self-Awareness

As clients interact in a novel relationship with a social worker and try out new interpersonal behaviors in their couple, family, or group contacts, they commonly experience unexpected emotions. Although managing such emotional reactions may require a temporary detour from goal attainment activities, these efforts frequently represent opportunities for growth in self-awareness. Self-awareness is the first step to self-realization. Many voluntary clients wish to understand themselves more fully, and they can benefit from becoming more aware of feelings that have previously been buried or denied expression.

Social workers can facilitate the process of self-discovery by employing additive empathic responses during the goal attainment phase. **Additive empathy responses** focus on deeper feelings than do **reciprocal empathy responses** (related to establishing rapport in the discussion of Phase I). Additive empathy, elaborated in Chapter 17, refers to making interpretations of what clients have shared.

Another technique used to foster self-awareness is **confrontation**. This technique helps clients become aware of growth-defeating discrepancies in perceptions, feelings, communications, behavior, values, and attitudes and then examine these discrepancies in relation to stated goals. Confrontation is also used in circumstances when clients act to violate laws or threaten their own safety or the safety of others.

Use of Self

As helping relationships grow stronger during the implementation and goal attainment phase, social workers increasingly use themselves as tools to facilitate growth and accomplishment. Relating spontaneously and appropriately disclosing one's feelings, views, and experiences ensure that clients have an encounter with an open and authentic human being. Modeling authentic behavior encourages clients to reciprocate by risking authentic behavior themselves, thereby achieving significant growth in self-realization and in interpersonal relations. Indeed, there is research showing that clients who perceive their social workers as acting in prosocial ways through actions such as returning telephone calls promptly have better outcomes than clients who perceive their social workers as less responsive (Trotter, 2015).

Social workers who relate in an authentic manner also provide their clients with experience that is transferable to the clients' real-world social relationships. A contrived, professional relationship lacks transferability to other relationships. Obviously, these issues should be covered in the educational process for social workers.

Assertiveness is another important aspect of the social worker using themself to help the client. In the social work context, assertiveness involves dealing tactfully but firmly with problematic behaviors. Social workers must sometimes relate assertively to larger client systems—for example, to focus on behavior of group members that hinders the accomplishment of goals. Using oneself to relate authentically and assertively is a major focus of Chapter 5.

Phase III: Termination

The terminal phase of the helping process involves three major aspects:

1. Assessing when client goals have been satisfactorily attained.
2. Helping the client develop strategies that maintain change and continue growth following the termination.
3. Successfully terminating the helping relationship.

Deciding when to terminate is relatively straightforward when time limits are specified in advance as part of the initial contact, as is done with the task-centered approach and other brief treatment strategies, or due to insurance limitations. Decisions about when to terminate are also simple when individual or group goals are clear cut (e.g., to get a job, obtain a prosthetic device, arrange for nursing care, secure tutoring for a child, implement a specific group activity, or hold a public meeting).

In other instances, goals involve growth or changes that have no limits. Thus, judgments must be made by the social worker and the client in tandem about when a satisfactory degree of change has been achieved. Today, many decisions about termination and extension involve third parties, as contracts for service and payers such as managed care may regulate the length and conditions of service (Corcoran & Vandiver, 1996).

Successfully Terminating Helping Relationships

Social workers and clients often respond positively to termination, reflecting pride and accomplishment on the part of both parties (Fortune et al., 1992). Clients who were required or otherwise pressured to see the social worker may experience a sense of relief at getting rid of the pressure or freeing themselves from the strictures of outside scrutiny. In contrast, because voluntary clients share personal problems and are accompanied through rough emotional terrain by a caring social worker, they often feel close to the social worker. Consequently, termination tends to produce mixed feelings for these types of clients.

Although clients are usually optimistic about the prospects of confronting future challenges independently, they sometimes experience a sense of loss over terminating the working relationship. Moreover, uncertainty about their ability to cope independently may be mixed with their optimism.

When they have been engaged in the helping process for a longer period, clients may develop a strong attachment to a social worker that may have inadvertently fostered dependency in their relationship. For such individuals, termination involves a painful process of letting go of a relationship that has satisfied significant emotional needs. Moreover, these clients often experience apprehension about facing the future without the reassuring strength represented by the social worker. Group members may experience similar painful reactions as they face the loss of supportive relationships with the social worker and group members as well as a valued resource that has assisted them to cope with their problems.

To effect termination with individuals or groups and minimize psychological stress requires both perceptiveness to emotional reactions and skills in helping clients to work through such reactions. The social worker must also be adept at modeling healthy endings to relationships.

Planning Change Maintenance Strategies

Social workers have voiced concern over the need to develop strategies that maintain clients' changes and continue their growth after formal social work service is terminated (Rzepnicki, 1991). These concerns have been prompted by findings that after termination many clients relapse or regress to their previous level of functioning. Consequently, more attention is now being paid to strategies for maintaining change after termination. Planning for follow-up sessions not only makes

it possible to evaluate the durability of results but also facilitates the termination process by indicating the social worker's continuing interest in clients, a matter we discuss in Chapter 19. Follow-up must be conducted mindfully because, in some cases, follow-up may trigger past dependency behaviors.

Evaluate Results

During Phase II of the helping process, interviewing skills are used to help clients accomplish their goals. Much of the focus during this phase is on identifying and carrying out actions or tasks that clients must implement to accomplish their goals. Not surprisingly, preparing clients to carry out these actions is crucial to successful implementation. Fortunately, effective strategies of preparation are available (see Chapter 13).

As clients undertake the challenging process of making changes in their lives, it is important that they maintain focus on a few high-priority goals until they have made sufficient progress to warrant shifting to other goals. Otherwise, they may jump from one concern to another, dissipating their energies without achieving significant progress. The burden, therefore, falls on the social worker to provide structure for and direction to the client. Toward this end, skills in maintaining focus during single sessions and continuity between sessions are critical.

As noted earlier, obstacles to goal attainment commonly arise during the helping process. Individual barriers typically include fears associated with change as well as behavior and thought patterns that are highly resistant to change efforts because they serve a protective function (usually at great psychological cost to the individual).

Summary

This chapter examined the three phases of the helping process from a global perspective and briefly considered the structure and processes involved in interviewing.

The remaining parts of the book focus in detail on the three phases of the helping process and on the interviewing skills and interventions employed during each phase.

Competency Notes

C1 Demonstrate Ethical and Professional Behavior

- Use supervision and consultation to guide professional judgment and behavior.

C2 Engage Antiracism, Diversity, Equity, and Inclusion in Practice

- Demonstrate anti-racist social work practice at the individual, family, group, organizational, community, research, and policy levels, informed by the theories and voices of those who have been marginalized.

- Demonstrate cultural humility applying critical reflexivity, self-awareness, and self-regulation to manage the influence of bias, power, privilege, and values in working with clients and constituencies acknowledging them as experts of their own lived experiences.

C6 Engage with Individuals, Families, Groups, Organizations, and Communities

- Use empathy, reflection, and interpersonal skills to effectively engage diverse clients and constituencies.

C7 Assess Individuals, Families, Groups, Organizations, and Communities

- Apply knowledge of human behavior and person-in-environment and other culturally responsive multidisciplinary theoretical frameworks when assessing clients and constituencies.

- Demonstrate respect for client self-determination during the assessment process collaborating with clients and constituencies in developing mutually agreed-on goals.

C8 Intervene with Individuals, Families, Groups, Organizations, and Communities

- Engage with clients and constituencies to critically choose and implement culturally responsive, evidenced-based interventions to achieve mutually agreed-on practice goals and enhance capacities of clients and constituencies.
- Incorporate culturally responsive methods to negotiate, mediate, and advocate, with and on behalf of clients and constituencies.

C9 Evaluate Practice with Individuals, Families, Groups, Organizations, and Communities

- Critically analyze outcomes and apply evaluation findings to improve practice effectiveness with individuals, families, groups, organizations, and communities.

Note

1. The idea of specific phases and their accompanying tasks in structuring casework was originally developed by Jessie Taft and Virginia Robinson and the Functional School. This concept was later extended by Reid (2000) and Epstein and Brown (2002) in the task-centered approach.

Chapter 4

Operationalizing Social Work Values and Ethics

Chapter Overview

Social work practice is guided by knowledge, skills, values, and ethics. This chapter introduces the guiding values of the profession and the ethical obligations that arise from those values. Because, in practice, values and ethics can exist in tension with each other, this chapter also describes some of these dilemmas and offers guidance about resolving them. As you read this chapter, you will have opportunities to place yourself in complex situations that challenge you to analyze your personal values and to assess their compatibility with social work values.

At the completion of your work on this chapter, you will be able to:

- Understand the core social work values and how they play out in practice.

- Develop self-awareness and professional competence by examining the tensions that

can occur when personal values intersect with professional values.

- Identify the roles ethics play in guiding professional practice.

- Learn about the structure and standards of the National Association of Social Workers (NASW) Code of Ethics.

- Be familiar with four core ethical issues: self-determination, informed consent, professional boundaries, and confidentiality.

- Know the steps for resolving ethical dilemmas and the ways in which these apply to a case.

- Understand the complexities of applying ethical standards to clients who are minors.

The EPAS Competencies in Chapter 4

This chapter will give you the information needed to meet the following EPAS competencies:

- Competency 1: Demonstrate Ethical and Professional Behavior

- Competency 2: Engage Antiracism, Diversity, Equity, and Inclusion in Practice

The Interaction Between Personal and Professional Values

Values are preferred conceptions or philosophies about how things ought to be. Values are the ideas, beliefs, and behaviors that are most important to people. For example, individuals may value adventure, hard work, family time, solitude, civic engagement, kindness, or money. Some values may be enduring and widely shared, and others may vary by culture, setting, and context. The list of values is endless because people can hold many values simultaneously. The profession of social work has values, too. Social workers must be attuned to their personal values and be aware when those values mesh or clash with those espoused by the social work profession. They must recognize that their clients also have personal values that shape their beliefs and behaviors, and these may conflict with the social worker's own values or with those of the profession. Further, the larger society has values that are articulated through cultural norms, policies, laws, and public opinion. These, too, can diverge from the values of the individual worker, social work clients, and the profession. Becoming a social worker means that regardless of your personal values, you are agreeing to promote and abide by the values of the profession. The deference of personal interests to professional obligations can be a rigorous and challenging process, but it is done in service of the people who rely on social workers to act on their behalf.

Self-awareness is the first step in sorting out these potential areas of conflict. The following sections describe the core values of the profession, provide opportunities to become aware of personal values, and describe the difficulties that can occur when social workers try to impose their values on clients.

The Cardinal Values of Social Work

The Code of Ethics developed by in the United States by the National Association of Social Workers (NASW, 2021) articulates the core values of the profession and the ethical principles that represent those values. They can be summarized as follows:

Service

All human beings deserve access to the resources they need to deal with life's problems and to develop their full potential. The value of service is embodied in this principle in that social workers are expected to elevate service to others above their own self-interest. Social workers are expected to use their knowledge and capacities to help people in need and address social problems through paid work, volunteerism, and the provision of pro bono (free) services.

Social Justice

The profession places a premium on working for social justice and social change. Social workers' "efforts are focused primarily on issues of poverty, unemployment, discrimination, and other forms of social injustice. These activities seek to promote sensitivity to and knowledge about oppression and cultural and ethnic diversity. Social workers strive to ensure access to needed information, services, and resources; equality of opportunity; and meaningful participation in decision making for all people" (NASW, 2021, p. 5).

Dignity and Worth

Social workers believe in the inherent dignity and worth of others. They demonstrate this value by treating each person in a caring and respectful fashion, remaining mindful of individual differences and cultural and ethnic diversity (NASW, 2021). Because social workers have a responsibility both to clients and to the broader society, they seek to resolve conflicts between clients' and systems' interests in an ethical and socially responsible manner.

Human Relationships

Social workers view interpersonal relationships as essential for well-being and as "an important vehicle for change" (NASW, 2021, p. 5). This value placed on human relationships affects the way social workers relate to others and the efforts they make to improve the well-being of client systems of all types.

Integrity

The value of integrity means that professional social workers behave in a trustworthy manner. They treat their clients and their colleagues in a consistently fair and respectful fashion. They are honest and promote responsible and ethical practices in themselves, their colleagues, and in their organizations.

Competence

The value of competence requires that social workers practice only within their areas of ability and continually develop and enhance their expertise. As professionals, they must take responsibility for assuring that their competence is not diminished by personal problems, substance use, or other difficulties. Similarly, they should act when confronted with incompetent, unethical, or impaired practice by other professionals.

What do these values mean? What difficulties can arise in putting them into practice? How can they conflict with social workers', clients', and society's values? The following sections describe these values and situations in which challenges can occur. Throughout this section, to enhance your awareness of situations in which you might experience such difficulties, we present ethical dilemmas that you may face as a social worker in the field. Imagine yourself in interviews with the clients in each of the following scenarios. You may even role play the scene with a classmate. Take note of your feelings and of possible discomfort or conflict. Pay attention to the following questions as we explore each value.

- What competing values are present?
- How did you become aware of a possible value conflict? What emotions, thoughts, or physical sensations alerted you to the experience?
- What assumptions did you make about the needs of the client(s) in each scenario?
- What actions would you take (or what information would you seek) to move beyond stereotypes in understanding your client(s)?

Valuing Service

A social worker's primary goal is to help people in need and to address social problems.

A historic and defining feature of social work is the profession's focus on individual well-being in a social context. Attending to the environmental forces that "create, contribute to, and address problems in living" is an essential part of social work theory and practice (NASW, 2021, p. 1). To embrace these values, social workers: (1) believe that people have the right to resources, (2) work to assure that adequate resources are available and accessible, (3) help secure needed resources, and (4) develop policies and programs to fill unmet needs. Although these values seem easy to embrace, actual cases can reveal conflicting priorities and biases that challenge the social worker. The United States has a long history of valuing self-sufficiency, productivity, hard work, and morality which is then reflected in policies and programs with little regard for people judged unworthy of services. As a result, many basic services (such as food and health care) that are considered fundamental rights in other countries are not universally available in the United States leading to real and perceived scarcity of resources. Social workers in broker roles may experience overt or covert pressure to ration services or judge a client's worthiness for a given service.

Service Scenario 1

You are a practitioner in a nonprofit agency that has received financial donations to assist clients to purchase essential devices such as eyeglasses, dentures, hearing aids, and other prosthetic items. Your client, Mr. Y, has a chronic psychiatric disorder. He requests special assistance in purchasing new glasses. He says he accidentally dropped his old glasses, and a passerby stepped on them. However, you have heard from other workers that, due to his confusion, Mr. Y regularly loses his glasses and has received emergency funds for glasses several times in the last year alone.

Service Scenario 2

Your 68-year-old client has been receiving treatment for terminal cancer for the past month. Appearing withdrawn and dramatically emaciated, the client reports that they have been in terrible pain. They request your assistance to pursue death with dignity through assisted suicide. The service is legal in your state.

Service Scenario 3

The broadband service in the rural county where you live is very weak, expensive, and unpredictable. During the COVID-19 pandemic, you had to park outside a McDonalds 20 miles away to have Wi-Fi access to check on your clients. You noticed many cars with local students trying to access their classes and realized how many other students were unable to keep up with classes remotely. The county commissioners have determined that broadband is not an essential service and will not support funds or tax incentives for companies to expand in your area, and the companies themselves say it is not financially prudent to expand. You are already overwhelmed with work and advocating for change seems like a hopeless cause.

Valuing Social Justice

Social workers challenge social injustice.

Injustice can present itself in many forms: oppressive policies and social structures, bureaucratic hurdles, judgmental services, inadequate resources, and the marginalization of vulnerable populations. While social work practice occurs in a wide array of settings, the profession's social change efforts target poverty, unemployment, discrimination, and other forms of injustice above all others. This means that social workers promote sensitivity to and awareness of oppression and cultural and ethnic diversity and "ensure access to needed information, services and resources; equality of opportunity; and meaningful participation in decision making for all people" (NASW, 2021, p. 5). Responding to clients' rights and needs speaks to the importance of social workers' altruism and dedication to serve others, acting beyond the worker's personal needs or interests. It also indicates the important role of macro practice and systems change skills to disrupt oppressive practices.

Social Justice Scenario 1

You and your coworkers have taken part in several marches to support the Black Lives Matter movement, antipoverty initiatives, and PRIDE parades. Participation is voluntary, and no work time is used for these events. You feel these efforts at large systems change should count as work, but the supervisor and the chair of the board have said these political events create conflicts of interest for the agency. Are they (and coworkers who refuse to join in) failing to follow social work values?

Social Justice Scenario 2

You are a military mental health provider treating a client with mild trauma symptoms. The client wants to be sent home from deployment, though their unit needs them to continue in combat. Some on the treatment team believe the client is genuinely experiencing trauma, though the commanding officer reports that the soldier is malingering. The psychiatrist argues that going home is ultimately more harmful for the client's mental health than staying and fulfilling commitments to the unit, the mission, and fellow personnel. Fear is common in combat: should everyone who is traumatized be allowed to go home? How should the client's self-determination be honored when they knew upon enlisting what the job would entail? (Simmons & Rycraft, 2010).

Social Justice Scenario 3

You are assigned to do a home study for a family interested in adoption. When you arrive at the home for the first interview, you observe that the applicants are significantly overweight and are older than most adoptive families. They live in a modest mobile home with a spare room to accommodate an adoptive child. This situation is so different than many of the home studies you conduct. You wonder if this couple will qualify or if the screening criteria are biased.

Valuing the Person's Dignity and Worth

Social workers respect the inherent dignity and worth of the person (NASW, 2021).

Respect for clients means that social workers believe that all people have intrinsic importance, whatever their past or present behavior, beliefs, way of life, or social status. Understanding these qualities is essential in involving clients as partners in change. These values embody several related concepts, sometimes referred to as "unconditional positive regard," "nonpossessive warmth," "acceptance," and "affirmation."

As you can see by the previous cases, the value that every person is unique intersects with the right to service and commitment to justice. Social workers should affirm the individuality of all whom they serve, entering that individual's world and understanding how that person experiences life. It is difficult to affirm individuality and self-worth when biases and stereotypes (either positive or negative) blind us to a particular person's uniqueness. Labels—such as "autistic," "unwed mother," "sorority girl," or "little old lady"—perpetuate stereotypes because they obscure the individual characteristics of the people assigned to those labels. Whether the preconceptions are positive or negative, professionals who hold them may fail to effectively engage with the person behind the label. They may overlook needs or capacities, and, as a result, their assessments, goals, and interventions will be distorted. Imagine an elderly client whose cognitive problems associated with a simple bladder infection are diagnosed as dementia or psychosis symptomatic of advanced age. Consider the person with developmental disabilities who is interested in learning about sexuality and contraceptives but whose social worker fails to address those issues, considering them irrelevant for members of this population. Perhaps the sorority member fails to disclose symptoms of a learning disorder or suicidal ideation to the social worker who presumes she has everything going for her.

Respect, curiosity, and nonjudgmental interactions are vital in helping build trust and mobilize capacities that are essential to change and to well-being. As a professional, you may inevitably confront the challenge of maintaining your own values without imposing them on your clients (Doherty, 1995). A first step toward resolving this issue is reflecting on and addressing your own judgments and first impressions.

Dignity and Worth Scenario 1

Your client is a 35-year-old married male who was referred for mental health services following his conviction for secretly videotaping women in restrooms at your college and other local establishments.

Dignity and Worth Scenario 2

A low-income family with whom you have been working recently received a substantial check as part of a settlement for delayed Social Security funds. During a visit in which you plan to help the family budget the funds to pay their past due bills, you find the settlement money is gone—spent on a large television and gambling at a local casino.

Dignity and Worth Scenario 3

You have been working for eight weeks with a 10-year-old boy who has experienced behavioral difficulties at school. During play therapy, he demonstrates with toys the process of strangling cats and dogs.

Valuing Human Relationships

Social workers recognize the central importance of human relationships (NASW, 2021, p. 5).

Like dignity and worth, this value also recognizes that respect is an essential element of the helping relationship. Before people risk sharing personal problems and expressing deep emotions, they must first feel fully accepted and trust the helpful intent of their service providers. Research affirms the importance of this value in findings that relationship factors such as warmth, empathy, encouragement, and acceptance account for 30% of change in the therapeutic process (Hubble et al., 1999). When asked to rank the factors they perceived as contributing to change, 35% of therapists selected the therapeutic relationship, again underscoring the importance of fostering strong rapport.

It is difficult to build a therapeutic alliance with clients who feel ashamed, inadequate, or powerless in seeking assistance. As a result, they may be especially alert to perceived judgments or condemnation on the part of the social worker. The worker's role is not to judge whether people are to blame for their problems. Rather, our role is to seek to understand clients' difficulties and assets and assist them in accessing solutions.

Human Relationships Scenario 1

Yanping, a Chinese student studying in the United States, has decided she wants to major in history, while her parents insist that she study business so that she can eventually take over the family company. You value Yanping's autonomy but understand the risk she faces in defying parental authority and tradition, so you suggest she also speak with your colleague who is from China. The Chinese social worker emphasizes values of family harmony and probes Yanping's individualistic insistence on choosing a major at odds with her parents' wishes.

Human Relationships Scenario 2

Your client, Mrs. O, was admitted to a domestic violence shelter following an attack by her husband in which she sustained a broken collarbone and arm injuries. This occasion is the eighth time she has contacted the shelter. Each previous time she has returned home or allowed her husband to move back into the home with her.

Human Relationships Scenario 3

You are a Latinx outreach worker. One Caucasian client has expressed appreciation for the help you have provided yet tells you repeatedly that she is angry at her difficulty finding a job, blaming it on "all these illegals."

Human Relationships Scenario 4

You are working with a high school senior, the eldest girl in a large family from a strict religious background. Your client wants desperately to get a job but has been told by her parents that she is needed at home to care for her younger siblings and assist in her family's ministry.

Valuing Integrity

The value of integrity means that professional social workers behave in a trustworthy manner.

Integrity has several dimensions. It refers to wholeness or compatibility with a person's essential character, consistency in one's words and actions, and steadfastness, where integrity is demonstrated despite the circumstances (Banks, 2010). As an ethical principle, integrity means that social workers act honestly, encourage ethical practices in their agencies, and take responsibility for their own ethical conduct (Reamer, 2018). In practice, it means that social workers present themselves and their credentials accurately, avoid other forms of misrepresentation (e.g., in billing practices or in presentation of research findings), and do not associate with fraud and deception. A recent addition to the Code indicates that trustworthiness is also related to worker well-being, and it asserts that social workers take care of themselves personally and professionally (NASW, 2021). Integrity also refers to the ways that social workers treat their colleagues. Professionals are expected to treat one another with respect, avoid involving clients or others in professional disputes, and be forthright in their dealings with fellow professionals. These expectations are important not only for our individual trustworthiness, but also because each of us serves as a representative of the larger profession, and we should act in ways that do not dishonor it.

This may seem to be a relatively straightforward expectation. However, challenges can arise when pressures from other colleagues or employing organizations create ethical dilemmas. In those cases, the challenge is not what is right but rather whether and how to do it. Professionals experience **moral distress** when institutional constraints prevent them from acting in ways that are congruent with their ethics codes and values (Mänttäri-van der Kuip, 2019; Papouli, 2019). This distress can be manifested I an array *of* emotional, physiological, and behavioral reactions that can be damaging to clients, employees, and organizations. Moral distress can be countered when workers cultivate **moral courage**; the ability act on behalf of principles, despite the possible personal harms or pressures to do otherwise (Strom-Gottfried, 2019). Moral courage is visible when people have "the capacity to overcome the fear of shame and humiliation in order to admit one's mistakes, to confess a wrong, to reject evil conformity, to renounce injustice, and also to defy immoral or imprudent orders" (Miller, 2000, p. 254). Following are examples of such dilemmas involving the principle of integrity and the possibility of moral distress. What additional strategies might you pursue to resolve these dilemmas and act with honesty and professionalism?

Integrity Scenario 1

Your agency was unprepared for the COVID-19 outbreak, and no personal protective equipment was available for staff working in the office or client homes. You and your colleagues determined that most clients could still be safely served by alternating in-person and phone appointments, but the administration insisted on regular (in-person) meetings because the reimbursement for phone services was too low.

Integrity Scenario 2

Your supervisor wants to discuss cases over lunch to save time in your busy schedules. Whether these weekly meetings are at local restaurants or the building's cafeteria, it is impossible to have a private space or avoid discussing details of the cases.

Integrity Scenario 3

Your roommate graduated from the social work program last year and is supposed to receive weekly supervision as a condition of their beginning license. You have learned that their sister-in-law (also a social worker) is signing the supervision paperwork without providing any oversight.

Valuing Competence

The value of competence requires that social workers practice only within their areas of ability and continually develop and enhance their professional expertise.

As with the value of integrity, this principle places the burden for self-awareness and self-regulation on the social worker. An expectation of practice is that professionals take responsibility for knowing their own limits and seek out the knowledge and experience needed to develop further expertise throughout the span of their careers. This principle means that social workers will decline cases where they lack sufficient expertise, and that they seek out opportunities for continuous self-examination and professional development. The commitment to utilizing evidence-based practices means that professionals must be lifelong learners, staying abreast of practice-related research findings, discarding ineffective or harmful practices, and tailoring interventions to the clients' unique circumstances (Gambrill, 2007). It also means learning to use novel tools for practice, including technology. Each of these elements speaks to developing and maintaining professional competence. The NASW Code of Ethics also includes cultural competence among its expectations for social workers, requiring cultural humility and critical self-reflection, knowledge of cultural diversity, dedication to anti-oppressive and empowerment-based practices, and skills for culturally informed interventions (NASW, 2021).

Self-regulation requires social workers to be alert to events or problems that affect professional competence. For example, does a health or mental health problem hinder the worker's services? Are personal reactions to the client (such as anger, partiality, or sexual attraction) impairing the social worker's judgment? Are family problems or other stressors detracting from the social worker's capacity to respond to the demands of a case? **Countertransference** refers broadly to the ways that a social worker's experiences and emotional reactions influence the perceptions of and interactions with a client or client system. Its correlate, **transference**, refers to the same dynamic when the client consciously or unconsciously associates the social worker with past experiences in such a way that perceptions and interactions with the social worker are affected. Later in this book, you will learn more about the ways that transference and countertransference can constructively or harmfully affect the helping process. It is important to be alert to such reactions and use supervisory sessions to examine and address their impact.

As noted earlier, supervision is an essential element in professional development and ongoing competence. In the helping professions, a supervisor is not someone looking over the employee's shoulder to catch and correct mistakes. More typically, supervisors can be thought of as mentors, teachers, coaches, and counselors all wrapped up into one role (Haynes et al., 2003). Successful use of supervision requires you to be honest and self-aware in seeking guidance, raising issues for discussion, sharing your challenges and successes, and being open to feedback, praise, critiques, and change. Effective supervisors help you develop skills to look clearly at yourself so that you understand your strengths and weaknesses, preferences, and prejudices and become able to manage these for the benefit of your clients.

Developing and maintaining competence is a career-long responsibility, yet it can be challenging to uphold. Consider the following scenarios.

Competence Scenario 1

You are a new employee at a small, financially strapped counseling center. The director of your agency just received a contract to do trauma-informed interventions with children. The director has assigned you to this unit and has emphasized how important the new funding is for the agency's survival. Although you took a human behavior course as a social work student, you have never studied or worked with children, especially those at risk.

Competence Scenario 2

For the past few weeks, you've found yourself attracted to one someone on your caseload, thinking about the client often and wondering what they are doing at different times of the day. You wonder if this attraction could affect your objectivity on the case but are reluctant to discuss the situation with your supervisor because you are embarrassed and worried about their reaction.

Competence Scenario 3

Your internship is at a busy metropolitan hospital. In one morning alone, you encounter a woman from the Ukraine whose dialect you are unfamiliar with, a Muslim woman reluctant to disrobe for the physical exam, and a Korean family at odds over the placement of their teenager's newborn infant. Your commitment to cultural humility is sound, but as you are called in to assist the medical team, you wonder how to effectively incorporate the cultural and individual differences in these cases within the pressure-packed schedule of the hospital workday without burdening your clients by asking them to teach you about the cultural implications of their situations.

Challenges in Embracing the Profession's Values

In the presentation of the social work profession's values, numerous scenarios have highlighted the potential for value conflicts. Uneasy or negative feelings may have arisen for you in these scenarios. Emotional or physical reactions are not unusual. Each of us may be tripped up by a situation that is new to us, challenges our embedded beliefs, or triggers emotions such as anxiety or anger. It can be challenging to look beyond differences, our comfort zones, distressing case information, or bureaucratic systems to suspend judgment and work for change. However, by focusing intentionally on the person within the troubling behavior or role, you can move beyond initial reactions and see others in full perspective. Safe and trusting supervisory relationships can also facilitate this process now and throughout your career. Skilled mentors, teachers, or colleagues can help probe your reactions, encourage reflection, share divergent perspectives, and promote accountability to change. Talk with other professionals about the value conflicts they initially experienced, and how they managed them. What value challenges still arise and what techniques do they use to stay resilient, self-aware, and client centered? How do they convey respect for clients, service providers, or public officials, even those whose actions or attitudes they disdain? How can strong relationships facilitate candid and difficult conversations that might be impossible without a trusting bond?

How does this acceptance play out in practice? Acceptance is conveyed by listening attentively, by responding sensitively to others' messages, and by using facial expressions, voice intonations, and gestures that convey interest and concern. Reaching beyond preconceptions or superficial interactions to understand others fosters humility, builds alliances, and increases appreciation for the life journeys we all bring to our interactions.

What if you have made these efforts, and your values continue to conflict with others' values? Social workers occasionally encounter situations in which they cannot conform to the profession's values or in which a person or agency's history, behaviors, or communications evoke such powerful reactions that a constructive helping relationship cannot be established. Personal experiences such as addictions, family conflicts, or struggles in school can be triggered by certain case situations. Regardless of their histories, some social workers maintain that they cannot work with clients accused of sex offenses (Grady & Strom-Gottfried, 2011). Some agency missions and personnel evoke strong negative reactions. Professionals with strong religious, political, or ideological convictions may find it difficult to engage with organizations or personnel that they perceive rejects or marginalizes their views. In such instances, it is important to acknowledge these reactions and to explore them through supervision or therapy. It may be feasible to overcome these

difficulties to be more fully available as a helping person. Righteous indignation may feel satisfying, but it may also impede the ability to act with or on behalf of the clients who need your help. If personal change is not possible or timely, or if the situation is exceptional, the social worker and their supervisor should explore the possibility of transferring the case to another practitioner who can effectively engage with the client or the necessary systems.

In such circumstances, it is vital to clarify that the transfer is because clients deserve the best service possible, and the particular social worker cannot provide that service. It is not necessary to go into detail about the social worker's challenges. A general explanation conveys goodwill and safeguards clients' well-being. When a transfer is not possible, the social worker is responsible for seeking intensive assistance and oversight to ensure that services are properly provided and that ethical and professional responsibilities are upheld. Practitioners who are consistently unable to accept clients' differences or carry out their roles in a professional manner owe it to themselves and to future clients to reflect seriously on their suitability for the social work field.

Values, Ethics, and Culture

C1

Are values such as justice and acceptance universally recognized guidelines for behavior, or should their application be tempered by local or regional norms? Is the embrace of individual rights insensitive to cultures in which duty to community, family, and tradition are more highly prized? Do social work codes reflect the values of entrenched powerful interests in wealthy nations and thus overemphasize individual pathology over structural change or emphasize independence over interdependence (Finn 2021; Jessop, 1998; Silvawe, 1995)? These are not merely philosophical disputes. Tensions in the embrace of values and ethics creates significant challenges for practitioners working amid international or cultural differences (Banks & Nohr, 2011; Gharaibeh, 2019). Cultural values shift and evolve over time, and social workers' systems change efforts may appropriately target stances that harm or disenfranchise certain groups, but how can social workers ensure that their efforts are proper and congruent with the desires of the particular cultural group and not a misguided effort born of paternalism and ethnocentrism?

Are ethics fixed guidelines that should be applied universally (a **deontological perspective**)? Are they flexible, depending on the place and population to which they are applied (a **relativist position**)? Do ethics depend on the worker having honorable personal characteristics, such as honesty, kindness, or integrity (**virtue ethics**)? (Reamer, 2019). Healy (2007) concludes that "social work is obligated to work for cultural change when equal rights are in jeopardy" (p. 6), labeling this position as "moderate universalism" (p. 24), where the human rights of equality and protection are promoted along with the importance of cultural diversity and community ties. As we have introduced already in this book, striving for cultural humility, curiosity, and lifelong learning are vital first steps to bridge competing values and norms (Barsky, 2019; Maschi & Liebowitz, 2018). Ultimately, striking this balance means that social workers, individually and collectively, must be aware of their values and those of their colleagues and clients and engage in ongoing education and conversation. This approach encourages exploration and discourse in order to determine where the ethical tensions reside and how much of an impediment they are to the helping process.

Ethics

Codes of ethics are the embodiment of a profession's values. They set forth principles and standards for behavior of members of that profession. Codes can be issued by employers, regulatory bodies, and professional associations. For example, in the United States, licensed social workers are governed by codes of conduct from their state regulatory board as well as general codes of the profession. The International Federation of Social Workers (IFSW) issues a code, as do associations of social workers in many nations (BASW, 2014; CASW, 2005; IFSW, 2018; JFSW, 2005). In each jurisdiction, the code reflects values and standards that embody the history, culture, and context in which it is written. The Indian Declaration of Ethics for Professional Social Workers emphasizes solidarity, peace and nonviolence, cooperation, and environmental ethics. Puerto Rico's code centers issues of economic and political disenfranchisement, human rights, release, and emancipation. The Canadian Association of Social Work code is explicitly linked to the Universal Declaration of Human Rights. Beyond national or regional variations, the auspices that issue codes demonstrate special emphases in values and standards. The National Association of Black Social Workers code accentuates political and social action for the security and well-being of the Black community. The Code of Ethics for Radical Social Service reflects a Marxist critique of capitalism and thus highlights the struggle for social transformation and revolutionary societal change (Finn, 2021).

Today in the United States, the most employed code of ethics is promulgated by the NASW. It addresses a range of responsibilities that social workers have as professionals to their clients, their colleagues, their employers, their profession, and society. This section addresses four primary areas of ethical responsibility for social workers: self-determination, informed consent, maintenance of client–social worker boundaries, and confidentiality. First, however, it details how ethics are related to legal responsibilities and malpractice risks. The section concludes by summarizing the resources and processes available for resolving ethical dilemmas.

The Intersection of Laws and Ethics

The practice of social work is governed by a vast array of policies, laws, and regulations. Whether established by court cases, the U.S. Congress, state legislatures, licensure boards, or regulatory agencies, these rules affect social workers' decisions and actions.

For example, state mandatory reporting laws require social workers to report cases in which child abuse is suspected. The Health Insurance Portability and Accountability Act (HIPAA) regulates the storage and sharing of patient records (U.S. Department of Health and Human Services, 2003). Some states' administrative rules forbid the placement of children with same-sex foster parents. Licensure board regulations may forbid social work practice by persons with felony convictions. Federal court cases may extend evidential privilege to communications with social workers (Reamer, 1999). Federal, state, or local laws may prohibit the provision of certain benefits to undocumented immigrants. Competent practice requires social workers to be aware of the laws and regulations that govern the profession and apply to their area of practice and the populations they serve. But knowing the laws is not enough. Consider the case of Alice on the following page.

This case neatly captures the clash of ethics, laws, and regulations and illustrates the stakes for social workers who make the wrong decision. In a scenario such as this one, the social worker needs a clear answer from a lawyer or a supervisor who will tell them exactly what to do. Unfortunately, matters are not that simple. Competent practice requires knowledge of both the applicable ethical principles and the relevant laws. Even with this knowledge, dilemmas may persist. In this case example, the ethical principles of self-determination and confidentiality are pitted against the principle to protect others from harm, which itself is derived from a court case (Barsky 2019; Reamer, 1995). The state or setting where the case takes place may have laws or regulations that govern the social worker's actions. Finally, the threat of civil litigation for malpractice looms large, even when the social worker's actions are thoughtful, careful, ethical, and legal.

When you think about the intersection of laws and ethics, it may be helpful to think of a Venn diagram with two ovals overlapping (see Figure 4-1). In the center are areas common to both ethics and laws; within each oval are items that are exclusive to laws and ethics, respectively.

Figure 4-1 The Relationship of Law and Ethics

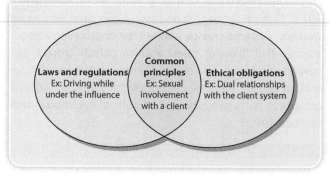

Case Example

Alice is a 38-year-old woman who has presented for treatment, filled with guilt as the result of a brief extramarital affair. In her third session, she discloses that she is HIV positive but is unwilling to tell her husband of her status because then the affair would be revealed, and she fears losing him and her two young daughters. You are concerned about the danger to her husband's health and press her to tell him or to allow you to do so. Alice responds that you seem more concerned about her husband than about her. She says if you keep pushing for telling him you will be breaking your promise of confidentiality and violating her privacy. She implies that she would sue you or report you to your licensing board and to your profession's ethics committee.

Some standards contained in the NASW Code of Ethics are not addressed by laws and regulations (such as the prohibition of sexual relationships with supervisees or standards on treating colleagues with respect). Similarly, some areas of the law are not covered by the Code of Ethics. For example, it is illegal to drive while intoxicated, but the Code of Ethics lacks a standard related to that act. Where the two realms intersect, there can be areas of agreement as well as areas of discord. As the Code of Ethics notes:

> Social workers' primary responsibility is to promote the well-being of clients. In general, clients' interests are primary. However, social workers' responsibility to the larger society or specific legal obligations may on limited occasions supersede the loyalty owed clients, and clients should be so advised. (NASW, 2021, p. 7)

Also:

> Instances may arise when social workers' ethical obligations conflict with agency policies or relevant laws or regulations. When such conflicts occur, social workers must make a responsible effort to resolve the conflict in a manner that is consistent with the values, principles, and standards expressed in this Code. If a reasonable resolution of the conflict does not appear possible, social workers should seek proper consultation before making a decision. (NASW, 2021, pp. 3–4)

Processes for ethical decision-making are addressed later in this chapter. For now, it is important to acknowledge that social workers must know both the law and ethical principles to practice effectively. They must also recognize that sometimes conflicts occur between and among ethical and legal imperatives. For example, state laws may prohibit the provision of services or resources to undocumented immigrants, but ethics would expect social workers to fill basic human needs. Thoughtful examination, consultation, and skillful application of the principles serve as guides when laws and ethics collide.

Key Ethical Principles

The NASW Code of Ethics contains 171 standards, addressing a variety of ethical issues (such as conflicts of interest, competence, or confidentiality) for social workers in a range of roles (such as supervisor, teacher, direct practitioner, or administrator). In this section, we examine four key areas of immediate relevance to direct practitioners: self-determination, informed consent, professional boundaries, and confidentiality.

Self-Determination

Biestek (1957) has defined self-determination as "the practical recognition of the right and need of clients to freedom in making their own choices and decisions" (p. 103). Self-determination is central to the social worker's ethical responsibility to clients:

> Social workers respect and promote the right of clients to self-determination and assist clients in their efforts to identify and clarify their goals. Social workers may limit clients' right to self-determination when, in their professional judgment, clients' actions or potential actions pose a serious, foreseeable, and imminent risk to themselves or others. (NASW, 2021, p. 7)

This value also embodies the perspective that individuals have the capacity to grow, change, and develop solutions to their difficulties, as well as the right and capacity to responsibly exercise free choice. Affirming someone's right to self-determination rests in large measure on the social worker's perceptions of the helping role and the change process. Social workers who rush to solutions or freely dispense advice may demean others by overlooking existing strengths and efforts, foster dependency, and discourage self-reliance or enable passive cooperation (or passive resistance). The type of relationship that affirms self-determination and supports growth is a partnership wherein the practitioner and the client (whether an individual, a couple, or a group) are joined in a mutual effort to search for solutions to problems and develop resources to enact them. As enablers of change, social workers facilitate clients' quests to view their problems realistically, consider various solutions and their consequences, implement change-oriented strategies, understand themselves and others more fully, gain awareness of previously unrecognized strengths and opportunities for growth, and tackle obstacles to change and growth. As helpful as these steps are, ultimately, the responsibility for pursuing these options rests with the client.

Just as fostering self-determination enhances client autonomy, exhibiting paternalism (i.e., preventing self-determination based on a judgment of the client's own good) infringes on autonomy. Linzer (1999) refers to paternalism as "the overriding of a person's wishes or actions through coercion, deception or nondisclosure of information, or for the welfare of others" (p. 137). A similar concept is paternalistic beneficence, wherein the social worker implements protective interventions to enhance the client's quality of life, sometimes despite the client's objections (Abramson, 1985; Murdach, 1996). Laws that allow professionals to override a client's wishes to administer antipsychotic medication are created in the notion that someone else knows best what another person needs.

Under what conditions might it be acceptable for a social worker to override a client's autonomy? Paternalism may be acceptable when a client is young or judged not to have sufficient decision-making capacity, when an irreversible act such as suicide can be prevented, or when the interference with the client's decisions or actions ensures other freedoms or liberties, such as preventing a serious crime (Reamer, 2018; Strom-Gottfried, 2008). Murdach (1996) suggests three gradations of beneficent actions, which vary in their level of intrusiveness depending on the degree of risk and the client's decision-making capacity. Even under these circumstances, social workers must weigh the basis for their decisions against the potential outcomes of their actions.

For example, if a psychiatric patient refuses medication, some would argue that the client lacks capacity to make such a decision, and forcing them to take the medication would be "for the client's own good," yet diagnosis or placement is not a sufficient basis for overriding a person's autonomy. For this reason, most states have developed elaborate administrative and judicial processes that must be traversed before an individual can be involuntarily hospitalized or medicated (Montross, 2014).

Even when clients have reduced ability for self-determination, social workers should act to ensure that they exercise their capacities to the fullest feasible extent. For example, self-determination can be extended to individuals who are terminally ill by educating them about their options and encouraging them to articulate their desires through advance directives that provide instructions to family members and health-care personnel regarding which medical interventions are acceptable. Diminished intellectual or cognitive capacity doesn't mean that people are unable to make any decisions regarding their lives, but competence may vary by the type and significance of the decision. Although child clients are not authorized to give consent for treatment, through the process of seeking assent, social workers can explain the proposed services to the child and seek their agreement for care.

Operationalizing clients' rights to self-determination can sometimes pose perplexing challenges. Adding to this complexity is the reality that in certain instances, higher order principles such as safety supersede the right to self-determination. To challenge your thinking about how you might affirm the value of self-determination in practical situations, we have provided scenarios based on our own experiences. As you read each scenario, analyze possible courses of action, and think of the laws, policies, and resources that you might consult as part of your decision-making. Consider how you would work with the client to maximize self-determination, taking care also to promote their best interests.

Self-Determination Scenario 1

In your work for the state welfare department, you oversee the care of numerous nursing home residents whose services are paid for by the state. Two of your clients, both in their 90s, reside in the same facility and are sexually involved with each other. The couple's family members oppose the union for various reasons, and the administrator of the facility strenuously protests that their behavior is disruptive and risky if either adult is incompetent or coercive.

Self-Determination Scenario 2

A 15-year-old who is four months pregnant has contacted you several times in regard to planning for her child. During her last visit, she confided that she is habituated to heroin. You have expressed your concern that the drug may cause prenatal damage, but she does not seem worried, nor does she want to give up use of the drug. You also know that she obtains money for heroin through prostitution and is living on the street.

Self-Determination Scenario 3

While making a visit to Mr. F, an elderly man living in a rural farmhouse, you discover that he is disheveled and thin, and the house is unclean, piled high with old newspapers and magazines, and occupied by more than a dozen cats. The homecare aides have been inattentive and untrustworthy, so Mr. F fired them, and he now reports that he is "managing fine on my own."

Self-Determination Scenario 4

As a rehabilitation worker, you have arranged for a young woman to receive training as a beautician in a local technical college, a vocation in which she expressed intense interest. Although initially enthusiastic, she now tells you that she wants to discontinue the program and go into nursing. According to your client, her supervisor at the college is critical of her work, and the other trainees tease her and talk about her behind her back. You are torn about what to do because you have seen the client antagonize others with quick or profane remarks. You wonder if, rather than change programs, she needs to learn more effective ways of communicating and relating to her supervisor and coworkers.

Providing Informed Consent

Nine standards in the NASW Code of Ethics address facets of **informed consent**. In essence, informed consent requires that social workers:

C1

> ...use clear and understandable language to inform clients of the purpose of the services, risks related to the services, limits to services because of the requirements of a third-party payer, relevant costs, reasonable alternatives, clients' right to refuse or withdraw consent, and the time frame covered by the consent. Social workers should provide clients with an opportunity to ask questions (NASW, 2021, pp. 7–8).

As discussed in Chapter 1, the growth in technology has led to additional considerations for ethics, including informed consent. For example,

> Social workers who use technology to provide social work services should obtain informed consent from the individuals using these services during the initial screening or interview and prior to initiating services. Social workers should assess clients' capacity to provide informed consent and, when using technology to communicate, verify the identity and location of clients. (NASW, 2021, p. 8).

> Social workers should obtain client consent before conducting an electronic search on the client. Exceptions may arise when the search is for purposes of protecting the client or other people from serious, foreseeable, and imminent harm, or for other compelling professional reasons. (NASW, 2021, pp. 7–8).

Timely and understandable informed consent sets the stage for social work services by acquainting the client with expectations for the process. For example, a common element of informed consent involves the limits on client privacy. Social workers explicitly state that in situations involving concerns about the client's danger to self or others, the social worker reserves the right to break confidentiality and seek appropriate help. Mandatory reporting requirements (for child and elder abuse and other circumstances, such as communicable diseases) are typically also covered at this time.

The Code of Ethics also indicates that clients should be informed when their services are being provided by a student. This can be an uncomfortable conversation, as interns may feel that acknowledging student status undermines their authority or the client's confidence in them. Nevertheless, from the service recipient's perspective, that is important information. Even if it leads the client to question the worker's competence, it is their right to do so and could be considered a sign of strength to insist on quality care. Providing and receiving informed consent can be awkard and time consuming, but consider the breach of trust and progress that could occur when a client learns, after three months of service, that their worker is a student who will be away for five weeks for holiday break from college.

In addition to respectfully educating clients about their rights and responsibilities, informed consent lays the groundwork for future actions the social worker might need to take. In the case example earlier in the chapter about the woman who refused to let her husband know about her HIV-positive status, informed consent would have alerted the client at the outset to the social worker's responsibility to protect others from harm and the duty to notify public health or other authorities about the risk created by the client's unprotected sexual activity.

Some professionals view informed consent as a formality to be disposed of at the first interview or as a legalistic form to have clients sign and then file away. In fact, informed consent should be an active and ongoing part of the helping process. Given the tension and uncertainty that can accompany a first session, clients may not realize the significance of the information being provided. In addition, new issues may emerge that require discussion of the client's risks, benefits, and options (Strom-Gottfried, 1998b). Therefore, it makes sense to revisit the parameters of service and invite questions throughout the helping process. Having a fact sheet that describes relevant policies and answers commonly asked questions can also help clients by giving them something to refer to between meetings, should questions arise (Houston-Vega et al., 1997; Zuckerman, 2008).

To facilitate informed consent for persons with hearing, literacy, or language difficulties, social workers should utilize interpreters and multiple communication methods as appropriate. When clients are temporarily or permanently incapable of providing informed consent, "social workers should protect clients' interests by seeking permission from an appropriate third party, informing clients consistent with the client's level of understanding," and "seek to ensure that the third party acts in a manner consistent with the client's wishes and interests" (NASW, 2021, p. 8). Even people who are receiving services involuntarily are entitled to know the nature of the care they will be receiving and understand their right to accept or refuse it.

Preserving Professional Boundaries

The term **boundaries** refers to norms of separation that are maintained between the social worker and the client in an effort to preserve the working relationship. They are intended to help prevent conflicts of interest, making the client's interests the primary focus and avoiding situations in which the social worker's professionalism is compromised. In part, boundaries help clarify that the client–social worker relationship is not a social one. Even though the helping relationship may involve a high degree of trust and client disclosure, the relationship is not an intimate one, such as might be experienced with a friend, partner, or family member. When clients can trust that boundaries exist and will be maintained by the social worker, they are more able to focus on the issues for which they are seeking help. They can freely share of themselves and trust that the social worker's reactions and statements—whether of support, confrontation, or empathy—are artifacts of the working relationship, not social or sexual overtures or personal reactions such as might arise when friends agree or disagree.

Sometimes social workers and other helping professionals have a difficult time with the notion of boundaries, perceiving that they establish a hierarchical relationship in which the client is deemed less worthy than the social worker. Some professionals may also feel that establishing such boundaries is a cold and clinical move, treating the client as an object instead of a fellow human deserving of warmth and compassion (Lazarus, 1994). Our viewpoint is that the two positions are not mutually exclusive. Social workers can have relationships with clients that are characterized by collaborative problem solving and mutuality, and they can react to clients authentically and kindly, without blurring the boundaries of their relationship or obscuring the purpose of their work.

The NASW Code of Ethics addresses boundaries through several provisions:

1. "Social workers should not take unfair advantage of any professional relationship or exploit others to further their personal, religious, political, or business interests" (NASW, 2021, p. 10).

2. "Social workers should not engage in dual or multiple relationships with clients or former clients in which there is a risk of exploitation or potential harm to the client. In instances when dual or multiple relationships are unavoidable, social workers should take steps to protect clients and are responsible for setting clear, appropriate, and culturally sensitive boundaries. (Dual or multiple relationships occur when social workers relate to clients in more than one relationship, whether professional, social, or business. Dual or multiple relationships can occur simultaneously or consecutively.)" (NASW, 2021, p. 10).

3. "Social workers should not engage in physical contact with clients when there is a possibility of psychological harm to the client as a result of the contact (such as cradling or caressing clients). Social workers who engage in appropriate physical contact with clients are responsible for setting clear, appropriate, and culturally sensitive boundaries that govern such physical contact." (NASW, 2021, p. 15).

4. "Social workers should under no circumstances engage in sexual activities, inappropriate sexual communications through the use of technology or in person, or sexual contact with current clients, whether such contact is consensual or forced." (NASW, 2021, p. 15).

5. "Social workers should not engage in sexual activities or sexual contact with clients' relatives or other individuals with whom clients maintain a close personal relationship....This has the potential to be harmful to the client and may make it difficult for the social worker and client to maintain appropriate professional boundaries. Social workers—not their

clients, their clients' relatives, or other individuals with whom the client maintains a personal relationship—assume the full burden for setting clear, appropriate, and culturally sensitive boundaries." (NASW, 2021, p. 15).

6. "Social workers should not engage in sexual activities or sexual contact with former clients because of the potential for harm to the client." (NASW, 2021, p. 15).

Although these standards of practice may seem self-evident, they represent an area fraught with difficulty within social work and other helping professions. Research on ethics complaints indicates that in NASW-adjudicated cases, boundary violations accounted for more than half of all cases in which violations occurred (Strom-Gottfried, 1999a). Most social workers cannot imagine developing sexual relationships with their clients, yet this outcome is often the culmination of a slippery slope of boundary problems that may include excessive self-disclosure on the part of the social worker, the exchange of personal gifts, socializing or meeting for meals outside the office, and arranging for the client to perform office and household chores or other favors (Barsky, 2019; Epstein et al., 1992; Gartrell, 1992).

The growth in electronic communications creates other considerations for professional boundary setting. Search engines, social networking sites, and electronic communications can blur private and professional boundaries for clients and workers. Rudimentary online searches usually reveal information about both service providers and service recipients, and the infusion of personal information into the helping relationship can create role confusion and divert the focus from therapeutic goals. The NASW Code cautions that "social workers should avoid communication with clients using technology (such as social networking sites, online chat, email, text messages, telephone, and video) for personal or nonwork-related purposes," "take reasonable steps to prevent client access to social workers' personal social networking sites and personal technology" and "be aware that posting personal information on professional websites or other media might cause boundary confusion, inappropriate dual relationships, or harm to clients" (2017, p. 11).

While social workers have the right to their personal lives, hobbies, political action, and memberships, these activities may become detectable through social media and may affect professional standing and effectiveness. For example, employers, supervisors, clients, and clients' families may discover the social worker's presence on websites, social media, and other forms of technology and censure or criticize the worker because

of it. In the words of the Code of Ethics, "Social workers should be aware that involvement in electronic communication with groups based on race, ethnicity, language, sexual orientation, gender identity or expression, mental or physical ability, religion, immigration status, and other personal affiliations may affect their ability to work effectively with particular clients" (NASW, 2021, p. 11).

Boundary issues can be both subtle and complex. For example, you may meet a neighbor in the agency waiting room or run into a consumer while doing your grocery shopping. You may decide to buy a car and find that the salesperson is a former client. You may visit a relative in the hospital and discover that their roommate is a current or former client. Friends in need of social work services may ask to be assigned to your caseload because you already know them so well. A client may ask you to attend their family event, such as a graduation or wedding. You may resonate with some clients and think what great friends they could be. You may have experienced a problem like the client's and wish to tell the client how you handled it. You may sympathize with a person's job search plight and consider referring them to a friend who is currently hiring new workers.

It is not uncommon for social workers to experience feelings of warmth, kinship, and even sexual attraction toward those with whom they work. When such feelings arise, however, it is crucial to raise them with faculty or supervisors so they can be acknowledged and examined. Such discussion normalizes and neutralizes these feelings and decreases the likelihood that the social worker acts on the attraction (Pope et al., 1993). These issues are explored further in Chapter 18 as we discuss relational reactions and their effects on the helping process.

Not all encounters with clients outside the helping relationship are unethical. Contacts with clients that are unplanned, manageable, temporary, and transparent may simply be boundary crossings rather than boundary violations (Barsky, 2019). Certain settings (such as rural practice) and types of work (such as home-based care and community-based interventions) may create special opportunities for boundary confusion (Strom, 2022; Strom-Gottfried, 2005, 2009). The possibilities for boundary complications are endless, and addressing them involves nuanced application of the standards on boundary setting and other ethical principles, such as maintaining confidentiality and avoiding conflicts of interest. Therefore, setting "clear, appropriate, and culturally sensitive boundaries" (NASW, 2021, p. 10) might mean different things in different settings.

Many social workers routinely discuss the possibility of public contact with clients during the first session, explaining, for example, that in deference to privacy, they will not acknowledge the client unless spoken to first should they encounter the client in a grocery store or on the street. A social worker invited to "friend" a client on a social networking site (or join the client in an in-person social activity) can sensitively explain the importance of not blurring the working relationship with other kinds of contact. Buying a car (or some other product or service with variable pricing) from a client or former client could be exploitive of either party and could complicate the working relationship if the product or service is flawed. Such arrangements should be avoided. If they cannot, boundary setting may mean ending the commercial relationship or the helping relationship if the two cannot be successfully merged. If neither choice is a possibility, consultation and intercession of a supervisor would be recommended to assure that neither the client nor the social worker is disadvantaged by the transaction.

An invitation to an event like a graduation or marriage ceremony should be processed with the client to explore the meaning of the offer. Ethical boundary setting might variously involve declining the invitation, accepting it, or attending the public portion of the event rather than the more private elements, such as a reception. The desire to disclose personal experiences with a client may be a form of authenticity (discussed further in Chapter 5) or an upsetting derailment where attention is switched from the client's experiences and needs to the social worker's. Social workers should always be mindful of what they are trying to accomplish in making a personal self-disclosure and consider alternate ways of achieving the same objective. For example, rather than the social worker saying, "When I have that kind of conflict with my mother, I do X," they could simply state, "Sometimes, people in conflict with their parents find that X is helpful."

Later in this chapter, we discuss strategies for more thoroughly examining and resolving ethical dilemmas. The key in managing boundaries is to be alert to **dual relationships**, seek advice from colleagues and supervisors, and take care that the primacy of the helping relationship is preserved in questionable boundary situations (Reamer, 2019). Consultation helps social workers determine whether dual relationships are avoidable and whether they are problematic. It is incumbent on the social worker to ensure that clients are not taken advantage of and that their services are not obscured or affected detrimentally when boundary crossings cannot be avoided.

Safeguarding Confidentiality

Confidentiality is essential to the helping process. Without the assurance of confidentiality, it is unlikely that anyone seeking services would risk disclosing private aspects of their lives that, if revealed, could cause shame or damage to their reputations. This is especially true when problems involve shameful events, troubling thoughts, and traumatic experiences. Implied in confidentiality is an assurance that the practitioner will never reveal such personal matters to others.

Social workers are bound by the NASW Code of Ethics to safeguard their clients' confidentiality. While numerous standards operationalize this principle, in essence, social workers are expected to respect clients' privacy, gather information only for the purpose of providing effective services, and disclose information only with clients' consent. Disclosure of information without clients' permission should be done only for compelling reasons, and even then, there are limits on what information can be shared and with whom. These exceptions to confidentiality are addressed later in this section.

An unjustified breach of confidentiality is a violation of justice and is tantamount to theft of a secret with which one has been entrusted (Biestek, 1957). Maintaining strict confidentiality requires a strong commitment and constant vigilance because people commonly reveal information that is shocking, moving, humorous, bizarre, or titillating. To fulfill your responsibility in maintaining privacy, you must guard against disclosing information in inappropriate situations. Examples include discussing details of your work with family and friends, having gossip sessions with colleagues or fellow students, doing dictation within the listening range of others, discussing client situations within earshot of other staff, posting pictures or case information from clients on social media sites, and making remarks about cases in elevators or other public places.

The emergence of technology that permits the electronic collection, transfer, and storage of information raises new complexities for maintaining client privacy (Barsky, 2019). When you leave a voice mail for a client, are you certain that only the client will receive the message? Will you agree to accept and send text messages to clients? When you post information in an electronic record system, can you be sure that others will not access and misuse the data? Further complexities arise in the electronic provision of services through video software, websites, online groups, and so on. There are many advantages to such interventions. They are commonly used methods of modern communication. They can efficiently offer reminders of appointments or tips for relapse prevention, and they can assist with symptom management and increase service access for homebound individuals and those who need access to services on a 24/7 basis (Kessler et al., 2009; Shapiro et al., 2009), yet they present challenges for confidentiality, informed consent, and professional liability (Reamer 2018).

Beyond ethical standards, the Health Insurance Portability and Accountability Act of 1996 (HIPAA) established federal standards to protect the privacy of personal health information. HIPAA regulations affect pharmacies, health-care settings, and insurance plans as well as individual health and mental health providers. The rules affect identifiable client information in all forms, including paper records, electronic data and communications, verbal communications, client files, and psychotherapy notes. There are several important provisions for social workers in HIPAA (CDC, 2018; Camper & Felton, 2020; Office of Civil Rights, 2008b; Theodos & Sittig, 2020):

- A general principle of the Privacy Rule is that if a person has the right to make a health-care decision, then that person has a right to the information associated with that decision.

- Although clients should have access to their records and the opportunity to seek corrections if they identify errors or mistakes, their access to psychotherapy notes is restricted.

- Clients must be given information on the organization's privacy policies, and they must sign a form or otherwise indicate that they have received the information.

- Client records or data should be protected from non-medical uses, such as marketing, unless the client gives specific permission otherwise.

- Clients should understand their rights to request other reasonable efforts to protect confidentiality, such as requesting to be contacted only at certain times or numbers.

- Organizations and their employees must take care to ensure that security standards are in place and that they are reinforced through staff development and agency policies.

- HIPAA recognizes the validity of professional standards, such as those contained in the NASW Code of Ethics, and in some cases, those provisions may be more stringent than HIPAA's.

- In the case of minors, parents are generally considered the personal representatives for their children and as such can have access to personal health information as well as make health-care decisions on behalf of their children. Some exceptions are: (1) when State law does not require parental consent for a minor to receive treatment, (2) when a court has appointed someone other than the parent as the child's guardian, and (3) if the parent agrees to a confidential relationship between the health care provider and the child.

- The health-care provider does not have to disclose information to the parent of a minor if (1) the provider has reasonable belief of abuse or neglect or that the information to be provided may endanger the child, or (2) using personal judgment, the provider decides that it is not in the minor client's best interest to treat the parent as the minor's individual representative.

The Family Educational Rights and Privacy Act (FERPA) is another significant privacy law that resembles HIPAA in empowering individuals to control their personal information (CDC, 2018). FERPA applies to public and private schools from kindergarten through universities. It gives parents (and, students, once they are 18) control over educational records allowing them to review and correct the records and requiring consent for the disclosure of information in the record, except under exceptional circumstances (CDC, 2019). As such, FERPA has significant implications for social workers employed in schools or college wellness centers and those who interface with schools through child welfare, juvenile justice, and family services (U.S. Department of Education, 2020).

What Are the Limits on Confidentiality?

Although social workers are expected to safeguard the information they collect in the course of their professional duties, there are several situations in which helping professionals are allowed or are compelled to share case information. These include when the social worker is seeking supervision or consultation, when the client waives confidentiality, when the client presents a danger to self or others, when the social worker is reporting suspicions of child or elder maltreatment, and when the social worker presented with a subpoena or court order.

Supervision and Consultation

The right to confidentiality is not absolute because case situations are frequently discussed with supervisors and consultants and may be presented at staff conferences. Disclosing information in these instances, however, is for the purpose of enhancing the provision of services, and clients generally consent to these uses when the purpose is clarified. The client has a right to be informed that such disclosures may occur, and practitioners seeking supervision have a responsibility to fully conceal the identity of the client and reveal no more personal information than is necessary to get assistance on the case.

Other personnel such as administrators, volunteers, clerical staff, consultants, board members, researchers, legal counsel, and outside persons who may review records for purposes of quality assurance, peer review, or accreditation may have access to files or case information. This access to information should be for the purposes of better serving the client, and these individuals should sign binding agreements not to misuse confidential information. It is essential that social workers promote policies and norms that protect confidentiality and assure that case information is treated carefully and respectfully.

Client Waivers of Confidentiality

Social workers are often asked by other professionals or agencies to provide confidential information about the nature of their client's difficulties or the services provided. Sometimes, these requests can be made with such authority that the recipient is caught off guard, inadvertently acknowledging a particular person as a client or providing the information requested about the case. It is important that case data be provided only with the written, informed consent of clients, as this releases the practitioner and the agency from liability in disclosing the requested information. Even when informed consent is obtained, it is important to reveal information selectively based on the essential needs of the other party.

In some exceptional circumstances, information can be revealed without informed consent, such as a bona fide emergency in which a client's life appears to be at stake or when the social worker is legally compelled to do so, as in the reporting of child or elder abuse. In other instances, it is prudent to obtain supervisory and legal input before disclosing confidential information without the client's written consent for release of information.

Danger to Self or Others

In certain instances, the right to confidentiality may be less compelling than the rights of others who could be severely harmed or damaged by actions planned by the client and confided to the practitioner. For example, if the client plans to commit kidnapping, injury, or murder, the social worker is obligated to disclose these intentions to the intended victim and law enforcement officials so that timely preventive action can be taken. Indeed, if practitioners fail to make appropriate disclosures under these circumstances, they may be liable to civil prosecution for negligence, a precedent established in the *Tarasoff* case (Reamer, 1994). This court decision has led to varying interpretations in subsequent cases and in resulting state laws, but two principles have consistently resulted from it

(Dickson, 1998; Houston-Vega et al., 1997): If the worker perceives a serious, foreseeable, and imminent threat to an identifiable potential victim, the social worker should (1) act to warn the victim(s) or (2) take other precautions (such as notifying police or placing the client in a secure facility) to protect the public from harm.

Another application of the duty to protect personal safety involves intervening to prevent a client's suicide. Social workers are not only permitted to breach a client's privacy to mobilize support and safety for a person with acute suicidal intentions, but they are also obligated to do so. The failure to act assertively to avoid lethal self-harm could be considered liability for wrongful client death. Knowing when the risk is sufficient to warrant breaking a client's confidence is both a clinical decision and an ethical matter. Chapter 9 offers guidelines for determining the risk of lethality in cases of suicidal threats or client aggression.

Suspicion of Child or Elder Abuse

The rights of others also take precedence over the client's right to confidentiality in instances of child abuse or neglect. In fact, all 50 states have statutes making it mandatory for professionals to report suspected or known child abuse. Statutes governing the mandatory reporting of child abuse may make it a crime if responsible parties fail to report abuse. States have established similar provisions for reporting the suspected abuse of the elderly or other vulnerable adults (Corey et al., 2014). The responsibility to report suspicions of abuse does not empower the social worker to breach confidentiality in other ways. That is, even though social workers are **mandated reporters**, they should still use caution in the amount of unrelated case information shared with child welfare authorities. Furthermore, the requirement is to report suspicions to specific protective agencies, not to disclose information to the client's family members, teachers, social media, or other parties.

Although afforded immunity from prosecution for reporting, practitioners must still confront the difficult challenge of preserving the helping relationship after having breached the client's confidentiality. One way of managing this tension is through informed consent. As noted earlier, clients should know at the outset of service what the ground rules for service are and what limits exist on what the social worker can keep private. When people understand that the social worker must report suspected child abuse, such a report may not be as damaging to the helping relationship. Similarly, the Code of Ethics states, "If social workers plan to disclose confidential information, they should (when feasible and to the extent possible) inform clients about the disclosure and the potential consequences prior to disclosing the information." (NASW, 2021, p. 12). With a trusting relationship, informed consent, and careful processing of the decision to file a child abuse report, social workers may prevent feelings of betrayal and preserve the working alliance.

Subpoenas and Privileged Communication

Yet another constraint on the client's right to confidentiality is that this right does not necessarily extend into courts of law. Unless social workers are practicing in states that recognize the concept of privileged communication, they may be compelled by courts to reveal confidential information and to produce confidential records. **Privileged communication** refers to communications made within a "legally protected relationship," which "cannot be introduced into court without the consent of the person making the communication," typically the patient or client (Dickson, 1998, p. 32). Statutes that recognize privileged communication exempt certain professions from being legally compelled to reveal content disclosed in the context of a confidential relationship.

Determining the presence and applicability of privilege can be complicated, however. As Dickson notes, "Privilege laws can vary with the profession of the individual receiving the communication, the material communicated, the purpose of the communication, whether the proceeding is criminal or civil, and whether the professional is employed by the state or is in private practice, among other factors" (1998, p. 33). At the federal level, the U.S. Supreme Court in *Jaffee v. Redmond* upheld client communications as privileged and specifically extended "that privilege to licensed social workers" (Social Workers and Psychotherapist-Patient Privilege: *Jaffee v. Redmond* Revisited, 2005).

Laws recognizing privileged communication are created for the protection of the client; thus, the privilege belongs to the client, not to the professional (Schwartz, 1989). Because subpoenas, whether for records or testimony, are orders of the court, social workers cannot ignore them. Whether the subpoena is legitimate or is issued for irrelevant or immaterial information, you should be wary about submitting privileged material, carefully reviewing the subpoena, and consulting with the client, and a supervisor and agency attorney before responding (Barsky, 2019).

Confidentiality in Various Types of Recording

Accreditation standards, funding sources, state and federal laws all may dictate how agencies maintain record-keeping systems. Because case records can be subpoenaed and because clients and other personnel have access to them, it is essential that practitioners develop and implement policies and practices that provide maximal confidentiality. To this end, social workers should adhere to the following guidelines (Barnett, 2009; Yale University, 2020).

1. Record no more than is essential to the services being provided. Identify observed facts and distinguish them from opinions. Use descriptive terms rather than professional jargon. Avoid using psychiatric and medical diagnoses that have not been verified.

2. Unconfirmed reports about a third party by the client; the personal judgments, opinions, or clinical hypotheses of the clinician; and sensitive information that is not relevant to treatment should be omitted from documentation.

3. Do not include verbatim or process recordings in case files.

4. Assure that records are accurate, relevant, timely, and complete.

5. Employ private and soundproof dictation facilities.

6. Keep paper records in locked files and issue keys only to those personnel who require frequent access to the files. Take similar privacy precautions, such as encryption, firewalls, and passwords to protect electronically stored and shared data.

7. Do not remove case files from the agency except under extraordinary circumstances and with special authorization.

8. Do not leave case files on desks, computer screens, or electronic devices where others might gain access observe them.

9. Inform clients of the agency's authority to gather information, the conditions under which that information may be disclosed, the principal uses of the information, and the effects, if any, of limiting what is shared with the agency.

Beyond case records, special precautions are needed for recordings of client interactions. As noted earlier, social workers sometimes record live interviews or group sessions so that they can analyze interactional patterns or group process at a later time or scrutinize their own performance with a view toward improving their skills and techniques. Recording is also used extensively for instructional sessions between students and practicum instructors and as evidence in investigations, for example, about child abuse. Yet another use of recordings is to provide first-hand feedback to clients by having them listen to or view their actual behavior in live sessions.

Before recording sessions for any of these purposes, social workers should obtain written consent from clients on a form that explicitly specifies how the recording will be used, who may listen to or view the recording, and when it will be erased. A recording should never be made without the client's knowledge and consent. People vary widely in their receptivity to having sessions recorded; if they indicate reluctance, their wishes should be respected. The chances of gaining consent are enhanced by discussing the matter openly and honestly, taking care to explain the right to decline.

Social workers who record sessions assume a heavy burden of responsibility in safeguarding confidentiality because live sessions can prove extremely revealing. Recordings should be guarded to ensure that copies cannot be made and unauthorized persons do not have access to them. When they have served their designated purpose, they should be promptly erased or destroyed. Failure to heed these guidelines may constitute a breach of professional ethics.

Beyond protecting files or recordings from misuse, the NASW Code of Ethics also addresses clients' rights with respect to records, stating that "social workers should provide clients with reasonable access" to their records (NASW, 2021, p. 14). It further notes that the social worker should provide "assistance in interpreting the records and consultation with the client" (p. 14) in situations where the social worker is concerned about misunderstandings or harm arising from seeing the records. Access to records should be limited "only in exceptional circumstances when there is compelling evidence that such access would cause serious harm to the client" (p. 14). In our exprience, the trend toward greater client access to records has enhanced client rights by avoiding misuse of records and has compelled practitioners to be more prudent, rigorous, and circumspect in their documentation.

The Ethics of Practice with Minors

A particular challenge in social work practice is interpreting ethical standards as they apply to clients under the age of 18 (Strom-Gottfried, 2008). Although minor clients have the right to confidentiality, informed consent, self-determination, and the protection of other ethical principles, their rights are limited by laws and policies, by differences in maturity and decision-making capacity, and by their very dependence on adults as their caretakers. As such, parents may retain the right to review a child's treatment record and to be kept informed of issues the child raises in therapy. A 15-year-old teen parent has the right to make decisions about their baby's health care that they cannot legally make about their own. Child welfare experts and other authorities are empowered to decide where to place children and when to move them based on their appraisal of the best interests of the child. A 10-year-old may resist medication or treatment but lacks the ability to withhold consent because of their age and cognitive capacities. As such, their parents or guardians can compel them to comply, even against their expressed wishes.

Minors' rights are also affected by the service setting and by their presenting problems. For example, youth seeking services for substance use would have privacy protections under federal regulations that assure confidentiality (42-CFR) even if their parents insisted on service information (Strom-Gottfried, 2008). Similarly, minors in need of prenatal care or treatment for sexually transmitted diseases could offer their own consent for services and be assured of confidentiality. Emergency services may be provided for a minor if delaying for parental consent could jeopardize the minor's well-being. School districts that accept abstinence only funding for health care can limit the information that social workers and nurses can share with students about contraception and HIV prevention, even if students ask explicitly about those issues.

As you can see, practice with minors is a complex tangle of legal, developmental, ethical, and social issues (Konrad, 2019). Unsnarling this web requires a thorough understanding of child development and the physical, emotional, and cognitive capacities that emerge over the first two decades of the life span. It also requires an understanding of ethical standards, so that the worker appreciates the areas in which tensions might arise between legal and developmental limits to a minor's rights and the expectations of the profession for honoring clients' prerogatives, irrespective of age. Professionals in child-serving settings should be familiar with the policies and practices that govern services for their clientele. Through supervision, staff consultation, and careful decision-making, social workers must consider various factors on a case-by-case basis to ensure that minors' rights are maximized, even amid constraints on those rights.

Understanding and Resolving Ethical Dilemmas

Social workers sometimes experience quandaries in deciding which of two values or ethical principles should take precedence when a conflict exists. In the foregoing discussions of self-determination and confidentiality, for example, we cited examples of how the rights of clients and ethical obligations of social workers are sometimes superseded by higher-order values (e.g., safety, child protection). Thus, the right to confidentiality takes second place when people confide child abuse or when they reveal imminent and serious plans for harmful acts that would jeopardize the health or safety of themselves or other people. Dilemmas can also arise if you find that certain policies or practices of your employing agency seem detrimental to clients. You may be conflicted about your ethical obligations to advocate for changes because doing so may jeopardize your employment or pose a threat to your relationships with certain staff members. Situations such as these present social workers with agonizingly difficult choices about how to uphold professional responsibilities amid the competing rights and prerogatives. Sound ethical decision-making helps assure that all perspectives are carefully considered and opportunities for positive outcomes are maximized (Strom-Gottfried, 2019).

Steps in Ethical Decision-Making

Social workers encounter many situations that inevitably involve uncertainty and ambiguity. Dilemmas are difficult because they pit competing goods or rights against each other. It is not only good to secure safe and loving homes for children in foster care, but it is also good to protect their dignity and privacy by not advertising their availability for adoption in newspapers or online sites. While ethical standards and agency policies can guide decisions, they cannot address the context of every situation. Further, ethical standards themselves contain elastic language such as "compelling," "feasible," or "appropriate" that can be interpreted differently in different scenarios.

What should you do when you find yourself confronted with an ethical dilemma? Ethical decision-making models are as yet untested for their capacity to yield high-quality outcomes. Nevertheless, a list of recommended steps can be used to ensure thoughtful and thorough examination of options (Corey et al., 2014; Marson & McKinney, 2019; Strom-Gottfried, 2008, 2015):

1. Identify the problem or dilemma, gathering as much information about the situation from as many perspectives as possible, including that of the client.
2. Determine the core principles and the competing issues.
3. Review the relevant codes of ethics.
4. Review the applicable laws and regulations.
5. Consult with colleagues, supervisors, legal experts, or professionals with special practice knowledge related to resources and options.
6. Consider the possible and probable courses of action and examine the consequences of various options.
7. Decide on a course of action, weighing the information you have and the impact of your other choices.
8. Develop a strategy for effectively implementing your decision.
9. Evaluate the process and the results to determine whether the intended outcome was achieved and consider modifications for future decisions.

These procedures need not be followed in the order listed. For example, consultation can prove useful in revealing options, identifying pros and cons, and rehearsing strategies for implementing the decision. Laws, ethical standards, and values can be examined after options are developed. Even decisions that must be made on the spot with little planning or consultation can be evaluated after the fact using this model so that critical thinking is brought to bear for future dilemmas and actions. The key is to go beyond mere intuition or reactionary decision-making to mindful, informed, shared, and critically examined choices (Gallagher, 2020).

Beyond these steps, you should be sure to carefully document the input and the considerations taken into account at each phase of the decision-making process. This documentation may be in the client's formal record, your informal notes, or in the notes from supervisory sessions.

Applying the Ethical Decision-Making Model

To apply this model, let's use the case of Alice from earlier in the chapter. As you may recall, Alice is 38 years old and is reluctant to notify her husband of her HIV-positive status for fear of revealing her extramarital affair.

The dilemma for the social worker in the case arises from Alice's disclosure about her HIV-positive status and her refusal to tell her husband, which places him at risk for infection. The social worker has a loyalty to Alice's needs and wishes but also a responsibility to prevent her from harming another person (her husband). If the social worker reveals the truth, they may save the husband's health (and ultimately his life) but in so doing is violating Alice's trust and right to privacy and potentially putting the marriage at risk by exposing the affair. On the other hand, maintaining the secret, although protecting Alice's privacy, could put the unwitting husband at risk for contracting a serious disease and hinder his ability to get treatment for the condition. The social worker may also worry about legal liability for actions or inaction in the case. In fact, either party who is disgruntled or damaged in the case could seek to hold the social worker accountable: Alice for the breach of privacy, or the husband for negligence in failing to protect him from harm.

Several provisions in the NASW Code of Ethics (2017) speak to this dilemma:

Social workers should protect the confidentiality of all information obtained in the course of professional service, except for compelling professional reasons. The general expectation that social workers will keep information confidential does not apply when disclosure is necessary to prevent serious, foreseeable, and imminent harm to a client or others. In all instances, social workers should disclose the least amount of confidential information necessary to achieve the desired purpose; only information that is directly relevant to the purpose for which the disclosure is made should be revealed. (1.07c)

If social workers plan to disclose confidential information, they should (when feasible and to the extent possible) inform clients about the disclosure and the potential consequences prior to disclosing the information. This applies whether social workers disclose confidential information on the basis of a legal requirement or client consent. (1.07d)

Social workers should discuss with clients and other interested parties the nature of confidentiality and limitations of clients' right to confidentiality. (1.07e)

Social workers should review with clients circumstances where confidential information may be requested and where disclosure of confidential information may be legally required. This discussion should occur as soon as possible in the social worker-client relationship and as needed throughout the course of the relationship. (1.07e)

Embedded in these provisions are important ethical concepts: respect for client self-determination, the importance of informed consent, and the significance of discretion around private information. It would be helpful to know how the social worker handled informed consent with Alice at the outset of services. Did Alice understand the social worker's responsibilities should she prove to be a danger to herself or someone else? If so, the question of notifying her husband should not come as a surprise or betrayal but rather as a possible consequence of the conditions of service and the established limits of confidentiality.

Beyond ethical standards, social workers must be familiar with the laws, regulations, practices, and policies that apply in their jurisdictions and practice settings. The disclosure of HIV-positive status is one example where laws and policies vary widely across states. Some states explicitly shield health professionals from liability for making disclosures to protect the health of another if they do so following established procedures. Other states view partner notification as a public health responsibility and require professionals to alert health departments in cases such as Alice's so that health authorities can undertake necessary disclosures. Preferably, the agency where Alice sought services was already aware of the laws and had incorporated them into policies and informed consent procedures for all clients prior to the outset of service. The social worker should also consider how Alice knows she is HIV positive and the partner notification policies in the jurisdiction where she was diagnosed. Depending on where and how she was diagnosed, Alice's condition may have already been processed by medical personnel to initiate notification of her husband, her paramour, and any other individuals who may be at risk by contact with her.

Supervisory guidance is essential in this case. Alice's social worker needs help thinking through the implications for the helping relationship and everyone involved, including the social worker's employer). Supervisory consultation can help the social worker identify alternatives and the various pros and cons involved, anticipate reactions and prepare to address them, and think through ways to improve practices in the future. Beyond talking with the supervisor, the social worker may seek consultation from legal and medical experts to address specific questions about the options, legal liability, and best practices in working with clients with infectious diseases. In these conversations, the social worker should protect the client's identity, focusing on the issues that gave rise to the dilemma rather than details of this particular case.

Options for Action

As a result of these discussions, the social worker may identify at least six options that can be employed singly or in combination:

1. Honor Alice's wishes and keep the secret.

2. Work with Alice to institute safe-sex practices and other control procedures to limit her husband's exposure to her disease.

3. Educate Alice about the virus, learn more about her fears in sharing her diagnosis, and explore her thoughts about the benefits and the complications in not telling her husband.

4. Offer to assist Alice in telling her husband and processing the information.

5. Offer Alice the chance to tell her husband and let her know that if she does not, the social worker will.

6. Make a report (anonymously or not) to the public health authorities about the risk to Alice's husband.

Regardless of what option the social worker pursues, she should make sure that Alice understands the nature of her disease, is getting proper care, and is taking precautionary steps to protect others from contracting HIV. This is congruent with the ethics of putting the client's needs first and has the pragmatic effect of mitigating damage resulting from Alice's secrecy about her illness.

To Tell or Not to Tell

The question, however, remains: to tell or not to tell? The options that ultimately involve alerting Alice's husband will protect his health and well-being, clearly an advantage of these choices. These options comply with ethical standards, principles, and policies that require social workers to protect others from significant, foreseeable harm. Alerting the husband will probably make the social worker feel more comfortable if she is worried about her complicity and her liability should she keep Alice's secret and he contracts HIV as a result.

The hazards of telling include violating Alice's expressed desire for privacy, rupturing the trust that is central to the helping relationship, and possibly putting Alice's marriage at risk if the secret of her affair is revealed. Alice may make good on a threat to file a regulatory board complaint or lawsuit against the worker or agency for breach of confidentiality. The options in which the social worker encourages Alice to tell may take time to employ, but they have the advantage of empowering her to take control of the situation and face her dilemma head on. Her ability to rely on the social worker is essential in this process. The social worker can help her look at the long-term effects of deception in contrast to the short-term effects of revealing her condition and how she contracted HIV. The social worker can help Alice anticipate and plan for that difficult conversation with her husband and family and can be a support to her after the fact, whatever the husband's reactions are. All the advantages of working with the client on this challenging problem are lost if the social worker decides to abruptly override Alice's wishes and notify the husband.

Honoring Alice's demands for secrecy without considering the husband's needs and interests fits with the principle of client self-determination but may be at odds with laws and policies about protecting the safety of others. It may also be at odds with Alice's own best interests. Social workers must often navigate between clients' wishes and the steps needed to adequately address their problems. Alice's desire to avoid telling her husband in the short run will not spare anyone pain or harm in the long run. In fact, her insistence on silence now may keep her stuck while her health and family relationships suffer. The social worker who can empathize with her and help her forthrightly address her fears and problems will be carrying out both ethical and professional responsibilities. Should this process fail, the social worker may resort to notification against Alice's will. Given the greater expertise and experience of public health authorities in notifications, the social worker might refer the case to them for assistance.

Self-awareness and self-evaluation are important elements of competent, ethical, and professional practice. | **C1** |
Throughout this process, Alice's social worker should examine their own motivations, decisions, and actions. Fear of liability, judgments about Alice's behavior, or other factors might lead the social worker to act precipitously or thoughtlessly. In doing so, they may make a decision that is more in their own interest than Alice's.

Supervision is also an important element in self-evaluation. An adept and involved supervisor can help the social worker walk through the decision-making process, identify positive and problematic outcomes, and work on areas for improvement and skill development. Did the decision adequately resolve the dilemma? If it created unplanned or problematic results, what can be done to remedy them? For example, if the social worker's efforts to get Alice to inform her husband of her illness result in Alice's withdrawal from treatment, evaluation helps the social worker determine next steps as well as assess her past actions.

Summary

This chapter introduced the ethics and the values that support the social work profession and highlighted the ways these values may create conflicts in professional practice. It provided guidelines for supporting self-determination, respecting confidentiality, obtaining informed consent, maintaining boundaries, and resolving ethical dilemmas. The chapter suggested steps to aid in resolving ethical dilemmas and applied these steps to a case in which self-determination and client confidentiality conflicted with another's safety. Throughout, the chapter considered the importance of self-understanding and self-regulation so that social workers learn to be intentional in their statements and actions and assure that clients' needs and the working relationship are given precedence. In the following chapters, we move toward putting these insights into action as you learn beginning skills for effective communication with and on behalf of clients.

Competency Notes

C1   Demonstrate Ethical and Professional Behavior

- Demonstrate professional demeanor in behavior, appearance, and oral, written, and electronic communication.
- Use supervision and consultation to guide professional judgment and behavior.
- Manage personal and professional value conflicts and affective reactions.
- Make ethical decisions by applying standards of the National Association of Social Workers Code of Ethics, relevant laws and regulations, models for ethical decision-making, ethical conduct of research, and additional codes of ethics as appropriate to context.

C2   Engage Antiracism, Diversity, Equity, and Inclusion in Practice

- Demonstrate cultural humility applying critical reflexivity, self-awareness, and self-regulation to manage the influence of bias, power, privilege, and values in working with clients and constituencies acknowledging them as experts of their own lived experiences.
- Demonstrate anti-racist social work practice at the individual, family, group, organizational, community, research, and policy levels, informed by the theories and voices of those who have been marginalized.

Skill Development Exercises

Operationalizing Social Work Values

To assist you in developing skills in operationalizing the cardinal values of social work in specific practice situations, we have provided several exercises with modeled responses. As you read each one, note which values are germane to the situation. To refresh your memory, the values are as follows:

1. Service
2. Social Justice
3. Dignity and Worth of the Person
4. Importance of Human Relationships
5. Integrity
6. Competence

Next, assume you are the client's service provider and formulate a response that implements the relevant social work value. After completing each exercise, compare your response with the modeled response that follows the exercises. Bear in mind that the modeled response is only one of many possible acceptable responses. Analyze it and compare it with your own. Also, remember that vocal tone is an essential component of effective, congruent communications. Imagine the modeled responses that follow spoken with different verbal and emotional tones: sensitivity, tentativeness, anger, impatience, pity, kindness, and conceit. Which feel genuine to you? Which can help achieve your objectives with the client? Which are congruent with professional values of respect and support for client dignity? By carefully completing these exercises, you will improve your competence in putting values into action in the varied and challenging situations encountered in direct social work practice.

Client Statements

1. Group member [in first group session]: Is this a safe space? I need to be sure what I say isn't spread around to other people. [Turning to social worker.] How can I be sure that won't happen?

2. Inmate in correctional institution [after social worker's introduction]: So, you want to help me, huh? I'll tell you how you can help. You can get me out of this effing place—that's how!

3. Female [initial interview in family counseling center]: I'm looking for help from someone who understands and values my faith. Being a Seventh Day Adventist is important to me, but a lot of my stress is coming from that.

4. Teenager [caught with contraband in her possession by a supervisor–counselor in a residential treatment center]: Please don't report this. I've been doing better lately, and I've learned my lesson. You won't need to worry about me. I won't mess up anymore.

Modeled Social Worker Responses

1. "Jeanine raises a good point that concerns all of you. So you can feel more comfortable about sharing personal feelings and experiences with the group, we need an agreement about how private information is handled. What are your thoughts about Jeanine's concern? How do we build trust?"

2. "I hear you. It's what I'd want if I were in your situation. As a matter of fact, that's what I want for you, too, but the review board won't release you until they feel you're prepared to make it in the community. I can't get you out, but with your cooperation, I can help you to make changes that will get you ready for release."

3. "I have to confess I know only a little bit about your religion, which may make you wonder if I can appreciate your problems. I'll do my best to learn and understand more, and I might need you to help me with that. The most important thing, though, is your comfort about my ability to help you with your stress. Shall we talk some more and revisit it at the end of the appointment?"

4. "I'm sorry you're still using, Joy, because of the difficulties it's caused you. I don't like to see you get into trouble, but I have no choice but to report this. If I didn't, I'd be breaking a rule myself. That wouldn't help you in the long run."

Skill Development Exercises

Managing Ethical Dilemma

The following cases will give you practice in applying ethics concepts and ethical decision-making to specific practice situations. Note that the appropriate response or course of action is rarely cut and dried. Reflection and discussion with others help you build on your initial reactions and identify or weigh other viable choices. After reading each case, answer the following questions:

1. What conflicting principles and values are in play in the case?

2. What are the pros and cons of the various courses of action?

3. What guidelines are applicable in resolving this dilemma?

4. What resources could you consult to help you decide on an ethical course of action?

Ethics Case 1

A classmate has told you that they are Googling clients from their field agency as well as looking them up on Facebook. They state that the information is public, so there is no confidentiality involved, and the more they learn about them the better they can help them. In your own placement, workers send Snapchat messages to each other of the wacky ways clients dress and behave. They say it builds camaraderie in the team and is harmless since the photos and comments go away after only a few seconds.

Ethics Case 2

You are forming a youth group in a state correctional facility. From past experience, you know that members sometimes make references in the group to previous offenses that they have committed without being apprehended. You also know that they may talk about indiscretions or misdemeanors they (or others) may have committed or plan to commit within the institution, such as smoking marijuana, engaging in sexual encounters, receiving contraband from visitors, or stealing supplies or property from peers or staff. Are you required to share all the information you learn in the group? How can you encourage trust and sharing if there are limits to confidentiality?

Ethics Case 3

In conducting an intake interview with a young woman in a family agency, you observe that both of her young children are withdrawn and listless. Throughout the interview, the client seems defensive, suspicious, and appears ambivalent about having come for the interview. At one point, she states that she feels overwhelmed with her parenting responsibilities and is having difficulty in coping with her children. She also alludes to her fear that she may hurt them but then abruptly changes the subject. As you encourage her to return to the discussion of her problems with the children, your client says that she has changed her mind about wanting help, takes her children in hand, and hastily leaves the office.

Ethics Case 4

You have seen a husband and wife and their 15-year-old daughter twice regarding relationship problems between the parents and the daughter. The parents are both angry and fed up with their daughter, stating that they never had such problems with their other children and that she just needs to "shape up." Today your received a text from the girl that she is pregnant and knows her parents will explode if they find out, and she needs to see you without her parents present to talk about her plans.

Ethics Case 5

You have been working in a mental health agency with a middle-aged male who has a history, when angered, of becoming violent and physically abusive. He has been under extreme psychological pressure lately because of increased expectations at work. In an interview today, he is extremely angry, clenching his fists as he tells you that his boss is giving him a hard time, singling him out for criticism, and threatening that he will lose his job. "If that happens," he says, "they'll be sorry."

Ethics Case 6

A murder was reported tonight on the evening news. You recognize the victim as a woman who had numerous brief stays at the domestic violence agency where you work. You suspect that her boyfriend was the perpetrator and wonder if you should contact the police with this information.

Ethics Case 7

You are working with a 17-year-old to stay on track for graduation. Today he acknowledged that he was sleeping in class because he sometimes sneaks out of his house after his father is asleep to go hang out with his girlfriend. You do not know who she is, but you know that she is under 16.

Part 2

Exploring, Assessing, and Planning

Part 2 of this book deals with processes and skills involved in the first phase of the helping process. In this phase, you will engage clients in relationship, will learn about the problem(s) that prompts their involvement with a social work helping system, identify stressors and resources that bear on the problem, and develop intervention goals and an agreement to work together. Throughout, the

Continued

orienting perspectives presented in Chapter 2 and the values and ethics presented in Chapter 4 will orient your work toward social justice and empowerment outcomes.

Chapter 5 begins this exploration by setting the context and developing skills for building effective working relationships with clients, one of the two major objectives of initial interviews.

Chapter 6 shifts the focus to skills required to explore clients' difficulties and recognize and enhance strengths.

Chapter 7 identifies verbal and nonverbal patterns of communication that impede the development of effective working relationships and suggests positive alternatives.

Chapters 8 and **9** focus specifically on the process of assessment. Chapter 8 deals with explaining the process, sources of information, delineation of clients' problems, and questions to be addressed during the assessment process. Chapter 9 highlights the many dimensions of ecological assessment, delineating the intrapersonal, interpersonal, cultural, and environmental systems and noting how they reciprocally interact to produce and maintain problems.

Chapter 10 narrows the focus of assessment to family systems. It discusses various types of family structures and considers the dimensions of family systems that must be addressed in assessing family functioning, including the cultural context of families.

In **Chapter 11**, the focus changes to groups. Here, the discussion hones in on purposes of groups, selection of group members, and ways to begin group process. It then points out various factors to be considered in assessing the functioning of groups.

Part 2 concludes with **Chapter 12**, which deals with negotiating goals and contracts with both voluntary and involuntary clients. Included in this chapter are theory, skills, and guidelines that address these processes, which lay the foundation for the process of goal attainment.

Chapter 5

Building Blocks of Communication: Conveying Empathy and Authenticity

Chapter Overview

The development of strong working relationships is central to effective social work practice in all settings. Research on treatment outcomes in therapy demonstrates the importance of the client–social worker relationship. Relationship factors like emotional closeness and mutual agreements about the change process account for as much as 30% of therapeutic outcomes, compared to the use of specific treatment models that account for just 15% of therapeutic outcomes (Adams et al., 2008; Miller et al., 2013). This means that the therapeutic alliance is equally, if not more, important than the treatment model. Client–social worker relationship quality is important for nontherapeutic settings characterized by brief encounters and for telesocial work settings as well (Irvine, et al. 2020). For involuntary clients, relationships that are experienced as trusting, respectful, transparent, and fair are essential to the change process (Schwalbe, 2012; Skeem et al., 2007). For this reason, social workers engaged in direct practice have long invested substantial efforts at establishing meaningful working relationships with their clients.

This chapter presents skills and strategies necessary to establish strong working relationships with clients, whether they be voluntary or involuntary. The specific skills addressed in this chapter include preparing clients for the helping process, communicating with empathy, and communicating with authenticity.

As a result of reading this chapter and learning and applying skills, you will be able to:

- Prepare clients for the helping process by explaining the roles of the social worker and client and explaining client rights, including limits to confidentiality.

- Convey empathy, including attentiveness to surface and deeper feelings.

- Respond to clients with authenticity, including with effective self-disclosure and positive feedback.

The EPAS Competencies in Chapter 5

This chapter will give you the information needed to meet the following practice competencies:

- Competency 1: Demonstrate Ethical and Professional Behavior

- Competency 2: Engage Anti-Racism, Diversity, Equity, and Inclusion in Practice

- Competency 6: Engage with Individuals, Families, Groups, Organizations, and Communities

- Competency 7: Assess Individuals, Families, Groups, Organizations, and Communities

Roles of the Participants

Social work relationships begin with purpose where social workers and clients have unique and specific tasks to accomplish, and fulfilling these tasks is central to the success of the helping relationship. While your role may include activities like case management, counseling, and teaching, your clients' roles often include activities like sharing sensitive information about their lives, participating in the intervention planning process, seeking out and obtaining resources, complying with rules, and using new skills and behaviors. You need to guide the process of problem solving, while your clients need to participate fully and intentionally. To be successful, both you and your clients need to have a shared understanding of how your roles complement one another.

Unfortunately, social workers and clients do not always communicate openly about their roles. For voluntary clients, mutual understanding is vital to align yours and your clients' problem-solving activities. For involuntary or mandated clients, mutual understanding is the foundation of a fair process in which the obligations and potential consequences for noninvolvement are transparent and fully acknowledged. For this reason, role preparation, what we have in the past referred to as "role induction," is a critical first step when establishing new relationships with clients.

Role preparation is the process of developing a shared expectation for the helping process, a shared role definition of the social worker and of the client, and a mutual understanding of client rights and obligations, including informed consent and limitations to the right to confidentiality. When successful, role preparation establishes the foundation for a trauma-informed approach to practice by ensuring client comfort and safety, promoting collaboration and empowerment, and demonstrating the transparency of the helping process. Research demonstrates that role preparation increases client participation and sustained involvement in the helping process (Delgadillo & Groom, 2017; Koksvik, et al., 2018) and is associated with successful outcomes with clients who are mandated to services (Rooney & Myrick, 2018; Trotter, 2015).

Our role preparation guidelines include three general stages:

1. Determining your client's expectations for the helping process
2. Discussing the helping process
3. Discussing informed consent, confidentiality, and agency policies

As you read more detail about these stages, bear in mind that your choice of language and detail should be in line with your client's developmental level and understanding, should be presented in reference to your client's culturally informed view of the helping process, and should be tailored to the needs and purposes of your agency. For some, this three-stage process will unfold over a lengthy period of time. For others, it will be concluded in less than five minutes. Throughout the discussion, we recommend adopting a spirit of collaboration and a strengths perspective, communicating respect and helpful intent. Following these recommendations, begin your role preparation conversation by exploring your client's expectations for the helping process.

Determine Your Client's Expectations for the Helping Process

In many (if not most) social work encounters, the place to begin is to learn what the client expects or hopes to experience as a result of their work with social work helping systems. Early on, ask questions such as, "how do you hope I can help you?" or "when you thought about coming here, what were your ideas about the kind of help you wanted?" For clients who are mandated to participate in services, this discussion should also include questions such as, "what does your probation officer expect from us?" or "how does your teacher want things to change?" The shared understanding that results from a discussion of these questions forms the basis of a collaborative working relationship, emphasizing the orienting frameworks that we presented in Chapter 2 (Horvath & Bedi, 2002), and serves as a backdrop to assessment and goal development phases of the helping process taken up later in this book.

Clients sometimes state their expectations in terms of change. For example, clients seeking services in various settings have said, "I don't want to hear these voices anymore," "I don't want to be scared," or "I want to go back to the way it was." At other times, clients state expectations about what the social worker or helping system will do to facilitate change. For example, our clients have responded with statements such as, "we were hoping you could talk with him and help him understand how much he is hurting us," "I need someone to help me with my rent," or "can you talk to the judge?" Either type of response can be a useful springboard to discussions that follow about the nature of the helping process and your role as social worker.

However, it is not unusual for clients to hesitate when responding to questions about their hopes and expectations. On the one hand, hopes and expectations are often an intimate revelation. Clients may not be ready to share deeply in the early stages of a relationship. You may need to be patient, trusting that your genuine interest and expressions of helpful intent will foster a relationship that supports more intimate sharing. On the other hand, clients may not know what to expect. Although many of your clients may have previous exposure to social work helping systems, some will encounter professional social workers for the first time. For these people, the role as a client in an unknown helping process can bring uncertainty, leading you to discuss the nature of the helping process and how your encounter can lead to positive outcomes.

Additionally, clients may hesitate to discuss their hopes and expectations because of powerful sociocultural forces that have a direct bearing on the helping process. Most social work service settings are associated with social stigma. Stigmas are negative judgements that are made about people based on membership in socially constructed categories. Mental health and criminal justice system stigmas have received some of the most research attention, but stigma and labeling processes are relevant in numerous helping systems and should always be considered when engaging clients in role preparation. Be alert to those times where clients signal unease with how they will be judged (e.g., "I don't know what my friends will think if they knew I was here."), when they may resist participating to avoid stigmatized identities (e.g., "I'm not like one of 'those' people. I don't need to be here."), or when they are concerned with preserving their dignity or "saving face." When clients signal a stigma-related concern, your genuine concern should communicate your awareness of stigma and labeling and commitment to help them navigate these forces.

Discuss the Helping Process

An open discussion about what the client hopes to achieve or expects to experience is an important first step in the role preparation process, but it is often not complete. Evidence-based models of role preparation follow with a discussion and sometimes a negotiation about the helping process itself. By the end of this discussion, you should have (1) negotiated an agreement about the basic expectations and hopes for the types of helping provided by you and your agency, (2) shared information about the methods of helping provided by you and your agency, (3) discussed the process of change, and (4) discussed yours and your client's role in the helping process.

Negotiating Agreement about Expectations

Most often, expectations that clients have shared about the helping process are reasonably well matched to the expectations that social workers and their agencies have. However, it is helpful to clarify the social workers' role. For example,

> **Client:** I just want someone to listen to me without any judgement. My family is so judgmental. I just need to feel support, and I also like advice and solutions about how to fix the situation at work.
>
> **Social worker:** I hear that you want to be heard and not judged. I am here to listen to you without judgement. I can provide support with the situation at work, and together we can try and come up with a solution.

Occasionally, however, people express hopes or anticipate helping actions by the social worker that are inconsistent with the practice of their agencies. For instance, they may come with the stated hope that social workers can give advice (e.g., "I was hoping you could tell me what to do."). While there are occasions where the social worker has information or experience that lends itself to credible advice, advice-giving as a general helping strategy is not featured in most theories of helping or most programs. At other times, clients ask social workers to force behavior change in others (e.g., the example given previously, "we were hoping you could talk with him and help him understand how much he is hurting us."). Social workers rarely have that kind of power. In these instances, social workers should educate clients about how their stated expectations match with those of the social worker and agency and give information about ways in which the helping process can achieve goals that are implied by client stated expectations.

Teach Clients about Methods of Helping in Your Agency or Program

As you gain experience in direct social work practice, you will develop a way of describing what you and your agency can do to achieve the hopes and expectations of your clients. What you say depends entirely on the nature of your program and services and what theoretical orientation you adopt. Regardless, the ethical principle of informed consent requires that you provide information to all clients about your services in a way that can be understood depending on their developmental level. For example, a social worker conducting an intake interview in a shelter for victims of battering might say:

> **Social Worker:** Our job is to make sure that you and your children are safe and give you space to figure out what you want to do next. We do that by protecting your privacy and by creating a comfortable, homelike space for your children. We also have counselors here 24 hours per day to monitor who comes into the house and who

will be here when you need support. Finally, we know the decisions you are making are complicated and that you can't do this alone. Our case managers will meet with you after you have settled in to walk you through a planning process. How does that sound to you?

However, a school social worker may say the following to an elementary-aged child:

Social worker: My name is Julie, and I am the school social worker. That means that I talk to kids who may have problems at school or at home, and I help them think about ways to solve their problems. I'd like to talk to you about what you're feeling and thinking. Sometimes the principal will be part of our talks when it comes to discussing discipline issues, but my role is to help you learn to better solve your problems. While you're here, please play with the items on my desk like my squishy balls and paperclips if that will make you feel more comfortable. Kids can feel nervous around new adults, and that might make you feel better.

In these examples, the social workers provided a brief summary of their programs. The summary provides information that educates clients about what they can expect in the helping process and leads to a discussion of the process of change that can occur next.

Discuss the Process of Change

The process of change is rarely straight forward. If it were, clients would not be meeting with you. On the other hand, the process of change is not mysterious. The role preparation process provides a space to briefly outline how your agency or program envisions the change process and helps clients anticipate its challenges. Your goal is to lend your confidence that, in partnership with you and your agency, clients can overcome these challenges and resolve their presenting problems. For example:

Social Worker: We take a task-centered approach to case management. That means that our meetings are like planning sessions. When we meet, we will talk about the specific things that we can do in the upcoming week to make progress toward your goals. Our clients find that it is easier to achieve their goals when we take it a little bit at a time, so that's what we try to do. Do you have any questions about that?

Include in this discussion some of the specific challenges that may be faced in the process of problem solving. For example:

Social Worker: We can do this, but it will take work and effort. Sometimes people forget to do what they agreed to do, and sometimes the things we plan don't have the outcomes we expect. Sometimes it can be painful or disappointing, and to be honest, sometimes we just get unmotivated, but I think that if we work together, we can face these kinds of challenges and figure them out. (Pause) What concerns do you have?

Talking about My Agency's Anti-oppressive, Antiracism Practices

C2

Implementing an anti-oppressive style is difficult under any circumstance and is more so in the absence of agency and social support. We encourage you to talk about your personal stance and your agency's stances about anti-oppressive and antiracism practices during role preparation. Agency-based equity initiatives are necessarily rooted in local agencies and local communities, usually following a series of ad-hoc and deliberate steps toward organizational transformation (The Annie E. Casey Foundation, 2014; Soler, 2005). When talking about racial equity in social work agencies, it may be helpful to focus on these five questions:

1. What are your agency's explicit goals regarding racial equity?

2. What data about racial inequities in your agency exist or are being collected?
3. How is the agency holding itself accountable to the communities it serves?
4. What racial equity trainings have been conducted?
5. What anti-oppressive equity policies and practices have been launched?

If you are unable to answer any of these questions, we recommend that you seek support inside and outside of your agency for your own efforts to implement an anti-oppressive approach, and act internally to support anti-oppressive and social justice-related organizational change efforts.

Discuss the Roles of the Social Worker and Client

Finally, the role preparation process allots time to clarify what you are able and not able to do in the helping process and engage clients in a conversation about what they can do to facilitate the helping process. You can briefly describe the purpose of your work (e.g., "my role is to learn about your goals and needs and to help you navigate the housing system. I can also advocate to make sure that your voice is heard"). It is often helpful to stress the collaborative aspects of your role and your intent to partner with clients. You may also solicit your clients' views about what they can do to promote the helping process (e.g., "based on what I've shared about us and our services, what are things that you may need to do to get the most out of what we can offer to you?"), and address topics relevant to your agency or program such as attendance, completion of tasks, and sharing openly and honestly.

While important for all clients, this conversation is of particular importance for those mandated to services and illustrates the need for transparency in the working relationship (Trotter, 2015). Often, social workers who work with mandated clients balance two competing roles – helping and social control. The helping roles are familiar to social workers. They assess needs and make referrals. They help clients in their decision-making process. They teach skills, but the social control role can seem contradictory. Social workers often have a reporting requirement, say, to a judge or other referring authority, and sometimes social workers have a direct role in enforcing rules with consequences, such as recommending removal of children to foster care or the imposition of coercive legal sanctions. Social workers in all settings need to have a clear understanding of how their work fits into both systems, helping and social control. For example:

> **Social worker:** My job will be to develop a case plan with you. I won't be the one to say, "This is what you need to do." I want you to have input in that decision and to say, "Well, I feel I can do this." I will be willing to share ideas with you as we decide what to work on and how to do it. I will need to include any court-mandated requirements, such as our need to be meeting together, in the agreement, and we need to remember that the probation officer is going to ask me for progress updates from time to time. However, I want you to have a lot of say in determining what we work on and how.

Communicating Informed Consent, Confidentiality, and Agency Policies

The encounter between the social worker and the client exists within a context of **C1**

limits, possibilities, and rights. In this regard, the social worker must share the rights and limits to communication discussed in Chapter 4: discuss confidentiality and its limits, obtain informed consent, and share agency policies and legal limits. A social worker might share the following:

> **Social worker:** What you say to me is private in most circumstances. I will share what we have discussed with my supervisor. In certain circumstances, however, I might have to share what we have discussed with others. For example, if you threaten to seriously harm another person, I would have a duty to warn, which would mean that I could not keep that information private. For example, if your children were in danger, I am a mandated reporter, and I would have to share that information. Similarly, if you were to seriously consider harming yourself, I would have to share that information. If a judge were to subpoena my records, they could gain access to a general summary of what we have done together. Do you have any questions about this?

It is important that this section of the initial interview be presented in language that the client readily understands so that the discussion embodies the spirit of informed consent. With children, the complexity of informed consent and confidentiality policies and laws needs to be conveyed forthrightly and in a manner in which they can understand, usually using their preferred language and avoiding jargon (see Ethics of Practice with Minors, Chapter 4). It is important that you carry out this duty in a genuine fashion rather than presenting it as a ritualistic sharing of written forms that has the appearance of obtaining informed consent but ignores its intent. In hurried agency practice, sometimes this principle is violated. Discuss with your supervisor what information needs to be shared with clients and how that is done in ways that are useful to those clients.

Facilitative Conditions

Whether you are working with clients in the beginning, middle, or ending phases of a social work intervention, relational communication skills are the primary means through which you will engage clients in a working relationship. Evidence points to three relational communication skills that we call the facilitative conditions: empathy, authenticity, and respect. These conditions or skills were originally conceptualized by Carl Rogers (1957) as *empathy*, *unconditional positive regard*, and *congruence*, forming the basis of evidence-based interventions such as client-centered treatment and later motivational interviewing (Mason, 2009).

Our experience suggests that the facilitative conditions generalize to form the foundation of social work practice in nearly any setting in which you encounter clients. The facilitative conditions help create relationships that are focused on clients' experiences, circumstances, and needs. They foster a collaborative approach that recognizes the expertise and agency of the client and the limits of the power of the social worker. Relationships built on the facilitative conditions are collaborative and strengths based. Because we addressed respect as a foundation of ethical practice in Chapter 4, the remainder of this chapter elaborates the skills of communicating with empathy and authenticity.

Empathic Communication

Empathic communication involves the ability of the social worker to perceive accurately and sensitively the inner feelings of the client and to communicate their understanding of those feelings in language attuned to the client's experiencing of the moment. Empathy is the basis of active listening and the emotional connections between people and underlies the perception that one has been understood. Most people have had this experience. Think of a time when you believed that a person with whom you were speaking truly and fully understood what you were saying on an emotional level. The positive associations you felt in that moment suggests that your listener had accurate empathy for you and your experience.

Contemporary theory and research in neuropsychology and social work practice point to three interrelated components of the empathy experience. First, empathy is initiated by an affective response, called mirroring in the neuropsychological research literature (Clark, 2020). The affective response is an emotional and physiological experience whereby the listener vicariously experiences the speaker's emotions. By experiencing these emotions, social workers have a powerful clue about the emotions and feelings that clients carry. Second, empathy requires self-awareness and emotional regulation. Self-awareness and emotion regulation enable the listener to perceive their own internal emotional experience and its source while recognizing that the listener and speaker are separate individuals. Finally, empathy entails empathic action. In direct practice, empathic action is often a verbal process of communicating what the social worker understands about the emotions and feelings being experienced by clients, but empathic action could also mean a shift in body language and physical attending behaviors, such as we discuss in Chapter 7, or engaging in social action and allyship with clients as part of a broader change agenda.

Empathic communication is distinguished from sympathetic responding in the cognitive processes of self-awareness and emotion regulation. Sympathetic responses occur when the social worker experiences significant emotional reactions (i.e., mirroring) but focus on their own experiences rather than those of the clients (i.e., fail to exercise emotion regulation and self-control). In ways subtle and not, social workers sometimes fail to recognize that their experience is separate from that of the client. Contrast responses such as, "I'd feel the same way if I were in your position" or "I think you are right" with "I sense that you are feeling ..." or "you seem to be saying ...." The former reflects a shift in focus from the client's point of view to that of the social worker, while the latter two responses show how the social worker is using their own affective responses to understand the client's feelings and emotions. Taken to an extreme, the failure to separate one's own from another's feelings can contribute to compassion fatigue, which can interfere with the social worker's capacity for empathy and contribute to burnout (Conrad & Kellar-Guenther, 2006), topics we address in more depth in Chapter 18.

Because people never experience events and circumstances in exactly the same way, empathy includes the elements of objectivity and imagination (Clark & Butler, 2020), what some people refer to as perspective taking (Linker, 2015). Objectivity refers to the knowledge about emotions and feelings that social workers gain from personal and vicarious experiences and from study, and imagination refers to educated guesses about the emotional experiences that might be associated with people's experiences.

Perspective taking becomes increasingly important as the social worker's base of personal experiences diverges from that of their clients. Cross-racial and cross-cultural relationships present special instances that highlight the importance of perspective taking in the process of establishing empathic relationships. Because of the power differences arising from the positionality of social workers relative to their clients, social workers may not recognize the presence of traumas, both personal and historical, that impact on the emotional lives of their clients. They may not recognize the nuances of how repeated exposure to racism and discrimination impact clients' experiences. They may not see how their position as "helper" can reinforce and sustain marginalizing and oppressive hierarchies. Under these circumstances, perspective taking is critical.

Empathic communication plays a vital role in nurturing and sustaining the helping relationship. It fosters a sense of emotional closeness and trust between people and is a core skill to deploy when deescalating conflict (Hallett & Dickens, 2017). For telesocial work, empathic communication enables the development of a working relationship despite the communication challenges inherent in computer-aided communication (Irvine et al., 2020). With involuntary clients, conveying empathic understanding reduces the level of threat perceived by clients and mitigates their defensiveness, conveys interest and helpful intent, and creates an atmosphere conducive to behavior change (Trotter, 2013).

Developing Perceptiveness to Feelings

To accurately perceive how clients are feelings, social workers need a rich vocabulary of words and expressions to match how they perceive their own affective responses. For example, dozens of descriptive feeling words may be used to express anger, including "furious," "aggravated," "provoked," "put out," "irritated," and "impatient"—all of which express different shades and intensities of this feeling. However, it has been our experience that many beginning social workers use a limited range of feeling words when conveying empathy. For instance, repeatedly using the words "upset" or "frustrated" when more nuanced language could lead to a deeper understanding

of client anger. The repetitive use of feeling words limits the social worker's ability to reflect the full intensity and range of feelings experienced by clients, whereas a broad range of feeling words give sharp and exact focus to clients' feelings and serve to deepen the empathetic experience for both social workers and for their clients.

The accompanying emotional vocabulary list illustrates the wide range of expressions social workers can use when responding to clients' feelings. Although the emotional vocabulary list is not exhaustive, it encompasses many of the feelings and emotions frequently encountered in the helping process. Feeling words are subsumed under 11 categories, running the gamut of emotions from intense anguish and pain (e.g., grieved, terrified, bewildered, enraged, and powerless) to positive feeling states (e.g., joy, elation, ecstasy, bliss, and pride in accomplishment) to feeling words related to competence and strength (e.g., brave, undaunted, confident, inspired).

Note that particular word usages can vary over time, in different regions, and with different populations. Similarly, some of the expressions in the accompanying lists may be unfamiliar to some of the people you work with. Select those that are compatible with your clients.

Affective Words and Phrases

Competence/Strength		Happiness/Satisfaction		Caring/Love	
Convinced you can	Confident	Elated	Superb	Adore	Loving
Sense of mastery	Powerful	Ecstatic	On cloud nine	Infatuated	Enamored
Potent	Courageous	On top of the world	Organized	Cherish	Idolize
Resolute	Determined	Fantastic	Splendid	Worship	Attached to
Strong	Influential	Exhilarated	Jubilant	Devoted to	Tenderness toward
Brave	Impressive	Terrific	Euphoric	Affection for	Hold dear
Forceful	Inspired	Delighted	Marvelous	Prize	Caring
Successful	Secure	Excited	Enthusiastic	Fond of	Regard
In charge	In control	Thrilled	Great	Respect	Admire
Well equipped	Committed	Super	In high spirits	Concern for	Taken with
Sense of accomplishment	Daring	Joyful	Cheerful	Turned on	Trust
		Elevated	Happy	Close	Esteem
Undaunted	Effective	Light-hearted	Wonderful	Hit it off	Value
Sure	Sense of conviction	Glowing	Jolly	Warm toward	Friendly
Trust in yourself	Self-reliant	Neat	Glad	Like	Positive toward
Sharp	Able	Fine	Pleased	Accept	Enchanted by
Adequate	Firm	Good	Contented		
Capable	On top of it	Hopeful	Mellow		
Can cope	Important	Satisfied	Gratified		
Up to it	Ready	Fulfilled	Tranquil		
Equal to it	Skillful	Serene	Calm		
On top of it	Resourceful	At ease	Awesome		

Depression/Discouragement

Anguished	In despair
Dreadful	Miserable
Dejected	Disheartened
Rotten	Awful
Horrible	Terrible
Hopeless	Gloomy
Dismal	Bleak
Depressed	Despondent
Grieved	Grim
Broken hearted	Forlorn
Distressed	Downcast
Sorrowful	Demoralized
Pessimistic	Tearful
Weepy	Down in the dumps
Deflated	Blue
Lost	Melancholy
In the doldrums	Lousy
Kaput	Unhappy
Down	Low
Bad	Blah
Disappointed	Sad
Below par	Unnerved

Inadequacy/Helplessness

Worthless	Depleted
Good for nothing	Washed up
Powerless	Helpless
Impotent	Crippled
Inferior	Emasculated
Useless	Finished
Like a failure	Impaired
Inadequate	Whipped
Defeated	Stupid
Incompetent	Puny
Inept	Clumsy
Overwhelmed	Ineffective
Like a klutz	Lacking
Awkward	Deficient
Unable	Incapable
Small	Insignificant
Like a wimp	Unimportant
Over the hill	Incomplete
Immobilized	Like a puppet
At the mercy of	Inhibited
Insecure	Lacking confidence
Unsure of self	Uncertain
Weak	Inefficient
Unfit	Feeble

Anxiety/Tension

Terrified	Frightened
Intimidated	Horrified
Desperate	Panicky
Terror-stricken	Paralyzed
Frantic	Stunned
Shocked	Threatened
Afraid	Scared
Stage fright	Dread
Vulnerable	Fearful
Apprehensive	Jumpy
Shaky	Distrustful
Butterflies	Awkward
Defensive	Uptight
Tied in knots	Rattled
Tense	Fidgety
Jittery	On edge
Nervous	Anxious
Unsure	Hesitant
Timid	Shy
Worried	Uneasy
Bashful	Embarrassed
Ill at ease	Doubtful
Uncomfortable	Self-conscious
Insecure	Alarmed
Restless	Frenzied

Confusion/Troubledness

Bewildered	Puzzled
Tormented by	Baffled
Perplexed	Overwhelmed
Trapped	Confounded
In a dilemma	Befuddled
In a quandary	At loose ends
Going around in circles	Mixed-up
Disorganized	In a fog
Troubled	Adrift
Lost	Disconcerted
Frustrated	Floored
Flustered	In a bind
Torn	Ambivalent
Disturbed	Conflicted
Stumped	Feeling pulled apart
Mixed feelings about	Uncertain
Unsure	Uncomfortable
Bothered	Uneasy
Undecided	Overwhelmed

Rejection/Offensive

Crushed	Destroyed
Ruined	Pained
Wounded	Devastated
Tortured	Cast off
Betrayed	Discarded
Knifed in the back	Hurt
Belittled	Abused
Depreciated	Criticized
Censured	Discredited
Disparaged	Laughed at
Maligned	Mistreated
Ridiculed	Devalued
Scorned	Mocked
Scoffed at	Used
Exploited	Debased
Slammed	Slandered
Impugned	Cheapened
Mistreated	Put down
Slighted	Neglected
Overlooked	Minimized
Let down	Disappointed
Unappreciated	Taken for granted
Taken lightly	Underestimated
Degraded	Discounted
Shot down	Disrespected

Anger/Resentment

Furious	Enraged
Livid	Seething
Could chew nails	Fighting mad
Burned up	Hateful
Bitter	Galled
Vengeful	Resentful
Indignant	Irritated
Hostile	Pissed off
Have hackles up	Had it with
Upset with	Bent out of shape
Agitated	Annoyed
Got dander up	Bristle
Dismayed	Uptight
Disgusted	Bugged
Turned off	Put out
Miffed	Ruffled
Irked	Perturbed
Ticked off	Teed off
Chagrined	Griped
Cross	Impatient
Infuriated	Violent

Loneliness	
All alone in the universe	Isolated
Abandoned	Totally alone
Forsaken	Forlorn
Lonely	Alienated
Estranged	Rejected
Remote	Alone
Apart from others	Shut out
Left out	Excluded
Lonesome	Distant
Aloof	Cut off

Guilt/Embarrassment	
Sick at heart	Unforgivable
Humiliated	Disgraced
Degraded	Horrible
Mortified	Exposed
Branded	Could crawl in a hole
Like two cents	Ashamed
Guilty	Remorseful
Crummy	Really rotten
Lost face	Demeaned
Foolish	Ridiculous
Silly	Stupid
Egg on face	Regretful
Wrong	Embarrassed
At fault	In error
Responsible for	Goofed
Lament	Blew it

Using the Lists of Affective Words and Phrases

The lists of affective words and phrases may be used with the exercises at the end of the chapter to formulate responses that capture the nature of feelings expressed by clients. After you have initially practiced responding to messages in which clients convey feelings, check the lists to determine whether some other words and phrases might more accurately capture the client's feelings. Also, scan the lists to see whether the client's message involves feelings in addition to those you identified.

To illustrate, consider the following situation in which a client describes an experience of racism. The client is currently in a drug aftercare program and has returned to work as a residential gas meter reader. He reports that when he knocked on the door in a predominantly white suburb neighborhood intending to read the meter, an elderly white woman would not let him in, despite him wearing his picture identification name tag on his uniform: "I was so low down and depressed. What can you do? I am doing my thing to keep straight, and I can't even do my job because I'm Black." On the surface, this client might be feeling disheartened, demoralized, and deflated (see the depression/discouragement words), but there is likely a deeper level to his emotional experience as well. While his confidence may be shaken (see the competence/strength words), he may also be striving to retain a sense of hopefulness (see the happiness/satisfaction words) and determination (see the competence/strength words).

In the following exercise, identify both the apparent surface feelings and the probable underlying feelings embodied in each of the four client statements. To complete the exercise, read each statement carefully and write down the apparent feelings and probable deeper feelings involved. Scan the lists of affective words and phrases to see whether you might identify additional feeling words. After you have responded to all four statements, check the feeling words and phrases you identified with those given at the end of the chapter. If the feelings you identified were similar in meaning to those identified in the answers at the end of the chapter (see page 106), consider your responses to be accurate. If they were not, review the client statements for clues about the client's feelings that you overlooked.

Client Statements

1. **An elderly client:** I know my children have busy lives. It is hard for them to have time to call me.

   Apparent feelings:
   Probable deeper feelings:

2. **A LGBTQ client referring to partner who has recently come out to their family:** When I was at your brother's wedding, and they wanted to take family pictures, nobody wanted me in the pictures. In fact, nobody wanted to talk to me.

   Apparent feelings:
   Probable deeper feelings:

3. *Tearful client who is a mother:* When I was a teenager, I thought that when I was married and had my own children, I would never yell at them like my mother yelled at me, yet here I am doing the same things.

Apparent feelings:

Probable deeper feelings:

4. *Client in child welfare system:* The system is against people like me. People think that we drink, beat our kids, lay up on welfare, and take drugs.

Apparent feelings:

Probable deeper feelings:

Accurately Conveying Empathy

Empathic responding is a fundamental skill that requires extensive effort and practice. Skill in empathic communication has no limit or ceiling; rather, this skill is always in the process of "becoming." When listening to their recorded sessions, even highly skilled professionals discover feelings they overlooked. Many social workers, however, do not fully utilize empathic responding. They fail to grasp the versatility of this skill and its potency in influencing clients and fostering growth in moment-by-moment transactions.

We find it helpful to conceptualize empathic responses in a range of levels. Earlier editions of this textbook outlined a range of empathic responses in five or six levels (Duan & Hill, 1996; Truax & Carkhuff, 1967). However, recent scholarship has advanced to more parsimonious frameworks for understanding the process of conveying empathy (see Miller & Rollnick, 2013). Moreover, our own experience in the classroom points to the utility of just three levels: surface empathy, reciprocal empathy, and additive empathy.

Surface Empathy

Empathic responses at the **surface** level are a direct reflection of the feelings and concerns that clients express, usually using the same vocabulary. Your use of surface-level responding conveys your attentiveness to what clients are saying and signals that you are listening carefully. Surface-level responses are usually brief. For example:

Client: I've been on the street for three months. Budget cuts, layoffs, and I did not have seniority. I had plans, but I'm down now. Way down.

Social Worker: I hear you saying that you are way down?

Client: As down as you can go.

Surface-level empathic responses can be helpful, especially in the beginning stages of a helping relationship where the working relationship is being formed. Accurate responses at this level create a teaching and learning process in which clients convey the language that is important to them and prepare you for the cognitive aspects of perspective taking that underpins empathic communication. Surface-level empathic responses can lead clients to feel heard, understood, and valued, and when used strategically, surface-level responding can reinforce client participation in the interviewing process and help you to focus interviews, as we discuss later in Chapter 6.

On the other hand, surface-level empathic responding can sound robotic and inauthentic when overused. While a well-timed surface response can encourage clients to elaborate and provide more information, surface responses risk an emotional retreat by clients, as when they feel compelled to say: "yes, I just said that." Therefore, we encourage you to experiment with surface-level responses as part of an overall pattern of empathic communication and interviewing, paying attention to its effect on clients and on the pattern of your conversations.

Reciprocal Empathy

Like surface-level empathic responses, reciprocal empathic responses focus on the direct feelings that clients express to you. However, reciprocal responses extend perspective taking into empathic communication by expanding the language of feelings that are used in a conversation. While surface-level responses adhere closely to the specific words and phrases that clients express, reciprocal responses speculate about feelings and emotions by adding feeling words and expressions that the client may not have considered. For example:

Client: Goodness, I know that I need more help, but the more I think of moving, the more scared I get. I have neighbors here who look after me, and I won't know a soul there. I'm afraid I'll be all alone.

Social Worker: It sounds as though you have some mixed feelings about moving. Part of you wants to go because you could live more comfortably, but another part of you is afraid you'll feel alone and lost and wants to cling to people you know care about you.

In this example, the social worker introduced feeling words that clients did not originally share. In doing so, they sent a strong signal of their effort to understand. Notice too that the social worker used multiple feeling words to address the complexity of their clients' emotional states. This added complexity opened opportunities for conversations to reveal more detail about the client's experience and potentially created new learning for a client who may not have considered the intensity and the range of their own emotional experiences. In this way, reciprocal responses encourage a more nuanced view of people's emotional reactions to the situations and the problems that bring them in contact with social workers and social work helping systems.

Oftentimes, new social workers express two concerns about empathic responses at this level related to the inherent speculation involved. First, what happens when your empathic response is inaccurate? Second, can't the power difference between social workers and clients mute their willingness to correct reciprocal responses that are inaccurate? The answer to both questions lies in part with the approach social workers take toward the working relationship.

Social workers who convey authenticity, strengths orientation, cultural humility, and sensitivity to the effects of trauma will have established collaborative relationships that empower clients. In this context, an occasional inaccurate empathic response will most often provide an opportunity for correction, strengthening the power of clients in the helping relationship, and deepen the relationship through a dialog that leads to greater understanding.

However, routine or frequent inaccurate empathic responses can interfere with the helping process and signal limited understanding by the social worker. It may be that social workers in this circumstance are simply distracted and not listening carefully. Their distractedness may interfere with their capacity for a mirroring affective response, or it may be that social workers have a minimal capacity for perspective taking with some clients. Perspective taking requires cognitive effort and is based on a repertoire of prior experiences gained from personal as well vicarious experience. When your reciprocal responses are inaccurate, and especially if they are repeatedly inaccurate, we recommend that you strive for greater self-awareness and seek consultation with a supervisor or trusted colleague. You may need to address the distractions that make empathic responding difficult or gaps in your knowledge that keep you from understanding certain clients on an emotional level.

How do you know what kind of words to incorporate into your reciprocal responses? It is through the full experience of empathy where your own affective response or emotional mirroring join with the cognitive activities of perspective taking and imagination to consider how a client might be feeling or experiencing their emotional life. Reciprocal empathy is a skill and discipline requiring work on your part. That work includes expanding your own vocabulary and repertoire of feeling words such as we presented previously. It also includes active listening in the moment when you deliberately reflect on what the client is saying. Accurate reciprocal responses depend on your growing relationship with your clients. In that way, reciprocal responses are more intentional than surface-level empathic responses. Over time and with practice, reciprocal responding will become part of a natural and authentic repertoire of strategies you employ to communicate empathically.

Additive Empathy

Additive empathy is the process of reflecting the full range and intensity of the surface and underlying feelings that clients convey through verbal and nonverbal communication. This form of responding is "additive" in the sense that the social worker contributes both an extended language of emotions and feelings described in reciprocal responding but also speculates about connections between clients' surface-level feelings with their unstated underlying feelings and with prior experiences or feelings. Additive empathy is sometimes used to reveal patterns, themes, goals, and directions for personal growth. Responding empathically at this high level facilitates the client's exploration of feelings and problems in much greater breadth and depth than responding at lower levels. For example:

Client: I don't see the sense in having to come here every [expletive] week. I haven't been in any trouble now since I went to court a month ago. You should know by now you can trust me.

Social Worker: Having to come here each week irritates you, and I gather you may be pissed off that I keep encouraging you to follow the judge's order.

Client: It's because I don't need it!

Social Worker: You don't need it.

Client: No!

Social Worker: I get the sense that you value this about yourself, that you know what your needs are, and that you are tired of people telling you what to do. (pause) It would be such a relief to be left alone to make these decisions for yourself.

This example illustrates how different levels of empathic responding have been woven together into an experience of additive empathy. The social worker's first response is reciprocal in the sense that they are responding to two aspects of the client's message (i.e., anger at the courts order and with the social worker's support for the court order). Then, the social worker follows with a surface level empathic response (i.e., "you don't need it."), followed by a response that is additive. The additive response here introduces a richer conversation about trustworthiness and freedom. Further conversation might endorse these as client strengths and use them to negotiate how to conduct their relationship within the context of the court order, including the possibility of advocating for the court order's modification.

The use of additive empathy is conditioned by factors associated with the relationship, its purpose, and the service system context. The use of additive empathy usually requires a working relationship characterized by higher levels of intimate sharing on the part of the client and a well-developed assessment by the social worker. Therefore, it is best used as a transition to the middle and ending phases of the helping process. Moreover, it is usually considered a core skill of the therapeutic process of behavior change. Therefore, while one would never preclude the use of additive empathy in any setting where it can advance the helping process, additive empathy is ordinarily associated with psychotherapy and clinical social work settings.

Responding with Reciprocal Empathy

Because reciprocal responding is an essential skill used frequently to meet the objectives of the first phase of the helping process, we recommend that you first aim to achieve mastery of empathic responding at this level. Extended practice with reciprocal empathy should significantly increase your effectiveness in establishing viable helping relationships, interviewing, and gathering data. Although responding at additive levels represents an extension of the skill of reciprocal responding, it is an advanced skill that we address with other advanced change-oriented or "action" skills presented in Part 3 of the book.

C6

Constructing Reciprocal Responses

Reciprocal empathic responses accurately capture the content and surface feelings in client messages but do so in a way that does not merely restate what clients have said. The following paradigm is one way to construct reciprocal empathic responses:

You feel _____ about _____ because _____

> accurately
> identifies
> or describes
> feelings.

The following excerpt from a session involving a social worker and a 17-year-old female illustrates the use of the preceding paradigm in constructing an empathic response:

> **Client:** I can't talk to my father without feeling scared and crying. I'd like to be able to express myself and to disagree with him, but I just can't.
> **Social worker:** It sounds as though you just feel panicky when you try to talk to your father. You feel down on yourself because, at this point, you can't say what you want without falling apart.

This message reflects the client's current feeling but implies that it could change at another point when she acquires more confidence and skill (Greene et al., 2005).

Many times, client messages contain conflicting or contrasting emotions, such as the following: "I like taking drugs, but sometimes I worry about what they might do to me." In such cases, each contrasting feeling should be highlighted:

- You feel ___, yet you also feel ___.
- I sense that you feel torn because while you find taking drugs enjoyable, you have nagging thoughts that they might be harmful to you.

Remember that to respond empathically at a reciprocal level, you must use language that your clients readily understands. Abstract, intellectualized language and professional jargon create barriers to communication and should be avoided. It is also important to vary the language you use in responding. Many professionals tend to respond with stereotyped, repetitive speech patterns, commonly using a limited variety of leads to begin their empathic responses. Such leads as "You feel …" and "I hear you saying …" repeated over and over not only distract the client but also seem phony and contrived. This kind of stereotyped responding draws more attention to the social worker's technique than to the message.

Below you will find a list of varied introductory phrases that can help you expand your repertoire of possible responses. We encourage you to read the list aloud several times and to review it frequently while practicing the empathic communication training exercises in this chapter. The reciprocal empathic response format ("You feel ___ because ___") is merely a training tool to assist you in focusing on the affect and content of client messages. The leads list below will help you respond more naturally.

Leads for Empathic Responses

Could it be that …	You're feeling …
I wonder if …	I'm not sure if I'm with
What I guess I'm hearing	you but …
is …	You appear to be feeling …

Correct me if I'm wrong, but I'm sensing …
Perhaps you're feeling …
Sometimes you think …
Maybe this is a long shot, but …
I'm not certain I understand; you're feeling …
As I hear it, you …
Is that the way you feel?
The message I'm getting is that …
Let me see if I'm with you; you …
If I'm hearing you correctly …
So, you're feeling …
You feel …
It sounds as though you are saying …
I hear you saying …
So, from where you sit …
I sense that you're feeling …
Your message seems to be …
I gather you're feeling …
If I'm catching what you say …
What you're saying comes across to me as …

It appears you feel …
Maybe you feel …
Do you feel …
I'm not sure that I'm with you; do you mean …
It seems that you …
Is that what you mean?
What I think I'm hearing is …
I get the impression that …
As I get it, you felt that …
To me it's almost like you are saying …
So, as you see it …
I'm picking up that you …
I wonder if you're saying …
So, it seems to you …
Right now, you're feeling …
You must have felt …
Listening to you, it seems as if …
You convey a sense of …
As I think about what you say, it occurs to me you're feeling …
From what you say …
I gather you're feeling …

A review of the list of leads for reciprocal empathy points to an important discipline in the use of empathic communication, that empathic responses should be offered tentatively. Checking out the accuracy of responses with appropriate lead-in phrases such as, "Let me see if I understand …" or "Did I hear you right?" is helpful in communicating a desire to understand and a willingness to correct misperceptions. Empathic responding is part of a dialog in which the client clarifies their feelings for the social worker to promote their deeper understanding. Perhaps even more important than accuracy is the commitment to understand conveyed by your genuine efforts to perceive the client's experience. If you consistently demonstrate your goodwill and intent to help through attentive verbal and nonverbal responding, an occasional lack of understanding or faulty timing will not damage the client–social worker relationship.

Exercises designed to help you to develop Level 3 reciprocal empathic responses appear at the end of the chapter. Included in the exercises are a variety of client statements taken from actual work with individuals, groups, couples, and families in diverse settings. In addition to the skill development exercises, we recommend that you record the number of empathic responses you employ in sessions over several weeks to determine the extent to which you are applying this skill. We also suggest that either you or a knowledgeable associate rate your responses and identify patterns in your use of reciprocal empathy when you meet with clients. If you find (as most beginning social workers do) that you are underutilizing empathic responses or responding at low levels, you may wish to set a goal to improve your skill.

Employing Empathic Responding

How you weave empathic responses into conversations with clients will vary depending upon the phase of the problem-solving process and setting in which you work. While empathic responses in the beginning phase of the helping process may be focused on surface-level feelings and more closely adhere to the actual words chosen by clients, empathic responses in the middle and ending phases are more likely to be reciprocal and additive in conjunction with a deeper working relationship. In settings where brief encounters are the norm and services are focused on concrete resources and social support, empathic responses may primarily be used to facilitate the working relationship. In longer-term relationships and therapeutic relationships, additive empathic responses may be used to foster client insight. In general, we suggest starting with simple empathy, restating clients' expressions using their same or similar words, then progressing toward reciprocal and then additive empathy as appropriate to your setting as your relationship deepens.

It is also important to remember that empathic understanding is conveyed by nonverbal cues such as body language and tone of voice as much as it can be conveyed by the actual words you express and language you employ. When working with clients in person, self-awareness about how you react physically can provide clues to your clients' emotional states and experiences and will help you to convey empathic responses authentically. When communicating with clients by telephone, video conferencing, or other electronic method, much of your nonverbal communication may be filtered out. Nevertheless, empathic responding remains important, so social workers should be more deliberate in asking directly about the emotions that clients may be experiencing and listen carefully for tone of voice, pace of speech, and silences, for clues into the emotional lives of their clients (Grondin & Lomanowska, 2019).

Finally, it is important to recognize that the emotional lives of people who identify as members of historically marginalized and oppressed groups are deeply affected by racism and discrimination. Historical traumas associated with systemic racism in health, education, social welfare, and criminal justice systems persist in many inequities present today, whether they be in health disparities, disparities in educational outcomes, disproportionate minority contact with the justice system, or disproportionate rates of foster care placement among children of color in the child welfare system. The ongoing presence of these traumas are faced by people in a myriad of ways, including protective reactions like wariness and mistrust, painful reactions like despondency and fatigue, and strength-based reactions like determination and resolve.

To deepen your capacity for empathy in cross-racial and cross-cultural relationships, we recommend that you sensitize your capacity for perspective taking by educating yourself about the histories of racism and discrimination that have affected your clients. All social workers need to recognize how their and their clients' positionality sustains racism and discrimination. Moreover, social workers are called on to take empathic action both through empathic communication and concrete actions that convey understanding and that seek to dismantle systems of oppression that continue to disadvantage their clients.

Multiple Uses of Empathic Communication

Earlier in the chapter, we referred to the versatility of empathic communication. To this point, our main focus has been on the importance of empathic communication for conveying understanding and for developing strong relationships. In this section, we delineate additional ways in which you can employ reciprocal empathic responding.

Facilitating the Intervention Process

Skilled social workers recognize that clients have feelings about the helping process in addition to those feelings associated with their presenting problems. Emotional states like excitement, anticipation, and interest can motivate client participation in services. Emotional states like wariness, anxiety, and disappointment can lead people to back away from the helping process and hesitate to participate fully. Reciprocal empathy during Phase I of the helping process can enable clients who harbor negative feelings about the helping process to feel understood, a critical element of procedural justice, and amplify the hopeful anticipation of clients who are eager to begin.

Reciprocal empathy during the intervention planning activities of Phase II point to emotions and feelings that can signal the need to revise tasks and plans and demonstrate the social worker's understanding of client perspectives, and empathic responses during Phase III termination activities can reinforce gains made by clients and help them to navigate the complex process of ending relationships. Throughout the intervention process, empathic responses help the social worker "start where the client is" and tune into how their clients perceive the helping process.

Along with emotions and feelings about the helping process, clients also have emotions and feelings about social workers themselves. Some client emotions and feelings are a direct response to the interviewing strategies and skills that social workers employ. Others are in response to client perceptions about the ability of the social worker to be helpful because of positionality and social status differences associated with age, gender, race, or other marker of shared or divergent experience. The use of reciprocal empathy about how clients feel about the approaches used with them both demonstrate a social worker's commitment to be helpful and open dialogue that can provide learning opportunities for both the social worker and client.

Accurately Assessing Client Problems

The levels of empathy offered by social workers are likely to correlate with their clients' levels of self-exploration. That is, high-level empathic responding should increase clients' exploration of self and problems. As the social worker moves "with" clients by frequently using empathic responses in initial sessions, clients will begin to lay out their problems and to reveal events and relevant data. Figuratively speaking, clients then take social workers where they need to go by providing information crucial to making an accurate assessment. Such an approach contrasts sharply with sessions that emphasize history taking and in which social workers, following their own agendas rather than the clients', spend unnecessary time asking hit-or-miss questions and gathering extraneous information.

C7

Understanding Anger and Deescalating Risk of Violence

While empathic communication is necessary in response to the full range of client emotional experiences, the expression of anger can pose challenges for social workers, especially when anger is directed at the social worker or associated with an increased risk of violence or aggression. Research on de-escalation strategies in high-tension environments such as psychiatric hospital wards and emergency rooms point to a set of strategies to help reduce the risk of violence and the need for coercive control measures (Bowers, 2014; Hallett & Dickens, 2017; Spielfogel & McMillen, 2017). Chief among these is empathic communication.

At the outset, it is important to recognize that anger is a multifaceted emotion that serves multiple purposes in human communication. Anger provides energy and motivation for productive goal-directed change and often forms the basis of a healthy response to trauma and injustice. When presented with a client's expression of anger, social workers do not use empathic communication or any other strategies to remove anger or to eliminate it, or to reduce its intensity. Rather, reciprocal empathy can be used to convey understanding of the presence and intensity of client anger and to notice and give voice to the multiple feelings that co-occur alongside anger. In a way, reciprocal empathy helps you and your client to be aware of the complexity of the anger your client expresses. For instance:

- "I can see that you are pissed off. The message I'm getting is that you are worried that your children are going to be taken away from you and that you are determined to not let that happen."
- "What I've heard you say is that you are as angry as you have ever been and frustrated that you can't seem to make people understand you."
- "You seem to be seething and feeling very vulnerable right now."

By empathizing with the multiple circumstances and feelings that surround client anger, you demonstrate a deeper and richer understanding of your clients and set the stage for productive problem solving and de-escalating violence risk when necessary.

For many social workers, the expression of anger by clients shines a light on challenging aspects of empathic communication involving self-awareness and emotion regulation, as discussed earlier. Self-awareness and emotion regulation enable social workers to recognize and manage their own emotional states while maintaining a persistent focus on their clients. When working with clients who express intense anger, it is not unusual to experience a sense of threat, anxiety, or fear. In these moments, it is important to evaluate your responses in light of the observations you make of your immediate environment. Best practices in de-escalation highlight the importance of paying attention to your body language and conveying a sense of calm and confidence, while at the same time taking action to ensuring the safety of everyone involved, including yourself (Spielfogel & McMillen, 2017). While this can be a difficult challenge, it is incumbent on you to manage your own defensiveness and anxiety so that you can sustain your full attention on clients, their emotions, and their safety.

Authenticity

Authenticity, the third of the facilitative conditions, is the sharing of self by relating in a natural and genuine manner. When you are authentic in relationships, clients encounter you as sincere rather than contrived, trust that what you say is congruent with your actual feelings and thoughts and experience you as a real person. Authentic social workers assume responsibility for their thoughts and feelings rather than denying them or blaming others. Authenticity also involves being nondefensive and human enough to admit one's errors to clients. Realizing that clients are usually expected to relate openly, social workers who demonstrate authenticity model humanness and openness and avoid hiding behind a mask of "professionalism." In short, authenticity means presenting your true self rather than a contrived false self.

What does authenticity require? Social workers who strive for authenticity pay attention to the feelings and thoughts they experience during the course of their professional relationships (Kernis & Goldman, 2006). They recognize when their thoughts reflect acceptance and when their thoughts reflect judgement. Authenticity does not mean that social workers always like what they see. Like all people, social workers are prone to corrosive implicit biases and racism (Hall et al., 2015) as well as idiosyncratic preferences and prejudices that lie at the root of judgmentalism. Authenticity requires that we observe and reflect on our interior experiences, even negative ones, rather than deny or minimize them. We can do this in supervision, in private disciplines like journaling, and in psychotherapy. Social workers who strive for authenticity seek to deepen their self-awareness and grow through their explorations.

Authenticity also requires that social workers act in a manner that is congruent with their internal selves as they understand them in light of the profession's ethical boundaries and constraints (Kernis & Goldman, 2006; Wickham et al., 2015). Sometimes, some of the internal states you experience can interfere with the helping process, while other internal states promote it. Thus, authenticity entails decisions about what aspects of our true selves we choose to reveal and the way we choose to express them. Usually, we express our true selves indirectly through the communication skills we use at any given moment. For example, reciprocal and additive empathy can reveal the depth of our emotional connections with clients, while open-ended questions, as we discuss later in Chapter 6, often reveal our priorities and interests. Other times, aspects of our true selves are revealed passively by the way we dress, how we decorate our workspaces, and by the cars we drive. Passive disclosures can reveal our style preferences and present powerful symbols of our cultures, social class, and values. Sometimes, authenticity refers to the choices we make to directly reveal our own thoughts, feelings, and experiences. In the remainder of this section, we address two discrete skills that are often used in social work to present an authentic self: self-involving statements and personal self-disclosure.

Types of Authentic Responses

Lee (2014) defines self-involving statements as any message that expresses the social worker's personal reaction to the clients. Often, these are expressions of pride, worry, excitement, or sadness. The following are examples of self-involving statements:

- "I'm impressed with the progress you've made this past week. You applied what we discussed last week and have made another step toward learning to control angry feelings."

- "I want to share my reaction to what you just said. I feel sad for you because you are very hard on yourself."

- "You know, as I think about the losses you've experienced this past year, I am impressed with how well you have coped."

In contrast, personal self-disclosure messages present information about social workers' lives and experiences. Personal self-disclosure includes structural information (e.g., age, race/ethnicity, gender expression, marital status, education) as well as experiential information that may or may not be similar to those described by clients. The following are examples of this type of self-disclosure:

- "As you talk about your problems with your children, it reminds me of similar difficulties I had with mine when they were that same age."

- "I hear that some of your concerns relate to being a first-generation college student without family role models for this kind of coping. I can relate to that, having also been a first-generation college student."

Research findings comparing the effects of different types of authentic responding have been mixed (Farber, 2006). Self-involving statements and personal self-disclosures can convey empathic understanding and also be a source of ideas for problem solving strategies. However, these types of authentic responses also place the focus on the social worker rather than the client, leaving clients to wonder "who is being helped here?" As one client said, "My case

worker wanted to tell me all about their weekend and their significant other and so on. And I said, 'TMI: too much information. I don't need to know this, and I don't want to know this." Given the current state of research and practice, social workers should use authentic responding, and especially personal self-disclosure, sparingly. When used, disclosures should be relatively brief, carefully linked to the context of the client's circumstances, and avoid sending the message that "you can do it" (Hanson, 2005).

Cross-cultural and cross-racial relationships present particular challenges and opportunities for authenticity. Careful analysis of conversations between therapists and clients affirms that cultural differences are constantly negotiated in these interactions, even when cultural differences themselves are not discussed directly (Lee, 2014). Unstated and unexplored differences in cultural norms and in social positionality with respect to racism and other systems of oppression can create barriers to the helping process and nurture conditions that reinforce oppression and marginalization. Perhaps for this reason, evidence in the study of cultural humility, discussed previously in Chapter 2, favors authentic and open discussion with clients about cultural identities, cultural differences, and how the forces of racism, discrimination, and marginalization can hamper the helping process. Usually, these conversations are undertaken from a "not knowing" position (Yan, 2008) and include a statement of resolve by social workers to remain open to further discussion and commitment to take antiracist and anti-oppressive action to facilitate the helping process when needed (Fisher-Borne et al., 2015; Hook et al., 2017; Owen et al., 2016). For example:

- "I identify as [insert relevant identity characteristics] who is committed to antiracism and anti-oppression. My experiences have taught me that it is important to talk about these things directly and openly. My experiences have also taught me that while I can probably relate to you in many ways, there may be ways that I can't relate to your experiences, and this can affect how we work together. I'll do my best to own my mistakes. What has your experience taught you?"

- "I identify as [insert relevant identity characteristics] who is committed to antiracism and anti-oppression. We are working together in a system that affects families differently based on their race. Because of this, it is important to talk about these things directly and openly. I'll try to relate to your experience as best as I can, but I'll probably make mistakes and will own them when I do. Overall, my goal is to help you move past this system. Can you share your perspective with me?"

Personal self-disclosures about your positionality with regards to race, gender expression, sexual orientation, and other social identities are called **broaching** in the cultural humility literature (Day-Vines et al., 2020). Most evidence and scholarship on broaching suggests its importance whenever there are significant differences in social identities between the social worker and client. How and what you self-disclose about your positionality depends on your positionality itself, the positionality of your clients, and about characteristics of the service system in which you work.

A Paradigm for Self-Involving Statements

Beginning social workers (and clients) may learn the skill of relating authentically more readily if they have a paradigm for formulating effective self-involving statements. The paradigm presented shares similarities with others described as "assertive communication" and includes four elements:

1. Personalize messages by using the pronoun "I"
2. Share feelings that lie at varying depths
3. Describe the situation or behavior in neutral or descriptive terms
4. Identify the specific impact of the situation or behavior on others

The following example involving a social work student intern illustrates the use of this paradigm (Larsen, 1980). The social work student described the situation: "Don and I had a hard time together last week. I entered the living unit only to find that he was angry with me for some reason, and he proceeded to abuse me verbally all night long. This week, Don approached me to apologize."

> **Don:** I'm really sorry about what happened the other night. I didn't mean to diss you.
>
> **Student social worker:** Well, you know, Don, I'm sorry it happened, too. I was hurt and puzzled that night because I didn't understand where all your anger was coming from. You wouldn't talk to me about it, so I felt frustrated, and I didn't quite know what to do or make of it. One of my real fears that night was that this was going to get in the way of our getting to know each other. I really didn't want to see that happen.

Note that the social work student used all of the elements of the paradigm: taking responsibility for their reaction with an I-statement; identifying specific feelings (hurt, puzzlement, frustration, fear); describing the events that occurred in a neutral, nonblaming manner;

and identifying the impact they feared these events might have on the client–social worker relationship.

As you consider the paradigm, note that we are not recommending that you use it in a mechanistic and undeviating "I-feel-this-way-about …" response pattern. Rather, we suggest that you learn and combine the elements of the paradigm in a variety of ways as you practice constructing authentic messages. Later, as you incorporate authentic relating into your natural conversational repertoire, you will no longer need to refer to the paradigm.

Note that this paradigm is also applicable in teaching clients to respond authentically. We suggest that you present the paradigm to clients and guide them through several practice messages, assisting them to include all elements of the paradigm in their responses. For example:

Specific "I" Feelings	Description of Event	Impact
I get frustrated	when you keep looking at your phone while I'm speaking	because I feel very unimportant to you.

As you practice authentic responding and teach clients to respond authentically in their encounters with others, we suggest you keep in mind the following guidelines related to the four elements of an authentic message.

Use "I" Statements

Personalize messages by using the pronoun "I." When attempting to respond authentically, people commonly make the mistake of starting their statements with "you." This introduction tends to focus a response on the other person rather than on the sender's experiencing. In contrast, beginning messages with "I" encourages senders to own responsibility for their feelings and to personalize their statements.

Share Feelings that Lie at Varying Depths

Social workers must reach for those feelings that underlie their immediate experiencing. Doing so is particularly vital when social workers experience strong negative feelings (e.g., dislike, anger, repulsion, disgust, boredom) toward a client because an examination of the deeper aspects of feelings often discloses more positive feelings toward the client. Social workers need to be in tune with their feelings, positive and negative, and learn when and how sharing such emotions appropriately can be useful to clients. Expressing these feelings preserves the client's self-esteem, whereas expressing superficial negative feelings often poses a threat to the client, creating defensiveness and anger.

For example, in experiencing feelings of anger and perhaps disappointment toward a client who is chronically late for appointments, the social worker may first connect their feelings of anger to feeling inconvenienced. In reaching for the client's deeper feelings, however, the social worker may discover that the annoyance derives from a concern that the client may not find the sessions useful. At an even deeper level may lie hurt in not being more important to the client. Further introspection may also uncover a concern that the client is exhibiting similar behavior in other areas of life that could adversely affect their relationships with others. The fact is that the social worker does not know why the client is late for appointments, and overt exploration of the obstacles can lead the social worker and the client into a more productive discussion on how to resolve the issue. The social worker may discover multiple and sometimes conflicting feelings that may be beneficially shared with the client, as illustrated in the following message:

> **Social worker [to client]:** I would like to check some things out with you. You apologized for being late for the session, and I appreciate that. However, this has occurred before, so I wanted to check out with you how things are going for you about our sessions. You lead a busy life, balancing many commitments. I am not sure what part these sessions are playing for you in addressing the issues you brought in. I would also like to know what you're feeling just now about what I said.

Describe the Situation or Behavior in Neutral or Descriptive Terms

When responding authentically, social workers should carefully describe specific events that prompted their responses, particularly when they wish to draw clients' attention to some aspect of their behavior or to a situation of which they may not be fully aware. The following social worker's message illustrates this point:

> **Social worker:** I need to share something with you that concerns me. Just a moment ago, I gave you feedback regarding the positive way I thought you handled a situation with your partner. (Refers to specific behaviors manifested by client.) When I did that, you seemed to discount my response by (mentions specific behaviors). Actually, this is not the first time I have seen this happen. It appears to me that it is difficult for you to give yourself credit for the positive things you do and the progress you are making.

Social workers constantly need to assess the specificity of their responses to ensure that they give clients the benefit of behaviorally specific feedback and provide positive modeling experiences for them. It is also vital to coach clients in giving specific feedback whenever they make sweeping generalizations and do not document the relationship between their responses and specific situations.

Identify the Specific Impact of the Situation or Behavior on Others

Authentic messages often stop short of identifying the specific effects of the situation on the sender or on others, even though such information would be very appropriate and helpful. This element of an "I" message also increases the likelihood that the receiver will adjust or make changes, particularly if the sender demonstrates that the receiver's behavior is having a tangible effect on them. Consider a social worker's authentic response to a member of an adult group:

> **Social worker:** Sometimes I sense some impatience on your part to move on to other topics. (Describes situation that just occurred, documenting specific messages and behavior.) At times, I find myself torn between responding to your urging us to "get on with it" or staying with a discussion that seems beneficial to the group. It may be that others in the group are experiencing similar mixed feelings and some of the pressure I feel.

Here, the social worker first clarifies the tangible effects of the client's behavior on themselves and then suggests that others may experience the behavior similarly. Given the social worker's approach, others in the group may be willing to give feedback as well. The client is then free to draw their own conclusions about the cause-and-effect relationship between their behaviors and the reactions of others and to decide whether they wish to alter their way of relating in the group.

Social workers can identify how specific client behaviors impact not only the social worker but also the clients themselves (e.g., "I'm concerned about [specific behavior] because it keeps you from achieving your goal"). Further, they may document how a client's behavior affects others (e.g., their spouse) or the relationship between the client and another person (e.g., "It appears that your behavior creates distance between you and your child").

Cues for Authentic Responding

The impetus for social workers to respond authentically with self-involving statements or personal self-disclosure may emanate from (1) clients' request for self-disclosure or (2) social workers' decisions to share perceptions and reactions they believe will be helpful. Next, we consider a variety of common situations arising in social work practice that call for direct authentic responses.

Requests for Personal Information

Clients often request personal information, such as "How old are you?", "Do you have any children?", "What is your religion?", "Are you married?", and "Are you a student?" It is natural for clients to be curious and to ask questions about a social worker in whom they are confiding, especially when their well-being and future are at stake.

The decision to self-disclose in these circumstances depends upon the social worker's assessment of the client's motivation for asking a particular question. When questions appear to be prompted by an attempt to be sociable, such responses are usually appropriate and helpful. On the other hand, client requests for information can be a signal of deeper needs or concerns related to the helping process. For example, it is appropriate for clients to want to know whether you are likely to be helpful. They often want to know "Are you any good at what you do?" and "Can I relate to you?" Their way of assessing this may take the form of asking about your personal experience, whether it be drug use or raising children. Consider the following exchange from an initial session involving a 23-year-old student social worker and a 43-year-old client who requested help in dealing with their marital problems:

> **Client:** Are you married?
> **Student social worker:** No, I am not. Is it important to you to work with a married helper?
> **Client:** Oh, I don't know. I just wondered.

Given the context of an older adult with a much younger student, the client's question was likely motivated by a concern that the student might lack life experience essential to understanding marital difficulties or the competence needed to assist in resolving them. In this instance, immediate authentic disclosure by the student was probably inappropriate because it did not facilitate exploration of the feelings underlying the client's inquiry.

Such an exchange may yield information vital to the helping process if the social worker avoids premature self-disclosure and begins with a deeper exploration of what the question means to the client. It is sometimes very difficult to distinguish whether clients' questions are motivated by a natural desire for information or by deeper concerns or feelings. As a rule of thumb, when clients request information from you that may be

motivated by their concerns about the helping process, precede your self-disclosure with open-ended questions or empathic responses about their request. Continuing with our earlier example:

> **Student social worker:** When you say you wondered whether I was married, please help me understand how knowing that could be helpful to you.
> **Client:** Well, I guess I was thinking that someone who is married could understand my situation. I hope it doesn't offend you.
> **Student social worker:** Not at all. In fact, I appreciate your frankness. It's natural that you want to know whether your social worker might be able to help you. I know there's a lot at stake for you. Tell me more about your concerns.

Notice how the social worker's question led to a discussion of their client's underlying concerns. Responses like this can foster confidence in clients and greatly facilitate the establishment of a helping relationship. The fact that the student "leans into" the situation by inviting further exploration rather than skirting the issue may also be read by the client as an indicator of the student's own confidence in his or her ability to help. After fully exploring the client's concerns, the student can respond with an authentic response identifying personal qualifications:

> **Student social worker:** I do want you to know that I believe I can be helpful to you. I have worked with other clients whose difficulties were similar to your own. I also consult with my supervisor regularly. Of course, the final judgment of my competence rests with you. It is important for us to discuss any feelings you may still have at the end of the interview as you decide about returning for future sessions.

It is not necessary to answer all questions from clients in the service of authenticity. If you feel uncomfortable about answering a personal question or deem it inadvisable to do so, you should feel free to decline answering. When doing so, it is important to explain your reason for not answering directly, again utilizing an authentic response. If a teenage client, for example, asks whether the social worker had sexual relations before they married, the social worker may respond as follows:

> **Social worker:** You are asking about a very private part of my life. Asking me took some risk on your part. I have an idea that your question probably has to do with a struggle you're having, although I could be wrong. Can you tell me what sparked your question?

Requests for Social Worker's Opinions, Views, and Feelings

Clients may also pose questions that solicit the social worker's opinions, views, or feelings. Typical questions include "How do I compare to your other clients?" "Do you think I need help?" "What would you do?" and "Do you think there's any hope for me?" Such questions can pose a challenge for social workers, who must consider the motivation behind the question and judge whether to disclose their views or feelings immediately or to employ other responses such as empathy or open-ended questions. While there are no concrete rules, social workers in this situation commonly seek to learn more about clients' deeper concerns before providing an authentic response. For example, in response to the question "Do you think there's any hope for me?", the social worker may respond:

> **Social worker:** Can you tell me about your question?

Depending upon the client's response, the social worker may explore in more depth the client's sense of hope and hopelessness or may choose to make a self-involving statement, such as:

> **Social worker:** Although you do have some difficult problems, I'm optimistic that if we work hard together, things can improve. You've shown a number of strengths that should help you make changes.

Disclosing Personal Past Experiences

On occasion, you may recognize lessons from your prior experiences that you think may helpfully relate to the circumstances in which your clients find themselves. Perhaps it was in the way you overcame a challenge or was as aspect of your past that you share in common with your clients. The experience may be painful, traumatic, or mundane. This urge to disclose personal information with the intention of imparting helpful advice or to strengthen the helping relationship is one shared by many social workers.

In general, we advise against disclosing personal experiences in this manner. Sharing our personal experiences puts us at risk of using the helping process to serve our own needs, whether they be a need for validation or the need to process the effect of our own traumas. Partly for this reason, the profession has a long history of avoiding self-disclosures of this type. Moreover, evidence discussed above suggests that personal self-disclosure should be minimal. Finally, if your impulse is to share experiences that you or your client recognize as traumatic, seek supervision and personal therapeutic support to ensure that you are not unintentionally leaning on clients for support.

Nevertheless, there may be times when an authentic response involving self-disclosure seems important. When you do, take care to limit your self-disclosure to a minimal set of details and immediately follow up to check out whether your client sees this experience as comparable or helpful. Throughout, maintain your focus on this client and the helping process.

Providing Feedback

A key role of the social worker in the change-oriented phase of the helping process is to act as a candid feedback system by revealing personal thoughts and perceptions relevant to client problems (Hammond et al., 1977). Such responding is intended to further the change process in one or more of the following ways:

1. To heighten clients' awareness of dynamics that may play an important part in problems
2. To offer a different perspective regarding issues and events
3. To aid clients in conceptualizing the purposes of their behavior and feelings
4. To bring clients' attention to cognitive and behavioral patterns (both functional and dysfunctional) that operate at either an individual or a group level
5. To share the social worker's here-and-now affective and physical reactions to clients' behavior or to processes that occur in the helping relationship
6. To share positive feedback concerning clients' strengths and growth

After responding authentically to achieve any of these purposes, it is vital to invite clients to express their own views and draw their own conclusions. Sharing perceptions with clients does involve some risk. In particular, clients may misinterpret the social worker's motives and feel criticized, put down, or rebuked. Clarifying the social worker's helpful intent before responding diminishes this risk somewhat. Nevertheless, it is critical to watch for clients' reactions that may indicate a response has struck an exposed nerve. For example:

> **Social worker:** I can see that what I shared with you hit you hard and that you're feeling put down right now. (Client nods but avoids eye contact.) I feel bad about that because the last thing I'd want is to hurt you. Please tell me what you're feeling.

Experiencing Discomfort in Sessions

Sometimes intense discomfort may indicate that something in the session is going awry and needs to be addressed. It is important to reflect on your discomfort, seeking to identify events that seem to be causing or exacerbating it (e.g., "I'm feeling very uneasy because I don't know how to respond when my client says things like, 'You seem to be too busy to see me' or 'I'm not sure I'm worth your trouble'"). After privately exploring the reason for the discomfort, the social worker might respond as follows:

> **Social worker:** I'd like to share some impressions about several things you've said in the last two sessions. (Identifies client's statements.) I sense you're feeling unimportant—as though you don't count for much—and that perhaps you're imposing on me just by being here. I want you to know that I'm pleased you had the courage to seek help in the face of all the opposition from your family. It's also important to me that you know that I want to be helpful to you. I am concerned, however, that you feel you're imposing on me. Could you share more what contributes to that feeling for you?

Social workers also must learn to respond authentically when clients express anger, as we discussed earlier. Consider a situation in which an adolescent states during an initial interview, "I don't want to be here. You social workers are all assholes." In such instances, social workers should share their reactions, as illustrated in the following response:

> **Social worker:** It sounds as though you're really angry about having to see me and that your previous experiences with social workers haven't been good. I respect your feelings and don't want to pressure you to work with me. I want you to know that I am interested in you and that I would like to know what you are facing.

Intertwining empathic and authentic responses in this manner often defuses clients' anger and encourages a deeper examination of their situations.

Sharing Feelings Frustration, Anger, and Hurt

Although social workers should be able to take most client behaviors in stride, sometimes they can experience feelings of frustration, anger, or even hurt. In one case, a client acquired a social worker's home phone number from another source and began calling frequently about daily frustrations. In another instance, an intoxicated client called the social worker in the middle of the night "just to talk." In yet another case, an adolescent client let the air out of a social worker's automobile tires.

In such situations, social workers should share their feelings with clients—if they believe they can do so constructively. In the following case example, note that the student social worker interweaves authentic and empathic responses in confronting an adolescent in a correctional institution who had maintained they were innocent of hiding drugs that staff had found in their room. Believing the youth's story, the student social worker went to bat for them, only to find out later that the client had lied. Somewhat uneasy at their first real confrontation, the student social worker tries to formulate an authentic response. In an interesting twist, the client helps the social worker to be "up front" with them:

> **Student social worker:** There's something I wanted to talk to you about, Randy … (Stops to search for the right words.)
>
> **Randy:** Well, come out with it, then. Just lay it on me.
>
> **Student social worker:** Well, remember last week when you got that incident report? You know, I really believed you were innocent. I was ready to go to the hearing and tell staff I was sure you were innocent and that the charge should be dropped. I guess I'm feeling kind of bad because when I talked to you, you told me you were innocent, and, well, that's not exactly the way it turned out.
>
> **Randy:** You mean I lied to you. Go ahead and say it.
>
> Student social worker: Well, yes, I guess I felt kind of hurt because I was hoping that maybe you had more trust in me than that.
>
> **Randy:** Well, let me tell you something. Where I come from, that's not lying—that's what we call survival. Personally, I don't consider myself a liar. I just do what I need to do to get by. That's an old trick, but it just didn't work.
>
> **Student social worker:** I hear you, Randy. I guess you're saying we're from two different worlds, and maybe we both define the same thing in different ways. I guess that with me being white, you can't really expect me to understand what life has been like for you.

Several minutes later in the session, after the student has further explored the client's feelings, the following interchange occurs:

> **Student social worker:** Randy, I want you to know a couple of things. The first thing is that when social workers work with clients, they must honor what they call confidentiality, so I can't share what we talk about without your permission in most cases. An exception to this relates to rule or law violations. I can't keep that confidential. The second thing is that I don't expect you to share everything with me. I know there are certain things you don't want to tell me, so rather than lying about something that I ask you about, maybe you can just tell me you don't want to tell me. Would you consider that?

Randy: Yeah, that's okay. (Pause.) Listen, I don't want you to go around thinking I'm a liar now. I'll tell you this, and you can take it for what it's worth, but this is the truth. That's the first time I've ever lied to you, but you may not believe that.

Student social worker: I do believe you, Randy. (He seems a little relieved, and there is a silence.)

Randy: Well, that's a deal, then. I won't lie to you again, but if there's something I don't want to say, I'll tell you I don't want to say it.

Student social worker: Sounds good to me. (Both start walking away.) You know, Randy, I really want to see you get through this program and get out as fast as you can. I know it's hard starting over because of the incident with the drugs, but I think we can get you through. (This seemed to have more impact on Randy than anything the social worker had said to him in a long time. The pleasure was visible on his face, and he broke into a big smile.)

Noteworthy in this exchange is that the social worker relied almost exclusively on the skills of authenticity and empathy to bring the incident to a positive conclusion. Ignoring their feelings would have impaired the student's ability to relate facilitatively to the client and would have been destructive to the relationship. In contrast, focusing on the situation proved beneficial for both.

Responding to Positive Feedback

Social workers sometimes have difficulty responding receptively to clients' positive feedback about their own attributes and/or performance. We suggest that social workers model the same receptivity to positive feedback that they ask clients to demonstrate in their own lives, as illustrated in the following exchange:

Client: I don't know what I would have done without you. I'm just not sure I would have made it if you hadn't been there when I needed you. You've made such a difference in my life.

Social worker: I'm touched by your gratitude and pleased you are feeling so much more capable of coping with your situation. I want you to know, too, that even though I was there to help, your efforts have been the deciding factor in your growth.

Giving Positive Feedback

Positive feedback, in the form of affirmations, praise, and complements, is a form of authentic responding that reinforce client strengths, coping efforts, and growth. Think of times when you have received positive feedback. It is likely that you experienced pride, an increase in confidence, an increase in motivation, or some combination of each of these. When used in social work settings, positive feedback can foster these same outcomes and reinforce the potential for change and hope for the future.

Many opportune moments occur in the helping process when social workers experience warm or positive feelings toward clients because of the latter's actions or progress. When appropriate, social workers should share such feelings spontaneously with clients, as illustrated in the following messages:

- "You have what I consider exceptional ability to pay attention to your own behavior and to analyze the part you play in relationships. I think this strength will serve you well in solving the problems you have identified."

- "I've been touched several times in the group when I've noticed that, despite your grief over the loss of your spouse, you've reached out to other members who needed support."

- [To newly formed group]: "In contrast to our first session, I've noticed that this week we haven't had trouble getting down to business and staying on task. I've been pleased as I've watched you develop group guidelines for the past 20 minutes with minimal assistance from me. I had the thought, 'This group is really moving.'"

The first two messages acknowledge strengths of individuals. The third lauds a behavioral change the social worker has observed in a group process. Both types of messages sharply focus clients' attention on specific behaviors that facilitate the change process, ultimately increasing the frequency of such behaviors. When sent consistently, positive messages also have the long-range effect of helping people who have low self-esteem to develop a more positive self-image. When positive feedback is employed to document the cause-and-effect relationship between their efforts and positive outcomes, individuals also experience a sense of satisfaction, accomplishment, and control over their situation.

Saying No and Setting Limits

Many tasks that social workers perform on behalf of their clients are quite appropriate. For example, negotiating for clients and conferring with other parties and potential resources to supplement and facilitate client action are tasks that are rightly handled by social workers (Epstein, 1992). In contracting with clients, however, social workers must occasionally decline requests or set limits. This step is sometimes difficult for beginning social workers to take, as they typically want to demonstrate their willingness to help others. Commitment to helping others is a desirable quality, but it must be tempered with judgment as to when acceding to clients' requests is in the best interests of both social worker and client.

Some clients may have had past experiences that led them to believe that social workers will do most of the work required out of sessions. However, clients are often more likely to experience empowerment by increasing the scope of their actions than by having social workers perform tasks on their behalf that they can learn to do for themselves. Consequently, if social workers unthinkingly agree to take on responsibilities that clients can perform now or could perform in the future, they may reinforce passive client behavior.

Setting limits has special implications when social workers work with involuntary clients where relationships are negotiated (Cingolani, 1984). In **negotiated relationships,** social workers assume the roles of compromiser, mediator, and enforcer in addition to the more comfortable role of counselor. For example, when an involuntary client requests a break related to performance of a court order, the social worker must be clear about the client's choices and consequences of making those choices. They must also clarify what the client should expect from the social worker.

> **Rory (member of domestic violence group):** I don't think that it is fair that you reported I didn't meet for eight group sessions. I could not get off work for some of those sessions. I did all I could do.
>
> **Social worker:** You did attend seven of the sessions, Rory, and made efforts to attend others. However, the contract you signed, which was presented in court, stated that you must complete eight sessions to be certified as completing the group. I do not have the power to change that court order. Should you decide to comply with the court order, I am willing to speak with your employer to urge him to work with you to arrange your schedule so that you can meet the court order.

In their response, the social worker made it clear that they would not evade the court order. At the same time, the social worker assured Rory that if he chose to comply with the court order, the social worker would be willing to act as a mediator to assist with difficulties in scheduling with the employer.

Being tactfully assertive is no easier for social workers with excessive needs to please others than it is for other persons. These social workers have difficulty declining requests or setting limits when doing so is in the best interests of clients. To remedy this, such social workers may benefit by setting tasks for themselves related to increasing their assertiveness. Participating in an assertiveness training group and delving into the popular literature on assertiveness may be highly beneficial as well. We suggest that you consult with your supervisor about requests that pose special questions. In some cases, this can lead to problem solving around where else a client might be assisted to find a resource, rather than dwelling only on whether it is appropriate to get that resource from the social worker. The following are a few of the many situations in which you may need to decline clients' requests:

1. When clients invite you to participate with them socially or through social media such as Facebook or Instagram
2. When clients ask you to grant them preferential status (e.g., set lower fees than are specified by policy)
3. When clients request physical intimacy
4. When clients ask you to intercede in a situation they should handle themselves
5. When clients request a special appointment after having broken a regular appointment for an invalid reason
6. When clients ask to borrow money
7. When clients request that you conceal information about violations of probation, parole, or institutional policy
8. When spouses request that you withhold information from their partners
9. When clients disclose plans to commit crimes or acts of violence against others
10. When clients ask you to report false information to an employer or other party

In addition to declining requests, you may need to set limits with clients in situations such as the following:

1. When clients make excessive phone calls or text messages to you at home or in the office
2. When clients cancel appointments without giving advance notice
3. When clients express emotions in abusive or violent ways
4. When clients habitually seek to go beyond designated ending points of sessions
5. When clients consistently fail to abide by contracts (e.g., not paying fees or missing numerous appointments)
6. When clients make sexual overtures toward you or other staff members
7. When clients come to sessions while intoxicated or under the influence of drugs

Part of maturing professionally means learning to decline requests, set limits, and feel comfortable in doing so. As you gain experience, you will realize that you help clients as much by ensuring that they have reasonable expectations as you do by providing a concrete action for them.

Summary

This chapter introduced you to the process of role clarification, and to the facilitative conditions of empathy and authenticity. By the conclusion of this chapter, you should be able to prepare clients for the helping process, convey accurate empathy at multiple levels, and respond to clients with authenticity, including effective self-involving statements and personal self-disclosures. Throughout, we have discussed how these skills can help you engage clients across cultural and other differences and how they can help you implement an anti-oppressive, empowering approach to the helping process. In Chapter 6, you will build on these skills by developing more advanced skills in listening, focusing, and exploring. First, we encourage you to practice your new skills by completing the exercises in this chapter.

Competency Notes

C1 Demonstrate Ethical and Professional Behavior

- Manage personal and professional value conflicts and affective reactions.

C2 Engage Anti-Racism, Diversity, Equity, and Inclusion in Practice

- Demonstrate anti-racist social work practice at the individual, family, group, organizational, community, research, and policy levels, informed by the theories and voices of those who have been marginalized.
- Demonstrate cultural humility applying critical reflexivity, self-awareness, and self-regulation to manage the influence of bias, power, privilege, and values in working with clients and constituencies acknowledging them as experts of their own lived experiences.

C6 Engage with Individuals, Families, Groups, Organizations, and Communities

- Use empathy, reflection, and interpersonal skills to effectively engage diverse clients and constituencies.

C7 Assess Individuals, Families, Groups, Organizations, and Communities

- Apply knowledge of human behavior and person-in-environment and other culturally responsive multidisciplinary theoretical frameworks when assessing clients and constituencies.
- Demonstrate respect for client self-determination during the assessment process collaborating with clients and constituencies in developing mutually agreed-on goals.

Skill Development Exercises

Responding with Empathy and Authenticity

The purpose of this exercise is to provide you with practice in responding with empathy and authenticity. What follows are 20 statements made by clients in a variety of direct practice settings. For each statement, put yourself in the role of a social worker and construct responses representing surface empathy, reciprocal empathy, and self-involving statements. You may wish to use the list of affective words (page 83) to broaden your feelings vocabulary, the list of leads for empathic responses (page 88) to vary how you convey empathy, and the paradigm for self-involving statements (page 93) as a guide for structuring authentic responses. Remember, surface responses are usually simple statements that adhere closely to the feeling words that clients use, whereas reciprocal responses use synonyms to add depth and complexity to how feelings are communicated and understood. Self-involving statements, as a form of authenticity, generally focus on how your clients' statements affect you, and how sharing your thoughts, feelings, or disclosures may influence your clients' thoughts or feelings.

When you are done, we invite you to compare your responses to the modeled responses that follow. As you compare your responses to those presented in this section, keep in mind that empathic communication involves perspective taking, and authentic responding involves high levels of self-awareness. For these reasons, the responses you develop may differ from those presented here. While there may be responses that are more specific or more accurate, this exercise does not have correct or incorrect answers, as long as you are responding to client emotions at the surface and reciprocal levels, and your self-involving statements communicate your reactions in a way that strengthens your relationships and helpfully advances the problem-solving process.

Client Statements

1. Father of 14-year-old adolescent with developmental disabilities: We just don't know what to do with Henry. We've always wanted to take care of him, but we've reached the point where we're not sure it's doing any good for him or for us. Henry has grown so strong—we just can't restrain him anymore. He hit my wife last week when she wouldn't take him to the store late at night—I was out of town—and she's still bruised. She's afraid of him now, and I have to admit I'm getting that way, too.

2. Recent immigrant: My children miss school because they do not feel comfortable there. Teachers are often mean to them because we are Hispanic. They do not give them a chance. I don't think there is anything I can do

3. Employee assistance program client: They complain that I get too many personal calls at work. They all know that I have kids at home, but they still complain, and lately, they've been leaving me out of luncheons. They never ask. They all go, except for me. It feels, [pause] not good

4. Parent: Who'd want to make trouble for me by accusing me of not taking care of my kids? [Tearfully.] Maybe I'm not the best parent in the world, but I try. There are a lot of kids around here that aren't cared for as well as mine.

5. Person in counseling: I've really felt irritated with you after our last session. When I brought up taking the correspondence course in art, all you could talk about was how some correspondence courses are rip-offs and that I could take courses at a college for less money. I knew that, but I've checked into this correspondence course, and it's well worth the money. You put me down, and I've resented it

6. Member of battered women's group: Last month I was living in mortal fear of Art. He'd get that hateful look in his eyes, and I'd know he was going to let me have it. The last time I was afraid he was going to kill me, and he might have, if his brother hadn't dropped in. I'm afraid to go back to him, but what do I do? I can't stay here much longer!

7. Elderly person grieving the death of a spouse: I'm feeling just alright. Since the funeral, I've not had a lot of energy. I don't feel like doing a lot of things, so I don't, [pause] I don't go out.

8. Young adult: I'm willing to take the chance on moving out of transitional housing into a new home even with this new temp job because it pays actually kind of good, and it has maybe an opportunity to move into a full-time job with benefits. I feel like things are looking up.

9. Client in a state prison: They treat you like an animal in here—herd you around like a damn cow. I know I've got to do my time, but sometimes I feel like I can't stand it any longer—like something's building up in me that's going to explode.

10. Adult: I don't have any pleasant memories of my childhood. It seems like just so much empty space. I can remember my father watching television and staring at me with a blank look as though I didn't exist.

11. Patient in hospital: I know the doctor is a skilled surgeon and tells me not to worry—that there's very little risk in this surgery. I know I should feel reassured, but to tell you the truth, I'm just plain panic-stricken.

12. Female group member: We have some debt. Actually, we have a lot of debt from the house and from our credit card. We fight about it, and I get so angry. It's a lot, but we didn't have the money, and I had to feed the kids.

13. Man on probation: They already decided exactly what I was when I walked in; didn't make a difference in what I said. That's why I left. I couldn't stand in front of people I didn't know and say I was a man who battered. I don't know what I am! They

wouldn't let my try to figure out what I was. I had to be what they wanted me to be

14. Adolescent on probation: I used to get to school early. At the beginning of the school year, I got here a lot earlier, but then something happened. I started getting up late. I get up really late. I can't wake up, so then my parents get on me, and my sister be like 'why don't you get up on time,' but I don't know what to do about it.

15. Isaiah, referred by court (see Chapter 2): I was scared, but I got so mad that I pushed the cop. Then, the two cops pushed me to the ground, put hand-cuffs on me, and put me into the police car. They took me to juvie, and I could not get out until the next morning. The problem is the cops are always harassing us. I don't want to go to no group. I don't have an anger problem. I don't need a group.

16. Adult: It's not that I have to drink all the time. It's that I am so tired of people telling me that I have a drinking problem and telling me what to do about it. They don't control me.

17. Adolescent girl in foster care with her baby: When I come in, my foster mom leaves suckers and stuff on the table, and my baby be wanting a sucker, and I be telling her no, and my foster mom still keeps giving my baby the candy, and I be wondering why she not listen what I'm saying. She just gives her the candy.

18. Blind client: You know, it really offends me when people praise me or make a fuss over me for doing something routine that anyone else could do. It makes me feel like I'm on exhibition. I want to be recognized for being competent, not for being blind.

19. High school student: School is easier now. 'Cause, before, I wasn't really doin' that good in school, but as I looked, I like want to be somethin' in life, I want to better myself. Then we [with teacher] started havin' a good relationship and I started pushin' myself to do better things.

20. Female-identified young adult: How do you think I felt? When I came out to my parents, I mentioned to them that I wanted to talk to them. I was really scared about how they would react. I told them I was dating somebody, and her name was Anna. They both just nodded. Then my dad got up and started watching TV, and my mom changed the subject. They didn't hug me, but at least they didn't yell at me or kick me out.

Modeled Social Worker Responses

1. Surface empathy: "I hear you saying that you and your spouse have become afraid of Henry."
Reciprocal empathy: "I hear you saying that you are uncertain about how to care for Henry right now and that his violence frightens you."
Self-involving statement: "I think that it makes sense that your worries about caring for Henry are growing right now. As he gets older, his needs will change."

2. Surface empathy: "I understand that you are feeling powerless right now."
Reciprocal empathy: "It sounds like you are struggling to help your children. I imagine that it must be painful to watch them face racism in school."
Self-involving statement: "You are facing difficult challenges at school. I want you to know that you are not alone. We support you."

3. Surface empathy: "You feel pretty bad."
Reciprocal empathy: "Perhaps you are feeling isolated or maybe rejected by your coworkers?"
Self-involving statement: "I'm beginning to feel defensive for you, like this is not fair. Do you feel defensive too?"

4. Surface empathy: "You're feeling angry."
Reciprocal empathy: "I get the feeling that this is so hurtful, to be accused of neglecting your children when you in fact work so hard."
Self-involving statement: "I know that you are working very hard to care for your children. Who else knows this about you?"

5. Surface empathy: "My reaction angered you and left you feeling resentful of me."
Reciprocal empathy: "What I hear you saying is that you were irritated by my reactions and that you felt unheard given how excited you were about the class."
Self-involving statement: "I can understand how that would have made you feel irritated. Looking back, I guess I was responding to the negative experiences that people I've known had in correspondence courses. I was feeling protective. How do you think this has affected our relationship?"

6. Surface empathy: "I get the feeling that you are still afraid of him."

Reciprocal empathy: "Am I hearing you correctly, that you are still terrified of him but afraid that you have nowhere else to go."

Self-involving statement: "I am concerned that your safety with him depends so much on the presence of others. That doesn't seem right. What are your thoughts and feelings about this?"

7. Surface empathy: "You are feeling just alright."

   Reciprocal empathy: "From what you are saying, it sounds as though you are grieving pretty hard and perhaps feeling somewhat depressed."

   Self-involving statement: "It is entirely natural to grieve. What you are experiencing sounds completely normal to me, and healthy."

8. Surface empathy: "It sounds like there are reasons to be hopeful."

   Reciprocal empathy: "I gather that you are feeling hopeful, excited even."

   Self-involving statement: "At the same time, I am a little worried what will happen to you and your partner if the temp job doesn't pan out. Having a backup plan would seem to be a good idea. Have you given any thought to a backup plan?"

9. Surface empathy: "You feel like you might explode."

   Reciprocal empathy: "If I understand you correctly, you feel degraded by the way you're treated, as though you're less than a human being and that you are reaching a boiling point."

   Self-involving statement: "I know that it is hard for me to understand because I've not lived in prison, but I do worry about what can happen to you here if you do explode. What worries do you have?"

10. Surface empathy: "It sounds like you felt invisible."

    Reciprocal empathy: "I sense that memories of your childhood, especially your father, leave you feeling depressed and worthless or maybe invisible. It sounds lonely."

    Self-involving statement: "When you tell your story like that, I feel an emptiness inside of me, a vacant space that has no floor. Is that what this feels like to you?"

11. Surface empathy: "I hear you saying that you are scared."

    Reciprocal empathy: "Intellectually, you tell yourself not to worry, that you're in good hands. Still, on another level, you have to admit you're terrified of that operation."

    Self-involving statement: "I agree with the doctor, but reassurance doesn't always help. Would you like to talk about strategies you can use to relax while you prepare for the surgery?"

12. Surface empathy: "It sounds like a very stressful situation."

    Reciprocal empathy: "Correct me if I'm wrong, but I hear you saying that you are frustrated about your debt situation, and I am wondering if you might also feel trapped or boxed in, like you don't have any good choices?"

    Self-involving statement: "I agree, feeding your kids was important. I probably would have done the same thing, but you are learning that managing your debt load is important too. I think that we can find ways to do both. What are your thoughts?"

13. Surface empathy: "It sounds like you were angry."

    Reciprocal empathy: "Correct me if I'm wrong, but it sounds like you felt demeaned and criticized and that it was important for you to remain in control."

    Self-involving statement: "I'm impressed by how seriously you take services like this. If you are going to be involved in a program, you are not going to fake it. What kind of program would work best for you?"

14. Surface empathy: "You are feeling uncertain about how to get up on time?"

    Reciprocal empathy: "You seem to be saying that you are not entirely in control of when you get up in the morning and that you are not happy about it the pressure you are getting from your parents and your sibling."

    Self-involving statement: "I am concerned that your grades may suffer if you continue to arrive late. How realistic is my concern?"

15. Surface empathy: "It sounds like you are upset about being sent to this group."

    Reciprocal empathy: "I get the picture that police harassment in your neighborhood makes you angry, really angry, and that the court order for the anger management group feels unfair and makes you really upset."

    Self-involving statement: "I'm impressed by the way that you share your perspective. My job requires me to talk to you about anger, but it does not require me to agree with the court about your need for an anger management group. What is your goal for our meeting today?"

16. Surface empathy: "Your message seems to be that you are in control."

    Reciprocal empathy: "It sounds like you are feeling criticized or maybe insulted or controlled, by people who are talking about how you should change your drinking habits."

    Self-involving statement: "I believe that only you are in control of yourself. Can you tell me more about the pressure that you feel from others?"

17. Surface empathy: "Sounds like you might be frustrated or angry with your foster mother."
Reciprocal empathy: "I get the sense that you are beginning to resent your foster mother and that you feel capable of deciding whether or not your baby should be given candy."
Self-involving statement: "I think that it is important that your questions are answered. You are wondering why your foster mom gives candy to your baby even when you have said 'no.' I suggest that we ask her. What do you think of that?"

18. Surface empathy: "It offends you when people praise you for doing routine things."
Reciprocal empathy: "I get the sense that praise can leave you feeling insulted and that you find it demeaning."
Self-involving statement: "This sounds similar to what other blind people have said. I worry that without meaning to I may have made you or others here feel the same way. Have there been times when you have felt this way in our group conversations?"

19. Surface empathy: "It sounds like school has gotten easier."
Reciprocal empathy: "Maybe this is a long-shot, but I get the sense that you have been feeling a sense of determination to do better in school and might even be feeling more hopeful now than you were before."
Self-involving statement: "I'm so impressed that you started pushing yourself to do better at school. When did you decide to make this change?"

20. Surface empathy: "I hear you saying that telling your parents was a scary thing to do."
Reciprocal empathy: "It sounds complicated. You started feeling very anxious, then relief but perhaps not fully satisfied."
Self-involving statement: "That was a brave thing you did to tell your parents. What does your bravery say about you?"

Answers to Exercise in Identifying Surface and Underlying Feelings (page 85)

1. Apparent feelings: unimportant, neglected, disappointed, hurt. Probable deeper feelings: rejected, abandoned, forsaken, deprived, lonely, depressed.

2. Apparent feelings: unloved, insecure, confused, embarrassed, left out, or excluded. Probable deeper feelings: hurt, resentful, unvalued, rejected, taken for granted, degraded, doubting own desirability.

3. Apparent feelings: chagrined, disappointed in self, discouraged, letting children down, perplexed. Probable deeper feelings: guilty, inadequate, crummy, sense of failure, out of control, fear of damaging children.

4. Apparent feelings: frustrated, angry, bitter. Probable deeper feelings: afraid, depressed, discouraged, hopeless.

Chapter 6

Verbal Following, Exploring, and Focusing Skills

Chapter Overview

Chapter 6 introduces verbal following skills and their uses. This chapter includes discrete skills such as reflective listening, open-ended questions, and summaries, as well as higher-order skills like seeking concreteness and establishing a focus for interviews that blend discrete skills. These skills are the building blocks for communicating with empathy and authenticity, two topics we addressed in Chapter 5. Throughout this chapter, you will see references to the orienting frameworks for practice that were discussed in Chapter 2. In addition to being helpful in direct practice, verbal following skills are useful at the mezzo level in work on behalf of clients through advocacy and in work with colleagues and other professionals.

As a result of reading this chapter, you will be able to:

- Construct reflective responses that respond to content and emotions, including both simple reflections and double-sided reflections
- Construct furthering responses
- Construct open-ended questions
- Construct closed-ended questions
- Construct summarizing responses
- Construct responses to seek concreteness
- Construct responses to provide and maintain focus

The EPAS Competencies in Chapter 6

This chapter will give you the information needed to meet the following practice competencies:

- Competency 2: Engage Anti-Racism, Diversity, Equity, and Inclusion in Practice

- Competency 6: Engage with Individuals, Families, Groups, Organizations, and Communities

- Competency 7: Assess Individuals, Families, Groups, Organizations, and Communities

Verbal Following Skills

Verbal following skills are the communication strategies that you use to encourage people to share information about themselves and about their circumstances. In this chapter, we outline seven distinct verbal following skills:

C6

1. Furthering responses
2. Reflection responses
3. Closed-ended responses
4. Open-ended responses
5. Summarizing
6. Seeking concreteness
7. Providing and maintaining focus

When blended with empathic and authentic responses (see Chapter 5), verbal following skills can strengthen your relationships and facilitate the helping process across all its stages. Verbal following skills demonstrate helpful intent and the desire to understand and facilitate the helping process by fostering exploration of problems and by maintaining a sustained focus on the tasks and objectives of the helping process at each phase.

This chapter includes exercises to help you master verbal following. As you practice, pay attention first to the ways in which you construct your verbal following responses. Then, when you understand how each is structured, pay attention to the patterns that you use in conversation with clients. Many beginning social workers overuse closed-ended questions, for example, creating the sense of interrogation in their interviews, or they routinely ask open-ended questions immediately following reflections, thereby failing to allow space for the client to respond to the reflection. With feedback about your own communication patterns, you will become increasingly adept at using verbal following skills, along with empathic responses and authentic responses, purposefully.

One lesson that you will observe over time is the contingent use of verbal following skills. Interviewing is not a random process but rather entails choice. Choice in how and what questions to ask. Choice in what aspects of client communication to reflect. Choice in when you seek concreteness and choice in how you focus the interviewing process. These choices will be informed by a mix of factors, including the purpose of your relationships as determined by the agency context, the helping models you employ, by your clients' values and priorities, and by the values and biases that you bring to the relationship.

It should be clear, then, that use of verbal following skills is not a value-free or neutral endeavor. Therefore, it is imperative that you understand the values that you bring to your relationships. Direct social work practice is conducted within a set of commitments to social justice and a particular emphasis on empowerment practice with marginalized and oppressed populations. Informed by these commitments, your use of the skills presented in this chapter will enable you to adopt an empowering approach to practice where you engage clients in dialogue about matters such as positionality and power, racism and discrimination, the effects of trauma, and the hopefulness that comes with an awareness of their strengths and resources.

C2

The deliberate use of verbal following skills requires a keen sense of self-awareness, the ability to observe yourself, and practice with feedback. It is to this last objective that we turn to next as we outline each verbal following skill in turn.

Furthering Responses

Furthering responses are those utterances and actions that, rather than convey a complete thought, send the message that you are listening attentively and invite further sharing. Think about those times when you observe others saying things like "uh-huh" and "hmm." Although these utterances add nothing of their own to a conversation, they do send a specific signal in the interaction – "please continue." By paying attention to your furthering responses, you will gain control of these important and natural elements of communication.

C6

There are two types of furthering responses: minimal prompts and accent responses. **Minimal prompts** signal the social worker's attentiveness and encourage the client to continue verbalizing (e.g., "mmm hmm"). **Nonverbal minimal prompts** consist of nodding the head, using facial expressions, or employing gestures that convey receptivity, interest, and commitment to understanding. They implicitly convey the message, "I am with you; please continue." **Verbal minimal prompts** consist of brief messages that convey interest and encourage or request expanded verbalizations along the lines of the client's previous expressions. These messages include "Yes," "I see," "But?", "Tell me more," "And then what happened?", "And?", "Please go on," and other similar brief messages that affirm the appropriateness of what the client has been saying and prompt them to continue. **Accent responses** (Hackney & Cormier, 2005) involve repeating, in a questioning tone of voice or with emphasis, a word or a short phrase. Suppose a client says, "I've really had it with the way my supervisor at work is treating me." The social worker who replies, "Had it?" is employing an accent response.

Reflection Responses

Reflective listening, what earlier editions of this textbook referred to as "paraphrasing," is a bedrock skill of active listening in direct social work practice. In its most basic form, reflections restate for the client what they have communicated, both in terms of content as well as emotion. Like surface-level empathic responses, reciprocal responding, and additive empathy presented in Chapter 5, reflective listing signals to the client that you are listening carefully and provides clients with an opportunity to correct your misunderstandings. As you hone this skill, you will also find that reflective listening acts in place of direct questions as this skill often encourages greater elaboration by clients.

Forms of Reflections

Simple reflections restate what clients have said using the same or similar language. When reflecting emotions, simple reflections are the same as surface-level empathic responses. Their purpose is to convey understanding and encourage further exploration. In a conversation with Rhonda, a high-school-aged student who has an infant son and whose friends are frequently in trouble with the law, simple reflections may sound like this:

> **Rhonda:** My friends are like family to me.
> **Social worker:** You are really close to them.
> **Rhonda:** That's it! They are always there for us. They love my son. It's so cute how they coo and cuddle with him.
> **Social worker:** You like how they play with your son.

Complex reflections go beyond what the client has directly stated or implied, adding substantial meaning or emphasis to convey a more complex picture. When reflecting feelings, complex reflections are complementary to empathic responses at the reciprocal and additive levels. Complex reflections *add content* that focuses on meanings or feelings that the client did not directly express (Moyers et al., 2003). For example:

> **Rhonda:** I don't want trouble anymore. It was fun when we used to go out and mess around.
> **Social worker:** It sounds as though you may be changing.

Often, complex reflections highlight ambivalence, or those times when clients feel uncertainty about their goals or planned tasks, as in this example:

> **Rhonda:** I've got to stay in school for my son. That's our future, but that means that I can't see my friends as much.
> **Social worker:** I hear you saying that you want what's best for your son, but it's hard to know if that means committing to school or staying with friends who are like family to you.

Complex reflections that suggest new ways of thinking about problems and problem solving can be used to **reframe** client's understanding in terms of strengths or possibilities. For example:

> **Rhonda:** I don't want to choose, but I'm supposed to choose. Why can't I just figure this out?
> **Social worker:** I hear you saying that you are loyal to both. You want to commit to school, and you want to stay connected with your friends. I get the picture that loyalty is important to you.

Contingent Reflective Listening

How does one decide what aspects of client speech to reflect and whether to use simple or complex reflections? There are no prescribed formulas to guide these choices, and much is context dependent. Guided by our orienting perspectives presented in Chapter 2, perhaps the first guideline is to listen carefully and reflect what you hear, allowing clients to lead your reflections. This helps establish a collaborative approach to interviewing. Self-awareness is also important when using reflective listening, as what we hear depends in part on our positionality and the blinders we can carry about the experience of others, particularly when our clients have experienced traumas, including traumas associated with discrimination and marginalization. Make your reflections tentative to allow clients the opportunity to correct any misperceptions that your reflections may convey. Further, reflective listening can be a powerful strategy for identifying and affirming strengths, so reflect strength and assets whenever possible. Finally, our discussion of empathy in Chapter 5 suggests listening carefully to the emotions that clients convey alongside the concrete information they may present during conversation. While this is a lot to think about when you are with clients in the moment, sustained deliberate practice enables you to weave simple and complex reflections into your interviews.

Exercises in Reflective Listening

In the following exercises, read each client/colleague statement and formulate written responses that reflect the content and the emotions of the statement. Strive to develop simple and complex reflections. Modeled responses for these exercises appear at the end of the chapter (see page 124).

1. "I can't talk to people. I just completely freeze up in a group."

2. "It wasn't so difficult to adjust to this place because the people who run it are helpful and friendly, and I am able to make contacts easily—I've always been a people person."

3. "When it comes right down to it, I think I'm to blame for a lot of her problems."

4. "I just don't see how putting more services into this family makes sense. The parents are not motivated, and the kids are better off away from them. This family has been messed up forever."

5. "I don't know how they can expect me to be a good mother and make school appointments, supervise my kids, and put in all these work hours."

6. "Some days I am really angry because I'm only 46 years old, and there are so many more things I wanted to do. Other days, I feel kind of defeated, like this is what I get for smoking two packs of cigarettes a day for 25 years."

7. "Kids pick on me at school. They are mean. If they try to hurt me, then I try to hurt them back."

Closed- and Open-Ended Questions

Asking questions is the foundation of much of the interview process in social work. On the surface, questions are an invitation to clients to teach us about important aspects of their lives and experience as they relate to the helping process, but questions do more. They let people know that you are attending to them and reveal your priorities about the helping process. Questions create an experience for clients that can feel warm and welcoming or like a test or an interrogation. The manner with which you compose and ask questions is a critical skill for your social work practice.

Closed-ended questions define a topic and restrict responses to a few words or a simple yes or no answer (e.g., "How old are you?" "Did you know your teacher

was angry?"). They are ordinarily a direct appeal for narrow information. **Open-ended questions**, on the other hand, cannot be answered with single-word answers and invite an elaborated, expanded answer (e.g., "How did you find out when you were expected at home?").

General advice under most practice settings favors the more frequent use of open-ended questions than closed-ended questions. Closed-ended questions are useful for soliciting factual information, as when social workers assist clients in the completion of intake forms, or when social workers request details that fill in a story. However, when overused, closed-ended questions create an interrogation-like experience that diminishes the strength of the working relationship. Well-constructed open-ended questions, on the other hand, typically lead people to share high levels of detail and nuance. They foster a spontaneous interaction and permit the client to direct the flow of the interview, creating a more collaborative experience.

While favoring the use of open-ended questions, it can be quite useful to weave closed-ended questions into your interviews. For example, a client may relate certain relationship problems that have existed for many years, and the social worker might ask parenthetically, "And how long have you been in this relationship?" Similarly, a parent may explain that a child began to have irregular attendance at school when the parent started to work six months ago, to which the social worker might respond, "I see. Incidentally, what type of work do you do?" It is vital, of course, to shift the focus back to the problem. If necessary, the social worker can easily maintain focus by using an open-ended question to pick up the thread of the discussion. For example, the social worker might comment, "You mentioned that Ernie began missing school when you started to work. I'd like to hear more about what was happening in your family at that time."

Because open-ended responses elicit more information than closed-ended ones, frequent use of the former technique increases the efficiency of data gathering. In fact, the richness of information revealed by the client is directly proportional to the frequency with which open-ended responses are employed. Frequent use of open-ended responses also fosters a smoothly flowing session; consistently asking closed-ended questions, by contrast, may result in a fragmented, discontinuous process.

Formulating Open-Ended Questions

Open-ended questions in social work practiced in the English language ordinarily begin with the question words *who*, *what*, *where*, *when*, and *how*. Questions like "Who is most helpful?", "What kinds of support do they provide?", "Where do they obtain their resources?", "When are they most available?", and "How do you feel when you are with them?" might be useful for elaborating on the availability and impact of members of a social support network, for example. Open-ended questions like these provide clients with ample opportunities to share important aspects of their experience.

Open-ended questions vary in their directedness. Some open-ended responses are nondirective, leaving the topic to the client's choosing (e.g., "What you would like to discuss today"). Other open-ended responses are structured such that the social worker defines the topic to be discussed but leaves the client free to respond in any way that they wish (e.g., "How did the conflict with your son affect you?").

Open-ended questions in social work usually do not begin with "why." Why? Because like closed-ended questions, they can lend an air of interrogation to a conversation and sometimes can convey judgment and provoke defensiveness. When you decide that it is important to learn "why," pause to reformulate your question with an alternative question word. For example, if you are interested to learning why a client refuses to take prescribed medication, you might instead ask "How does the medication make you feel?" or "What led you to decide to stop taking your medications?"

Many open-ended questions can also take the form of a polite directive. In social work, it is common for social workers to say things like "Tell me more about the effect that medications have on your sleep," "I'm curious what your family thinks about your medications," or "I'm wondering what you might tell your doctor about your medications." Often, polite directives have the same effects as more formal questions in that they lead clients to share elaborated information. Interspersed with other open- and closed-ended questions, polite directives can be a useful approach to an interview.

Exercises in Identifying Closed- and Open-Ended Responses

The following exercises will assist you in differentiating between closed- and open-ended questions. Identify each statement with either a C for a closed-ended question or an O for an open-ended question. Turn to the end of the chapter (see Table 6-1, page 124) to check your answers.

1. "Did your parents ask you to see me because of the problem you had with the principal?"

2. "When John says that to you, what do you experience inside?"

3. "You said you're feeling fed up, and you're just not sure that pursuing a reconciliation is worth your trouble. Could you elaborate?"

4. "When is your court date?"

Now read the following client statements and respond by writing open-ended responses to them. Avoid using *why* questions. Examples of open-ended responses to these messages appear at the end of the chapter (see page 124).

1. **Client:** Whenever I'm in a group with Ralph, I feel like I have to let him know I am smart too.

2. **Client:** I have always had my parents call for me about appointments and other things I might mess up.

3. **Client:** He sure let me down, and I really trusted him. He knows a lot about me because I spilled my guts.

4. **Group nursing home administrator:** I think we are going to have to move Gladys to another, more suitable kind of living arrangement. We aren't able to provide the kind of care that she needs.

The next sections of this chapter explain how you can blend open-ended and reflective responses to keep a discussion focused on a specific topic. In preparation for that, respond to the next two client messages by formulating a reflection followed by an open-ended question that encourages the client to elaborate on the same topic.

5. **Teenage girl seeking abortion:** I feel like you are all tied up with my mother, trying to talk me out of what I have decided to do.

6. **Client:** Life is such a hassle, and it doesn't seem to have any meaning or make sense. I just don't know whether I want to try figuring it out any longer.

When you incorporate open-ended responses into your repertoire, you will experience a dramatic positive change in your interviewing style and confidence level. To assist you to develop skill in blending and balancing open-ended and closed-ended responses, we have provided a recording form to help you examine your own interviewing style (see Figure 6-1). This form may be used as part of your training through role play exercises, or it may be completed by supervisors or colleagues during observations of your meetings with clients. If your agency supports the use of audio recording for training purposes, and with client consent, you may also use this form to rate your own use of open-ended and closed-ended questions.

Figure 6-1 Recording Form for Open- and Closed-Ended Responding Seeking Concreteness

Social Worker's Responses	Open-Ended Responses	Closed-Ended Responses
1.		
2.		
3.		
4.		
5.		
6.		
7.		

Directions: Record your discrete open- and closed-ended responses and place a check in the appropriate column. Agency time constraints will dictate how often you can practice it.

Summarizing Responses

Summaries are an extended form of reflective listening that social workers use to review key details and highlight patterns or themes shared by clients. Summaries are one way that social workers and clients collaborate on the creation of a coherent story. Sometimes that story is related to the presenting problem. At other times, that story is on how the helping process is progressing. By summarizing, clients are afforded the opportunity to confirm or correct social workers' understanding and can also lead to new insights as complicated stories are woven together into a coherent whole.

Summaries are versatile. They can be used to refocus a conversation (see focusing, which follows) in the middle of a meeting. They can be used at transition points between phases of the helping process. They can also be used in the beginning of a meeting to create continuity between meetings and at the end of a meeting to ensure that the social worker and the client have a shared understanding of tasks and responsibilities. Here, we discuss in detail the following three specific uses of summaries:

1. Highlighting problems, strengths, and resources
2. Clarifying lengthy messages
3. Facilitating transitions

Highlighting Problems, Strengths, and Resources

During the phase of an initial session in which problems and resources are explored in moderate depth, summaries tie together and highlight central elements of clients' stories before proceeding to explore additional concerns and strengths. For example, the social worker might describe how the problem appears to be produced by the interplay of several factors, including external pressures, overt behavioral patterns, unfulfilled needs and wants, and covert thoughts and feelings. Connecting these key elements assists clients in gaining a more accurate and complete perspective of their own circumstances.

Employed in this fashion, summarization involves fitting pieces of the problem together to form a coherent whole. Those concerns can also be matched with a discussion of values and current and potential resources and strengths. Seeing the situation in a fresh perspective often proves beneficial because it expands clients' awareness and can generate hope and enthusiasm for tackling an issue that has hitherto seemed insurmountable.

Summarization that highlights problems and resources is generally employed at a natural point in the session when the social worker believes that relevant aspects have been adequately explored and clients appear satisfied in having had the opportunity to express their concerns. The following example illustrates this type of summary. In this example, the client, an 80-year-old widow, has been referred to a program for aging adults to explore alternative living arrangements because of her failing health, isolation, and recent falls. As the social worker and the client have worked together to explore alternative living arrangements, the pair has identified several characteristics that would be important for the client in an improved living situation. Highlighting the salient factors, the social worker summarizes the results to this point:

Social worker: It sounds as if you are looking for a situation in which there is social interaction, but your privacy is also important to you. You want to maintain your independence. You also want to have someone available to help in emergencies and some assistance with cooking and cleaning. Does this sound about right?

Summarizing responses of this type serve as a prelude to the process of formulating goals, as goals flow naturally from problem formulations. Moreover, highlighting various dimensions of the problem facilitates the subsequent identifications of subgoals and tasks that must be accomplished to achieve the overall goal. In the preceding example, to explore an improved living situation, the social worker helps the client analyze the specific form of privacy (whether living alone or with someone else) and the type of social interaction (how much and what kind of contact with others) they desire.

Summarizing salient aspects of problems and resources is also a valuable technique in sessions with groups, couples, and families. It enables the social worker to stop at timely moments and highlight the difficulties experienced by each participant. In a family session with a pregnant adolescent and her mother, for example, the social worker might make the following statements:

> **Social worker:** [To adolescent]: "You feel as if deciding what to do about this baby is your decision—it's your body, and you have decided that an abortion is the best solution for you. You know that you have the legal right to make this decision and want to be supported in making it. You see your mother as a potential resource and know that your mother wants to help. You value your independence in decision-making and know that she can't tell you what decision to make."

> **Social worker:** [To mother]: "As you spoke, you seemed saddened and very anxious about this decision your daughter is making. You are saying, 'I care about my daughter, but I don't think she is old enough to make this decision on her own.' As you have noted, women in your family have had a hard time conceiving, and you wish that she would consider other options besides abortion."

Such responses synthesize in concise and neutral language the needs, concerns, and problems of each participant for all other members of the session to hear. This type of summarization underscores the fact that all participants are struggling with and have responsibility for problems that are occurring, thus counteracting the tendency of families to view one person as the exclusive cause of family problems.

Clarify Lengthy Messages

Clients' messages range from one word or one sentence to lengthy monologues. Although the meaning and significance of brief messages are often readily discernible, lengthy messages challenge the social worker to encapsulate and tie together diverse and complex elements. Linking the elements together often highlights and expands the significance and meaning of the client's message. For this reason, such messages represent one form of additive empathy, a skill discussed in Chapter 17.

Because lengthy client messages typically include emotions, thoughts, and descriptive content, you need to determine how these dimensions relate to the focal point of the discussion. In the following example, Valerie is in a first meeting with a social worker through her employee assistance program. After discussing issues around informed consent, mandated reporting, and after responding to Valerie's questions about the social worker's knowledge and experience working with Native American families, the social worker asked:

> **Social Worker:** What brings you here today?
>
> **Client:** My boss gave me a performance review about two weeks ago. I didn't agree with it, and, um, I refused to sign it. He told me that signing the form didn't mean that I agree with it, just that we had a review. (*Sigh*) In some of the ratings, he rated me below average. I was mad and left his office crying.

Later, near the end of a discussion about the interpersonal dynamics of the workplace, the conversation continued:

> **Client:** Lately, they've been leaving me out of their lunches. They all go out for lunch, and they never ask me. The whole office except for me.
>
> **Social Worker:** How does it make you feel when they do that?
>
> **Client:** Not good.
>
> **Social Worker:** That sounds like it might be painful. (*Pause*). Since you came back after taking a week off to take care of family things, they changed their attitude toward you and quit inviting you to lunch and including you in social things.
>
> **Client:** They complain that I'm getting too many personal calls at work, and they all know that I have kids at home, but they still complain.
>
> **Social Worker:** It sounds like an uncomfortable, hurtful situation you are in. It sounds like you're not getting much support. Is that pretty close?

The interaction above features open-ended questions ("How does it make you feel when they do that"), empathic responses ("That sounds like it might be painful" and "it sounds like an uncomfortable, hurtful situation you are in …"), and a summary (starting with "since you came back after taking a week off …").

This sequence of skills sent the strong message that the client was heard and understood. The summary itself was pivotal, as it ensured that the social worker had an accurate and factual understanding of the critical events that have led Valerie to feel hurt and possibly isolated from others in her office. Moreover, the summary lent organization to the flow of the interview, which can be crucial when clients are sharing information and emotions about complicated and challenging circumstances.

Facilitating Transitions

Summaries are useful during meetings when transitioning between phases of the helping process. Summaries provide a signal to clients that the nature of their work with you will change (e.g., between initial engagement activities to assessment or between assessment to goal formulation and intervention planning) and ensure that your forward progress in the helping process is based on a mutual understanding of what has transpired before. For example, the summary that follows occurred during an initial session between a case manager and a client who was preparing for discharge from a skilled nursing facility where they received nursing and physical therapy. By this point, the client had been involved in the mental health system for many years and was vocal in their belief that the mental health system was unresponsive and overcontrolling. Just prior to this meeting, the social worker assigned to the client's care had been changed abruptly and without warning. Trust was an early theme in the meeting. The social worker summarized their discussion of trust and mistrust, creating a bridge to a conversation about discharge planning.

> **Social worker:** We have spoken about several really important things. You have worked with a lot of social workers who you have trusted and that you want to trust, but you haven't felt that it was reciprocated. Why trust now when in the past it hasn't worked for you? That's going to be an enduring issue for us, so I hope that when we are working together that you feel that your trust is not misplaced. Let's keep that in mind. (*Pause*) My job is to help you figure out where you can live now and make sure that you are successful. You told me that you want something like an adult foster home for you and Lexie [a service dog] in a small town. If you could envision an environment where it would be a good place for you to be, what would it be like?

Summaries are helpful when used at the end of a meeting to provide an overview of progress and, importantly, agreements for moving forward. This is a time to review plans to make sure that everyone understands clearly and precisely what is expected. In these and all summaries, it is important to use specific language so as to avoid misunderstandings. For example:

> **Social worker:** To sum up, I want to make sure that I've captured what you've talked about. My sense is that you are describing a living environment that will work for you is a small community like you had before, in a small group home or adult foster home, and that Lexie [service dog] is an important part of that. It's got to feel safe and stable, where stable means that you can live there at least three months if not longer. You need access to backup services, but we need to determine what those are because there has been some disagreement about backup services in the past. Last, I need to look into how payment for the services is going to follow you because, in your experience, people can promise you things, and then the money won't be there. Is there anything you would like to add?

Finally, summaries of prior work can be useful ways to open an interview. These summaries review accomplishments and agreements made during prior sessions and serve to create agendas for your ongoing work. As with all of the verbal following skills presented in this chapter, summaries should be incorporated into a collaborative and empowering approach to practice. Thus, summaries at the beginning of your meetings should provide opportunities for client input, as in this example:

> **Social worker:** The last time we met we started to talk about the kinds of places you might go after you leave the rehab center, and I had agreed to look into options and funding. We also talked about your feeling that prior social workers had not been completely honest with you and that they have not been here when you've needed them. This is really important now that we are working on your discharge plan. The third thing we talked about is your social support, which will be important when you move, and the last thing that you mentioned was about how you wanted to go to the summer camp program. Does this sound accurate?
>
> **Client:** I guess so. You are the one keeping notes.
>
> **Social worker:** Has anything changed in the past week that we should talk about today?

Seeking Concreteness

Asking clients to communicate with specificity, a skill that we call seeking concreteness, is critical to the helping process. Seeking concreteness means helping people give rich,

C7

descriptive accounts of their experiences, behaviors, and feelings, countering our tendency to think and talk in generalities. It is the difference between saying, "I'm depressed" and saying, "I have low energy all the time and pretty much feel like the future is hopeless." As increasingly specific details are added, our capacity for empathy increases, as does the depth of our understanding. When we seek concreteness with clients, we use the skills of open- and closed-ended questions, reflections, summarizing, empathic responding, and authentic responding to help clients elaborate on the details of their experiences. For example, a client might say:

Client: I did not like my last social worker.
Social worker: Would you tell me more about that?
Client: They didn't answer my calls.

When we seek concreteness, we validate the importance of what clients are telling us through careful attending and reveal opportunities for empathic responses and complex reflections. In the preceding example, the social worker was able to reflect the client's deeper feelings only after they made a request for more specificity. Moreover, seeking concreteness advances the helping process. Again, the preceding example suggests that the client values timely responses from their social worker, a message that the social worker can attend through an authentic response such as:

Social worker: I know getting a call back is important to you. It also bugs me when people take a long time to return my calls. I will do my best to return your calls as quickly as possible. Most of the time I can do this within 24 hours. If you need to reach me quickly, though, the best way to do that is by sending a text message. How does that sound to you?

Learning to seek concreteness is surprisingly difficult. Your first challenge is to recognize clients' overgeneralized statements and to assist them to reveal specific information related to their feelings and experiences. A second challenge is to help clients learn how to respond more concretely in their relationships with others. A third challenge is to describe your own experience in language that is precise and descriptive.

The remainder of our discussion on the skill of seeking concreteness is devoted to assisting you in meeting these three challenges. We find it helpful to consider the following five circumstances in which social workers commonly seek concreteness:

1. Check perceptions
2. Clarify vague or unfamiliar terms

3. Elicit specific feelings
4. Focus on the here and now
5. Elicit sequence of events

Check Perceptions

Responses that help social workers clarify and check whether they have accurately heard clients' messages (e.g., "Do you mean..." or "Are you saying...") are vital in building rapport with clients and in communicating the desire to understand their problems. Such responses also minimize confusion in the helping process. Clients benefit from social workers' efforts to understand because clarifying responses assist clients in sharpening and reformulating their thinking about their own feelings and other concerns, thereby encouraging self-awareness and growth.

Sometimes, perception checking becomes necessary because clients' messages are incomplete, ambiguous, or complex. Occasionally, social workers may encounter people who repeatedly communicate in highly abstract or metaphorical styles, or clients whose thinking is scattered and whose messages just do not track or make sense. In such instances, social workers might spend considerable time sorting through clients' messages and clarifying perceptions.

At other times, the need for clarification arises not because the client has conveyed confusing, faulty, or incomplete messages but rather because the social worker has not fully attended to the client's message or comprehended its meaning. Fully attending throughout each moment of a session requires intense concentration, which can be especially challenging when you are working with families or small groups, where a myriad of transactions occur and competing communications bid for the social worker's attention.

It is important that you develop skill in using clarifying responses to elicit ongoing feedback regarding your perceptions and to acknowledge freely your need for clarification when you are confused or uncertain. Rather than reflecting personal or professional inadequacy, your efforts to accurately grasp the client's meaning and feelings will most likely be perceived as signs of your genuineness and your commitment to understand.

To check your perceptions, try asking simple questions that seek clarification or try combining your request for clarification with a reflection or empathic response that reflects your perception of the client's message (e.g., "I think you were saying ___. Is that right?"). Examples of clarifying messages include the following:

- "You seem to be really irritated, not only because they didn't respond when you asked them to help but because they seemed to be deliberately trying to hurt you. Is that accurate?"

- "I'm not sure I'm following you. Let me see if I understand the order of events you described..."
- "Would you expand on what you're saying so I can be sure I understand what you mean?"
- "Could you go over that again and perhaps give an example that might help me understand?"
- "I'm confused. Let me try to restate what I think you're saying."
- "As a group, you seem to be divided in your approach to this matter. I'd like to summarize what I'm hearing, and I would then appreciate some input regarding whether I understand the various positions that have been expressed."

Clarify Vague or Unfamiliar Terms

When expressing themselves, people often employ terms that have multiple meanings or use terms in idiosyncratic ways. For example, in the message "The kids in this school are mean," the word *mean* may have different meanings to the social worker and the client. If the social worker does not identify what this term means to a particular client, they cannot be certain whether the client is referring to behavior that is violent, unfriendly, threatening, or something else. The precise meaning can be clarified by employing one of the following responses:

> **Social worker:** "Tell me about the way that some kids are mean in this school."
> **Social worker:** "I'm not sure I know what is happening when you say that some kids act in a mean way. Could you clarify that for me?"
> **Social worker:** "Can you give me an example of something mean that has happened at this school?"

Many other words also lack precision, so it is important to avoid assuming that the client means the same thing you mean when you use a given term. For example, "codependent," "irresponsible," "selfish," and "careless" conjure up meanings that vary according to the reference points of different persons. Exact meanings are best determined by asking for clarification or for examples of events in which the behavior alluded to actually occurred.

Elicit Specific Feelings

Social workers often find it helpful to seek concreteness when clients are sharing feelings and emotions because certain "feeling words" denote general states of feeling rather than specific feelings. For example, in

the message, "I'm really upset that I didn't get a raise," the word "upset" helps clarify the client's general frame of mind but fails to specify the precise feeling. In this instance, "upset" may refer to feeling disappointed, discouraged, unappreciated, devalued, angry, resentful, or even incompetent or inadequate because of failing to receive a raise (see Chapter 5). Until the social worker has elicited additional information, they cannot be sure of how the client actually experiences being "upset."

Other feeling words that lack specificity include *frustrated, uneasy, uncomfortable, troubled,* and *bothered.* When clients employ such words, you can pinpoint their feelings by using responses such as the following:

> **Social Worker:** "How do you mean, 'upset'?"
> **Social Worker:** "I'd like to understand more about that feeling. Could you clarify what you mean by 'frustrated'?"
> **Social Worker:** "Can you say more about in what way you feel 'bothered'?"

Focus on the Here and Now

Another aspect of concreteness takes the form of responses that shift the focus from the past to the present. Messages that relate to the immediate present are usually high in concreteness, whereas those that center on the past are often low in concreteness. Many of us are prone to dwell on past feelings and events. Unfortunately, precious opportunities for promoting growth and understanding may slip through the fingers of social workers who fail to focus on emotions and experiences that unfold in the immediacy of the interview. Focusing on feelings as they occur enables you to observe reactions and behavior firsthand, eliminating any bias and error caused by reporting feelings and experiences after the fact. Furthermore, the helpfulness of your feedback is greatly enhanced when this feedback relates to the client's immediate experience.

The following exchange demonstrates how to achieve concreteness in such situations:

> **Client [choking up]:** When they told me it was all over, that they were in love with someone else—well, I just felt—it's happened again. I felt totally alone, like there just wasn't anyone.
> **Social worker:** That must have been terribly painful. [Client nods; tears well up.] I wonder if you're not having the same feeling just now—at this moment. [Client nods in agreement.]

Not only do such instances provide direct access to the client's inner experience, but they also may produce lasting benefits as the client shares deep and painful emotions in the context of a warm, accepting, and supportive relationship. Here-and-now experiencing that involves emotions toward the social worker (e.g., anger, hurt, disappointment, affectional desires, fears) is known as relational immediacy. Skills pertinent to relational immediacy warrant separate consideration and are dealt with in Chapter 18.

Focusing on here-and-now experiencing with groups, couples, and families is a particularly potent technique for assisting members of these systems to clear the air of pent-up feelings. Moreover, interventions that focus on the immediacy of feelings bring buried issues to the surface, paving the way for the social worker to assist members of these systems to clearly identify and explore their difficulties and (if appropriate) to engage in problem solving.

Elicit Sequence of Events

Concrete responses are also vital in accurately assessing interactional behavior. Such responses pinpoint what actually occurs in interactional sequences—that is, what circumstances preceded the events, what the participants said and did, what specific thoughts and feelings the client experienced, and what consequences followed the event. In other words, the social worker elicits details of what happened, rather than settling for clients' views and conclusions. The following is an example of a concrete response to a client message:

> **High school student:** My teacher really lost it yesterday. They were so mad, and I didn't do anything to deserve it.
> **Social worker:** Can you describe for me what happened?
> **High school student:** They just grabbed the papers off my desk and told me to go to the office.
> **Social worker:** Ok, let's start from the beginning. What was happening just before your teacher "lost it?"

In such cases, it is important to keep clients on topic by continuing to assist them to relate the events in question, using responses such as "Then what happened?", "What did you do next?", or "Then who said what?" The goal of seeking concreteness in this sequence is to visualize behavioral sequences as they unfold. Often, the process of seeking concreteness reveals key moments in a sequence where people can take responsibility for change or reveal patterns that increase clients' understanding about the difficulties and challenges that they face.

Specificity of Expression by Social Workers

It has been our experience that mastery of the skill of communicating with specificity requires extended and determined effort. The task becomes more complicated if you are unaware of your own vague communication patterns. We recommend that you carefully and consistently monitor your meetings with clients and your everyday conversations with a view toward identifying instances in which you did or did not communicate with specificity. Paying close attention to your own communication patterns enables you to recognize when you might not communicate clearly, and you can set goals for yourself to improve your communication. We also recommend that you enlist your practicum instructor to provide feedback about your performance level on your communication skills.

When communicating with clients, specificity often relates to the precision of your questions. Contrast these open-ended questions:

> **Social Worker:** What can you do to make progress on your goal?
> **Social Worker:** What can you do this week to make progress on your goal?

The second question is more precise by anchoring the question with the dimension of time. Specificity also relates to the precision of your empathic responses. Contrast these empathic responses:

> **Social Worker:** That sounds hard.
> **Social Worker:** It sounds like you are facing a lot of frustrating barriers.

The second response is more precise by naming a feeling (frustrating) and describing its apparent source (barriers). In both instances, the social worker's concrete communication enables clients to elaborate with greater specificity. Both of these examples are reflective of an exchange that would be common in a task-centered approach to problem solving, which we introduce in Chapter 13.

An additional challenge for social workers striving for specificity is the overuse of professional jargon and stereotyped labels. Unfortunately, jargon and labeling pervade professional discourse and runs rampant in social work literature and case records. Their use reinforces social stigma and is, therefore, antithetical to the social work value of dignity and worth of the individual. Furthermore, labels tend to conjure up images of clients that vary from one social worker to another, thereby injecting a significant source of error into communication.

We recommend that you avoid using professional jargon wherever possible, instead defaulting to plain language descriptive language. For example, saying "the client seems to forget the medium- and long-term consequences of their decisions" rather than "the client lacks judgment." The word "judgment" in this context refers in part to decision-making with forethought and is evaluated as a part of a mental status exam (see Chapter 9).

We also recommend discretion in the use of identify-first and person-first language in place of stigmatizing labels when referring to groups of people and problems (Kansas University Research and Training Center on Independent Living, 2020). Person-first language conscientiously separates people's identities from their problems and circumstances. For example, your clients may prefer to be referred to as "someone who is diagnosed with a mental health disorder" rather than as a "mentally ill person." The same may be said for people who are formerly incarcerated (rather than "convict," "felon," or "criminal"), people who receive income supports from Temporary Assistance for Needy Families (TANF) (rather than "welfare recipient," "poor person"), and people who inject heroin (rather than "addict"). On the other hand, some of your clients may prefer identity-first language, particularly when the descriptors or labels identify clients as members of recognizable communities and cultures. Examples may include "deaf" and "autistic," as well as the language people use to identify their race, ethnicity, and gender. For many, identity-first language is empowering. In all cases, avoid language that is patronizing or demeaning and default to the preferences of your clients.

Exercises in Seeking Concreteness

In the following exercises, read each client statement and then formulate a written response that elicits concrete data regarding the client's problems. You may wish to combine your responses with either an empathic response or a reflection. After you have finished the exercises, compare your responses with the modeled responses at the end of the chapter (see page 125).

Client Statements

1. *Client:* It really seems weird to be back here.
2. *Client:* You can't depend on friends. They'll stab you in the back every time.
3. *Client:* They've got a terrible temper—that's the way they are, and they'll never change.
4. *Client:* My supervisor is so insensitive; you can't believe it. All they think about are reports and deadlines.

5. *Client:* I was upset after I left your office last week. I felt you really didn't understand what I was saying and didn't care how I felt.
6. *Client:* My dad's 58 years old now, but I swear he still hasn't grown up. He always has a chip on his shoulder.
7. *Client:* My rheumatoid arthritis has affected my hands a lot. It gets to be kind of tricky when I'm handling pots and pans in the kitchen.
8. *Client:* I just have this uneasy feeling about going to the doctor. I guess I've really got a hang-up about it.
9. *Client:* You ask why I don't talk to my teacher about why I'm late for school. I'll tell you why. Because she's white, that's why. She's got it in for us Black students, and there's just no point talking to her. That's just the way it is.
10. *Client:* John doesn't give a damn about me. I could die, and he wouldn't lose a wink of sleep.

Maintaining Focus

Focusing is the act of sustaining attention to the problem-solving process. When you and your clients focus effectively, your activities will generally correspond to the needs of the helping process at any given moment. For example, during the Phase I process of role preparation (see Chapter 5), discussions about the helping process and about client rights and needs helps you to achieve the relational goals of transparency and collaboration, while brainstorming solutions would often be premature and eclipse the full development of a working relationship. Similarly, when negotiating goals (see Chapter 12), educating clients about the purpose of goals and assessing their readiness to establish goals advances the goal-setting process, whereas side conversations about unrelated topics can delay the process of establishing shared goals and objectives that are crucial for the later selection, implementation, and success of interventions. At every stage, distractions may surface to derail the helping process. Your responsibility is to ensure that yours and your clients' efforts contribute to the helping process and the resolution of client concerns and problems.

The task of focusing can be difficult. New social workers, and experienced social workers who are learning new skills and new models for helping, may not remember critical steps or may feel awkward adopting new approaches. For clients, the helping process can seem risky or unfamiliar. Others may have lingering ambivalence about the need for change or may simply disagree about the need for change, and still others may distrust the helping systems that you represent, perhaps because of the historic role of social welfare agencies in the oppression and marginalization of people of color (Park, 2019). For these and many other reasons, clients and social workers can wander aimlessly through the helping process in a haphazard fashion, avoiding or forgetting key tasks, and ultimately reducing its effectiveness.

Focusing skills blend reflections and empathic responding, open- and closed-ended questions, summarizing, authentic responding, and seeking concreteness to sustain attention to the three phases of the helping process. In general, what you choose to focus on is itself a negotiation informed by a host of contextual factors and constraints. Chief among these are the clients' needs, desires, and aspirations, agency mandates and purpose, and the framework for helping that you adopt in practice. Ideally, the result is a collaborative process in which you and your clients together identify priorities for the helping process to which you can be mutually accountable.

To assist you in learning how to focus effectively, we consider three ways in which social workers use the skills of focusing with clients:

1. Selecting topics for exploration
2. Exploring topics in depth
3. Managing obstacles to focusing

Selecting Topics for Exploration

Areas relevant for exploration vary from situation to situation. Nevertheless, with experience, you will notice similarities in discussion topics between you and clients in your agency setting. Clients newly admitted to nursing homes often share a concern for loss of independence and about their rehabilitation. Parents who are involved in the child welfare system often have overpowering feelings about state intrusion into family life. Adults with disabilities living in a group home often wonder about when they might be able to live in their own apartments. People in treatment for drug or alcohol addictions wonder how they can feel ok when they do not have a way to "take the edge off." The similarities you see among people who share problems in common will lead to a cadence or pattern to the topics that focus your interviews. In effect, you will adopt a structure or routine that guides your selection of questions and discussion topics.

This structure is important because of its effect on focusing. Wholly unstructured interviews usually lack focus. They have a wandering quality that lends uncertainty to the helping process. To prevent this, many social workers find it helpful to enter into their meetings with a flexible outline or list of questions and topic areas. Indeed, some agencies prescribe interview outlines as part of their intake practices. Outlines that you may use will be informed by agency policies and mandates, expert advice such as we provide on assessments in Chapters 8 and 9, and also by the helping models that you adopt. For instance, the task-centered model, presented in Chapter 13, emphasizes task planning, a process that itself provides tremendous focus to your conversations with clients at later stages of the helping process.

At the same time, it is important to recognize the importance of client choice. Outlines should not be rigid, and forms should not be completed at the expense of opportunities for spontaneous discussion. Given the demands of the helping process, there are usually multiple avenues that can be explored with clients, even in structured conversations guided by an outline or an intake form. In the spirit of collaboration, you should bring clients into the focusing decisions to the greatest extent possible. For example:

> **Social worker:** Prior to our meeting, I was thinking about what we should talk about. My supervisor and I had three ideas [*share list*]. What other areas would you like to discuss?

Mandated clients, and those under pressure to participate in social work services, often feel disempowered. However, the process of focusing can highlight opportunities to exercise choice, as in this example:

> **Social worker:** I understand that your parents are hoping that we can talk about your goals at school. What would you like to talk about?

When transitioning between phases of the helping process, it may be helpful to combine summaries with a closed-ended question, such as:

> **Social worker:** We've been talking about [*list related to the presenting problem*]. Which area is most important to you?

Exploring Topics in Depth

When social workers and clients focus effectively on the presenting problem, their exploration of important topics moves from generality and superficiality to greater depth and meaning, but this is no easy task. Beginning social workers often wander in individual or group interactions, repeatedly skipping across the surface of vital areas of content and feelings, eliciting largely superficial information. This tendency is illustrated in the following excerpt from a first session with an adolescent in a school setting:

> **Social worker:** Tell me about your family.
>
> **Client:** My father is ill, and my mother is dead, so we live with my sister.
>
> **Social worker:** How are things with you and your sister?
>
> **Client:** Good. We get along fine. She treats me pretty good.
>
> **Social worker:** How about your father?
>
> **Client:** We get along pretty well. We have our problems, but most of the time things are okay. I don't really see him very much.
>
> **Social worker:** Tell me about school. How are you getting along here?
>
> **Client:** Well, I don't like it very well, but my grades are good enough to get me by.
>
> **Social worker:** I notice you're new to our school this year. How did you do in the last school you attended?

By focusing superficially on the topics of family and school, this social worker misses opportunities to explore potential problem areas in the depth necessary to illuminate the client's situation. Not surprisingly, this exploration yielded little information of value, in large part because the social worker failed to employ responses that focused in depth on topical areas. In the next sections, we further delineate the skills that considerably enhance a social worker's ability to maintain focus on specific areas.

Open-Ended Responses

As we discussed earlier, social workers may employ open-ended questions to focus on desired topics. Earlier we noted that some open-ended responses leave clients free to choose their own topics, whereas others focus on a topic but encourage clients to respond freely to that topic. The following examples, taken from an initial session with a mother of eight children who experienced major depression, illustrate how social workers can employ open-ended responses to define topical areas that may yield a rich trove of information vital to grasping the dynamics of the client's problems.

> **Social worker:** What have you thought that you might like to accomplish in our work together?

> **Social worker:** You've discussed many topics in the last few minutes. Could you pick the most important one and tell me more about it?
>
> **Social worker:** You've mentioned that your oldest son doesn't come home after school as he did before and help you with the younger children. How has this change affected you?
>
> **Social worker:** Several times you've mentioned your concern that your spouse may leave you, your voice has trembled. I wonder if you could share what you are feeling.
>
> **Social worker:** You've indicated that your partner doesn't help you enough with the children. You also seem to be saying that you feel overwhelmed and inadequate in managing the children by yourself. What happens as you try to manage your children?
>
> **Social worker:** You indicate that you have more problems with your 14-year-old child than with the other children. What are some of the unique challenges you experience?

In the preceding examples, the social worker's open-ended questions progressively moved the exploration from the general to the specific. Note also that each response or question defined a new topic for exploration. To encourage in-depth exploration of the topics defined in this way, the social worker must blend open-ended questions with other facilitative verbal following responses that focus on and elicit expanded client expressions. After having defined a topical area by employing an open-ended question, for instance, the social worker might deepen the exploration by weaving other open-ended responses into the discussion. If the open-ended responses shift the focus to another area, however, the exploration may suffer a setback. Note in the following exchange how the social worker's second open-ended response shifts the focus away from the client's message, which involves expression of intense feelings:

> **Social worker:** You've said you're worried about retiring. I'd appreciate you sharing more about your concern.
>
> **Client:** I can't imagine not going to work every day. I feel at loose ends already, and I haven't even quit work. I'm afraid I just won't know what to do with myself.
>
> **Social worker:** How do you imagine spending your time after retiring?

In this example, the social worker's follow-up question shifts the focus away from the client's emotions (i.e., fear, feeling at loose ends). It may be important to discuss what the client imagines daily life in retirement to be, but raising that question now shortchanges a deeper exploration of the client's feelings in the moment. Later, the social worker may return to this topic with the following:

> **Social worker:** Earlier, you said that you were feeling at loose ends and were afraid that you wouldn't know what to do with yourself. I'd like to understand how you are feeling more specifically. What are you afraid of?

Reflective Listening

As noted earlier, reflective listening serves a critical function by enabling social workers to focus in depth on troubling feelings, as illustrated in the next example:

> **Client:** I can't imagine not going to work every day. I feel at loose ends already, and I haven't even quit work. I'm afraid I just won't know what to do with myself.
>
> **Social worker:** You seem to be saying, "Even now, I'm apprehensive about retiring. I'm giving up something that has been very important to me, and I don't seem to have anything to replace it." I gather that feeling at loose ends, as you do, you worry that when you retire, you'll feel useless.
>
> **Client:** I guess that's a large part of my problem. Sometimes I feel useless now. I just didn't take time over the years to develop any hobbies or to pursue any interests. I guess I don't think that I can do anything else.
>
> **Social worker:** It sounds as if part of you feels hopeless about the future, as if you have done everything you can do, and yet I wonder if another part of you might think that it isn't too late to look into some new interests.
>
> **Client:** I do dread moping around home with time on my hands. I can just see it now. My partner will want to keep me busy doing things around the house all the time. I've never liked to do that kind of thing. I suppose it is never too late to look into other interests. I have always wanted to write some things for fun, not just for work. You know, the memory goes at my age, but I have thought about just writing down some of the family stories.

Note how the client's problem continued to unfold as the social worker utilized reflections and empathic responding, revealing rich information in the process. The social worker also raises the possibility of new solutions, not just dwelling in the feelings of uselessness.

Blending Open-ended Questions with Reflections

After employing open-ended questions and reflections to focus on a selected topic, social workers should use a mix of reflections and additional closed- and open-ended questions to maintain focus on that topic. In the following excerpt, observe how the social worker employs both open-ended and empathic responses to explore problems in depth, thereby enabling the client to move to the heart of their struggle. Notice also the richness of the client's responses elicited by the blended messages.

> **Social worker:** As you were speaking about your child, I sensed some pain and reluctance on your part to talk about them. I'd like to understand more about what you're feeling. Could you share with me how it is for you to be talking about them? *[Blended empathic and open-ended response that seeks concreteness.]*
>
> **Client:** I guess I haven't felt too good about coming this morning. I almost called and canceled. I feel I should be able to handle these problems myself. Coming here is like having to admit I'm no longer capable of coping with my child.
>
> **Social worker:** So, you've had reservations about coming *[reflection]*—you feel you're admitting defeat and that perhaps you've failed or that you're inadequate—and that hurts. *[Empathic response.]*
>
> **Client:** Well, yes, although I know that I need some help. It's just hard to admit it, I think. My biggest problem in this regard, however, is my spouse. They feel much more strongly than I do that we should manage this problem ourselves, and they really disapprove of my coming in.
>
> **Social worker:** So, even though it's painful for you, you're convinced you need some assistance with your child, but you're torn about coming here because of your spouse's attitude. I'd be interested in hearing more about that. *[Blended empathic and open-ended response.]*

In the preceding example, the social worker initiated a discussion of the client's here-and-now experiences through a blended open-ended and empathic response, following it with other empathic and blended responses to explore the client's feelings further. With the last response, the social worker narrowed the focus to a potential obstacle to the helping process (the spouse's attitude toward therapy), which could also be explored in a similar manner.

Open-ended and empathic responses may also be blended to facilitate and encourage discussion from group members about a defined topic. For instance, after using an open-ended response to solicit group feedback regarding a specified topic ("I'm wondering how you feel about..."), the social worker can employ empathic or other facilitative responses to acknowledge the contribution of members who respond to the invitation to comment. By utilizing open-ended responses, the social worker can also successively reach for comments of individual members who have not contributed ("What do you think about…?").

Managing Obstacles to Focusing

There will be times when you and your clients may find it difficult to sustain your focus on the problem-solving process. For example, your attention may wander. Clients may avoid topics that you think are important. Other distractions may get in the way. You may find yourself avoiding certain topics and changing the directions of conversations. When this happens, you need to assess the source of the focus challenges and then collaborate with your clients to return attention to the presenting problem. Fortunately, the skills you have learned already are the same ones you can use to overcome these challenges. Here, we emphasize three challenges – personal distractions, mistrust in the helping process, and client avoidance.

Personal Distractions

Sometimes focus-related challenges originate in your own distractedness and avoidance. As should be clear by now, active listening and attentiveness demand significant emotional and cognitive effort by social workers. Fatigue and sleepiness can make it hard for you to pay attention. Worries and anxiety that you carry can be intensely distracting. Occasionally, you may have strong emotional reactions to your clients. This process, called **countertransference** in the psychotherapy literature, happens when clients' behaviors and their own stories trigger emotions in social workers. Sometimes countertransference reactions can be helpful, as when they inform the social worker's capacity for empathy, but in the context of focusing challenges, we recognize that some emotional reactions lead to avoidance, as when, for example, a client's trauma history reminds a social worker of their own experience of trauma.

Whatever its source, focus problems that originate with you send a strong signal to seek supervision and to attend to your self-care needs. The cardinal values of the profession, especially the values of service and competence (see Chapter 4), create an ethical obligation for all of us to ensure that we can prioritize client needs over our own and provide effective services. This may mean taking time to address your own physical and emotional well-being. It may also mean seeking consultation with your supervisor and trusted colleagues to understand how clients can trigger your own emotional reactions in ways that are unhelpful to the helping process.

What can you do in the moment to restore focus when you are distracted? First, an effective response requires self-awareness about the source of your distractedness. Second, it may be appropriate to simply acknowledge having been distracted and use an open-ended question to get back on track, as in:

> **Social Worker:** I'm sorry. I don't think that I heard you fully. Can we go over again what happened the last time you were in treatment?

However, we would ordinarily not recommend a full self-disclosure of your self-care needs or complex emotional reactions. As discussed previously (see Chapter 5), self-disclosure takes the focus of a conversation off clients. While, in general, we support authentic responses as a strategy for establishing strong relationships, self-disclosures about your countertransference reactions and your self-care needs creates a burden for clients and does not usually result in more focused interviews.

Mistrust in the Helping Process

Mistrust can present a potent challenge to the process of focusing for social workers. Clients who mistrust you or the agency may not engage fully in the helping process and may avoid discussing the nuances of their presenting problem. Many social workers practice in systems with which clients have prior traumatic experiences, in systems that involve an underlying threat of state intrusion and social control, and in systems that have been implicated in the historical trauma of people of color. Under these circumstances, avoidance, which in our formulation is the opposite of focus, may be a rational approach to self-preservation and protection.

Following the orienting frameworks presented in Chapter 2, and especially cultural humility, anti-oppressive practice, and trauma-informed practice, your focusing strategy should include an historical perspective on the service system in which you work. In what ways has your service system disempowered and overcontrolled Black people, Indigenous nations, and people of color, people who experience poverty, people with disabilities, and people who identify as LBGTQ+?

Next, your focusing strategy continues with an understanding of your client's positionality relative to yours and to the helping system. What are the limits of client choice? In what ways does your client have the opportunity to exercise agency and power? Finally, your focusing strategy should include a direct conversation about potential sources of mistrust while taking a nondefensive, supportive stance. An expression of understanding and empathy may strengthen your relationship and enable you to engage clients in the helping process.

Client Avoidance

Sometimes focus-related challenges manifest in clients as avoidance. Avoidance itself can have many sources. Avoidance can be a function of mistrust, as discussed previously, or the result of ambivalence about the helping process, or as a strategy to hide emotionally painful and stigmatized aspects of our behaviors and presenting problems. When people practice avoidance, they may shift from topic to topic, engage in superficial discussions, offer overgeneralized or abstract answers, or refrain from answering questions or participating in a dialogue. While avoidance is a natural strategy that most people use from time to time to regulate their emotions and their public face, you should be attentive to patterns in your interactions with clients where avoidance seemingly derails the helping process.

When you suspect that a client may be practicing avoidance, we recommend that you begin with an assessment of the helping process itself. Is it possible that your client's goals or reasons for seeking services have changed? Is it possible that your clients disagree with the mandates that compelled them into service in the first place? If so, you may need to reengage clients in a process of role clarification as discussed in Chapter 5 or reengage clients in the process of contracting and goal setting, as discussed later in Chapter 12. This strategy assumes that client avoidance is a signal that the helping process is no longer meeting their expectations or needs. By reestablishing common purpose and goals, you can refocus the helping process in a way that engages clients in areas about which they will be more motivated.

Alternatively, you may suspect that avoidance is helping clients manage difficult emotions. Much of social work practice engages clients in topics and challenges that have roots in trauma or in experiences that involve shame and stigma. Not surprisingly, people who seek help, even when wholly voluntary, confront aspects of themselves or the helping process about which they feel ambivalent or, perhaps, afraid. When this happens, it may be important to focus on the here and now to explore how the expectations for intimate and revealing conversations may be affecting your client.

Analyzing Your Verbal Following Skills

Learning to blend minimal prompts, reflections, open- and closed-ended questions, and summaries, along with empathic responses and authentic responses discussed in Chapter 5 to seek concreteness and focus interviews is no small feat. Most people, even those trained in social

work, are not naturally inclined to use these communication skills consistently and purposefully. We all have habits of communication and values that, in conjunction with our emotional state at any given moment, can interfere with intentional and purposeful use of skills. The urgency we feel can lead us to provide directives or commands rather than rely on a more patient approach using reflections and open-ended questions, for example, or our worries may lead us to poorly formed questions and inaccurate summaries that increase confusion rather than promote clear communication and appropriately focused interviews. For this reason, the development of sustained interviewing skillfulness requires attention to multiple dimensions of competence (Bogo et al., 2014), including the mechanics of operationalizing the skill, background knowledge about the skill, judgment about when to use a skill, and self-awareness that enables you to exercise choice and discretion about when a skill is deployed.

Achieving the competence you seek across all these dimensions requires practice with feedback. We can't learn new communication skills simply by reading a book or participating in a workshop or lecture. Evidence from training evaluation studies in the evidence-based practices is clear on that point (Herschell et al., 2010; Schwalbe et al., 2014). In addition to knowledge about skills, sustained implementation and continued growth depends on reflection and feedback, such as can be gained from clinical supervisors and consultants.

Feedback can come from a variety of sources. Ideally, feedback originates in live observations of practice by your supervisor or a joint review of audio- or video-recorded interviews between you and your clients. The feedback that you gain from watching, reflecting, and engaging discussions about your use of practice skills can strengthen your awareness about your interviewing habits and idiosyncrasies and also help you to see directly how your communication style affects clients. Generations of students have learned that overcoming the difficulties inherent in watching your own performance of skills and opening yourself to the direct feedback of others are potent sources of information that help you shape your practices and achieve mastery.

The ethical use of audio and video recordings were addressed in Chapter 4 and bears repeating here. Recordings can be an important strategy for meeting our ethical obligation for practice competence. Despite their potential value, clients nevertheless deserve the right to decline to have their sessions recorded, with informed consent acting as the overriding ethical consideration. Clients have the right to know that any given session is being recorded, the uses of the recording, and who in addition to the social worker

Figure 6-2 Recording Form for Verbal Following Skills

Client Message	Open-Ended Responses	Closed-Ended Responses	Empathic Responses	Level of Empathy	Concrete Responses	Summarizing Responses	Other Types of Responses
1.							
2.							
3.							
4.							
5.							
6.							
7.							

Directions: Categorize each of your responses from a recorded session. Where responses involve more than one category (blended responses), record them as a single response, but also check each category embodied in the response. Excluding the responses checked as "Other Type of Responses," analyze whether certain types of responses were utilized too frequently or too sparingly. Define tasks for yourself to correct imbalances in future sessions. Retain a copy of the form so that you can monitor your progress in mastering verbal following skills over an extended period of time.

may access the recording. Related, of course, is the heavy burden of responsibility that recording places on the social worker and the agency to safeguard client privacy and confidentiality. Recordings should not be made on your personal devices and should be structured to remain within the secure ecosystem of your agency's records.

Short of direct observation of your work with clients, there is, of course, a long tradition in social work training for creating analog practice experiences via role play, and more recently, using simulated client actors (Bogo et al., 2014). Evidence suggests that feedback through these methods can translate into practice, especially when the role play scenarios match closely with the structure and the relational dynamics in which the skills are implemented with clients (Healy & Bourne, 2012).

Finally, clients can be a potent source of feedback, though perhaps not directly. It is not likely that your clients will say "that was a well-developed open-ended question. I'm wondering why you chose to use that approach rather than a simple or complex reflection?" However, you may notice moments in your interviews in which your working relationship achieves greater intimacy and depth, or when clients react with confusion. These may be signals to you about the effectiveness of your verbal following skills. Your obligation is to adopt a reflective approach to practice in which you strive for self-awareness and conscious control of your questions and reflections. For example, in an interview between a social worker and a man referred to a batterers' treatment program:

> **Social worker:** It seems to me that you left the program once already, which was confusing to me, when you had the chance to get through the legal process, and so I wonder why did you decide to leave the program, and what do you think will be different this time?
> **Client:** um
> **Social worker:** Sorry, that was confusing. Let's take this one step at a time. What led you to leave the program when you did?

To facilitate your observations, either self-observations or those of your supervisors or colleagues, we have developed a recording form for verbal following skills (see Figure 6-2). Use the form to keep a tally of how often you use various communication skills, paying special attention to the patterns you use during the course of an interview. Then, explore in supervision how your communication patterns affected clients and the ways in which the interviewing skills you employed either promoted or interfered with the purposes of the interview.

Summary

This chapter has helped you learn how to explore, reflect, and appropriately use closed- and open-ended responses as means to better focusing, following, and summarizing in your social work practice. These skills may be applied both with clients and with other persons and colleagues on behalf of clients. Importantly, consideration of these verbal following skills reminds us that the conscientious use of these skills entails choice. Social workers need to be mindful of how our professional values and ethics, in conjunction with the orienting frameworks that ground our approach, can help us use these communication skills in the service of social justice and empowerment. In Chapter 7, we will explore some common difficulties experienced by beginning social workers and some ways to overcome them.

Competency Notes

C2 Engage Anti-Racism, Diversity, Equity, and Inclusion in Practice

- Demonstrate anti-racist social work practice at the individual, family, group, organizational, community, research, and policy levels, informed by the theories and voices of those who have been marginalized.
- Demonstrate cultural humility applying critical reflexivity, self-awareness, and self-regulation to manage the influence of bias, power, privilege, and values in working with clients and constituencies acknowledging them as experts of their own lived experiences.
- Apply self-awareness and self-regulation to manage the influence of personal biases and values in working with diverse clients and constituencies.

C6   Engage with Individuals, Families, Groups, Organizations, and Communities

- Apply knowledge of human behavior and person-in-environment, and other multidisciplinary theoretical frameworks to engage with clients and constituencies.
- Use empathy, reflection, and interpersonal skills to effectively engage diverse clients and constituencies.

C7   Assess Individuals, Families, Groups, Organizations, and Communities

- Apply knowledge of human behavior and person-in-environment and other culturally responsive multidisciplinary theoretical frameworks when assessing clients and constituencies.

Exercises in Reflective Listening

1. Simple reflection: "You just freeze. You don't say anything."

   Complex reflection: "Something about being in the group makes your mind go blank, and you don't know what to say."

2. Simple reflection: "It sounds like you have adjusted easily."

   Complex reflection: "It seems that being a 'people person' makes adjusting easier for you, especially when people are friendly."

3. Simple reflection: "You blame yourself."

   Complex reflection: "It seems important that you take responsibility for their problems."

4. Simple reflection: "This family struggles when they are together."

   Complex reflection: "Their struggles have been so long lasting. You don't seem to have much hope for them."

5. Simple reflection: "It doesn't seem fair to you."

   Complex reflection: "You work so hard, yet it is hard to imagine that you could accomplish all of this while still raising your children."

6. Simple reflection: "I hear you saying that you feel angry and defeated."

   Complex reflection: "You feel angry and defeated, like you have cheated yourself out of more time."

7. Simple reflection: "Kids at school have been mean to you."

   Complex reflection: "It sounds like you are not going to take it anymore, and it is important that you stand up and defend yourself."

Answers to Exercises

Table 6-1   Identifying Closed- and Open-Ended Responses

Statement	Response
1	C
2	O
3	O
4	C

Exercises in Closed- and Open-Ended Responses

1. "Could you tell me more about your wanting to impress Ralph?"

2. "What are you afraid you'd do wrong?"

3. "Given your experience with that probation officer, how would you like your relationship with me to be?"

4. "Can you describe the kind of care you believe they need?"

5. "It sounds like you are worried that I'm not on your side. Can you tell me what I have done that has caused you to think that your parent and I are against you?"

6. "You sound as if you are at a pretty hopeless point right now. When you say you don't know if you want to keep trying to figure it out, can you tell me more about what you are thinking about doing?"

Exercises in Seeking Concreteness

1. "Can you tell me how it feels weird to you?"

2. "I gather you feel that your friends have let you down in the past. Could you give me a recent example in which this has happened?"

3. "Could you tell me more about what happens when they lose their temper with you?" or "You sound like you don't have much hope that they will ever get control of their temper. How have you concluded they will never change?" [A *social worker might explore each aspect of the message separately.*]

4. "Could you give me some examples of how they are insensitive to you?"

5. "Sounds like you've been feeling hurt and disappointed over my reaction last week. I can sense you're struggling with those same feelings right now."

6. "It sounds as if you feel that your parent's way of communicating with you is unusual for someone their age. Could you recall some recent examples of times you've had difficulties with how they communicate with you?"

7. "It sounds as if the arthritis pain is aggravating and blocking what you normally do. When you say that handling the pots and pans is kind of tricky, can you tell me about recent examples of what has happened when you are cooking?"

8. "Think of going to the doctor just now. Let your feelings flow naturally. *[Pause.]* What goes on inside you—your thoughts and feelings?"

9. "You see it as pretty hopeless. You feel strongly about your teacher. I'd be interested in hearing what's happened that has led you to the conclusion they've got it in for Black students."

10. "You feel as if you're nothing in their eyes. I'm wondering how you've reached that conclusion?"

Eliminating Counterproductive Communication Patterns and Substituting Positive Alternatives

Chapter Overview

Chapter 7 explores common communication difficulties that arise in social work practice and suggests alternatives to these patterns. Being alert to these difficulties, you can focus your attention on developing new skills for effective communications. In addition to direct practice applications, the chapter provides numerous communication examples related to both mezzo- and macro-practice.

As a result of reading this chapter and practicing with classmates, you will be able to:

- Identify counterproductive patterns in your verbal and nonverbal behavior.

- Identify constructive alternatives in those instances.

The EPAS Competencies in Chapter 7

This chapter will give you the information needed to meet the following practice competencies:

- Competency 1: Demonstrate Ethical and Professional Behavior

- Competency 2: Engage Antiracism, Diversity, Equity, and Inclusion in Practice

- Competency 6: Engage with Individuals, Families, Groups, Organizations, and Communities

- Competency 7: Assess Individuals, Families, Groups, Organizations, and Communities

- Competency 9: Evaluate Practice with Individuals, Families, Groups, Organizations, and Communities

Impacts of Counterproductive Communication Patterns

All social workers experience counterproductive communication patterns. These can happen in interviews, team meetings, tele social work sessions and referral calls. We all want to experience error-free learning. However, each of the authors have made communications errors in their social work practice. We, however, examined our practice through self-assessment, supervision, and client feedback and have improved. Competence includes being able to recognize our errors, taking ownership of them, and working toward improvement. In this chapter, we will help you become aware of potential communication errors and explore ways to deal with those errors by replacing them with more productive patterns. In some cases, this means referring to content in earlier chapters.

Previous research provides direction for identifying communication errors and suggests that improvements can occur. At the end of this chapter, it is our hope that you will both be aware of the communication errors that you need to work on *and* feel increasingly confident in your abilities to replace those errors with more productive responses.

Identifying and Improving Nonverbal Barriers to Effective Communication

Nonverbal behaviors strongly influence interactions between people, and social workers' nonverbal interview behavior contributes significantly to ratings of their effectiveness. Social work practice in the time of the coronavirus pandemic has frequently entailed telesocial work. Attentiveness to nonverbal cues is as important in telesocial work as it is with in-person practice. There may be incongruence between what the social worker intends to communicate and the resulting impact of their behavior. There may be "leakage"—the transmission of information about feelings and responses that the sender did not intend to communicate to the receiver. Facial expressions—such as a furrowed brow or a look of dismay—may convey more about the social worker's attitude toward the client or the client's message than what is said aloud. In fact, if there is a discrepancy between the social worker's verbal and nonverbal communication, the client is more likely to discredit the verbal message and consider the nonverbal cues to indicate feelings more accurately. Note that, as a social worker, you are more likely to attend to these errors if you have opportunities to view your practice in videos.

Clients need to perceive that the social worker is concerned about their situation. Social workers must be aware of nonverbal behaviors that may convey a lack of concern for the client. For example, staring vacantly, looking out the window, frequently glancing at the clock, yawning, and fidgeting suggest a lack of attention; trembling hands or rigid posture may communicate hurriedness or anxiety. These and other behavioral cues that convey messages such as inattention or lack of interest can be readily perceived by most clients, many of whom are sensitive to criticism. Social workers must also pay attention to societal preoccupation with checking cell phones for messages, as social workers are not immune to this habit. Doing so in a client's presence could readily convey inattention and disrespect. Voluntary clients with sufficient resources and self-esteem are not likely to accept social worker behavior that they consider disrespectful, nor should they. Involuntary clients with fewer choices, fewer resources, and possibly lower self-esteem may believe that they have little recourse to accepting such behavior.

Physical Attending

The purpose of physical attending in interviews is to convey empathy and understanding to the client. How those physical attending behaviors are received is conditioned in part based on culture. For example, in cross-cultural relationships, some common advice given in textbooks may not apply. For example, the emphasis on strong eye contact and facing the client directly may reflect norms in white contexts. In other contexts, avoiding direct eye contact may convey respect or deference. Similarly, clients with traumatic histories may be triggered by nonverbal behaviors including eye contact.

Attending also requires social workers to be fully present—that is, to keep in moment-to-moment contact with the client through disciplined attention. Attending in a fully present (though perhaps not relaxed) fashion is expected of beginning social workers, despite their typical anxiety about what to do next, how to help, and how to avoid harming clients. Such skill is more likely to evolve with greater experience after novice social workers have engaged in considerable observation of expert social workers, role-playing, initial interviews with clients, and viewing of their own practice.

Social workers should consider the possibility of differences in assumptions about helping professionals as authorities who can solve problems by providing advice. For instance, some clients might not be forthcoming unless they are spoken to by the social worker. The social worker in turn may mistakenly perceive the client's behavior as passive or reticent. Such gaps in communication can engender anxiety in both parties that may undermine the development of rapport and defeat the helping process. Further, failure to correctly interpret the client's nonverbal behavior may lead the social worker to conclude erroneously that the client has flat affect (i.e., limited emotionality). Given these potential hazards, social workers should strive to understand the client's frame of reference. Clarifying roles and expectations should also be emphasized.

C1

Taking Inventory of Nonverbal Patterns of Responding

To assist you in taking inventory of your own styles of responding to clients, Table 7-1 identifies recommended and not recommended nonverbal behaviors. You may find that

C9

you have a mixed repertoire of nonverbal responses, some of which have the potential to enhance helping relationships and foster client progress. Other less desirable behaviors of the beginning social worker may include nervousness that may block your clients from freely disclosing information and otherwise limit the flow of the helping process. You thus have a threefold task: (1) to assess your repetitive nonverbal behaviors; (2) to eliminate nonverbal styles that hinder effective communication; and (3) to sustain and perhaps increase desirable nonverbal behaviors. As noted earlier, it is helpful to make a video recording of your practice to assess your behavior.

At the end of this chapter, you will find a checklist intended for use in supervision to obtain feedback on nonverbal aspects of behavior. Given the opportunity to review a videotape of your performance and/or to receive behaviorally specific feedback from supervisors and peers,

Table 7-1 Inventory of Practitioner's Nonverbal Communication

Recommended	Not Recommended
Facial Expressions	
Direct eye contact (except when culturally proscribed)	Avoidance of eye contact
Warmth and concern reflected in facial expression	Staring or fixating on person or object
Eyes at same level as client's	Lifting eyebrow critically
Appropriately varied and animated facial expressions	Eye level higher or lower than client's
Mouth relaxed; occasional smiles	Nodding head excessively
	Yawning
	Frozen or rigid facial expressions
	Inappropriate slight smile
	Pursing or biting lips
Posture	
Arms and hands moderately expressive; appropriate gestures	Rigid body position; arms tightly folded
Body leaning slightly forward; attentive but relaxed	Body turned at an angle to client
	Fidgeting with hands
	Squirming or rocking in chair
	Leaning back or placing feet on desk
	Hand or fingers over mouth
	Pointing finger for emphasis
Voice	
Clearly audible but not loud	Mumbling or speaking inaudibly
Warmth in tone of voice	Monotonic voice
Voice modulated to reflect nuances of feeling and emotional tone of client messages	Halting speech
	Frequent grammatical errors
Moderate speech tempo	Prolonged silences
	Excessively animated speech
	Slow, rapid, or staccato speech
	Nervous laughter
	Consistent clearing of throat
	Speaking loudly
Physical Proximity	
Three to five feet between chairs	Excessive closeness or distance
	Talking across desk or other barrier

you should be able to adequately master physical aspects of attending in a relatively brief time.

A review of your taped performance may reveal that you are already demonstrating many of the desirable physical attending behaviors listed in Table 7-1. You may also possess personal nonverbal mannerisms that are particularly helpful in establishing relationships with others, such as a friendly grin or a relaxed, easy manner. As you take inventory of your nonverbal behaviors, solicit feedback from others regarding these behaviors. Try to note your behaviors when you are and are not at ease with clients. When appropriate, increase the frequency of recommended behaviors that you have identified.

As you review videotapes of your sessions, pay particular attention to your nonverbal responses at those moments when you experienced discomfort with what the client was saying or you noticed differences that surprised you. This assessment will assist you in determining whether your responses were counterproductive. All beginning interviewers experience moments of discomfort in their first contacts with clients, and nonverbal behaviors serve as an index of their comfort level. To enhance your self-awareness of your own behavioral patterns, develop a list of the verbal and nonverbal behaviors you display when you are under pressure. When you review your videotaped sessions, you may notice that under pressure you respond with humor, fidget, change voice inflection, assume a rigid body posture, or manifest other nervous mannerisms. Becoming aware of and eliminating obvious signs of anxiety is an important step in achieving mastery of your nonverbal responding.

Eliminating Verbal Barriers to Communication

Many types of ineffective verbal responses inhibit clients from sharing freely with the social worker. We will first present seven barriers that emerge from social worker verbal behaviors that can have a negative effect on communication. Later, we present 11 additional barriers that emerge from inappropriate interviewing techniques. In each case, we explore positive alternatives to these barriers.

Social Worker Verbal Behavior Contributing to Communication Barriers

1. Reassuring, sympathizing, consoling, or excusing
2. Advising and giving suggestions or solutions prematurely

3. Using sarcasm or employing humor that is distracting or makes light of clients' problems
4. Judging, criticizing, or placing blame
5. Trying to convince the client about the right point of view through logical arguments, lecturing, instructing, or arguing
6. Making a declaration rather than inviting a discussion about options
7. Threatening, warning, or counterattacking

The first three behaviors are mistakes that beginning social workers commonly make across a variety of populations and settings, often reflecting their nervousness and an abounding desire to be immediately helpful. Numbers four through seven are also common but are more likely to occur when the social worker is working with clients in situations in which there is a power differential, and the client cannot readily escape. An underlying theme of these behaviors can be that the social worker and the agency reflect a sense of superiority over people whose behavior or problem solving has been harmful to themselves or others. This is obviously inconsistent with the anti-oppressive practice perspective introduced in Chapter 2.

1. **Reassuring, Sympathizing, Consoling, or Excusing**
   - "You'll feel better tomorrow."
   - "Don't worry, things will work out."
   - "You probably didn't do anything to aggravate the situation."
   - "I really feel sorry for you."

A pattern found in 90% of the taped interviews completed by beginning social work students was that they would reassure clients their responses were normal, and they were not responsible for the difficulty they were concerned about (Ragg et al., 2007). When used selectively, well-timed reassurance can engender much needed hope and support, but glib reassurance that "things will work out" can cause the social worker to be out of touch with the clients' feelings. Situations faced by clients may present no immediate relief. Social workers must explore those distressing feelings and assist clients in acknowledging painful realities rather than glossing over clients' feelings. It is important for the social worker to develop awareness of their own reactions to clients' strong feelings. Beginning social workers need to convey that they hear and understand their clients' difficulties as they experience them. They will also want to convey hope while exploring prospects for change at the appropriate time in the dialogue.

Reassuring clients prematurely or without a genuine basis for hope often serves the social worker's purposes more than the client's purposes and may dissuade clients from revealing their troubling feelings. That is, reassurance may serve to restore the comfort level and the equilibrium of social workers rather than to help clients. Instead of fostering hope, glib statements convey a lack of understanding of clients' feelings and raise doubts about the authenticity of social workers. Clients, in turn, may react with thoughts such as, "It's easy for you to say that, but you don't know how very frightened I really am," or "You're just saying that so I'll feel better." In addition, responses that excuse clients (e.g., "You're not to blame") or sympathize with their position (e.g., "I can see exactly why you feel that way; I think I would probably have done the same thing") often have the effect of unwittingly reinforcing inappropriate behavior or reducing clients' anxiety and motivation to work on problems.

In place of inappropriate reassurance, more positive and useful responses can come from reflecting that you heard and understood what the client was conveying and, in some cases, positive reframing, which does not discount concerns but places them in a different light.

2. Advising and Giving Suggestions or Solutions Prematurely

- "I suggest that you move to a new place because you have had so many difficulties here."
- "I think you need to try a new approach with your child. Let me suggest that...."
- "I think it would be best for you to try using timeout."

Barriers that prevent the social worker from staying in psychological contact with the client can be caused by a self-inflicted pressure to seek immediate solutions to the client's problems. In fact, many beginning social workers have prior experience in positions in which their job was to quickly assess a situation and provide a rapid solution. Such skills are valuable but not overly generalized such that you limit exploration of client concerns and prematurely move to solutions. Sufficient time must be given to engagement and assessment before moving into intervention planning.

The strength perspective introduced as a guiding perspective in Chapter 2 suggests that many people have access to their solutions within them so exploring how they have thought about addressing their concerns is always a good idea to help you both assess your available resources. Such advising can fit particular positions that require sharing expert information. However, in many cases, a skill can be shared in learning how to access expert information. The above prior suggestions or advice could be useful if you have together explored client resources and ideas and examined ways to get information about useful resources and solutions. A frequent pattern found in the Ragg et al. (2007) study was that

in 90% of the videos of beginning social workers, they would appear at times to turn off from listening to the client and seem to be engaging in an internal dialogue related to formulating a solution to concerns raised. Such patterns may have been fostered in previous work positions and exchanges with friends where the pattern was to move quickly to problem-solving solutions without grasping the larger situation. We do not mean to discount the social worker's capacity to think about a problem and possible solutions. Rather, we want to stress the importance of waiting until the social worker has fully grasped the situation and empathized with the client before moving into a mutual examination of alternatives.

Little is known about the actual provision of advice in terms of its frequency or the circumstances in which it occurs. Clients often seek advice, and appropriately timed advice can be an important helping tool. Conversely, untimely advice may elicit opposition. Even when clients solicit advice in early phases of the helping process, they often react negatively when they receive it because the recommended solutions, which are invariably based on superficial information, often do not address their real needs. Further, because clients are frequently burdened with conflicting pressures in their lives, they are not ready to act on their problems at this point. For these reasons, after offering premature advice, social workers may observe clients replying with responses such as "Yes, but I've already tried that," "That won't work," or "I could try that" with little enthusiasm. In fact, these responses can serve as feedback clues that you may have slipped into the habit of giving premature advice.

Although many clients seek advice from social workers because they see the social workers as expert problem solvers, social workers can (wrongly) seek to expedite problem solving by quickly comparing the current situation to other similar ones encountered in the past and recommending a solution that has worked for other clients or themselves. In such cases, social workers may feel pressure to provide quick answers or solutions for clients who unrealistically expect magical answers and instant relief from problems that have plagued them for long periods of time.

Beginning social workers may also experience inner pressure to dispense solutions to clients' problems, mistakenly believing that their new role demands that they, like physicians or advice columnists, prescribe a treatment regimen. They thus run the risk of giving advice before they have conducted a thorough exploration of clients' problems. Instead of dispensing wisdom, a major role of social workers is to create and shape processes with clients in which they engage in mutual discovery of problems and solutions—work that takes time and concentrated effort.

Beginning social workers who are working with involuntary clients may feel justified in "strongly suggesting" their opinions because of their assessment of presumed past inappropriate behaviors that might have contributed to their current predicament. While assessing clients' performance and capabilities in certain circumstances can be appropriate, judging them as people is not appropriate. Assisting clients through modeling and reinforcement of prosocial behavior can be appropriate alternatives to judging clients and imposing social workers' own opinions (Trotter, 2015).

The timing and form of recommendations are all-important in the helping process. Advice should be offered sparingly and only after thoroughly exploring the problem and the client's ideas about possible solutions. At that point, the social worker may serve as a consultant, tentatively sharing ideas about solutions to supplement those developed by the client and assisting the client in weighing the pros and cons of different alternatives. This can be a time for sharing information about the personal expertise of the social worker and the function of the agency that contributes to this expertise as a source for advice. The social worker can work with clients to discover and tailor solutions to fit their unique problems.

Clients may expect to receive early advice if social workers have not appropriately clarified roles and expectations about how mutual participation in generating possible solutions will further the client's own growth and self-confidence. Inappropriate advice also minimizes or ignores clients' strengths and potentials, and many clients respond with resentment to such treatment. In addition, clients who have not been actively involved in planning their own courses of action may lack motivation to implement the social worker's advice. Moreover, when advice does not remedy a problem, clients may blame social workers and disown any responsibility for an unfavorable outcome.

Rather than say, "I suggest that you move to a new place because you have had so many difficulties here," a more productive response would be to say, "You have had a lot of difficulties in your current place. What have you considered doing about your living situation?" Based on that response, you could assist the client either in considering ways to improve that situation or in looking for alternative living arrangements.

3. Using Sarcasm or Employing Humor Inappropriately

- "Did you get up on the wrong side of the bed?"
- "It seems to me that we've been through all this before."
- "You really fell for that line."

Humor can be helpful, bringing relief and sometimes perspective to work that might otherwise be tense and tedious. Pollio (1995) has suggested ways to determine appropriate use of humor. Are you a social worker capable of telling something that is humorous? Do others, including clients, think so? Does the comment fit the situation? Is something needed to unstick or free up a situation in a way that humor might help? What do you know about the client's sense of humor? Similarly, van Wormer and Boes (1997) described ways that humor permits social workers to continue to operate in the face of trauma. Using plays on words or noting a sense of the preposterous or incongruous can help social workers and clients face difficult situations. Humor also allows clients to express emotions in safe, less emotionally charged ways. Caplan (1995) described how in group work facilitation of humor can create a necessary safety and comfort level in work with men who batter. Teens have been described as using irony, sarcasm, mocking, and parody as ways of coping with difficult situations (Cameron et al., 2010). Similarly, humor can be used in ways to diffuse conflict (Norrick & Spitz, 2008).

Excessive or untimely use of humor, however, can be distracting, keeping the content of the session on a superficial level and interfering with mutual objectives. Sarcasm often emanates from unrecognized hostility that tends to provoke counter-hostility in clients. Similarly, making a comment such as "you really win the prize for worst week" is demeaning and offensive when a client recounts a series of serious or painful events. It runs the risk of conveying that the difficulties are not taken seriously. A better response would be to empathize with the difficulties of the week and compliment the client on persisting to cope despite them.

Rather than saying, "Did you get up on the wrong side of the bed?" a more descriptive response that does not run the risk of diminishing the client's experience would be to say, "It sounds as if today was difficult from the time you got up."

Use of humor should not be forced and should only be considered when rapport has been established. Should the social worker misjudge and make a comment that the client appears to not appreciate, the social worker should explore what occurred and apologize.

4. Judging, Criticizing, or Placing Blame

- "You're wrong about that."
- "Running away from home was a bad mistake."
- "One of your problems is that you're not willing to consider another point of view."
- "You're not thinking straight."

Clients do not feel supported when they perceive the social worker as critical, moralistic, and defensive rather than warm and respectful (Coady & Marziali, 1994; Wolgien & Coady, 1997; Safran & Muran, 2000). Responses that evaluate and show disapproval can be detrimental to clients and to the helping process. Clients often respond defensively and sometimes counterattack when they perceive criticism from social workers. Some may simply cut off any meaningful communication with social workers. When they are intimidated by a social worker's greater expertise, some clients also accept negative evaluations as accurate reflections of their poor judgment or lack of worth or value. In making such negative judgments about clients, social workers violate the basic social work values of nonjudgmental attitude and acceptance.

Such responses are unlikely to be tolerated by voluntary clients with adequate self-esteem or enough power in the situation to have alternatives. Such clients are likely to "fire" you, speak to your supervisor, or put you on notice if you act in such seemingly disrespectful ways. Others may shut down, perceiving you as having some power over them. Such responses are antithetical to the anti-oppressive practice and cultural humility perspectives

Involuntary clients often face what they believe to be dangerous consequences for not getting along with the social worker. Hence, some clients with substantial self-control and self-esteem may put up with such browbeating without comment. Others may respond in kind with attacks of their own that then appear in case records as evidence of client resistance.

Judging in the situation is not useful and is often counterproductive. On the other hand, it could be useful in some circumstances to help the client reflect about actions that might be a danger to themself or others or about violations of the law. In such circumstances, asking about the client's awareness of consequences and alternatives can be useful. For example, the social worker might ask, "How do you look now at the consequences of running away from home?" or "How would this appear from your partner's point of view?" The social worker might also provide a double-sided reflection, as described in Chapter 6.

5. **Trying to Convince Clients about the Right Point of View through Logic, Lecturing, Instructing, or Arguing**

   - "Let's look at the facts about drugs."
   - "You have to take some responsibility for your life, you know."
   - "Running away from home will only get you in more difficulty."
   - "That attitude won't get you anywhere."

Collaboration was presented as a guiding principle in Chapter 2. Clients sometimes consider courses of action that social workers view as unsafe, illegal, or contrary to the clients' goals. However, attempting to convince clients through lecturing or instructing often provokes a boomerang effect. That is, clients are not only unconvinced of the merits of the social worker's argument but may also be more inclined to hold onto their beliefs. As noted earlier, according to reactance theory, clients attempt to defend their valued freedoms when these privileges are threatened (Brehm & Brehm, 2013). For some clients (especially adolescents, for whom independent thinking is associated with a particular developmental stage), deferring to or agreeing with social workers is tantamount to giving up their individuality or freedom. The challenge when working with such clients is to learn how to listen to and respect their perspective at the same time while making sure they are aware of alternatives and consequences. Compare the two ways of handling the same situation described in the following.

Teen parent client: I have decided to drop out of high school for now and get my cosmetology license.

Social worker: Don't you know that dropping out of high school is going to hurt you and your children, both now and in the future? Are you willing to sacrifice hundreds of thousands of dollars less that you would earn over your lifetime for you and your children just to buy a few little knickknacks now?

Teen parent client: But this is my life! My babies need things now. You don't know what it is like to scrape by. You can't tell me what to do! You are not my mom! I know what is best for me and my children.

Rather than escalate into what has been called the confrontation–denial cycle (Murphy & Baxter, 1997), a better alternative is to respond to the teen parent client with an effort to understand her perspective before exploring alternatives and consequences.

Teen parent client: I have decided to drop out of high school for now and get my cosmetology license.

Social worker: So, you have been going to high school for a while now with some success, and now you are considering that going in a different direction and getting your cosmetology license may work better for you. Tell me about that.

Teen parent client: Well, it is true that I have been working hard in high school, but I need more money now, not just far off in the future. My babies and I don't have enough to get by.

Social worker: And you feel that getting a cosmetology license will help you do that?

Teen parent client: I do. I still want to finish high school and get my diploma. I know that I will earn more for my kids and myself with a diploma than if I don't finish. If I get my cosmetology degree, it will take a little longer to get my high school diploma, but I think I am up to it.

Social worker: So, your longer-term plan is still to get your high school diploma but just to delay it. You think that getting your cosmetology degree will help you and your kids get by better now. Are there any drawbacks to withdrawing from high school at this time?

Teen parent client: Only if I get distracted and don't return. I could kind of get out of the habit of going to school, and I might be around people who haven't finished school.

Social worker: Those are things to consider. How might you be sure that your withdrawal from high school was only temporary?

In the first example, the social worker attempts to vigorously persuade the client about the course of action they deem wisest. Such efforts, while well meaning, often create power struggles, thereby perpetuating dynamics that have previously occurred in clients' personal relationships. By confronting before attempting to understand the client's perception, social workers ignore their clients' feelings and views, focusing instead on the social worker "being right;" this tactic may engender feelings of resentment, alienation, or hostility in clients. Such efforts are both unethical and ineffective. Persuasion in the sense of helping clients to obtain accurate information with which to make informed decisions can be an ethical intervention. When clients contemplate actions that run contrary to their own goals, or may endanger themselves or others, then an effort to persuade can be an ethical intervention. Such efforts should not focus on the one "pet" solution of the social worker, however, but rather should assist the client in examining the advantages and the disadvantages of several options, including those with which the social worker may disagree (Rooney & Myrick, 2018). Hence, the effort is not to convince but rather to assist clients in making informed decisions. By not being confrontational with the client in the second example, the social worker is able to support the client's right to make decisions for themself and to do so considering alternatives and consequences.

6. Making a Declaration Rather than Inviting a Discussion about Options

- "You're behaving that way because you're angry with your partner."
- "Your attitude may have kept you from giving their ideas a fair hearing."

- "You're acting in a passive–aggressive way."
- "You're really hostile today."

When used sparingly and timed appropriately, interpretation of the dynamics of behavior can be a potent change-oriented skill (see Chapter 17). However, even accurate interpretations that focus on purposes or meanings of behavior substantially beyond clients' levels of conscious awareness tend to inspire client opposition and are likely to fail.

When stated dogmatically ("I know what's wrong with you," or "how you feel") interpretations can threaten clients, causing them to feel exposed or trapped. When a glib interpretation is thrust upon them, such as in the prior examples, clients often expend their energies in disconfirming the interpretation, making angry rebuttals or passively acquiescing rather than working on the problem at hand.

Using social work terms such as *fixation*, *resistance*, *reinforcement*, *repression*, *passivity*, *neuroticism* to describe the client's behavior in their presence can be destructive to the helping process. Indeed, it may confuse or bewilder clients and provoke opposition. These terms can also oversimplify complex phenomena and stereotype clients, thereby obscuring their uniqueness. In addition, generalizations provide no operational definitions of clients' problems, nor do they suggest avenues for behavior change. If clients accept the social worker's restricted definitions of their problems, they may define themselves in the same terms as those used by social workers (e.g., "I am a passive person" or "I have a borderline personality disorder"). Stereotypic labeling can cause clients to view themselves as "sick" and their situations as hopeless, providing them with a ready excuse for not working on their problems.

It is important to help clients identify their feelings and behaviors as a means toward increasing client self-awareness and coping. Introducing terminology to describe behavior and feelings should be done as a suggestion, while inviting the client to correct the social worker if they are incorrect: "Correct me if I'm wrong, but it seems as if you are uncomfortable with what we're talking about. Perhaps it makes you feel vulnerable."

Inviting a discussion about areas in which the client feels conflict and, examining what attract them about different options can be part of a process of eliciting change talk described in Motivational Interviewing and described in more detail in Chapter 17 (Miller & Rollnick, 2012). Instead of making a declaration about a relationship, as described previously, a more collaborative response would be to ask, "When you experience these conflicts with your partner, what do you think about doing?" When the alternatives are suggested, you can help the client look at what they see as the possible advantages and disadvantages of each option. Such a process can help them move closer to making a decision rather than blaming them for not making a decision.

7. Threatening, Warning, or Counterattacking

- "You'd better ... or else!"
- "If you don't..., you'll be sorry."
- "If you know what's good for you, you'll..."

Each of these behaviors is antithetical to the collaborative stance we proposed in Chapter 2. Sometimes, clients consider actions that would endanger themselves or others or are illegal. In such instances, alerting clients to the potential consequences of those actions is an ethical and appropriate intervention. Conversely, making threats of the sort described often produce oppositional behavior that exacerbates an already strained situation.

Even the most well-intentioned social workers may occasionally bristle or respond defensively under the pressure of verbal abuse, accusations, or challenges to their integrity, competence, motives, or authority. For example, a social worker was scheduled to offer services to a veteran who was entering hospice care. The veteran exploded with a series of expletives and insults to the effect that they had no need of such services. Rather than choose this as a time to inform the client of proper respect and boundaries, the social worker made a better choice to ask if they could come at another time to explain the possible services so that the client could be sure about whether they might be helpful. The veteran became calmer and averred that coming at another time would be fine.

Whatever the dynamics behind clients' provocative behavior, responding defensively is counterproductive, as it may duplicate the destructive pattern of responses that clients have typically elicited and experienced from others. To achieve competence, therefore, you must learn to master your own natural defensive reactions and develop effective ways of dealing with negative feelings, putting the client's needs before your own. Paying attention to your own emotional reaction is important without immediately acting on it can create an opportunity to examine the interaction. For example, should a client say: "I am not sure if I want to keep coming to see you because I don't know if it is helping," your first internal response might be to think, "You know you have dropped out of counseling in the past and not dealt with the issues we have discussed." A better response might be to note, "It makes sense for you to assess with me what is and is not working about our meeting together".

Empathic communication produces a cathartic release of negative feelings, defusing a strained situation and permitting a more rational exploration of factors that underlie clients' feelings. For example, replying to a client, "You have difficult decisions to make and are caught between alternatives that you don't consider very attractive. I could perhaps help you weigh those options, as you decide what to do."

The negative effects of certain types of responses are not always immediately apparent because clients may not overtly demonstrate negative reactions at the time or because the dampening effect on the helping process cannot be observed in a single transaction. To assess the effect of responses, the social worker must determine the frequency with which they issue the dampening responses and evaluate the overall impact of those responses on the helping process. Frequent use of some types of responses by the social worker indicates the presence of counterproductive patterns of communication such as the following (note that this list is a continuation of the list of problematic social worker behaviors).

Inappropriate Interviewing Technique Barriers

In addition to the seven social worker behaviors that contribute to verbal barriers, the following are 11 additional inappropriate interviewing techniques that contribute to communication barriers.

1. Stacking questions
2. Asking leading questions
3. Interrupting inappropriately or excessively
4. Dominating the interaction
5. Keeping discussion focused on safe topics
6. Responding infrequently
7. Parroting or overusing certain phrases or clichés
8. Vague effusive positivity
9. Dwelling on the remote past
10. Tangential exploration
11. Failing to be aware of implicit and cognitive bias

Individual responses that fall within these patterns may not be ineffective when used occasionally. When they are employed extensively in lieu of using varied response patterns, however, they inhibit the natural flow of a session and limit the richness of information revealed. The sections that follow expand on each of these verbal barriers and detrimental social worker responses.

8. Stacking Questions

In exploring problems, social workers should use facilitative questions that assist clients in revealing detailed information about specific problem areas. Asking multiple questions at the same time, or **stacking questions**, diffuses the focus and confuses clients. Consider the vast amount of ground covered in the following messages:

- "When you don't feel you have control of situations, what goes on inside of you? What do you think about? What do you do?"
- "Have you thought about where you are going to live? Is that one of your biggest concerns, or is there another that takes priority?"
- "How satisfied are you with the housing situation and your case worker?"

Stacking questions is a problem frequently encountered by beginning social workers who may feel an urgent need to help clients by providing many options all at one time. Adequately answering even one of the foregoing questions would require a client to give an extended response. Rather than focus on one question, however, clients often respond superficially and nonspecifically to the social worker's multiple inquiries, omitting important information in the process. Stacked questions thus have low yield and are unproductive and inefficient in gathering relevant information. Slowing down and asking one question at a time is preferable. If you have asked stacked questions (and all social workers have at many points), and the client hesitates in response, you can correct for the problem by repeating your preferred question.

9. Asking Leading Questions

Leading questions have hidden agendas designed to persuade clients to agree with a particular view or to adopt a solution that social workers deem to be in clients' best interests. For example:

- "Do you think you've really tried to get along with your partner?"
- "You don't really mean that, do you?"
- "Don't you think that dropping out of school is going to hurt you in the long run?"
- "Aren't you too young to move out on your own?"
- "Don't you think that arguing with your parent may provoke them to come down on you as they have done in the past?"

These types of questions often obscure legitimate concerns that social workers should discuss with clients. Social workers may conceal their feelings and opinions about such matters, however, and present them obliquely in the form of solutions (e.g., "Don't you think you ought to ...") in the hope that leading questions guides clients to desired conclusions. It is an error, however, to assume that clients will not see through such maneuvers. Indeed, clients often discern the social worker's motives and inwardly resist having views or directives imposed on

them under the guise of leading questions. Nevertheless, to avoid conflict or controversy with social workers, they may express feeble agreement or simply divert the discussion to another topic.

By contrast, when social workers authentically assume responsibility for concerns they wish clients to consider, they enhance the likelihood that clients will respond receptively to their questions. In addition, they can raise questions that are not slanted to imply the "correct" answer from the social worker's viewpoint. For example, "How have you attempted to reach agreement with your partner?" does not contain the hint about the "right" answer found in the first question given. Similarly, the last question could be rephrased as follows: "I am not clear how you see arguing with your parent is likely to be more successful than it has proved to be in the past."

10. Interrupting Inappropriately or Excessively

Beginning social workers often worry excessively about covering all items on their own and their agency's agenda ("What will I tell my supervisor?"). To maintain focus on relevant problem areas, social workers must sometimes interrupt clients. To be effective, however, these interruptions must be purposeful, well timed, and smoothly executed. Interruptions may damage the helping process when they are abrupt or divert clients from exploring pertinent problem areas. For example, interrupting to challenge a client's account of events or to confirm an irrelevant detail can break the flow and put the client on the defensive. Frequent untimely interruptions tend to annoy clients, stifle spontaneous expression, and hinder exploration of problems.

Identifying and prioritizing key questions in advance with an outline can assist in avoiding this pattern. Appropriate interruptions can occur if you want to convey that you have heard what a client has to say. For example, some clients seem to repeat certain stories and accusations about bad things that have occurred to them as a key part of a prized narrative. A more useful response is to provide an empathic summary. For example, "Let me interrupt you to see if I am getting what you are saying. You are not opposed to having home health care. In fact, you welcome it. However, timing has been a problem for you. Aides often come early in the day when you are not yet up for the day. Is that correct?" Such an empathic summary can free some clients from needing to repeat the story and move on to consider what feasible options to their dilemma there might be.

11. Dominating the Interaction

Social workers should guide discussions. They should not dominate the interaction by talking too much or by asking too many closed-ended questions. Such behavior discourages clients from expressing themselves and fosters a one-up, one-down relationship in which clients feel at a great disadvantage and resent the social worker's supercilious demeanor.

Social workers should monitor the relative distribution of participation by all participants (including themselves) involved in individual, family, or group sessions. Although clients naturally vary in their levels of verbal participation and assertiveness, all group members should have equal opportunity to share information, concerns, and views in the helping process. Social workers have a responsibility to ensure that this opportunity is available to them.

Sometimes social workers defeat practice objectives in group or conjoint sessions by dominating the interaction through such behaviors as speaking for members, focusing more on some members than on others, or giving speeches. Even social workers who are not particularly verbal may dominate sessions that include reserved or nonassertive clients, as a means of alleviating their own discomfort with silence and passivity. Although it is natural to be more active with reticent or withdrawn clients than with those who are more verbal, social workers must avoid seeming overbearing.

Using facilitative responses that draw clients out is an effective method of minimizing silence and passivity. When a review of one of your taped sessions reveals that you have monopolized the interaction, it is important that you explore the reasons for your behavior. Also, examine the clients' style of relating for clues regarding your own reactions and analyze the feelings you were experiencing at the time. Based on your review and assessment of your performance, you should then plan a strategy for modifying your own style of relating by substituting facilitative responses for ineffective ones. You may also need to focus on and explore the passive or nonassertive behavior of clients with the objective of contracting with them to increase their participation in the helping process.

12. Keeping Discussions Focused on Safe Topics

Keeping discussions focused on safe topics that exclude feelings and minimize client disclosures is contrary to the helping process. Social chitchat about the weather, news, hobbies, mutual interests or acquaintances, and the like tends to foster a social rather than a productive relationship. In contrast to the lighter and more diffuse communication characteristic of a social relationship, helpful, growth-producing relationships feature sharp focus and high specificity. Another frequent pattern found in the Ragg, Okagbue-Reaves, and Piers (2007) was that beginning practitioners would attempt to ressions of high emotion such as anger, dismay,

or sadness rather than reflect them, as indicated in the following example:

> **Parent:** I have had about all I can take from these kids sometimes. They are so angry and disrespectful that it is all I can do to keep from blowing up at them.
> **Social worker:** Kids nowadays can be difficult.

A more appropriate response would be:

> **Social worker:** You sometimes feel so frustrated when your kids act disrespectfully. You want to do something about it without exploding.

In general, such "safe" social interaction in the helping process should be avoided. Two exceptions to this rule exist, however:

- Discussion of "safe" topics may be utilized to help children or adolescents lower their defenses and risk increasing openness, thereby assisting social workers to cultivate a quasi-friend role with such clients.
- A brief discussion of conventional topics may be appropriate and helpful as part of the getting-acquainted or warm-up period of initial sessions or during early portions of subsequent sessions. A warm-up period is particularly important when you are engaging clients from ethnic groups for which such informal openings are the cultural norm, as discussed in Chapter 3.

Even when you try to avoid inappropriate social interaction, however, some clients may resist your attempts to move the discussion to a topic that is relevant to the problems they are experiencing and to the purposes of the helping process. Techniques for managing such situations are found in Chapter 18. For now, simply note that it is appropriate for the social worker to bring up the agreed-upon agenda within a few minutes of the beginning of the session.

13. Responding Infrequently

Monitoring the frequency of your responses in client sessions is an important task. As a social worker, you have an ethical responsibility to utilize the time you have with clients in pursuing your practice objectives. To be maximally helpful, social workers must structure the helping process by developing contracts with clients that specify the respective responsibilities of both sets of participants. For their part, they engage clients in identifying and exploring problems, formulating goals, and delineating tasks to alleviate clients' difficulties.

Inactive social workers can contribute to counterproductive processes and

C1

failures in problem solving. One deleterious effect, for example, is that clients lose confidence in social workers when they fail to intervene in situations that are destructive to the client or to others.

Although social workers' activity, per se, is important, the quality of their moment-by-moment responses is critical. Social workers significantly diminish their effectiveness by neglecting to utilize facilitative responses.

Self-assessment of your sessions and discussions with your supervisor can be helpful in determining whether you are modeling an appropriate level of interaction with the client. For example, some beginning social workers may welcome highly verbal clients. However, overly talkative clients may come to dominate the session. While catharsis can be useful, usually such clients are coming in because there is an issue they wish to address. The client would be better served by refocusing the discussion and coming back to the concern that brought the client in.

14. Parroting or Overusing Certain Phrases or Clichés

Parroting a message irritates clients, who may issue a sharp rebuke to the social worker: "Well, yes, I just said that." Rather than merely repeating clients' words, social workers should use fresh language that captures the essence of clients' messages. In addition, social workers should avoid punctuating their communications with superfluous phrases. The distracting effect of such phrases can be observed in the following message:

> **Social worker:** You know, a lot of people wouldn't come in for help. It tells me, you know, that you realize that you have a problem, you know, and want to work on it. Do you know what I mean?

Frequent use of such phrases as "you know," "Okay?" ("Let's work on this task, okay?") can annoy some clients if used in excess. The same may be said of clichés such as "awesome," "sweet," "cool," "tight," or "dude."

Another mistake social workers sometimes make is trying to over-relate to youthful clients by using adolescent jargon to excess. Adolescents tend to perceive such communication as phony and the social worker as inauthentic, which hinders the development of a working relationship. It can be part of the learning process, however, to discover the meaning of terms unfamiliar to the social worker, so that in some cases you can translate concepts using terms you have learned from the client.

15. Vague Effusive Positivity

Another error can come from a misapplication of the strengths perspective to be overly positive in a vague fashion that does not convey the specific positive

feedback intended. For example, rather than saying "I just think you are doing awesome," a client would be more benefited by specific feedback such as, "I am very impressed by how you have persisted in studying for this exam when I know it is difficult for you."

16. Dwelling on the Remote Past

Social workers' verbal responses may focus on the past, the present, or the future. Helping professionals differ regarding the amount of emphasis they believe should be accorded to gathering historical facts about clients. Focusing largely on the present is vital, however, because clients can only change their present circumstances, behaviors, and feelings. Dwelling on the past may avoid dealing with painful aspects of present difficulties and with possibilities for change.

Messages about the past may reveal feelings the client is currently experiencing related to the past. For example:

> **Client [with trembling voice]:** He used to make me so angry.
> **Social worker:** There was a time when he really made you mad. As you think about the past, even now it seems to stir up some of the anger and hurt you felt.

As in this excerpt, changing a client's statement from past to present tense often yields rich information about clients' present feelings and problems. The same may be said of bringing future-oriented statements of clients to the present (e.g., "How do you feel now about the future event you're describing?"). It is not only possible but often productive to shift the focus to the present experiencing of clients, even when historical facts are being elicited, in an effort to illuminate client problems.

17. Tangential Exploration

Another counterproductive interviewing strategy is pursuing content that is only tangentially related to client concerns, issues of client and family safety, or legal mandates. Such content may relate to unfamiliar language of social workers or agencies and be puzzling to clients. Confusion may arise if the connection between these theories and the concerns that have brought clients into contact with the social worker is not clear. A wise precaution, therefore, would be to avoid taking clients into tangential areas if you cannot readily justify the rationale for that exploration. If the social worker feels that the exploration of new areas is relevant, then an explanation of its purpose is warranted. For example, if a social worker was concerned that a client's social interactions are largely through the Internet and texting and proposed to the client that excessive use of social media is unhealthy, it would be better not to impose such a judgment but rather to remain focused on the client's satisfaction with their social interactions. If lack of in-person socialization was the presenting problem, the social worker could first join with the client about the positive parts of online communication and validate and acknowledge the client's satisfaction, and then the worker could help the client think about other ways of socializing and about experimenting with other behavior.

18. Failing to Be Aware of Implicit and Cognitive Biases

Social workers can be subject to implicit bias when they are not consciously aware of mental associations they are making about clients on the basis of irrelevant characteristics such as race or gender (FitzGerald & Hurst, 2017). Research on implicit bias suggests that people can act based on prejudice and stereotypes without intending to do so. That is, a social worker could believe that they hold egalitarian views about gender and race when it would appear from their actions that an implicit bias could be affecting judgment (Brownstein, 2015).

Meanwhile, cognitive bias refers to seeking out information that confirms our understanding, preferences, or perceptions while ignoring information that contradicts these biases. Cognitive biases may have both positive and negative influences on clients. Social workers may influence clients to make decisions that confirm the social worker's bias about how humans should function in the world. A social worker who is biased toward individualism, for example, may attempt to counsel a client from a collectivist culture to make decisions that align with individualistic lifestyles, or social workers may screen out negative assessments of themselves while paying attention only to positive assessments, even when the negative assessments may contribute to growth. These types of biases influence how we as social workers interact with clients and require substantial self-awareness to change and address. It is, therefore, important for social workers to recognize how personal experiences and cognition shape our understanding of the world and the manner in which we engage with clients.

Gauging the Effectiveness of Your Responses

The preceding discussion should assist you in identifying ineffective patterns of communication you may have been employing. Because most learners ask too many closed-ended questions, change the subject frequently, and recommend solutions before completing a thorough

exploration of clients' problems, you should particularly watch for these patterns. In addition, you will need to monitor your interviewing style for idiosyncratic counterproductive patterns of responding.

As noted earlier, one way of gauging the effectiveness of your responses is to carefully observe clients' reactions immediately following your responses. Because multiple clients are involved in group and family sessions, you may often receive varied verbal and nonverbal cues regarding the relative effectiveness of your responses when engaging clients in these systems. As you assess your messages, keep in mind that a response is probably helpful if clients react in one of the following ways:

- They continue to explore the problem or stay on the topic.
- They express pent-up emotions related to the problematic situation.
- They engage in deeper self-exploration and self-experiencing.
- They volunteer more personally relevant material spontaneously.
- They affirm the validity of your response either verbally or nonverbally.

In contrast, a response may be too confrontational, poorly timed, or off target if clients react in one of the following ways:

- They reject your response either verbally or nonverbally.
- They change the subject.
- They ignore the message.
- They appear mixed up or confused.
- They become more superficial, more impersonal, more emotionally detached, or more defensive.
- They argue or express anger rather than examine the relevance of the feelings involved.

In analyzing social worker–client interactions, keep in mind that the participants mutually influence each other. Thus, a response by either person in an individual interview affects the expressions of the other person.

In summary, your task is twofold: You should monitor and seek to eliminate your own ineffective responses while simultaneously modifying ineffective responses by your clients. Bear in mind that this is a career-long task, as we have ineffective actions despite more experience. We hope and expect that we come to spot our errors more quickly and have a larger repertoire of options to consider.

You will make faster progress if you test out your new communication skills in your private life. To master these essential skills and to fully tap into their potential for assisting clients, social workers must promote their own interpersonal competence.

The Challenge of Learning New Skills

Because of the unique nature of the helping process, establishing and maintaining a productive relationship requires highly disciplined efforts on the social worker's part. Moment by moment, the social worker must sharply focus on the needs and problems clients. The success of each transaction is measured in terms of the social worker's adroitness in consciously applying specific skills to move the process toward the therapeutic objectives.

A major threat to learning new skills comes from students' fear that in relinquishing their old styles of relating they are giving up an essential part of themselves. Similarly, students who previously engaged in social work practice may experience fear related to the fact that they have developed methods or styles of relating that have influenced and moved clients in the past; abandoning these response patterns may mean surrendering a hard-won feeling of competency. These fears are often exacerbated when instruction and supervision in the classroom and practicum primarily strive to eliminate errors and ineffective interventions and responses rather than to develop new skills or enhance positive responses or interventions with clients. In such circumstances, students may receive considerable feedback about their errors but inadequate input regarding their effective responses or styles of relating. Consequently, they may feel vulnerable and stripped of their defenses (just as clients do) and experience more keenly the loss of something familiar.

As a beginning social worker (and throughout your career), you must learn to receive constructive feedback openly and nondefensively about your styles of relating or intervening that have not been helpful in the past. Effective supervisors should not dwell exclusively on shortcomings but rather be equally focused on identifying your expanding skills (Rooney & De Jong, 2011). If they do not do so, then you should take the lead in eliciting positive feedback from educators and peers about your growing strengths. Remember that supervision time is limited, and the responsibility for utilizing that time effectively and for acquiring competency necessarily rests equally with you and your practicum instructor. It is also vital that you take steps to monitor your own growth systematically by reviewing audio and video recordings, by counting your desirable and undesirable responses in client sessions, and by comparing your responses with the guidelines for constructing effective messages found in this book. Perhaps the single most important requirement for you in furthering your competency is to assume responsibility for advancing your own skill level by consistently monitoring your responses and practicing proven skills.

Most of the skills delineated in this book are not easy to master. In fact, competent social workers spend years perfecting their ability to sensitively attune themselves to the inner experiences of their clients; in furthering their capacity to share their own experiencing in an authentic, helpful manner; and in developing a keen sense of timing in employing these and other skills.

In the months ahead, as you forge new patterns of responding and test your newly developed skills, you may experience a sense of disequilibrium as you struggle to respond in new ways and, at the same time, to relate warmly, naturally, and attentively to your clients. Sometimes you may feel that your responses are mechanistic and experience a keen sense of transparency: "The client will know that I'm not being real." If you work intensively to master specific skills, however, your awkwardness will gradually diminish, and you will eventually incorporate these skills naturally into your repertoire.

Summary

This chapter outlined a series of nonverbal and verbal barriers to effective communication that are often experienced by beginning social workers. As you become alert to these potential obstacles and more skilled in applying more productive alternatives, you will become more confident in your progress. Chapter 8 asks you to apply your communication skills to one of the most important tasks you will face: conducting a multisystemic assessment.

Assessing Verbal Barriers to Communication				
Directions: In reviewing each 15-minute sample of recorded interviews, tally your use of ineffective responses by placing marks in appropriate cells.				
15-Minute Recorded Samples	1	2	3	4
1. Reassuring, sympathizing, consoling, or excusing				
2. Advising and giving suggestions or solutions prematurely				
3. Using sarcasm or employing humor that is distracting or makes light of clients' problems				
4. Judging, criticizing, or placing blame				
5. Trying to convince the client about the right point of view through logical arguments, lecturing, instructing, or arguing				
6. Making a declaration rather than inviting a discussion about options				
7. Threatening, warning, or counterattacking				
8. Stacking questions				
9. Asking leading questions				
10. Interrupting inappropriately or excessively				
11. Dominating the interaction				
12. Keeping discussion focused on safe topics				
13. Responding infrequently				
14. Parroting or overusing certain phrases or clichés				
15. Vague, effusive positivity				
16. Dwelling on the remote past				
17. Tangential exploration				
18. Failing to be aware of implicit and cognitive bias				
Other responses that impede communication. List:				

Assessing Physical Attending Behaviors	
	Comments
1. Direct eye contact 0 1 2 3 4	
2. Warmth and concern reflected in facial expression 0 1 2 3 4	
3. Eyes at same level as client's 0 1 2 3 4	
4. Appropriately varied and animated facial expressions 0 1 2 3 4	
5. Arms and hands moderately expressive; appropriate gestures 0 1 2 3 4	
6. Body leaning slightly forward; attentive but relaxed 0 1 2 3 4	
7. Voice clearly audible but not loud 0 1 2 3 4	
8. Warmth in tone of voice 0 1 2 3 4	
9. Voice modulated to reflect nuances of feeling and emotional tone of client messages 0 1 2 3 4	
10. Moderate speech tempo 0 1 2 3 4	
11. Absence of distracting behaviors (fidgeting, yawning, gazing out window, looking at watch) 0 1 2 3 4	
12. Other 0 1 2 3 4	

Rating Scale:
0 = Poor, needs marked improvement
1 = Weak, needs substantial improvement
2 = Minimally acceptable, room for growth
3 = Generally high level with a few lapses
4 = Consistently high level

Competency Notes

C1 Demonstrate Ethical and Professional Behavior

- Demonstrate professional demeanor in behavior, appearance, and oral, written, and electronic communication.

C2 Engage Antiracism, Diversity, Equity, and Inclusion in Practice

- Demonstrate cultural humility applying critical reflexivity, self-awareness, and self-regulation to manage the influence of bias, power, privilege, and values in working with clients and constituencies acknowledging them as experts of their own lived experiences.

C6 Engage with Individuals, Families, Groups, Organizations, and Communities

- Use empathy, reflection, and interpersonal skills to effectively engage diverse clients and constituencies.

C7 Assess Individuals, Families, Groups, Organizations, and Communities

- Demonstrate respect for client self-determination during the assessment process collaborating with clients and constituencies in developing mutually agreed-on goals.

C9 Evaluate Practice with Individuals, Families, Groups, Organizations, and Communities

- Select and use appropriate methods for evaluation of outcomes.

Assessment: Exploring and Understanding Problems and Strengths

Chapter Overview

Assessment involves gathering information and formulating it into a coherent picture of the client and their circumstances. Assessments serve as the basis for ongoing client–social worker interactions, including goal setting, intervention implementation, and progress evaluation. This chapter focuses on the fundamentals of assessment and the strategies used in assessing presenting problems and strengths. Chapter 9 describes the characteristics considered when examining and portraying a client's functioning and their relationships with others and with the surrounding environment. Together, Chapters 8 and 9 explain how to effectively assess the client's interpersonal functioning and their related social systems and environments. All the skills introduced in the preceding chapters are employed when creating a comprehensive assessment. As you learn about assessment, keep these prior skills in mind and refer to them as needed.

As a result of reading this chapter, you will be able to:

- Understand that assessments involve both gathering information and synthesizing it into a working hypothesis.

- Identify the distinctions between *assessment* and *diagnosis*.

- Explain what the *Diagnostic and Statistical Manual of Mental Disorders*, Fifth Edition (*DSM-5*) is and how it is organized.

- Explain how to utilize the strengths-based perspective to capture client capacities and resources in assessment.

- Recognize the risks of ethnocentric assessments and the importance of cultural humility and anti-oppressive practice.

- Identify the roles that knowledge and theories play in framing assessments and the structural implications of those approaches.

- Identify the sources of data from the client's ecosystem that may inform the social workers' assessments.

- Identify questions to bear in mind while conducting an assessment.

- Understand how to conduct a telesocial work assessment.

- Recall the various elements of problem analysis.

The EPAS Competencies in Chapter 8

This chapter will give you the information needed to meet the following practice competencies:

- Competency 1: Demonstrate Ethical and Professional Behavior

- Competency 2: Engage Antiracism, Diversity, Equity, and Inclusion in Practice

- Competency 4: Engage in Practice-Informed Research and Research-Informed Practice

- Competency 7: Assess Individuals, Families, Groups, Organizations, and Communities

The Multidimensionality of Assessment

Human problems—even those that appear to be simple at first glance—involve a complex interplay of many factors. Rarely do sources of problems reside solely within one individual or within a single source from that individual's environment. Therefore, a comprehensive assessment should use the ecological perspective introduced in Chapter 2 to address individual functioning while also considering the larger social context (e.g., family, work/school, social conditions, racism, oppression, cultural factors) that impact the client. For example, the social worker should consider dynamic interactions among the individual's biophysical, cognitive, emotional, cultural, behavioral, familial, and community systems and the relationship between those systems and the client's problems. Not every system plays a significant role in your client's situation. However, overlooking relevant systems may result in an assessment that is incomplete at best and irrelevant or erroneous at worst. Interventions based on poor assessments may be ineffective, misdirected, or even harmful.

In addition to considering the multiple ecological systems impacting the client, social workers should conduct a culturally humble assessment rooted in anti-oppressive practice (AOP). The social work value of competence demands that social workers have the knowledge, skills, and values to practice effectively with a wide array of potential clients. This includes being familiar with the history and the effects of oppression, racism, and trauma. You should also examine your own positionality and understand how your race, gender, education, and role as a social worker give you opportunities and power that your client may lack. In addition to this foundation, before meeting with a client and conducting an initial assessment, you should familiarize yourself with the cultural implications of your client's experiences. For example, if your clientele includes immigrants or refugees, you might research their countries of origin and possible events or injustice that could have necessitated their relocation (e.g., genocide, oppressive governmental regimes, gang violence). If your clientele includes gender-diverse individuals, you should learn about historic and ongoing mechanisms of oppression that effect the access to and quality of employment, housing, and health care. Cultural humility reminds social workers to have conversations about differences, discrimination, and racism. For some clients, these conversations may need to occur even before the assessment to encourage trust and confidence in the social worker. In summary, while attending to the client's immediate concern or presenting problem, you should also consider the multiple systems that impact the client and be alert to your own positionality relative to them and their concerns.

Defining Assessment: Product and Process

The word assessment has two central meanings in the social work context. First, the term *assessment* refers to the written products that result from the process of understanding the client. Although assessments are commonly written after the first one to two sessions, they can be written at any time to synthesize a case. A written assessment summarizes the client's presenting problem(s); current functioning including mood, affect, and cognition; treatment goals; social, medical, and mental health history; sources of strength and adversity; possible resources; and factors contributing to the problem. Because assessments must constantly be updated and revised, it is helpful to think of an assessment as a complex working hypothesis based on the most current data available.

Written assessments range from comprehensive biopsychosocial reports to brief analyses about very specific topics, such as the client's mental status, substance use, capacity for self-care, or suicidal risk. An assessment may summarize progress on a case or provide a comprehensive overview to facilitate client transfer to another resource or termination of the case. The scope and the focus of the written product and of the assessment itself varies depending on three factors: the *role* of the social worker, the *setting* in which the social worker works, and the *needs* presented by the client. For example, a school social worker's assessment of an elementary school student may focus on the history and the pattern of disruptive behaviors in the classroom, as well as on the classroom environment itself. A social worker in a family services agency seeing the same child may focus more broadly on the child's developmental history and their family's dynamics, as well as on the troubling classroom behavior. A social worker evaluating the child's eligibility to be paired with an adult mentor would look at the family situation, the child's existing social supports, and other information to determine their interest and readiness for a prospective match.

In addition to a written product, assessment also refers to the ongoing process that occurs between a social worker and a client in which the social worker is constantly gathering information and analyzing and synthesizing it in order to maintain an accurate and updated picture of the client and their needs and strengths. Social workers engage in the process of assessment from the beginning of their contact with the client until the relationship's termination, which may occur days, weeks, months, or even years later. Thus, assessment is a fluid and dynamic process that involves receiving, analyzing, and synthesizing new information as it emerges during the entire course of a given case. In the first session, the social worker generally elicits abundant information and then assesses the information's meaning and significance as the client–social worker interaction unfolds. This moment-by-moment assessment guides the social worker in deciding which information is salient and merits deeper exploration and which is less relevant to understanding the client and the presenting problem. After gathering sufficient information to illuminate the situation, the social worker analyzes it and, in collaboration with the client, integrates the data into a tentative formulation of the client's problem. Some potential clients do not proceed with the social worker beyond this point. If their concerns can be best handled through a referral to other resources, if they do not meet eligibility criteria, or if they choose not to continue the relationship, contact often stops here.

Should the social worker and the client continue to work together, assessment continues, although it is not a central focus of the work. Clients often disclose new information as the problem-solving process progresses, casting the original assessment in a new light. Sometimes this new insight emerges as the natural result of coming to know the client better. In other cases, individuals may withhold vital information until they are certain that the social worker is trustworthy and capable. As a result, preliminary assessments often turn out to be inaccurate and must be discarded or drastically revised.

In settings in which social work is the primary profession, the social worker often conducts assessments independently or in consultation with colleague(s) including members of other disciplines. Assessments also represent opportunities to determine whether the agency and the particular social worker are best suited to address the client's needs. The social worker may identify the client's eligibility for services (based, for example, on the client's needs, insurance coverage, or enrollment criteria) and make a referral to other resources if either the program or the social worker is not appropriate to meet the person's needs.

In settings in which social work is not the only (or not the primary) profession (e.g., schools, hospitals, correctional facilities), the social worker may be a member of an **interdisciplinary** team. As a member of an interdisciplinary team, social workers collaborate with other professionals to provide comprehensive client care. In these situations, the assessment may be a collaborative effort between team members. While the social worker often compiles the assessment, various team members provide information for the assessment. For example, in a school setting, an interdisciplinary team might be comprised of the social worker, school psychologist, occupational therapist, school nurse, teachers, administrators, and parents. In this case, the school nurse would provide the health history for an initial assessment, while the teacher would provide information an academic ability, and the psychologist would provide information on testing and so on. The assessment process may take longer because of the time required for all team members to complete their individual assessments and reach collective agreement during group meetings. However, the collaboration and unique knowledge contributed from each team member can enhance treatment and improve client outcomes.

Assessment Focus

Although some information is commonly gathered in all assessments, the focus of a particular assessment interview and assessment formulation varies according to the social worker's task, mission, theoretical framework, and the client's presenting problem. For example, a social worker who is investigating an allegation of child endangerment will ask questions and draw conclusions related to the level of risk and safety in the case. A social worker whose expertise lies in cognitive behavioral theory will structure the assessment to address the effects of misconceptions or cognitive distortions on the client's feelings and actions. A social worker using the AOP framework will focus on social hierarchies and be cognizant of their own power and positionality. The AOP framework influences the direction of the discussion, and questions focus on how oppressive hierarchies impact clients' lives and their presenting problem(s) and on how privilege, oppression, identity, context, and power impact client diagnosis and treatment (Veltman & La Rose, 2016). For example, a social worker might ask about how experiences of racism, oppression, and/or sexism have impacted the client's presenting problem. These examples do not mean that in these cases the social worker focuses only on those topics but rather that the interview and the written assessment are guided by the social worker's mission, theory, setting, and clinical focus.

Typically, an initial social work assessment, conducted with new clients over the first one or two sessions, takes the form of a biopsychosocial assessment and is global in nature. The purpose of initial assessments is to paint a comprehensive picture of the client and their presenting problem and strengths. Information on the nature and the root of the presenting problem is included as well as physical and mental health history, family and social history, substance use, past work and education, mental and emotional functioning, trauma and developmental history, and strengths and resources. As noted previously, this initial assessment is often revised as additional information surfaces over the course of treatment.

Assessment and Diagnosis

It is important to clarify the difference between diagnoses and assessments. Diagnoses are labels or terms that may be applied to an individual or their situation. A diagnosis provides a shorthand categorization based on specifically defined criteria. It can reflect a medical condition (e.g., end-stage renal disease, type 2 diabetes), mental disorder from the DSM-5 (e.g., depression, agoraphobia), or other classification (e.g., student with a learning disability). Diagnostic labels serve many purposes. For example, they provide a language through which professionals and patients can communicate about a commonly understood constellation of symptoms. The use of accepted diagnostic terminology facilitates research on problems, identification of appropriate treatments or medications, and linkages among people with similar diagnosis. For example, diagnosing a set of troubling behaviors as bipolar disorder helps the client, their physician, and the social worker identify necessary medication and therapeutic services, including group supports (discussed in Chapters 11 and 16). The diagnosis may comfort the individual by helping put a name to their experiences. It may also help the client and family members learn more about the condition, locate support groups, and stay abreast of developments in understanding the disorder.

However, there is a negative side to diagnoses. Although such labels provide an expedient way of describing complex problems, they do not tell the whole story. Diagnoses can become self-fulfilling prophecies, wherein clients, their families, and their helpers begin to define the person only in terms of the diagnostic label. This distinction is highlighted by comparing the use of diagnostic labels and saying, "Joe is schizophrenic" to using person first language and saying, "Joe has schizophrenia," or "Joe was diagnosed with schizophrenia." Although diagnostic labels hold a lot of power, they can sometimes be bestowed in error (the result of misdiagnosis or diagnostic categories that change over time), and they may obscure important information about the client's difficulties and capacities. Referring to a client

as having an "intellectual developmental disability," for example, may speak only to that individual's score on an IQ test, not to their level of daily functioning, interests, goals, joys, and challenges.

At this point, assessment steps in. Assessments describe the symptoms that support a particular diagnosis but also help us understand the client's history and background, the effect of the symptoms on the client, the available support and resources to manage the problem, and so on. In other words, diagnoses may result from assessments, but they tell only part of the story.

The Diagnostic and Statistical Manual (DSM-5)

The *Diagnostic and Statistical Manual,* Fifth Edition (*DSM-5*) is an important tool for understanding and formulating mental and emotional disorders (American Psychological Association, 2013b). New to the *DSM-5* is the inclusion of the International Classification of Diseases, 11th Revision (ICD-11) in parenthesis following each *DSM-5* diagnostic. The ICD-11 is a commonly used system to codify both health and mental health disorders and determine the incidence and the prevalence of symptoms, factors that influence health status, and causes of injury or illnesses (World Health Organization, 2020). ICD codes are commonly needed for insurance reimbursement. Thus, social workers should be familiar with this resource.

Diagnostic systems such as the *DSM-5* have come under fire for several reasons, including excessive focus on individual pathologies rather than strengths and/ or societal and environmental factors. Critics suggest that the manual is bound by time and culture (e.g., included research focuses on North America), throwing the validity of the categorizations into dispute. The latest revision, *DSM-5,* was released in May 2013, and although the *DSM* provides useful language for common understanding, it must be employed with caution and humility.

Criticisms notwithstanding, the *DSM-5* is widely used by professionals and consumers. Assessments and DSM diagnoses are often required for insurance reimbursement and other forms of payment for services, and many social workers work with individuals who have received mental health diagnoses from a previous provider. You will need specialized knowledge and training to be thoroughly familiar with the *DSM* system and apply it to the complexities of human behavior and emotions. This section will acquaint you with the features of the classification system and serve as a reference point for discussions in Chapter 9 about prominent cognitive and affective diagnoses.

DSM disorders are assigned a three- to five-digit code, with digits after the decimal point specifying the severity and course of the disorder. Thus, for example, 296.21 would represent major depressive disorder, single episode, mild (American Psychological Association, 2013a). For each disorder, the manual uses a standardized format to present relevant information. The sections contain:

- Diagnostic criteria
- Subtypes/specifiers
- Recording procedures
- Diagnostic features
- Associated features supporting diagnosis
- Prevalence
- Development and course
- Risk and prognostic factors
- Specific culture, gender, and age features
- Functional consequences of the specific diagnosis
- Differential diagnosis
- Comorbidity

The manual attempts to describe the conditions it covers. It does not use a specific theoretical framework, recommend appropriate treatments, or address the causation or etiology of a disorder except in unique circumstances. Resources such as *The Synopsis of Psychiatry* (Sadock et al., 2021) and *DSM-5 Clinical Cases* (Barnhill, 2014) are helpful materials to prepare for regular use of the manual and to develop the clinical acumen for making and using diagnoses.

Sources of Information for Assessments

Where do social workers get the information on which they base their assessments? Numerous sources can be used individually or in combination. The following are the most common:

1. Information provided by the client

   - Background sheets or other intake forms the clients complete
   - Interviews with clients (e.g., explanation, history, and views about the problem, significant contributing events)
   - Client self-monitoring (e.g., keeping a journal of anxious thoughts)

2. Collateral information (e.g., relatives, friends, physicians, teachers, employers, and other professionals)

3. Tests or assessment instruments
4. Social workers personal experiences with the client

   - Direct observation of clients' nonverbal behavior
   - Direct observation of interactions between partners, family members, and group members
   - Personal experiences of the social worker based on direct client interactions

We go over each of these sources in more depth below.

Information Provided by the Client

The information obtained from client interviews is usually the primary source of assessment information. The skills described in Chapters 5 and 6 for structuring and conducting effective interviews help in establishing a trusting relationship and acquiring the information needed for assessment. It is important to respect clients' feelings and reports, to use empathy to convey understanding, to probe for depth, and to check with the client to ensure that your understanding is accurate. Interviews with child clients may be enhanced or facilitated by playing games, drawing and art activities, and other play therapy techniques.

Client self-monitoring is also a potent source of information (Bronson, 2022), that produces a rich and quantifiable body of data and empowers the client by turning them into a collaborator in the assessment process. In self-monitoring, clients track symptoms in logs or journals, write descriptions, and record feelings, behaviors, and thoughts associated with particular times, events, symptoms, or difficulties. The first step in self-monitoring is to recognize the occurrence of the event (e.g., signs that lead to anxiety attacks, temper tantrums by children, episodes of drinking or gambling). Using self-anchored rating scales (Jordan & Franklin, 2003) or simple counting measures, clients and/or those around them can keep a record of the frequency or intensity of a behavior. How often was Charles late for school? How would Shayla rate the severity of her anxiety in the morning, at noon, and in the evening? Which nights did Louis have difficulty sleeping? Did this difficulty relate to events during the day, medications, stresses, or anything he ate or drank?

A major advantage of self-monitoring is that the process itself requires the client to focus attention on patterns. As a result, clients gain insights into their situations and the circumstances surrounding their successes or setbacks. The process of recording also assists in evaluation because progress can be tracked more precisely by examining data that show a reduction of problematic behaviors or feelings and an increase in desirable characteristics. Client self-monitoring is an example of the ongoing nature of assessment. A social worker would ask a client to begin self-monitoring after the initial social work assessment was conducted and would use the data to refine the treatment plan.

Collateral Contacts

Another source for assessment data is collateral contacts—that is, information provided by relatives, friends, teachers, physicians, child-care providers, and others who possess essential insights about relevant aspects of clients' lives. Collateral sources are of particular importance when the client's ability to generate information may be limited due to developmental capacity or functioning. For example, parents, guardians, and other caregivers are often the primary source of information about a child's history, functioning, resources, and challenges. Similarly, assessments of individuals with memory impairment or cognitive limitations are enhanced by the data that collaterals (family members, caregivers, or friends) can provide.

Social workers must exercise discretion when deciding that such information is needed and in obtaining it. Clients can assist in this effort by suggesting which collateral contacts might provide useful information. Their written consent (through agency release of information forms) is required prior to contacting these sources.

In weighing the validity of information obtained from collateral sources, it is important to consider the nature of their relationship with the client and the ways in which that might influence these contacts' perspectives. For example, members of the immediate family may be emotionally involved or exhausted by the individual's difficulties and unconsciously skew their reports accordingly. Individuals who have something to gain or to lose from pending case decisions (e.g., custody of a child, residential placement) may be less credible as collaterals than individuals who do not have a conflict of interest or are further removed from case situations. Conversely, individuals who have limited contact with the client (such as other service providers) may have narrow or otherwise distorted views of the client's situation. As with other sources of information, input from collateral contacts must be viewed critically and weighed against other information in the case.

Assessment Instruments

Assessment instruments, including psychological tests, screening instruments, and assessment tools are another possible source of information. Some of these tests are administered by professionals such as psychologists or educators who have undergone special training in the administration and scoring of assessment tools. In these cases, social workers might receive reports of the testing and incorporate these findings into their psychosocial assessments or treatment plans. In other cases, social workers can administer assessment tools. For example, the Patient Health Questionnaire (PHQ-9; Kroenke et al., 2001) and the Beck Depression Inventory (BDI-II; Beck et al., 1996) have well-established validity and reliability, can be effectively administered and scored by clinicians from a variety of professions, and can assist practitioners in evaluating the seriousness of a client's condition. Importantly, both tools have been rigorously tested and are functional measures of depression for a wide variety of race/ethnicities (Keum et al., 2018; Makhubela, 2016).

Tests and screening instruments are useful and expedient methods of quantifying data and behaviors. They are also essential components in evidence-based practice in that they "enhance the reliability and validity of the assessment and provide a baseline for monitoring and evaluation" (O'Hare, 2015, p. 7). Consequently, tests and screening instruments play an important role in case planning and intervention selection. To use these tools effectively, however, practitioners must be well grounded in test theory and in the characteristics of specific tests. Instruments can be biased and have poor reliability or poor validity; some are ill-suited for certain populations and thus should be used with extreme caution. For example, many instruments were tested on white, middle-class samples and thus may be ineffective for racially and culturally diverse samples (Aisenberg, 2008). To avoid the danger of misusing these tools, social workers should thoroughly understand any instruments they are using or recommending and seek consultation in the interpretation of test administered by other professionals. It is vital to ensure the chosen tool is suitable for the demographics of your specific client (e.g., gender, age, race/ethnicity, presenting problem). Sources such as Fischer, Corcoran, and Springer (2020) can acquaint social workers with an array of available instruments and their proper use.

Social Worker's Personal Experience with the Client

A final source of information for assessment is the social worker's personal experience based on direct interaction with the client. You may react in different ways to different people, and these insights can prove useful in understanding how others respond to the client. For example, you may view certain individuals as withdrawn, personable, dependent, caring, manipulative, seductive, assertive, overbearing, or determined. These impressions should be considered in light of other information you are gathering about the client and their circumstances. For instance, a client who reports that others take them for granted and place unreasonable demands on them may appear to you to be meek and reluctant to make their needs known, even in stating what they want from counseling. These observations may provide you with clues about the nature of the client's complaint about being exploited by others.

Direct observation of nonverbal behavior adds information about emotional states and reactions such as anger, hurt, embarrassment, and fear. The social worker must be attentive to nonverbal cues such as tone of voice, tears, clenched fists, vocal tremors, quivering hands, a tightened jaw, pursed lips, variations of expression, and gestures and link these behaviors to the topic or the theme during which they arise. The social worker may share these observations in the moment ("Your whole body deflated when you were telling me what they said") or note them to be included with other data ("The client's voice softened, and they had tears in their eyes when talking about their spouse's illness").

Observations of interactions between spouses or partners, family members, and group members are also often enlightening. Social workers may be surprised at the differences in people's reports of their relationships and the behaviors they demonstrate in those relationships. A social worker may observe a father interacting with his daughter, impatiently telling her "I know you can do better." In an earlier session, however, the father may have described his behavior to her as "encouraging." Direct observation may reveal that his words are encouraging whereas his tone and gestures are not. Social workers must also be cognizant of reciprocal interactions, the interactions between a person and their external world; the person acts upon and responds to the world, and those actions affect the external world's reactions (and vice versa). For example, a parent may complain about having poor communication with an adolescent, attributing the difficulty to the fact that the teenager is sullen and refuses to talk. The adolescent, in turn, may complain that it is pointless to talk with the parent because the latter consistently pries, lectures, or criticizes. Each participant's complaint about the other may be accurate, but each unwittingly behaves in ways that have produced and now maintain their dysfunctional interaction. After noting these transactions, the social worker can then help the family recognize and change these patterns.

Chapter 10 includes guidance about observing family interactions and gathering information about family system functioning.

Some cautions are warranted in relying on your own observations as clients may not behave with the social worker as they do with other people. Apprehension, involuntariness, and the desire to make a good impression may all skew a person's presentation. Also, initial impressions can be misleading and must be confirmed by other sources of information or additional contact with the person. All human perceptions are subjective and may be influenced by our own interpersonal patterns and perceptions. Your reactions to clients may be affected by your own life experiences. Before drawing even tentative conclusions, scrutinize your reactions to identify possible biases, distortions, or actions on your part that may have contributed to the behavior you are observing. Self-awareness and understanding implicit bias are indispensable to drawing valid conclusions from your interactions with others.

Assessments that draw from multiple sources of data can provide a thorough, accurate, and helpful representation of the client's history, strengths, and challenges. However, social workers must be attuned to the advantages and disadvantages inherent in different types of input and weigh those carefully in creating a comprehensive picture of the client. Each source plays a pivotal role in addressing the many areas a thorough assessment should cover.

Areas of Focus in Assessments

As noted in earlier chapters, good practice requires you to use a variety of communication methods to encourage the client to tell their story. The questions presented under each heading in this section are not necessarily intended to be asked in the assessment but instead are meant to be used as a guide or checklist to ensure that you have not overlooked a significant factor in your assessment of the problem.

Priorities in Assessments

Although an assessment is guided by the setting in which it is conducted, certain priorities in assessment influence all social work settings. Without prioritization, social workers run the risk of conducting unbalanced, inefficient, or misdirected evaluations. Initially, three questions should be assessed in all situations:

1. *What does the client see as their primary concerns or goals?*

The first question to consider when meeting with a client is: what is the client's presenting problem or concern? Assuming there are no pressing health/safety concerns (e.g., suicidality) or legal mandates, the social worker should then assess the presenting problem in more depth. You should begin by exploring the client's presenting problem. Sometimes this question is a simple, open-ended inquiry: "What brings you in to see me today?" or "I'm glad you came in. How can I help you?" Sometimes referred to as "starting where the client is," these questions highlight social work's emphasis on self-determination and commitment to assisting individuals (when legal, ethical, and possible) to reach their own goals. Questions such as these allow the client an opportunity to express their concerns and help give direction to the questions that follow.

2. *What (if any) current or impending legal mandates must the client and social worker consider?*

If clients are mandated to receive services or face other legal concerns (e.g., a probation requirement or the consequence of a child maltreatment complaint), this factor may shape the nature of the assessment and the way that clients present themselves. For example, an adult protection worker must assess the risk of abuse, neglect, or other danger to an older client, regardless of whether the client shares those concerns. Further, the nature of the mandate, referring information, and the client's perception of the referral frames the early part of the first interview.

3. *What (if any) potentially serious health or safety concerns might require the social worker's attention?*

Social workers must be alert to health problems and other conditions (e.g., suicidality, homicidally) that may place clients at risk. For example, if the client were currently suicidal, assessing that would take precedence over other presenting problems. An assessment focused on a client's employability following incarceration may need to take a different direction if the client reports self-destructive thoughts, hazardous living conditions, substance use, untreated injuries, predatory roommates, or other issues of more immediate concern. Although the profession places high value on self-determination, social workers must act—even if it means overruling the client's wishes—in situations that present "serious, foreseeable, and imminent harm" (NASW, 2021).

Another consideration at the first interview is whether any danger exists that the client might engage in self-harm or harm someone else. Some referrals—for example, in emergency services—clearly involve the risk for harm, which should be discussed and evaluated at the outset. In other instances, the risk may be more subtle. For example, a client may open an interview by saying, "I'm at the end of my rope ... I can't take it any longer." The social worker should respond to this opening by probing further: "Can you tell me more ...?" or "When you say you can't take it, what do you mean by that?" If additional information raises the social worker's concerns about the danger for suicidal or aggressive behavior, more specific questioning should follow, geared toward assessing the lethality of the situation.

Whatever the client's presenting problem, if shared information gives rise to safety concerns, the social worker must redirect the interview to focus on the degree of danger. If the threats to safety are minor or manageable, the practitioner may resume the interview's focus on the presenting problem that brought the person in for service. However, if the mini assessment regarding harm to self or others reveals serious or imminent risk, the focus of the session must be on ensuring safety rather than continuing the more general assessment. Chapter 9 describes the process for conducting a suicide lethality assessment and other sources offer additional guidelines for interviewing about self-harm and assessing the degree of risk in various situations (Erbacher, Singer, & Poland, 2015; The American Psychological Association, 2020a).

After answering these three fundamental questions, the social worker goes on to explore the client's functioning, interactions with their environment, problems and challenges, strengths and resources, developmental needs and life transitions, and key systems related to the case.

Identifying the Presenting Problem

Your initial contacts with clients will concentrate on identifying the presenting problem, uncovering the sources of this problem, and engaging the client in planning appropriate remedial measures. In Chapter 9, we will discuss the other elements to assess in biopsychosocial assessment; however, here, we focus mainly on how to assess the presenting problem.

It is important to find out the specific indications of the problem, how the problem manifests itself, and what the consequences are. When asked to describe their problems or concerns, people often respond in generalities. The description typically involves a deficiency of something needed (e.g., health care, adequate income or housing, companionship, harmonious family relationships, self-esteem) or an excess of something that is not desired (e.g., fear, guilt, temper outbursts, marital or parent–child conflict, addiction). In either event, the presenting problem often results in feelings of disequilibrium, tension, and apprehension. The emotions themselves are often a prominent part of the problem configuration, which is one reason

Working with Minors

When working with children and adolescents, it is helpful to first meet with the caregiver and the child together to discuss your role, confidentiality, and the general presenting problem. It is then important to meet alone with the caregiver to obtain a more in-depth understanding of the presenting problem; caregivers might not feel comfortable talking openly in front of the child, and it is, therefore, necessary to meet with caregivers alone. Finally, the social worker should then meet alone with the child/adolescent to assess their view of the presenting problem. Caregivers and children/adolescents might have differing opinions and views about the nature of the presenting problem and might be more likely to express their honest views alone with the social worker. Throughout work with minors, it is vital that the social worker continually check in with caregivers about the client's behavior and any changes at home; this allows for an accurate and comprehensive ongoing assessment of the child/adolescent.

why empathic communication is such a vital skill during the interview process.

Accurately understanding the presenting problem is significant because it reflects the client's impetus for seeking help. The presenting problem is distinct from the **problem for work** (e.g., the problem that the social worker and the client ultimately focus on). The problem(s) that bring the client and the social worker together initially may not, in fact, end up being the focus of goals and interventions later in the relationship. As the helping process progresses, increased information sharing, insights, and trust may reveal factors that change the focus of work and goals for service. The assessment process may reveal to you and the client whether the problem for work differs from the one that brought them to your service. For example, a client may come in seeking help for ongoing anxiety. However, as work unfolds, it may become apparent that a history of childhood trauma is the root of this anxiety, and the problem for work shifts from addressing symptoms of anxiety to working through past trauma. The anxiety is not disregarded or ignored, but it is no longer the focus of therapy sessions.

The presenting problem is also important because it suggests areas to be explored in assessment. If the difficulty described by parents involves their adolescent's truancy and rebellious behavior, for example, the exploration includes the family, school, and peer systems. As the exploration proceeds, it may also prove useful to explore the parental system if difficulty in the marital relationship appears to be negatively affecting the parent–child relationship. If learning difficulties appear to contribute to the truancy, the cognitive and perceptual subsystems of the adolescent may need to be assessed as part of the problem. The presenting problem thus identifies systems that are constituent parts of the predicament and suggests the resources needed to ameliorate it.

Severity of the Problem

Assessing the severity of the problem involves answering the question: How severe is the problem, and how does it affect the client? You may also assess factors that increase or decrease problem severity. It is important to assess severity in order to evaluate whether clients have the capacity to continue functioning in the community or whether hospitalization or other strong supportive or protective measures are needed. When functioning is temporarily impaired by extreme anxiety and loss of emotional control, such as when people experience acute posttraumatic stress disorder, short-term hospitalization may be required. The intensity of the situation will necessarily influence your appraisal of the client's stress, the frequency of sessions, and the speed at which you need to mobilize support systems.

Meanings that Clients Ascribe to Problems

The next element of assessment involves understanding and describing the client's perceptions and definitions of

C2

the problem. What meaning does the client ascribe to the problem(s)? The meanings people place on events (**meaning attributions**) are as important as the events themselves because they influence the way people respond to their difficulties. For example, a parent might attribute their child's suicide attempt to their grounding the child earlier in the week. A job loss might mean shame and failure to one person and a routine and unavoidable part of economic downturn for another. Determining these views is an important feature of assessment. Exploratory questions such as the following may help elicit the client's meaning attributions:

- "What do you make of their behavior?"
- "What were the reasons for your parents' disciplining you?"
- "What caused the eviction?"
- "What are your views as to why you didn't get a promotion?"

Discovering meaning attributions is also vital because these beliefs about cause and effect may represent powerful barriers to change. It is, therefore, important to understand client perceptions about why events have occurred. For example: "My family has the gene for lung cancer. I know I'll get it, and there's nothing we can do about it," or "I've never been an affectionate person. It's just not in my character."

Fortunately, many attributions are not permanent. People are capable of cognitive flexibility and are open—even eager—to examine their role in problematic situations and want to modify their behavior. When meaning attributions such as those listed previously are encountered, it is vital to explore and resolve them before attempting to negotiate change-oriented goals or to implement interventions. When working with children and adolescents, it is vital to assess the meaning that both the client and their caregiver ascribe to the problematic behavior and to investigate any potential distorted thought attributions. Although the child is the identified client, the caregiver's view of the problem will significantly affect the child and their success in therapy.

Sites of Presenting Problems

Determining where the presenting problem occurs may provide clues about which factors trigger it. For example, children may have tantrums in certain locations but not in others. Adults may be anxiety-free in certain environmental contexts but not in others. Some older individuals become more confused in community settings than at home. Determining where the presenting problem occurs can assist you in identifying patterns that warrant further exploration and in pinpointing factors associated with the behavior in question.

Identifying where the presenting problem does not occur is also valuable because it provides clues about the features that might help in alleviating the problem and identify situations in which the client experiences relief from difficulties. For example, a child may act out in certain classes at school but not in all of them. What is happening in the incident-free classes that might explain the absence of symptoms or difficulties there? How can it be replicated in other classes? A client in residential treatment may gain temporary respite from overwhelming anxiety by visiting a cherished aunt on weekends. In other instances, clients may gain permanent relief from intolerable stress by changing employment, discontinuing college, or moving out of relationships when tension or other unpleasant feeling states are experienced exclusively in these contexts.

Temporal Context of Presenting Problems

Determining when problematic behaviors occur also offers valuable information. The onset of a depressive episode, for example, may coincide with a season or the anniversary of a loved one's death. Family problems may occur when one parent returns from work or travel, at bedtime for the children, at mealtimes, when visitations are beginning or ending, or when children are getting ready for school. Similarly, couples may experience severe conflict when partners are working different shifts, after participation by either partner in activities that exclude the other, or when one or both have been drinking. These clues can shed light on the patterns of clients' difficulties, indicate areas for further exploration, and lead to helpful interventions.

In addition, certain circumstances or behaviors may typically precede problematic behavior. A family member may say or do something that precipitates an angry, defensive, or hurt reaction by another. Pressure from the landlord about past due rent may result in tension and impatience between family members. A child's outburst in the classroom may follow certain stimuli, such as teasing by a classmate. Events that precede problematic behavior are referred to as antecedents. Antecedents often give valuable clues about the behavior of one participant that may provoke or offend another participant, thereby triggering a negative reaction, followed by a counter negative reaction, thus setting the reciprocal interaction in motion. In addition to finding out about the circumstances preceding troubling episodes, it is important to learn about the consequences or outcomes associated with problematic behaviors. These results may shed light on factors that perpetuate or reinforce the client's difficulties.

Frequency of Presenting Problems

The frequency of problematic behavior provides an index to both the pervasiveness of a problem and its effects on the participants. As with the site and timing of symptoms, information on frequency helps you assess the context in which problems arise and the pattern they follow in the client's life. Services for clients who experience their problems on an ongoing basis may need to be more intensive than for clients whose symptoms are intermittent. Determining the frequency of problematic behaviors thus helps to clarify the degree of difficulty and the extent to which it impairs the daily functioning of individuals and their families. Assessing the frequency of problematic behaviors also provides a baseline against which to measure behaviors targeted for change. Making subsequent comparisons of the frequency of the targeted behaviors enables you to evaluate the efficacy of your interventions.

Duration of the Problem

Another important dimension vital to assessing problems relates to the history of the problem—namely, how long it has existed. In addition, it is important to find out why the client is seeking help now. Knowing when the problem developed and under what circumstances assists in further evaluating the degree of the problem, unraveling psychosocial factors associated with the problem, determining the source of motivation to seek assistance, and planning appropriate interventions. Often, significant changes in life situations, including even seemingly positive ones, may disrupt a person's equilibrium to the extent that they cannot adapt to changes.

Events that immediately precede decisions to seek help are particularly informative. Sometimes referred to as **precipitating events**, these antecedents often yield valuable clues about critical stresses that might otherwise be overlooked. Clients often report that their problems have existed longer than a year. Why they chose to ask for help at a particular time is not readily apparent, but uncovering this information may cast their problems in a somewhat different light. For example, a parent who complained about their teenager's long-standing rebelliousness did not seek assistance until they became aware (one week before calling the agency) that their child was engaging in an intimate relationship with a person in their 20s. The precipitating event is significant to the call for help and would not have been disclosed had the practitioner not sought to answer the critical question of why they were seeking help now. In some instances, people may not be fully aware of their reasons for initiating the contact, and it may be necessary to explore what events or emotional experiences occurred shortly before their decision to seek help.

Determining the duration of problems is also vital in assessing clients' levels of functioning and in planning appropriate interventions. This exploration may reveal that a person's adjustment has been marginal for many years and that the immediate problem is simply an exacerbation of long-term multiple problems. In other instances, the onset of a problem may be acute, and clients may have functioned at an adequate or high level for many years. In the first instance, modest goals and long-term intermittent service may be indicated; in the second instance, short-term crisis intervention may suffice to restore them to their previous level of functioning.

Assessing Strengths

In addition to thoroughly assessing the client's presenting problem, it is also vital to assess client strengths. Indeed, the process of assessment is often criticized for being overly focused on client deficits because a specific diagnosis is often needed in order to receive reimbursement for services (Aboraya, 2007). As noted in Chapter 2, the strengths perspective counters the focus on pathology and highlights the importance of attending to clients' strengths, including available supports, coping mechanisms, and problem-solving abilities. Social workers should infuse their assessments with the strengths-based perspective and ask questions such as:

1. How have you been coping with your presenting problem?
2. What resources or supports have you been using?
3. What qualities do you have that have enabled you to keep going in the face of such difficulty and stress?

The following list emphasizes strengths that are often overlooked or taken for

C7

Central Questions to Assess the Presenting Problem

1. How **severe** is the problem?
2. What **meaning** does the client ascribe to the problem?
3. **Where** does the problem occur?
4. **When** does the problem occur?
5. **How often** does the problem occur?
6. **How long** has the problem existed?

granted during assessment. In addition to the prior questions, these strengths can be highlighted by the social worker as a means of bolstering client confidence and illustrating their capacity for overcoming their presenting problem.

1. Facing problems and seeking help
2. Taking a risk by sharing problems with the social worker—a stranger
3. Persevering under difficult circumstances
4. Being resourceful and creative in making the most of limited resources
5. Seeking to further knowledge, education, and skills
6. Expressing caring feelings to family members and friends
7. Asserting one's rights rather than submitting to injustice
8. Being responsible in work or financial obligations
9. Seeking to understand the needs and feelings of others
10. Having the capacity for introspection or perspective taking
11. Demonstrating self-control
12. Functioning effectively in stressful situations
13. Demonstrating the ability to consider alternative courses of actions and the needs of others when solving problems

Another way to incorporate strengths into your assessment is to use Resources, Options, Possibilities, Exceptions, Solutions (ROPES; Graybeal, 2001). Assessing **resources** focuses on your client's personal resources and strengths as well as those embedded in their family, social environment, and community. Examining **options** emphasizes the choices your client has and focuses on the present by looking at accessible resources and available resources that have not yet been leveraged. Assessing **possibilities** helps your client creatively imagine their future and think about possible options they have not yet tried. An assessment of **exceptions** asks the client about moments when the problem does not happen or is different and how the client has survived and endured their difficult circumstances. Finally, assessing **solutions** helps the client think of creating solutions by asking them about what is currently working, what their successes have been, and what they are doing that they will continue to do (Graybeal, 2001). Whatever checklists or mnemonic devices you use, attending to strengths, assets, and power provide a more balanced and hopeful assessment.

The Interaction of Other People or Systems

Exploring the presenting problem usually identifies key individuals, groups, or organizations that are part of the client's situation. Relying on the ecological framework, it is important to find out what persons or systems are involved in the problem(s). An accurate assessment must consider all these elements and determine how they interact. An effective intervention plan should take these same elements into account, even though it is not always feasible to involve all participants in the change effort.

To understand more fully how the client and other involved systems interact to produce and maintain the problem, you must elicit specific information about the functioning and interaction of these various systems.

People commonly interact with the following ecological systems:

1. The family and extended family or kinship network
2. The social network (friends, neighbors, coworkers, associates, and acquaintances from faith communities, cultural or social groups)
3. Public institutions (educational, recreational, law enforcement and protection, mental health, social service, health care, employment, economic security, legal and judicial, and various governmental agencies)
4. Personal service providers (doctor, dentist, barber or hairdresser, bartender, auto mechanic, nursing aide, landlord, banker)
5. The faith community (religious leaders, lay ministers, fellow worshipers)

Understanding how the interaction of these elements plays out in your client's particular situation requires detailed information about the behavior of all participants, including what they say and do before, during, and after problematic events.

It is important to ensure that assessments are sensitive to the racism and the marginalization that exist across these ecological systems. For example, an assessment using the AOP framework would center racism and oppressive hierarchies as a main explanatory factor for the presenting problem. The assessment would examine how racism and discrimination present at the various ecological systems in the client's life cause and/or exacerbate the presenting problem. Rather than problematizing the individual's behavior and making the client responsible for change, the focus would be changing oppressive systems and discriminatory practices.

Assessing Needs and Wants

Problems commonly involve unmet needs and desires that result from a poor fit between these needs and the resources available. What unmet needs and/or wants impact the presenting problem? Determining unmet wants and needs is the first step in identifying which resources must be tapped or developed. If resources are available, but clients have been unable to access those resources, it is important to determine the barriers to utilization. Some people, for example, may suffer from loneliness not because of an absence of support systems but because their interpersonal behavior alienates others and leaves them isolated, or their loneliness may stem from shame or other feelings that keep them from asking for assistance from family or friends. Still other clients may appear to have emotional support available from family or others, but closer exploration may reveal that these potential resources are unresponsive to clients' needs. The task in such instances is to assess the nature of the negative transactions and to attempt to modify them to the benefit of the participants so that resources can be unblocked to address the client's wishes.

Human wants and needs include universal necessities (e.g., adequate nutrition, safety, clothing, housing, and health care) but also include personal changes (e.g., feel less depressed, improve social skill) or changes at other ecological levels (e.g., get along better with parents/friends/partner, get a new job, finish college). In determining clients' unmet needs and wants, it is essential to consider the developmental stage of the individual, couple, or family. For example, the psychological needs of an adolescent—for acceptance by peers, sufficient freedom to develop increasing independence, and development of a stable identity (including a sexual identity)—differ markedly from the typical needs of older persons—for

health care, adequate income, social relationships, and meaningful activities. As with individuals, families go through developmental phases that include both tasks to be mastered and needs that must be met if the family is to provide a climate conducive to the development and well-being of its members.

Although clients' presenting problems often reveal obvious needs and wants (e.g., "Our unemployment benefits have expired, and we have no income"), sometimes the social worker must infer what is lacking. Presenting problems may reveal only what is troubling the person on the surface, and careful exploration and empathic "tuning in" are required to identify unmet needs and wants. A couple, for example, may initially complain that they disagree over virtually everything and fight constantly. From this information, one could safely conclude that the pair wants a more harmonious relationship. Exploring their situation on a deeper level, however, may reveal that their ongoing disputes are a manifestation of unmet needs of both partners for trust, caring, appreciation, or companionship.

Identifying needs and wants also serves as a prelude to the process of negotiating goals. Expressing goals in terms that address needs and wants enhances the motivation to work toward goal attainment, as the payoff for goal-oriented efforts is readily apparent. Even though some desires may seem unachievable considering the individual's capacities or the opportunities in the social environment, these aspirations are still worthy of discussion. Goal setting is addressed in detail in Chapter 12.

Stresses Associated with Life Transitions

In addition to developmental stages that typically correspond to age ranges, individuals and families commonly must

C2

Common Client Wants and Needs

- To have less family conflict
- To feel valued by one's spouse or partner
- To be self-supporting
- To gain more self-confidence
- To have more freedom
- To control one's temper
- To overcome depression

- To have more friends
- To be included in decision-making
- To get discharged from an institution
- To make a difficult decision
- To master fear or anxiety
- To cope with children more effectively

adapt to other major transitions that are less age specific. Some transitions (e.g., geographical moves and immigrations, divorce, untimely deaths) can occur during virtually any stage of development. Many of these transitions can be traumatic, and the adaptations required may temporarily overwhelm the coping capacities of individuals or families. Separations (from a person, homeland, or familiar role) or transitions that are involuntary (job reassignment) or abrupt (a home is destroyed by fire) are highly stressful and may temporarily impair social functioning.

The person's history, concurrent strengths and resources, and past successful coping can all affect the adaptation to these transitions. The environment plays a crucial role as well. People with strong support networks (e.g., close relationships with family, kin, friends, and neighbors) generally have less difficulty in adapting to traumatic changes than do those who lack strong support systems. Assessments and interventions related to transitional periods, therefore, should consider the availability or lack of essential support systems.

The following are major transitions commonly encountered in across the life span:

Role and Developmental Transitions

- Work, school, career choices
- Health impairment
- Parenthood
- Geographic moves and migrations
- Marriage or partnership commitment
- Retirement
- Separation or divorce
- Single parenthood
- Death of a spouse or partner
- Military deployments

Many of these major transitions would also affect children or adolescents. In addition to these transitions, other milestones affect specialized groups. For example, in the LGBTQ+ community, the decision of how and when to come out to others is a significant experience. Life events such as graduations, weddings, and holidays may be more emotionally charged and take on greater complexity when there has been divorce or death in the family of origin. The parents and siblings of individuals with severe illnesses or disabilities may experience repeated losses if typical milestones such as sleepovers, graduations, dating, proms, marriage, and parenthood are not available to their loved ones. Retirement may not represent a time of release and relaxation if it is accompanied by poverty, poor health, or new responsibilities such as caring for ill family members or raising grandchildren (Gibson, 1999). Military deployments

and returns may be easier for service members than for reservists, in that the former typically have formal and informal supports on base, whereas reservists may deploy from decentralized communities. Migration to a new country, whether to escape violence and human rights violations in one's home country or to pursue better educational or employment opportunities, is also a stressful transition.

Clearly, life transitions can be differentially affected by individual circumstances, culture, socioeconomic status, and other factors. Social workers must be sensitive to these differences and take care not to make assumptions about the importance or unimportance of a transitional event or developmental milestone.

Cultural, Societal, and Social Class Factors

As we noted earlier, ethnocultural factors influence what kinds of problems people experience, how they feel about requesting assistance, how they communicate, how they perceive the role of the professional, and how they view various approaches to solving problems. It is, therefore, vital to consider how ethnocultural, societal, and social class factors bear on the problem(s). It is important to consider the degree to which the client experiences a goodness of fit with the culture in which they are situated. Social workers should rely on the ecosystems perspective and assess functioning and cultural fit at each ecological level, including individual, family, peer group, community, and larger cultural context. For example, an adolescent who has recently immigrated might feel comfortable at home surrounded by familiar language, food, and cultural practices but might struggle at school and in the larger community when faced with unfamiliar language and cultural practices. Many people are members of multiple cultures, so their functioning must be considered in relationship to both their predominant cultural identity and the majority culture. For example, an older lesbian may feel alienated or accepted depending on how the culture around her views her age, gender, and sexual orientation. This goodness of fit is a consideration when examining any person in the context of their environment. Individuals from the same ethnic group may vary widely in the degree of their acculturation or their comfort with biculturalism, depending on several factors—for example, the number of generations that have passed since their original emigration, the degree of socialization to the majority culture, and interactions with the majority culture.

C2

Cultures vary widely in their prescribed patterns of child rearing, communication, family member roles, mate selection, and care of the elderly—to name just a few areas of differentiation. For example, to whom in a Latinx family would you properly address concerns about a child's truancy? What are normative dating patterns in the gay and lesbian communities? At what age is it proper to allow a child to babysit for younger siblings? What are appropriate expectations for independence for a young adult with Down syndrome? How might Laotian parents view their child's educational aspirations? Answers to these questions vary across clients. Knowing about Laotian parents is not the same as knowing about the specific Laotian parents you are serving. Thus, being knowledgeable about a given group is necessary but not sufficient for understanding the behavior of individual members of the group. It is important to remember that social work practice must be tailored to meet the cultural needs of each individual client (Substance Abuse and Mental Health Services Administration, 2014).

While your client is the expert in their own culture, you should still seek out knowledge of your client's cultural norms. Otherwise, you may make serious errors in assessing both individual and interpersonal systems because patterns that are functional in one cultural context may prove problematic in another and vice versa.

Errors in assessment can lead to culturally insensitive interventions that may aggravate rather than diminish clients' problems. The necessary knowledge about cultural norms is not easy to obtain. It requires a baseline understanding of historical experiences, religious traditions and spiritual beliefs, individual and group oppression, world views, cultural customs and practices, and beliefs about wellness and illness. Social workers must acknowledge their own position of power and examine personal biases and stereotypes (National Association of Social Workers, 2015). It is important to note that being a member of the same racial/ethnic group as the client does not preclude social workers from engaging in these steps of cultural humility and learning.

Other Issues Affecting Client Functioning

Numerous other circumstances and conditions can affect the client's presenting problem and their capacity to address it.
For this reason, it is often wise to specifically explore the use of alcohol or other substances; exposure to abuse, violence, or other trauma; the presence of health problems, depression, or other mental health problems; and the use of prescription medication. For example,

`C7`

Assessments with Immigrant and Refugee Populations

Broadly speaking, both immigrants and refugees were born in one country and moved to another country; however, immigrants left their home country voluntarily (often due to violence or lack of economic opportunities), and refugees were forced to leave their country due to human rights violations (Potocky & Naseh, 2019). These clients may present with a unique constellation of presenting problems given possible personal and/or intergenerational trauma, assimilation and acculturation challenges, language barriers, discrimination, oppression, and limited social and financial supports. Immigrant and refugee clients often experience problems not only at the individual level (e.g., poor mental health, trauma) but also at the larger community level including discrimination and lack of access to health are or employment (Potocky & Naseh, 2019).

The following questions can help guide assessments with immigrant and refugee populations:

1. What led them to leave their country and come to the United States?

2. Did they experience abuse or violence in their home country, including seeing others get hurt?

3. Did they spend time in a refugee camp and what was that experience like?

4. What language do they speak at home? In the community? In the community? How are they managing interacting in the English-speaking community?

5. What clubs, groups, religious, or faith community do they belong to? (Learn about rival groups, or differences within a cultural group, as appropriate; Clemons, 2014).

It is also important to assess for personal and/or intergenerational trauma and to assess for any trauma that occurred in the process of coming to the United States. All assessments should include a trauma assessment, but this is especially true when working with immigrant and refugee populations. Trauma is often the reason people leave their home county, and then they encounter more trauma during their journey and once they arrive in the United States.

have other risk factors (e.g., alcohol or substance abuse, physical or sexual abuse) affected the functioning of the client or family members? Depending on the setting, purpose of the interview, and the information gathered, the social worker may focus the interview specifically on the client's medical history, past trauma, substance use, or mental health. Further information on these assessments is included in Chapter 9.

It is particularly important to assess for trauma including interpersonal trauma (e.g., sexual, physical, and/or emotional abuse; childhood neglect; witnessed abuse; sexual assault), other trauma (e.g., natural disaster that destroyed a home; immigration; seeking asylum; racism; poverty), and adverse childhood experiences (ACES). ACES are traumatic events that occur prior to age 18 and include experiencing violence, abuse, or neglect; witnessing home or community violence; having a family member attempt or complete a suicide; living in a family with substance misuse, mental health problems, parental separation or divorce, or family member incarceration (CDC, 2020). ACES are associated with long-term negative effects on health and well-being, including increased risk of injury, sexually transmitted infections, maternal and child health problems, teen pregnancy, involvement in sex trafficking, disease, and mental health problems, including suicide (CDC, 2020). Therefore, assessing for past (adult clients) or present (children/adolescent clients) ACES is an important part of the assessment process.

It is important to note that ACES were established using a mostly white (75% white) sample (Dube et al., 2001), and, therefore, the role of racism, oppression, and historical trauma were not considered, though their significance is undeniable (Sacks & Murphey, 2018). Historical trauma refers to trauma extending across multiple generations of a specific cultural, racial, or ethnic group and is related to oppressive events that harmed the group such as slavery, racial and religious caste systems, the Holocaust, and the colonization of Native Americans (Administration for Children & Families, n.d.). Although the current ACE questionnaire does not assess historical trauma, social workers can employ specific assessment skills to explore this impact. Using a genogram may help reveal the influence of historic patterns on current functioning. In addition, social workers should "attend to the ways in which the personal story provides insights into the broader social and historical story" (Finn, 2021; p 208). In doing so, social workers encourage clients to elaborate on their experiences and emotional responses, demonstrate curiosity and humility, and honor resistance when it arises.

Emotional Reactions

When people encounter problems in daily living, they typically experience emotional reactions to those problems. What are the client's emotional reactions to the problem(s)? It is important to explore and assess these reactions for three major reasons. First, people often gain relief simply by expressing troubling emotions. Common reactions to problem situations are worry, agitation, resentment, hurt, fear, and feeling overwhelmed, helpless, or hopeless. Being able to express painful emotions in the presence of an understanding and concerned person is a source of great comfort.

C7

Trauma Assessment

Given the ubiquity of trauma and the fact that failing to address trauma specific symptoms can impede successful treatment, it is important to screen all clients for trauma (SAMHSA, 2014). While the specifics of trauma-informed care are discussed in Chapter 13, here we provide important guidelines for trauma assessment (SAMHSA, 2014):

- All clients should be asked about a history of trauma, including ACES (CDC, 2020). Consider using a validated screening instrument, which can be less overwhelming for some clients than an interview.

  - Trauma symptom checklist (Elliot & Briere, 1992)
  - PTSD checklist (Weathers et al., 2013)

  - Adverse Childhood Experiences Questionnaire (Got your ACE score, n.d.)

- Do not ask clients to give a detailed description of traumatic events.

- Focus on how trauma symptoms impact the clients' current functioning and how the client has coped with these symptoms.

- Let the client know you will use this information to create a treatment plan for them.

- Ensure the client feels safe and contained before leaving.

Second, because emotions strongly influence behavior, the emotional reactions of some people impel them to behave in ways that exacerbate or contribute to their difficulties. In some instances, people create new difficulties because of emotionally reactive behavior. Burdened by financial concerns, an individual may become impatient and verbally abusive, behaving in ways that frighten, offend, or alienate employers, customers, or family members. An adult experiencing unremitting grief may cut themselves off from loved ones who cannot stand to see them cry. Powerful emotional reactions may thus be an integral part of the overall problem configuration.

Third, intense reactions often become primary problems, overshadowing the antecedent problematic situation. A parent may become depressed over an unwed daughter's pregnancy; a person may react with anxiety to unemployment or retirement; and culturally dislocated persons may become angry following relocation, even though they may have fled intolerable conditions in their homeland. Other individuals may react to problematic events by experiencing feelings of helplessness or panic that can become immobilizing. In these instances, interventions must address the overwhelming emotional reactions as well as the situations that triggered them.

Coping Efforts and Needed Skills

"What have you tried to address this problem?" "How has it worked?" The coping methods that people employ give valuable clues about their levels of stress and functioning. Exploration may reveal that a person has few coping skills but rather relies on rigid patterns that are unhelpful or cause further problems. Some people follow avoidance patterns—for example, dealing with trouble at home by immersing themselves in tasks or work, withdrawing, or numbing with drugs or alcohol. People may cope with interpersonal conflict through controlling behavior or by passivity and submissiveness. Others demonstrate flexible and effective coping patterns which prove insufficient under extreme or cumulative stressors.

Examples of strengths-based questions that could guide your assessment of coping include:

C7

1. How has the client coped with the problem(s), and what are the required skills to resolve the problem?
2. What are the client's coping skills, strengths, and resources?
3. What support systems exist or need to be created to enhance client coping?
4. What additional external resources could enhance client coping?

Important insights from exploring coping efforts emerge when you are discussing mechanisms and skills that have worked in the past but no longer work. In such instances, it is important to explore carefully what has changed. For example, a person may have been able to cope with the demands of one supervisor but not with a new one who is more critical and aloof or who is of a different generation, race, or gender. A parent may have skillfully raised an infant but be stymied by a toddler.

By exploring the different circumstances, meaning attributions, and emotional reactions, you should be able to identify subtle differences that account for the varied effectiveness of your clients' coping patterns in different contexts. This part of assessment is also essential before exploring treatment goals or service options. Offering premature interventions may be rejected by a client who says, "I did that already, and it didn't work." Without understanding what the client has tried and when, how, and how much it helped, it is risky to jump to conclusions about what assistance is needed now.

Support Systems

C7

An essential part of understanding individuals involves understanding the systems with which they interact. This can include formal systems such as schools, medical clinics, mentors, or home health aides, and natural or informal systems such as neighbors, family, or friends. These systems are also important parts of problem and strengths assessments. Formal support systems may be part of the problem (the school that cannot provide adequate educational resources to help a child with disabilities or the child welfare service plan that is too demanding for the client to manage along with part-time work and adequate child care). Natural support systems may also be part of the problem configuration (the family member whose criticism fuels a client's despair or the peer network that encourages theft and drug use). On the flip side, formal and informal networks can be part of coping and client strengths ("I can always go to my caseworker when I'm feeling overwhelmed;" "My neighbor watches my kids when I get called into work;" "Our church helped us with food and companionship when my mother was sick").

Resources Needed

When people request services, you must determine (1) whether the services requested match the function of the agency and (2) whether the staff possesses the skills required to provide high-quality service. If not, a referral is needed to assure that the individual receives the highest-quality service to match the needs presented. Referrals may also be required to complement services within your agency or to obtain a specialized assessment that are factored into your services (e.g., "Are the multiple medications that the client is taking causing the recent cognitive problems?"; "Are there neurological causes for these outbursts?"). In such instances, the practitioner performs a broker or case manager role, which requires knowledge of community resources or at least knowledge of how to obtain relevant information. Fortunately, many communities have online resource information centers that can help clients and professionals locate needed services. Irrespective of the presenting problem, people can often benefit from help in a variety of areas—from financial assistance, transportation, and health care to child or elder care, recreation, and job training. Problem exploration helps identify possible needs.

Assessing Children and Older Adults

Social workers are often employed in settings serving children and older adults. Assessment with these populations utilizes many of the skills and the concepts noted elsewhere in this chapter and in earlier sections. However, children and older clients also present unique requirements because of their respective life stages and circumstances. This section is intended to acquaint you with some of the considerations that can shape assessments with these populations.

Because children and older adults often present for service in relation to systems of which they are already a part (e.g., hospitals, schools, families, assisted living facilities), your assessment may be bound by those systems in a multidisciplinary team. This can present a challenge for creating an integrated assessment, as several caregivers, agencies, and professionals may hold pieces of the puzzle while none possesses the mandate or the capacity to put all the pieces together.

Children and older adults typically appear for service because someone else (e.g., parents/caregivers, teachers, neighbors, health-care providers) has identified a concern. This factor does not automatically mean that the client will be resistant but indicates that they may disagree about the presence or nature of the problem or be unmotivated to address it.

Data Sources and Interviewing Techniques

In working with children and older adults, particularly very young children or the frail elderly, you may need to rely more than usual on certain data sources (e.g., collateral contacts or observations) and less than usual on other sources (e.g., the client's verbal reports). A trusting relationship with the client's primary caregivers is vital to your access to the client and dramatically affects the rapport you achieve with them. Depending on the child's level of development or the older adult's capacities, they may have difficulty helping you construct the problem analysis or identify strengths or coping methods. Data sources, such as interviews with collateral contacts (e.g., parents/caregivers, teachers, family members, service providers), may be essential in completing an assessment, although these can be open to various distortions.

Assessment Techniques Specific to Children and Adolescents

Child assessments differ from adult assessments and, in addition to collecting information via interviews and observation, expressive modalities (e.g., artwork, games, dolls, puppets), may also serve as sources of information for the assessment (Konrad, 2019). Watching a child play or create art can provide important information. For example, are the child's interests and skills age appropriate? What mood is reflected in the child's play, and is it frequently encountered in children of that age and situation? Do themes in the child's play relate to possible areas of distress? How often do those themes recur? How does the child relate to you and to adversity (the end of play, losing, or a wrong move in a game)? How well can the child focus on the task? In this context, play is not a random activity meant for the child's distraction or enjoyment. Instead, you must use it purposefully and be attentive to the implications of various facets of the experience. Your impressions of the significance and meaning of the play activities should be evaluated based on other sources of information.

A developmental assessment may be particularly relevant for understanding the child's history and current situation. With this type of assessment, a parent or other caregiver provides information about the circumstances of the child's delivery, birth, and infancy; achievement of developmental milestones (e.g., language, motor development); family description and atmosphere (e.g., ages of family members, who lives in the home, financial situation, family relationship dynamics); interests (e.g., hobbies, friends); significant life transitions (e.g., separations from caregivers, loss of loved ones to death); presenting problem including history of the problem; and school history (Jordan & Hickerson, 2003; Konrad, 2019; Levy & Frank, 2011). This information helps form impressions about the child's experiences and life events, especially as they may relate to their current functioning.

As with other forms of assessment, you must organize and interpret what you discover from all sources to paint a meaningful picture of the child's history, strengths, and needs. This assessment then serves as the basis of your goals and interventions. Knowledge of child development is useful to help gauge whether the child is in the developmentally appropriate range (Konrad, 2019).

Assessment Techniques Specific to Older Adults

Comprehensive, competent assessments for geriatric clients also involve items that go beyond the typical multidimensional assessment. For example, functional assessments would address the client's ability to perform various tasks, typically activities of daily living (ADLs)—those things required for independent living such as dressing, hygiene, feeding, and mobility. Instrumental ADLs (IADLs) involve measuring the client's ability to perform more intricate tasks such as managing money, taking medicine properly, completing housework, shopping, and preparing meals (American Psychological Association, 2020b). Because some of the IADL skills may be traditionally performed by one gender or another, you should ascertain the client's baseline functioning in these areas before concluding there are deficits or declines in IADLs. For example, driving is a complex skill, an area of significant risk and a powerful symbol of independence, and the potential loss of this freedom often evokes strong emotions in the elderly population; thus, assessment of driving capacity is a specialized and important aspect of functioning (Gallo, 2005).

Aging is not synonymous with decline and death. However, the inevitability of decline and death are often on the minds of older adults and are thus worthy of exploration. Assessments in these areas might include reminiscence and discussion of spirituality and beliefs, all of which examine how the older client derives purpose and meaning in his or her life (Richardson & Barusch, 2006). Clients may have significant concerns about incapacitation and death and find that they have few outlets with which to share those thoughts. Too often, family, friends, and helping professionals shut down such conversations as morbid or signs of giving up. Social workers can effectively open these conversations with questions such as:

1. How would you describe your philosophy of life? How satisfactory is this philosophy to you now?

2. How do you express your spirituality? What kinds of practices enhance your spirituality?

3. How do you understand hope? What do you hope for?

4. What helps you the most when you feel afraid or need special help?

5. What is especially meaningful to you now? What do you live for? What is most important to you now?

6. How has being sick made any difference for you in what or how you believe?

7. What do death, being sick, suffering, pain, and so on mean to you?

8. How do you handle feelings such as anger, doubt, resentment, guilt, bitterness, and depression? How does your spirituality influence how you respond to such feelings? Do you want to receive spiritual support to deal with such feelings or thoughts about them?

9. Where do you get the love, courage, strength, hope, and peace that you need? (Dudley et al., 1995)

These questions may be appropriate for clients at the end of life and in other situations where traumatic experiences or existential crises are part of the presenting problem.

Physical examinations and health histories also take on particular importance in the assessment of older clients. These assessments must consider the impact of limitations in vision and hearing, restricted mobility and reaction times, pain management, sexual functioning, and medication and disease interactions. Specialized and comprehensive evaluations require interdisciplinary teams with expertise in geriatric care. Assessing physical health is particularly important when working with older clients, as poor physical health is a significant risk factor for depression in this population.

For both very young and very old clients, direct observation of functioning may yield more reliable results than either self-reports or information from collateral sources. This may mean classroom visits, home visits, and other efforts to view the client in their natural setting. Specialized expertise is required to ensure that assessments are properly conducted and interpreted for these and other especially vulnerable populations.

Maltreatment

Children and older adults are both at particular risk for maltreatment at the hands of caregivers. Therefore, it is important for all professionals to understand the principles for detecting abuse or neglect and their responsibilities for reporting it. For both minors and older adults, mistreatment can be categorized into four areas: neglect, physical abuse, sexual abuse, and emotional or verbal abuse. For older persons, additional categories include self-neglect and financial exploitation (Bergeron & Gray, 2003; Donovan & Regehr, 2010). The specific definitions of various forms of abuse vary by jurisdiction (Rathbone-McCuan, 2008; Wells, 2008). Sometimes abusive individuals or their victims report abuse to the social worker. More commonly, abuse is covered by fear, confusion, and shame, and thus, the professional must be alert to signs of abuse, such as:

- Physical injuries: Burns, bruises, cuts, or broken bones for which there is no satisfactory or credible explanation; injuries to the head and face
- Lack of physical care: Malnourishment, poor hygiene, unmet medical or dental needs
- Unusual behaviors: Sudden behavioral changes, withdrawal, aggression, sexualized behavior, self-harm, fearful behavior at the mention of or in the presence of caregiver
- Financial irregularities: For the older client, missing money or valuables, unpaid bills, coerced spending (Donovan & Regehr, 2010; Mayo Clinic, 2007).

Social workers (including student workers) are mandated to report suspicions of child abuse to designated child protective agencies. Most jurisdictions also compel workers to report elder abuse, although it may be voluntary in some regions. All professionals should know the steps required in their setting and state for making an abuse report. It is often helpful for social workers, especially new social workers, to first discuss the case with a supervisor prior to making a report.

The Role of Knowledge and Theory in Assessments

"What you see depends on what you look for." This saying captures the roles that knowledge and theory play in shaping the questions that are asked in the assessment and the resulting hypotheses. Competent, evidence-based practice requires that assessments be informed by problem-specific knowledge (O'Hare, 2015). As a result, the social worker should consider the nature of the problem presented by the client at intake (e.g., explosive anger, hoarding, parent–child conflict, truancy) and refer to available research to identify the factors that contribute to, sustain, and ameliorate those problems. This knowledge helps the social worker know the relevant information to collect during the assessment.

For example, the literature might suggest that truancy is caused by a poor fit between the student's needs and the classroom environment or the teacher's attitude and methods, or it might stem from chaos at home in which children are not awakened for school, prepared for the day, or even expected to attend school. Truancy or poor academic performance could be due to vision or hearing problems, attention deficits, or learning disabilities. It may also arise from shame on the child's part about hygiene, dress, worthiness, bullying, or other negative peer experiences. Regardless of the factors involved, there is rarely a strictly linear, cause-and-effect explanation for truancy. Instead, the influence of some factors (e.g., poor vision or hearing) leads to behaviors (e.g., acting out or truancy) that distance the child from peers, irritate the teacher, and lead to a withdrawal by the student that puts them even further behind and, in turn, more likely to act out or withdraw further—a reciprocal interaction. Your understanding of the research and the theories on human behavior will help focus the assessment on those elements that are involved in a particular client's difficulties.

Theories

Theories shape social work assessments. The areas you explore in your interviews and the resulting impressions, goals, and interventions are guided by the theoretical orientation(s) you embrace. In Chapter 2, you were introduced to six perspectives that influence the approach to direct practice contained in this book. One of those perspectives, ecosystems theory, provides an overarching framework for conducting assessments. It takes into account intrapersonal systems (physical, emotional, cognitive, behavioral) and the surrounding environment such as social structures and institutions, community conditions, and formal and informal support systems. Like assessments influenced by other theoretical orientations, these multidimensional assessments look at role transitions, strengths and capacities, and patterns in thoughts, actions, and interpersonal relationships.

Other theoretical orientations with demonstrable efficacy shape the entire assessment. For example, behavioral theories focus on identifying and altering the antecedents and consequences that cause and maintain problematic behavior. As such, an assessment rooted in behavioral theory would focus on the conditions surrounding troubling behaviors, the conditions that reinforce the behavior, and the consequences and secondary gains that might result (Bronson, 2022; Sundel & Sundel, 2017). Behavioral theories have also expanded to include a focus on the maladaptive thoughts that contribute to problematic behaviors (e.g., cognitive behavioral therapy; Bronson, 2022). Assessments derived from these theories focus on the nature of the client's thoughts and schemas (cognitive patterns), causal attributions, the basis for the client's beliefs, and antecedent thoughts in problematic situations (Walsh, 2010).

Understanding human functioning has always included a focus on physical and biological factors. Specifically, neurobiology seeks to uncover the ways that the nervous system mediates behavior. A burgeoning area of research and theory development examines the neurobiological changes that occur when people are exposed to adversity and trauma (Rosenzweig & Sundborg, 2022). Employing this theory in practice requires knowledge of brain architecture and the ways it is activated and changed by toxic stress. Assessments from a neurotrauma lens also depend on understanding mind–body stress response systems and polyvagal theory, which describes the ways that the vagus nerve affects emotional regulation, social connection, and fear responses (Rosenzweig & Sundborg, 2022). Beyond the application to toxic stress, neurobiology has been applied to theories of aging, addictions, eating disorders, attention deficit and hyperactivity disorder, and other conditions.

While influential theories can focus on microscopic cellular changes, as in neurobiology, they can also focus on historic institutional conditions that shape behavior, opportunities, policies, and social systems. For example, critical theories focus on dismantling socially constructed identities (e.g., race, gender, sexual orientation) that create hierarchies of power, privilege, and oppression (Albritton et al., 2022). Critical race theory (CRT), feminist theory, and queer theory are examples of critical theories (Albritton et al., 2022; Finn, 2021). These theories fit well with the anti-oppressive practice (AOP) framework, as AOP encourages social workers to analyze their own positionality in social hierarchies and then counter the tendency to reenact societal oppression. A CRT-informed assessment, for example, would include questions about the role of racism and discrimination on client well-being and opportunities. As part of client psychoeducation, a CRT-guided social worker would present information and research regarding the negative impact of discrimination and racism on mental health (Kolivoski et al., 2014). An assessment might explore how this research and information relates to the clients' own experience, providing space for them to discuss their own experiences of oppression (Kolivoski et al., 2014). Assessments conducted from a social justice lens may center interventions away from the individual and instead lead to systems change to address inequities in power and opportunities (Finn, 2021).

Caveats about Using Knowledge and Theories

Naturally, there are cautions about the degree to which existing knowledge or theories influence assessment. Although they are helpful in predicting and explaining client behaviors and in structuring assessments and interventions, when applied too rigidly, theories may oversimplify the problem and objectify the individual client (Walsh, 2010). Adhering to a single preferred framework may obscure other relevant factors in the case, blind the practitioner to limits in existing theory or knowledge, and inhibit the pursuit of promising new knowledge and interventions, yet practicing from a multitheoretical perspective is more complicated than simply claiming to have an eclectic approach. Integrating the philosophies, empirical findings, and procedural techniques of several theories into a coherent approach is a sophisticated undertaking, though several approaches have been developed to assist with theoretical pluralism (Borden, 2021). Whether practicing from a single theory or one that incorporates multiple theories, you must employ proper training and critical thinking to effectively evaluate and apply the framework on behalf of your clients (O'Hare, 2015).

Telesocial Work

Although it is ideal to conduct assessments in person, electronically delivered social work has become increasingly common in the past decade, and its use escalated in 2020 because of the coronavirus (COVID-19) pandemic. Telesocial work via phone, video, and text allows clients to be treated in their own homes, which is especially helpful for residents of remote areas, older adults, and people who are homebound due to caregiving responsibilities, illness, or the lack of transportation. Indeed, the benefits of telesocial work include decreased barriers to treatment access, cost effectiveness, and a broad service availability (Racine et al., 2020). In addition, telesocial work creates a more intimate environment then the office by providing the social worker a window into the client's home. This offers clinicians a front-row seat to family interactions and provides information about client resources (e.g., comfortable furniture, TV) and safety in the home. The client also has a window into the social worker's home, which might enhance their feeling of connection to the social worker and increase trust. However, this can also engender boundary tensions, as home and family are revealed through the conversation.

Accompanying the convenience and efficiency of telesocial work services are unique limitations and complications. Telesocial work requires access to the internet and an electronic device such as a computer, laptop, tablet, or smart phone. Although 82% of U.S. households have an internet subscription (Ryan, 2018), people of color, older adults, rural residents, and individuals with lower levels of education and income are less likely to have internet service at home (Pew Research Center, 2020). Even with internet service, not all households have plans with unlimited access or the quality of connection needed for video meetings. Another challenge of teleservices is the absence of private, quiet, and safe spaces for social work interviews. Ideally, clients would be alone in a room with a closed door; however, this might not be possible in residences with shared or limited space; for example, during COVID-19 pandemic, many family members were working and/or taking online classes at home (Racine et al., 2020). This lack of privacy could impact a client's behavior, making an accurate assessment difficult for the social worker. Further, it is impossible for a telesocial worker to ensure that the client is alone, which is particularly troubling in cases of child abuse and/or domestic violence. The abuser could be in the room with the client, out of sight of the video monitor, which would hinder a client's ability to speak honestly and, therefore, make it impossible for the social worker to conduct a comprehensive assessment (Banks et al., 2020). The social worker should ask clients if they are in a safe and secluded area; however, not being with the client in person, it is impossible to ensure the client is alone, and, therefore, the social worker cannot ensure confidentiality. The limited scope of the camera and the quality of audio connections further restrict what mannerisms, intonations, and other communication cues the client conveys. Home studies for child placement or elder safety are particularly challenging due to the restricted range of vision and the lack of access to the sounds, smells, and other environmental features of the home. It is, therefore, difficult to conduct a thorough risk assessment via telesocial work.

It can also be difficult to assess client affect, especially with children, via telesocial work (Racine et al., 2020). For example, assessing dissociation can be particularly complex over video, as it can be difficult to ascertain if certain behaviors are a result of dissociation from trauma or a result from difficulty establishing rapport and connection with the social worker via electronic means. Given these difficulties, the social worker may need to ask additional questions when assessing affect electronically. For example, "I'm having a difficult time interpreting your facial expression. Could you explain how you're feeling right now?" or "I'm not sure how to interpret your facial expression. Can you help me?" It is important to remember that many people are uncomfortable with technology, which might limit their engagement, cause irritation or frustration, or otherwise affect the way they present themselves. Because disruptions in treatment may occur due to weak internet connections or malfunctioning technology, you should discuss contingency plans with clients prior to service engagement.

Assessments are important, complex, and multifaceted. They can be influenced by an array of factors that affect the ways that clients reveal themselves and their information and the ways social workers interpret what they hear and see. Deep knowledge helps social workers understand and synthesize information. For instance, understanding cultural practices, historic and contemporary forms of marginalization, the challenges of help-seeking, and other contextual features influence the questions that are asked and the meaning that is made of the answers.

Social workers need to approach assessments with humility and recognize that they are fluid and speculative. As such, you should treat clients' information with grace and generosity and avoid making pathologizing conclusions.

Summary

This chapter introduced the knowledge and the skills entailed in multidimensional assessment. A psychiatric diagnosis may be part of but is not the same as a social work assessment. The discussion in this chapter emphasized strengths and resources in assessments and the importance of relying on AOP and cultural humility. A framework for prioritizing what must be done in assessment was presented, along with the components of problem exploration and their application to specific populations. In Chapter 9, we will consider the assessment of intrapersonal and environmental systems and the terms and concepts used to describe their functioning, as well as the processes for writing effective assessments.

Competency Notes

C1 Demonstrate Ethical and Professional Behavior

- Use technology ethically and appropriately to facilitate practice outcomes.

C2 Engage Antiracism, Diversity, Equity, and Inclusion in Practice

- Demonstrate anti-racist social work practice at the individual, family, group, organizational, community, research, and policy levels, informed by the theories and voices of those who have been marginalized.
- Demonstrate cultural humility applying critical reflexivity, self-awareness, and self-regulation to manage the influence of bias, power, privilege, and values in working with clients and constituencies acknowledging them as experts of their own lived experiences.

C4 Engage in Practice-Informed Research and Research-Informed Practice

- Apply research findings to inform and improve practice, policy, and programs.

C7 Assess Individuals, Families, Groups, Organizations, and Communities

- Apply knowledge of human behavior and person-in-environment and other culturally responsive multidisciplinary theoretical frameworks when assessing clients and constituencies.
- Demonstrate respect for client self-determination during the assessment process collaborating with clients and constituencies in developing mutually agreed-on goals.

Skill Development Exercises

Exploring Strengths and Problems

On April 16, 2007, 23-year-old Seung-Hui Cho killed 32 people on the campus of Virginia Tech University before turning the gun on himself. In the months leading up to the murders, Cho had numerous encounters with mental health professionals. He had been declared an "imminent danger to self or others as a result of mental illness" on a temporary detention order from a Virginia District Court. Two students had filed complaints against him for bizarre phone calls and emails he had sent. Another student, his former roommate, called campus police stating that Cho could be suicidal. A poetry professor at the school recalled that he was menacing in class, and other students stopped attending after he began photographing them. This professor later removed Cho from the class and worked with him one on one. They also reported that the content of his poems and other writings was disturbing and seemed to have an underlying threat.

A South Korean national, Cho moved with his family to the United States at the age of 8. As a youngster, he was diagnosed with depression and selective mutism, a condition associated with social anxiety, and received therapy and special education services as a result. He was a successful elementary school student, but by middle school, he was apparently subject to mockery from fellow students because of his speech abnormalities, his accent, and his isolation.

Imagine that you worked in a setting where Seung-Hui Cho presented for service at age 10, 15, or 22, and address the following questions:

1. What sources of information would you use to better understand your client, their problems, and their strengths?

2. What cross-cultural concerns should you be aware of in this case?

3. What questions would you ask as part of problem analysis?

4. What transitional and developmental issues might be of particular interest?

5. What role would your client's diagnoses play in your assessment?

6. What environmental and interpersonal interactions are relevant in this case?

7. What consultation would be helpful to you in completing this assessment?

Note

1. See the U.S. Department of Health and Human Services Substance Abuse and Mental Health Services Administration (www.samhsa.gov), the North Carolina Evidence Based Practice Center (www.ncebpcenter.org), the National Institute of Mental Health (www.nimh.nih.gov), the Cochrane Collaboration (www.cochrane.org), and the Campbell Collaboration (http://www.campbell collaboration.org) for toolkits and other resources for evidence-based practice in an array of problem areas.

Chapter 9

Assessing Individual and Environmental Factors and Their Interaction

Chapter Overview

Chapter 9 reviews three key aspects of a comprehensive assessment: the client's personal functioning (physical, emotional, behavioral, and cognitive), the client's environment, and the transactions between the two. The chapter introduces these areas for examination and helps you develop an understanding of the difficulties and the assets to consider in all these systems. It also discusses how social worker–client differences can affect these factors.

As a result of reading this chapter, you will be able to:

- Understand how assessments capture the reciprocal nature of client systems.

- Learn the elements of intrapersonal functioning, including physical, emotional, cognitive, and behavioral.

- Assess the spiritual and environmental factors affecting the client system and evaluate how racism and oppression impact these factors.

- Know the questions to ask to assess substance use.

- Learn the diagnostic criteria for common thought and affective disorders.

- Recognize the elements of a mental status exam and a social history.

- Understand how to evaluate suicide risk and risk for violence.

- Know the do's and don'ts for writing assessments and examine examples of assessments.

The EPAS Competencies in Chapter 9

This chapter will give you the information needed to meet the following practice competencies:

- Competency 1: Demonstrate Ethical and Professional Behavior

- Competency 2: Engage Antiracism, Diversity, Equity, and Inclusion in Practice

- Competency 7: Assess Individuals, Families, Groups, Organizations, and Communities

The Interaction of Multiple Systems in Human Problems

Problems, strengths, and resources encountered in direct social work practice result from interactions among intrapersonal (e.g., internal functions, thoughts, perceptions, or reactions), interpersonal (e.g., communication and interactions between two or more people), and environmental systems (e.g., work, home, school, community). Difficulties are rarely confined to one of these systems. A functional imbalance in one system typically contributes to an imbalance in others. For example, individual difficulties (e.g., illness, feelings of worthlessness, depression) invariably influence how one relates to other people (e.g., withdrawal, irritability,). Interpersonal difficulties (e.g., job strain, parent–child discord) likewise affect individual functioning (e.g., stress, difficulty concentrating). Similarly, environmental deficits (e.g., racial microaggressions, inadequate housing, hostile working conditions, social isolation) affect individual and interpersonal functioning (e.g., stress, anger, relationship tensions).

The reciprocal effects among the major systems embodied in the person and environment are not limited to the negative effects of functional imbalance and system deficits. Assets, strengths, and resources also have reciprocal positive effects. A supportive environment may compensate for intrapersonal difficulties; similarly, strong interpersonal relationships may provide positive experiences that more than offset an otherwise impoverished environment.

A comprehensive assessment of the individual considers a variety of elements, including biophysical, cognitive/perceptual, affective (emotional), and behavioral factors and examines the ways that these interact and affect interactions with people and institutions in the individual's environment (see Figure 9-1). Keeping this in mind, the social worker's assessment may focus more sharply on some of these areas than others, depending on the nature of the client's difficulties, the reason for the assessment, and the setting in which the assessment is taking place. It is important to remember, however, that an assessment is just a snapshot of the client system's functioning at any point in time. As we noted in Chapter 8, the social worker's beliefs and actions and the client's feelings

Figure 9-1   Overview: Areas for Attention in Assessing Individual Functioning

---

INDIVIDUAL SYSTEMS

Biophysical Functioning

Physical characteristics and presentation

Physical health

Use and abuse of medications, alcohol, and drugs

Alcohol use and abuse

Use and abuse of other substances

Dual diagnosis: comorbid addictive and mental disorders

Cognitive/Perceptual Functioning

Intellectual functioning

Judgment

Reality testing

Coherence

Cognitive flexibility

Values

Beliefs

Self-concept

Affective Functioning

Emotional control and range of emotions

Appropriateness of affect

Suicidal risk

Depression and suicidal risk with children and adolescents

Depression and suicidal risk with older adults

Behavioral Functioning

Risk of aggression

Motivation

about seeking help impact the assessment. For all these reasons, care and respect are required when collecting and synthesizing assessment information into a working hypothesis for intervention.

Implicit Bias

Implicit bias refers to mental associations or stereotypes that are unconsciously triggered when thinking about or meeting people from different social groups (Payne et al., 2019). Implicit racial biases are the unconscious beliefs about people from different racial groups. Skin color is part of everyone's physical appearance. When we first see someone, whether a client or a person on the street, our brain immediately perceives race (Contreras et al., 2013). This means that before you have even exchanged words with a client, your brain has identified their race (and they yours), which could activate a host of implicit biases.

Everyone has implicit biases, but because they are unconscious, they can be difficult to detect. Recent research indicates that 54.4% of the population has a small level of self-reported preference for white, while 74.5% of the population has an implicit preference for white (Greenwald & Lai, 2020). In addition, research with social work students suggests that this group has biases against specific social problems (e.g., poverty) as well racial/ethnic minorities (Wahler, 2012). Implicit biases can also revolve around gender and gender identity, including transgender individuals. If you have not yet begun to examine your own implicit biases, it is vital that you begin this lifelong work now. Using the acronym IMPLICIT, the following eight steps serve as a useful guide (Edgoose et al., 2019):

1. *Introspection:* You must acknowledge that implicit bias exists and then learn about your own implicit bias. Taking the Implicit Associations Tests (Project Implicit, 2011; https://implicit.harvard.edu/implicit/selectatest.html) is a good first step.

2. *Mindfulness:* Stress increases our use of cognitive shortcuts, including implicit biases. Thus, practicing mindfulness (e.g., yoga, meditation, focused breathing) is one way to decrease the likelihood that you will rely on implicit racial biases during moments of stress.

3. *Perspective Taking:* Try to walk in someone else's shoes by considering experiences from the perspective of a person from stereotyped groups. Read novels, watch documentaries, listen to podcasts, and engage in positive interactions with stereotyped group members to increase psychological closeness to that group.

4. *Learn to Slow Down:* To recognize our own implicit biases, we must stop, think, and reflect.

When you interact with someone from a stereotyped group, examine your response, identify what responses are based on stereotypes, and reflect on why that response occurred. Think about how that biased response could be avoided in the future and replaced with an unbiased response.

5. *Individuation:* Use individual personal characteristics, not group stereotypes, to evaluate clients. Connect with individuals over common interests, shared experiences, or mutual purpose.

6. *Check Your Messaging:* Instead of trying to be color- or gender-blind, use evidence-based statements that decrease implicit bias such as welcoming and embracing multiculturalism and gender diversity.

7. *Institutionalize Fairness:* It is not enough for individuals to take actions to reduce their own implicit racial bias. Organizations must also commit and work to overcome it. A checklist to help an organization examine blind spots and biases can be helpful. Organizations can also display images that counter stereotypes.

8. *Take Two:* Counteracting implicit bias and working toward cultural humility is lifelong work and must be practiced consistently and constantly.

Understanding and examining your own implicit biases, especially regarding race and gender, enables you to engage more effectively with your clients and conduct just and thorough assessments.

Assessing Biophysical Functioning

Biophysical functioning encompasses physical characteristics, health factors, and genetic factors, as well as the use and abuse of drugs and alcohol.

Physical Characteristics and Presentation

People's physical characteristics and appearance may be either assets or liabilities. In many cultures, physical attractiveness is highly valued, and unattractive people may be disadvantaged in terms of their social desirability, employment opportunities, or marriageability. Social workers should take care to observe distinguishing physical characteristics that may affect social functioning. Attributes that merit attention include body build, dental health, posture, facial features, gait, and any physical anomalies that may create positive or negative perceptions about the client, affect their self-image, or pose a social liability.

How people present themselves is worthy of note before attributing meaning to their presentation. Individuals who walk slowly, display stooped posture, talk slowly and without animation, and show minimal changes in facial expression may be depressed, in pain, or overmedicated. Dress and grooming often reveal much about a person's morale and living conditions. The standard for assessing appearance is generally whether the dress is appropriate for the setting. Is the client barefoot in near-freezing weather or wearing a helmet and overcoat in the summer sun? Is the client dressed seductively, in lacy pajamas, or overdressed by wearing a prom dress for an appointment with the social worker? While attending to these questions, social workers should be cautious in the conclusions they reach. Cultural and societal norms and values dictate what is considered normal or appropriate. A disheveled appearance may indicate poverty, depression, the effects of the client's job, or a fashion statement. Being clothed in bright colors may indicate mania or simply a culture that favors wearing bright colors. As with other elements of assessment, your description of what you observe (collared shirt, dress pants, clean-shaven) should be separate from your assessment of it (well-groomed and appropriately dressed).

Other important factors associated with appearance include hand tremors, facial tics, rigid or constantly shifting posture, and tense muscles of the face, hands, or arms. Sometimes these characteristics reflect the presence of an illness, physical problem, or overmedication. They may also indicate a high degree of tension or anxiety, warranting exploration by the social worker. During the assessment, an effective social worker determines whether the anxiety displayed is normative for the given situation or whether it is excessive and might reveal an area for further discussion.

Physical Health

Poor physical health can contribute to depression, sexual difficulties, irritability, low energy, restlessness, anxiety, poor concentration, and a host of other problems. It is, therefore, important for social workers to consider their clients' state of health during the intake session. Social workers should determine if clients are under medical care and when they last had a medical examination. They should ensure that medical problems are not the source of difficulty by referring clients for medical evaluations, when appropriate, before attributing problems solely to psychosocial factors. However, social workers who are part of an integrated care team would rely on the team's medical personnel to conduct a physical and to learn about the client's health history.

A health assessment may also entail gathering information about illnesses in the client's family. Chapter 10 introduces genograms, similar to a family tree, which can be helpful in mapping out familial mental and physical health history. You may also find out about family history simply by asking. For example, "Has anyone else in your family ever had an eating disorder?" "Are you aware of other family members who have experience infertility?" or "How did your grandparents die?"

Assessing Use and Abuse of Medications, Alcohol, and Drugs

An accurate understanding of a client's biophysical functioning must include information on their use of both legal and illicit drugs. First, it is important to determine which prescribed and over-the-counter medications the client is taking, whether they are taking medication as instructed, and whether the medication is having the intended effect. You can assess this directly by asking: "What medications do you take?" and "How do these medications work for you?"

The second reason for evaluating drug use is that even beneficial drugs can produce side effects or unwanted reactions that affect the functioning of various biopsychosocial systems. Common side effects from medications include drowsiness, dry mouth, or stomach pains (FDA, 2018). However, side effects can be more severe and include disorientation, confusion, or muscle rigidity which may necessitate a referral for evaluation and medication changes.

Alcohol is a legal drug, but its abuse can severely impair health, disrupt family life, and create serious workplace and community problems. Similarly, the use of illicit drugs may have detrimental consequences for users and their families, and drug abuse brings further problems due to its connotation as a banned or illegal substance. In addition, users may engage in dangerous or illegal activities, such as prostitution or theft, to support their habits. Variations in the purity of the drugs used or the methods of administration (e.g., sharing needles) may expose users to risks beyond those associated with the drug itself. The following sections discuss how to assess use and dependence.

Alcohol Use and Abuse

Understanding a person's alcohol use is essential for a number of reasons. Clearly, problematic use may be related to problems in meeting work, school, and family obligations. Even moderate use may be a sign of escape or self-medication and lead to impaired judgment and risky behavior, such as driving while intoxicated. According to the Centers for Disease Control and Prevention (CDC, 2019), alcohol should be consumed in moderation, including up to one drink per day by women and two drinks per day by men. Indeed, heavy drinking for women is considered eight drinks or more per week and 15 or more drinks per week for men (CDC, 2020). You can assess alcohol use in the initial session by asking: "Now, I'd like to know about some of your habits. First, in an average month, on how many days do you have at least one drink of alcohol?" If alcohol is an element of the presenting problem, you might consider probing further by asking, for example: "What role do you see your alcohol use playing in this relationship conflict?"

Heavy drinking moves into alcoholism when an individual becomes preoccupied with making sure that the amount of alcohol necessary for intoxication always remains accessible. As a result, individuals may affiliate with other heavy drinkers to escape observation. As alcoholism advances, individuals may try to conceal use, as they hide bottles or other evidence, drink alone, and/or cover up drinking binges. It is vital that social workers assess client substance use as part of a routine biopsychosocial assessment.

There are validated instruments to assess alcohol or drug use that can be administered by the social worker or self-administered by the client. For example, commonly used tools include the Michigan Alcoholism Screening Test (MAST; Pokorny et al., 1972; Selzer, 1971) and the Drug Abuse Screening Test (DAST; Gavin et al., 1989). Some instruments use mnemonic devices to structure assessment questions. For example, the CRAFFT utilizes six questions to assess problematic alcohol use in adolescents (Knight et al., 2002), and the CAGE (Ewing, 1984) consists of four items in which an affirmative answer to any single question is highly correlated with alcohol dependence:

1. Have you ever felt you should **cut** down on your drinking?
2. Have people **annoyed** you by criticizing your drinking?
3. Have you ever felt bad or **guilty** about your drinking?
4. Have you had an **eye opener** first thing in the morning to steady your nerves or get rid of a hangover?

Additional questions for alcohol and substance abuse assessment are included in Table 9-1.

`C7`

Use and Abuse of Other Substances

People abuse many types of drugs in addition to alcohol. Because immediate medical care may be essential in instances of acute drug intoxication, and because abusers often attempt to conceal their use of drugs, it is important that practitioners recognize the signs of abuse of commonly used drugs (e.g., excessive drowsiness, dilated/constricted pupils, agitation). Common general indications of drug abuse include the following:

- Changes in attendance at work or school
- Decrease in normal capabilities (e.g., work performance, efficiency, habits)
- Poor physical appearance, neglect of dress and personal hygiene
- Use of sunglasses to conceal dilated or constricted pupils and to compensate for inability to adjust to sunlight
- Unusual efforts to cover arms to hide needle marks
- Association with known drug users
- Involvement in illegal or dangerous activities to obtain drugs

In assessing the possibility of drug abuse, it is important to elicit information not only from the client (who may not be a reliable reporter for several reasons) but also from people who are familiar with the habits and lifestyle of the individual. Likewise, the social worker should assess problems of alcohol and drug abuse from the ecosystems perspective and identify reciprocal interactions between the individual's use and the (conscious and unconscious) actions of their family, social contacts, health-care provider, and others.

Assessing the misuse and abuse of drugs by older adults is especially important due to increased social isolation, metabolic and health changes, and the likelihood of multiple prescribed medications. It is, therefore, vital to obtain an accurate account of the clients' medications through their self-reports and records or information from their health-care providers. Patients might take unprescribed medications, miss doses, take incorrect medication combinations, or consume incorrect dosages; the risk for this medication mismanagement is of particular concern for the elderly (O'Quin et al., 2015). Having the older client sign a release of information allows the social worker to consult directly with collateral contacts such as the prescriber or family members, obtain an accurate list of medications and dosages, and talk with caregivers who are responsible for monitoring and dispensing medications.

Dual Diagnosis: Addiction and Mental Health Disorders

Because alcohol and other drug abuse problems can co-occur with a variety of health and mental health problems (known as comorbidity), accurate assessment is important for proper treatment planning. To assess

Table 9-1 Interviewing for Substance Abuse Potential

The First Six Questions Will Help Guide the Direction of Your Interview, the Questions You Ask, and Your Further Assessment
1. Do you—or did you ever—smoke cigarettes? For how long? How many per day?
2. Do you drink alcohol?
3. What do you drink? (Beer, wine, liquor?)
4. Do you take any prescription medications regularly? If yes, which ones? What dosage? How do they make you feel?
5. Do you use any over-the-counter medications regularly? If yes, which ones? What dosage? How do they make you feel?
6. Have you ever used any other drugs (e.g., marijuana, cocaine, heroin)?
7. When was the last time you consumed alcohol and/or used drugs?
8. How much did you have to drink/use?
9. When was the last time before that?
10. How much did you have?
11. Do you always drink/use approximately the same amount? If not, is the amount increasing or decreasing?
12. (If it is increasing) Does that concern you?
13. Do most of your friends drink/use?
14. Do (or did) your parents drink/use?
15. Have you ever been concerned that you might have a drinking/drug problem?
16. Has anyone else ever suggested to you that you have (or had) a drinking/drug problem?
17. How does drinking/using help you?
18. Do other people report that you become different or change when you have been drinking/using (for example, more careless, angry, or out of control)?
19. Do you drink/use to get away from your troubles?
20. (If so) What troubles are you trying to get away from?
21. Are you aware of any way in which drinking/using is interfering with your work?
22. Are you having any difficulties or conflict with your spouse or partner because of drinking/using?
23. Are you having financial difficulties? Are they related in any way to your drinking/using?
24. Have you ever tried to stop drinking/using? How?

Source: From *Where to Start and What to Ask: An Assessment Handbook* by Susan Lukas. Copyright © 1993 by Susan Lukas. Used by permission of W. W. Norton & Company, Inc.

for co-occurring disorders (COD) social workers should address (SAMHSA, 2005):

- Background (e.g., family, trauma history, marital status, medical problems, education, housing status, education, employment, strengths, and resources)
- Substance use (e.g., age at first use, primary drugs used, patterns of drug use, past treatments, family history of substance use problems)
- Mental health problems (e.g., family history of mental health problems; client history of mental health problems, including diagnosis, hospitalizations, and other treatments; current symptoms and mental status; medications, medication adherence)

Depending on the combination of factors that affect them, clients may have difficulty seeking out and adhering to treatment programs. Furthermore, an understanding of the reciprocal interaction of mental health, social problems, and substance use may affect the social workers' assessment and resulting intervention. Some psychiatric problems (e.g., paranoia, depression) may emerge because of substance use. Social problems such as joblessness or incarceration may limit the client's access to needed treatment for substance abuse, and substance use may limit job and housing opportunities. Problems such as personality disorders may impede the development of ongoing trusting and effective treatment relationships needed to treat drug addiction.

If a client with a perceived substance use disorder attends treatment due to family pressure or court mandates, they might not perceive substance use as a problem. Even if a person seeks help voluntarily, they

American Society of Addiction Medicine Criteria

The American Society of Addiction Medicine (ASAM) criteria is a set of guidelines outlining the placement, continued stay, transfer, or discharge of clients with addiction and co-occurring conditions. These criteria provide health-care professions with a nomenclature for discussing the continuum of addiction services (ASAM, 2020). There are six dimensions that create a complete, biophysical assessment used for treatment planning across all levels of care:

1. Acute intoxication and/or withdrawal potential
   - Explore client's past and current experiences with substance use and withdrawal
2. Biomedical conditions and complications
   - Explore client's medical/health history and current physical conditions

3. Emotional, behavioral, or cognitive conditions and complications
   - Examine client's thoughts, emotions, and mental health issues
4. Readiness to change
   - Assess client's readiness, interest, and motivation to change
5. Relapse, continued use, or continued problem potential
   - Explore client's relationship with relapse and/or continued use
6. Recovery/living environment
   - Assess client's recovery or living situation and the surrounding people, places, and things

might not view substance use as the root of their problems. People may deny that illicit or licit substances are a problem and attempt to conceal the abuse by blaming others, lying, arguing, distorting, attempting to intimidate, diverting the interview focus, or verbally attacking the social worker. The social worker needs to express empathy and sensitivity, recognizing that such behaviors are often a subterfuge behind which lie embarrassment, hopelessness, shame, ambivalence, or anger.

When asking about alcohol use, be forthright in explaining why you are pursuing that line of questioning. Vague, wordy, or indirect questions tend to invite evasions and unproductive responses. The questions listed in Table 9-1 should be asked in a direct and compassionate manner. They address the extent and effects of the client's substance use, and the impact on their environment.

Assessing Cognitive/ Perceptual Functioning

People's perceptions of others, themselves, and events largely determine how they feel and respond to problems and other life experiences. Perceptions of identical events or circumstances vary widely according to the complex interaction of an individuals' belief systems, values, attitudes, state of mind, self-concept, and past experiences. A trauma-informed lens is particularly important when assessing client perceptions because past trauma impacts perceptions of the external world. For example, many trauma survivors experience hyperarousal, which can lead them to perceive danger and react strongly, even when the situation is safe (SAMSHAS, 2014). If someone accidently bumps into a child who has experienced trauma, that child may perceive a threat and react by sobbing inconsolably or by attacking the perceived offender. Both reactions seem extreme until the child's traumatic past is considered.

To understand and influence human behavior, you must be knowledgeable about how people think. Our thought patterns are influenced by a variety of factors addressed in this section:

- Intellectual functioning
- Judgment
- Reality testing
- Coherence
- Cognitive flexibility
- Values
- Beliefs
- Self-Concept

In the following sections, we briefly consider each of these factors and demonstrate their use in a mental status assessment (see Figure 9-2).

Intellectual Functioning

Understanding the client's intellectual capacity is essential for a variety of reasons. Your assessment of intellectual functioning allows you to adjust your verbal expressions to a level that the client can readily comprehend, and it will help you in assessing strengths and difficulties, negotiating goals, and planning tasks commensurate with the client's capacities. In most instances, a rough estimate of level of intellectual functioning is sufficient. In making this assessment, you may want to consider the client's ability to grasp abstract ideas, to engage in self-expression, and to analyze or think logically. Additional criteria include level of educational achievement and vocabulary employed, although these factors must be considered in relation to the person's previous educational opportunities, primary language, cognitive decline, or learning difficulties and other factors that can mask intellectual capacity.

When communicating with clients who have marked intellectual limitations, use simple and easily understood words and avoid abstract explanations. To avoid embarrassment, many people pretend that they understand when, in fact, they do not. Therefore, you should make keen observations and actively seek feedback to determine whether the client has grasped your intended meaning. If you are concerned that a client does not understand what you are saying, you could gently ask them to repeat back in their own words what you just said.

Judgment

Judgment is the ability to accurately identify the consequences of a given action (Snyderman & Rovner, 2009). People who have adequate or even keen intellect may nevertheless encounter difficulties in life because of deficits in judgment. Examples of decisions based on poor judgment include being duped by phone or internet scams, quitting jobs impulsively, leaving small children unattended, rushing into relationships without adequate information, or failing to safeguard personal property.

Deficiencies in judgment generally come to light when you explore problems and the patterns surrounding them. You may find that a client acts with little forethought, fails to consider the probable consequences of their actions, or engages in wishful thinking. When people fail to learn from past mistakes, they appear to be driven by intense impulses that overpower consideration of the consequences of their actions. Impulse-driven individuals may lash out at authority figures, write bad checks, misuse credit cards, or take other actions that provide immediate gratification but ultimately lead to adverse consequences such as the loss of a job, housing, or relationships.

Reality Testing

Reality testing provides insight on a person's mental health. Strong functioning on this dimension means meeting the following criteria:

1. Being properly oriented to time, place, person, and situation
2. Reaching appropriate conclusions about cause-and-effect relationships
3. Perceiving external events and discerning the intentions of others with reasonable accuracy
4. Differentiating one's own thoughts and feelings from those of others

Several conditions could impair reality testing. These include psychosis (e.g., disturbed thoughts and perceptions making it difficult to discern what is real and what is not (National Institute of Mental Health, 2019), drug or alcohol use, or pathological brain syndromes such as Alzheimer's disease. Disorientation is usually easily identifiable, but when doubt exists, questions about the date, day of the week, current events that are common knowledge, and recent events in the client's life will usually clarify the matter.

Perceptual patterns that involve distortions of external events are common but may cause difficulties, particularly in interpersonal relationships. **Mild distortions** may be associated with stereotypical perceptions (e.g., "All social workers are Democrats" or "The only interest men have in women is sexual"). **Moderate distortions** often involve marked misinterpretations of the motives of others and may severely impair interpersonal relationships (e.g., "My boss told me I was doing a good job and that there is an opportunity to be promoted to a job in another department; he's only saying that to get rid of me" or "My wife says she wants to take an evening class, but I know what she really wants is to meet other men"). In instances of **extreme distortions**, individuals may have **delusions** or false beliefs— for example, that others plan to harm them when they do not. On rare occasions, people suffering from delusions may take violent actions to protect themselves from their imagined persecutors.

Dysfunctions in reality testing of psychotic proportions occur when clients hear voices or other sounds (**auditory hallucinations**) or see things that are not there (**visual hallucinations**). In these instances, the people affected cannot distinguish between thoughts and beliefs that emanate from themselves and those that originate from external sources. Consequently, they may present a danger to themselves or others when acting in response to such commands or visions. Social workers must be able to recognize such severe cognitive dysfunction and respond with referrals for medication, protection, and/or hospitalization.

Coherence

Social workers occasionally encounter individuals who demonstrate major thought disorders, which are characterized by rambling and incoherent speech. For example, successive thoughts may be highly fragmented and disconnected from one another, a phenomenon referred to as looseness of association or derailment in the thought processes. The social worker can understand the words the client uses, but the sequence of words is not dictated by logic but by rhymes, puns, other rules that are not apparent to the clinician (Morrison, 2016). Another form of derailment is flight of ideas, in which the client's response seems to "take off" based on a particular word or thought, unrelated to logical progression or the original point of the communication. These difficulties in coherence may be indicative of head injury, mania, or thought disorders such as schizophrenia. Incoherence, of course, may also be produced by acute drug intoxication, so practitioners should be careful to rule out this possibility.

Cognitive Flexibility

People who are receptive to new ideas and able to analyze many facets of problematic situations are highly adaptable and capable of successful problem solving. Individuals with cognitive flexibility generally seek to grow, to understand the part they play in their difficulties, and to understand others. These individuals can also ask for assistance without perceiving such a request to be an admission of weakness or failure. Many people, however, are rigid and unyielding in their beliefs, and their inflexibility poses a major obstacle to progress in the helping process. In line with the strengths-based approach, social workers should highlight moments when clients demonstrate cognitive flexibility to reinforce this behavior and support clients in becoming more flexible thinkers.

A common pattern of cognitive inflexibility is thinking in absolute terms (e.g., a person is good or evil, a success or a failure, responsible or irresponsible— there are no in-betweens). People who think this way are prone to criticize others who fail to measure up to their stringent standards. The resulting relationship problems, workplace conflict, or parent–child disputes can then become a presenting problem for social work intervention.

Negative cognitive sets (i.e., the lens through which you view the world) is fixed thinking that can include biases and stereotypes about certain groups (e.g., authority figures, ethnic groups, gender-diverse individuals) or individuals. Severely depressed clients often have another form of tunnel vision, viewing themselves as helpless or worthless and the future as dismal and hopeless. They may selectively attend to their own negative

attributes, have difficulty feeling good about themselves, and struggle with being open to other options.

Values

Values are an integral part of the cognitive/perceptual subsystem because they strongly influence human behavior and often play a key role in the problems presented for work. For this reason, you should seek to identify your clients' values, assess the role those values play in their difficulties, and consider ways in which clients' values can be deployed to create incentives for change. Your ethical responsibility to respect the client's right to maintain their values and to make choices consistent with them requires you to become aware of those values. Because values result from our cultural conditioning, understanding the client's cultural reference group is important, particularly if it differs from your own. In line with cultural humility, you should not only learn about your client's culture but also understand how your client feels their culture impacts their values.

Examples of questions that will clarify values include:

- "You say you believe your parents are old fashioned about sex. What are your beliefs?"
- [To a couple]: "What are your beliefs about how couples should make decisions?"
- "You feel you're not succeeding in life. To you, what does being successful involve?"

Beliefs

Cognitive theory holds that thought patterns fuel psychological problems (American Psychological Association, 2017). Sometimes, beliefs are not misconceptions but rather are unhelpful, though accurate, conceptions. Examples of common destructive beliefs and contrasting functional beliefs include: "The world is a dog-eat-dog place; no one really cares about anyone except themselves" versus "There are all kinds of people in the world, including those who are ruthless, and those who are caring; I need to seek out the latter and strive to be a caring person myself;" or "All people in authority use their power to exploit and control others" versus "People in authority vary widely—some exploit and control others, while others are benevolent; I must reserve judgment, or I will indiscriminately resent all authority figures."

It is important to identify misconceptions and their sources to create a comprehensive assessment. Depending on how central these beliefs are to the client's problems, the goals for work that follow may involve modifying key misconceptions, thereby paving the way to behavioral change. As with other areas, client strengths may derive from the absence of misconceptions and from the ability to accurately, constructively, or positively perceive and construe events and motivations.

Cognitive dissonance may result when people discover inconsistencies among their beliefs and behaviors. Examining these contradictions can help reveal whether this tension is problematic or self-defeating. For example, consider an individual coming to terms with their sexuality or gender identity within a religious faith that condemns nonheterosexual orientations. Tension, confusion, and distress can result as this client and others attempt to reconcile disparate beliefs. The social worker may help by identifying and labeling the cognitive dissonance and working with the client to reconcile the differences or create options so that they are no longer mutually exclusive.

Self-Concept

Convictions, beliefs, and ideas about the self (that is, one's self-concept) have been generally recognized as crucial determinants of human behavior. Thus, there are strengths in having good self-esteem and in being realistically aware of one's positive attributes, accomplishments, and potential as well as one's limitations and deficiencies. A healthy person can accept limitations as a natural part of human fallibility without being overly distressed or discouraged. People with high self-esteem, in fact, can joke about their weaknesses and mistakes.

Many people, however, are tormented with feelings of worthlessness, inadequacy, and helplessness. These and similarly self-critical feelings pervade their functioning in diverse negative ways, including the following:

- Underachieving in life because of imagined deficiencies

Ideas In Action

Cognitive or Thought Disorders

As you assess cognitive functioning, you may note signs and symptoms of thought disorders and developmental delays. Three disorders to be alert to are intellectual disability, schizophrenia, and major neurocognitive disorder (*DSM-5;* American Psychiatric Association, 2013a).

Intellectual disability is typically diagnosed in infancy or childhood. It is defined as lower-than-average intelligence and "deficits in general mental abilities and impairment in everyday adaptive functioning, in comparison to an individual's age-, gender-, and socioculturally matched peers" (American Psychiatric Association, 2013a, p. 37). General intellectual functioning is appraised using standardized tests, and other measurement instruments may be used to assess the client's adaptive functioning, or ability to meet common life demands. Four levels of intellectual disability are distinguished: mild, moderate, severe, and profound.

Schizophrenia is a psychotic disorder that causes marked impairment in social, educational, and occupational functioning. Its onset typically occurs during adolescence or young adulthood, and development of the disorder may be abrupt or gradual. It is signified by a combination of positive and negative symptoms. In this context, these terms do not refer to whether something is good or bad but rather to the presence or absence of normal functioning. For example, **positive symptoms** of schizophrenia include delusions (i.e., fixed beliefs that cannot be altered even in the presence of conflicting evidence), hallucinations (i.e., perception experiences of sound, sight, touch, or taste in the absence of external stimuli), disorganized thinking and/or speech, and grossly disorganized behavior (e.g., switching rapidly between topics) or abnormal motor behavior (e.g., catatonia, agitation; American Psychiatric Association, 2013a). **Negative symptoms** include flattened affect, restricted speech, and **avolition**, or limited initiation of goal-directed behavior.

Major neurocognitive disorder (NCD) is characterized by "evidence of significant cognitive decline from previous level of performance in one or more cognitive domains (complex attention, executive function, learning and memory, language, perceptual-motor, or social cognition" (American Psychiatric Association, 2013a, p. 602). These deficits must be of sufficient severity to affect one's daily functioning to warrant a diagnosis of NCD (Corcoran & Walsh, 2010).

Treatment of individuals with these diagnoses is specialized and varied but may include use of medication as well as vocational, residential, and case management services. Understanding the features of these and other cognitive or thought disorders can assist you in better understanding clients, in planning appropriate treatment, and in considering how your role on cases meshes with that of other service providers.

- Passing up opportunities because of fears of failing
- Avoiding social relationships because of expectations of being rejected
- Permitting oneself to be taken for granted and exploited by others
- Excessive drinking or drug use to fortify oneself because of feelings of inadequacy
- Devaluing or discrediting worthwhile achievements
- Failing to defend one's rights

People may spontaneously reveal how they view themselves, or their description of patterns of difficulty may convey a damaged self-concept. An open-ended query, such as "Tell me how you see yourself," often elicit rich information. Because many people have not actually given much thought to the matter, they may hesitate or appear perplexed. An additional query, such as "What comes into your head when you think about the sort of person you are?" is usually all that is needed to prompt the client to respond.

Assessing Affective Functioning

People often seek help because they are experiencing strong emotions, or they feel that their emotions are out of control. Some individuals, for example, are emotionally volatile and engage in aggressive behavior while in the heat of anger. Others are emotionally unstable, struggling to stay afloat in a turbulent sea of feelings. Some people become emotionally distraught as the result of stress associated with the death of a loved one, divorce, severe disappointment, or another blow to self-esteem. To assist you in assessing emotional functioning, the following sections examine vital aspects of this dimension and the related terms and concepts. Figure 9-2 demonstrates the use of these concepts in a mental status exam.

Emotional Control and Range of Emotions

People vary widely in the degree of control they exercise over their emotions, ranging from emotional constriction to emotional excesses. Individuals who are experiencing emotional constriction may appear unexpressive and withholding in relationships. They do not appear to permit themselves to feel joy, hurt, enthusiasm, vulnerability, and other emotions that might otherwise invest life with zest and meaning. These individuals may be comfortable intellectualizing but retreat from expressing or discussing feelings. They often favorably impress others with their intellectual styles but sometimes have difficulties maintaining close relationships because their emotional detachment thwarts them from fulfilling the needs of others for intimacy and emotional stimulation. It is important to unpack why the client is emotionally restricted. Is a mental health diagnosis such as depression at the root of this constriction? A lack of self-confidence? A trauma history? An intellectual disability? You should also consider the role of oppression on clients of color and gender diverse clients. Emotional constriction may be an attempt to avoid attracting unwanted attention from police or others, an internalization of years of discrimination and oppression, or a manifestation of the client not trusting or feeling safe with the social worker.

A person with emotional excesses, on the other hand, may have "a short fuse," losing control and reacting intensely to even mild provocations. This behavior may involve rages and escalate to interpersonal violence. Excesses can also include other emotions such as irritability, crying, panic, despondency, helplessness, or giddiness. The key to assessing whether the emotional response is excessive is determining whether the response is appropriate and proportionate to the situation.

Emotionally healthy people experience the full gamut of human emotions within normal limits of intensity and duration. The capacity to experience joy, grief, exhilaration, disappointment, and the rest of the full spectrum of emotions is, therefore, an area of strength.

As discussed in Chapter 8, your assessment may stem from your personal observation of the client, feedback from collateral contacts, or the client's own report of their response to a situation. As always, your appraisal of the appropriateness of the response must factor in the client's social and cultural context and the nature of their relationship with you. Both may lead you to misjudge the client's normal emotional response and what is considered appropriate emotional regulation.

Cultures vary widely in their approved patterns of emotional expression. Nevertheless, emotional health in any culture shares one criterion: it means having control over emotions to the extent that one is not overwhelmed by them. Emotionally healthy persons also enjoy the freedom of experiencing and expressing emotions appropriately. Likewise, strengths include the ability to bear painful emotions without denying or masking feelings or being continually incapacitated by them. Emotionally healthy persons can discern the emotional states of others, empathize, and discuss painful emotions openly without feeling unduly distressed—recognizing, of course, that a certain amount of discomfort is natural. Finally, the ability to mutually share deeply personal feelings in intimate relationships is also considered an asset.

It is important to note that the presence of persistent traumatic stressors such as racism, homophobia, and discrimination impact people's emotional expression. Systems of oppression and personal experiences can intensify emotions and should be considered before social workers erroneously label an emotional reaction as overly intense or problematic. For example, a client may have what the social worker deems an inappropriately strong emotional reaction to their child being suspended from school. However, an assessment of this response must consider the client's identities and history. Past or repeated experiences of racism and disproportionate treatment may influence their current reaction, and the social worker must understand the client's emotional expression from within the larger context.

Appropriateness of Affect

Direct observation of clients' affect (emotionality) usually reveals valuable information about their emotional functioning. Healthy functioning involves spontaneously experiencing and expressing emotion congruent with the context and the material being discussed. However, labeling affect as appropriate is subjective and may be impacted by your own background and your clients' circumstances. Practicing with humility and an anti-oppressive lens means accounting for historic and structural factors in assessing the way that people express themselves. Suspicion, discomfort, or irritation may be entirely appropriate affect for a first session with a stranger (social worker) whose intentions are unknown, but power is clear. People who have experienced traumatic events often describe them matter-of-factly, with blunted and flat affects (discussed later). This could be a form of self-protection from intense recollections and feeling or the result of having to repeatedly tell the story to various investigators, counselors, or concerned or nosy others.

Inordinate apprehension—often demonstrated by muscle tension, constant fidgeting or shifts in posture, hand wringing, lip biting, and similar behaviors—usually indicates that a person is fearful, suspicious, or exceptionally uncomfortable in unfamiliar interpersonal situations. Such extreme tension may be expected in involuntary situations. In other cases, it may be characteristic of a client's typical demeanor. For clients of color or transgender clients, a high level of apprehension may result from previous experiences receiving culturally insensitive care. Racism, oppression, and discrimination are ubiquitous in health-care settings, and clients from

marginalized groups should not be labeled as having inappropriate affect for expressing reticence at trusting a new social worker.

Emotional blunting is what the term suggests: a muffled or apathetic response to material that would typically evoke a stronger response (e.g., happiness, despair, anger). For example, emotionally blunted individuals may discuss, in a detached and matter-of-fact manner, traumatic life events or conditions such as the murder of one parent by another, deprivation, or physical and/or sexual abuse. Emotional blunting can be indicative of a severe mental disorder, a sign of drug misuse, a side effect of medications, or an indication of past trauma, so it always warrants special attention.

Inappropriate affect can also appear in other forms, such as laughing when discussing a painful event (gallows laughter) or smiling constantly regardless of what is being discussed. Elation or euphoria that is incongruent with the individual's life situation, combined with constant and rapid shifts from one topic to another (flight of ideas), irritability, expansive ideas, and constant motion, also suggests mania.

Appropriateness of affect must always be considered in light of cultural differences. Measures to assure appropriate interpretation of affect include understanding the features of the client's culture, consulting others who are familiar with the culture or the client and evaluating the client's current presentation with their demeanor in the past. Clients may feel uncomfortable if certain personal attributes related to their culture (e.g., race/ethnicity, sexuality, gender identity, religion) do not match up with that of the social workers. Social workers should take make sure to understand those cultural elements.

Suicidal Risk

Part of assessing affect may include a suicide assessment based on client demeanor and if the client endorses suicidal thoughts. Not all individuals with depressive symptoms are suicidal, and not all suicidal individuals are depressed. Nevertheless, whenever clients exhibit depressive symptoms or hopelessness, it is critical to evaluate suicidal risk so that precautionary measures can be taken when indicated. With adults, the following factors are associated with high risk of suicide:

- Feelings of despair and hopelessness
- Previous suicide attempts
- Concrete, available, and lethal plans to commit suicide (when, where, and how)
- Family history of suicide

- Perseveration about suicide
- Lack of support systems and other forms of isolation
- Feelings of worthlessness
- Belief that others would be better off if the client were dead
- Advanced age (especially for white males)
- Substance abuse

When a client indicates, directly or indirectly, that they may be considering suicide, it is essential that you address those concerns through careful and direct questioning. Beginning social workers often worry that asking a client about suicide will plant the idea in the client's head. This is not the case. If a client is considering suicide, asking them about it gives them the space to discuss their thoughts and conveys to them that you care about them. You may begin by stating, "You sound pretty hopeless right now. I wonder if you might also be thinking of harming yourself?" or "When you say, 'They'll be sorry' when you're gone, I wonder if that means you're thinking of committing suicide?" An affirmative answer to these probes should be followed with a frank and calm discussion of the client's thoughts about suicide. Has the client considered how they might do it? When? What means would be used? Are those means accessible? In asking these questions, you are trying to determine not only the lethality of the client's plans but also the specificity. If a client has a well-thought-out plan in mind, the risk of suicide is significantly greater. An understanding of the client's history, especially regarding the risk factors mentioned and previous suicide attempts, will also help you decide the degree of danger and the level of intervention required. Standardized scales can also be used to evaluate suicidal risk.

When the client's responses indicate a potentially lethal attempt, it is appropriate to mobilize client support systems and arrange for psychiatric evaluation and/or hospitalization if needed. Such steps provide a measure of security for the client who may feel unable to control their impulses or who may become overwhelmed with despair.

Depression and Suicidal Risk with Children and Adolescents

Children and adolescents may experience depression which can lead to suicidal thoughts and/or attempts (National Institute of Mental Health, 2020). Indeed, most of the children and adolescent who attempt suicide have a mental health disorder, most commonly depression (American Academy of Child & Adolescent Psychiatry, 2018). In 2019, 18.8% of U.S. high school students contemplated attempting suicide, and 8.9% actually attempted (CDC, 2020).

Given the connection between depression and suicide, it is important to recognize the symptoms of depression in adolescents and the behavioral manifestations that may be reported by peers, siblings, parents, or teachers. The symptoms of depression in adolescents are similar to those in adults, though irritability and somatic complaints may be more prominent with children and teens (American Psychiatric Association, 2013a; Dulcan, 2009).

Because parents, teachers, coaches, and friends often do not realize that the child or adolescent is depressed, it is important to alert them to the following potentially troublesome symptoms (Mayo Clinic, 2018):

- Deterioration in personal habits
- Decline in school achievement or attendance
- Marked increase in sadness, moodiness, and sudden tearful reactions
- Changes in appetite such as decreased appetite and weight loss or increased appetite and weight gain
- Use of drugs or alcohol
- Talking and/or thinking about of death, dying, or suicide (even in a joking manner)
- Withdrawal from friends and family and/or increased conflict with these groups
- Making final arrangements, such as giving away valued possessions
- Sudden or unexplained departure from past behaviors (from shy to thrill-seeking or from outgoing to sullen and withdrawn)

Specific subgroups of children and adolescents may experience additional, unique risk factors related to their gender, race/ethnicity, or sexual orientation and the ways that these interact with the environments around them (Drescher, 2014; Mayo Clinic, 2019). Given the tumultuous nature of adolescence, it may be difficult to distinguish warning signs of depression from normative actions and behavior. Cautious practice would suggest taking any changes seriously rather than minimizing them or writing them off as typical teen behavior. Regardless of whether these changes are indicative of depression and suicide risk, changes in behavior and patterns such as these indicate that something is going on that is worthy of

Ideas In Action

Affective Disorders

The *DSM-5* (American Psychiatric Association, 2013a) contains extensive information on the criteria for diagnosing bipolar and related disorders and depressive disorders. Treatment of these diagnoses generally includes medication, often with concurrent cognitive or interpersonal psychotherapy. Understanding these diagnoses is important for treatment planning and detection of suicidal ideation and other serious risk factors (Corcoran & Walsh, 2010).

Bipolar Disorder

The dominant feature of **bipolar disorder** is the presence of manic episodes (mania) with intervening periods of depression. Among the symptoms of mania are "a distinct period of abnormally and persistently elevated, expansive or irritable mood" (American Psychiatric Association, 2013a, p. 124) and at least three of the following:

- Inflated self-esteem or grandiosity
- Decreased need for sleep
- More talkative than usual or pressure to keep talking
- Flight of ideas or subjective experience that thoughts are racing
- Distractibility (i.e., attention too easily drawn to unimportant or irrelevant external stimuli), as reported or observed
- Increase in goal-directed activity (either socially, at work or school, or sexually) or psychomotor agitation (i.e., purposeless non-goal-directed activity)
- Excessive involvement in pleasurable activities with a high potential for painful consequences, such as unrestrained buying sprees, sexual indiscretions, or unwise business investments

Full-blown **manic episodes** require that symptoms be sufficiently severe to cause marked impairment in job performance or relationships or to necessitate hospitalization to protect patients or others from harm.

If exploration seems to indicate a client has the disorder, immediate psychiatric consultation is needed for two reasons: (1) to determine whether hospitalization is needed and (2) to determine the need for medication. Bipolar disorder is biogenetic, and various compounds containing lithium carbonate may produce remarkable results in stabilizing and maintaining affected individuals. Close medical supervision is required,

however, because commonly used medications for this disorder have a relatively narrow margin of safety.

Major Depressive Disorder

Major depressive disorder, in which affected individuals experience recurrent episodes of depressed mood, is far more common than bipolar disorder. Major depression differs from the "blues" in that painful emotions (**dysphoria**) and the absence of pleasure in previously enjoyable activities (**anhedonia**) are present. The painful emotions are commonly related to anxiety, mental anguish, an extreme sense of guilt (often over what appear to be relatively minor offenses), and restlessness (agitation).

To be assigned a diagnosis of major depressive disorder, a person must have evidenced depressed mood and loss of interest or pleasure as well as at least five of the following nine symptoms for at least 2 weeks (American Psychiatric Association, 2013a, pp. 160–161):

- Depressed mood for most of the day, nearly every day
- Markedly diminished interest or pleasure in all or almost all activities
- Significant weight loss or weight gain when not dieting or decrease or increase in appetite
- Insomnia or hypersomnia
- Psychomotor agitation or retardation nearly every day
- Fatigue or loss of energy
- Feelings of worthlessness or excessive or inappropriate guilt
- Diminished ability to think or concentrate or indecisiveness
- Recurrent thoughts of death or suicidal ideation or attempts

As noted in Chapter 8, several scales are available to assess the presence and degree of depression. When assessment reveals that clients are moderately or severely depressed, psychiatric consultation is indicated to determine the need for medication and/or hospitalization. Antidepressant medications have proven to be effective in accelerating recovery from depression and work synergistically with cognitive or interpersonal psychotherapy.

In assessing depression, it is important to identify which factors precipitated the depressive episode. An important loss or series of losses may lead to depression associated with bereavement.

adult attention, as well as professional consultation and evaluation.

Depression and Suicidal Risk with Older Adults

In addition to the signs noted for depression and suicidal ideation in adults, adolescents, and children, older adults warrant particular attention in screening for these conditions. Risk factors for older persons include isolation, ill health, hopelessness, and functional and social losses. Older clients may be reluctant to appear for mental health services, and psychiatric conditions may be overlooked by primary care providers and loved ones or minimized as typical features of aging. Commonly used instruments to assess depression, such as the Geriatric Depression Scale, may provide insufficient screening for suicidal ideation (Heisel et al., 2005). The assessment of suicidality in elder clients requires discernment to distinguish between suicidal intent and the awareness of mortality or preparedness for death, which may be hallmarks of that developmental phase (Heisel & Flett, 2006).

Assessing Behavioral Functioning

In direct social work practice, change efforts frequently target behavioral patterns that impair the client's social functioning. Because behavioral change is commonly the focus of social work interventions, you must be skillful in discerning and assessing both dysfunctional and functional patterns of behavior. In individual sessions, you can directly observe clients' social and communication patterns as well as some personal habits and traits. In conjoint interviews and group sessions, you can observe these behavioral patterns as well as the effects that these actions have on others. Figure 9-2 demonstrates the use of these concepts in a mental status exam.

In assessing behavior, it is helpful to think of problems as consisting of excesses or deficiencies. For excess-related problems, interventions aim to diminish or eliminate the behaviors, such as temper outbursts, too much talking, arguing, competition, and consumptive excesses (e.g., food, alcohol, sex, internet use, gambling, shopping). For behavioral deficiencies, when assessment reveals the absence of needed skills, interventions aim to help clients acquire the skills and behaviors to function more effectively. For example, a client's behavioral

repertoire may not include skills in expressing feelings directly, engaging in social conversation, listening to others, solving problems, managing finances, parenting, planning nutritious meals, being a responsive sexual partner, or handling conflict. Sometimes problems can result from a combination of behavioral excesses and deficiencies.

In addition to identifying dysfunctional behavioral patterns, it is important to be aware of those behaviors that are effective and represent strengths. In assessing behavior, it is vital to specify actual problem behaviors. For example, rather than assess a person's behavior as abrasive, a social worker might describe the behaviors leading to that conclusion: "the client constantly interrupts his fellow workers, insults them by telling them they are misinformed, and boasts about his own knowledge and achievements." It will be easier for you and the client to focus your change efforts when detrimental behavior is specified and operationalized.

Risk of Aggression

A particular behavioral concern is the risk of aggression. Aggression can take many forms, from making threats and bullying to assaults and gun violence. It may be directed at the social worker or at others in the client's environment, such as siblings, classmates, dating partners, parents, or bosses. Although there is significant variability in the definition and measurement of risk factors among these tools, there are several risk factors that have been consistently related to violent behavior (Andrade, 2009). The most consistently predictive of these factors is past violent behavior or criminal behavior. Additional risk factors include early age of first criminal offense, substance abuse, gender (violence by men generally exceeds that by women), and psychopathy. several dynamic risk factors such as impulsiveness, anger, psychosis, interpersonal problems, and antisocial attitudes that may impact violence, but no predictive conclusions can yet be drawn (Andrade, 2009). For youth violence, there are a variety of risk factors, including prior history of violence, early initiation of violence, school achievement problems, abuse, maltreatment and neglect, substance use problems, impulsivity, negative peer relationships, and community crime and violence (Broum & Verhaagen, 2006).

Motivation

Evaluating and enhancing client motivation are integral parts of the assessment process. When working

Figure 9-2   Mental Status Exams

One specialized form of assessment is the mental status exam. This exam is intended to capture and describe features of the client's mental state. The terminology developed for use in a mental status exam facilitates communication among professions for both clinical and research purposes.

The mental status exam typically consists of the following items, which are described elsewhere in this chapter and in other sources (Gallo et al., 2000; Lukas, 1993):

Appearance
- How does the client look and act?
  - Note client's stated age
  - Describe dress and clothing
  - Describe psychomotor movements, tics, facial expressions

Reality Testing
- Assess judgment
- Describe dangerous, impulsive behaviors
- Assess insight
  - To what extent does the client understand their problem?
  - How does the client describe the problem?

Speech
- Volume: low, inaudible versus very loud
- Rate of speech: rapid versus slow
- Amount: poverty of speech versus talking very quickly and at length

Emotions
- Mood: how the client feels most of the time
  - Anxious, depressed, overwhelmed, scared, tense, restless, euthymic, euphoric

Affect:
- How the client appears to be feeling currently
  - Variability (labile)
  - Intensity (blunted, flat)

Thought
- Content: What does the client think about?
  - Delusions: unreal belief, distortion
  - Delusions of grandeur: unusual or exaggerated power
  - Delusions of persecution: unreal belief that someone is after the client
  - Delusions of control: someone else is controlling the client's thoughts or actions
  - Somatic delusions: unreal physical concerns
- Other thought issues
  - Obsessions: unrelenting, unwanted thoughts
  - Compulsions: repeated behaviors, often linked to an obsession
  - Phobias: obsessive thoughts that arouse intense fears
  - Thought broadcasting: belief that others can read the client's mind

- Ideas of reference: insignificant or unrelated events that have a secret meaning to the client
- Homicidal ideation: desire or intent to hurt others
- Suicidal ideation: range from thought, desire, intent, or plan to die
- Process: how the client thinks
  - Circumstantiality: lack of goal direction
  - Perseveration: repeated phrase, repeated topic
  - Loose associations: move between topics without connections
  - Tangentiality: barely talking about the topic
  - Flight of ideas: rapid speech that is unconnected

Sensory Perceptions
- Illusions
  - Misperception of normal sensory events
- Hallucinations
  - Experience of one of the senses: olfactory (smell), auditory (hearing), visual (sight), gustatory (taste), tactile (touch)

Mental Capacities
- Orientation times four: oriented to time (date and/or time of day), person (who they are), place (where they are), and situation (why client is in current place, such as attending a doctor's appointment)
- General intellect: average or low intelligence
- Memory: remote (past presidents), recent (what the client ate yesterday for breakfast), and immediate (remember three items)
- Concentration: Distraction during interview, count backward by 3s

Attitude Toward Interviewer
- How the client behaves toward the interviewer: suspicious, arrogant, cooperative, afraid, reserved, entertaining, able to trust and open up, forthcoming

Sample Mini Mental Status Report
Mr. Stewart presents as unshaven, thin, with unkempt hair, and older than his stated age. No abnormal body movements or tics are noted. Mr. Stewart is alert and oriented times four. His thought content and processes appear normal, although there are no specific questions to address delusions, hallucinations, or intellect. He describes his mood as euthymic, and his affect is guarded. Although he is inquisitive about the clinician's notes and he provides only brief answers, Mr. Stewart is cooperative. His judgment is impaired, as seen by his driving while intoxicated and missing work. Mr. Stewart's insight appears limited, as he has come for evaluation to appease his wife and does not see his drinking as heavy or problematic. He denies thoughts or plans of suicide or homicide.

with family members or groups, social workers are likely to encounter a range of motivation levels within a single client system. People who do not believe that they can influence their environments may demonstrate a kind of learned helplessness, a passive resignation that their lives are out of their hands. Others may be at different phases in their readiness to change. Involuntary clients my express less motivation to change given that they are being forced into treatment. For example, if a someone does not see their drinking as problematic but has been coerced into attending treatment by their family, motivation to change may be low. Asking clients about their goals and what changes they would like to make is a good way to start assessing motivation. Specific frameworks (e.g., motivational interviewing) for addressing motivation are discussed in depth in Chapter 13.

Assessing Environmental Systems

As noted in Chapter 2, taking the ecological approach is a cornerstone of social work. After evaluating the history [C7] and the pattern of the presenting problem and various facets of individual functioning, the social worker must assess the client in the context of their environment (see Figure 9-3). This assessment focuses on the transactions between the two, or the goodness of fit between the person and their environment. Problem-solving efforts may be directed toward assisting people

to adapt to their environments (e.g., supporting them in improving interpersonal skills), altering environments to more adequately meet the needs of clients (e.g., enhancing both the attractiveness of a nursing home and the quality of its activities), or a combination of the two (e.g., enhancing the interpersonal skills of a withdrawn, chronically ill person as well as moving that person to a more stimulating environment). This part of assessment goes beyond the evaluation of resources described in Chapter 8 to take a holistic view of the client's environment and examines the adequacy of various aspects of the environment to meet the client's needs.

In assessing environments, you should give the highest priority to those aspects that are most salient to the client's individual situation. The adequacy of the environment depends on the client's life stage, physical and mental health, interests, aspirations, and other resources. For example, a family may not be concerned about living in a highly polluted area unless one of their children suffers from asthma that is exacerbated by the physical environment. Another family may not worry about the availability of day treatment programs for an adult child with developmental disabilities until a crisis (e.g., death of a parent or need to return to work) forces them to look outside the family for accessible, affordable services.

You should tailor your assessments of clients' environments to their varied life situations, weighing the individual's unique needs against the availability of essential resources and opportunities within their environments. In addition to noting the limitations or problems posed by inadequate physical or social environments, it is important to acknowledge the strengths at play in the person's life—the importance of a stable, accessible, affordable residence or the value of a support system that mobilizes in times of trouble.

The following list describes basic environmental needs. You can use this list in evaluating the adequacy of your client's environments.

1. A physical environment that is adequate, is stable, and fosters health and safety (this includes housing as well as surroundings that are free of toxins and other health risks)

2. Adequate social support systems (e.g., family, relatives, friends, neighbors, organized groups)

3. Affiliation with a meaningful and responsive faith community

4. Access to timely, appropriate, affordable health care (e.g., vaccinations, physicians, dentists, medications, and nursing homes)

Figure 9-3   Areas for Attention in Assessing Person-in-Environment Fit

Environmental Systems

Physical Environment
- Adequacy
- Health
- Safety

Social Support Systems
- Missing
- Affirming
- Harmful

Spirituality and Affiliation with a Faith Community
- Spirituality
- Religion
- Cognitive, affective, and behavioral dimensions of faith

5. Access to safe, reliable, affordable child and elder care services

6. Access to recreational facilities

7. Transportation—to work, socialize, utilize resources, and exercise rights as a citizen

8. Adequate housing that provides ample space, sanitation, privacy, and safety from hazards and pollution (both air and noise)

9. Responsive police and fire protection and a reasonable degree of security

10. Safe and healthful work conditions

11. Sufficient financial resources to purchase essential resources (e.g., food, clothing, housing)

12. Adequate nutritional intake

13. Predictable living arrangements with caring others (especially for children)

14. Opportunities for education and self-fulfillment

15. Access to legal assistance

16. Employment opportunities

This list must be viewed through the framework of anti-oppressive practice. It is important to consider how the items on this list are impacted by social hierarchies and systems of oppression. Institutional racism, for example, limits the quality and availability of many items on this list for people of color. Institutionalized racism refers to the policies, practices, and rules in every system of our society (e.g., health care, educational, judicial) that unfairly disadvantage people of color. In light of the institutionalized racism inherent in policing, high rates of police brutality toward people of color make it extremely difficult for people of color to view the police as safe and responsive. Accessing adequate housing with privacy, safety, and clean air is difficult for individuals in low-income neighborhoods because the government chooses to locate major highways near low-income neighborhoods as opposed to near higher income neighborhoods. Receiving adequate health care can be difficult for people of color given the presence of racial health-care disparities. The items on this list must be viewed in the context of racism and oppression.

In this chapter, we will address the first three areas on the list—physical environment, social support systems, and faith community—in depth, in light of their particular importance for individual functioning. This discussion may also help you generalize some of the complexities of environmental assessment to the other 13 areas.

Physical Environment

Physical environment refers to the stability and adequacy of one's physical surroundings and whether the environment fosters or jeopardizes the client's health and safety. A safe environment is free of threats such as personal or property crimes. Assessing health and safety factors includes considering sanitation, space, and heat. Extended families may be crammed into small homes or apartments without adequate beds and bedding, homes may not be designed for running water or indoor toilets, or access to water may be broken or shut off. Inadequate heat or air conditioning can exacerbate existing health conditions and lead to danger during periods of extreme weather. Further, families may take steps to heat their residences in ways that can create further health dangers (such as with ovens or makeshift fires). Sanitation may be compromised by insect or rodent infestations or by owner or landlord negligence in conforming to building standards and maintaining plumbing. The home may be in an area with exposure to toxic materials or poor air quality. The role that institutionalized racism plays in an inadequate physical environment should be considered and discussed with your client.

Assessing physical environment is particularly important for older clients and should consider whether the person's living situation meets their health and safety needs (Garner & Holland, 2020). If an older adult lives alone, does the home have adequate resources for the individual to meet their functional needs? Can the client use bathroom and kitchen appliances to conduct their daily activities? Does clutter contribute to the client's confusion or risk (e.g., not being able to find bills or stumbling over stacked newspapers)? Is the home a safe environment, or do some aspects of the building (e.g., stairs or loose carpeting) pose a danger to less mobile clients? If the client resides in an institution, are there mementos of home and personal items that bring comfort to the individual? Tools such as the Instrumental Activities of Daily Living Screen (Gallo, 2005) and Direct Assessment of Functioning Scale (DAFS; Lowenstein et al., 1989) can assess functional ability, screen for and address risk factors, and evaluate changes in functioning.

Social Support Systems

Social systems across the various ecological levels of your client's life constitute the second item on the list of needed resources. Social support systems fill a variety of needs to improve quality of life. To assist you in

Figure 9-4   Diagram of Ecological Social Systems

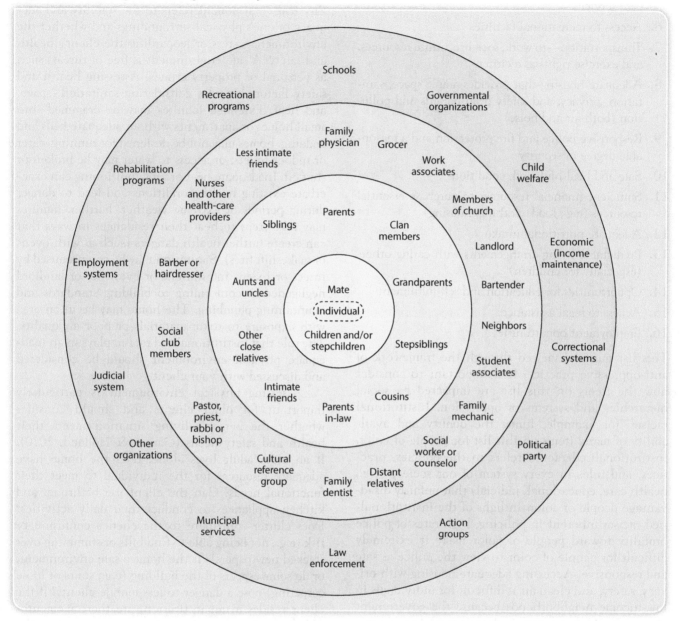

identifying pertinent social systems, Figure 9-4 depicts interrelationships between individuals and families and other systems (Hartman, 1994). Systems that are central in a person's life appear in the center of the diagram. These systems typically play key roles both as sources of difficulties and as resources that may be tapped or modified in problem solving. Moving from the center to the periphery in the areas encompassed by the concentric circles are systems that are progressively distant from individuals and their families. There are exceptions, of course, such as when an individual feels closer to an intimate friend or a faith leader than to family members. Moreover, if clients' situations require frequent contacts with institutions or organizations (e.g., child protective services, income maintenance programs, judicial systems), those institutions may no longer occupy a peripheral position because of how dramatically they affect individuals and families at such times. The intensity of affiliation with extended family or kinship networks may vary by cultural group and reflect the effects of migration and cultural dislocation (Taylor et al., 2013). Reciprocal interactions thus change across time, and diagrams depicting these interactions should be viewed as snapshots that remain accurate only within limited time frames.

Social support systems are increasingly recognized as playing a crucial role in determining the level of social functioning. Theorists have long recognized the critical importance of a nurturing environment to healthy development of infants and children, but it is now clear that adults also have vital needs that can be met only through affiliation with supportive systems. Consequently, the lack of adequate social support systems is considered an area of vulnerability and may represent a source of distress, whereas adequate social support systems reduce the effects of stressful situations and facilitate successful adaptation. Knowing what the social support systems are and what roles they play with clients is essential for assessment and may even be the focus of interventions that tap into the potential of dormant social support systems or mobilize new ones. What benefits accrue from involvement with social support systems?

C7

1. Attachment, provided by close relationships that give a sense of security and sense of belonging

2. Social integration, provided by memberships in a network of people who share interests and values

3. The opportunity to nurture others, which provides incentive to endure in the face of adversity

4. Physical care when persons are unable to care for themselves because of illness, incapacity, or severe disability

5. Validation of personal worth (which promotes self-esteem), provided by family and colleagues

6. A sense of reliable alliance, provided primarily by kin

7. Guidance, child care, financial aid, and other assistance in coping with difficulties as well as crises

When assessing supports, the trauma-informed care framework should be invoked. Trauma can disrupt a person's ability to form and maintaining close attachments. Thus, minimal social support may not be due to a lack of availability but because of a client's reaction to past trauma.

To this point, we have highlighted the positive aspects of social support systems. It is also important to note that some social support systems may foster and sustain problems in functioning. For example, overprotective parents may stunt the development of competence, autonomy, and personal responsibility in their children. Gangs, cliques, and other antisocial peer groups may foster violence and

C2

criminality, even as they provide a sense of belonging and affiliation. Friends may ridicule or sabotage a person's aspirations, thereby undermining that individual's confidence and capacity for success. Family members may rally to support a person during joyous events (e.g., graduation, childbirth) but not be available in times of need or sadness.

You should be aware of the various social networks at play in a client's life and assess the roles that those social support systems play in the person's difficulties or in their ability to overcome hardships. Sometimes, a negative support system can be counteracted by the development of prosocial or positive networks. At other times, the system itself may be the focus of intervention as you strive to make the members aware of their roles in the client's problems and progress.

Spirituality and Affiliation with a Faith Community

Spirituality shapes beliefs and often provides strength during times of adversity. The link to a faith community, whether spiritual or religious, can be a tangible source of assistance and social support. Spirituality and religion are often considered to be synonymous, but they are distinct (Darrell & Rich, 2017).

C7

Spirituality reflects the "human search for transcendence, meaning and connectedness beyond the self" and religion refers to a "more formal embodiment of spirituality into relatively specific belief systems, organizations and structures" (Sherwood, 1998; p. 80). A spiritual assessment may help the social worker better understand the client's belief system and resources. While spirituality is almost always a part of religion, individuals may consider themselves to be spiritual without prescribing to religious doctrines or belonging to a specific religious group.

Questions such as "What are your sources of strength and hope?", "How do you express your spirituality?", "Do you identify with a particular religion or faith?", and "Is your religious faith helpful to you?" can begin to elicit information about the client's spiritual and/or religious beliefs. A variety of guides for gathering information about clients' spiritual beliefs and religious affiliations are available (Crisp, 2017; Saguil & Phelps, 2012; Starnino et al., 2014).

At times, religion and spirituality issues may be central to the client's presenting problems. For example, parents may disagree about the spiritual upbringing of their children, couples may be at odds over proper gender roles and expression, or families may be in conflict about behaviors proscribed by certain religions, such as premarital sex, contraceptive use, alcohol use, divorce, or homosexuality.

Spirituality involves three relevant areas: cognitive (the meaning given to past, current, and personal events), affective (one's inner life and sense of connectedness to a larger reality), and behavioral (the way in which beliefs are affirmed, such as through group worship or individual prayer; Thibault et al., 1991). Thus, spiritual beliefs may affect the client's response to adversity, the coping methods employed, the sources of support available (e.g., the faith community may form a helpful social network), and the array of appropriate interventions available. Particularly when clients have experienced disaster or unimaginable traumas, the exploration of suffering, good and evil, shame and guilt, and forgiveness can be a central part of the change process. Social workers must be aware of their own spiritual journeys and understand the appropriate handling of spiritual content, depending on the setting, focus, and client population involved (Ellor et al., 1999). Social workers are also advised to involve clergy or other faith leaders to work jointly in addressing the personal and spiritual crises faced by clients (Grame et al., 1999).

Written Assessments

The assessment phase is a critical part of the helping process. It provides the foundation on which goals and interventions are based. It is also an ongoing part of the helping process, as appraisals are reconsidered and revised based on new information and understanding. As a written product, assessments may be done at intake, following a period of interviews and evaluations, and at the time of transfer or termination (a summary assessment). Assessments may be brief and targeted (such as an assessment for referral), or longer, as with a social history, a detailed report for the court or another entity, or a comprehensive biopsychosocial assessment. Whichever form it takes, several standards must be followed to craft a sound document that clearly conveys accurate information and credible depictions of the client (Kagle & Kopels, 2013).

C1

1. Remember your purpose and audience. These can help you decide what should be included and maintain that focus. Know the standards and the expectations that apply in your work setting and understand the needs of those who may review your document.

2. Be precise and accurate. It is important that any data you include be accurate. Erroneous information can take on a life of its own if what you write is taken as fact by others. If you are unclear on a point, or if you have gathered conflicting information, note that in your report.

Document your sources of information and specify the basis for any conclusions and the criteria on which a decision was based (for example, to refer the client to another agency, to recommend a custody placement, or to conclude that suicidal risk was slight).

Present essential information in a coherent manner. An assessment is intended to be a synthesis of information from a variety of sources, including observation, documents, collateral contacts, and client interviews. Organizing that material so that it paints a comprehensive picture of the client's situation, strengths, and challenges at that moment is not easy. Avoid going off on tangents or piling up excessive details that derail the clarity of your document. Keep details that illustrate your point, document your actions, or substantiate your conclusions.

3. Avoid the use of labels, subjective terminology, and jargon. In assessing the social functioning of individuals, social workers often make global judgments—for example, "Mr. A's job performance is marginal." Such a sweeping statement has limited usefulness because it fails to specify how the client's functioning is inferior, and it emphasizes deficits. Instead of using labels ("Alice is a kleptomaniac"), use the client's own reports or substantiate your conclusion ("Alice reports a three-year history of shoplifting on a weekly basis" or "Alice has been arrested five times for theft and appears unable to resist the compulsion to steal small items"). Be factual and descriptive rather than relying on labels and subjective terms.

Various resources are available to help in honing your skills and expanding your assessment vocabulary (e.g., Kagle & Kopels, 2013; Wiger, 2009). It is also important to remember that anything that is part of the client's record, including your written assessment, can be subpoenaed by a court. Thus, when you are writing an assessment, imagine that it could be brought before a judge and jury.

Biopsychosocial Assessments

Assessments are often referred to as **biopsychosocial assessments** or **evaluations**. The term **biopsychosocial** refers to the notion that when social workers or other mental health professionals such as psychologists or psychiatrists assess clients, they evaluate the biological, psychological, and social domains and how these domains both influence and are influenced by disease, disorder, or illness. Assessing biology includes obtaining information about the clients' physical health, psychological functioning, biochemical functioning, nutritional choices, and genetic heritage. Assessing the psychological domain includes evaluating emotional well-being, affective presentation, cognitive functioning, general behavior, spiritual preferences, and personality. Assessment of the social domain includes examining interpersonal relationships and interactions, environment, culture, family, work, and faith community (Peterson et al., 2015).

Typically, biopsychosocial assessments include the following (Ross, 2000):

- Identifying information (e.g., name, age, referral source, brief overview of the presenting problem)
- A history of the present circumstances (i.e., the presenting problem, symptoms)
- The past psychiatric and medical history of the client and the client's family (e.g., injuries, operations, medical conditions, medication, ongoing medical treatment)
- The client's social history (e.g., overview of client's childhood, family structure, living situation, employment and employment history, educational history, hobbies, daily routine, religious or spiritual preferences, friends, past trauma, substance use)
- A mental status exam (see Figure 9-2, p. 181) and *DSM-5* diagnosis
- A **formulation** (e.g., a statement that summarizes and synthesizes the most important aspects of the case to create a story of the client and their past and presenting problems)

For children and adolescents, a brief overview of developmental milestones may be included, addressing the age at which they began crawling, walking, talking, toilet training, and so on.

The assessment in Figure 9-5 demonstrates how the concepts described in Chapter 8 and this chapter are incorporated into different written documents, based on the needs and norms of the setting in which they were conducted.

Case Notes

In addition to more comprehensive assessments, direct practitioners record information in client charts based on each meeting or contact with the client and after other significant contacts about the case, such as the receipt of test results or information from a collateral contact. Record-keeping policies are often specific to the setting. For example, in schools, social work notes would be kept separate from the child's educational record. In some settings, notes are dictated, and in others they are handwritten. Well-crafted **case notes** "provide accountability, corroborate the delivery of appropriate services and support clinical decisions" (Cameron & Turtle-Song, 2002, p. 1).

Although there are many different practices in record keeping, one commonly used practice is worthy of attention. **SOAP notes** include subjective observations, objective data, assessments, and plans (Kettenbach, 2003). A variation on this, DAP, combines subjective and objective information under one heading: data. SOAP notes refer to the most recent assessment, problem list, and treatment plan. The subjective section in SOAP notes includes information shared by the client or significant others such as recent events, emotions, changes in health or well-being, and changes in attitude, functioning, or mental status. Information in this section is typically paraphrased and presented as, for example, "The client reports...", "The patient's mother states...", "She indicates...", or "Patient's husband complains of..." Direct client quotes should be kept to a minimum (Cameron & Turtle-Song, 2002).

The objective section in SOAP notes should be factual, precise, and descriptive, based on your observations or written material, and presented in quantifiable terms—factors that "can be seen, heard, smelled, counted or measured" (Cameron & Turtle-Song, 2002, p. 2). In such notes, the advice for writing proper assessments applies. Avoid conclusions, judgments, and jargon, and substitute descriptions that would lead to such conclusions with more objective commentary. Rather than saying, "The client was resistant," an objective statement might read, "The client arrived 20 minutes late, sat with her coat on and her arms folded, and did not make eye contact with this writer."

The assessment section of SOAP notes is the place to include diagnoses, judgments, and clinical impressions based on both the subjective and objective data that precede the assessment. "The client is

Figure 9-5   Example of a Biopsychosocial Assessment

Identifying Information

Dan is a 10-year-old White male who presented at the community mental health center with his parents following a serious car accident that occurred 3 months ago. His pediatrician referred Dan after his parents mentioned that following the car accident, Dan has been having nightmares about the accident and has difficulty sleeping, a decreased appetite, refusal to ride in the car, and apparent preoccupation with thoughts of the accident.

History of Presenting Problem

Dan and his parents were in a serious car accident about 3 months before their intake appointment. The parents report that prior to this accident, Dan was a normal kid who enjoyed playing soccer with his friends, did well in school, completed household chores without complaining, was on a regular sleep schedule, and had a healthy appetite. Following the accident, they report Dan has been having nightmares about the accident a few times a week, does not want to be alone, insists on sleeping on his parents' floor (although he often does not fall asleep until after midnight), eats very little, has stopped playing soccer, is very irritable and argumentative with his parents and siblings, is very tearful, and has difficulty concentrating at school and on his homework, resulting in lower grades. Dan's parents also report that Dan now hates riding in the car and avoids the car at all costs. They state that if he must ride in the car, he often cries and screams at whoever is driving to slow down and be careful. Dan states that since the accident, "I can't stop thinking about it." He reports constantly worrying about his parents because they both drive to work, and he is terrified of one of them being in an accident. Dan states that he finds it difficult to play with his friends and have a good time because he is always thinking about the accident. As a result, Dan reports that he has been feeling very alone since the accident.

Past Psychiatric and Medical History

Dan's parents deny any previous mental health problems and state that prior to the accident Dan was happy and healthy. In terms of family psychiatric history, Dan's parent reports that they have been treated for depression and anxiety in the past but notes no other family psychiatric history. Dan has never been hospitalized for any medical issues, is not taking any medications, and has never had any serious injuries or operations. The parents deny any significant family medical history.

Social History

Dan currently resides with his mother (age 40), father (age 41), older sister (17), and older brother (14). Dan's mother was a stay-at-home mom, but recently returned to work because of family financial stress. Dan's father works as a landscaper during the week and tries to pick up odd jobs such as painting or construction on the weekends. Dan's sister is a senior in high school, and his brother is in the eighth grade. Dan's parents report that the family has no religious affiliation. Both sets of grandparents live nearby, and Dan is especially close with his paternal grandfather. Dan's father reports that he has two brothers in the area, and Dan's mother states that her sister lives out of state. The parents describe the family as close knit and supportive.

Dan's mother reports that when she was pregnant with Dan, it was a normal pregnancy and delivery. Dan hit all developmental milestones at the appropriate times: he crawled at about 10 months of age, walked at 14 months, began talking at 18 months, and was out of diapers by the time he was two and a half.

Dan is currently in fourth grade at the local elementary school. Prior to the accident, Dan and his parents report that he got almost all As; however, those grades have now slipped to Bs, Cs, and some Ds. Dan used to enjoy playing with his friends but states that now he mostly watches TV because he prefers to stay at home so he can be near his parents, and he does not have the energy or desire to be with his friends. Dan also used to belong to a club soccer team but has refused to attend practice since the accident. Dan's parents state that Dan has always been popular among his peers but has really distanced himself from his friends since the accident. Dan and his parents deny any past trauma and any substance use.

Mental Status Exam

Dan presents as alert and oriented times four (oriented to time, person, place, and situation). He looks his stated age of 10 and was dressed appropriately in jeans and a sweatshirt and was well groomed and clean. Dan made minimal eye contact and fidgeted almost constantly as he sat in his chair, either shaking one or both legs or twisting his sweatshirt in his hands. His rate of speech was normal, but he spoke in a very quiet voice. Dan was a bit shy at first but after a while began talking at greater length and depth about his experience with the car accident. Dan has good insight into his problems and was able to clearly identify how his life has changed following the accident. He reports feeling sad, down, and without energy. He also reports worrying all the time that another car accident will occur. Dan's downcast eyes, flat affect, and quiet and monotone voice match his reported mood. Dan denies auditory and visual hallucinations, self-harming behaviors, suicidal ideation, past and present suicide attempts, and homicidal ideation.

(Continued)

Figure 9-5   Continued

DSM-5 Diagnosis

Based on Dan's reported symptoms of traumatic nightmares, recurrent and intrusive memories of the car accident, constant trauma-related thoughts and feelings, constantly being reminded of the trauma when riding in a car, diminished interest in activities that he previously enjoyed, inability to experience positive emotions, sleep disturbances, difficulty concentrating, and irritability, Dan is diagnosed with post-traumatic stress disorder (PTSD; 309.81).

Formulation

Dan is a 10-year-old White male who presented with his parents following a serious car accident. Dan and his parents report that following the car accident Dan has consistently displayed several concerning symptoms (e.g., constant thoughts about the accident,

refusal to ride in the car, traumatic nightmares, sleep disturbance, difficulty concentrating), all of which are consistent with a diagnosis of PTSD. Dan comes from a very supportive and nurturing family and has a close bond with both of his parents and his paternal grandfather. He is a well-liked child, and both he and his parents report that he has many friends. However, since the accident, Dan has distanced himself from his friends, is often quiet and withdrawn at home, and does not engage with the family as much as he used to. This social isolation has likely exacerbated Dan's PTSD symptoms and contributes to his feelings of loneliness. Further, Dan's mother recently began working outside the home and has not been home as much as Dan is used to. This is another change that might be affecting his emotions.

struggling to maintain her sobriety in light of pressure from friends and stress at school." The last section, the plan, addresses following appointments, next steps, referrals needed, and actions expected of both the client and the worker: "The client will attend at least one AA meeting per day, review relapse triggers and self-care plan."

Each SOAP entry should begin with the date and end with the social worker's name, credentials, and signature. Entries should be completed as soon as possible after the actual contact to ensure they are accurate and up to date. Again, it is important to remember that your notes could be subpoenaed by court. Notes should not include every single detail of what you discuss with your client. They should be used to document the general themes that arise, changes in the clients presentation/behavior, and any other important changes.

Summary

This chapter discussed assessment of physical, cognitive/perceptual, emotional, and behavioral functioning, as well as motivation and environmental factors. Although each of these factors was presented as a discrete entity, these factors are neither independent nor static. Rather, the various functions and factors interact dynamically over time, and from the initial contact, the practitioner is a part of that dynamic interaction. Each factor is, therefore, subject to change, and the social worker's task is not only to assess the dynamic interplay of these multiple factors but also to instigate changes that are feasible and consonant with clients' goals.

Assessment involves synthesizing relevant factors into a working hypothesis about the nature of

problems and their contributory causes. You need not be concerned in every case with assessing all the dimensions identified thus far. Indeed, an assessment should be a concise statement that embodies only the most pertinent factors.

This chapter's scope was limited to intrapersonal and environmental dimensions. It excluded conjoint, family, and group systems, not because they are unimportant components of people's social environments but rather because they generally are the hub of people's social environments. To work effectively with interpersonal systems, however, requires an extensive body of knowledge about these systems. Therefore, we devote the next two chapters to assessing couple and family systems and therapeutic groups.

Competency Notes

C1 Demonstrate Ethical and Professional Behavior

- Demonstrate professional demeanor in behavior, appearance, and oral, written, and electronic communication.

C2 Engage Antiracism, Diversity, Equity, and Inclusion in Practice

- Demonstrate anti-racist social work practice at the individual, family, group, organizational, community, research, and policy levels, informed by the theories and voices of those who have been marginalized.
- Demonstrate cultural humility applying critical reflexivity, self-awareness, and self-regulation to manage the influence of bias, power, privilege, and values in working with clients and constituencies acknowledging them as experts of their own lived experiences.

C7 Assess Individuals, Families, Groups, Organizations, and Communities

- Demonstrate respect for client self-determination during the assessment process collaborating with clients and constituencies in developing mutually agreed-on goals.
- Apply knowledge of human behavior and person-in-environment and other culturally responsive multidisciplinary theoretical frameworks when assessing clients and constituencies.

Chapter 10

Assessing Family Functioning in Diverse Family and Cultural Contexts

Chapter Overview

Social workers encounter families in many service settings. For example, social workers in child welfare and child protective services agencies focus on reducing maladaptive family patterns that contribute to child maltreatment and neglect (Wodarski et al., 2015). Social workers who serve adult clients with severe cognitive impairments associated with traumatic brain injuries or dementia are concerned with the support that the client's family can provide (Albert et al., 2002; McGovern, 2015). Psychiatric social workers often implement psychoeducational interventions to families to increase support for psychiatric patients and reduce relapse (Singer et al., 2012). Forensic social workers and probation officers evaluate the quality of family support to reduce reoffending (Maschi et al., 2009). Social workers also work with families in the role of family counselor, family therapist, and family case manager. An example of a family counselor is a generalist youth or family counselor who is not providing specific ongoing assessment and intervention therapeutic strategies. Instead, a counselor would be doing a quick assessment and first-order intervention strategies to help the family return to immediate functioning while referring the family to additional services to achieve ongoing stabilization. A family therapist is someone who may provide long- or short-term services in a therapeutic setting to assist the family in developing skills to maintain ongoing functioning. A family case manager typically works with the family to connect the family to services in the role of a case manager.

Social workers who work with families often use skills from evidence-based family therapy models rooted in systems theory that have been in development in the United States and around the world since the 1950s such as family systems theory (Nichols & Schwartz, 2012; Papero, 1990). Some examples include brief strategic family therapy (Szapocznik & Hervis, 2020), structural family therapy (Minuchin, 1974), and family systems theory (Bowen, 1978). Social workers must develop the skill to view families as systems and be able to apply concepts from systems theory in their work with families as demonstrated in family systems theory. Family systems theory, developed by Murray Bowen (1978), utilizes concepts from systems theory such as boundaries, patterns, roles, and equilibrium to assess and understand family functioning.

This chapter provides strategies for how to effectively assess families. It presents concepts for understanding how family functioning and individual functioning are interrelated. It also provides a basis for understanding how the family itself can be treated as a unit, approaching problems of individual members within a context of family dynamics that themselves can become the target of change. Finally, the chapter provides an eclectic framework for family assessment consisting of several models used in social work practice with families. The chapter avoids using a normative template for family structure and strives to discuss family dynamics from the vantage point of the cultures within which family formation and family development occur.

As a result of reading this chapter, you will be able to:

- Take a broad view of how families are defined and how family functioning is understood.

- Understand the role of self-awareness and cultural humility in family assessment and how cultural values influence beliefs and values about family membership and family functioning.

- Describe the dimensions of family structure, including homeostasis, boundaries, power and decision-making, roles, rules, life cycle, and sociopolitical environment.

Continued

- Discuss family adaptive capacity, including stress and resilience.

- Use an anti-oppressive approach by describes the role of culture, human rights, and social justice

in the definition and expression of family system characteristics.

- Develop skills and strategies to assess patterns of interactions that underlie family functioning.

The EPAS Competencies in Chapter 10

This chapter will give you the information needed to meet the following practice competencies:

- Competency 2: Engage Anti-Racism, Diversity, Equity, and Inclusion in Practice

- Competency 3: Advance Human Rights and Social, Racial, Economic, and Environmental Justice

- Competency 7: Assess Individuals, Families, Groups, Organizations, and Communities

Defining Family and Family Functions

There is considerable diversity in family forms, including two-generation married parent-headed households, heads of household who are not married and caring for children, blended families (e.g., stepparents, stepchildren), same-sex couples, single-parent households, multigenerational households (e.g., grandparents, parents, children), foster families, grandparent-led households, and families not necessarily bounded by biology. In addition, values about family and how family is expressed are influenced by the family's cultural heritage, as well as by popular culture and dominant social views about family. In view of the diversity of family forms, how families define their members and membership is best articulated by the family members themselves.

Debates about definitions of family are not without consequences for all clients served by social workers. When families do not conform to prevailing dominant cultural norms about family definitions, the conflict that results can burden families with significant strain, exacerbating stress and affecting family member functioning. Pregnancy among unmarried adolescents is a provocative example. In some communities, pregnancy before marriage can ostracize and exclude adolescents from community life, whereas in other communities, pregnancy brings increased family support along with its hardships associated with increased roles and responsibilities, and marriage is delayed until the realization of other life goals (Edin & Kefalas, 2005). Therefore, understanding the transactions between client definitions of family and the cultural milieu in which families are imbedded can be critical to the social work

assessment process. Underlying the definition of family is a shared understanding of two elements of family structure: how family membership is composed and the various functions that the family serves as an enduring social institution. It is important to consider the extent to which the family has the capacity to perform the essential functions that contribute to the development and well-being of its members as well as the individual contributions to family functioning. There is a reciprocal relationship between individual family members and the family system itself.

Family functions refer to the ways that families are organized to solve problems of evolutionary survival. In essence, the family performs certain functions and has responsibilities, such as attending to family members' social and educational needs, health and well-being, and mutual care of its members that are unlike those of any other social systems. Family provides identity and a sense of community and belonging to individuals (Zakiei et al., 2020). It is largely through the family that character is formed, attachments are developed, vital roles are learned, and members are socialized for participation in their culture and the larger society.

Self-Awareness in Family Assessment

There is reason to be concerned about oppressive practices in social work with families. Social workers, as individuals from a vast array of cultural backgrounds, hold values and beliefs about families and what constitutes family. Lack of self-awareness and implicit bias can cause social workers to impose their own values and beliefs

Case Example 1: Home for the Holidays

In "Home for the Holidays," Jackie and Anna scheduled a couples' therapy session at Jackie's request. Both women are Caucasian and appear to be close in age (25 to 35 years old). Jackie, a chef, owns the restaurant where she works. The couple have been together for five years and have lived together for the past year. They initiated couples' therapy because of disagreements about their holiday plans. They both would like to spend the time together. Jackie, however, feels pulled to visit her family during the holidays because they live in another state, and she has not seen them in some time. Anna states that she does not feel completely comfortable at the home of Jackie's parents. She perceives them as distant and avoiding meaningful contact because of their discomfort with their relationship. In fact, when they attended a family wedding, Anna was not invited to stand with the family when pictures were taken.

Jackie recently came out to her parents as a lesbian. When she disclosed to them that she was moving in with her significant other, Anna, her parents were quiet and took up other activities. This withdrawal behavior is normalized in Jackie's family. She explained that in her family, "there is little outward expression, and we don't make a big deal about everything." Nonetheless, Jackie does recognize her parents' discomfort with her sexuality. Anna acknowledged a difference between their family styles, remarking that in her family, "there were no secrets" and "everyone's situation was open for discussion." Anna would like Jackie to broach the subject of her sexuality with her parents a second time to "strengthen the connection between Jackie and her parents, to hasten Jackie's parents' acceptance of our relationship."

When asked to explore the meaning that this conversation would hold for her, Jackie expressed feeling pushed by the request and that it felt like an ultimatum. For Jackie, there was too much at stake for her to risk another conversation with her parents. In her mind, the worst-case scenario would be that her parents would shut her out. Hearing Jackie's interpretation of the request as an ultimatum and the pressure that Jackie

was feeling, Anna clarified and softened her position. To Anna, the conversation "would help Jackie open up more." Anna also stated that, as is the case in her family of origin, "Jackie does not communicate at home."

Concerning their plans for the holiday, Anna agreed to go to Jackie's house. The two made plans to cook a meal together for the family and give gifts from both of them as a sign of unity. Jackie agreed to consider plans to hold hands with Anna at dinner; she requested time to discuss this at the next session. Their overall goal was to improve their communication with each other.

Congruence may also be related to a goal to which not all family members agree. For example, in the case "Home for the Holidays," the dialogue between Jackie and Anna in their session with Kim, the social worker, illustrates the concepts of congruence in communication. Consider how you would describe the congruency of Anna's messages. For example, Anna would like Jackie to broach the subject of her sexuality with her parents. The content of her message is clear, but Jackie and Anna's goals are dissimilar, which causes tension in their relationship.

Family rules, interactions, and communication patterns often accompany couples and play out in their relationship with each other. For example, in the case "Home for the Holidays," Anna states, "In my family, there are no secrets, everyone's situation is open for discussion." Jackie, on the other hand, wishes to maintain homeostasis in her family by adhering to the family rule of "We don't make a big deal about everything." Clearly, Jackie and Anna have had prior conversations about their relationship and the response from Jackie's parents. They are in different stages of coming out. In their sequence of interactions, Anna appears to perceive Jackie and her family as the problem in their relationship. For example, Anna pushes Jackie to talk to her parents again, which in her mind is a premium in their relationship. Jackie is understandably reluctant to have this conversation with her parents, so the repetitive, patterned interactional cycle between the couple continues.

onto families. In the 1980s, feminist scholars began to criticize the burgeoning family therapy movement for reinforcing patriarchal family structures (Goldner, 1985). Often, mothers were directly and indirectly blamed for the presenting problems of their children, including children who later developed schizophrenia

and children who came to identify as nonheterosexual. The relative silence of prevailing family systems theories and theorists about the social construction of normative family system structures, such as the nuclear family, provided indirect support to patriarchal family arrangements. Thanks to feminist scholarship and critical scholarship in allied disciplines, social work with families today is generally understood within a broader conception of family structure and functioning, and social workers have a more highly developed sense of how their roles interact with client worldviews about how families are defined.

To achieve this understanding, social workers need to grapple with their own assumptions about what constitutes a healthy and functional family. In doing so, social workers, through supervision, study, and reflection, need to understand their own worldviews and beliefs about families, including how unexamined binary thinking and cultural bias that may result in subjective responses to questions such as "How should families be organized?", "What is the best way for families to raise children?", and "What are the proper roles of elders, parents, and children in a family?" Furthermore, social workers need to assess client views about families, their perspectives about family structure, and their beliefs about how families work. When social workers encounter clients whose family worldviews differ in meaningful ways from their own, they must redouble their efforts to understand the strengths of client worldviews and perspectives on family structure and the opportunities those strengths provide to promote growth and problem solving.

Although social workers are called on to view cultural differences among families through a nonjudgmental lens, they are not required to accept client family worldviews at face value, nor are they required to change their own family worldviews when they conflict with those of their clients. In both extreme and subtle ways, culturally sanctioned family structure and family function practices can be oppressive, warranting social work interventions based on cultural humility, anti-oppressive, and empowerment principles. Social workers are advised to consult a variety of frameworks, including professional codes of ethics, legal codes, public policy, and the social work agency's values and mission, as well as human rights frameworks. Social workers must not hesitate to advocate for the needs of families whose configurations may be different from the dominant cultural norm.

The implications for social work practice because of differing views about family between social worker and client are important to keep in mind, as these differing views may influence service delivery. The most difficult challenges for social workers and their clients arise when different views about family have unclear impacts on family members or on society. Family values related to the use of corporal punishment as a child-rearing tool are illustrative. The prevailing view of most who write about parenting practices mirrors the thrust of evidence-based programs such as **parent management training (PMT)**, emphasizing the reinforcement of positive child

behaviors, minimizing the use of punishing parenting practices including corporal punishment, and resorting to time-outs when corrective parenting interventions are needed (Kazdin, 2005). However, evidence suggests that the use of timeouts may not be compatible with family beliefs about discipline across all cultures, particularly those families who value family and community membership over and above individual needs and wants (Hoagwood et al., 2006). In such cultures, time-outs can be experienced as a highly abusive banishment, whereas a spanking provides a negative consequence for misbehavior without the implied separation from the family group. However, studies on childhood trauma categorize spanking as an adverse childhood experience (ACE) (Afifi et al., 2017; Merrick et al., 2017). Considering conflicts such as these, it is necessary for the social worker to consult many frameworks and perspectives before concluding about family behavior, with decisions being made in collaboration with the family.

The Family Systems Framework

Family assessment in social work is conducted within a systems framework. The family systems framework shows how families are organized to achieve their goals and perform their functions. The family systems framework defines properties and characteristics of families rather than of any particular individual within the family. These properties provide social workers with areas for assessment as they seek to understand the family. These properties include factors such as the family life cycle, homeostasis, family decision-making, hierarchy, and power, adaptive capacity, and the social environment. These factors point to an important difference between the assessment of individual clients and the assessment of families. Unlike assessments of individuals, family assessment focuses social work attention on the family as a system, with communication norms and patterns among and between individuals providing clues about the properties of the family system. The language of family assessment also includes words that emphasize the collective rather than individuals such as family life cycle, social environment, family decision-making, power, and hierarchy. Although individual family members may be described by their moods and actions, a family assessment describes families according to their roles, rules, boundaries, and subsystems.

The shift from individual to collective has important implications for family interventions, as we will discuss in Chapter 15. When assessing family functioning, problematic behaviors are viewed as symptoms of family functioning, as opposed to being blamed on individual pathology. In addition, responsibility for change is shared among all family members simultaneously.

When assessing families using the concepts presented here, it is important to bear in mind that a family assessment does not ordinarily occur in isolation from an assessment of the presenting problem. Presenting problems assessed within the family systems framework also need to be understood in the context of their onset, severity, frequency, precipitating and perpetuating factors, and the needs and conditions of individual family members, including mental health function, physical health, and social functioning. In addition, social work and family interaction typically occur as a result of an individual referral for service. For example, the referral may be for an individual client, resulting in the initial intake consisting of an assessment of the individual client's presenting problem, history, and goals for treatment. However, using family systems theory, we recognize that individuals do not exist in isolation. Thus, with the consent of the individual client, the family is included in the planned change process, as well as in the social worker–client relationship. The family's history, family dynamics, and goals of the family are included in the provision of services. The inclusion of family, by consent of the client, is especially important for many clients who may align with collectivist values which emphasize the role of the family in the decision-making process.

Homeostasis

Homeostasis is a systems concept that describes the tendency of a system to maintain or preserve equilibrium or balance. In essence, homeostasis is a conservative property of family systems that strives to maintain the status quo and avoid change. When faced with a disruption, a system tends to try to regulate and maintain homeostasis (Kim & Rose, 2014). Families may try to maintain the status quo in response to family transitions in the life cycle or stressors associated with abrupt change to the family system itself (e.g., death, divorce, a new addition to the family, an abrupt move), or environmental events such as immigration or move to a new location, or changes in daily routines. For example, during the COVID-19 pandemic, many families had to transition to work and school from home, resulting in increased stressors on the family system because of the disruption to homeostasis. Stressors and difficulty adjusting to the change may often look like resistance. For example, a family may wish for life to go back to normal following a death of a family member. Instead, the loss of a member from the family system requires realignment of roles, rules, and boundaries among the remaining family members, resulting in substantial changes from the accustomed norms within

the family. The death of a parent may result in the addition of a new adult to the household to ameliorate the loss of the role functions served by the deceased parent, or often, the oldest adult child may assume more authority in place of the deceased parent. As systems, families develop mechanisms that serve to maintain balance in their structure and operations. They may restrict the interactional repertoires of members to a limited range of familiar behaviors and develop mechanisms for restoring equilibrium whenever it is threatened, in much the same way that the thermostat of a heating system governs the temperature of a home.

Homeostasis operates through a pattern of feedback loops to reinforce the status quo and preserve the family structure. Feedback loops are cycles of interactions or expected interactions that are used to exert influence over families and family members. Ordinarily, feedback loops preserve one or more aspects of family system structure, such as family boundaries, roles, rules, and hierarchy. Feedback loops occur when children seek a rule change and are pushed back by their parents; when, in nuclear family arrangements, elders seek to have influence over parents, and parents act to set boundaries to minimize elder influence; and when adult couples negotiate changes to family responsibilities. Fear of violence or of deportation may cause families to strengthen their boundaries and ask that some members assume additional roles (e.g., teenage children may need to be employed while undocumented parents are unable to find work), while other members may reduce some behaviors (e.g., undocumented parents may face isolation) in order to protect the family system. Sometimes feedback loops are quite dramatic, involving aversive, coercive, forceful, and loud communication strategies (e.g., yelling, threats of violence), whereas other times feedback loops are subtle, quiet, subversive, and difficult to detect (e.g., not following through on agreements).

It should be noted that all family systems are characterized by feedback loops that preserve the status quo and maintain homeostasis. This property of family system structure explains what social workers have come to understand: changes to family system structure are often slow and difficult to achieve. Thus, the force of homeostasis can be a major frustration to social workers and family members who may wish to see change or improvement happen quickly, yet it is also important to recognize that homeostasis, and the associated feedback loops that preserve it, is an important source of family strength. It is because of the force of homeostasis that families can provide a stable and predictable environment for development and decision-making. It is because of homeostasis that the family is recognized by outsiders as a distinct social system and that it is not easily changed.

Just as feedback loops operate internally to sustain the status quo of internal family functioning, feedback loops also regulate family relationships with external environments. Families themselves receive feedback from their external environments that send messages, such as "You are a good family" or "You are not a good family." Often, these messages reflect the community's values, representing its views about human rights, justice, and shared obligations, while at other times these messages can be a conduit for injustice and oppression. In many instances, social workers embody community feedback loops as they represent community standards about child rearing in the case of child protective services and about proper education in the case of school social work.

Although the focus of our discussion about homeostasis emphasizes the conservative nature of family systems, this should not be taken to suggest that homeostasis or the tendency of families to maintain the status quo is the opposite of flexibility or adaptation. In fact, families are in a constant state of adaptation to forces in the external environment, as well as to changes among members in the internal family structure. Under most circumstances, and for most families, the tendency of family systems toward homeostasis helps families adapt in ways that preserve the integrity of the family as a distinct unit. Under such circumstances, feedback loops help guide change and adaptation in the face of sometimes overwhelming challenges and obstacles.

Boundaries and Boundary Maintenance

Boundaries, a central concept in family systems theories, can be likened to abstract dividers that function between and among other systems or subsystems within the family. Boundaries delineate family and individual family members' expectations around personal, physical, and psychological space as well as privacy and individual decision-making preferences. Boundaries act as abstract dividers between the family and the environment and serve as invisible lines that identify people, groups, or entities as insiders and as outsiders. Boundaries can be detected or observed by behaviors and communication patterns, both blatant and subtle, that signify who belongs within an identifiable family or subsystem within a family, whose input into the family system may be accepted, or who may or may not receive information about the family system.

External Family Boundaries

Because family systems are part of larger systems (e.g., neighborhood, school, church, community), families engage in diverse transactions with the environment. Boundaries change over time as the family system as a whole and its members experience various developmental levels. For example, when a child begins school, the boundaries of the family system expand to permit interactions with the educational system.

Families can widely differ in the degree to which they are flexible and accepting of transactions with other systems. In operational terms, flexibility means the extent to which outsiders are permitted or invited to enter and become part of the family system and whether members are allowed to invest emotionally and engage in relationships outside the family. Flexibility also means the extent to which information and materials are exchanged with the environment. A family system with rigid, inflexible boundaries is characterized by strict regulation that limits its transactions with the external environment and restricts incoming and outgoing people, objects, information, and ideas. Rigid boundaries can serve important functions for the family by preserving territoriality, protecting the family from undesired intrusions, and safeguarding privacy. A family of color may have less trust of outside mainstream institutions and be less open to input from institutions due to negative experiences with social workers or law enforcement. Similarly, certain families may prefer alternative methods of healing and be less open to sharing information about their health practices with Western medical institutions. Some families may not be as open to accepting recommendation from Western doctors due to lack of trust. It is necessary for social workers to build rapport with families in order to understand their boundaries and gain acceptance and trust from families. Rigid boundaries can also limit family members' access to social support, opportunities, and expansion of self in the external environment.

When assessing the boundary patterns of families related to outside influences, it is essential that you consider the family's unique style, cultural preferences, strengths, needs, and the functionality of a family's chosen boundary preference. Families may have more flexible boundaries with extended family members, perhaps including well-defined obligations and responsibilities to one another. In collectivist cultures, the boundaries between a family, friends, and their extended family may be more flexible due to the collectivist nature of their culture. Conversely, boundaries may appear less flexible when external influences intrude upon family traditions and values and are seen as a source of conflict or disruption to the family system. For example, the behavior of a youth that results in the entry of a juvenile probation officer into the family can be disruptive, but the family system, out of necessity, can reluctantly accommodate this intrusion. At other times, the family may change to accommodate new inputs over the course of the life cycle or during transitions. For example, during the COVID-19 pandemic, family boundaries changed to accommodate virtual interaction with teachers or health-care providers within the home setting.

Internal Boundaries and Family Subsystems

All families develop networks and relationships between coexisting subsystems that can be formed based on gender, interest, generation, or functions that must be performed for the family's survival (Minuchin, 1974). Members of a family may simultaneously belong to numerous subsystems, entering into separate and reciprocal relationships with other members of the nuclear family, depending on the subsystems they share in common (e.g., parents, parent/child, older sibling/younger sibling), or with the extended family (e.g., grandmother/granddaughter, uncle/nephew, mother/son-in-law). Each subsystem can be thought of as a natural coalition between participating members. Of course, while some coalitions may be enduring, many of the coalitions or alliances are situation related and temporary in nature. For example, a teenager may be able to enlist one parent's support in asking another parent's permission for a special privilege. A grandparent living in a home may voice disagreement with their adult child and their spouse regarding their discipline of children, thus temporarily forming a coalition with their grandchildren. Such passing alliances are characteristic of temporary subsystems. In addition, several subsystems or coalitions may exist within a family, with individual family members belonging to more than one coalition at one time. For example, a parent may be in coalition with the other parent yet also be in a coalition with a child, creating a triangle. Several triangles may impact one other at the same time. Bowen refers to these as interlocking triangles (Bowen, 1978).

Subsystems such as partner/spouse, parental, and sibling subsystems are more enduring in nature. Minuchin's (1974) seminal work in family therapy proposed the structural family systems model, which states that the formation of stable, well-defined coalitions between members of these vital subsystems is critical to the well-being and health of the family. Unless there is a strong and enduring coalition between the executive system, such as parents, for example, conflict will reverberate throughout a family, and children may be co-opted into one faction or another as executive subsystems struggle for power and control. In general, the boundaries of these subsystems must be clear and defined well enough to allow members sufficient differentiation to carry out

functions without undue interference (Minuchin, 1974). At the same time, they must be permeable enough to allow contact and exchange of resources between members of the subsystem.

Minuchin (1974) points out that the clarity of the subsystem boundaries has far more significance in determining family functioning than the composition of the subsystem. For example, a parental subsystem that consists of a grandmother and an adult parent/child may function adequately. The relative integrity of the boundaries of spouse/partner, parental, and sibling subsystems is determined by family rules. A parent clearly defines the role of the parental subsystem, for example, by telling the oldest child not to interfere in the conversation when a younger child is being disciplined. The message or rule is that an older child is not a co-parent. A parent, however, may delegate caretaking of younger child to an older child in the parent's absence. In this instance, the boundaries of the parental and sibling subsystems are clearly delineated.

Enmeshment and Disengagement

The clarity of boundaries within a family is a useful parameter for evaluating family functioning. Minuchin (1974) conceives of all families as falling somewhere along a continuum of extremes in boundary functioning, where the opposite poles are disengagement (diffused boundaries around the family unit and rigid boundaries around the individual) or enmeshment (diffused boundaries between family members and inappropriately rigid boundaries between the family and outside systems). Family closeness in an enmeshed family system is defined as everyone thinking and feeling alike and relationships that require a major sacrifice of autonomy, in which members are discouraged from developing their own identity and independent explorations or behaviors. Enmeshment and disengagement are not necessarily indicative of dysfunctional relationships. Depending on the cultural, racial, or socioeconomic groups, these concepts may appear differently as cultural values around interdependence, collectivism, and individuality and can vary among families. In collectivist cultures, multiple generations may live together in one household, share bedrooms, food, and financial resources. In collectivist cultures where family is prioritized and connection to a family or group system is a prominent feature of individual identity, the discussion and resolution of individual problems or relationship problems are handled as a family system with perhaps the inclusion of extended family members in the problem-solving process.

According to Minuchin (1974), every family experiences enmeshment or disengagement between its subsystems as the family passes through various developmental phases.

During a family's early developmental years, for example, a caretaker and a young child, out of necessity, are an enmeshed subsystem. A cultural variant, however, is that a child's relationship can involve several caretakers with close ties. Sharing the parental bed until a certain age or sleeping in the same room with parents are common practices in some cultures (Fontes, 2005). In the United States, many parents prefer this arrangement as well; however, the risk of co-sleeping with a young child is a prominent concern of medical professionals.

In many cultures, adolescents gradually disengage from the parent–child subsystem as they move toward young adulthood and perhaps prepare to leave home. In some cultures, young adults may continue living with parents and eventually assume the care of aging parents. The period of adolescence and its behavioral markers are subject to cultural norms. In some cultures, adolescents may be engaging in marriage and family formation, while in some cultures, the stage of adolescence may extend well into their 20s. Differing cultural norms can be seen in other areas of family life as well. For example, in many different cultures, there is a high level of interdependence between family members whereby individual resources are pooled in which the adult children and parent(s) share financial resources toward the purchase of a home, food is community property regardless of who purchased it, and all members, when able, share the financial burden of household expenses. This should not be confused with enmeshment. Therefore, fluid roles, bonding patterns, and rules as framed in Western society may not signal that a relationship is enmeshed or that a member is disengaged. However, it is necessary for social workers to consult various frameworks around family roles, function, and individual well-being. Parentified children may indicate a lack of parenting capability on the part of the executive system, indicating interventions meant to strengthen the parental subsystem through various supports that allow the family system to develop healthy boundaries for each subsystem.

Family Decision-Making, Hierarchy, and Power

Decision-making authority and power constitute an important dimension of the family system structure. Indeed, all social systems have some form of hierarchy and differentiation of power that is suited to their functions. In families, power is ascribed to certain members and subsystems to enable the system to achieve its goals, described as family functions. Power arrangements and family decision-making authority should create an environment in which primary attachments can flourish, the economic needs of the group can be met, social status

can be preserved, and the emotional and developmental needs of all members can be nurtured. For most families, power alignments and decision-making structures serve as a source of strength. For some, power alignments and decision-making structures interfere with successful family functioning and serve to exacerbate presenting problems.

Formal family decision-making authority ordinarily rests with the executive subsystem. The executive subsystem has the right and the obligation to provide overall direction to a family, allocate resources, manage boundaries, protect the integrity of the family system in its external relations, and assign roles to individual members. Membership of the executive subsystem has strong cultural determinants, usually being restricted to the parents of children in nuclear families, adult members of a household, differentiated to include elders in multigenerational families, or delegated to the eldest child in some family systems. The membership and functioning of executive subsystems are also negotiated within individual families depending on the idiosyncratic circumstances that each family faces. For example, families that include divorced parents negotiate executive decision-making and leadership, often with the aid of mediators and the courts. Blended families must figure out how to form new decision-making patterns within preexisting patterns of family relations, and families with limited or strained resources often incorporate children in the decision-making process, as can be seen in some families with one or more older children assuming some amount of care for younger siblings. Regardless of composition, executive subsystems exist to provide leadership to the family system. Variations in the composition of the executive system can be considered strengths on the part of the family to realign roles and responsibilities among individual family members to promote the functioning of the family system while also creating room for individual family members to pursue goals and activities outside of the family system.

The composition and functioning of the executive subsystem can be observed in the way that power and authority functions within the family and in relation to its external environment. Power is displayed in different forms within families, and it is important to recognize the multiple expressions that power takes. Executive power is the concentration of formal decision-making authority into the position of a recognized leader or set of leaders. Family members can usually tell who is in charge of a family. These are members of the executive subsystem.

Alternatively, power can be distributed to family members based on tasks. Such task-specific power is evident when members of the family make decisions about which other members conform or follow. Power also exists covertly in families. Such **covert power** is held by family members who, for example, enter into coalitions to challenge or circumvent executive power or task-specific power. It also can be expressed by family members who employ their own strengths and agency to influence family decision-making.

Of course, power or the ability of one or more persons to affect the behavior and worldviews of others is rarely distributed according to explicit rules, and herein lies the complexity of understanding how decision-making power and leadership exist within families. Although power and leadership may formally reside with the executive subsystem, shifts in power can depend on the specific circumstances faced by families. Crises, chronic stress, and external forces can elevate the influence of children on the decisions of the parental subsystem, amplifying their role in the family's power structure. Developmental changes over the life course also influence the distribution of power in a family system, as can be seen when members of an executive subsystem succumb to the effects of chronic health problems and when parental authority is challenged by adolescents. Power may be held both overtly and covertly. For example, one individual may be formally acknowledged as the central figure in the family and thus have more power in family decision-making, as in families that conform to patriarchal traditions. Even so, other, less visible members or subsystems can have significant covert power in the family. For example, an individual can hold power because of a disability or chronic condition. Another can gain power because of their level of literacy, including literacy with technology, or attainment of a level of education or income.

The distribution of power and the exercise of leadership within a family are not value-free. How families organize decision-making authority, or how they wish to organize power, often expresses deeply held values that may or may not be culturally sanctioned. For this reason, it is important to understand family power and decision-making within the frameworks of social justice and human rights (McDowell et al., 2012). While human rights conventions and treaties embody a strong presumption of family privacy to guard against government intrusion and government-sanctioned oppression (Convention on the Rights of the Child, September 2, 1990), there is increasing recognition that the exercise of power within families can systematically oppress its members. This is particularly evident when families organize along patriarchal values to limit educational opportunities to its members or expect certain levels of accomplishment by gender, limit access to employment outside the home to some members, or sanction intimate partner abuse or child abuse. Family-level oppression can also be expressed as ageism, whereby family elders are exploited either intentionally or unintentionally because of their diminished capacity to care for themselves.

How power and decision-making authority are organized within a family should maximize social justice and human rights. In your assessment of family power and decision-making, you must determine not only how power is distributed but also who, if anyone, is formally designated as the leader and to what extent covert power is exercised by individual members. It is equally important to assess the extent to which family rules allows the family system to reallocate power so that members can adjust their roles to meet changing circumstances. Finally, you must assess whether family members are satisfied with the distribution or shifts in power.

Family Roles

Roles are generally understood patterns of behavior that are accepted by family members as part of their individual identities. Usually, roles can be identified by their labels, which denote both formal roles that are socially sanctioned (e.g., grandparent, mother, father, brother, sister) and idiosyncratic roles that evolve over time within a specific family context (e.g., comedian, scapegoat, caregiver). Role theory, when applied to the family system, suggests that each person in a family fulfills many roles that are integrated into the family's structure and represent certain expected, permitted, or forbidden behaviors (Collins et al., 2021). Family roles are not independent of each other. Rather, role behavior involves two or more persons engaging in reciprocal transactions. Roles within the family system may be assigned based on legal or chronological status or cultural and societal scripts. In some families, role assignments are based on gender or age. At the same time, as with power and decision-making, roles may be flexible and diffused throughout the family system. In sorting out roles in the family system, individual role behavior may be enacted, prescribed, or perceived. In an **enacted role**, a mother, for example, engages in the actual behavior—such as care-taking—relative to her status or position. A **prescribed role** is influenced by the expectations that others hold regarding a social position. For example, despite the changes in families, in a family's interaction with a bank officer, a male is almost always presumed to be the head of a household or the primary decision maker in the family. A **perceived role** involves the expectations of self, relative to one's social position. These expectations of self may be a result of social norms around identities such as age and gender.

Roles are both learned and acquired over time. The role of parent, for example, is acquired, but it is also learned from others and through experience. Similarly, the various roles that exist between couples in a relationship are learned based on interactions over time. Satisfaction with the respective role behavior indicates a level of harmony in interpersonal family relationships. In addition, roles may be complementary or symmetrical. The role relationship between a parent and a child, for example, is a complementary relationship (or an independent–dependent role relationship) in which the needs of both are satisfied. In contrast, in a symmetrical relationship, both parties function as equals—for example, the division of household or child-rearing responsibilities or decision-making are shared instead of based on gender roles.

Roles for the most part are not static. Rather, they can evolve because of family interactions and negotiations. Consequently, they often defy traditional stereotypical role behaviors. In actuality, role relationships in most families operate along a continuum and may be characterized as complementary, symmetrical, or quid pro quo because of negotiation.

Life transitions and conflict often demand changes, flexibility, and modifications in role behavior. A family may experience role transition difficulties in making the necessary adjustments when, for example, an older relative comes to live in their home. The aging parent may experience difficulties in adjusting to becoming dependent on adult children. For example, older people who are no longer able to drive can feel that they are a burden and even resent the loss of their independence. Another significant change for some parents is adjusting to the void when children leave the home.

Conflict in the family may occur when individuals become dissatisfied with their roles, when there is disagreement about roles, or when individuals holding certain or multiple roles become overburdened. Interrole conflict can occur when an individual is faced with excessive, competing, and multiple role obligations, especially when two or more roles are incompatible—for example, wife/partner, mother, daughter, employee. Fulfilling the responsibilities associated with these enacted and perceived roles can cause an individual to experience conflict in juggling multiple role demands.

Understanding the roles and the role behavior within the family, including the way in which roles are defined as well as role conflict, is important in the assessment of the family role dimension. In the assessment, you want to determine what role assignment in the family is based on—for example, age or gender rather than such factors as abilities, need, and interest. As you assess the role behavior in any family, you may probably note several individual and family strengths, such as how well members flexibly adapt to changing roles and their role-performance behavior. Because each culture or family form has its own definitions of roles, social workers must determine and assess the goodness of fit with the needs of family members. Assessment then must consider whether members are satisfied with their respective roles and, if a member is dissatisfied, whether the family is amenable to modifying or changing determined roles.

Communication Patterns in Families

There is a plethora of terminology to describe communication patterns in families such as open communication, communication that emphasizes emotions or beliefs of members, blame seeking, direct communication, and indirect communication. In this chapter, we examine concepts such as congruence, clarity, mystification, negative communication patterns, fault-defend communication, dual monologues, and sender and receiver patterns. We also consider the levels of communication such as verbal, nonverbal, and context. One pattern that cuts across many cultural groups is that of discouraging the open expression of feelings often resulting in considerable difficulty asserting oneself or confronting others, particularly in ways that are facilitative. In all instances, you must first determine the impact of family's communication patterns and styles on its members and the relationships therein, and whether change is desirable, including considerations of the cultural implications.

Another aspect of communication that transcends culture, which may be generational, is the multiple ways in which people communicate with each other. Youth, for example, use particular words, phrases, and abbreviations in their communications. Today's youth are more likely to rely on text messaging or social networks as primary means of interacting with each other. These modes of communication may differ from communication rules that existed before technology became widely use. Differing modes of communication can be identified when working with families, especially when there are miscommunications between adults and younger family members.

Whether family communication patterns are culturally influenced or otherwise determined, they may be faulty, causing significant problems for family members. In assessing the impact of a family's communication style, you must be aware of the complexities of communication and the influence of culture or technology and be prepared to assess the functionality of members' communication patterns and the extent to which there is congruence and clarity in how members communicate with each other.

Congruence and Clarity of Communication

Family members convey messages through both verbal and nonverbal channels and qualify those messages through other verbal and nonverbal messages. A task for social workers is to assess the congruency of messages—that is, whether there is correspondence between the various verbal and nonverbal elements.

According to Satir (1967) and other communication theorists, messages may be qualified at any one of three communication levels. At the verbal level or metacommunication level, people explain the intent of their messages verbally. Metacommunication happens when people discuss the content and topics of communication. Note that implied messages are also a form of metacommunication. At the nonverbal level, people reinforce or contradict their verbal messages nonverbally, through gestures, facial expressions, tone of voice, posture, eye contact, and so on. At the contextual level, the situation in which communication occurs, such as environment, culture, political, and other factors, can reinforce or disqualify a speaker's verbal and nonverbal communications. Social workers must be able to assess communication patterns and identify discrepancies between levels of communication and seek clarification when a person's words and expressions are incongruent. In addition to considering the congruence of communications, it is important to assess the clarity of messages. (See Case Study 1 Home for the Holidays.) Notice how Jackie's parents used nonverbal messages to communicate their opinions about Jackie's new living arrangement; however, their communication lacked clarity. Considering contextual factors and the parent's nonverbal behavior, one may be able to fairly assess the parents' emotional state in that moment and further assess the communication patterns between Jackie and her parents. Jackie's lack of disclosure about her emotional response to that experience also warrants further assessment to gain clarity about how Jackie and her family norms around communication.

The term mystification (Laing, 1965) describes how some families befuddle or mask communications and obscure the nature and the source of disagreements and conflicts in their relationships. Mystification of communication can be accomplished by myriad kinds of maneuvers, including disqualifying another person's experience, addressing responses to no one in particular even though the intent of the speaker is to convey a message to a certain person, using evasive responses that effectively obscure knowledge of the speaker, or utilizing sarcastic responses that have multiple meanings. Some couples also use their children or pets to convey messages to each other, such as, "I think your behavior is upsetting to the children."

Barriers to Communication

In Chapter 7, we identified several barriers to communication that, when utilized by social workers, block client communications and hamper the therapeutic progress. Likewise, family members use these and similar responses in their communications with each other, thereby preventing meaningful exchanges and creating tension in relationships. The assessment of communication barriers also includes nonverbal behaviors such as affect and facial expressions, hand placement, eye contact, fidgeting, etc.

All families have communication barriers within their conversational repertoires. Members of some families, however, monitor their own communications and adjust their manner when their response has an adverse impact on another person. As you observe the communication patterns of families, it is important to assess three issues:

- The presence of patterned negative communications
- The pervasiveness of such negative patterns
- The relative ability of individual members of the system to modify their communication patterns

In addition to assessing these factors, it is vital to ascertain the various combinations of communication patterns that occur repetitively as family members relate and react to one another. For example, one individual may frequently dominate, criticize, attack, or accuse the other, whereas the other may defend, apologize, placate, or agree. In an exchange in which one member continues to attack or accuse another member, the other tends to continue to defend their position, thus manifesting a fault–defend pattern of communication. Attacks or accusations generally take the form of "You never ...," in which case the other defends themself by providing examples that contradict the accusation. In such situations, even though the topic of conflict or the content of the discussion may change, the way couples or family members relate to each other and orchestrate their scenario remains unchanged. Furthermore, the same types of exchanges tend to occur across many other areas of the family's interaction. The thematic configurations that occur in families' or couples' communication tend to be limited, but they reinforce tensions in the relationships. Your task as a social worker is to assess the thematic communication pattern, including the context in which the fault–defend sequence occurs.

Receiver Skills

A critical dimension of communication is the degree of receptivity or openness of family members to the inner thoughts and feelings of other members in the system.

Receptivity is manifested using certain receiver skills, which we will discuss shortly. Again, a caution: These skills are in keeping with Western traditions, and, therefore, the assessment should include the extent to which these skills are consistent with the preferences of the family systems with which you interact.

You may observe response patterns in some families that convey understanding and demonstrate respect for other members' messages. In other families, messages can be met with response patterns such as ridicule, negative evaluations, or depreciation of character. In still other families, members may engage in dual monologues—that is, members communicate simultaneously, which to the casual observer might appear to be a free-for-all. Family members may also use words, sayings, or gestures specific to their family or reference group.

In general, facilitative receiver skills invite, welcome, and acknowledge the views and perceptions of others. For example, free-for-all conversations invite and even encourage responses but perhaps not in the way that may be most familiar to you. In such situations, family members feel free to express agreement or disagreement, even though doing so may sometimes spark conflict. Facilitative responses that convey understanding and acceptance include the following:

- Physical attending (direct eye contact may or may not be encouraged, receptive body posture, hand gestures, attentive facial expressions)
- Listening or paraphrasing responses by family members that restate in fresh words the essence of a speaker's message (e.g., "Man, you said ...," or as a youth might say, "I feel you ...")
- Responses by receivers of messages that elicit clarification of messages (e.g., "Tell me again. I'm not sure what you meant" or "Am I right in assuming you meant ...?")
- Brief responses that prompt further elaboration by the speaker (e.g., "Oh," "I see," "Tell me more")

Sender Skills

Another facet of assessing communication patterns and skills is assessing family members' sender skills—that is, the extent to which family members can share their inner thoughts and feelings with others in the system. Becvar and Becvar (2000b) refer to such sender skills as the ability of family members to express themselves clearly as feeling, thinking, acting, valuable, and separate individuals and to take responsibility for their thoughts, feelings, and actions. "I" messages are messages phrased in the first person that openly and congruently reveal either pleasant or unpleasant feelings, thoughts, or reactions experienced by the speaker ("I feel ...," "I think ...,"

"I want ..."). For the social worker, an essential task is to assess the extent to which the climate in the family allows family members to be candid, open, and congruent in their communications.

A positive communication climate stands in sharp contrast to situations in which family communications are indirect, vague, and guarded and individuals fail to take responsibility for their feelings, thoughts, or participation in events. Instead of "I" messages, family members are likely to use "you" messages that obscure or deny their responsibility or that attribute responsibility for the feelings to others (e.g., "You've got me so rattled. I forgot"). Such messages are barriers to communication and are often replete with injunctions concerning another's behavior (e.g., "you should" or "you ought") or negatively evaluate the message of the sender (e.g., "You shouldn't feel that way").

In assessing communication patterns of families, social workers must gauge the extent to which individual members have the skills to utilize the facilitative responses identified in the preceding list. So that the social worker and the family understand their communication style, part of the assessment can include asking family members to keep track of the extent to which individual members (and the group as a whole) utilize facilitative communication skills. A simple grid with the relevant indicators can be developed, and responses can be rated as a plus or minus by other family members.

Critical to assessing family communication patterns is the extent to which messages contribute to the development of self-confidence and consistently validate a person's worth and potential. In contrast, consider whether the patterns and the repertoires that you observe consist of constant negative messages (e.g., putdowns, attacks, or criticism) or otherwise humiliate or invalidate the experience of others in the family. It is also advisable to keep in mind that a family experience with internal and external stressors may, in fact, challenge even previously effective communication skills.

Family Life Cycle

The family life cycle encompasses the developmental stages through which families must pass and varies depending on the family's culture. Knowledge of stages in family development helps social workers assess and understand changes experienced by families as the family develops and changes over time. Families may often experience difficulties during normal changes in the family system. For example, as young children develop into adolescents, they may experience stress during the growth and change process which is normal; however, parents may perceive this time to be a stressful period in the family life cycle. Social workers are able to assess the problems identified by the family and help develop interventions or solutions that help the family understand and cope with the stage of development in which they find themselves.

Duvall (1977) and other theorists such as Carter and McGoldrick (1988) developed a conceptual framework of the family life cycle that represents changes in the family over time that some families may experience. For example, these models identify normal family changes such as birth, marriage, retirement, and launching of children. Carter and McGoldrick (1988, 2005) identified six stages of family development (unattached young adult, new couple, family with young children, family with adolescents, family that is launching children, and family in later life), all of which address nodal events related to changes in family composition over time.

In addition to these types of changes, families may also experience death in the family, divorce, adoption, a move, job loss, income loss or income gain. Using systems theory, the social worker assesses family problems by identifying any changes in the family system that may be precipitating factors. For example, a new couple may experience more conflict after moving in with each other as they adjust to a new living arrangement. The change is the new living arrangement which requires negotiation of space, preferences, schedules, and adoption of new patterns of daily living. The same can be said for almost all changes in the family life cycle such as marriage, the addition of a new baby, when young children become teenagers, when children move out, and divorce. Roles must realign, and norms must be renegotiated. Variations in the life cycle are, of course, highly likely to occur in today's world. Families can change, readjust, and cope with stressful transitions that occur within the life cycle. In much of our society, education, work, love, marriage or a committed relationship, childbirth, and retirement do not follow a linear fashion. For example, older adults return to school. Adult children live with their parents, and childbirth is no longer within the exclusive realm of the traditional family form.

Variations also occur in the family life cycle among cultures. Every culture marks off stages of living, each with its appropriate expectations, defining one's own sexuality, defining what it means to be an adult, to be young, to grow up and leave home, to find a partner or not, and to have children or not. Exploring the meaning of the life cycle with diverse families is particularly critical to determine important milestones from their perspective. Cultural variants that have a negative connotation in Western society include the legal versus the culturally derived age for marriage, as well as family responsibilities and roles for children. Families from other countries, therefore, may experience adverse reactions to practices that were common in their country of origin. Because culture plays an important role in family progression and life-cycle expectations, it cannot be avoided as an essential dimension in the assessment of family functioning at a particular development stage in the life cycle.

Family Rules

Family rules, which underlie all aspects of family system structure, prescribe the rights, duties, and range of appropriate behaviors of members within a family. They govern how boundaries are established and maintained, the distribution of family roles, the execution of power and decision-making, how families adapt in the face of family life-cycle changes, and, in short, strive to maintain family system homeostasis. As with all dimensions of family system structure, family rules have strong cultural determinants. In general, family rules can be explored across two dimensions: explicit/ implicit rules and flexible/rigid rules.

Explicit and Implicit Rules

Explicit rules are those rules that family members readily recognize and can articulate. These include expectations for behavior that parents impose on children, both prescribed behavior (e.g., complete your chores) and proscribed behavior (e.g., don't hit your brother), as well as negotiated agreements among members of the executive subsystem (e.g., who manages money) and across subsystems (e.g., elders are expected to spoil their grandchildren). Explicit rules are important because they express family values. These rules represent family efforts to meet important goals and obligations and to respond to demands imposed on the family from both internal and external forces. Very often, explicit rules are the subject of family fights and contests.

Implicit rules are different. In general, implicit rules are hidden from family members' awareness, similar to the way in which elements of an individual's personality may be hidden in the subconscious. Being hidden, implicit rules can be difficult to detect without careful observation of behavior that tends to reveal their content, but once revealed, implicit rules showcase their importance. Implicit rules govern how family members unwittingly collaborate to maintain the status quo in the family system structure. Although explicit rules are often the topic of a family feud, implicit rules govern how family feuds are fought and resolved. While explicit rules dictate how order is maintained, implicit rules dictate how rule changes are negotiated, and whereas explicit rules establish expected behavioral repertoires, implicit

Case Example 2: Shon Family

Teng Shon, 56, is married and lives with his wife, age 53, his five adult children ages 36, 35, 32, 28, and 22, and both his parents. Teng's oldest son, Xue, age 36, is married to Lyla, age 24. Xue and Lyla have three children under the age of 6. Xue's wife and children also live in the home with Teng. Teng's mother is age 72, and his father is 85. You have been called to the home to do an early childhood assessment for Xue's oldest child, who will be entering kindergarten in the fall. Social workers must practice self-awareness about their own values and worldview regarding family. Social workers who practice from only a Western perspective may have several questions about this family. However, it is important to think broadly about definitions of family and consider the client's culture and worldviews that may differ from one's own. Questions you may have about this family might be the following:

1. Why do the adult children still live with their parents?

2. Do they have enough space in their home for such a large family?

3. What circumstances surround the age difference between Xue and Lyla and the fact that Lyla began having children at a young age?

4. Are Teng's parents' needs being met at their advanced ages?

Points to consider for each question:

1. Teng may come from a family where children remain living in the home well into adulthood and often do not leave the home until they are married. Xue, as the eldest son, remains living in the home even after marriage so that he may take care of his parents in their old age and eventually take over the head of the household role.

2. There are values in a first-world country such as the United States that shape our impressions of how much living space each person must have. This perspective comes from a privileged place in which one can afford to provide individual rooms for each family member. In many communities, especially in those facing economic oppression and in holistic cultures, shared and communal spaces are more common. Providing separate bedrooms for each family member is not prioritized.

3. Early marriage is still a common practice in many cultures in the United States. Cultural marriages that take place outside of the American courts is also common. It may be the case that early marriage occurred for Lyla, at which point she began birthing her children soon after the marriage.

4. For many cultures, families prefer to care for aging parents within the home rather than placing them in a nursing home. Social workers are positioned to provide and refer community supports to families caring for aging parents in the home.

rules explain why family members do not always conform to expectations.

Family rules, both explicit and implicit, can be detected by the real or expected consequences suffered when rules are violated, what we earlier defined as feedback loops. Feedback loops are thought of as an escalation of some aversive behavior, such as raising voices, imposing punishments, and, in extreme cases, using violence. It should be recognized that feedback loops are not limited to aversive behavior, and all family members are involved in the regulation of family rules through the use of feedback loops. Feedback loops that occur from within the family system related to the preservation of explicit and implicit rules can be observed by answers to questions like "What happens when [a given rule is violated]?", or "What would happen if [a given rule were violated]?" In some family systems, for example, explicit and implicit rules are developed to manage the anxiety of fragile family members, being governed by expectations about the threat of decompensation in the face of stress. In such cases, the expectation of decompensation is the feedback mechanism that promotes adherence to a set of explicit and implicit rules.

Herein lies a key property of family rules: Explicit rules are often conditional, depending on circumstances, and the salience of conditions on feedback loops depends on the simultaneous expression of implicit rules. Consider a parent who sometimes imposes consequences for a curfew violation but sometimes does not, depending on the level of stress and strain experienced within the family. Implicit rules involving the regulation of stress are often revealed after careful examination of such instances.

Flexible and Rigid Rules

The explicit and implicit rules found in a family system may be either flexible or rigid, depending on context and time. In tense conflicted situations, family members may monitor what they say and how they behave, such as "Be careful what you say around Mom." However, at other times, speaking freely is acceptable. Flexible rules enable the family system to respond to family stressors as well as to the developmental needs of individual members. As you observe families, you will want to assess the extent to which rules provide members with opportunities to explore solutions that utilize individual and collective family capacities. For example, an open discussion of member differences can facilitate an understanding of acceptable behavior. Similarly, openly discussing touchy subjects can be instrumental in bringing the family together in stressful times. Rules that permit the system to respond flexibly are usually optimal and vary by culture.

As you observe family processes, keep in mind that all families have flexible rules as well as rigid rules. The latter can undermine positive family dynamics, but flexible rules allow the family to work out disagreements and encourage participation because everyone's ideas are important. Of course, variations in both types of rules can of course occur depending on the age and cognitive ability of family members.

Many family rules change over the course of the family life cycle. The developmental stage of minors, for example, often means that they press for redefinition or modification of family rules that are appropriate to their age. An individual may also pursue interests and choose values that are alien to those embraced by the family. Rules that govern the behavior of minors are by necessity modified when they become adults. Elders, however, accustomed to a certain set of rules vis-à-vis their status may be disinclined to accept modifications. It is often difficult for elders to cope with situations in which they feel acted upon by rules set forth by their adult children, professionals, or institutions. These dynamics cause "disequilibrium within the family system, a sense of loss, and perhaps a feeling of strangeness until new transactional patterns are in place to restore family balance" (Goldenberg & Goldenberg, 1991, p. 40).

In addition to assessing the stresses on rules caused by developmental changes and internal events (inner forces), it is important that you also assess the extent to which a family's rules allow the system to respond flexibly to dynamic societal stresses (outer forces) such as job loss, concerns about neighborhood safety, family relocation, natural disaster, or family uprooting experienced by immigrants or refugees.

Families may also construct rigid rules that function as protective factors to minimize real or potential risks, such as telling minors to avoid certain people, places, or situations. For immigrants or refugee families, further complicating dynamics are the vast contrasts between rules of the culture of origin and that of the host society. Immigration and the related cultural transition require significant life changes over a short period of time, including material, economic, and educational changes; changes in roles; and the loss of extended family, support systems, and familiar environments (Green, 1999). These families may adopt a mix of rules from their new and old cultures.

Responding successfully to inner and outer stresses requires constant transformation of the rules and the behaviors of family members to accommodate ongoing changes while maintaining family continuity. Families often seek help because of an accumulation of events that have strained the coping ability of the entire family or of individual members. Even when these changes are for the better, they may overwhelm the coping mechanisms and resilience of individual members or an entire family system.

Social Environment

A key dimension of family system structure is the depth and the nature of its involvement in the social environment. Like all social systems, families require inputs of energy and resources from external environments for their survival. Without such transactions with the environment, families suffer from entropy or the tendency of systems to wither over time. An example is the breakdown of a family system when mental health concerns go unaddressed for a long period of time. Often, relations of families with their external environments can be a source of stress and strain, threatening family functioning and even survival. Most often, the social environments that families inhabit provide both strain and facilitative support.

The social environment of families can be described as a set of broad social sectors that catalog the various ways that all families engage with the outside world. These include the economic sector and the labor market, educational institutions, public health and mental health systems, public safety and corrections institutions, nongovernmental organizations, religious institutions, familial networks, and informal support networks. Within each, families may experience advantages conferred through rich formal and informal networks of relationships but also may suffer disadvantages by virtue of sparse social networks. Moreover, family social status itself confers advantages as well as disadvantages. Within each social sector, prejudice and discrimination linked to minority group identity, socioeconomic status, and gender present serious challenges for families. Workplace discrimination, mass incarceration, and interreligious conflict are just a few of the problems associated with prejudice and discrimination that social workers may encounter in their work with families.

Family mobility and migration illustrate the importance of the social environment in overall family functioning (Sluzki, 2008). Family relocation can threaten family functioning or create excitement as people are drawn to new opportunities and challenges. It threatens family functioning first through the depletion of social resources immediately available to help families achieve their goals (e.g., meeting the attachment, economic, social status, and emotional health needs of family members). Simple problems like access to friendship networks and alternative child care arrangements can strain families who remain isolated from social support resources in their new communities.

The COVID-19 pandemic introduced a plethora of challenges to family functioning, including transition to virtual schooling from home, work from home, loss of regular child care, technology challenges, as well as job loss and income loss for many. These changes caused stress and conflict as families struggled to adjust.

Relocation can also strain families through the cultural conflicts that can attend movement across regional and international boundaries. Refugee and immigrant families frequently experience intergenerational conflict as children and adults adjust differently to the new culture. In the face of resource challenges and cultural conflicts, families sustain their functioning through active engagement in their new social environment, collecting local social capital to enable them to access local resources and institutions while also sustaining their engagement with social support networks from their communities of origin (Smokowski & Bacallao, 2011).

How families manage their engagement with the social environment brings the interrelationship of family system structures (e.g., boundaries, rules, roles, power, and decision making) into strong focus. When navigating their external environments, families are managing boundaries, reinforcing rules, and exercising role differentiation, all at the same time. Who within a family is responsible for participation in the labor market? How do parents and siblings react when one of the children is facing disciplinary problems at school? Where can family members go for health-care and mental health services that respect their cultural heritage? How do family rules and norms facilitate or impede access to formal and informal networks that may be available to support coping? Answers to these questions and others illustrate both how families are embedded within the social

environment and how family system structure dynamics are operating to manage the transaction between the family and its environment.

Family Adaptive Capacity

The adaptive capacity of any given family refers to the extent to which the family can achieve its functioning goals, given the demands of family and social life. As the family faces demands from its environment and challenges from its members, its capacity to adapt is a central property of the ability to maintain itself as a cohesive unit. The concept of adaptive capacity brings to light two additional concepts that are relevant to family life: family stressors and family strengths and resilience.

Family Stressors

A family stressor is something that threatens existing family structures and patterns or that interferes with a family's capacity to achieve its goals. For example, a job loss can strain a family's capacity to assure the economic viability of the family unit. A family member's refusal to continue playing an accepted role in the family (e.g., negotiator) can strain family functioning by altering the family's usual pattern of activity, and a social worker's entry into a family can strain family definitions as to who is and is not a member of the family's executive subsystem.

The source of stress within the family system can be internal—the result of family dynamics, roles and relationships, communication patterns, or life-cycle transitions or separations. The source of stress can also be external, including the neighborhood in which the family lives, inequality, racial or economic discrimination, or public policy—any one of which can marginalize families. It is quite possible to encounter reciprocal pressures between internal and external stressors. For example, stressful internal dynamics within a family system may be the result of economic pressures.

Family stressors can be classified in several ways. First, stressors can be classified based on their relationship to the family life cycle. From this perspective, stressors are considered to be normative—disruptive events (e.g., marriage) that are predictable based on expected patterns of growth and development of family members but that nevertheless provoke a change in prevailing family routines—or non-normative—disruptive events (e.g., an accident) that are unexpected and not necessarily associated with the family life cycle. Classification of family stressors into normative and nonnormative categories showcases how life-cycle transitions can strain families and force adaptations that are often resisted as family systems strive toward homeostasis.

However, classifying stressors into normative/non-normative categories misses the central features of stressors that may be routinely experienced, and thus may be normative but are not directly the result of the family life cycle. For example, systematic exclusion from the labor market because of discrimination or strained relations between families and key social institutions such as schools or child welfare systems are not easily described through the normative/non-normative classification.

Alternatively, stressors can be classified according to their frequency and duration, for example, by using a three-category typology that describes stress as acute, episodic, or chronic. **Acute stressors** are usually single occurrence events. They may be relatively minor yet disruptive health problems that force family system adjustments (e.g., a sick child who cannot attend day care or school) or large events that permanently change family system structure (e.g., marriage, birth of a child, divorce, death). **Episodic stressors** are those stressors that have an ending but are repeated periodically. Some serious mental health conditions, such as major depressive disorder, can be episodic in nature, requiring families to adapt during the period of illness. Finally, **chronic stress** persists over a long period of time. Poverty and economic insecurity, for example, are often associated with diminished family cohesion and marital discord, along with coercive and aggressive parenting and unstable housing. Poverty can determine where a family lives, the condition of the housing where they reside, their access to resources such as a full-service grocery store, the safety of their neighborhood, and the quality of education that their children receive.

Stressors can also be characterized in terms of magnitude and number. **Stressful life events** are generally considered major disruptions that, in some cases, may be traumatic, whereas **daily hassles** are the pressures and the responsibilities that family members must face daily. Although the impact on family functioning of serious stressful life events such as job loss, death of a close associate, and violence may seem evident, daily hassles like the burden of household chores, monitoring children, minor health problems, problematic relations at work, concern for job security, and countless others can also have a negative impact on family functioning.

This points to the final way that stressors can be described: Stressors can be characterized in terms of number. A consistent finding in research on risk and resilience is that, for most people, exposure to a single risk factor does not strongly predict negative impacts. However, as exposure to hardships increase in number, a property called **cumulative risk**, the likelihood of a host of negative outcomes increases exponentially (Fraser, 2004).

Thus, family stress—the events and challenges that threaten family homeostasis—can be described in a variety of ways. However described, families seen by social workers often face significant levels of stress that threaten families' capacity to achieve their goals and perform critical family functions. In assessing families, it is, therefore, useful to pay attention to the sources of family stress and determine whether and how stressors pose a risk to family functioning. How families cope with and adapt to stressors may depend on their resources, strengths, or resilience, bolstered by family networks, social supports, spirituality, and relational caregiving. It is also important to recognize that not all stress leads to debilitating family problems, and not all families succumb to stress, as will be made clear in the next section.

Family Strengths and Resilience

Resilience is the capability of individuals and families to sustain their functioning and thrive when threatened by risk and adversity. It is the answer to the question, "Why do some families succeed even when they suffer significant adversity?" Although resilience as a concept has been developed and operationalized by developmental psychologists, psychiatrists, and social workers at the individual level (Fraser, 2004), a small number of scholars have extended resilience to the study of families. For example, important contributions to our understanding of resilient family functioning and family strengths have been made in the United States through the study of families of different identities (Bell-Tolliver et al., 2009; Walsh, 2016) and families involved in the child welfare system (Lietz, 2006, 2007).

Research on family resilience has used primarily qualitative methods, resulting in a limited list of **resilience factors**. These factors provide families with resources for problem solving and patterned ways of approaching challenges that promote growth and successful adaptation. In no way do resilience factors keep problems from happening, nor does it minimize the structural stressors placed on families. However, by including resilience factors in an assessment of family system functioning, social workers and families can have a full appreciation of the myriad ways that families attempt to cope with difficult problems.

A current synthesis of research on family resilience suggests the following potential strengths or resilience factors to include in family assessments (Bell-Tolliver et al., 2009; Lietz, 2006, 2007; Walsh, 2016):

1. Social support from the community as well as from kinship bonds. Families who have active and vital social support networks have ready access to coping resources.

2. Internal cohesion and commitment. Families are able to adapt to adversity when family members have a strong sense of dedication to each other and when their patterns of communication lend themselves to mutual understanding of family members' thoughts, ideas, and feelings regarding adversity.

3. Creativity and flexibility. Families that strive for creative solutions to problems, including demonstrating flexibility in role assignments, enable families to find solutions to stressful situations.

4. Appraisal, insight, and meaning. When families strive to understand their difficulties and find affirmative meaning in them, they have an increasing ability to sustain their problem-solving efforts under stress. Very often, appraisal and insight are linked to family spirituality and belief systems.

5. Initiative and achievement. Families who are action oriented tend to approach problem solving using positive coping strategies such as cognitive coping, problem solving, and constructive emotional regulation strategies.

6. Boundary setting. Families with a strong sense of family structure will seek to shield its members from unhelpful, unhealthy, and destructive influences.

As you are perhaps aware, assessing strengths in families is not easy. One difficulty with a strengths-based perspective is that helping professionals and the agencies in which they work, as well as funding resources and policymakers, have deeply entrenched views about the pathology of families who experience problems. Some agencies and practitioners purport to embrace a strengths perspective; however, family strengths seem to be an abstract idea, as their assessment tools can attest. Families themselves are not always comfortable with a strengths focus. Having been socialized to focus on their problems in exchange for receiving services, they can be reluctant and indeed suspicious when social workers talk about strengths. Further, family members may not recognize that their capacity to cope with adversity, their support and celebration of each other, and their talents and aspirations are strengths. Once the conversation about family strengths takes place, you can ask family members to highlight other family strengths.

Assessment Skills and Strategies

Social workers assess family system structure in a variety of ways. For example, they may observe patterns of interaction as they unfold over the course of an interview. Of course, the interview process itself is a primary source of data about family boundaries, hierarchy, rules, roles, and strengths. Finally, a host of standardized scales have been developed to describe family functioning. In the sections that follow, we describe specialized family assessment strategies, including the use of direct observation, interviewing with circular questioning, genograms, and selected standardized scales. To illustrate these strategies in practice, we will use an assessment with the Diaz family as a case example.

Problems occur in a person or family and situational context. In this case example, the problems occurred in part because of Mr. Diaz's living situation, his access to alternative living environments, and the availability of a continuum of care that could include in-home supports. For example, income and health insurance coverage may be external factors that can influence the alternative care arrangements that are available to a family.

Case Example 3: Diaz Family

Carlos Diaz, 66, lives with his 16-year-old son John in a subsidized apartment on the second floor of a three-story building. Mr. Diaz is diabetic, is visually impaired but not legally blind, and has a history of heavy alcohol use, although he has abstained from alcohol for the last seven years. Mr. Diaz's companion of 18 years, Ann Mercy, recently died of a massive stroke. She had provided emotional support, given Mr. Diaz his insulin injections, and managed the household. Mr. Diaz has difficulty walking, has fallen several times in the past year, and is now hesitant to leave his apartment. In addition to John, Mr. Diaz has eight children from an earlier marriage who live in nearby suburbs, though only one, Maria, calls him regularly. Mr. Diaz's physician considers his current living arrangement to be dangerous because of the need for Mr. Diaz to climb stairs. The physician is also concerned about his capacity to administer his own insulin. A medical social worker convenes a family meeting with Mr. Diaz, his son John, his daughter Maria, and his stepdaughter Anita.

External factors should always be accorded prominence in the assessment to avoid the assumption that problems are caused solely by factors internal to the family system. In this case, both internal and external factors may impinge upon and disrupt family functioning. When families experience a disruption, dynamics in the family tend to be directed toward maintaining homeostasis and restoring equilibrium.

Observing Patterns of Interaction

To assess family system structure, social workers first assess the sequences of interaction that occur between members. All families play out scenarios or a series of transactions in which they manifest redundancies in behavior and communication. Learning about these repetitive patterns of verbal communication, nonverbal communication, and behavior among family members provides clues about the presence and the strength of family system boundaries, decision-making authority and power, roles, rules, and adaptive capacity. In their assessments of family system structure, social workers use interviewing skills, asking questions to reveal repeated sequences of interactions surrounding a presenting problem, and also observe family interactions that occur in the presence of the social worker.

To illustrate how this works, consider the following script from the first minutes of a session with the Diaz family. The medical social worker involved with this family has convened a family group conference to consider health and safely alternatives for Mr. Diaz (Carlos), who is being considered. In this example, Mr. Diaz, daughter Maria, son John, and stepdaughter Anita demonstrate sequential verbal and nonverbal behaviors that have a powerful impact on the family system.

> **Anita [to social worker]:** Carlos can't maintain himself or John. John runs wild, with no appropriate adult supervision, and Carlos can't take care of himself now that Mother has died. [Anita looks earnestly at the social worker but signals a relational distance between herself and Mr. Diaz by using his first name. In response, Mr. Diaz sits stoically, arms folded, glowering straight ahead.]
>
> **Maria [to social worker]:** Dad is having trouble with John and hasn't taken care of himself all these years with Ann Mercy doing the cooking and cleaning and injecting his insulin. [To Mr. Diaz]: Dad, I respect you and want to help you in any way that I can, but things just can't continue like they are [attempting to reason with her father].
>
> **Mr. Diaz** [to social worker]: These children "no tienen respeto." They don't give me the respect they should give the father as the head of the family. They want to put me in a nursing home and take John away from me

> [appealing to the social work to notice the unfair, disrespectful way that he is being treated].
>
> **Anita:** Maybe that would be for the best, since you can't take care of yourself or John [triumphant facial expression, resembling a smile].
>
> **Maria [showing frustration, explains to social worker]:** Dad is used to having his own way and we do respect him, at least I do, but he won't listen to how some things have to change.
>
> **Mr. Diaz:** Maria, you have been a good daughter, and I am surprised at your behavior. I would think that you would be the loyal one and stick by your father if anyone would.
>
> **John:** Dad, you know I stick by you, and I can help with some things, too. I want to stay with you. We have been getting along okay, and I want to be a good son and take care of you [asserting his loyalty and attempting to maintain equilibrium by supporting the father].
>
> **Anita:** John, you have been running in the streets, in trouble with the law, taking money from your father. You are no help to him, and he can't be a good parent to you [reasserting her point of view].
>
> **Maria:** John, I know you want to help, and you are close to your dad, but you have made a lot of problems for him, and I, too, wonder if you can take care of him or he can take care of you.

In the preceding example, the Diaz family members play out a discordant yet repetitive thematic interaction that, with slight variation, can be observed over and over in their transactions. Families may discuss an endless variety of topics or content issues, but their processes often have a limited number of familiar behaviors. It is as though the family is involved in a screenplay, and once the curtain is raised, all members participate in the scenario according to the family script. It is important to understand that family scripts rarely have beginnings or endings; that is, anyone may initiate the scenario by enacting their lines. The rest of the family members almost invariably follow their habitual styles of relating, editing their individual scripts slightly to fit different versions of the scene being acted out by the family. In sequenced interaction scenes, the subjects discussed will vary, but the roles taken by individual family members and the styles of communicating and behaving that perpetuate the scenario tend to fluctuate very little. Notice the sequenced interactions that occurred in this family:

1. Anita speaks forthrightly about her concerns about John and Mr. Diaz's capacity for parenting him because of Mr. Diaz's medical condition. Responding nonverbally [folding his arms and glowering], Mr. Diaz declines to openly respond [a patterned behavior when his authority is questioned or when there is disagreement].

2. Maria affirms some of Anita's concerns but also speaks directly to her father [affirming her respect for him as father and head of the family].

3. Mr. Diaz asserts that his children "no tienen respeto," and their motivation is to put him away [maintaining his authority].

4. Anita does not deny that a nursing home might be the best solution [reasserting her position that he cannot care for himself].

5. Maria reasserts her respect for her father yet notes that some things must change.

6. Mr. Diaz addresses Maria and questions whether she is, in fact, showing proper respect for him as her father.

7. John joins the fray and tries to identify himself as a good son with "respeto," which adds another dimension to the transactions.

8. Anita puts John in his place by doubting whether he has acted as a good son or whether Mr. Diaz can be a good parent to him.

9. Maria supports John's desire to be a good son but agrees that there are persistent problems with Mr. Diaz and his care of John.

10. Maria expresses concerns about whether or not John is getting what he needs as a minor residing with Mr. Diaz

11. Six of Mr. Diaz's eight children are not active participants in the meeting. Indeed, background information suggests that Maria may be most actively involved among the sibling subsystem.

These patterned behaviors are suggestive of family system structure. First, it is clear that the family is contemplating a significant life-cycle change in which Mr. Diaz's traditional position of authority is threatened by a looming family decision regarding placement in a nursing home. He employs both the overt power of his position (invoking the authority of the head of the family) and covert power (splitting Maria away from Anita by expressing surprise at her behavior) to resist this family system change. Second, overt family rules regarding respect for elders continue to be invoked, and active feedback loops are in place to preserve this important rule. Feedback loops include Mr. Diaz's complaints about his children's lack of respect as well as Maria's affirmation of the importance of respect. Third, subsystem boundaries are revealed in the manner in which Maria and Anita echo each other's concerns about both Mr. Diaz and John, while John is excluded from this sibling subsystem. Additional subsystem boundaries are suggested in the way that Maria and John both seek emotional closeness

with Mr. Diaz, while Anita and Mr. Diaz remain emotionally distant. Fourth, a mediating role is suggested by Maria's attempt to acknowledge Anita's expressed concerns while attempting to reason with her father.

Interviewing Skills and Circular Questioning

Following on these observations of family system functioning, the social worker may use a variety of interviewing strategies to selectively confirm aspects of family system structure that are relevant to the resolution of the presenting problem. For example, it may be useful to learn more about the rules governing power and decision-making in the family. Also, the social worker will likely be interested in the roles and the positions of nonparticipating family members as well. The social worker will want to take a strengths perspective with the family, striving to identify family resilience factors that may provide resources for problem solving. In this case, Anita's active involvement and coalition with Maria, despite being a stepdaughter, suggests a source of cohesion and commitment that may exist within the family despite the lack of involvement from other children in the family.

Social workers have available a variety of interviewing strategies to assess family system structure. Interviewing skills presented in Chapter 6, including verbal following, exploring, and focusing skills, can, of course, provide the basis for most if not all assessment strategies that social workers employ. In general, it is important that the social worker listen carefully to all family members who participate in family meetings. Thus, reflective listening and summarizing are two skills that are especially featured in family meetings. The complexity of a family meeting, given the multiple people present, usually requires that the social worker manage the interview process carefully, liberally seeking concreteness and using focusing skills to ensure that the conversation stays on track.

Circular questioning is a specialized interviewing strategy that is often employed to elicit information about the repetitive transactions that take place among family members (Brown, 1997; Patrika & Tseliou, 2015). As the name implies, circular questions suggest the concept of circular causality, in which an antecedent produces an outcome or effect only insofar as the antecedent itself is embedded in a cyclical or repetitive chain of events. Any given sequence of events occurs within a multilayered context of actions and inactions by others, which serve to support, dampen, or alter the sequence. Circular questions treat family members as perceivers of family life, eliciting information from them about the interrelatedness of family members and relationships that are often external to the perceiver. The nature of circular questions will become clear through our description of three types of circular questions below.

First are circular questions that elicit member perceptions about the presenting problem. A question as simple as, "What is the problem as you understand it?" can initiate a circular dialogue when it leads to a discussion of similarities and differences among family members. Importantly, a social worker employing circular questions usually adopts a neutral stance, avoiding the temptation to judge the truth or the validity of family member perspectives except as these themes emerge through contrasts highlighted in the perspectives of others. The following is an exchange that took place between the social worker and the Diaz family:

Social worker: Mr. Diaz, I understand you to be saying that you do not want to go to an assisted living facility, and you want to continue to take care of John. Is that correct?

Mr. Diaz: Yes, I don't want to go to one of those places. You have no freedom. You go there to die.

Social worker: Thank you, Mr. Diaz. Later, I would like to talk with you about how assisted living facilities help people manage health problems like diabetes and about how many, many people who live in these kinds of places are quite happy, but now, I would like to stay focused on how you and members of your family are understanding the problem. What is going on here? What is the problem as you see it?

Mr. Diaz: My children want to take over. This is plain.

Social worker: I notice that John did not want to take over. He said that he wants to keep living with you.

Mr. Diaz: Yes. John is a good boy. He has some trouble some time, but he is a good boy.

Social worker: John, how does your dad's definition of the problem—that the children are trying to take over—compare with your older sisters' definition of the problem?

John: He wants to be in charge, and they want him to give up his apartment and move.

Social worker [to everyone]: It seems that members of this family are operating from two different problems. First, the children are seeking to take control of Mr. Diaz's affairs, and second, that Mr. Diaz needs significant support to care for his health and for John, and he may not be able to do these two things well while living alone in his apartment.

Among the skills that stand out in this vignette, it should be noticed that the social worker invited family members to provide their perceptions of what other family members might think or believe about the presenting problem. This is a signal characteristic of circular questioning,

that family members external to the exchange can be recruited to provide their observations. Circular questions can also be used speculatively or as a simulation by invoking the perspectives of members who are not present in the interaction. For example, consider the following interaction, which took place approximately five minutes later, after further discussion of the presenting problem:

Social worker: Maria, let's imagine that your older brother is having a conversation with the doctor about your father's health-care needs. What would he tell the doctor?

Maria: My brother is not helpful at all in this. He keeps his distance and tries not to get involved. I don't know what he would say.

Social worker: The purpose of my question is not to figure out exactly what he thinks. Only he can do that, but questions like this help me to understand family dynamics. What do you imagine that he would say to the doctor?

Maria: I'm not saying that he would ever meet with the doctor, but if he were forced, he would say that we should leave dad alone.

Mr. Diaz: He is a good boy with many responsibilities. He is successful in his life. He can't be bothered by this.

Maria: But Dad, he is not helping. He has never helped.

Social worker [interjecting]: Maria, let's extend the pretend question one step further. Say that the doctor expressed concerns about your father's health and ability to care for himself. What would your brother say then?

Anita [interjecting]: What does he have to do with this? He's not even here.

Social worker: Anita, I would like to learn more about your perspective as well and will turn to you in a moment. For now, it is important to let Maria share hers. Maria, what might your brother say?

Maria: He would tell the doctor that my dad is proud and would never agree to move into assisted living, no matter how bad it got.

Social worker: Anita, I want to ask for your impressions of something I've noticed. It appears that the men of this family are all supporting independence for Mr. Diaz. On the other hand, it is the women of the family, you, Maria, and especially your mother, who have focused their energy on making sure that Mr. Diaz's health-care needs are taken care of. What is your perspective?

Anita: This has always been the case. My mother went out of her way to make sure that Carlos was taken care of.

Social worker: Mr. Diaz, what is your perspective?

Mr. Diaz: Women should take care of things like this. This is the natural way of things, but it should be done with proper respect.

Social worker: So, Maria and Anita are fulfilling their roles.

The social worker uses circular questions not to identify the truth of any of a competing number of problem definitions but rather to showcase family system functioning. In the example, several features of the Diaz family system structure are suggested, including the nature of subsystem coalitions and strong values about gender roles. Additionally, it is interesting to note how the family is struggling to reorganize itself to account for the loss of Mr. Diaz's partner, Ann Mercy. Such family system functioning came to light because the social worker observed patterns of responses by family members as they reported their perspectives and reflected together about similarities and differences.

Second are questions to establish sequences of events related to a presenting problem. Beginning at a point in time, the social worker asks variations of the question "What happened next?" repetitively to obtain a concrete version of how a series of events unfolded. For the Diaz family, the social worker might have established a sequence of events when members of the family first discussed with Mr. Diaz the possibility of moving into an assisted living apartment. Although the initial sequence may appear linear, a social worker who employs circular questioning seeks to understand how all members of the family relate to the event sequence. This includes members who are directly involved in the sequence as well as members who are silent or who are not apparently involved. As with problem definitions, information about the positions and the reactions of family members are often elicited from peripheral actors. For example, the social worker might inquire about John's presence and behavior while the discussion of an assisted living placement took place and might ask John to describe his perceptions of the discussion as it happened.

Finally, social workers can use rating and ranking questions to highlight differences and similarities. In the context of family assessment, ranking and rating questions are often used to compare members on key family system dynamics such as boundaries, roles, rules, and power. Rating and ranking questions may be used to highlight subsystem boundaries (e.g., Who is the most involved in the family? Who is least involved? On a scale of 1 to 10, how strongly does Maria agree with Anita?); role differences (e.g., Who is the funniest person in the family? Who gets things done?) or repetitive feedback loops (e.g., Who is first to express respect for father? Who is most likely to challenge father?). Social workers generally adopt a neutral stance when seeking circular explanations for a family presenting problem, and often the questions are framed to allow peripheral actors to provide perspectives on family system structure.

Genograms

The genogram is an interviewing tool commonly employed in social work interventions with families (McGoldrick et al., 2008). In essence, a **genogram** is a pictorial representation of a family, resembling a family tree, which helps social workers and family members understand family traditions and family system structure across generations and over time. In therapeutic applications, genograms help family members understand how problems in living can be passed from generation to generation, identify problematic relationships that contribute to emotional and behavioral health problems, and point to family-based strategies to resolve presenting problems (Nichols & Schwartz, 2012). However, genograms can also be useful in nonclinical applications such as might be found in child welfare, health, educational, and forensic settings. In these settings, genograms help the social worker and the client quickly understand sources of stress that can exacerbate presenting problems and sources of support and resilient functioning that can serve as resources for problem solving.

Figure 10-1 presents a simplified genogram for a fictitious nuclear family. It shows three generations, including elders, adult children, and grandchildren. By convention, circles are usually used to identify females, boxes for males, and solid lines to denote birth and marriage relationships among members. Dashed lines are usually used to denote close relationships among unmarried partners. Deaths are indicated by an X, adoption is denoted as a line with an A above, and divorces are denoted using hash marks. Key dates (e.g., births, deaths, and marriages) are often included.

A genogram such as the one shown in Figure 10-1 can be used as the basis for an in-depth assessment of family functioning and family system structure. Were a genogram to be completed for the Diaz family, it could be used to assess family resources, decision-making patterns, and patterns in family life-cycle adaptations. Certainly, the life-cycle changes being faced by the Diaz family are complex, and it may be useful to identify how family traditions bear on their decisions. For example, where other family members have successfully navigated the transition to some form of supported living arrangements in the past, social workers may see potential sources of support and evidence of family resilience. Moreover, a genogram could help identify additional family members who can participate in the decision-making process.

However, the utility of genograms for other reasons should not be overlooked. For example, genograms can be a powerful tool to enhance engagement. As a

Figure 10-1 Genogram

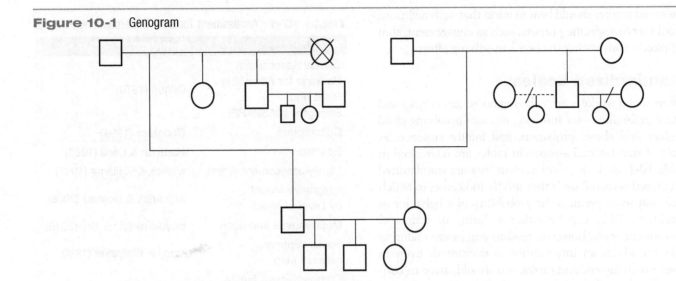

genogram interview proceeds, the process of elaborating on family membership, relationships, and events often begs for family storytelling. Stories have a way of drawing attention and enhancing involvement in a way that a simple statement of facts does not. Family storytelling can help family members become active participants in the social work process.

The genogram interview usually begins with a blank piece of paper and a pen, though some computer-based applications have also been developed. First, basic information about as many family members and their structural relationships as possible are arrayed on the paper, as in Figure 10-1. Often, experts recommend that genograms represent at least three generations of a family system to identify repetitive patterns (McGoldrick et al., 2008; Nichols & Schwartz, 2012). Next, the interview turns to questions related to family structure and process, depending on the purpose of the intervention and the needs of the assessment. For example, interview questions could include:

1. Circular questions about family relationships (e.g., "Who is closest to your dad?")

2. Drugs and alcohol, trauma, mental health and health (e.g., "Did anyone in your family ever use alcohol?)

3. Criminal/juvenile justice involvement (e.g., "Has anyone in your family had any interactions with the law?)

4. Resilience factors (e.g., "What did your family turn to in the past when you encountered stressful situations?")

5. Cultural factors (e.g., "What are some family traditions?")

The questions presented here are a limited set of examples. The specific questions you choose should be based on your assessment of what types of family patterns, what sets of relationships, and what historic events may be implicated in the presenting problem, either as sources of strain or as sources of resilient functioning.

Among the chief challenges when using genograms is the matter of time. Genograms can be highly detailed, and the storytelling involved can be time consuming, well beyond what is available to the social worker and family. Many social workers themselves feel drawn to family stories as a matter of curiosity and interest. Both factors, the time involved in storytelling and social worker curiosity, place an extra burden on social workers to manage time and maintain a strong focus on the purpose of the interview. In some settings, genograms may be developed over a series of several meetings with the family, but these settings are the exception rather than the rule in contemporary social work practice. Thus, most social workers who employ genograms need to discipline their curiosity and exercise informed judgment to focus genogram interviews on factors that are most likely to reveal information relevant to the presenting problem and its resolution.

That said, it is not the case that genograms must be weighty, problem-saturated dialogues. Indeed, the genogram interview can be playful even as it elaborates on important family system structure characteristics. For example, the conventional symbols used to denote family members and relationships are not fixed, and a creative social worker might include silly drawings of pets, when these are mentioned by family members, or other pictorial devices imagined by the social worker or by family members themselves to represent events or family patterns. When straying from genogram conventions, the social worker should bear in mind that such additions should serve a specific purpose, such as engagement, that is linked to advancing the problem-solving effort.

Standardized Scales

Often social workers are called upon to assess risks and safety in families—for instance, in cases involving child neglect and abuse, probation, and family violence. A table of standardized assessment tables are referenced in Table 10-1. Risk or safety assessments are standardized structured actuarial tools that specify indicators in which a certain score predicts the probability of a behavior or condition. Risks can be either enduring or transient. Assessment tools, however, tend to emphasize enduring risks for which an intervention is warranted. Even in cases involving enduring risks, you should strive to conduct a balanced assessment, including micro-, mezzo-, and macro-level strengths, protective factors, and resilience. In this way, risks are not overly emphasized at the expense of strengths, and contributing environmental factors as well as cultural factors are acknowledged.

Because it can be difficult to find the right tool for a family or its problem, multiple screening inventory tools may be more appropriate for assessing family strengths

Table 10-1   Assessment Tools for Understanding Families

Tools	Author(s)
Clinical Assessment Package for Assessing Risks and Strengths (CASPARS)	Gilgun (1970)
Culturagram	Congress (1994)
Ecomap	Hartman & Laird (1983)
Family assessment wheel	Mailick & Vigilante (1997)
Integrative Model by Level of Need	Kilpatrick & Holland (2008)
Multisystems approach	Boyd-Franklin & Bry (2019)
Social support network map	Tracy & Whittaker (1990)
Comprehensive family assessments	Schene (2005)

and stressors (Hudson & McMurtry, 1997). Jordan and Franklin (2011) is a resource for further study on family assessment tools; see also Fontes (2005) and Dubowitz and DePanfilis (2000).

Summary

The specialized family assessment skills and strategies presented in this chapter will help you understand clients and their families within the context of a family systems framework. As can be seen by the review presented in this chapter, many of the presenting problems your clients encounter are directly and indirectly influenced by family system arrangements and characteristics. When conducting family assessments, it is imperative that you identify those aspects of family system functioning that

are most influential on the presenting problem and that you also identify those aspects of family system functioning that represent sources of strength. It is critical that you maintain a constant awareness of the role of culture in the definition of proper or normative family functioning. Fortunately, the assessment tools described in the chapter, including direct observation, interviewing with circular questioning, genograms, and standardized scales, can help you handle with these tasks.

Competency Notes

C2   Engage Anti-Racism, Diversity, Equity, and Inclusion in Practice

- Demonstrate anti-racist social work practice at the individual, family, group, organizational, community, research, and policy levels, informed by the theories and voices of those who have been marginalized.
- Demonstrate cultural humility applying critical reflexivity, self-awareness, and self-regulation to

manage the influence of bias, power, privilege, and values in working with clients and constituencies acknowledging them as experts of their own lived experiences.

C3   Advance Human Rights and Social, Racial, Economic, and Environmental Justice

- Advocate for human rights at the individual and system levels.

C7   Assess Individuals, Families, Groups, Organizations, and Communities

- Apply knowledge of human behavior and person-in-environment and other culturally responsive multidisciplinary theoretical frameworks when assessing clients and constituencies.

- Demonstrate respect for client self-determination during the assessment process collaborating with clients and constituencies in developing mutually agreed-on goals.

Skill Development Exercises

Assessing Families

To develop your skills in assessing families, take some time to answer the following questions about your own family and experiences:

1. What are the preferred communication styles in your family?

2. Describe the different forms of power in your family and identify who the holders are. Specify how the power in your family, in whatever form, is culturally constructed.

3. Describe how boundary maintenance, internal and external, operates in your family.

4. How are decisions made in your family, and who is involved in the process?

5. Reflecting on marginalized or minoritized families that you have worked with, write a brief response to the assertion in this chapter that oppression is a normative experience for some families.

6. Review the guidelines for effective decision-making and assess your own family's adherence to these guidelines. If appropriate, identify cultural variants.

7. Put yourself in the position of a teen mother who is meeting with a social worker for the first time. What would you like to be the starting point in your initial contact?

8. Develop a set of questions or indicators that you could use to assess family strengths.

9. Think of ways in which client strengths may have a minor or major role in your experience with agencies, funding resources, and policy makers. How would you articulate the strengths perspective to any one or all these organizations?

Understanding Social Work Groups

Chapter Overview

Groups are powerful mechanisms for individual and collective change. They foster mutuality, raise consciousness, help people claim their voices, and invite awareness of power dynamics, social inequalities, and individual positionality. Being aware of the uncertainty that typically accompanies entrance into any type of new group (e.g., a class, club, or team) can equip members and facilitators with the humility and anticipatory empathy necessary to cocreate a successful group (Finn, 2021).

Social workers often engage in group work and support client participation in groups that may be conducted in person or electronically. Groups provide hope and encouragement, normalize and validate experiences, minimize isolation, teach coping skills, and provide members with role models and peer feedback (Toseland & Rivas, 2017). Groups are useful for supporting people who may be marginalized such as people of color, LGBTQ individuals, older adults, and those with stigmatizing illnesses or disabilities (Bateganya et al., 2015; Centers for Disease Control and Prevention, 2017, 2019; National Alliance on Mental Illness, 2020). Groups can provide a powerful mechanism for change, whether they are used as the only intervention or in conjunction with individual counseling, family work, community organizing, or other services.

Social workers plan and lead groups in a variety of settings and with an array of populations. Whatever type of group social workers lead, they must (1) facilitate a group that can effectively achieve members' goals, (2) accurately assess individual and group dynamics, and (3) intervene effectively to modify processes that are affecting the group's achievement of its goals. The success or the failure of a group frequently rests on the groundwork that takes place before the group even meets. Whether creating a group from scratch or facilitating existing groups, the social worker must thoughtfully and skillfully visualize a group and determine its purpose, structure, and composition. Without careful attention to group structure and atmosphere, assessment and intervention efforts may be jeopardized by the lack of a firm foundation.

This chapter describes the concepts for understanding groups, so that you can effectively start a group or join in facilitation of an existing group. As such, it describes the group purpose, formation, and structure, and provides a framework that enables you to accurately assess group processes, laying the foundation for effective group interventions, the subject of Chapter 16. Throughout these two chapters, you will find illustrative case vignettes based on a group called Healthy Eating, Attitudes, Relationships and Thoughts (HEART) for teenage females with obesity.

After reading this chapter, you will be able to:

- Describe the distinctions between treatment, self-help, and task groups, as well as different group subtypes

- Describe the steps in planning groups

- Describe the steps in recruiting and screening group members

- Develop individual and group goals

- Identify individual and group patterns in behaviors and communications

- Apply assessment concepts to treatment and task groups

The EPAS Competencies in Chapter 11

This chapter gives you the information needed to meet the following competencies:

- Competency 1: Demonstrate Ethical and Professional Behavior

- Competency 2: Engage Antiracism, Diversity, Equity, and Inclusion in Practice

- Competency 4: Engage in Practice-Informed Research and Research-Informed Practice

- Competency 6: Engage with Individuals, Families, Groups, Organizations, and Communities

- Competency 7: Assess Individuals, Families, Groups, Organizations, and Communities

- Competency 8: Intervene with Individuals, Families, Groups, Organizations, and Communities

Classification of Groups

A social work group is defined as three or more people with a common goal, shared beliefs (e.g., values or beliefs that distinguish group members from those outside the group), and interdependence (e.g., members work together to achieve their common goal; Glisson et al., 2012). Social workers are typically associated with three broad group types: treatment groups, self-help groups, and task groups. Treatment groups seek to enhance members' socioemotional well-being by developing social skills, providing psychoeducation, fostering mutual support, and engaging in therapy. In treatment groups, communications are generally open, and members are encouraged to interact and disclose personal feelings and experiences. Treatment groups are intended to be confidential, and success often is evaluated by individual treatment goal completion. For example, a treatment group for people with anxiety could teach mindfulness and cognitive restructuring skills, provide psychoeducation about ways to combat anxiety (e.g., exercise, meditation), and encourage members to discuss experiences with anxiety through talk therapy.

In self-help groups (SHG), members convene around shared concerns such as coping with addiction, illness, or grief. SHG are a prevalent and important part of the service delivery system. Though they share many features with task and treatment groups, SHG are distinct because they are typically consumer-led, though social workers may work in partnership with SHG and may assist in creating or providing support for them. SHG are based on mutual aid, often facilitated by peers who are experiencing the same issues as the other group members. As such, SHG benefit from internal rather than external expertise. This empowering shift makes

participants both beneficiaries and credible experts (Yalom & Leszcz, 2020).

In contrast to treatment and self-help groups, task groups focus on macro or external goals rather than individual members' goals or change. Communications are more structured, focusing on customary agenda items, with minimal self-disclosure. Group meetings or documents may be open to the public. Success is based on the accomplishment of the task or production of a product. For example, a social work task group comprised of representatives from local agencies, citizens, and community leaders might convene to assess gaps in services for adolescents in the community and to create an action plan to address these gaps. Table 11-1 summarizes treatment, self-help, and tasks groups.

Group Subtypes

There are many variations in treatment, self-help, and task groups, distinguished by their unique purposes. For example, treatment groups may focus on support, education, growth, therapy, or socialization. Self-help groups provide peer support for a specific problem or life situation (e.g., addictions and compulsions, emotional and mental health, bereavement). Task groups could refer to treatment teams, committees, governing boards, or community coalitions.

C6 and 7

Treatment Groups Subtypes

1. Support groups help members cope with life stresses by enhancing and teaching coping skills so that members can more effectively adapt to difficult life events (e.g., breast cancer survivors group, bereavement support group).

Table 11-1   Treatment and Task Groups (adapted from Toseland & Rivas, 2017)

Group Characteristic	Treatment Group	Self-Help Group	Task Group
Reason for group formation	Members' personal needs	Members' personal needs	Task to be completed
Facilitator	Mental health professional leads the group	Member led; there maybe be no appointed facilitator; a trained peer or group member may facilitate	Led by an agency employee, consumer, community member, or elected official
Group member roles	Develop organically through interaction	Develop organically through interaction	May be assigned, appointed, or develop organically through interaction
Communication patterns	Open, conversational interaction based on members' needs	Open, conversational interaction based on members' needs	Focused on the specific task to be accomplished.
Procedures	Flexible or formal, depending on the group	Flexible or formal, depending on the group	Set agenda. May be structured by by-laws or Roberts' Rules of Order
Group member composition	Based on members common concerns or presenting problems	Based on members common concerns or presenting problems	Based on positions, needed talents, knowledge, or expertise
Self-disclosure	Expected to be high	Expected to be high	Expected to be low
Confidentiality	Group content is generally private and kept within the group	Group content is generally private and kept within the group	Group proceedings may be private but can be open to the public
Evaluation of success	Based on members' meeting treatment goals	Determined by group members; survival of the group indicates success as member attendance is what keeps the group alive	Based on accomplishment of task or mandate, or producing a product

2. **Educational groups** focus on helping members learn about and cope with a specific topic that impacts them (e.g., an adolescent sexuality group, a diabetes management group, a heart attack recovery group, a psychoeducational group for relatives of people with major mental illnesses).

3. **Growth groups** stress self-improvement, offering members opportunities to expand their capabilities and self-awareness and make personal changes (e.g., a personal development group, a communication enhancement group for couples). Growth groups contrast with other types of groups in that they focus on promoting socioemotional health rather than alleviating socioemotional challenges.

4. **Therapy groups** help members change behavior, cope with or ameliorate personal problems, or recover from social or health trauma (e.g., addiction recovery group, an anger management group, an interpersonal violence survivors group). Support and growth are emphasized, using the group process and the social worker's interventions as catalysts for change.

5. **Socialization groups** increase members' communication and social skills, often using activities to improve interpersonal relationships. Field trips, social events, structured exercises, and/or role-plays are often utilized (e.g., a lunch club for formerly institutionalized persons, a social skills group for children who have difficulty making friends, a current events group for residents in an assisted living facility).

These group subtypes often overlap as they are designed to meet multiple purposes. For example, groups to assist people who are caregivers for loved ones provide support as well as education and resource exchanges. A men's cooking group at a community center is intended to educate recently divorced or widowed members, prepare them with skills, and provide socialization (Northen & Kurland, 2001). A group of teens convened after the shootings at Columbine High School helped to facilitate intergenerational communication and allowed youth the opportunity to articulate their fears and needs, in

C6

contrast to safety measures instituted by authorities without their input (Malekoff, 2006). Such groups offer the opportunity for social reform amid individual change.

Self-Help Group Subtypes

There are three common subtypes of self-help groups (Encyclopedia of Mental Disorders, 2021; Gluck, 2016):

1. **Twelve-Step Groups**
   The Twelve Steps and Twelve Traditions coined by Alcoholics Anonymous (AA) are probably the best-known type of self-help group. Twelve-step programs are based on turning one's life over to a personally chosen and meaningful higher power and admitting powerlessness in regard to a particular substance or behavior. In addition to AA, Narcotics Anonymous, Cocaine Anonymous, Gambler's Anonymous, Schizophrenics Anonymous, Emotions Anonymous, and Overeaters Anonymous are other common twelve-step self-help groups. Group members support one another as they as they work through the 12 steps to recovery.

2. **Support Groups**
   Self-help support groups address an array of issues and are often established for people coping with health problems (e.g., weight management, recovery from addiction), dealing with a medical diagnosis (e.g., cancer, HIV/AIDS, muscular dystrophy), or struggling with a mental health disorder (e.g., depression, schizophrenia, bipolar). Self-help groups also offer support for individuals whose family members are experiencing these issues. In addition, SHG focused on support can be established for other stressful life events such as expressing gender identity or sexual orientation, coping with bereavement, or caregiving for aging parents.

3. **Online Self-Help Groups**
   Online SGH are increasingly common, especially following COVID-19 pandemic. Many larger-scale consumer health-care websites have forums for patient discussions regarding diseases and disorders. While some online groups may be provider led, the majority are organized and maintained by peers. Examples include chat rooms, forums, and closed social networks all of which provide 24/7 support.

Task Group Subtypes

Social workers in direct practice commonly participate in task groups as members or facilitators. Task groups are generally organized into three different subtypes (Toseland & Rivas, 2017):

C6 and 7

1. **Groups that Are Created to Meet Client Needs**
   These include teams that collaborate on behalf of client services. Case coordination meetings or family group conferences, which organize and monitor treatment plans. Staff development teams are responsible educating staff to improve client care.

2. **Groups that Are Intended to Meet Organizational Needs**
   In contrast to client-focused task groups, organization-focused task groups are generally responsible for the governance and well-being of an institution. For example, all nonprofit organizations have boards of directors, trustees, or governors that run an organization, including fiduciary responsibilities (legal and financial accountability). All organizations utilize another form of task groups, committees, to get work done. Committees may be standing (established and ongoing) or ad hoc (time-limited). Examples of standing committees might include a grievance committee, the management team, a fundraising team, or government relations. Examples of ad hoc committees include search committees to fill vacant positions, planning groups for special events, or groups to prepare for accreditation, mergers, or other infrequent but significant occasions. Organizations may also have cabinets, which advises executive officers about future and/or current policies and procedures.

3. **Groups that Address Community Needs**
   In this context, "community" refers broadly to the needs of a geographic community or a community of interest or affiliation. Social workers may be members or facilitators of such groups. For example, social workers might facilitate a social action group to implement change tactics to address a pressing social problem such as hate crimes, community violence, or environmental disasters. Social workers may be members of multiagency coalitions (a group of social action groups with a common goal) convened to lobby for improved funding, examine service gaps, or coordinate programs. Finally, delegate councils represent different organizations or chapters. Social workers who are members of professional organizations, such as the National Association of Social Workers (NASW), may be on committees to change licensing laws, revise practice standards, or advocate for improved reimbursement for services. Chapter 14 addresses groups that focus on community needs more in depth.

Although group types may differ, several underlying principles are common to all forms of group work practice. We will now consider common features of creating and assessing treatment groups and task groups.

Online Groups

Although groups traditionally meet face to face, with advancements in electronic communications and challenges posed by the COVID-19 pandemic, electronically convened groups became increasingly common (Barbhuiya & Mazmuder, 2020; Datta & Deb, 2020; Lind, 2020). Indeed, any group subtype can utilize telesocial work and meet virtually online. The considerations for individual telesocial work discussed elsewhere in this text also apply to groups. However, confidentiality is of even greater importance with group telesocial work as the privacy of multiple participants is at stake. Therefore, group members should commit to being in a private location during the online group sessions, and if this is not possible, they should use earphones so people in the room or household do not hear what other group members say.

Developing Treatment Groups

The success or failure of a treatment group rests to a large extent on the thoughtful creation of the group and the careful selection and preparation of members for the group experience. In this section, you will learn the steps needed to foster a positive group outcome. Table 11-2 lists these steps.

Identifying the Need for the Group

The decision to offer services through groups can arise from several origins. Some agencies adopt group-based services to meet efficiency or cost-containment goals. Sometimes social workers or agencies determine that groups are best suited to meet the needs of their clientele. Sometimes group work is indicated when naturally existing groups lend themselves to social work interventions—for example, in communities or schools where disparate treatment brings people together to advocate for change.

Table 11-2   Considerations in Forming and Starting Treatment Groups

Identify the need for the group
Establish the group purpose
Decide on leadership
Determine group composition
Choose an open or closed group
Determine group size and location
Set the frequency and duration of meetings
Conduct preliminary interviews
Determine the group structure
Formulate preliminary group guidelines

Establishing the Group Purpose

Clarifying the overall purpose of a group is vital because the group's objectives influence all the processes that follow, including recruiting and selecting members, deciding on the group's duration, identifying its size and content, and determining meeting location and time. The overall

Appling Group Concepts

Chapter 2 introduces 14-year-old Isiah, who has been referred to social work and probation services following adjudication for resisting arrest. Specifically, he has been court-ordered to attend a group for anger management, which he characterizes as "bulls**t," contending that his reaction was appropriate given the situation and provocation by the police.

- How should his social worker respond to the mandate to attend group?

- If Isiah doesn't need an anger management group, what other type of group or group purpose be beneficial for him?

- If he must attend an anger management group, what steps should the facilitator take to align his mandate and wishes with the group purpose and the needs of other members?

purpose of a planned group should be established by the social worker in consultation with colleagues and clients prior to forming the group. The goals subsequently negotiated by the group should reflect the perspectives of those three stakeholders. If the agency's goals differ from the worker's or members' goals, those involved must negotiate a general group purpose that is agreeable to all parties. Failing to do so may lead to distress and ambiguity in the group, send mixed messages, and triangulate its members.

Individual or Co-Leadership

Once the group's purpose is established, group planners must consider whether individual or co-leadership is necessary to assist the group in meeting its aims. Two facilitators can provide additional eyes and ears for the group, with one facilitator specifically attending to content and the other taking note of the process and meta-messages (underlying messages) by group members. Co-leaders can bring different perspectives, backgrounds, and personalities to the group process, which can appeal to a wider array of members than a single facilitator might. They can also use their interactions to model effective communication and problem solving. In addition, two facilitators have greater capacity for observing communications and formulating responses and can support and strategize with each other (Luke & Hackney, 2007; Yalom & Leszcz, 2020).

Sometimes co-leadership is necessary for practical reasons. With two facilitators, one can check on a member who is missing or has left the room, while the other continues working with the group. Co-leadership can provide continuity if vacations, illness, or another emergency on the part of one facilitator might otherwise result in cancellation of a session. With some populations, two facilitators may help send a message of authority in an otherwise disruptive group; they may also provide a sense of physical safety and protection from harm by their very presence (Carrell, 2000).

Of course, co-facilitation is sometimes impractical because of the costs involved and the time needed to coordinate roles, plan the group sessions, and debrief together. In managing the cost concern, some agencies utilize volunteers or peer support—consumers who have had group training and can bring personal experiences to the group process.

Determining Group Composition

Composition refers to the group's membership. Composition may be heterogeneous, made up of people with of different ages, races, gender identities, or experiences with the problem at hand. Groups can also be homogeneous based on a given demographic or clinical characteristic of the members. Composition may be static, in that it is the same for the life of the group, or dynamic,

shifting from meeting to meeting as new members come and go. Let's consider some examples.

Composition may be heterogeneous and shifting, based on the setting—for example, when the group consists of all residents in a group home, all patients preparing for discharge, or all motorists mandated to attend due to charges of driving while intoxicated. A group of community members concerned about anti-Semitic hate crimes may ask for the help of a social work organizer. The members might have several things in common, such as their neighborhood location, place of worship, and Jewish identity, but also be heterogeneous in terms of gender and age or other characteristics. Further, the composition may shift if community members concerned about other forms of hate crimes join. Some groups may be explicitly homogeneous as a necessary condition of meeting the therapeutic goals, and social workers would play an important role in composing the ultimate membership by recruiting, selecting, and preparing potential members. For example, a group for people preparing for gender reassignment surgery would necessarily be homogeneous and static in its membership to support the safety and confidentiality of a vulnerable population and to also organize people around a common identity and life stage.

Factors in successful group composition include members' interest in the groups' mission, motivation to participate, and compatibility with other members in the group. Research suggests that "Ethnicity and culture can have a profound effect on treatment. The greater the mix of ethnicities in a group, the more likely it is that biases will emerge and require mediation" (Substance Abuse and Mental Health Services Administration, 2005, p. 52). Homogeneity in personal characteristics and purpose for joining the group can facilitate communication, feelings of belongingness, and the growth of supportive networks in addition to the group itself.

Sometimes, the group's purpose influences the decision for similarity among certain characteristics. For example, there are advantages to creating single gender groups when the issues differ by gender (e.g., interpersonal violence) or when mixed groups might inhibit member comfort or participation (Goode et al., 2020).

Characteristics such as age, development, stage of change, or the nature of the problem might also require homogeneity among members. For example, in composing a group for parents who have lost children, those members whose loved ones were very young when they died might have different needs and issues than those whose offspring were adults when they passed away. Membership in groups for recovery from substance use disorders should consider stage of recovery, progression of the disease, and readiness for change so that all members can "learn and grow without interfering with the learning and growth of others" (Substance Abuse and Mental Health Services Administration, 2005, p. 42).

Diversity among members with respect to coping skills, life experiences, and levels of expertise fosters learning and introduces members to differing viewpoints, problem-solving skills, and ways of communicating. To attain the desired outcomes of support, learning, and mutual aid, a treatment group, for example, might include members from different cultures, social classes, occupations, or geographic areas. Multicultural diversity in group membership offers a variety of perspectives and resources to the group's efforts and facilitates critical consciousness, empowerment, and advocacy (Anderson, 2007; Singh & Salazar, 2014). Heterogeneity is also vital in task group membership so that the group has sufficient resources to fulfill its responsibilities and efficiently divide the labor when completing complex tasks. The challenge in any type of group is to attain a workable balance between differences and similarities of members, given the group's purpose and avoid tokenism in the inclusion of marginalized community members (Singh & Salazar, 2014).

The practice of cultural humility by the group facilitator is also a salient consideration in composition. It may not be feasible to match leaders and members based on demographic characteristics. Therefore, social workers should value the cultural knowledge and the heritage expressed by clients and engage in continual self-assessment about their knowledge, skills, and attitudes in working with various groups. This includes familiarity with the cultural characteristics and experiences of oppression and discrimination by members of diverse groups, especially as they relate to the focus of the group, whether it be parenting, substance use, or illness. It requires an understanding of language differences, customs and beliefs, intragroup tensions, and views of gender and family roles. Facilitators should:

- Be prepared for and open to the expression of feelings and experiences involving racism, discrimination, and marginalization.

- Learn about their own culturally shaped assumptions to avoid imposing them on others

- "Work harder to recognize institutionalized racism than they do to perceive individual prejudice; that is, they should recognize how bias is structured into policies, practices, and norms in program relations.

- Question the knowledge base and theories that underlie their practice in order to eliminate prejudice and bias in that practice.

- Clinicians should look at their own feelings and reactions and listen to the feedback of others to recognize how their own ideas have been unconsciously shaped by discriminatory social dynamics" (Substance Abuse and Mental Health Services Administration, 2005, p. 49).

Choosing an Open or Closed Group

Related to the discussion about static or dynamic composition are the concepts of open and closed groups. Open format groups are open to enrolling new members, while in the closed format, no new members are added once the group gets under way. Typically, groups that are open or closed in terms of admitting new members are also open or closed regarding their duration. Alcoholics Anonymous and Weight Watchers are examples of open-ended and open membership groups. An ongoing symptom management group in an inpatient psychiatric setting would be open, as the census of the unit fluctuates daily with admissions and discharges. Alternatively, a 10-week medication management group, an eight-session grief group, and a semester-long social skills group could be considered closed membership and closed-ended.

Open-ended groups are generally used for helping clients cope with transitions and crises, providing support, acting as a means for assessment, and facilitating outreach (Schopler & Galinsky, 2006). Having open-ended groups ensures that a group is immediately available at a time of crisis. Open groups include the drop-in (or drop-out) model in which members are self-selecting, entry criteria are very broad, and members attend whenever they wish for an indefinite period. In the replacement model, the facilitator immediately identifies someone to fill a group vacancy. In the re-formed model, group members contract to attend for a set period, during which no new members are added, but original members may drop out. At the end of the contract period, a new group is formed consisting of some old and some new members.

The choice of format depends on the purpose of the group, the setting, and the population served. An open format provides the opportunity for members to leave when they have achieved their goals. New members can bring fresh perspectives to the group, and open formats offer immediate support for those in need, who come when they need to and stay as long as they choose. At the same time, the instability of this format discourages members from developing the trust and the confidence to openly share and explore their problems—a strong feature of the closed-ended group. Frequent changes of membership may also disrupt the work of the open-ended group, although the developmental patterns in such groups vary according to how many new members enter and the frequency of turnover (Alle-Corliss & Alle-Corliss, 2009). Facilitators of open-ended groups must be attuned to clients being at different places in the process and be able to work with core members to carry forward the group's traditions (Schopler & Galinsky, 2006).

Advantages associated with a closed group include higher group morale, greater predictability for role behaviors, and an increased sense of cooperation among members. Additionally, closed groups allow for all participants to begin treatment at the same time and at the same level and stage of the intervention. This allows for group members to move through treatment in cohesion in a potentially time-limited treatment context such as a 12-week closed group focused on dialectical behavioral therapy (Psychotherapy, 2019).

Disadvantages are that the group may not be admitting members when potential participants are ready to make use of it, and if too many members drop out, the group process may be drastically affected by the high rate of attrition. Closed groups also run the risk of having their effectiveness threatened if several members decide to abandon treatment, thus reducing the number of participants and limiting potentials for discussion and furthering diverse perspectives. Because group members take time to adjust to one another, participants dropping out and new members from the waitlist being added can restart the adjustment process which inevitably disrupts the treatment timeline (Tourigny & Hébert, 2007). Whether a group is closed or open, group facilitators must be aware of the period of the time necessary for group members to adjust to other group members and the treatment process.

Determining Group Size and Location

The size of the group depends in large part on its purpose, the age of clients, the type of problems to be explored, and the needs of members. Seven to ten members is usually an optimal number for a group with an emphasis on close relationships (Stewart et al., 2009). The group must be small enough that members feel safe and comfortable sharing confidential information but large enough that group members receive adequate support and relevant feedback. As such, educational and task groups may accommodate more members than would therapy and support groups, where cohesion is central to the group progress.

The location of in-person versus online group meetings should be selected with image and convenience in mind. Image refers to the impression that the site makes on members—the message it conveys that may attract them to the group or make them uncomfortable in attending. For example, a parenting group held at a school building may not be attractive to potential members if their own experiences with education or with the school system have been unfavorable. A parenting group that meets at a local Boys and Girls Club or community center may be perceived as comfortable to members who are used to going there for their children's sports or other neighborhood events.

Convenience refers to the accessibility of the site for those people whom the group chooses to attract. For example, is the site readily accessible to public transportation for those who do not own automobiles? Is it safe with plenty of parking and easy to find for those who may be uncomfortable venturing out at night? If the meeting is held online, will prospective members have the electronic device and broadband access needed to attend and interact with other members?

Setting the Frequency and Duration of Meetings

Closed groups benefit from having a termination date at the outset, which encourages focused work. Regarding the possible life span of a group, Corey and Corey (2006) note: "The duration varies from group to group, depending on the type of group and the population. The group should be long enough to allow for cohesion and productive work yet not so long that the group seems to drag on interminably" (p. 92). Attrition and other obligations may erode participation in long-term groups, and ending ahead of the planned time may lead to an unwarranted sense of failure. Shorter durations, during which attendance can be assured, may leave clients wanting more but with a sense of accomplishment and goal achievement at the group's conclusion. In general, short-term groups vary between one and 12 sessions, with the shorter-duration groups being targeted at crisis situations, anxiety alleviation, and educational programs (Northen & Kurland, 2001).

Conducting Preliminary Interviews

Before convening a treatment group, social workers often meet individually with potential group members to provide information, establish rapport, explore concerns, and clarify limits, mandates, and options for involuntary members. Interviews are helpful for optimizing group composition; they help ensure that the members are selected according to predetermined criteria and are likely to make effective use of the group experience. These meetings can:

1. *Orient potential members to proposed goals and purposes of the group, its content and structure, the facilitator's philosophy and style in managing group processes, and the roles of the facilitator and group members.* This is also a good time to identify expectations, such as attendance, confidentiality, and to focus and gauge the client's corresponding reactions and suggestions (Yalom & Leszcz, 2020; Singh & Salazar, 2014). With involuntary groups, you must distinguish between non-negotiable rules and policies, such as attendance expectations and general themes to be discussed, and negotiable norms and procedures, such as arrangements for breaks, food, and selection of topics and their order.

2. *Elicit information on the individual's prior group experiences*, including their style of relating in the previous groups and the goals that they accomplished. With people who may be uncomfortable or unfamiliar with group services, a pregroup orientation can answer questions, help them understand what to expect, reduce apprehension, and offer coaching on how best to participate (Chen et al., 2008).

3. *Elicit, explore, and clarify the clients' needs*, and identify those that fit with the proposed group. In some instances, either because people are reluctant to participate in the group or because their issues appear to be more appropriately handled through other settings or modalities, you may refer them to resources other than the group.

4. *Explore clients' hopes, expectations, and goals* regarding the proposed group (e.g., "What would you like to be different in your life as a result of your attending this group?"). This conversation may influence decisions in the construction of the group or may indicate that the proposed group is not the best fit for the client's interests.

5. *Mutually develop a profile of the client's strengths and attributes* and determine the ways they can contribute to the group and capacities that the client might like to enhance through work in the group. Preliminary interviews enable social workers to enter the initial group sessions with a previously established relationship with each member—a distinct advantage given that facilitators must attend to multiple communication processes at both individual and group levels.

6. *Identify and explore potential obstacles or reservations* about participating in the group, including shyness or privacy concerns, opposition from significant others about entering the group, a heavy schedule that might preclude attending all group meetings, or needs for transportation or child care.

7. *Ensure that screening for the group is a two-way process.* Potential members should have the opportunity to interview the social worker and determine whether the group meets their interests and whether the relationship with the facilitator will likely lead to a successful outcome. Further, establishing rapport with the facilitator is beneficial for members in that it enables them to feel more at ease and to open up more readily in the first meeting.

Planning Group Sessions

In addition to determining the group's purpose, goals, composition, duration, and other elements, social workers must consider how the time in group meetings will be used to meet the needs of participants most effectively. **Programming** refers to the content of group sessions and the processes, activities, or exercises that are used to meet group goals. Discussions foster group processing. Prompts from the facilitator can be used to check in on members' well-being, invite sharing, or inquire about the effects of content from past meetings. For example, "How have you been coping this week?", "Has anyone been able to use the mindfulness techniques we discussed last week? How did that go?" In addition to discussion, "content from games, play, structured exercises, role-playing, art, drama, guided imagery, cooking, hobbies, and other forms of creative self-expression are used to build group bonds and enhance the potential of the group to achieve group tasks and individual and social change" Garvin & Galinsky, 2008, p. 291). Activities should relate directly to the group's purpose and be introduced and concluded by discussions and debriefing that tie them to the group's goals.

With increased attention to evidence-based practices, **manualized curricula** have been developed that detail the sequence, content, and activities for various types of groups (DeSena et al., n.d.; Lotz, 2013; Margolin, 1999; Muñoz et al., 2007). These programmed approaches offer several advantages. They help to focus services, advance systematized practices, and support research on interventions. However, those who oppose manual-based practice are concerned that they promote paternalistic, one-size-fits-all approaches instead of the organic, empowerment-based changes that arise from members' and workers' dynamic interactions (Wood, 2007). A further concern is that they may be misused by workers who adopt curricula without supervision or sufficient appreciation for group dynamics and in the absence of group facilitation skills. Knowledgeable workers can integrate tested programming ideas with practice wisdom and emerging group needs to achieve group and individual purposes.

Whether conceived by the social worker or existing manuals, the results should be a clearly conceptualized format that provides the means for evaluating group and individual progress. The structure should also be flexible enough to accommodate differing group processes and the unique needs of members as they emerge. To ensure its continued functionality, review the format periodically throughout the life of the group.

The following activities will assist you and your members to focus your energies so as to achieve therapeutic objectives effectively and efficiently:

C6 and 7

1. Define group and individual goals in behavioral terms and rank them according to priority.

2. Develop an overall plan that organizes the work to be done within the number of sessions allocated by the group to achieve its goals. The facilitator or

Table 11-3 Example of Format for a Ninety-Minute Group

15 Minutes	1 Hour	15 Minutes
Checking in Reviewing and monitoring tasks	Focusing on relevant content (presentation and discussion) Mutual problem solving Formulating tasks Plan for the week	Summarizing plan for the week Evaluating group session

co-facilitators should have done preliminary work on this plan while designing the group.

3. Specify behavioral tasks (homework) to be accomplished outside the group each week that will assist individuals to make and sustain the desired changes.

4. Achieve agreement among members concerning the weekly format and agenda—that is, how time is allocated each week to achieve the group's goals. For instance, a group might allocate its weekly 1.5 hours to the format shown in Table 11-3.

Composition and programming may be complicated when some group members attend repeatedly while others cycle in and out. It can be a challenge to address the needs of those attending for the first time and those who have participated for several sessions. Studies suggest that single-session group meetings should be longer than typical treatment groups, as the membership may be larger, and time is needed within one session to create trust and facilitate sharing. As such, groups might meet for 90 to 120 minutes (Feigin et al., 1998; Keast, 2012; Ruffalo et al., 2011).

A further element to assess is whether group attendance is mandatory. As noted throughout this text, voluntariness and reactance have powerful implications for clients' quality and level of participation in services. Single-session groups may not afford the time to work through these issues, so facilitators must plan for this in structuring each session.

Formulating Preliminary Group Guidelines

Developing consensus about group guidelines (e.g., staying on task, adhering to confidentiality) is a vital aspect of contracting in the initial phase of the group.

Single-Session Groups

Groups whose membership is the same for only a single session are common in settings where the census of potential members fluctuates frequently, such as hospital medical and psychiatric units, inpatient substance abuse treatment settings, shelters, and other residential facilities. Some groups are simply designed to meet on only one occasion. For example, critical incident debriefing groups gather on a specific occasion to assist people affected by a traumatic event such as a workplace shooting (Davis, 2013; U.S. Department of Veterans Affairs, n.d.). The single-session group format is increasingly popular in light of reduced lengths of stay in treatment and the busy pace of life that may make it difficult for potential members to commit to attending ongoing groups. While single-session groups may sacrifice the cohesion and the reflection that can be characteristic of closed multisession groups, they have demonstrated effectiveness in education and in assisting members to resolve immediate challenges, restore equilibrium, and mobilize coping skills (Fried & Dunn, 2012). Some authors conceptualize single-session groups as services or workshops rather than therapeutic interventions (Ruffalo et al., 2011), and others view them as a variant of open membership groups (Turner, 2011).

With some modifications, the steps for establishing treatment groups also apply to single-session groups. Although extensive preliminary interviews are not feasible for single-session groups, facilitators may get acquainted with potential members through case staffing or their other therapeutic or supervisory roles in the residence or unit. This may provide the opportunity to educate clients or family members/caregivers about group offerings and determine what pressing issues the group might help to address. The format for single-session groups may be educational or didactic, but in either case, facilitators should be prepared to do on-the-spot assessments to make sure material is responsive to the needs of the individuals gathered for the session (Turner, 2011).

In formulating guidelines with the group, the social worker takes the first step in shaping the group's evolving processes to create a working group capable of achieving specific objectives. We offer the following suggestions to assist you in this aspect of group process:

1. If there are nonnegotiable expectations (e.g., confidentiality, no smoking policies, or rules about contact between members outside sessions), you should present them, explain their rationale, and encourage group discussion (Corey et al., 2013).

   C8

2. Introduce the group to the concept of **decision by consensus** on all negotiable items, and solicit agreement concerning adoption of this method for making decisions prior to formulating group guidelines.

3. Ask group members to share their vision for the group by responding to the following statement: "I would like this group to be a place where I could ...." Reach for responses from all members. Once this has been achieved, summarize the collective thinking of the group. Offer your own views of supportive group structure that assists members to work on individual problems or to achieve group objectives. Acknowledge that these initial wishes and agreements may be revisited as the group evolves.

4. Ask members to identify guidelines for behavior in the group that can assist them to achieve the kind of group structure and atmosphere they desire. You may wish to brainstorm possible guidelines at this point, adding your suggestions. Then, through group consensus, choose those that seem most appropriate.

The following items identify pertinent topics for treatment group guidelines, although each guideline's applicability depends on the specific focus of the group.

Help-Giving/Help-Seeking Roles

Groups can benefit from clarification of the help-giving and help-seeking roles that members play. The help-seeking role incorporates such behaviors as making direct requests for input or advice, authentically sharing one's feelings, being open to feedback, and demonstrating willingness to test new approaches to problems. The help-giving role involves such behaviors as listening attentively, refraining from criticism, clarifying perceptions, summarizing, maintaining focus on the problem, and pinpointing strengths and incremental growth. This guideline helps the group avoid moving prematurely to giving advice and offering evaluative suggestions about what a member

ought or ought not to do. The facilitator can further help the group appropriately adopt the two roles by highlighting instances in which members have performed well in either of these helping roles.

New Members

Procedures for adding and orienting new members may need to be established. In some cases, the group facilitator may reserve the prerogative of selecting members. In other instances, the group chooses new members based on certain criteria and consensus regarding the selections. In either case, procedures for adding new members and the importance of the group's role in orienting those entrants should be clarified.

Individual Contacts with the Social Worker

Whether you encourage or discourage individual contacts with members outside the group depends on the purpose of the group and the anticipated consequences or benefits of such contacts. In some cases, individual contacts serve to promote group objectives. For example, planned meetings with an adolescent between sessions may provide opportunities to focus on behaviors in the group, support strengths, and develop an individual contract with the youth. When the outside contact is not planned or routine, it may derail issues that should be brought to the group rather than addressed one on one, and it may alienate other group members who do not have access to the facilitator.

Member Contacts Outside the Group

Contacts by members outside the group can be constructive or harmful to individuals and the group's purpose, and thus, the practice literature contains differing views on this topic. Group sessions are but one activity in peoples' lives; and it is, therefore, unreasonable to expect members to follow rules that extend outside the temporal and special boundaries of the group. The nature and the benefit of collaborative support is limited if members are forbidden to make contact outside of session (Shulman, 2009).

Toseland and Rivas (2017) list possible drawbacks to contact between members outside the group, including diversions from the group's goal, the effect of coalitions on the other members' interactions in the group, and arguments stemming from the dissolution of an alliance or friendship formed outside the group. With the advent of online search engines and social networking, members

Confidentiality in the HEART Group

First Session

- **Dave (facilitator):** Good evening, everyone, and thank you for joining this group. I am glad to see you all again, and I want to start this session by saying a few words about housekeeping, things about how I'd like the group to go, or what I'd like to see us get out of the group, and also talk about confidentiality requirements for this setting.

  To begin, I hope that we can create a safe space for you all to talk about any concerns that you have about symptoms of depression or anxiety and concerns you have about being overweight and about behaviors that might contribute to that for you. I would like for us to decide how we are going to accomplish that as a group. It's a process that we call consensus decision-making so together we'll come up with the rules for how we're going to operate for the next 12 weeks that will determine how business is conducted, how each member takes time, and how we support each other and interact to make this group work. As a consideration for everybody, and as required by law, everything that happens in the group has to stay in the group. You are allowed to talk about what you say in group outside, but we're not allowed to talk about anybody else's business outside of the group. I'd like to see, just by the nods of your heads, that this is something that you understand and agree with. One exception to that rule is that if I find that someone appears to be in danger either from somebody else or in danger of harming themselves, then I have a duty to report that, to keep everybody safe, and I would like to know that everybody understands and is comfortable with that. [*Group nods.*] Okay, terrific.

To start, then, I'd like to ask you to introduce yourselves to the group. I'm okay to take a volunteer if somebody wants to volunteer to go first; otherwise, I'll need to choose somebody. Would anybody like to lead and introduce themselves to the rest of the group?

> **Amelia:** I'll start.
>
> **Dave:** Terrific, Amelia. Go ahead.
>
> **Amelia:** Okay. Can I actually ask a question?
>
> **Dave:** Of course.
>
> **Amelia:** When you say you must tell people if you're going to hurt yourself, what if you've already hurt yourself—is that an issue that you would have to tell?
>
> **Dave:** I would want to know if you currently feel like you're not safe physically. If you're in harm's way, however that may happen, I have to take steps to keep you safe, even if that means breaking our confidentiality agreement.
>
> **Maria:** So, if I say, Vanessa told me, "Oh, you can eat wraps in this certain place, and they're good for you," I shouldn't tell that to anybody?
>
> **Dave:** You shouldn't tell anybody that Vanessa told you that.
>
> **Maria:** Okay. I can say that wraps are good.
>
> **Dave:** You can say that. I'm particularly focused on personal information about members of the group, so information about eating and exercise and dieting you can share; just don't say who said it.
>
> **Amelia:** So, like, what's said in group stays in group, right?
>
> **Dave:** Yes, that's it.

may research each other and threaten boundaries and comfort by uncovering information and connections the individual has not shared in the group. Online relationships can give rise to problematic alliances or become an avenue for dealing with concerns that should be brought to the group.

Yalom and Leszcz (2020) acknowledge the various causes and effects of contacts outside the group. Their analysis suggests that outside group contact should be disclosed to the entire group, as clandestine contacts risk harming group unity. Particularly in time-limited groups, it is feasible and appropriate for members to limit outside contact for the duration of the group unless there are therapeutic reasons for supporting such communications.

Use of Recording Devices and Phones

Given the subtlety of current recording technology and the risks posed by inappropriate video or audio recording, this is an important topic for members and facilitators alike. Members should be reminded of confidentiality rules, and recording should be prohibited as part of their ground rules. If there is a therapeutic or professional purpose for recording the group, the social worker should always ask for the group's permission before doing so (NASW, 2021). Before asking for such a decision, the social worker should provide information concerning how the recording may be used outside the session, how it will be kept, and when it will be destroyed. Members' reservations regarding recording the session should be thoroughly aired, and the group's wishes should be respected.

A related issue involves the use of cell phones, tablets, and other handheld electronic devices. In addition to recording and photo capabilities, these devices, even when only emitting pings and notifications, are distracting to the members checking them and to the other people around them. Groups must discuss and construct norms about the use of electronic equipment: Must all items be turned off during meetings? Can they be on but not checked if they go off? What should members do if urgent calls are expected?

Eating and Drinking

Opinions vary among group facilitators concerning these activities in groups. Some groups and facilitators believe that they distract from group process; others regard them as comforting and thus beneficial to group operation. Some groups may intentionally provide meals as an incentive to encourage group attendance (Wood, 2007). You may wish to elicit members' views about these activities and develop guidelines with the group that meet member needs, conform to organization or building policies, and facilitate group progress. A related conversation involves the configuration and care of the room where the group meets. Making group decisions regarding care of the physical space (e.g., food, furniture, trash) fosters shared responsibility for the group meeting area.

Profanity

A related issue is the use of profanity in the group. Some social workers believe that group members should be allowed to use whatever language they choose in expressing themselves (Howes, 2012). However, swearing may be offensive to some participants, and the group may wish to develop guidelines concerning this matter, particularly if slurs have religious, racial, or gendered connotations.

Attendance

Discussing the importance of regular attendance and soliciting commitments from members can solidify membership and prevent the challenges that arise from attrition or absences. Involuntary groups often have attendance policies that permit a limited number of absences and late arrivals. Late arrivals and early departures by group members can typically be minimized if the group develops norms about this behavior in advance and if the facilitator starts and ends meetings promptly. Exceptions may be needed, of course, to accommodate crises affecting the schedules of members or to extend the session to complete an urgent item of business if the group concurs. However, individual and group exceptions to time norms should be rare.

Touching

The sensitive nature of some group topics may lead to expressions of emotion, such as crying or angry outbursts. It is important to have group guidelines that provide physical safety for members, such as no hitting. It is also important to set a climate of emotional safety to sanction the appropriate expression of feelings. Some group guidelines prohibit members from touching one another with hugs or other signs of physical comfort. Sometimes these rules are included to protect members from unwanted or uncomfortable advances. Other groups maintain that touch is a feeling stopper when one is tearful and insist that group members can display their empathy in other ways—through words or through eye contact and attention to the other, for example. Whatever the group's policy, it is important to explain the expectation and the rationale and to address member concerns rather than impose the guideline unilaterally.

Guidelines are helpful only to the extent that they expedite the development of the group and further the achievement of the group's goals. They should be reviewed periodically to assess their functionality in relationship to the group's stage of development. Outdated guidelines should be discarded or reformulated. When the group's actions are incompatible with the group guidelines, the facilitator should describe what is happening in the group (or request that members do so) and, after thoroughly reviewing the situation, ask the group to consider whether the guideline in question is still viable. If used judiciously, this strategy not only helps the group to reassess its guidelines but also places responsibility for monitoring adherence to those guidelines with the group itself rather than casting the facilitator as enforcer.

Assessing Group Processes

In group assessment, social workers must attend to processes that occur at both the individual and the group levels, including emerging themes or patterns, to enhance the functioning of individuals and the group. This section describes the procedures for accurately assessing the processes for both individuals and groups, and Table 11-3 summarizes the variables you should consider. A systems framework facilitates the identification and impact of such patterns. Group formation is often viewed in five phases, which will be briefly presented here and then discussed in more depth in Chapter 16. It is important to assess group dynamics as they evolve through these phases:

1. *Preaffiliation.* During this stage, the group is forming, and members can be quiet and hesitant.

Some members may test group guidelines or each other to determine how much the facilitator will intervene.

2. *Power and control.* During this stage, groups transition into an intimate system of relationships and struggle with autonomy, power, and control.

3. *Intimacy.* Group members' interactions become more familiar and comfortable as members recognize the significant of the group experience.

4. *Differentiation.* The fourth stage is marked by cohesion as members bond and come to see their group as a distinct entity separate from those outside the group.

5. *Separation.* Members begin to separate as the group draws to an end and their tight bond begins to weaken.

A Systems Framework for Assessing Groups

Like families, groups are social systems characterized by repetitive patterns. Chapter 10 extensively discusses a system framework as related to family functioning. These same concepts can be applied to groups. All social systems share an important principle—namely, that persons who compose a given system gradually limit their behaviors to a relatively narrow range of patterned responses as they interact with others within that system. Groups thus evolve implicit rules or norms that govern behaviors, shape patterns, and regulate internal operations.

A systems framework helps facilitators to assess group processes. They can attend to the repetitive interactions of members, infer rules that govern those interactions, and weigh the functionality of those rules and patterns. For example, a group may develop a habit in which one person's complaints receive a great deal of attention while others' concerns are dismissed. The rules leading to such a pattern may be "If the group doesn't attend to Richard, he might drop out or become angry," or "Richard is hurting more than anyone else," or "Richard's issues resonate with those of others, so he deserves the additional attention, whereas the other concerns that are raised aren't shared concerns and don't deserve group time." This pattern may result in the disenfranchisement of the members who feel marginalized, or it may lead to relief that some members can recede while the spotlight is on Richard. More constructively, the other members may concur that Richard's issues are symptomatic of the group and thus be glad that he is bringing them to the surface for discussion.

Conceptualizing and organizing group processes into response patterns enables social workers to make systematic, ongoing, and relevant assessments. This knowledge can help make sense of seemingly random and chaotic interactions. In addition to identifying patterned behaviors, facilitators must concurrently attend to individual and group behaviors. Observing processes at both levels is difficult, however, and social workers may default to attending more to individual dynamics than to group dynamics (or the converse) Recognizing this dilemma, we discuss strategies for accurately assessing both individual and group patterns in the remainder of this chapter.

Assessing Individuals' Patterned Behaviors

Some of the patterned behaviors that group members display are constructive in that they enhance the well-being of individual members and the quality of group relationships. Other patterned behaviors are problematic in that they erode the capacities of members and are destructive to relationships and group cohesion. Sometimes, people join groups specifically because some of their patterned behaviors are producing distress in their interpersonal relationships, although they may not be aware of the patterned nature of their behavior or the impact it has on their ability to achieve their goals. A major role of group workers is to help members become aware of their patterned behavioral responses, determine the effects of these responses on themselves and others, and choose whether to change such responses. To carry out this role, social workers can formulate a profile of the recurring responses of each member, utilizing the concepts of content and process. Content refers to verbal statements and related topics that members discuss, whereas process involves the ways members relate or behave as they interact in the group and discuss content. As with other assessments, social workers must first observe phenomena and then make meaning or working hypotheses about the significance of the observation.

It is at the process level that facilitators may discover members' thematic behaviors or patterned responses. In the HEART example, we might infer that Maria is jockeying to establish an exclusive relationship with the facilitator and bidding for an informal position of co-facilitator in the group, or perhaps she is uncomfortable with her peers and finds the facilitator to be a safe ally who will not reject her. Viewed alone, none of Maria's discrete behaviors provides sufficient information to justify drawing a conclusion about a possible response pattern. Viewed collectively, however, the repetitive responses indicate that a pattern does, in fact, exist, and may create difficulty for Maria in the group and in other aspects of her life.

Example of Patterned Group Behavior

In the first group meeting, Maria moved her chair close to the facilitator's chair. Maria complimented the facilitator when giving her introduction to the group and made a point to verbalize her agreement with several of the facilitator's statements. In subsequent meetings, Maria again sat next to the facilitator and offered advice to other group members, referring to opinions she thought were jointly held by her and the facilitator. Later, Maria tried to initiate a conversation with the facilitator concerning what she regarded as negative behavior of another group member in front of that member and the rest of the group.

During assessment, group facilitators should be attentive to the cognitive and behavioral qualities demonstrated by members whether constructive or problematic. These profiles and patterns are opportunities for the facilitator to intervene, raise awareness, reinforce strengths, and enhance group process and safety. Examples might include "monopolizes conversation," "gives advice prematurely," "is open to other perspectives," "supports others," "deflects attention to others," "quick to anger," or "distressed by strong expressions of emotion."

Identifying Roles of Group Members

In identifying patterned responses of individuals, facilitators also need to attend to the various roles that members assume in
the group. For example, members may assume leadership roles that are formal (explicitly sanctioned by the group) or informal (emerging as a result of group needs). Further, a group may have several members who serve different functions or who head rival subgroups.

Some members may assume task-related or instrumental roles that facilitate the group's efforts to define problems, implement solutions, or carry out tasks. These members may propose goals or actions, suggest procedures, request pertinent facts, clarify issues, or offer an alternative or conclusion for the group to consider. Other members may adopt maintenance roles that are oriented to altering, maintaining, and strengthening the group's functioning. Members who take on such roles may offer compromises, encourage and support the contributions of others, comment on the emotional climate of the meeting, or suggest group standards.

Some members may emerge as spokespersons around concerns of the group or enact other expressive roles. Rather than interpret those behaviors as a negative influence, you may consider whether that member is representing concerns held by others in the group or identifying issues that are lingering below the surface in group sessions. Still other members may assume self-serving roles, seeking to meet their own needs at the expense of the group. Such members may attack the group or its values, resist the group's wishes, continually disagree with or interrupt others, assert authority or superiority, display lack of involvement, pursue extraneous subjects, or find various ways to call attention to themselves.

Members may also receive informal labels from other members, such as "clown," "critic," "uncommitted," "lazy," "silent one," "rebel," "overreactor," or "good mother." These stereotypes can make it difficult for individuals to relinquish the set of expected behaviors or to change their way of relating to the group.

One or more members may also be assigned the role of scapegoat, bearing the burden of responsibility for the group's problems and the brunt of teasing or negative responses from other members. Such individuals may attract this marginalized role because they are socially awkward and repeatedly make blunders in their attempts to elicit positive responses from others (Moreno, 2007), or they may assume this role because they fail to recognize nonverbal cues that facilitate interaction in the group and thus behave without regard to the subtle nuances that govern the behavior of other members (Moreno, 2007). Individuals may also unknowingly perpetuate the scapegoat role they have assumed in other groups such as their family, workplace, school, or social system. Although group scapegoats demonstrate behaviors that attract the hostility or mockery of the group, the presence of the role signals a group phenomenon and pattern whose maintenance requires the tacit cooperation of all members.

Individuals may also assume the role of an isolate—being ignored by the group, not reaching out to others, or doing so but being rejected. The isolate differs from the scapegoat in that the latter gets attention, even if it is negative, whereas the former is simply disregarded.

Some members, of course, assume roles that strengthen relationships and enhance group functioning. Reinforcing these positive behaviors both encourages the individual who demonstrates them and helps other members to emulate them. It is important to identify all the roles that members assume because those roles profoundly affect the group's capacity to respond to the individual needs of members and its ability to fulfill the treatment objectives. Identifying roles is also vital because members tend to play out in treatment or task groups the same roles that they assume in other social contexts. Members need to understand the impact of functional and dysfunctional roles on themselves and others.

Assessing the Group's Patterned Behaviors

Social workers attend to group patterns as well as those of individuals, identifying those that are constructive for group goals and processes and those that are problematic. The examples in Table 11-4 are characteristic of a mature

C7

therapeutic group, though constructive group behaviors may also emerge in the initial stages of development. Positive behaviors that emerge early in the life of a group include:

- The group responds positively the first time a member takes a risk by revealing a personal problem.
- Members of the group are supportive toward other members or demonstrate investment in the group.
- The group works harmoniously for a time.
- Members effectively make a decision together.
- Members adhere to specific group guidelines, such as maintaining focus on work to be accomplished.
- The group responsibly confronts a member who is dominating interaction or interfering in some way with the group accomplishing its task.
- Members are willing to discuss difficult issues.

The group may also display transitory negative behaviors in initial sessions, particularly in regard to power and decision-making. Groups are sometimes torn apart because the exercise of power or privilege prevent the group from being a safe space and from meeting

Table 11-4 Examples of Group Behaviors

Constructive Group Behavior	Problematic Group Behavior
• Members openly communicate personal feelings and attitudes and anticipate that other members will be helpful.	• Members continue to keep discussions on a superficial level or avoid revealing their feelings and opinions.
• Members listen carefully to one another and give all ideas a fair hearing.	• Members are critical and evaluative of each other. They rarely acknowledge or listen to contributions from others.
• Decisions are reached through group consensus after considering everyone's views and feelings.	• Dominant members dismiss or bully other members in decision-making
• Members make efforts to incorporate the views of dissenters or less powerful members rather than to dominate or override these views.	• Members make decisions prematurely without identifying or weighing possible alternatives.
• Members recognize and give feedback regarding others' strengths and growth.	• Members are critical of others' differences.
• Members use "I" messages to speak for themselves, owning their own feelings and positions on matters.	• Members do not personalize their messages but use indirect forms of communication to express their feelings and positions.
• The guidelines established in initial sessions become norms.	• Members act in distracting or disruptive ways.
• Members share responsibility for the group's functioning and success.	• Members avoid talking about the here and now or addressing personal or group problems.
• The group works out problems that impair group functioning.	• Members show little awareness of the needs and feelings of others; emotional investment in others is limited.
• Members are attuned to the needs and feelings of others and give emotional support.	

the needs of some members (Singh & Salazar, 2014). Gender, racial, and other dynamics can be manifested in the group when people from dominant populations enact familiar behaviors in the therapeutic setting. Facilitators need cultural competence and a commitment to social justice to "bring others into the process of dialogue and to structure that process so participants have opportunities to listen as well as to speak. They serve as teachers in preparing group member to listen to, question, validate, challenge, and respect one another…learning to bear witness" to each other's stories (Finn, 2021, p. 244). This fosters a climate where power is distributed, and decisions are made collectively.

When social workers assess groups, they need to identify the current capacity of members to share power and resources and implement problem-solving steps that ensure mutually beneficial solutions. Facilitators must help the group make each member count if the group is to advance through stages of development into maturity.

Assessing Group Alliances

As members of new groups find other members with compatible attitudes, interests, and responses, they develop patterns of affiliation and relationship with these members. Subgroup formations may include pairs, triads, and foursomes. Larger subgroups may develop subdivisions influencing "who addresses whom, who sits together, who comes and leaves together, and even who may meet or talk together outside of the group" (Hartford, 1971, p. 204).

The subgroupings that invariably develop do not necessarily impair group functioning. Members may derive strength and support from subgroups, in turn enhancing their participation and investment in the larger group. Indeed, it is through the process of establishing subgroups or natural coalitions that group members achieve true intimacy. Problems may arise, however, when members develop exclusive subgroups or cliques that disallow intimate relationships with other group members or inhibit members from supporting the goals of the larger group. Subgroups that meet online or in person outside of group sessions can have a particularly pernicious effect on the functioning of the group. Competing factions can often impede or destroy a group.

Facilitators must be skilled in identifying subdivisions and assessing their impact on the group. This may involve constructing a sociogram of group alignments. Credited to Moreno and Jennings (Jennings, 1950), a sociogram graphically depicts patterned affiliations and relationships between group members by using symbols for people and interactions. Figure 11-1 illustrates a sociogram that captures the predominant connections, attractions, and tensions among members of the HEART group for teens with obesity.

Sociograms are representations of group alliances at a given point because alliances

C8

Figure 11-1 Sociogram

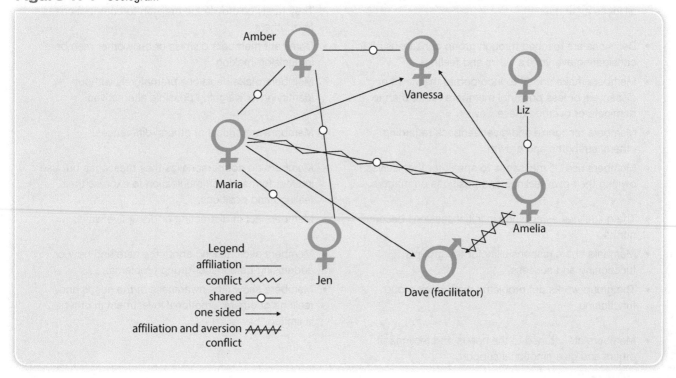

inevitably shift and change, particularly in the early stages of group development. Charting the transitory bonds that occur early in group life can prove valuable to facilitators in deciding where and when to intervene to modify, enhance, or stabilize relationships between members.

Assessing Group Norms

Norms are regulatory mechanisms that give groups a measure of stability and pre- dictability by letting members know what they can expect from the group and from one another. Norms may define the specific behaviors that are appropriate or permissible for individuals, or they may define the range of behaviors that are accept- able in the group. Norms represent the internalization of the group guidelines discussed earlier in this chapter.

Groups develop formal and informal sanctions to reduce behaviors that are considered divergent and return the system to its prior equilibrium. For example, an implicit group norm may be that everyone gets a chance to talk. If a new group member treads on this norm by interrupting or monopolizing discussion, other members may explicitly or subtly react by speaking up to encourage silent members to contribute or by directly asking the new member to let others have a turn. As in this example, people often learn about the norms of particular groups by observing situations in which norms have been violated. Members watch the behavior of other members as they reinforce some behaviors and discourage others. Whether the norms are constructive or problematic, reinforcement or sanctions are powerful in shaping subsequent group behavior.

All groups develop norms that influence the group's response to situations and determine the extent to which the group offers its members therapeutic experiences. A major role for the facilitator, then, is to identify emergent norms and influence them in ways that create a positive climate for inclusion, cohesion, and change. This skill also enables facilitators to identify patterned behaviors, in that those are always undergirded by supporting norms.

Facilitators may be able to identify norms by asking themselves key questions such as the following:

1. What subjects can and cannot be talked about in the group?
2. What kinds of emotional expressions are allowed or avoided in the group?
3. What is the group's pattern regarding working on problems or staying on task?
4. Do group members consider it their own responsi- bility or the facilitator's responsibility to make the group's experience successful?

5. What is the group's stance toward the facilitator?
6. What is the group's attitude toward feedback?
7. How does the group view the contributions of indi- vidual members? What kind of labels and roles does the group assign to them? Do the labels disempower other members?

Another strategy for identifying norms is to explain the concept of norms to group members and ask them to identify those that influence their behavior in the group. This strategy invites members to bring to a con- scious level the norms that are developing and make choices in favor of those that advance the group's goals. Facilitators who join existing groups should also solicit this feedback to better understand the group.

Table 11-6 provides examples of both constructive and problematic norms.

Assessing Group Cohesion

In the initial phases of the group's life, facilitators must also assess and foster the development of cohesion in groups. Defined as the degree to which members are attracted to one another, cohesion is correlated, under certain conditions, with productivity, participa- tion in and out of the group, self-disclosure, risk taking, attendance, and other vital concerns (Harpine, 2011). Cohesion in groups positively affects members' satisfac- tion and personal adjustment. Greater cohesiveness leads to increased self-esteem, more willingness to lis- ten to others, freer expression of feeling, better reality testing, higher self-confidence, and more effective use of other members' evaluations in enhancing a member's own development (Toseland & Rivas, 2017; Yalom & Leszcz, 2020).

Cohesion is inextricably linked to the development of norms in a beginning group. Norms that may poten- tially interfere with both group formation and cohesion include irregular attendance, cliques, changing member- ship, interpersonal aggression, excessive dependence on the facilitator, dominance by a few members, and general passivity in the interaction (Harpine, 2011). Research on negative group experiences indicates that the indi- viduals who are damaged by the group may be those very members who are too timid to help contribute to group rules and thus have little investment in the norms that have been negotiated between the facilitator and more vocal members (Smokowski et al., 2001). These detri- mental norms require the attention of both the facilita- tor and the group members because failure to address them discourages group development and jeopardizes the group itself.

Self-Help Groups

Self-help groups operate without facilitation by professionally trained leaders, either from social work or other fields. They may be organized and led by more experienced members or trained peer-support specialists who have had personal experience with mental health issues, trauma, or addictions and have been trained and credentialed (Tracy & Wallace, 2016). Many of the features of treatment groups will apply to self-help groups (SHG). These include roles and norms, opening and closing rituals, sharing, and eliciting support. Twelve-step groups, for example, typically have patterned programming wherein meetings start with a standard greeting and a moment of silence or recitation of the Serenity Prayer, followed by readings and discussion, and closing with prayer or meditative silence (AANAPA, n.d.). SHG member recruitment and composition is typically organic, changing, and less formally controlled than in social work-facilitated groups. SHGs benefit from spontaneity and the authenticity of shared experiences. Formal concepts in group functioning such as individual and group goals and guidelines will be less central to the functioning of SHGs.

Task Groups

We move now from consideration of treatment and self-help groups to task groups. Although all group types have features in common, task groups are differentiated by their purposes, composition, and format. These unique characteristics and common themes are highlighted in the following sections.

Task Group Purpose

As described earlier in this chapter, task groups are organized to meet client, organizational, and community needs, all of which focus on generating products, planning activities, developing policies, and making decisions rather than on enhancing the personal growth of members (Toseland & Rivas, 2017). Important early steps in forming and assessing task groups are planning for the group and structuring initial sessions to the group purpose.

Task Group Membership and Planning

Membership in task groups may be dictated by the needs of the group or the task to be accomplished, or it may be determined by organizational structure, bylaws, or regulations. For example:

- Agency rules may stipulate that all committees have two consumer members.

C6 and 7

- An association board may select members based on expertise, philanthropic capacity, passion for the cause, and geographic representation.
- A committee to assist with accreditation at a school of social work might include representatives of students, alumni, community facilitators, field instructors, faculty, and staff.
- Members of a treatment team may include all professionals involved in the case, or all individuals whose knowledge is needed to evaluate the case (e.g., speech therapist, teacher, social worker, behavior specialist).

Depending on the values of the organization and the culture of the team, clients, their family members, and representatives of other nondominant groups may be routinely involved as members of the team. Too frequently, however, their participation may be limited as a percent of the membership or in the power their voices are accorded. Social workers' embrace of social justice values and anti-oppressive practices plays an important role in influencing the true inclusions of marginalized and underrepresented people, not as tokens but as fully franchised members and leaders of task groups.

Task group composition may be voluntary, by appointment, or by election, but it should always be responsive to the group's purpose and goals. For example:

- A treatment conference may have the purpose of coordinating the efforts of members of a team involved in serving a particular client or family.
- An ad hoc committee may be recruited to work on a fundraising event for an agency.
- A board of directors is appointed or elected to provide guidance and accountability to an organization.
- A community crime prevention panel may consist of citizen advocates from the neighborhood who want to work for increased services and police reform.

The initiation of a task group and the determination of its purpose may come from many sources. For example, nonprofit agencies are required to have boards of directors as part of their nonprofit status. A staff member might propose a resident council in a halfway house. The director of an agency might initiate a committee to develop better agency communications, or residents of a housing development might suggest a social action group to deal with neighborhood safety.

Members of any task group should have the interest, information, skills, and power needed to accomplish the purpose of the group. The specific purpose of the group suggests sources for its membership. For example, a group formed to study how managed care affects service delivery should include consumers, providers, and representatives from insurance groups and regulatory agencies. A group formed to plan a new teen pregnancy program might include teen parents, their families, health-care providers, teachers, public health researchers, and child welfare workers.

Membership should be large enough and sufficiently diverse to represent the major constituencies affected by the problem being targeted, and participants should possess adequate skills and knowledge for addressing the group's purposes. Task groups that are too large make it difficult for members to have meaningful involvement. A board that has 45 members sends the message that individual viewpoints and attendance do not matter. Conversely, task groups that are too small may have insufficient membership to complete their responsibilities and may have insufficient diversity in viewpoints and expertise.

As with treatment groups, organizers should ensure that no individual is an isolate. For example, a special education advisory committee should not consist of a group of professionals plus a token parent. When consumers or those whose personal experience is valuable to the task group's purpose are included, multiple representatives should be recruited for the group and, if possible, should serve as representatives of other consumers. For example, in a committee on mental health reform, multiple consumers and parents might be involved, and some should represent groups, such as the National Alliance for the Mentally Ill. Taking these steps will help enhance the comfort, power, and legitimacy of group members.

Effective planning in this stage is reflected by accurately and clearly communicating the group's purposes and expectations to prospective members. The level of clarity achieved has important implications for whether those prospective members decide to attend and, later, how well they perform the functions of the group. How often does the group meet? How much time, outside of meetings, is required of members? Are members expected to make financial donations to the organization? How long are the terms of service?

As with treatment groups, task groups may be open or closed in time and in membership. Formal boards or committees generally are ongoing but have structures that provide for the rotation of membership in and out of the group, allowing for staggered terms to assure continuity. Other groups may be time limited and relatively closed in membership (e.g., a task force to review an incident in which a resident was injured, a committee to plan an agency's anniversary celebration, a search committee for a new employee). Some groups may be ongoing but have closed membership (e.g., an ethics committee that hears different cases each month as brought to them by members of the hospital staff).

Beginning the Task Group

The agenda for a beginning session of a task group is like that for a treatment group. It includes facilitating introductions, clarifying the purpose of the group, discussing ground rules, helping members feel a part of the group, setting goals, and anticipating obstacles (Toseland & Rivas, 2017). An opening statement, including the host agency's function and mission as it relates to the group purpose, should be shared so that members understand why they have been called together. Members can then be assisted to find commonalities in their concerns and experiences and identify shared goals for group participation. Some members may know one another from previous roles and have positive or negative preconceptions from that past. Ice breakers and other introductory activities can be used to facilitate communication and identify experiences and resources that members bring to the group (Corey et al., 2013).

Developing group rules and concurrence on decision-making (e.g., majority rule, consensus) then follows. A common rule involves adherence to confidentiality, as premature or distorted release of information might hinder the work and destroy the cohesion of the group. Other rules in task groups usually include expectations about attendance and preparation, processes for recusing oneself on items that may involve conflicts of interest, and structural issues such as timing of meetings, submission of agenda items, and effective communications (Levi, 2007). On boards of directors, a subcommittee may be responsible for recruiting and orienting new members, and the ground rules are specified in bylaws and board policies. New members may also be paired with veteran members who can help them prepare for and participate fully in meetings from the outset of their service (Thomas & Strom-Gottfried, 2018).

Task groups then proceed to goal setting. Such goals always include those mandated by the purpose of the group, such as revising agency policies, planning a conference, reviewing audit reports, implementing new regulations, or coordinating care. In addition, the group may generate its own goals—for example, generating a list of best practices in achieving its purpose or tailoring its response to the group's purpose based on the specific talents and assets available in the group.

As with treatment groups, task group members may take on or be assigned formal (e.g., secretary, chairperson, treasurer) and informal (e.g., timekeeper, devil's advocate, instrumental facilitator, expressive facilitator) roles. Whether these roles are constructive depends on how they are enacted and the extent to which they help the group fulfill its purpose. As with other types of groups, assessing the behaviors of individual members and the group helps identify functional and dysfunctional patterns. Many of the attributes listed in Table 11-4 applies to task groups as well as to treatment groups.

Other parallels with treatment groups include the evolution of subgroups, norms, cohesion, and the role of members' status in group dynamics. As with treatment groups, these phenomena can play either destructive or positive roles in the group's development. For example, a faction within a task group may form a voting bloc that inhibits the full participation of all members or hijacks the democratic decision-making of the group. Members' roles and statuses outside the group may play out in their behaviors and relationships in the group. For example, an agency director may be accustomed to deferential treatment and expect that from fellow group members, even though in the task group setting they are intended to be equals. Employees may be dismissive of or overly solicitous of the input of consumer or community representatives on a committee. Counterproductive norms may include "Attendance is optional," "My opinion doesn't matter," "We never get anything done," or "No one comes prepared." Constructive norms about attendance, active listening, respect, full participation, and honesty can help the group effectively and efficiently achieve its purpose. Although developing cohesion is less crucial in task groups, the presence of socioemotional ties between members can help develop the meaning, commitment, and participation members give to the group process.

Summary

This chapter presented guidelines for assessing and commencing work with treatment, self-help, and task groups, addressing group structure, such as format (open or closed), size, frequency, duration, and composition. We used a systems framework to examine the intersection of individual needs and behaviors with those of the group. We discussed common concerns for members at the outset of a group and the strategies for introducing and assessing group guidelines, norms, and values. In Chapter 12, we turn to considerations of how to build on the social worker's assessment knowledge to construct workable contracts with individuals. We return to consideration of groups in Chapter 16 to identify the skills needed to intervene at various stages of group development.

Competency Notes

C1 **Demonstrate Ethical and Professional Behavior**

- Make ethical decisions by applying the standards of the NASW Code of Ethics, relevant laws and regulations, models for ethical decision-making and ethical conduct of research, and additional codes of ethics as appropriate to context.

C2 **Engage Antiracism, Diversity, Equity, and Inclusion in Practice**

- Demonstrate anti-racist social work practice at the individual, family, group, organizational, community, research, and policy levels, informed by the theories and voices of those who have been marginalized.
- Demonstrate cultural humility applying critical reflexivity, self-awareness, and self-regulation to manage the influence of bias, power, privilege, and values in working with clients and constituencies acknowledging them as experts of their own lived experiences.

C4 **Engage in Practice-Informed Research and Research-Informed Practice**

- Apply research findings to inform and improve practice, policy, and programs.

C6 **Engage with Individuals, Families, Groups, Organizations, and Communities**

- Apply knowledge of human behavior and person-in-environment, and other multidisciplinary theoretical frameworks to engage with clients and constituencies.
- Use empathy, reflection, and interpersonal skills to effectively engage diverse clients and constituencies.

C7 Assess Individuals, Families, Groups, Organizations, and Communities

- Apply knowledge of human behavior and person-in-environment and other culturally responsive multidisciplinary theoretical frameworks when assessing clients and constituencies.
- Demonstrate respect for client self-determination during the assessment process collaborating with clients and constituencies in developing mutually agreed-on goals.

C8 Intervene with Individuals, Families, Groups, Organizations, and Communities

- Engage with clients and constituencies to critically choose and implement culturally responsive, evidenced-based interventions to achieve mutually agreed-on practice goals and enhance capacities of clients and constituencies.
- Incorporate culturally responsive methods to negotiate, mediate, and advocate, with and on behalf of clients and constituencies.

Skill Development Exercises

Planning Groups

Imagine that you are planning a group to assist one of the following populations:

1. People charged with domestic violence
2. Middle school students with diabetes
3. Teenage fathers
4. Families of people with schizophrenia
5. Elementary school children who have been exposed to family or community violence
6. Parents and community members who wish to change a school policy on suspensions
7. People newly admitted to an assisted living facility
8. Seventh and eighth graders who have no friends
9. Teens who want to start a Gay-Straight Alliance in their high school
10. Premarital couples
11. Widowers
12. People concerned about bullying in a **school**

Using the guidelines in this chapter, determine:

a. The name you will give the group
b. The type of group
c. A one-sentence statement of purpose
d. The size of the group
e. The length, structure, and format
f. The location where you will meet
g. Important factors in group composition
h. How you will recruit and screen members

Chapter 12

Developing Goals and Formulating a Contract

Chapter Overview

The idea of goals permeates social work practice. The programs and the agencies who employ social workers exist to improve the social welfare of disadvantaged people in some way. When you meet with a client for the first time, your goal is to establish a collaborative working relationship with a mutually understood purpose. When you express empathy and authenticity with clients, your goal is often to strengthen relationships and deepen your understanding about the effect of the presenting problem in their lives. The goal of assessment is to generate knowledge about strengths and challenges clients face with respect to their presenting problem and to point to possible avenues for assistance. Everything that you do with clients is done in relation to one or more goals, whether stated or unstated.

Goal formulation and contracting takes on a more formal character when you transition from Phase I to Phase II of the helping process. In this transition, you and your clients establish the formal targets of the helping process as they relate to their presenting problems. Your clients may be motivated to increase their access to financial and other material resources, expand and improve the quality of their social engagements, or increase their power and influence with important systems that affect their lives. They may be motivated

to adopt new behaviors or use new skills to increase their resilience in the face of adversity and difficult challenges like health and mental health problems, addictions, the effects of trauma, or violence, and mandated or involuntary clients are obligated to plan goals that meet the expectations of external authorities such as courts, schools, and parents.

The goal of this chapter is to equip you with the skills you need to formulate client-driven goals that advance the social justice mission of the profession, are aligned with agency and program requirements, satisfy externally imposed mandates, and motivate clients to participate actively in Phase II of the helping process.

As a result of reading this chapter, you will be able to:

- Understand the micro- and mezzo-level factors that influence the process of goal formulation

- Define the structural elements of effective goal statements

- Guide clients through the process of developing effective goal statements

- Monitor and measure progress toward goal attainment.

- Formulate a contract or service agreement.

The EPAS Competencies in Chapter 12

This chapter will give you the information needed to meet the following practice competencies:

- Competency 1: Demonstrate Ethical and Professional Behavior

- Competency 2: Engage Antiracism, Diversity, Equity, and Inclusion in Practice

- Competency 7: Assess Individuals, Families, Groups, Organizations, and Communities

- Competency 9: Evaluate Practice with Individuals, Families, Groups, Organizations, and Communities

Goals

All behavior is goal directed. That is, everything that we do helps us to achieve an end state that is valued, desired, or satisfies a perceived need or obligation. While many of our goals are subconscious, other goals are stated a priori and reflect a purposeful attempt to change our circumstances and solve important problems. Thus, you probably have goals for your professional education that you can state with some level of specificity (e.g., "I want to obtain employment as a child protection worker"), as well as goals in personal health care (e.g., "I want to avoid migraine headaches"), leisure activities (e.g., "I want my exercise to be fun"), and in other areas (e.g., "I want to use less plastic").

The act of formulating conscious goal statements is important for several reasons. First, well-constructed goal statements point to tasks and behaviors that lead toward goal attainment. For example, the long-term goal of employment in child protection suggests strategies such as obtaining a social work degree, taking specialized courses in child maltreatment, and learning state and local-level hiring policies. The linkage between goals and tasks is crucial for social work where, in the absence of clear goals, social work interventions can become unfocused and scattershot rather than purposeful and client centered.

Second, goals have a motivating force of their own. Goals reveal discrepancies between current conditions and desired end states, between current conditions and the vision that clients have for their future (Oyserman et al., 2017). The wider the discrepancy, the greater the motivating force of the goal. Interestingly, research on goal-setting theory demonstrates that, in addition to the emotional commitment that people have to their goals, goals that are perceived to be more difficult are more motivating (Locke & Latham, 2006). That is, where the discrepancy between the beginning and end states are largest, people tend to be more motivated, up to the point where they begin to perceive goals to be unreasonably difficult or not achievable.

One caveat to this discussion is that goal setting does not produce behavior change and problem solving all on its own. There are many factors that contribute to motivation and goal attainment, including the contexts in which people find themselves, their strengths and resources, constraints imposed by systems of oppression, and their competing commitments. Research does suggest, however, that attention to explicit goals makes a meaningful contribution to the change process (Levack, et al., 2015). Therefore, goals are a central element of direct social work practice linking assessment with the implementation of change strategies.

Purpose of Goals in Direct Social Work

The primary purpose of goals in social work is to make explicit the outcomes toward which you and your clients strive to achieve. Goals in social work link client desires and concerns to the tasks that you and they complete during the helping process. When goals are shared, that is, when your goals align closely with those of your clients, the focus of your work will more likely coordinate with theirs, thereby avoiding circumstances where you and they work at cross purposes. Of course, the major driver of social work goals are the target concerns identified by clients, regardless of age or status (Costa, et al., 2017; Vroland, et al., 2016). This is a critical aspect of the goal formulation process and bears repeating. Goal development should be a client-driven process where clients, to the greatest extent possible, determine their own goals based on their own values and their own assessment of need. Emphasizing client values in the goal-formation process maximizes the motivating force of goals and ensures that you and your clients are working in harmony toward the same outcome.

The orienting frameworks for social work practice are consistent with a client-driven approach for goals and goal development. Client-driven goals are more likely to reflect client strengths, be sensitive to their experience of trauma, and more likely to empower clients rather than marginalize or oppress them. Consistent with the social justice mission of social work, goals in direct social work practice specify client-level outcomes that enhance their capacity to overcome and adapt to challenges, increases their access to resources, and enables them to exercise self-determination while meeting their obligations and responsibilities.

We know that other stakeholders have interests that impinge on the goal formulation process as well. For instance, goals should fit with the mission and purposes of social work agencies and programs. All social work agencies and helping systems have program goals and objectives that are derived from their missions and sources of funding. It may be useful to think of **program goals** as general statements regarding the outcomes that are expected for all service recipients. For example, mental health programs funded through private or public managed care health plans may focus on the management of psychiatric symptoms and adherence to medical treatment, whereas other publicly funded programs may focus directly on vocational training and support. In that context, consider the following goal statements developed with a male-identified 47-year-old adult who was diagnosed with schizophrenia:

- **Goal statement #1:** [Name] will get a part-time job.
- **Goal statement #2:** [Name] will not be bothered by his voices (auditory hallucinations).
- **Goal statement #3:** [Name] will have people he can call when he is feeling nervous or anxious at work.

In this example, a careful assessment showed that the debilitating experience of auditory hallucinations was intensely stressful and impaired his ability to sustain a part-time job, which was prominent among his long-term goals. Although both programs, the mental health program and the vocational training program, might adopt obtaining a part-time job as a long-term goal, he and his social worker in the mental health program might be more likely to adopt the short-term goal statement #2 (not be bothered by voices) rather than goal statement #3 (have people to call when he is feeling nervous or anxious at work), which may instead be more appropriate to the vocational services program setting.

Goals are important for mandated and involuntary clients as well because goals demonstrate how clients can achieve mandates and requirements set by courts and other referring authorities. In general, intervention goals for involuntary clients should be consistent with the mandates that brought them into the service system in the first place. However, this can be a significant challenge for involuntary clients who disagree with the referring authority or who resent the loss of freedom and control represented by the imposition of treatment mandates. Goals that are perceived as a threat are less motivating (Locke & Latham, 2006) and the use of power over clients by referring authorities can itself engender resentment and resistance (Brehm & Brehm, 2013). In our experience, we find that a careful review of the mandates that began during the process of role preparation (see Chapter 5) and goal formulation skills elaborated later in this chapter often reveals discretion in how mandates can be fulfilled (Rooney & Myrick, 2018). This discretion can be expressed in the various ways that goals can be conceptualized, leaving room for clients to exercise self-determination and choice in a client-driven goal formation process.

Types of Goals

The first concern in the goal formulation process is for the specificity of the goal statements you develop with clients. You should strive for specific goal statements rather than general statements. Specific goals are usually elaborated

C7

statements that are precise in one or more of the following dimensions: behavioral description, person, place, and time. Guidance from research on goal setting is the source of popular mnemonics like SMART goals, where effective goals have the following qualities:

- **S**pecific
- **M**easurable
- **A**chievable
- **R**ealistic
- **T**ime-limited

Each of these qualities have research support both in and out of social work contexts. Specificity in goal setting is important because it points to tasks and activities that can promote goal attainment (Schwalbe & Koetzle, 2020); measurability enables monitoring and feedback, which is associated with motivation and goal attainment (Harkin et al., 2016); "achievable" and "realistic" ensure that goals fall within a person's perceived range of possibilities (Lovell et al., 2015); and time limits have been shown to be a central feature of effective social work interventions (Reid, 1997).

The case example of Bettina, an adolescent who resides in a group home with her daughter, provides examples of how goal statements can vary in their specificity (see case example). Compare the following goal statements:

- **Goal statement #4:** To get my own place.
- **Goal statement #5:** To get my own apartment for me and my daughter.
- **Goal statement #6:** To get my own apartment for me and my daughter by the time I'm 19.
- **Goal statement #7:** To get my own apartment for me and my daughter near her daddy's mother by the time I'm 19.

How do these goal statements compare to the qualities of SMART goals? Primarily, they become increasingly detailed and elaborated. Goal statement #5 adds a more precise description of the preferred end state (i.e., "apartment" rather than "place"). Goal statements #5 and #7 add relevant people (i.e., her daughter and daughter's grandmother). Goal statements #6 and #7 add a time dimension (by age 19), and goal statement #7 adds a location near her daughter's grandmother, presumably important for emotional and instrumental support.

Whether or not Bettina's goals are realistic and achievable cannot be known given the information available to us. It appears that the time frame for this goal may relate to program prerogatives as well as Bettina's own preferences, and the role of her daughter's grandmother signals the important role of social support

Case Example 1: Bettina

According to the case record summary about Bettina, age 17, she was removed from her home along with her siblings when she was six years of age. Each child was placed in a separate foster home. Bettina, the oldest child in the sibling group, has experienced multiple placements, and at age 16, she was on the run and pregnant. She is currently living with her child in a group home for pregnant or parenting teen mothers. She has lived in the home for the past year.

Multiple notes in the case record describe her as alternatively defiant/contrite, courteous/rude, uncooperative/cooperative, and motivated/unmotivated, depending on the day and her mood. Because of her behavior, staff have routinely initiated sanctions, and some believe that she should be placed in a more restrictive environment. Bettina's response to sanctions is unpredictable. At times, she may comply; at other times, she becomes explosive. The following is Bettina's story from her own point of view:

> I don't like people telling me what to do. I know my own mind! Everyone is always watching me, the mistakes that I make, like I care what they think. You know what I'm saying?

They never say, "Bettina, you are doing a good job caring for your baby." But you can be sure that they are just sitting around waiting and watching for me to mess up so they can come down on me. Sometimes I get confused and scared, but then my worker says, "Bettina, you can do it!" Then, we talk about stuff like what I want to do when I leave this place. Eventually, I want to live in my own place with my baby.

The other day I was angry and walking around cursing because I had missed an appointment with my worker. She and I had an appointment, but I had a chance to take my baby to see his daddy. Besides, the baby could also see his daddy's mother, who has been real helpful to me. I want my baby to have contact with his father's family. I could tell that my worker was unhappy, having driven across town for the appointment with me. I hate it when I mess up with my worker, but I did not know what else to do. I had a chance to take the baby to see his daddy and his daddy's mother, so I left, but as soon as she opened the door, I started cursing, in case she was angry. She let me go on for a while, and then she asked me, "What is going on in your head right now?" and I just started crying.

for her success. What can be inferred based on the difficulties faced by many adolescents who age out of foster care is that this might be a challenging goal to achieve. In general, goals should be achievable and realistic. This does not mean, however, that goals should be easy. Goal attainment takes work, and we know that motivated people with support can achieve difficult goals.

In addition to SMART goals, social workers need to bear in mind several other structural features of client-driven goals that influence goal attainment. Among these is goal time horizon. **Long-term goals** frame people's ambitions within their identities and values. Identity-based motivation theory suggests that people are more motivated to attain goals that are consistent with how they see themselves in their future and to avoid goals that reflect identities that they prefer to avoid or that they reject (Oyserman et al., 2017). While important, long-terms goals do not always motivate action in the absence of short-term goals, however. **Short-term goals** often reflect a partialized version of a long-term goal, possessing one or more of the SMART characteristics introduced earlier. They are important

because, as indicated earlier in this chapter, short-term goals help people make the link between tasks completed within a defined time window to help them make progress toward a long-term objective. Consider these two goal statements that may be applicable to Bettina (see case example):

- **Goal statement #8:** To have a job that will support me and my daughter when we have our own apartment
- **Goal statement #9:** To get a part-time job in a retail store in the next three months.

Goal statement #8 provides a context with which to understand why goal statement #9 is important. In this instance, Bettina is not only looking for a part-time job now but is starting to build an employment history that can help her as she later assumes the financial responsibility of caring for herself and her baby. Goal statement #9 can help Bettina transition to developing more immediate strategies for goal attainment. Finding employment that offers a living wage can be daunting in the absence of a series of short-term goals that build to this long-term objective. In general, we recommend that you work with clients to develop short-term goals that fit logically within the framework of their long-term goals (Schwalbe & Koetzle, 2020).

Second, goals can be classified as approach or avoidance. **Approach goals** identify a positive end state, usually emphasizing growth and change, whereas **avoidance goals** identify a future state to be avoided or minimized. For people who are in treatment for major depressive disorder, it is the difference between saying, "I want to be able to get up in the morning and look forward to the day" versus "I'm tired. I want the sadness and loneliness to go away." For Bettina, who feels heavily monitored and criticized by group home program staff (see case example), goal statement examples might include:

- **Goal statement #10:** To get staff to stop telling me what to do.
- **Goal statement #11:** To gain the freedom to make my own decisions about my schedule and how I care for my baby.

In general, social workers have taken the position that approach goals like goal statement #11 are stronger than avoidance goals like goal statement #10 because they activate hope in a future that can be visualized, and further because they point more directly to the kind of tasks that can help them make progress toward their goals. For people with major depression who want to "get up in the morning and look forward to the day," tasks and interventions may be developed to help them get out of bed and to anticipate activities in the day that could be pleasurable. For Bettina, an approach goal like gaining freedom suggest strategies like more effectively communicating her needs, strengthening relationships with one or more staff members to increase social and emotional support, or behavioral contracting with the program to enable her to more clearly see what steps she needs to take to increase her freedom to make choices. Avoidance goals provide less direction. Nevertheless, research in goal setting suggests that for many people avoidance goals may be important and that a balance of approach and avoidance goals may be a potent motivator for goal attainment (Chen, 2017; Oyserman, et al., 2017).

Third, goals can be classified in terms of performance or learning. **Performance goals** define a final outcome, whereas **learning goals** emphasize process and the acquisition of knowledge and skills that people can use to achieve short- and long-term goals. Consider these short-term approach goals:

- **Goal statement #12:** Bettina will have saved enough money to move into her own apartment (down payment plus first month's rent plus household supplies) by her 19th birthday.

- **Goal statement #13:** Bettina will know about the benefits and disadvantages of bank savings, bank loans, and credit cards.

Goal statement #12 is a performance goal, as it is focused on the ultimate outcome of developing assets that Bettina can use to promote secure, independent living for she and her daughter. Performance goals often have the advantage of measurability, where achievement can be determined by a preexisting criterion and can be motivating as people chart their progress toward goal attainment. However, for some clients, performance goals may be inappropriate on their own when your assessment reveals a lack of skill or knowledge needed to execute goal-related tasks. In these cases, research suggests that learning goals such as goal statement #13 may be most appropriate. Learning goals can be helpful when people are adopting new or novel behaviors and have the advantage of promoting skills that can be transferred to new contexts beyond the purposes of the social work intervention.

The foregoing goal characteristics—SMART, short-term versus long-term, approach versus avoidance, and performance versus learning create a menu of choices for you and for your clients to formulate client-driven goals according to their needs and values in the context of their referral mandates and the program's objectives. However, the social justice mission of the social work profession points to at least one additional characteristic of goals that you should consider when you formulate goals with clients: whether goals are empowerment-oriented, compliance/conformity-oriented, or risk-resilience oriented.

Empowerment-oriented goals are framed toward self-determination and agency. They operate at the sociopolitical level, often emphasizing dimensions of consciousness raising, education, social support, and access to resources. Achievement of empowerment goals can lead to an increase in self-determination, an increased capacity to change the condition of their sociopolitical environments, and an increase in their power to influence institutions and people in authority. Examples of empowerment-related approach goals from four prototypical social work settings include:

- **Goal statement #14 [child welfare]:** [parent's name] will obtain social support and advice from trusted advocates, friends, and family members by [date] about how to address accusations of neglect raised by the child protection report.

- **Goal statement #15 [juvenile justice]:** [adolescent's name] will learn strategies to avoid the effects of stigma and labeling that affect teenagers who are on probation.

- **Goal statement #16 [interpersonal violence]:** [partner's name] To identify role models for expressing masculinity without violence.
- **Goal statement #17 [mental health]:** [patient's name] will learn about the legal consequences for refusing to take psychotropic medications prescribed by psychiatrists.

You may observe that goal statements #14 and #16 focus on informal social support, and goal statements #15 and #17 focus on consciousness raising about community-level and system-level power dynamics. The social support goals are performance goals, and the consciousness raising goals are learning goals. All are short term. All start from the position that the client is involved in helping systems and programs with strong program objectives and mandates and, in part, are formulated with reference to these objectives and mandates. Empowerment goals are consistent with an anti-oppressive approach to practice that focuses on social, economic, and environmental justice outcomes and are based on a critical analysis of power relationships and power hierarchies in which the client and social worker are embedded.

Empowerment goals should not be confused with compliance and conformity goals. **Compliance and conformity goals** are usually responsive to the requirements of larger social systems and authority figures. They are represented in mandates and the prerogatives of program objectives and referring authorities. For example:

- **Goal statement #18 [child welfare]:** [parent's name] will maintain a clean, safe home environment for their children.
- **Goal statement #19 [juvenile justice]:** [adolescent's name] will avoid contact with law enforcement during their period of probation.
- **Goal statement #20 [interpersonal violence]:** [partner's name] will use alternatives to physical violence to resolve conflict with their partner.
- **Goal statement #21 [mental health]:** [patient's name] will take their medication in the morning and evenings as prescribed by their psychiatrist.

These goal statements are typical of those found in many social work settings. Like the empowerment goals earlier, they are short term but represent a mix of approach and avoidance goals. All are performance goals; none are learning goals. The defining feature of each is that they focus on outcomes that keep their respective clients in compliance with program objectives and mandates and correspond to convention social norms.

Risk-resilience goals occupies the space between empowerment goals and compliance/conformity goals. **Risk-resilience goals** identify changes in risk and protective processes that are likely to alleviate presenting problems. As such, they are often aimed at increasing self-efficacy, confidence, and skills associated with personal empowerment, but they also usually represent the prerogatives and mandates of social work programs and agencies. Behavior change is their frequent target. Staying with the four settings introduced in this section, examples of risk-resilience goals include:

- **Goal statement #22 [child welfare]:** [parent's name] will institute a schedule that includes times designated for family meals, bedtimes, and weekly mental health breaks.
- **Goal statement #23 [juvenile justice]:** [adolescent's name] will avoid after-school contact with peers who are actively using drugs.
- **Goal statement #24 [interpersonal violence]:** [partner's name] will learn to use grounding and mindfulness strategies when they are feeling triggered and upset when at home with their partner.
- **Goal statement #25 [mental health]:** [patient's name] will develop strategies to organize and keep track of their psychotropic medication adherence daily.

Risk-resilience goals are often evidence based and are, therefore, preferred by many social workers and social work programs to address serious problems such as child abuse and neglect, delinquency and criminal behavior, intimate partner violence, and mental health. Considering the examples here, goal statement #22 may address the consequences of emotional stress and psychiatric problems that can interfere with routine responsibilities of parenting and increase risk of neglect for some families (Mulder et al., 2018). Goal statement #23 addresses the effect of peer influence on delinquency and substance abuse among adolescents (Dishion & Tipsord, 2011). Goal statement #24 deals with the difficulties many perpetrators of intimate partner violence have with anger management and acute emotional frustration (Birkley & Eckhardt, 2015), and goal statement #25 addresses the important role of medication adherence to prevent the need for psychiatric hospitalization for many people with serious psychiatric problems (Conn & Ruppar, 2017). People who achieve goals such as these may experience an increase in competence, confidence, and self-determination. However, it is important to recognize that many risk-resilience goals are embedded within systems of control and that their underlying values emphasize program objectives and mandates. In a way, risk-resilience goals chart a pathway for clients' compliance and conformity; they do not challenge or change the sociopolitical structure, they reinforce it.

The orienting frameworks presented in Chapter 2 ordinarily suggest a preference for empowerment goals and risk-resilience goals rather than compliance and conformity goals. Empowerment goals maximize self-determination, a value underlying all the orienting frameworks and emphasize social justice outcomes in the sense that they address unequal access to material and social resources at the individual client level. Risk-resilience goals, while operating in tandem with referral mandates and program objectives, usually harness people's strengths and focus on factors in their personal and social environments that research evidence suggests can promote problem solving and resilience, yet compliance and conformity goals may be important in some cases. Often, involuntary clients face consequential legal mandates, and young people, especially children and adolescents, face considerable pressure for rule following behaviors in the home, school, and community. Short-term compliance goals that are aligned with long-term goals and objectives can motivate goal attainment (Schwalbe & Koetzle, 2020). Under these and similar circumstances, compliance and conformity may be the central reason for your work. To date, social work research has not provided a data-based solution to this challenge. Recognizing that compliance and conformity goals cannot always be avoided, in these instances we recommend a mix of empowerment, risk-resilience, and compliance/conformity goals in recognition of clients' obligations to referring authorities as well as their need to express self-determination and agency.

Factors Influencing Goal Formation

First and foremost, clients' preferences and their understanding of the assessment of their presenting problems and challenges **C2** should be the primary influence on client-driven goal formulation. Questions like "what is your goal" and "what would you like to change" should provide the major underpinnings for the goals you negotiate with clients. Of course, answers to these questions do not exist in isolation. In addition to personal factors such as preferences and an individualized assessment, and contextual factors such as program objectives and referral mandates, there are other sociostructural and personal factors that operate to promote and impinge on the process of goal formulation. This section addresses these factors, beginning with cultural influence.

The prominence of goals in social work is no doubt influenced by the Western orientation toward problem solving and individualism. Goals in social work traditionally focus on achievement, self-actualization, and autonomy, characteristic features of individualistic societies (Sue, 2006). The question "what is your goal" is usually quite natural in many Western-oriented social work contexts.

However, clients from non-Western cultures that are more strongly oriented toward collectivism may be most comfortable with an alternative approach to goals and goal formulation. The language of goals may prioritize the prevention of problems that create disharmony and emphasize responsibilities and obligations to others. Consistent with their emphasis on a relational mindset and interdependence, the content of goals may be oriented to the prevention or avoidance of problems that would affect the well-being of important kinship and community groups (Erez, 2013; Kurman et al., 2015), as suggested by the contrasting examples of these two goal statements for a person who experiences depression:

- **Goal statement #26:** To improve my mood.
- **Goal statement #27:** To restore my connections with friends and family.

Depression-type illnesses are commonly experienced by peoples around the world, although its manifestation varies across cultures (Haroz, 2017; O'Nell, 1996), with some cultures focused on the individual subjective experiences as in goal statement #26, and other cultures focused on the disruption depression can cause to important social ties as in goal statement #27. Consistent with the model of cultural humility that we advocate, you are encouraged to have direct conversations about how culture impacts the process of goal formulation, appreciate cultural differences that emerge in these discussions, and value your clients' cultural orientations by integrating those into the goal formulation process.

Goal formulation is a resource-intensive activity. Think about the goal **C7** statements you have read in this chapter. What resources are needed to envision a future in which these goals might be met? One type of resource common to all goal formulation exercise is the cognitive and emotional resources associated with self-control and self-management. These intraindividual resources include the capacity to regulate emotions, delay gratification, and focus on problem solving. In childhood and adolescence, self-control and self-management grow as rapid increases in short-term reward sensitivity are increasingly balanced by slower-growing increases in cognitive control (Steinberg, 2008). Until the balance of reward sensitivity and cognitive control reaches maturity in late adolescence and early adulthood, younger clients may be more focused on short-term goals that involve extrinsic reward systems such as social approval and concrete or material rewards. Research indicates that these and other cognitive and emotional resource enable people to focus on challenging goals and persist through obstacles.

However, the capacity to exercise cognitive and emotional control needed for goal formulation and goal pursuit depends not only on age and individual developmental factors but also on external resources such as social support, material resources, opportunities, and time. Social support is implicated in goal commitment and persistence (Strom, 2014) and these, along with material resources, can contribute to a sense of agency and mastery over goal attainment (Franklin, et al. 2019). For many clients, the emotional and instrumental support provided specifically by families and by significant others facilitate goal setting and goal attainment. For example, Ritter and Dozier (2000) found that although a court mandate to complete a drug treatment program was powerful, family support and involvement was equally important in preventing a relapse. Other studies have shown that family involvement and participation provide a cultural frame of reference that was essential to developing goals and ensuring goal attainment with adult and adolescent clients (Durlak et al., 2011; Gardner, 2000; Lum, 2007; Potocky-Tripodi, 2002; Sarkisian & Gerstel, 2004; Saulnier, 2002; Sue, 2006; Wong, 2007).

On the other hand, the strain of resource scarcity in one or more of these areas creates significant challenges in people's capacity to allocate resources, define goals, and meet competing obligations. People who have multiple resource deficits may have difficulty making connections between short- and long-term goals, feel powerless with respect to goals that may be encouraged or mandated, and experience a sense of hopelessness for the future (Franklin et al., 2019). They may be more likely to adopt avoidance goals rather than approach goals as part of a strategy to manage scarce resources (Schnelle et al., 2010), or because of sheer fatigue (Poortvliet et al., 2015). Discrimination in areas like housing and employment can have debilitating psychological effects that can hinder the goal formulation process through these same mechanisms (Dietz, 2000; Demby, 2013; Grote et al., 2007; Guadalupe & Lum, 2005). Consequently, social workers should assess the availability of resources in their clients' social environment, both as a source of strength to promote goal formulation but also as a source of strain, remembering that rarely do people have the luxury to focus on one or two immediate goals but that people most often are allocating social support, material resources, and time to multiple, competing goals and obligations.

At the micro level, goal formulation is also influenced by such factors as self-efficacy and goal commitment. Self-efficacy beliefs relate to people's confidence in their ability to learn new skills, complete a task, or achieve an outcome (Bandura, 1997). Self-efficacy develops through prior experience of success and failure in the same or similar tasks and by observing relatable role models who are more or less successful with the skill,

task, or outcome. Self-efficacy beliefs are distinct from self-esteem beliefs, which are generalized beliefs about a person's overall self-worth. Self-efficacy beliefs help people allocate their efforts toward goals that have a high likelihood of success and avoid effort and work in areas that are less likely to be successful.

Consider the following goal statements for a parent whose children were removed to foster care and whose long-term goal is reunification:

- **Goal statement #28:** [Parent's name] will learn how to reinforce positive behaviors and respond to negative behavior using a token economy.
- **Goal statement #29:** [Parent's name] will reduce alcohol consumption to no more than one alcoholic drink per day.

In what ways might self-efficacy be important to the adoption of either of these goals? For the first goal, self-efficacy beliefs about learning new skills may be paramount, whereas the second goal may be facilitated by self-efficacy beliefs developed in prior experience with similar tasks. When negotiating goals with clients, social workers should assess client confidence and self-efficacy beliefs about goal achievement and use this information to modify goal statements and to suggest additional goals that have as their aim to increase self-efficacy.

Self-efficacy interacts with values and commitments. People who are committed to a goal expend effort toward achieving the goal and persist in goal pursuit when faced with difficulties and challenges (Seijts & Latham, 2011). In the prior example, the parent's commitment to the goal of learning new parenting skills is a critical concern. Success requires that they choose to prioritize learning and that they give sustained effort to practice new skills in the face of temporary failures when predictable challenges arise. It is also important to remember that goals do not exist in isolation from one another, and many people express ambivalence about competing goals. In the previous example, the commitment of the parent to limit their alcohol use in a harm-reduction approach may enhance their willingness to address a complicated alcohol use problem that includes hidden goals related to stress reduction (Charlet & Heinz, 2017). While many people need to pursue more rigid abstinence goals for health and behavioral reasons, the client described here may have found the commitment to an abstinence goal to be too daunting, whereas a harm-reduction goal might enable the client to experience the valued ends of alcohol use while at the same time alleviating risks to the health and safety of their children.

In addition to these macro- to micro-level client factors, the power of the social work role also influences the goal formulation process. The degree to which you adopt a collaborative, transparent, and client-centered approach can empower people to adopt goals for which they have a strong desire and commitment to achieve. The resources you can offer by virtue of your role – social support as well as material resources – can be a significant source of help for clients who are negotiating multiple problems, responsibilities, and compounding resource constraints, and who waiver in their self-efficacy beliefs (Bagci, 2018). The knowledge you bring to the goal-formulation process can help clients think clearly about the end states they wish to achieve through the formation of approach versus avoidance goals, learning versus performance goals, and empowerment goals versus compliance goals versus risk-resilience goals.

The power of the social work role can also conspire against the goal-formulation process. When social workers pressure clients, clients may acquiesce to goals that they do not want or do not intend to act upon. This happens in voluntary service settings when social workers adopt a paternalistic position based on beliefs about client best interests and when social workers overidentify with treatment mandates and program objectives over and above client preferences and values. It is entirely reasonable to expect that your viewpoints about client goals can be discussed, including when you have concerns about client best interests, or when you have ethical and legal concerns about the goals that clients seek to attain. When your reservations are serious, you may wish to express them and then seek consultation with a supervisor or trusted colleague. Fortunately, this is a rare circumstance for most clients. Most often, your task is to collaborate with clients in the formation of client-driven goals that simultaneously satisfy their needs, program objectives, and external mandates rather than to pressure or to persuade them (Rooney & Myrick, 2018; Trotter, 2015).

Guidelines for Selecting and Defining Goals

The discussion to this point suggests a set of practice guidelines for client-driven goal formation. These guidelines are summarized in Table 12-1. Principle 1 sets the theme for all goal formulation in social work. When you develop goals with clients, they should be client-driven to the greatest extent possible. The goals you negotiate with clients should reflect the commitments and the values of your clients in the context of their culture, their personal and contextual resources, and be developed with recognition for their long-term goals and aspirations.

Goal formulation leverages the strengths of two experts: clients' expertise about the circumstances that

C1, 2, and 7

Table 12-1 Guidelines for Selecting and Defining Goals

1. Prefer client-driven short-term goals that are matched to their values, preferences, culture, and long-term goals.
2. Structure specific goals to enhance motivation
3. Balance short-term goals with long-term goals
4. Balance avoidance goals with approach goals
5. Balance performance goals with learning goals
6. Balance compliance-conformity goals with empowerment and risk/resilience goals
7. Maximize client choice within the constraints of program objectives and referral mandates

affect their lives and social workers' expertise about the role of goals in the helping process. Your respective roles in this process are outlined here:

Client: The client is the foremost expert in articulating what they would like to be different. Social work principles in support of clients' active involvement in goal decisions include empowerment, social justice, and the axiom "starting where the client is" (Finn & Jacobson, 2003; Marsh, 2002; Meyer, 2001; Smith & Marsh, 2002). Finn and Jacobson (2003) emphasize the social justice aspect of clients' involvement, stressing that "clients have a right to their reality and to have their reality be a part of their service provisions" (pp. 128–129).

Social worker: As the social worker, your professional expertise, knowledge, and skills facilitate the process by assisting clients to specify, prioritize, and define goals in measurable language. Also, as goals are discussed, you can help clients to assess feasibility, identify potential barriers, and become aware of resources and strengths related to goal attainment. Skills that you may utilize to elicit goal-directed information include the communication and facilitative skills discussed in Chapter 6.

Your sensitivity to and empathy for the reality of clients in goal decisions can be especially important in cross-cultural interactions. Without client participation, goals may be developed that are counterproductive to clients' needs or interests, cause stress, and potentially reinforce a sense of marginalization that mirrors the experience of oppression and inequality (Clifford & Burke, 2005; Guadalupe & Lum, 2005; Pollack, 2004; G. D. Rooney, 2009; Vera & Speight, 2003; Weinberg, 2006). Although your professional expertise is a vital resource, it is important that you acknowledge and respect clients' appraisals of life experiences to create an atmosphere of a mutual problem-solving partnership.

The remaining principles outline recommendations for goals that are structured to maximize motivation and goal attainment, are consistent with an anti-oppressive and trauma-informed perspectives, and recognize how program objectives and referral mandates place constraints on goal formulation. In general, preferred goals are more rather than less specific, approach rather than avoidance, and empowerment or risk/resilience rather than compliance-conformity focused.

However, there may be times when client preferences or program constraints lead to goals that do not meet all these guidelines. Clients may prefer avoidance goals or resist timelines, the nature of your service settings may require compliance-conformity goals, or clients may resist referral mandates despite their flexibility. In these circumstances, research supports, and we recommend, establishing a limited number of goals that balance less optimal goals with goals that are consistent with these guidelines. For instance, pair avoidance goals with complementary approach goals, or add empowerment goals emphasizing consciousness raising or social support to mandate-required compliance-conformity goals. When balancing goals, remember that the emphasis is not on what you think clients should strive to accomplish, but rather what clients want to accomplish (Principle 1).

Guidelines for Selecting and Defining Goals with Minors

Principles for the formulation of goals developed above generalize to all client groups irrespective of age, culture, or social position. Therefore, even young children and adolescents should be actively involved in the goal formulation process toward the objective of identifying client-driven goals. However, there are separate considerations when applying these principles in social work with children and adolescents. During childhood and adolescents, the context of goal formulation shifts depending upon normative developmental considerations that influence underlying self-control and self-management processes as well as the social context of childhood and adolescence that creates age-graded limits on their self-determination and agency. This section addresses some of these considerations.

Inherent power inequality marks the context of goal discussions with children and adolescents. Not only are children and adolescents disempowered in relation to adults by social custom and by formal legal statutes, but most children and adolescents you encounter will also have referral mandates and treatment pressure from some external authority. Often, disruptive or otherwise challenging behavioral problems can form the basis of the referral or mandates (Yeh et al., 2002). Parents and caregivers may bring their children for mental health treatment out of a mix of care, concern, frustration, and sometimes exhaustion. School officials may refer children and adolescents to social workers to remedy emotional or behavioral problems that disrupt classroom learning environments. Child welfare workers and probation officers leverage the power of the court and law to force children into therapy and adolescents into substance abuse treatment. In any case, it is rare that children or adolescents seek out social work services on their own. The implication is that, to a large extent, treatment goals are defined by others, not by the identified client.

In some respects, then, the practice of goal formulation with mandated clients apply to goal formulation with most children and adolescents. As with adults, it is important to clarify mandates and requirements with children and adolescents related to their intervention goals. Questions like "what does your [caregiver] want you to improve or change by coming to see me" are crucial, as are direct discussions with the referral sources to learn the parameters of the mandates as well as opportunities to individualize plans with client-driven, self-directed goals.

Nevertheless, inviting children and adolescents to join in the process of goal formulation is a central element of the goal formulation process. Research points to the effectiveness of setting client-driven goals, even with young children (Costa et al., 2017; Vroland-Nordstrand, 2015). Of course, the nature of your conversations with children and adolescents about goals may be influenced by their social, emotional, and cognitive development. Younger children may project a limited vision of themselves into the future and thus will be focused on more short-term goals, whereas adolescents have begun to establish preferences for their futures that provide a framework for their interests in short-term goals. Younger children may be concerned about rules and fairness, whereas older adolescents may express concerns about independence and rights (Palmer, 2016). Younger children may be apt to communicate about their short-term and immediate goals using expressive modes of communication like art and puppet play, whereas older adolescents are able to engage in adult-like conversations involving both short-term and long-term aspirations.

Additionally, it may be crucial to foster children's and adolescent's critical consciousness about power. Open and empathic conversations about the various normative hierarchies that constrain their range of choices and that influence their opportunities can help deepen your goal conversations with children and adolescents and reveal avenues for increased freedom and choice. For children of color, discussions about power may also include the ways that racism and other systems of oppression influence them. Healthy adolescent development, particularly for adolescents from marginalized and oppressed groups, includes a recognition of inequality and its sources and is a precursor to resilience, sociopolitical resistance, and activism (Anyiwo et al., 2020). For the goal-formulation process, a discussion about power, conducted openly and with empathy, can help children figure out what are fair and unfair expectations of them and figure out ways that they can influence their social environments.

Along with recognition of the power of others, it is also important to manage your own power and authority relative to children and adolescents. Two dimensions are relevant here. In the first place, you are likely to have informal social standing and power as an adult. Cultural norms can inform yours and your clients' expectations for deference, decision-making, and your status. In the second place, the social work setting influences your authority. School social workers, child welfare workers, staff in inpatient health and treatment facilities, and probation officers are roles in which the social worker carries institutional authority, often with direct responsibility for incentives, rewards, and consequences for clients. Social workers in settings such as outpatient therapy, community-based and advocacy organizations, and other community-based settings usually carry relatively less institutional authority while still holding power in their adult status. In all settings, your use of authority and power should be informed by the principles of procedural justice – fairness, transparency, and voice – as well as informed by the facilitative conditions of empathy, positive regard, and authenticity. Therefore, despite the nature of the mandates and pressures imposed on children and adolescents, goal formulation with children and adolescents starts with careful attentiveness and empathy for their perspectives and preferences.

The Process of Formulating Goals

The process of goal formulation rests on the engagement and assessment skills presented throughout this text. In it, you can refer to the client concerns, challenges, and strengths that you learned about during the assessment process, and throughout, you will convey empathy and authenticity, listen reflectively, use open-ended questions along with summaries and focusing strategies to engage clients fully in the process. The outcome should be a limited set of client-driven goal statements that can organize yours and your clients' activities during the work phase of the problem-solving process. To avoid overburdening clients with tasks and responsibilities, we recommend three goals or less in most circumstances.

Table 12-2 summarizes the tasks involved in goal formulation. While they are presented in a logical, linear order, you should bear in mind that they may occur

Table 12-2 Process of Goal Formulation

1. Determine clients' readiness for goal formulation.
2. Explain the purpose and function of goals.
3. Formulate client-driven goals.
4. Increase goal specificity.
5. Determine potential barriers and benefits.
6. Rank goals according to client priorities.

iteratively in a circular fashion and not necessarily in the order presented here. The important thing to remember is that these goal-formulation tasks can help you and your clients to establish client-driven empowering goals that motivate goal attainment, while at the same time satisfying program objectives and referral mandates.

Determine Clients' Readiness for Goal Formulation

Goal formulation is an inherently optimistic, future-oriented exercise. In it, social workers invite clients to consider a specific future state in which problems are resolved, problematic behaviors have been changed, and where relationships are supportive, yet these are complex undertakings. People, whether mandated to treatment or voluntary, are usually motivated by multiple goals that are sometimes competing. For this reason, assessing client readiness is an important early task in the goal formulation process.

Several strategies are available to you when assessing client readiness to formulate goals. You might simply combine summaries with closed-ended and open-ended questions such as what follows:

Social worker: Margaret, we've talked about some of the challenges that you are experiencing now that make living in your own home difficult and unsafe, your energy-level and stamina, and about the importance of independence. Which of these areas are you ready to tackle first?

Alternatively, you might also use a scaling question, such as:

Social worker: Margaret, on a scale of 1 to 10, where one means "not at all ready" and 10 means "completely ready," how ready are you to figure out the safety issues in your living situation?

Margaret: Oh, I don't know. I want to say 10, but I'm worried that I can't do anything about them, so I think my answer is five.

Social worker: A "five," so about half and half. Let's say that you were just a little bit more ready, and you answered "seven." What would you be able to do then that you are not quite able to do now?

Case Example 2: Margaret

Margaret is an 85-year-old widow who lives alone but is involved with a community-based multiservice senior center. Her four adult children live in other states. She is involved in activities offered by the center, including senior aerobics classes. She considers herself to be generally in good health. Because Margaret lives alone, regular contact with the senior center is an important part of her daily life. During the assessment interview, she talked about feeling unsafe in her home because she lacks a sustained level of energy to complete many of the activities of daily living. For example, she tires easily when doing housework, and at times, she has had difficulty getting in and out of the bathtub. Margaret prefers to remain in her own home because she is afraid that she will lose the level of independence that she now enjoys. She had considered home health services, but after hearing the complaints of friends, some of whom were conflicted about the benefit, she too is ambivalent about this resource. In fact, some her friends have emphasized that the scheduled visits of helpers limited their freedom. She laughed as she recounted the complaint of one friend, "You have to get up and out of bed on a schedule, and there are times when you just don't want people in your house." After a lengthy discussion with the social worker, Margaret identified her primary goal as living in a safe environment, preferably in her own home. However, she is open to considering other options, such as home health care or moving to an assisted living facility. Her second goal is to maintain her independence. Maintaining independence was defined as being able to make decisions about her life, continuing to be involved with social activities, and being able to do what she can for herself.

Margaret: I'd be less afraid. I'm afraid that I won't be able to do anything about this.

Social worker: Less afraid. Am I correct to understand that you would be more confident or hopeful that we could do something to help you with the safety issues in your home?

Note the use of the follow-up question. When clients respond low on a scaling question, it can be particularly informative to ask how circumstances would be different were then answer just a little bit higher, say two points.

When you have a sense that clients may feel ambivalent about more than one competing goal, reflective listening may be particularly useful, such as these two examples:

Social worker (1): I get the feeling that a part of you wants so badly to stay in your own home, but another part of you would feel more secure if you made a change to a new home with more support and where you had less work to do around the house.

Social worker (2): I get the feeling that you are hesitant to accept support because it means less independence in your daily schedule, but you are worried that without that support you won't be able to stay in your own home. I imagine you feel stuck between a rock and a hard place.

Assessing readiness to formulate goals may be a simple matter for many clients. However, it will not be unusual for you to encounter clients who express low readiness to think about goals. In those cases, it is important for you to assess the source of your clients' reluctance. In the spirit of client-driven goal formulation, consider the possibility that you are attempting to formulate goals in the wrong area and seek topics and problems for which they are more ready to establish goals.

Explain the Purpose and Function of Goals

Many elements of the helping process are educational. *Goals* and *objectives* are often associated with professional jargon, whereas many people talk about goals using more culturally meaningful colloquial language and metaphors. Some clients may be comfortable talking about short-term and long-term goals, while others might be more comfortable talking about "what they hope to be doing next year" and "what they want to be doing next month."

Take time to educate clients about goals using language that is suited to their culture and developmental level. For the most part, a brief explanation is all that is required, including an explanation about the match of their goals with program objectives and referral mandates. As your discussion of goal formulation deepens, clients may also find it helpful to learn about the importance of specificity (e.g., SMART goals, approach versus avoidance), and about the various types of goals that might be suited to their situations (e.g., performance versus learning, empowerment versus risk-resilience). For example:

> **Social worker:** Margaret, next I'd like to clarify your goals. This is important because goals make sure that we are working toward the same outcomes, and I want to make sure that I am helping you get to the outcomes that you want. What does the word "goal" mean to you?
>
> **Margaret:** It's like the endpoint. Like, when my kids were growing up, it was most important for them to grow up to be happy and kind.
>
> **Social worker:** Excellent. That is an example of a long-term goal. Together, you and I can think about your long-term goals as well as your short-term goals.

Formulate Client-Driven Goals

The heart of goal formulation is the dialogue with clients about their specific goals. Striving toward client-driven goals, a collaborative approach involving a simple open-ended question may be all that is required at this stage, as in this example:

> **Social worker:** I understand that one of your long-term goals is to feel safe, another is to be independent, and a third is to stay active. Which should we talk about first?
>
> **Margaret:** I am already staying active with the senior center. I think that the most important goal is to be safe because that will help me figure out independence.
>
> **Social worker:** What is your goal for staying safe?
>
> **Margaret:** I'm really afraid of falling when I get out of the bathtub. I guess I don't want to fall getting out of the bathtub. That's one thing.

Alternatively, you might combine reflective listening with tentative suggestions. Bear in mind that the objective is not for clients to agree with you or adopt your suggestion but to activate their imagination and participation in the goal-formulation process, as in this example:

> **Social worker:** When we did your ADL assessment earlier … remember when I asked you questions about daily tasks like bathing, dressing, and meal preparation? … I also heard you say that you are starting to notice that it is getting harder to get dressed, especially when you need to bend over to put on socks and shoes. You can still do it now, but you seemed worried about this too. Can I suggest that we set a goal about this too?

As you formulate goals with clients, it may also be helpful to encourage them to consider different types of goals in line with the guidelines for goal formulation presented earlier. For example, when clients give avoidance goals, you can reach for positive opposites, (Kazdin, 2005) as in:

> **Margaret:** I just don't want people telling me when I need to go to bed or get up in the morning.
>
> **Social worker:** Is that similar to saying that you want a flexible daily routine that you determine?

For client who express low confidence or efficacy beliefs about achieving a new or challenging goal, consider suggesting a learning goal, as in:

> **Social worker:** Can I suggest that it may be helpful to learn about how assistive technology can help you remain independent?

For clients who express a low goal commitment, consider a focus on their long-term goals before focusing explicitly on their short-term goals:

> **Social worker:** Let's take a step back for a moment. We've been talking about independence over the long-term. What does that mean to you?

Defining Client-Driven Goals with Mandated Clients

Goal formulation with mandated clients presents a unique challenge, where the key to success is to formulate goals with reference to the principle of motivational congruence. Motivational congruence occurs when target goals simultaneously meet long-term goals that are prioritized by clients and also satisfy the requirements of their mandates (Rooney & Myrick, 2018). Each of the strategies presented – open-ended questions, goal suggestions, and formulating alternative goal types – can be useful with mandated clients to formulate goals with high motivational congruence. However, referral mandates themselves create a context for goal formulation that should be acknowledged explicitly. Include the following in your goal-formulation dialog with involuntary clients:

1. What is the mandate? Use open-ended questions to invite clients to share their view of their mandates. The probation officer in the case of Mr. Morris (see case example) might ask, "Mr. Morris, what is your understanding of the requirements the court for you during your period of probation?" Evidence suggests that accurate client understanding is critical for goal attainment, so make sure that you and your clients both share the same understanding.

2. What is the rationale for the mandate? Mandates are usually associated with desirable social or health-related outcomes. Ask, for example (using the case of Mr. Morris), "What reason did the judge have to order you to refrain from alcohol," and "what do you suppose the judge wanted you to accomplish by completing a treatment program?" In what ways does your client agree or disagree with the rationale behind the mandate? This may be a source of common ground to facilitate the goals formulation process.

3. What options do clients have to satisfy the mandate? In this discussion, be persistent in finding those areas where clients can exercise freedom and self-determination. Often, when the context of mandates requires a compliance-conformity goal, clients are nevertheless free to supplement that goal with an empowerment goal, such as "To learn about treatment options for family counseling and addictions in addition to those recommended by the court."

Following mandate clarification, the formation of client-driven goals with mandated clients generally follows one of three strategies: agreeable mandate, "let's make a deal," and "getting rid of the mandate."

The **agreeable mandate** strategy entails a search for common ground that bridges the differing views of the involuntary client and the court (De Jong & Berg, 2001; Rooney & Myrick, 2018). Pursuing the agreeable mandate may also involve reframing the definition of the problem in such a way that it adequately addresses the concerns identified in the mandate or referral source while simultaneously responding to the concerns of the client. For Mr. Morris, an agreeable mandate might be situated within his long-term goal of "not wanting to hurt no body" (see case example). Within this long-term goal, he may be willing to adopt goals like "to maintain sobriety," "to learn new skills for anger management," or "to develop nonviolent conflict resolution strategies," which under his circumstances might be completed through a referral to a local program for batterers. Reframing is a useful technique for reducing reactance, facilitating a workable agreement, and increasing the client's motivation. The result of an agreeable mandate strategy is often risk-resilience goals that simultaneously satisfy the referral mandate and facilitate attainment of clients' long-term goals.

Negotiating goals with involuntary clients can include a bargaining strategy, or **"let's make a deal."** Essentially, clients and social workers agree to combine mandated goals with nonmandated goals in a reciprocal exchange. For example, a client may agree to work toward the mandated goal of completing a domestic violence program if the social worker also agrees to identify program options that Mr. Morris can select from. The "let's make a deal" strategy, while less reliant on motivational congruence, can result in a balanced package of compliance-conformity goals and empowerment goals.

Case Example 3: Mr. Morris

Mr. Morris is a 37-year-old man who was convicted of a second offense of fifth-degree domestic assault and ordered to two and a half years of probation. His conditions included that he pays court fees, avoid alcohol, and participate in a program for batterers in lieu of 90 days in jail. Three years prior, he was convicted of the same offense. At that time, he completed a period of probation but chose to serve 30 days in jail rather than finish a psychosocial batterers' program.

The assessment revealed that Mr. Morris and his wife argue frequently, and Mr. Morris was intoxicated during events leading to both of his convictions. On meeting with him, his probation officer learned that alcohol abuse was prevalent in Mr. Morris' family, and his father died of complications due to alcohol abuse several years prior. Mr. Morris believes that alcohol probably made it more likely that he would become violent toward his wife when they were arguing and fighting, which occurs on a weekly basis. He is uncertain about whether his wife will stay with him, but he does not want his children to be afraid of him. He is also concerned about his ability to run his farm and make a living. Among his goals, he stated that "I don't want to hurt nobody" and "I'm willing to listen to good advice."

He discontinued treatment three years ago because he disagreed with the treatment program. He stated "I had to stand up and say I was a man who batters in front of all these folks I didn't know. I don't know what I am! I had to be what they wanted me to be, so I left and did my 30 days." After assurances by the probation officer of alternative programs and a willingness to work with Mr. Morris on finding the right fit, Mr. Morris expressed a willingness to try a treatment program again.

With some involuntary clients, neither the agreeable mandate nor the "let's make a deal" strategies may be acceptable. In these instances, the "getting rid of the mandate" strategy may be the best approach. This strategy entails one of two directions, both intent on exercising influence over the referral authority. In the first, the client simply agrees to comply with the mandate in a bid to be free of the referring authority. For example, "Mr. Morris will complete a program for domestic violence that is recommended by his probation officer." The second direction follows from the anti-oppressive approach, to influence the referring authority directly to change or modify the mandate, whether that be to increase flexibility inherent in the mandate (e.g., "Mr. Morris will research treatment programs and recommend an acceptable program to the probation officer"), change the nature of the mandate (e.g., seeking court approval for an alternative goal, like "Mr. Morris will complete 200 hours of community service with a community-based antiviolence program"), or request that the mandate be dropped entirely (e.g., "Mr. Morris will petition the court to drop the mandate for treatment").

Increase Goal Specificity

For both voluntary and involuntary clients, the next step is to clarify goal language where necessary and reach for specificity using SMART principles. Goals are often described with imprecise, ambiguous language that relies on metaphor rather than behavioral description. While highly specific goals facilitate the intervention planning process by pointing to strategies and tasks to promote goal attainment, ambiguous goals are akin to telling people to "do their best" to achieve goals that have unclear targets. Unclear goals do little to motivate goal attainment under most circumstances (Lock & Latham, 2006).

Goal specificity is usually conceptualized in one or more of four dimensions: behavioral description, time, person, place. Often, goal specificity can be enhanced by simply asking clients to provide elaborated behavioral descriptions of metaphors and ambiguous words or phrases, such as

Social worker: Mr. Morris, I know that you don't want to hurt anybody. When you say "hurt," can you clarify what you mean?

Mr. Morris: Physically. I don't want to injure people.

Social worker: Often domestic assault can also include insults and emotional injuries. Do you mean those types of hurts as well?

Mr. Morris: I suppose so.

Social worker: What is the opposite of hurting people, do you suppose?

Mr. Morris: To resolve conflicts with words rather than with fists.

You may also ask directed open-ended questions that focus on time, as in:

Social worker: What times of the day do you need to be especially careful to resolve conflicts with words rather than with fists?

Mr. Morris: Well, like I told you, most of our fights happen in the evening.

You may seek greater specificity by asking about the dimensions of person or place related to their goals. For example:

Social worker: When you said that you want to resolve conflicts with words rather than with fists, who are we talking about?

Mr. Morris: My wife, mostly.

Social worker: Thanks Mr. Morris, this is very helpful. I hear us saying that one of your goals for your time on probation is to resolve evening conflicts with your wife with words rather than with fists. You want to avoid hurting your wife physically and emotionally. Am I hearing your correctly?

Determine Potential Barriers and Benefits

Barriers and benefits for goal attainment influence motivation and goal commitment. When you engage clients in a dialogue about barriers and benefits related to attainment of their goals, you anticipate circumstances in advance that can facilitate, inhibit, and motivate, goal attainment. These circumstances can be used to further refine goals or supplement goals with additional short-term goals that facilitate goal attainment.

One way to begin this discussion is with a scaling question about goal commitment (De Jong & Berg, 2012):

Social worker: Mr. Morris, on a scale of 1 to 10, where 10 means "highly motivated," how motivated are you to achieve the goal of resolving conflicts with your wife using words rather than physical or emotional violence?

Mr. Morris: I am, but it's hard to remember when we've been drinking and when she follows me when I'm trying to walk away.

Social worker: This will be a challenging goal, and we probably need to work on one or two other areas to help you to achieve it, but what about my question?

On a scale of 1 to 10, how motivated are you to achieve this goal?

Mr. Morris: Ok, I'll say seven.

Social worker: Thank you. Seven is pretty high. Let's say your motivation was a little bit stronger, like an eight or a nine. What would be different?

Mr. Morris: If I knew that my wife wants to stay with me, then that would make me more motivated.

Another way anticipates a future in which a barrier existed to goal attainment:

Social worker: Let's imagine for a moment that we are meeting, and you have not completed your goal and, in fact, hit your wife again. What are the kinds of things that probably got in the way of achieving your goal?

Mr. Morris: Like I said, drinking. We would be drinking.

Social worker: Your court order stipulates that you refrain from using alcohol. Should we shift over to figure out what your goals are for alcohol use?

A third strategy is to discuss benefits. Benefits of goal attainment are intrinsic or extrinsic rewards that function as incentives. Ideally, clients will identify their own benefits, rewards, or incentives for goal attainment:

Social worker: I'd like to list out the benefits of meeting your goal to resolve conflicts with your wife using words rather than physical violence. Can you think of what some of these might be?

In some settings, your role includes control of incentives and rewards:

Social worker: In our county, we can petition the court for an early dismissal of probation starting after 18 months when you successfully complete your treatment program.

Finally, a fourth strategy is to explicitly link short-term goals to client long-term goals. For example:

Social worker: I'd like to talk for a few minutes about how the goals we've talked about match with your long-term goals, which you said were to "not hurt nobody" and to "run your farm and make a living." How do these short-term goals help you to achieve your long-term goals?

Rank Goals According to Client Priorities

Following the identification of and client commitment to specific goals, it can be helpful to rank those goals in order of their priority. The purpose of identifying high-priority goals is to ensure that beginning change efforts are directed toward the goals of utmost importance to clients. Depending on the nature of the goals, the client's developmental stage, the resources available to the client, and the time required, settling on no more than three goals is advisable for most clients. In cases with multiple mandated goals, you can help the client to prioritize so that they are more manageable, emphasizing those that have a greater consequence. Participating in a drug treatment program, for example, may have priority. When working with larger systems, you might create a list of goals for both the clients and the systems involved and rank them for the client and the system. Where there are differences, your role is to assist all parties to negotiate and rank the priority of goals.

Case Example 4: Corning Family

Angela and Irwin Corning and their three children, Agnes (age 10), Henri (age 8), and Katrina (18 months), are homeless. Currently, they are residing in a transitional housing facility. Irwin lost his job eight months ago when the county agency that he worked for as a maintenance and cleaning specialist awarded the cleaning contract to a private contractor. Angela is employed in the evenings as a maid at a hotel. Prior to becoming homeless, the family had a comfortable living, owned their home, and were pleased with the neighborhood's diversity and their children's school. When Irwin became unemployed, the couple was unable to pay their bills or maintain their mortgage payments. For a time, they lived with Angela's sister's family. Angela and Irwin are concerned about the impact of their stressful situation on the two older children. To make matters worse, the school reports that Agnes and Henri are having difficulty at school. Both parents feel that the school situation will change once the family is stable. The social worker at the transitional housing facility referred them to a family service agency for help in finding housing and employment for Irwin. Their preference is to purchase another home, but they realize that at this point they need to move into an apartment until their financial situation has improved.

As a lead-in to the ranking process, when the client is voluntary, the following is an example of a summarizing message:

Social worker: So far, we have talked about several concerns and goals. Among the goals that you identified were moving from transitional housing and finding a full-time permanent job for Irwin. You also mentioned that you want your children to have a quiet place to study in the current housing situation. Now that you've settled on these goals, which one is the most important for you at this time? We'll get to all of the goals in time, but we want to start with the one that is most important.

With involuntary clients, you might use a message like this:

Social worker: While we have reached an agreement about which goals are most important to you, we also need to give priority to the goal established by the court. As you have said, you want the court out of your life. Your court order states that you need to enroll in a parenting class immediately, so this must be a priority. You also said that you feel alone and tired out by the demands of caring for four children and want to have time for yourself. You also mentioned wanting to return to school. Are you able to say which of these goals, in addition to the one required by the court, you would like to work on first?

It is up to you to help clients focus their effort by sorting out what is a priority for them so that they do not feel overwhelmed and become frustrated. When goals involve families or groups, different members may naturally accord different priorities to goals. In such cases, it is important that you take the lead in helping those involved to prioritize the goals.

Monitoring Progress and Evaluation

Monitoring and evaluating progress in goal attainment are essential components of the helping process. This section provides an overview of both quantitative and qualitative methods that may be used. For both methods, the following components are considered fundamental to this process:

- Identifying the specific problem or behavior to be changed
- Specifying measurable and feasible goals
- Matching goal and measurement procedures

- Maintaining a systematic record of relevant information
- Evaluating intermediate and final outcomes

Quantitative Measurements

Quantitative evaluation embodies the use of procedures that measure the frequency and/or severity of target problems. Measurements taken before implementing change-oriented interventions are termed **baseline measures** because they provide a baseline against which measures of progress can be compared. These comparisons provide quantitative data that make it possible to evaluate the efficacy of work with clients. The **single-subject design** is one example that can be used in a variety of settings, including mental health, family, and private practice. The method can be adapted so that you can integrate evaluation as a key element in your practice. In most cases, the simple Single Subject ABA can be used. Using this design is perhaps the most practical way in which you can track and evaluate progress over time.

Measuring Observable Behaviors

Observable behaviors often lend themselves to frequency counts. For example, Bettina's goal to save enough money to move into an apartment (goal statement #12), and a client's goal to take medication morning and evenings as prescribed by their psychiatrist (goal statement #21) can both be measured by counting things. By measuring pre-intervention rates of saving and medication adherence, social workers in these cases could help clients track changes over time. Frequency counts for these performance goals tracked over time can help clients see incremental changes as well as final outcomes.

Measurements obtained through self-monitoring often produces therapeutic effects of their own accord. For example, monitoring the rate of a desired behavior (i.e., raising one's hand before speaking) may act to increase the frequency of that behavior. Similarly, measuring the rate of negative behavior may influence a client to reduce its frequency.

The effects of self-monitoring on the target behavior are termed **reactive effects**. When viewed by a researcher, reactive effects represent a source of contamination that confounds the effects of the interventions being tested. From your viewpoint, however, self-monitoring may be employed as an intervention precisely because reactive effects tend to increase or decrease certain target behaviors. Although desired changes that result from self-monitoring may be either positive or negative, emphasizing positive behaviors is preferable because doing so focuses on strengths related to goals. It is advisable to use multiple measures or observations, of which self-monitoring is one source. In addition to a student's record of raising hands in class before speaking, for example, the classroom teacher along with a silent observer would be additional sources of information.

When baseline measures focus on observable behaviors, repeated frequency counts across specified time intervals are typically used. The time intervals selected should be those during which the highest incidence of behavioral excesses occur or the times in which desired positive behaviors are demonstrated. Focusing on the latter is preferable as it highlights a positive gain. It is also important to obtain measures under relatively consistent conditions. Otherwise, the measure may not be an accurate representation of the actual behavior you are attempting to measure (Bloom et al., 2009).

Retrospective Estimates of Baseline Behaviors

Baseline measurements are obtained before change-oriented interventions are implemented, either by having clients make retrospective estimates of the incidence of behaviors targeted for change or by obtaining data prospectively during the assessment process. Examples include paying rent on time, preparing nutritious meals, or being on time for school. Although it is less accurate, the former method often is preferable because change-oriented efforts need not be deferred pending the gathering of baseline data. This is a key advantage because acute problems or a crisis may demand immediate attention, and delaying the intervention for even one week may not be advisable. However, delaying interventions for one week while gathering baseline data in general does not create undue difficulty, and the resulting data are likely to be far more reliable than clients' estimates.

When determining the baseline of target behavior by retrospective estimates, it is common practice to ask the client to estimate the incidence of the behavior across a specified time interval, which may range from a few minutes to one day depending on the usual frequency of the target behaviors. Time intervals selected for frequent behaviors, such as nervous mannerisms (tapping a pencil on a desk), should be relatively short (e.g., 15-minute intervals). For relatively infrequent behaviors, such as speaking up in social situations, intervals may involve several hours or days.

Self-Anchored Scales

When goals involve subjective feelings or less observable outcomes, it is sometimes helpful to construct self-anchoring scales that denote various levels of an internal state. Self-anchoring scales might be useful for the depressed clients who seek an improved mood (goal statement #26) or restored connections with family and friends (goal statement #27). To anchor such scales, ask a client to imagine experiencing the extreme degrees of the given internal state and describe what they experience. You can then use these descriptions to define at least the extremes and the midpoint of the scale. Developing scales in this manner quantifies internal states in a unique manner for each client. In constructing self-anchoring scales, it is important to avoid mixing different types of internal states: Even though emotions such as "happy" and "sad" appear to belong on the same continuum, they are qualitatively different, and mixing them will result in confusion. Figure 12-1 depicts a seven-point anchored scale.

Clients can use self-anchoring scales to record the extent of troubling internal states across specified time intervals (e.g., three times daily for seven days) in much the same way that they take frequency counts of overt behaviors. In both instances, clients keep tallies of the target behaviors. A minimum of 10 separate measures is generally necessary to discern patterns among data, but urgent needs for intervention sometimes require that you settle for fewer readings. For example, the client, Mrs. Johnson, would complete the scale to record the varying levels and circumstances in which she was feeling blue and when she did not experience these feelings. The self-anchored scale and the incremental numeric changes can be augmented by the descriptive information based on Mrs. Johnson's narrative. For example, in reviewing her range of feeling blue from most to least, the discussion would focus on the events or situations that appeared to have triggered her feelings, plus or minus in each range.

Guidelines for Obtaining Baseline Measures

When you are obtaining baseline measures, it is vital to maximize the reliability and validity of your measurements (Berlin & Marsh, 1993; Bloom et al., 2009).

Figure 12-1 Example of a Self-anchored Scale

1	2	3	4	5	6	7
Least anxious (calm, relaxed, serene)		Moderately anxious (tense, uptight, but still functioning with effort)			Most anxious (muscles taut, cannot concentrate or sit still, could "climb the wall")	

Otherwise, your baseline measures and subsequent comparisons with those measures may be flawed and can lead to inappropriate conclusions. Adhering to the following guidelines can assist you in maximizing the reliability and validity of the data collected:

1. *Define the target of measurement in clear and operational terms.* Reliability is enhanced when the behavior (overt or covert) targeted for change is specifically defined using SMART criteria previously discussed. For example, measurements of compliments given to a partner are more reliable than general measurements of positive communications because the client must make fewer inferences when measuring the former than when counting instances of the latter.

2. *Be sure your measures relate directly and specifically to the goals targeted for change.* Otherwise, the validity of your measurements, both at the baseline and at subsequent points, may be highly suspect. For example, when a client's goal is increasing social skills, indicators of social skills should be used as measurement targets. Likewise, if a parent is to attend parenting classes to learn parenting skills, measures should be devised that specify observable behavioral changes. Similarly, measures of violent behavior and alcohol abuse should correspond to the frequency of angry outbursts (or control of anger in provocative situations) and consumption of alcohol (or periods of abstinence), respectively.

3. *Use multiple measures and instruments when necessary.* Clients typically present with more than one problem, and individual problems may involve several dimensions. For example, flat affect, fatigue, irritability, and anxiety are all frequent indicators of depression. Clients may also present with goals related to increasing self-confidence or improving their social skills, which would require the use of multiple measures and instruments to track.

4. *Measures should be obtained under relatively consistent conditions.* Otherwise, changes may reflect differences in conditions or environmental stimuli rather than variations in goal-related behaviors. For example, if a child's difficulty is that they do not talk while they are at preschool, measuring changes in this behavior while the child is at home, in church, or in other settings may be informative, but it is not as helpful as the indications of change at preschool, where the behavior primarily occurs.

5. *Baseline measures are not relevant when clients present with discrete goals.* Evaluating the efficacy of helping efforts in such instances is clear-cut because either a client has accomplished a goal or not. For example, when

with a goal of getting a job, the job seeker is either successful or not successful. By contrast, progress toward ongoing goals is incremental and not subject to fixed limits, as in the case of completing a job application. Employing baseline measures and periodic measures, therefore, effectively enables both you and the client to monitor incremental changes. Consider the following baseline measure for an ongoing goal: "Justin will sit in his seat during English class." If Justin's baseline has indicated that he is out of his seat (off task) 25 times per week, then improvement to 15 times per week would be significant.

Monitoring Progress

After obtaining baseline measures of targets of change, the next step is to transfer the data to a graph on which the horizontal axis denotes time intervals (days or weeks), and the vertical axis denotes the level of the measure being tracked. Simple to construct, such a graph makes it possible to observe the progress of clients and the efficacy of interventions. Figure 12-2 depicts the incidence of anxiety before and during the implementation of change using such a graph.

In Figure 12-2, note that the baseline period was seven days, and the time interval selected for self-monitoring was one day. Interventions to reduce anxiety were implemented over a period of four weeks. As illustrated in the graph, the client experienced some ups and downs (as usually occurs), but marked progress could nevertheless be observed.

In monitoring progress by taking repeated measures, it is critical to use the same procedures and instruments used in obtaining the baseline measures. Otherwise, meaningful comparisons cannot be made. It is also important to adhere to the guidelines for measurement listed in the preceding section. Repeated measurement of the same behavior at equal intervals enables practitioners not only to assess progress but also to determine variability in clients' behavior and to assess the effects of changes in the clients' life situation. For example, by charting measures of depression and increased social skills from week to week, it becomes possible to discern either positive or negative changes that correspond to concurrent stressful or positive life events. In this way, graphs of measured changes enable clients both to view evidence of their progress and to gain awareness of how particular life or environmental events contribute to their emotional states or behaviors.

Monitoring progress has several other advantages. Measures establish indicators, and monitoring tells both the client and you when goals have been accomplished, when the court mandate has been satisfied, and when the relationship can be terminated. For example, when

Figure 12-2 Example of a Graph Recording the Extent of Anxiety during Baseline and Intervention Periods

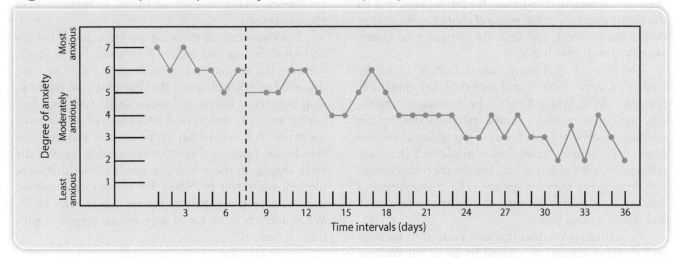

observable behaviors related to parenting skills—such as preparing three to four nutritious meals per week selecting from the five major food groups—have improved to the degree that they conform to explicit indicators, termination is justified. Similarly, termination is indicated when measurements of depression have changed to the range of nonclinical depression. Results of monitoring can also substantiate progress, justify continued coverage by third-party payers, and be used in reports to the court in the case of mandated clients. For clients, monitoring provides evidence of change, assuring them that they are not destined to remain forever involved with the social worker or agency. A final and critical advantage of monitoring is that if interventions are not achieving measurable results after a reasonable period, you can explore the reasons for this lack of progress and negotiate a different goal plan or intervention.

Receptivity of Clients to Measurement

You may feel hesitant to ask clients to engage in self-monitoring or to complete self-report instruments because of your concern that they may resist or react in a negative manner. To the contrary, research studies by Applegate (1992) and Campbell (1988, 1990) indicate that such concerns are not justified. These researchers found that clients generally were receptive to formal evaluation procedures. In fact, Campbell found that clients preferred being involved in the evaluation of their progress. In addition, clients preferred "the use of some type of systematic data collection over the reliance on social worker's opinion as the sole mean of evaluating practice effectiveness" (Campbell, 1988, p. 22). Finally, practitioners were able to accurately assess clients'

feelings about different types of evaluation procedures (Campbell, 1990).

Qualitative Measurements

Qualitative measure methods are viable options for monitoring progress and evaluating outcomes. Qualitative methods differ from quantitative methods in their philosophical, theoretical, and stylistic orientation (Jordan & Franklin, 2003; Shamai, 2003). The various types of qualitative measures are consistent with narrative and social constructivism approaches. Qualitative evaluation measures have advantages for monitoring progress, depending on the information that you are seeking. They can provide a more complete picture of the contextual conditions and dimensions in which change occurred (Holbrook, 1995; Shamai, 2003). Qualitative methods may be especially useful with minors in that they focus on subjective experiences and personal stories (Andrews & Ben-Arieh, 1999; Morgan, 2000).

In qualitative measures, the process of data collection is more open ended and allows clients to express their reality and experience, frame of reference, or cultural realities. For example, the findings of a study that examined the use of hospice care by African Americans revealed a difference in values that were barriers to hospice utilization (Reese et al., 1999). In essence, the client is the key informant or expert (Jordan & Franklin, 2003). Gilgun (1994) asserts that because qualitative measures focus on client perception, they are good fit with the social work value of self-determination.

In evaluating progress or outcomes using qualitative methods, descriptive information change can be expressed in graphs, pictures, diagrams, or narratives. For example, in the structural approach to family therapy, symbols are used to create a visual map of family relationships and interaction patterns. Narratives provided by the family members at the points of change, even change that is incremental, highlight the dynamics or events associated with the change.

The aim of qualitative information is to ensure credibility, dependability, and confirmability (Jordan & Franklin, 2003; Weiss, 1998). Like quantitative methods, qualitative measures require systematic observation and may involve multiple points of triangulated observations. For example, triangulation would include client self-reports, your observations, and descriptive information from other relevant systems. The triangulation of data replication establishes the credibility of information and guards against bias.

A qualitative method that may be used to measure and monitor change is referred to as an informative event or critical incidence. The method has some similarity to the logical analysis effects (Davis & Reid, 1988) in that both informative events and critical incidence established a linkage between context, intervention, and change.

Informative Events or Critical Incidences

An informative event, also referred to as a critical incidence, is a qualitative method that seeks to determine whether intended or unintended gains can be attributed to a particular event or action. These events or actions are also referred to as therapeutic effects, turning points, or logical analysis effects in that they are a significant link to goal attainment, thereby changing the status of the target problem (Davis & Reid, 1988; Shamai, 2003).

An advantage of informative event or critical incidence reports is that individuals can put their feelings and thoughts into words. For example, a group of mothers acknowledged that a session in which they reflected upon and discussed their grief and sadness about the removal of their children from their homes marked a change (critical incident) in their ability to move toward reunification with their child or children. Previously, many of the mothers had stored-up feelings of anxiety, fear, and even ambivalence about reuniting with their children. For many of the mothers, the discussion was a therapeutic and critical turning point because they were able to voice and subsequently release their feelings, helping them focus on the return of their children to their care. Morgan (2000, p. 91) suggests that significant turning points should be celebrated. For example, a certificate highlights such a turning point by naming the problem and the alternative story that emerged. For example, certificates for the mothers in the previous group would mark their movement from self-doubt to confidence and from guilt or shame to freedom from these feelings.

Tracking and monitoring progress need not be an ordeal, as you can use existing tools. For example, consider the ecomap, an assessment tool that we have discussed in other chapters that examines the relationship between a family and other social systems, identifying areas of tension or conflict as well as potential resources. For evaluation purposes, the ecomap may also be used pre- and postintervention to graphically track change in the tension or conflict lines that were identified as target problems. For illustration, examine the ecomaps presented in Figures 12-3a and 12-3b. What differences in social support are suggested with these ecomaps?

Combining Methods for Measuring and Evaluating

There are times when the depth of information you need is best obtained by combining qualitative and quantitative methods (Padgett, 2004; Weiss, 1998). For example, tracking the outcomes of a specific goal, such as learning new parenting skills, can be measured by using a quantitative pre/post design. In combining this method with qualitative indicators, you would be interested in determining at what point the new skill level occurred. For example, when did the parents' interactions with their children improve (turning point)? Likewise, frequency counts, such as the number of times that a student raised their hand before speaking in class, provide you with quantitative observations. You might also want to know whether the behavioral change was attributed to positive responses from the teacher related to the student's behavior, which provides you with qualitative information.

Obviously, each method can provide you with different information. Quantitative measures provide statistical data, and qualitative methods enrich the data with descriptive information. With young minors, monitoring and measuring progress can be facilitated by using pictures, stories, and conversation-related feelings (Morgan, 2000). These methods can easily be combined with quantitative methods such as pre/post designs, rating or behavioral scales, graphs, or grids.

Your practice setting may have methods for monitoring progress and measuring outcomes—for example, goal attainment scales. In some organizations such as schools and residential facilities, standardized behavioral contracts stipulate how progress is evaluated. Standardized tools or protocols, however, may place members of socioeconomic, cultural, and sexual minority groups at greater risk of appearing more "deviant or troubled" (Kagle, 1994, p. 96). The extent to

Figure 12-3a Preintervention Ecomap

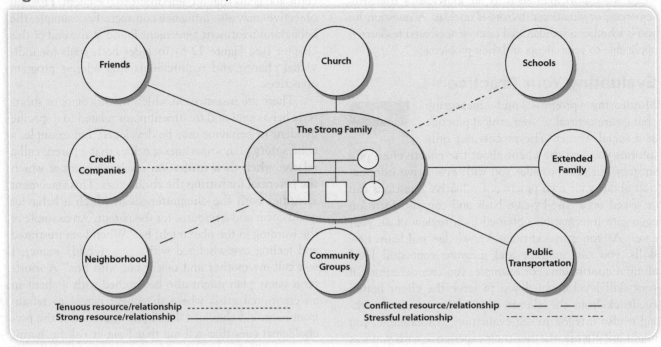

Figure 12-3b Postintervention Ecomap

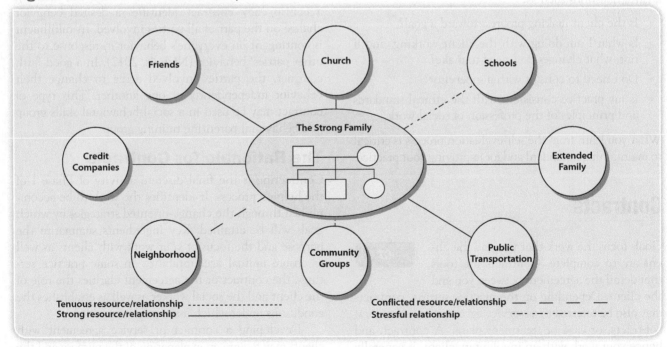

which standardize measures recognize and make use of the social work principles such as an individual's strengths, resources, or situational factors is unclear. A question for you is whether a standardized or evidence-based resource is applicable to your clients and their problems.

Evaluating Your Practice

Monitoring progress and measuring change are central to your ethical practice as a social worker. The process not only informs you and the client about the effectiveness of a strategy but also provides you with evaluative information about your own practice. Evaluative questions can be asked on a case-by-case basis and can also focus on aggregate information obtained by a review of all your cases. As you gain additional knowledge and learn new skills, you can monitor and measure your skill level along a continuum. For example, you can determine if your skill level enabled you to serve the client better. Feedback from the clients with whom you are working is also integral to self-evaluation. For example, you might ask clients whether their experience with you was culturally sensitive, what could be improved, and what elements proved to be the most helpful.

Evaluating your practice need not be intimidating. Many of the quantitative and qualitative methods can be used to provide you with evaluative information. Regardless of the method chosen, you should be able to answer questions such as:

- Is the client making progress toward a goal?
- Is what I am doing with the client working, and if not, what changes do I need to make?
- Do I need to consult with a supervisor?
- Is my practice consistent with the ethical standards and principles of the profession of social work?

What you learn from the self-evaluation process is critical to maintaining a standard and for improving your practice.

Contracts

Goals focus the work that you and the client are to complete. Contracts are tools that detail the agreement between you and the client. Depending on the practice setting, contracts may also be referred to as service agreements, behavioral contracts, or case or treatment plans. A contract, and hence your work with an involuntary client, is generally influenced by a court order or referral source. Contracts should not be confused with legal mandates. The legal mandate details the concern on which the contract is based and the expected outcome. It can also include concerns and goals that are important to the client. Program objectives may also influence contracts. For example, the behavioral treatment agreement found at the end of this chapter (see Figure 12-8) includes both goals for individual change and requirements that address program objectives.

There are instances in which intermediate or short-term behavioral and treatment plans related to a specific incident or behavior may be developed. For example, a child safety plan sometimes specifies that a parent call a relative when their frustration reaches a point at which the potential for hitting the child exists. This agreement identifies both the circumstances in which a behavior could occur and a resource for the parent. An example of the wording in the plan might be: "When I am frustrated and feeling overwhelmed with _____ (child's name), I will call my mother and talk it out with her." A short-term safety plan might also be reached with a client in an emotional crisis where the client agrees to refrain from harmful behavior ("I will pay attention to the psychological cues that tell me that I am at risk for harming myself"). Further, the agreement could include the condition that the client makes an appointment with a professional. The safety plan is signed by the social worker and the client.

Other types of short-term agreements include the contingency (quid pro quo) contract and good-faith contract. Used in cognitive behavioral family therapy, a contingency contract identifies a desired behavior change on the part of all parties involved. Its fulfillment is contingent on everyone's behavior in response to the other parties' behavior (Nichols, 2012). In a good-faith contract, the parties involved agree to change their behavior independently of one another. This type of contract may be used in a social-behavioral skills group or a behavioral parenting training group.

The Rationale for Contracts

Contracting is the final discrete activity of Phase I of the helping process. It identifies the work to be accomplished through the change-oriented strategies by which goals will be attained. Key ingredients summarize the purpose and the focus of your work with clients as well as ensure mutual accountability. In some practice settings, the contract or the agreement clarifies the role of the client and the social worker as well as establishes the conditions under which assistance is provided.

Developing a contract or service agreement with clients may require an explanation of the purpose and the rationale for the contract. Explanations may be particularly important for clients who are hesitant to sign a document without fully understanding its purpose. Involuntary clients may be suspicious or distrustful, perceiving the contract as further infringing on their freedom or that they are committing to a change with which they disagree. For minors, the concept of a contract may be a totally alien one regardless of their age and developmental stage. For this reason, you might frame the explanation as an agreement that describes expectations. In settings in which a minor's choice of whether to work with you is limited, specifying the required change and your role in supporting the minor to achieve goals, as well as clarifying rewards and benefits, can be especially important.

Formal and Informal Contracts

Contracts or service agreements can be developed with varying degrees of formality. Public agencies often require written service agreements in the form of case plans or behavioral contracts signed by clients. **Written contracts** provide space for entering the concerns or problems of a client situation and listing the expected intervention outcomes. Safety plans are almost always written, and they are a ready resource for clients in a crisis. Under some circumstances, signed contracts by you and your clients carry the same weight as a legal document. Some private agencies prefer **service agreements** to contracts, believing that contracts are more formal and administrative in nature.

Students often ask whether written or oral contracts are preferable. For some social workers, the rationale for using a written contract is that it provides a tangible reference to the commitments between themselves and their clients. In this way, the potential for a misunderstanding is minimized. In addition, the written contract assures accountability of services to supervisor and funders. Other social workers prefer **oral contracts** that include the same provisions but lack the formality, sterility, and finality of a written contract. If contracts or agreements are oral, questions may arise later regarding informed consent. A third option is to utilize a partially oral and partially written contract. The latter includes the basics—for example, the target concern or problem, goal, role expectations, time limits, and provisions for revision. With minors, either oral or written contracts, or some combination of the two, may be appropriate.

Whether the contract is oral or written, at a minimum, clients should have a clear understanding of what is to be accomplished because of your work together. Contracts that are specific and clearly articulated ensure that clients are informed; otherwise, clients may believe they are justified in filing suit for malpractice if they do not achieve their goals (Houston-Vega et al., 1997; Reamer, 1998).

Contracts or agreements with either a written or oral description, as well as any changes, are documented in the case record. This documentation is consistent with the requirements of record keeping and informed consent (Reamer, 1998; Strom-Gottfried, 2007).

Developing Contracts

Generally, contracts should include certain elements, which are outlined in the Agreement for Service found at the end of this chapter (see Figure 12-5). In making use of this resource, you can adjust the various elements to fit the needs of your practice setting and the particulars of your work with clients. Keep in mind, however, that certain elements are essential. The following is a brief discussion of each element.

Goals to Be Accomplished

First and foremost, the goals to be accomplished in relation to the target concern are ranked by priority, as goals provide the focus for working over the course of ongoing sessions. At the same time, goals are fluid. They can be expanded or modified as situations change and new information that has a bearing on the initial goals emerges. Of course, there must be a valid reason for changing goals. Although the continuous shifting of target concerns and goals during the contracting process would be unusual, a client may signal that they are not ready to proceed. At this point, you would return to the process of identifying goals.

Roles of Participants

In Chapter 5, the process of role clarification was discussed. These roles may need to be revisited during the contracting process. Role clarification may be especially pertinent with involuntary clients who have a mandated case or treatment plan, in which case your role and that of the client are specified in writing. Whether the client is voluntary or involuntary, the identification of roles affirms the mutual accountability and commitment of all parties, including that of the agency involved.

Socialization about the purpose of contract roles may be required and be especially important with certain clients. For example, involuntary clients may feel particularly vulnerable, and a contract may increase their feelings of being pressured or controlled. Potocky-Tripodi (2002) points out that some immigrants or refugees may experience fear and apprehension about contracts, depending on their past experiences. Because of the client's past experiences, the contract may be "perceived as an instrument of authoritarian coercion" (p. 167).

Minors may also feel vulnerable. With this group, the socialization process may require you to review what is expected of them and how you can assist them. For example, "I have written down that I will help you return to the classroom" or "Your role is to attend group sessions and to learn different ways of behaving in the classroom."

In all instances, taking the time to explain the function and the purpose of contracts and the client's role facilitates an individual's remaining active in the helping process.

Interventions or Techniques to Be Employed

This aspect of the contract involves specifying the interventions and the techniques that will be implemented to accomplish the stated goals. During initial contracting, it is often possible to identify interventions only on a somewhat global level. For example, group or family sessions may involve a combination of strategies. In some instances, depending on the identified goals, you and the client can discuss intervention strategies with greater specificity—for example, decreasing the occurrence of irrational thoughts, beliefs, and fears (cognitive restructuring) and developing skills (e.g., using tasks or solution to accomplish goals). In cases where you are the case manager, you would also indicate the various coordinated services to be involved in the case (e.g., home-delivered meals, home health services). Implementing an intervention strategy requires a discussion with the client in which you provide an overview of the intervention and your rationale to elicit clients' reactions and gain their consent.

Time Frame, Frequency, and Length of Sessions

Specifying the time frame, frequency, and length of sessions is an integral part of the contract. Most people tend to intensify their efforts to accomplish a given goal or task when a deadline exists. Consider the last-minute cramming students do before an examination. A time frame stated in the contract counters the human tendency to procrastinate.

Yet another argument that supports the development of a definite time frame is that most of the gains are achieved occur early in the change process. In working with families, Nichols (2012) notes that treatment has historically been established as brief and within a limited time period based on the rationale that change occurs quickly, if it occurs at all. Whatever the intended length, most contact with clients turns out to be relatively brief, the median duration being between five and six sessions (Corwin, 2002; Reid & Shyne, 1969).

Overall, clients respond favorably to services that are offered when they need them the most and when they experience relief from their problems. This is not to say that clients will not seek help for concrete or daily living concerns that they may have. Clients may value time-limited contracts because they make a distinction between talking and actual change, and within this particular time frame, the focus is on a specific concern.

Questions have been raised about the brevity of time limits. Are time-limited contracts, for example, effective across all cultures? Some theorists believe that time limits are inconsistent with perspectives of time held by some cultural groups (Chazin et al., 2000; Devore & Schlesinger, 1999). Other theorists cite outcome studies that emphasize time-limited contracts as preferable with racial and ethnic minority clients because they focus on immediate, concrete concerns. Devore and Schlesinger (1999), Ramos and Garvin (2003), and James (2008) note that in stressful situations, persons of color respond best to a present- and action-oriented approach. Corwin (2002) points out the advantages of time-limited, brief treatment by noting that these approaches are "congruent with how many minority clients understand and utilize mental health and social services" (p. 10). Of course, it would be presumptuous to assert hard-and-fast rules about a relationship between time limits and cultural identity. As highlighted in the previous discussion, brief contact with a specific focus appears to be a preference with most clients, irrespective of their status or background.

A second question relates to whether time limits are appropriate to all client populations and situations. Certainly, time-limited contracts may be inappropriate in some instances. For example, as an outpatient mental health case manager, your responsibility can be ongoing and time limits impractical. Nonetheless, you may find that time-limited contracts can be used with circumscribed problems of living or concrete needs defined as goals. In these instances, time-limited contracts can be effective when they are divided into multiple short-term contracts related to specific problems or episodes. A brief contract may, for example, involve a safety agreement, finding housing, or taking medication.

Decisions about specified time frames may be imposed on the work to be completed between you and clients. Managed care demands, specifically the brevity of the period in which outcomes are expected to be achieved, have dramatically influenced practice in both the private and the public sectors of social welfare services. In addition, agency resources, purchase of service (POS) contracts, funders, public policy, or the courts may stipulate a time frame and the duration of contact. In child welfare, for example, under the 1997 Adoption and Safe Family Act, parents are required to meet their case plan goals within a definitive period. Time pressures result in tensions for many parents. For some, this pressure is a decisive factor in the eventual reunion with their children. Prior to COVID-19 outbreak, there were long wait lists for services, limiting parents' ability to comply within the required time frame. In the age of COVID-19 pandemic, this is an even more precarious situation that could cause harm to those families who are unable to access services not available during the pandemic. Nonetheless, these time limits would be included in the contract. Within the contract, you can help clients with the ticking of the clock by helping them focus their efforts on responding to the most pressing concerns.

The helping process, as presented in this text, relies on the time frame being brief. The time period used is one that is commonly associated with the task-centered social work model, where specific target concerns and goals are identified. The action-oriented emphasis in the social work model and other brief treatment models can foster a conductive mindset that can facilitate change. The expectation of a change in the target concern within a specific time can have a positive influence on self-direction and motivation.

Research done in various settings and with various groups, including minors, supports the efficacy of 6 to 12 sessions conducted over a time span of two to four months. The flexibility inherent in this time frame, however, means that you can negotiate with the client regarding the specific number of sessions to be undertaken (Nichols, 2012).

Means of Monitoring Progress

Early discussions between you and the client have focused on the specific methods for monitoring and measuring progress. At this stage of the contracting process, a brief review may be all that is needed. For example, when baseline measures on target problems have been obtained, you would explain that the same measuring device would be used at specified intervals to note change. Clients can also be asked to rate their progress on a scale of 1 to 10, where one represents no progress, and 10 represents the highest level. Comparing ratings from one session to the next and over time provides a rough estimate of progress.

The frequency of monitoring may be negotiated with the client. Whichever method of monitoring is chosen, devoting some time at least every other session to review progress is advisable. Of course, you can be flexible, but no more than three sessions should pass between discussions of progress.

Stipulations for Renegotiating the Contract

Contracting within a brief time frame assumes that when goals are met, a change or significant reduction in the target problem occurs. Contracting continues during the entire helping process. Renegotiating a contract with clients can occur when their circumstances change, or new facts emerge, and the process evolves. For this reason, it is important to clarify for clients that conditions in the contract are subject to renegotiation at any time. Above all, the contract should be continually reviewed and updated to ensure its relevance and fit. When contracting with involuntary clients, any circumstances that would cause a unilateral change in the contract (e.g., evidence of new legal violations) should be specified.

Housekeeping Items

Talking with clients about such issues as provisions for canceling or changing scheduled sessions and financial arrangements is necessary but can be awkward and mundane. Perhaps discussing fees may be the most awkward for you and uncomfortable for the client. Your discomfort is understandable, given that your basic instinct as a social worker is to help people. Even so, most private agencies have policies that require payment for services, and many clients expect to pay, albeit on a sliding-scale fee arrangement. In addition, private insurance providers often have copayment requirements for services.

Financial arrangements, where required, are a fundamental part of the professional agreement between you and the client. A component of a social worker's competency is being able to effectively discuss financial arrangements, openly and without apology, when payment for services is expected. When clients fail to pay fees according to the contract, you should explore the matter with them promptly. Avoidance and procrastination just make matters worse and may result in you developing negative feelings toward the client. A failure to pay fees may derive from the client's passive, negative feelings toward the professional, financial strains, or irresponsibility in meeting obligations, any of which merits immediate attention.

There are situations with exceptions to a discussion of fees. Examples in which fees are not prominent include purchase of service agreement contracts with your agency or if the service is funded by a grant. This would also include services provided to minors in school settings. When the client is a minor in an agency setting, any discussion of fees is a conversation between you and the minor's parent or legal guardian.

Having an agreement about schedules and keeping appointments is also advisable. In making home visits, nothing is more frustrating than showing up at an agreed-upon time only to find that the client or the family is not at home or is unprepared for the visit. You should have the same expectations of yourself as you have of the client. Whether contact with a client is in your office or in their home, clients should be able to rely on your being available and attentive to their concerns. Of course, there are legitimate reasons that you or a client can have for changing or canceling an appointment. Discussing the "what ifs" in advance clarifies expectations about keeping appointments and prevents misunderstandings.

Sample Contracts

To assist you in developing contracts, we have included sample contracts at the end of this chapter. Each example includes most of the components discussed in preceding sections, although some are emphasized more than others. The first contract, Agreement for Professional Services (Figure 12-4), includes elements of ethical guidelines for work with clients and for managing malpractice risks articulated in the work of Houston-Vega, Nuehring, and Daguio (1997). Before using any of the contracts or agreements, you should clear them with your agency supervisor.

Figure 12-4 Agreement for Professional Services

Agreement for Professional Services

Name(s) of Client(s) _____ Name _____

Address _____ City _____ State _____ ZIP Code _____

Outline for the agreement to work collaboratively in achieving goals, and joint planning in carrying out activities for the achieving goals.

I. **Problem(s) or/Concern(s):** Defined and Specified

II. **Prioritized Goals & General Tasks:**

Goals _____ General Tasks _____

_____ _____

III. Conditions under which goals might change or be revised or others added.

IV. **Time Limits Applicable to Case:** Time frame that may influence the rate at which goals may need to be accomplished or where significant progress toward goals may need to be documented.

V. **Sessions:** Meeting times, frequency and durations, location, beginning and ending dates, and the total number of sessions.

VI. **Who is involved:** Individual, couple or family, group, or a combination?

VII. **Fees:** For service, and method and arrangement of payment.

VIII. **Evaluation:** How progress will be monitored and measured, including client participation, evaluating progress each session by reviewing the goal plan, and the steps taken to achieve goals and final evaluation at termination.

IX. **Reports and Records:** Confidentiality of records and consent of Release of Information. Specifies who will receive reports about progress (e.g., court, third-party payer, referral source).

X. **Requirements of Mandated Reporting:**

XI. **Agreement:** Affirmation of the review of the terms of the agreement, and that an understanding that the agreement can be renegotiated at any time.

Signature (Client /Family/Group Member)

Name _____ Name _____ Date _____

XII. **Social Worker:**

a. I agree to work collaboratively with _____ to achieve the goals outlined in this service agreement and others that we may subsequently agree upon.

b. I agree to adhere to the conduct that _____ agency expects of its staff and to abide by the regulatory laws and ethical codes that govern my professional conduct.

c. I have provided a copy of agency information about the rights of clients, available agency services, and information about the agency.

d. I have read the above terms of the service agreement, and pledge to do my best to assist the client(s) to achieve the goals listed and others that we may subsequently agree upon.

Professional's Signature: _____

Date: _____

Figure 12-5 Sample Contract: The Back Door, Making Change

the back door
MAKING CHANGE

Name: _____ Date: _____

File #: _____

❏ Housing   ❏ Planning   ❏ Drugs/Alcohol
❏ Employment   ❏ Volunteering   ❏ Problem Solving
❏ Education   ❏ Finances   ❏ Identification
❏ Personal   ❏ Leadership   ❏ Legal
                                               ❏ Other

CONTRACT STEP: _____ Step #: _____

WHAT I WANT TO WORK ON TODAY (i.e., WHERE I AM TODAY IN MY LIFE):

_____

_____

WHAT RESULT(S) I WOULD LIKE TO SEE (i.e., WHERE I WOULD LIKE TO BE):

_____

_____

WHAT I NEED TO MAKE IT WORK:

_____

_____

MY STEPS:

1. _____

2. _____

3. _____

4. _____

Contractor: _____ Paid by: _____

The following principles and questions reflect how *the back door* hopes to work. Please take time to think about how they worked for you in THIS contract step.

1. Principle: INTEGRITY/DIGNITY
   How did contracting this step contribute positively to your self-esteem?
2. Principle: LIFE IS SUCH THAT THINGS DO NOT ALWAYS WORK
   In attempting the above step, how did you find this to be so?
3. Principle: ACCEPTANCE WITHOUT JUDGMENT OR PREJUDICE
   How did contracting this step allow you to experience positive input from another person?
4. Principle: FORGIVENESS: EVERY DAY IS A NEW DAY
   How did contracting this step give you the freedom to learn from the past and try again?
5. Principle: PEOPLE WHO LISTEN TO EACH OTHER LEARN FROM EACH OTHER
   How did planning/working on this step help you to understand another person's point of view?
6. Principle: ALL ACTIONS/CHOICES AFFECT OTHER PEOPLE
   Did your working on this step have any effect on other people in your life?

Source: Used by permission of *The back door* © 2000.

The Agreement for Professional Services is presented in outline form. The agreement for the social worker is much more detailed, committed to observing ethical standards of practice.

The second contract (Figure 12-5) was developed to be used with participants of the agency called "the back door" (DeLine, 2000). This agency is committed to helping homeless and runaway youth get off the streets. The contract outlines the program objective and the services the agency provides. In addition, the role of youth clients is amplified because the focus is exclusively on how they can use the agency's services to alter their situation. The intent of the contract is to identify priorities and the most manageable tasks.

The remaining examples illustrate a treatment plan (Figure 12-6) and two behavioral contracts (Figures 12-7 and 12-8). Figure 12-7 is used by a county mental health center for men in a domestic violence program. Note that program requirements and objectives are a part of each client's treatment plan. Figure 12-8 is an example of a behavioral contract used in a juvenile facility, adapted from Ellis and Sowers (2001).

Figure 12-6 Sample Treatment Plan

Sample Treatment Plan

Areas of Concern	Short-Term Goals/Objectives	Long-Term Goals	Treatment Plan

Source: Adapted from Springer, D. W. (2002). Treatment planning with adolescents. In A. R. Roberts & J. J. Green (Eds.), *Social Worker's Desk Reference*. New York: Oxford University Press.

Figure 12-7 Behavioral Treatment Agreement

Behavioral Treatment Agreement

Name _____ Client # _____ Date _____ Therapist _____

1. Progress

Summary _____

_____

2. New Treatment Goals
1. Increased awareness of individual cues that trigger getting angry
2. Increased awareness of no abusive alternative ways of expressing anger
3. Increased use of support networks
4. Accepting responsibility for past abusive behavior

3. Plan

Attend 18 educational themes/complete 9 tasks

4. Outcomes
1. Side effects of treatment discussed ☐ yes ☐ no
2. Outcomes of treatment discussed ☐ yes ☐ no
3. Treatment options discussed ☐ yes ☐ no
4. Cost of treatment explained to client ☐ yes ☐ no
5. Client and staff rights form provided to client ☐ yes ☐ no
6. Is client considering:
   - Chemotherapy ☐ yes ☐ no
   - Hospitalization ☐ yes ☐ no
   - Other medical treatment ☐ yes ☐ no

If the answer is yes to any of the above, the physician or consulting psychiatrist shall inform the client of the treatment alternatives, the effects of the medical procedures, and the possible side effects.

All clinical services shall be provided according to the individual treatment plan.

5. Expected Duration of Treatment

18 weeks/dependent on task completion. You need to begin completing the required tasks within the first 4 weeks of the program.

6. Frequency of Treatment

Weekly

7. Collateral Resources and Referrals

_____

I understand the terms of this treatment agreement as well as my responsibilities in implementing the same. I have received a copy of this treatment plan.

Client _____ Date _____

Therapist _____ Date _____

Clinical Director _____ Date _____

Figure 12-8   Sample Behavioral Contract

Behavioral Contract

Name _____

Date _____

Responsibilities (activities, counseling sessions, behaviors to avoid):

Privileges (outlines privileges associated with meeting responsibilities):

Bonuses (meeting requirements for a certain time period):

Sanctions (circumstances in which privileges are lost, and possible action if requirements are not met):

Monitoring (identifies who is responsible for monitoring whether requirements are met):

Client's Signature _____

Social Worker's Signature _____

Source: Adapted from Ellis & Sowers (2001).

Summary

This chapter focused on the purpose and the function of goals and the process involved in goal development with voluntary clients, involuntary clients, and minors. Methods for monitoring and measuring the progress and outcome of goals were also discussed.

The contract examples provided in this chapter are intended as guides that can be adapted to situations or settings. Settings and client situations or status may dictate the inclusion of some elements over others. Also, including or omitting certain information in a contract can depend on the developmental age and stage of minors or a client situation.

Competency Notes

C1   Demonstrate Ethical and Professional Behavior

- Make ethical decisions by applying standards of the National Association of Social Worker Code of Ethics, relevant laws and regulations, models of ethical decision-making, ethical conduct of research, and additional codes of ethics as appropriate in context.

- Demonstrate professional demeanor in behavior, appearance, and oral, written, and electronic communication.

C2   Engage Anti-racism, Diversity, Equity, and Inclusion in Practice

- Demonstrate anti-racist social work practice at the individual, family, group, organizational, community, research, and policy levels, informed by the theories and voices of those who have been marginalized.

- Demonstrate cultural humility applying critical reflexivity, self-awareness, and self-regulation to manage the influence of bias, power, privilege, and values in working with clients and constituencies acknowledging them as experts of their own lived experiences.

C7 Assess Individuals, Families, Groups, Organizations, and Communities

- Apply knowledge of human behavior and person-in-environment and other culturally responsive multidisciplinary theoretical frameworks when assessing clients and constituencies.

- Demonstrate respect for client self-determination during the assessment process collaborating with clients and constituencies in developing mutually agreed-on goals.

C9 Evaluate Practice with Individuals, Families, Groups, Organizations, and Communities

- Select and use appropriate methods for evaluation of outcome.
- Critically analyze outcomes and apply evaluation findings to improve practice effectiveness with individuals, families, groups, organizations, and communities.

Skill Development Exercises

Developing Goals

To advance your skills in developing goals, complete the following exercises.

1. Develop a goal for yourself. Assess the feasibility of your goal, potential barriers, and risks and benefits. Also, determine which of the measurement and evaluation procedures discussed in the chapter you would use to observe goal attainment.

2. Using the same goal that you developed for yourself, rate your level of readiness. Now develop general and specific tasks or objectives that help you meet your goal.

3. Reread the case of Bettina, the adolescent in the group home. What is your reaction to the ongoing

staff pattern of punishment? Based on what you have read about involuntary clients, her developmental stage, and motivation theory, how would you work with Bettina to develop goals?

4. Review motivational congruence as a strategy for working with involuntary clients. What are ways in which you could make use of this strategy?

5. What values that you hold have the potential to create tension between what you believe and the goals that a client might want to pursue? Other than using a referral resource, which may or may not be an option, how would you deal with the differences between you and the client?

Notes

1. In addition to the procedures for measurement and monitoring discussed in this book, we recommend Jordan and Franklin (2003), Bloom, Fischer, and Orme (2009), Fischer and Corcoran (2007), and Thyer (2001b) for more in-depth information on standardized instruments and methods to evaluate practice.

2. For those interested in further study on single-subject research, informative resources are Bloom, Fischer, and Orme (2009), Fischer and Corcoran (2007), and Thyer (2001b). These informative resources describe a wide variety of methods that may be used to evaluate practice.

The Change-Oriented Phase

After formulating a contract, service agreement, or treatment plan, the social workers and the client begin Phase II of the helping process, the goal attainment or change-oriented phase. In Phase II, social workers and clients plan and implement strategies to accomplish goals related to the identified problem or concern. Implementing these strategies involves utilizing interventions and techniques specified in the contract or service agreement and contracting to use other strategies as indicated by changing circumstances. Before considering these factors further, a preview of Part 3 is in order.

Chapter 13 begins with a discussion of choosing and implementing interventions to facilitate change and includes eight therapeutic approaches for work

Continued

with individuals, families, and groups. Chapter 14 focuses on macro practice. Its coverage is enriched by case examples from social workers addressing environmental or institutional barriers in which macrolevel interventions were indicated. In Chapter 15, social work interventions with families are discussed by building on family assessment discussed in Chapter 10. Similarly, Chapter 16 presents group interventions, which builds on the discussion of group formation and assessment in Chapter 11. Techniques to expand self-awareness and to pave the way to change (additive empathy, interpretation, and confrontation) are considered in Chapter 17. Finally, Chapter 18 identifies barriers that can impede the change effort and discusses skills for addressing and resolving issues that can occur between the social workers and the client.

Chapter
13

Choosing and Implementing Interventions to Facilitate Change

Chapter Overview

Thus far, you have gained the knowledge and skills needed to complete a multidimensional assessment, develop goals, formulate a contract or treatment plan, and select methods for monitoring and measuring progress. The next step in the process requires you to select an intervention and create a plan for its use, which is associated with Phase II of the helping process.

After reading this chapter, you will be able to:

- Select a change strategy to facilitate goal attainment.
- Explain the importance of matching the strategy to the problem by utilizing a person-in-situation and person-in-environment framework.
- Describe the major tenets and procedures of the interventions outline in this chapter.

The EPAS Competencies in Chapter 13

This chapter will give you the information needed to meet the following practice competencies:

- Competency 1: Demonstrate Ethical and Professional Behavior

- Competency 4: Engage in Practice-Informed Research and Research-Informed Practice

- Competency 6: Engage with Individuals, Families, Groups, Organizations, and Communities

- Competency 7: Assess Individuals, Families, Groups, Organizations, and Communities

- Competency 8: Intervene with Individuals, Families, Groups, Organizations, and Communities

- Competency 9: Evaluate Practice with Individuals, Families, Groups, Organizations, and Communities

Interventions to Facilitate Change

Interventions enable social workers to help voluntary and involuntary clients attain their goals and facilitate change with individuals, families, and groups. Each intervention is supported by research and uses empirically grounded techniques or procedures that have demonstrated effectiveness with clients of different ages, backgrounds, and needs. The interventions are organized around the systematic, interpersonal, and structural elements of the helping process and follow the distinct phases of engagement, assessment, goal planning, intervention, and termination. The approaches are:

- The task-centered model
- The crisis intervention model
- The solution-focused brief treatment model
- Case management practice
- Motivational interviewing
- Cognitive-behavioral treatment
- Trauma-informed care
- Mind–body interventions

Regardless of whether social workers use a single intervention or a combination of approaches (i.e., eclectic approach), there are essential elements that should be part of every intervention. Many of these elements are what distinguishes social work from other disciplines such as psychology and sociology.

Person-in-Environment

Person-in-environment (PIE) is social work's distinctive principle and primary contribution to behavioral and social sciences (Green & McDermott, 2010). Person-in-environment recognizes that to truly understand an individual, family, group, organization, or some other entity you must also understand the environmental context (i.e., social, economic, political, communal, historical, religious, physical, cultural, and familial) in which the entity is embedded (Kondrat, 2008). PIE suggests that there is a reciprocal relationship between a person and their environment in that the individual can impact various elements within an environment and the environment can affect the individual (Kondrat, 2008). Social work's knowledge and ways of explaining the world, as well as our skills and purpose, 'are substantially constructed in, and through the environments in which we live' (Healy, 2005, p. 4).

Change Happens through the Helping Relationship

The helping relationship is one of the most important factors that contribute to client change (Fluckiger et al., 2020;

Wampold, 2017). A good helping relationship consists of mutual respect, acceptance, trust, warmth, and a focus on strengths, empowerment, and collaboration (Lambert & Ogles, 2009).

Strengths Perspective

Identifying and maximizing strengths can contribute to change, recovery, and improved well-being. The underlying beliefs of a strengths-based approach are:

- Everyone has strengths.
- People can and do change.
- People change and grow through the utilization and building upon of strengths and capacities.
- Problems can interfere with people's ability to identify their strengths.
- People can solve their problems (Pulla, 2017).

Building on these inherent strengths consists of "asking clients three simple but pertinent questions: (1) What has worked for you before? (2) What does not work for you? (3) What might work in the present situation for you (Pulla, 2017, p. 99). These three questions can assist social workers and clients in the process of goal attainment.

Empowerment

Empowerment is a process in which social workers develop a "mutual relationship between them and clients, whereby each is viewed as possessing unique knowledge and perspectives to share" (Lustick et al, 2020, p. 95). Empowerment is about helping people take control of their lives. Empowerment focuses on increasing the personal, interpersonal, and political power of people paying particular attention to oppressed and marginalized identities that historically have been disenfranchised or systemically disadvantaged by individuals and systems (Turner & Maschi, 2015).

The interventions highlighted in this chapter are process oriented and problem solving in nature and well suited to the helping process. The interventions adhere to the principles of social work practice, which emphasize mobilizing individuals, families, and groups toward positive action. Each strategy or intervention supports collaboration with clients by utilizing their strengths and increasing self-efficacy, which are critical aspects of empowerment.

Choosing an Intervention or Approach

There are several factors you should consider when selecting an intervention (Cournoyer, 2011). It is important to keep in mind that as your work progresses with clients, you may have to change your approach, which is why it is important to be flexible and follow the clients lead.

1. **What is the problem(s) you are trying to solve?**

   During Phase I, you collected information that provided a picture of the client as a person and their problem, situation, strengths, and goals. The method selected to address these, however, requires an understanding of context, circumstances, and nature of the problems and timing. To achieve a desired goal, the change strategy must be directed to the problem specified by the client and/or a mandate, as well as to the systems or the environmental issues that are implicated in the problem. For example, a school truancy problem and the reason the child is missing school necessitates involving the child, the family, and the educational system.

2. **Does the intervention make sense given the client context?**

   At this point, you may wonder how to go about selecting a change strategy. Change strategies should be chosen based on the needs, cultural background, and context, which is defined as the circumstances and broader range of relationship surrounding an event. The life cycle, human development, and ecological framework is not the same for everyone (Salazar, 2018). The intent behind this question is to prompt you to critically examine the appropriateness of a particular approach given the context.

   Discovery and cultural humility are two concepts that can help you understand contexts and ultimately select a change strategy in harmony with clients' values and beliefs. A spirit of discovery involves eliciting clients' view of the problem at hand; the related symbolic, cultural, and social nuances of their concerns; and their ideas about an approach as a remedy to their difficulties (Isaacson, 2014). Cultural humility requires you to place yourself in a learner role in which you are open to the client(s) as a teacher. Together, you and the clients are working together to understand and clarify the relevance of the change effort to their problem (Isaacson, 2014). Moreover, "cultural humility involves a change in overall perspective and way of life. Cultural humility is a way of being. Employing cultural humility means being aware of power imbalances and being humble in every interaction with every individual" (Foronda et al., 2016, p. 214).

3. **Does the selected intervention prioritize client choice and invite the kind of participation that will lead to a quality experience?**

   For some people, the act of asking for help, whether formally or informally, is unpopular. Narratives or suspicions about change strategies often are shaped by myriad experiences. These dynamics can be so prominent that problems or feelings may be minimized or ignored for fear of being perceived as vulnerable or giving the appearance of weakness (Sue, 2006). Involving clients in the process and providing explanations along the way can help clients be more at ease and lead to a quality experience.

4. **Do I have the best available information obtained from assessments and other reliable sources regarding the client's strengths, positive attributes, and resources, as well as problematic behaviors?**

   As you plan and select a change strategy, we encourage you to allow clients to consider the cost–benefit tradeoff of seeking help, which essentially means finding ways for clients to retain a sense of self and minimize any threats to the client's values and beliefs (Sue, 2006; Williams, 2006). As Sudeall and Richardson (2019) explained, individuals with little or no prior experience with formal helping systems may perceive an intervention as a threat, especially if past experiences involved traumatic, forceful, or repressive tactics. Some clients may struggle with change strategies that require them to make changes and confront deeply held beliefs. It is important to recognize despite current circumstances, all individuals have coped successfully with problems in their lives and overcome adversity of some kind (Connolly, 2013; Guadalupe & Lum, 2005; Sousa et al., 2006). It may be important to remind clients of past successes as they may need to be reminded that change is possible

5. **Does the approach safeguard the client's right to self-determination?**

   Promoting self-determination upholds a client's right to make decisions about their life. In your work with clients, they should feel empowered to fully participate in decisions related to their situation. Although some clients have limitations and may be unable to make decisions about certain aspects of their lives, the clients' limitations are not the sum total of who they are, nor does this mean they lack the ability to process task-specific information. The focus should be on the client's capacity rather than limitations. Above all, you are cautioned to refrain from acting in a paternalistic or beneficent manner to achieve your perception of the client's best interest. In a crisis, respecting self-determination can be overshadowed by a strong desire to help, so much so that the client's rights and the outcome sought may be unintentionally overlooked (Fullerton & Ursano, 2005; Sommers-Flanagan, 2007).

We acknowledge that the work setting in which you are employed may determine the approach utilized with a certain client population and, therefore, may limit decision-making about an intervention approach. In other settings, professionals acting as proxies can presume a particular client or client population lacks the capacity for self-direction. Best interest, in many instances, has become a means to sacrifice self-determination in which social workers act in a paternalistic manner. Consequently, fostering self-determination in certain settings may present a challenge for social workers. Whatever the circumstances might be, the defining question for which you may need to seek supervision is: What is the justification for ignoring a client's rights in making decisions about an intervention strategy?

6. **Does the approach safeguard the client's right to informed consent?**
Ensuring clients understand informed consent is essential to ethical and collaborative practice. Social workers should present information about the benefits, risks, and evidence of the approach's effectiveness with their problem in language that is easily understood by clients to ensure clients are fully informed. This same information should be provided to involuntary clients, even though they may be unable to withhold consent or to refuse a goal or service plan. They can, however, be given information about their options and the consequences of their choices.

Some clients such as minors and individuals who have cognitive and reasoning limitations have limited ability to give informed consent (Strom-Gottfried, 2008). Informed consent presumes clients not only understand a proposed approach but also are able to weigh potential outcomes. Parents or legal guardians are presumed to act in the best interest of minor's or individuals who have cognitive and reasoning limitations, and, therefore, they also should be consulted regarding the approach whenever possible (Strom-Gottfried, 2008). Although minors or individuals who have cognitive and reasoning limitations may be unable to provide informed consent, they should be given information about the approach and asked whether they assent; that is, they can give an "affirmative agreement" (Strom-Gottfried, 2008, p. 62).

7. **Do I have the knowledge and skill to use the identified approach and what professional expertise do I need to enhance my ability to serve clients?**
The complexities of clients' problems often necessitate having the knowledge and the competence to blend strategies and techniques of multiple approaches. In many respects, techniques can transcend models. Some social workers use an eclectic approach, which consists of drawing from multiple approaches to meet the needs of each client (Peterson & Fuller, 2021). In deciding to blend tactics or techniques, an essential question is whether you have the requisite knowledge, skills, and level of competence to use an eclectic approach. Eclectic practice does not mean you select a little bit of this and a little bit of that from various intervention approaches irrespective of your skill level. Ethically, in combining one approach with techniques from another, you must consider whether this is appropriate for the problem or the situation at the time. In instances where you lack the requisite skills or competence, you should seek ongoing supervision or consultation or refer the client to a professional with the applicable skill level (Karvinen-Niinikoski, 2016).

8. **What kind of support would the client find most helpful or desirable?**
Some clients may feel supported by more directive communication, while other clients may find encouragement and open-ended questions supportive. Some clients value emotive and affective expression, while others believe it is best to be rational and objective. All clients view the world differently and may find certain kinds of behaviors supportive (Swift et al., 2017). There are multiple ways of getting to the same place, and no one way is the right way; it is just different. For example, Swift et al., (2017) found that the same behaviors some clients find supportive, other clients find to be unhelpful. They state:

> Listening was deemed helpful when clients were expressing important emotions, but it was deemed hindering when clients were discussing less meaningful things. In these situations, the clients may have preferred the therapist to offer more structure and guide them to topics that are more impactful. However, if the therapist attempted to structure the session in a manner that did not fit the clients' preferences, then this was again seen as hindering. This finding illustrates the delicate balance that therapists must obtain while conducting therapy. To obtain this balance, it seems that a high level of therapist

attunement is needed. Expressions of empathy were also rated as both helpful and hindering. The difference may have been in the quality of empathy that was provided. Rather than feeling understood, clients reported that they felt judged or that the therapist was off track at the times when empathy was perceived to be unhelpful. Thus, therapists should work to convey accurate and genuine empathy to their clients (p. 1554).

9. **Are there any rules based on your practice setting that need to be considered?**
The approach social workers use may be determined by your practice setting. When planning and selecting an approach, it can be helpful to talk it over with a colleague or bring it up in supervisory consultation, so you clarify or affirm your decision. Organizational barriers can heavily influence practice. Williams et al. (2015) identified organizational barriers to implementing evidenced based practice. They found that workload, other staff/management not supportive, lack of resources, lack of authority to change practice, and workplace culture led to resist change (p. e38). While you may be bound by organizational context, it is important to keep in mind that your clients deserve the best services possible, which means sometimes you may have to push your organization in ways that could lead to change.

Evidence-Based, Evidence-Informed, Empirically Supported Treatments, and Practice Wisdom

For over 30 years, there has been a movement toward evidence-based practice (EBP), which is considered the gold standard of practice. According to Wall (2008), "evidence-based practice, which generally refers to the direct application of scientific (i.e., understood as quantitative/experimental) research findings to professional practice" (p. 37). Sackett and colleagues (1996) define "evidence-based practice as the conscientious, explicit, and judicious use of current best evidence in making decisions regarding the welfare of service users and careers" (as described in Pollack, 2013, p. 107). Within social work, there are three kinds of evidenced based practice:

Evidence-based practices are approaches to prevention or treatment that are validated by some form of documented scientific evidence, which include findings based on randomized controlled clinical studies, single-case experimentation, and double-blind studies.

Evidence-based programs and interventions use a defined curriculum or a set of services that, when implemented with fidelity, has been validated by some form of scientific evidence. Evidence-based practices and programs may be described as "supported" or "well-supported," depending on the strength of the research design. **Evidence-informed practices** use the best available research and practice knowledge to guide program design and implementation. This informed practice allows for innovation while incorporating the lessons learned from the existing research literature (Children's Bureau, 2011, p.16).

One of the major critiques of evidence-based and evidenced-informed practice particularly as it relates to anti-oppressive practice is that evidence-based practice is the only way of knowing or the only knowledge that counts. Practitioners who fail to use evidence-based practices often are taken less seriously (Wall, 2008). According to Pollack 2013, embedded within EBP is the explicit assertion that this type of research is superior to all other forms of knowledge acquisition and evaluation (p.107). Qualitative research methods, lived experience, and traditional, indigenous wisdom are not considered valid forms of knowledge because they do not meet the scientific gold standards of EBP such as randomized control trials (Pollack, 2013).

Non-White cultural groups such as Native Americans, African American, Latin-X, and Asian Americans believe in other ways of knowing. Table 13-1 highlights the differences between indigenous ways of knowing versus Western science (White ways of knowing). According to Simonds and Christopher (2013), "indigenous knowledge describes local, culturally specific knowledge unique to a certain population...often transmitted orally" (p. 2185). "True science" often relegates indigenous ways of knowing as folklore or mythical, furthering marginalizing indigenous voices (Wilson, 2008).

Most social work practitioners are trained to believe in research and other kinds of scientific evidence, as it provides research-supported practice and increases the likelihood of providing the best care possible to individuals, families, and groups (Woodbury & Kuhnke, 2014). While many of the interventions discussed in the chapter are supported by research and empirically grounded techniques, we also recognize evidence-based practices inadvertently "marginalizes different ways of knowing and perpetuates a belief in the superiority of experimental science" (Wall, 2008, p. 37). We embrace the continuum of practice, including practice wisdom and cultural practices that embrace multiple ways of knowing.

Table 13-1 Qualities Associated with Traditional (Indigenous) Knowledge Systems and Western Science

	Indigenous Ways of Knowing	Western Science	Common Ground
Organizing Principles	Holistic includes physical and metaphysical worlds linked to moral code. Emphasis on practical application of skills and knowledge.	Limited to evidence and explanation within physical world. Emphasis on understanding how.	Universe is unified body of knowledge stable but subject to modification.
Habits of Mind	Trust inherited wisdom. Respect for all ways of knowing.	Skeptical of everything that cannot be seen or measured.	Honesty, inquisitiveness, perseverance, open-mindedness.
Skills and Procedures	Practical experimentation, qualitative oral record, local verification, communication metaphor, and story connected to life, values, and proper behavior.	Tools expand scale of direct and indirect observation and measurement. Hypothesis falsification. Global verification. Quantitative written record. Communication of procedures, evidence, and theory.	Empirical observation in natural setting, pattern recognition, verification through repetition, inference, and prediction.
Knowledge	Integrated and applied to daily living and traditional subsistence practices.	Discipline based. Micro and macro theory. Mathematical models.	Plant and animal behavior, cycles habitat needs, interdependence. Properties of objects and material. Position and motion of objects. Cycles and changes in earth and sky.

Source: Barnhardt and Kawagley (2005, p. 16).

Different Types of Interventions

C8

Having described guidelines for planning and selecting a change approach, we now turn our attention to the major tenets and theoretical frameworks of interventions that new social workers are likely to use in their field placements and beginning practice

The Task-Centered Model

The task-centered (TC) model is a social work practice model developed by William Reid and Laura Epstein (1972). The model's contribution to social work practice is its specific focus on short-term problem solving as clients define them (Fortune et al., 2015). TC privileges clients' right to self-determination with an emphasis on tasks and the collaborative responsibilities between the client and the social worker (Bolton et al., 2021).

Tenets of the Task-Centered Approach

C4

The core tenets of the TC model are as follows:

- **Short time frames can produce maximum benefit** The development of the task-centered model (TC) challenged the idea that the more time you spend working with someone, the greater impact you could have (Marsh & Doel, 2005). TC is intended to reduce and, if possible, ameliorate problems (i.e., interpersonal conflicts, difficulties in social relations or role performance, reactive emotional distress, inadequate resources, and difficulties with organizations) in living within a brief, time-limited period (Bolton et al., 2021). Problems can overwhelm us, but if we break the problem down into smaller parts (i.e., tasks), they become more manageable. In keeping with the model's action orientation and brevity, termination begins at the initial point of contact, facilitated by specific goals with the primary focus on the development, and completion of tasks. The foundation of the TC model is empowerment. Through prioritizing problems identified by the client and using your vast knowledge, you empower the client to understand the problem in a deeper way and see solutions that they did not realize existed (Marsh & Doel, 2005).

- **The client's views, preferences, and concerns are paramount and should consistently drive the process.** The TC's emphasis is on the right of clients to identify preferences and concerns, including clients who are involuntary (Ramos & Tolson, 2008). One of social worker's primary roles is helping clients identify and express their preferences and concerns. The model is based on the explicit acceptance of the client's view of the problem and a here-and-now action orientation, rather than insightful talking. It is through the clarifying and shared understanding of problems, preferences, and concerns that clear, manageable tasks can be accomplished (Marsh & Doel, 2005). The only time clients' views, preferences, and concerns should not drive the process is if they involve abuse, are illegal, or are unethical.

- **Change is brought about through the identification and completion of tasks** Client problems are brought about through the completion of a series of tasks (Corcoran & Roberts, 2015). When the social worker and the client meet, they talk through the problem and the steps needed to solve the problem. These tasks are completed by clients and social workers (when applicable) outside of their work together. Once a task is complete, the social worker and the client identify the next step and create a plan to complete that task. This process

goes on until the problem has been addressed, or the client no longer wishes to work on the problem.

- **Lends itself to an eclectic approach** The TC is designed to be eclectic. The TC model makes use of different theories (e.g., cognitive-behavioral, problem-solving, and family structural approaches) that are relevant to the client's situation (Bolton et al., 2021; Ramos & Tolson, 2008). It TC techniques and strategies can be used with other approaches (Corcoran & Roberts, 2015).

- **The basic principles of the task-centered model are "cross culturally applicable" (Coady & Lehmann, 2016, p. 283)** TC practitioners are respectful of diverse lifestyles, views, cultures, and ethnic origins (Marsh & Doel, 2005). TC is used worldwide in countries such as Australia, Germany, Great Britain, Hong Kong, Israel, Japan, the Netherlands, Norway, Spain, South Korea, Switzerland, and Taiwan. It has been translated into several languages and has been adapted for different practice settings, such as family and group work (Chou & Rooney, 2010; Bolton et al., 2021; Ramos & Tolson, 2008; Rooney, 2010). It is incumbent on social workers to find ways to work with varied cultural views, allowing clients to educate them in cultural nuisances they may not understand.

Application of the Task-Centered Model

The task-centered approach involves a sequence of discrete steps to reduce and ameliorate problems. The steps (summarized in Figure 13-1) involve the major elements generally

C8

Figure 13-1 Task-Centered Process

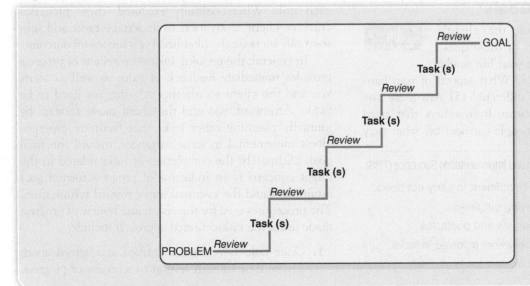

associated with successful change efforts. Research studies suggest that clients were more successful in accomplishing tasks when task planning and implementation sequence (TPIS) was implemented than when it was not (Reid, 1975, 2000). To implement TPIS systematically, the sequence is flexible and permits adaptations or modifications that are appropriate to the circumstances of each client situation.

Consequently, each step in the TPIS (see Table 13-2) is intended to increase the potential for a successful outcome. Identifying obstacles and possible challenges is built into the process and, when possible, resolved in advance. If necessary, behaviors involved in the task can be rehearsed. It may also be useful to identify incentives or rewards associated with task completion.

Procedures of the Task-Centered Model

The initial phase begins with the client identifying and prioritizing a target problem. In keeping with the model's action orientation and brevity, termination begins with the first session. Specifically, you and the client agree to work together for a particular number of sessions (e.g., six to eight weeks), although there is potential to extend contact or negotiate a new contract for a different problem. During the period of contact, progress toward the identified goal is monitored and reviewed in each session as the client moves toward termination.

Priority concerns and goals should be limited to a maximum of three. Goals are agreed upon, and general and specific tasks to achieve goal attainment are developed. Let's explore aspects of developing general and specific tasks and monitoring progress in more detail.

Goal Development and Partializing Goals

This process is based on the client's responses to some version of these questions: (1) What aspects of your life would you like to be different? (2) What aspects of your family would you like to be different? (3) Are there any legal requirements or pressure from others that need to be considered? While people can identify what they

Table 13-2 Task Planning and Implementation Sequence (TPIS)

1. Enhance the client's commitment to carry out tasks.
2. Plan the details of carrying out tasks.
3. Analyze and resolve barriers and obstacles.
4. Rehearse or practice behaviors involved in tasks.
5. Summarize the task plan.

would like to be different, they may need some help brainstorming possible ways to accomplish their goals. Brainstorming tasks involves a process in which you and the client mutually focus on generating a broad range of possible task options from which the individual, family, or group may choose. When you suggest tasks during the brainstorming process, it is critical to check with the client to ensure they agree with and are committed to the tasks. Most clients are generally receptive to your suggestions. It is critical clients dictate the focus of your work together as much as possible (Bolton et al., 2021).

Once you have brainstormed and identified possible goals, you must begin narrowing and prioritizing concerns. Let us explore aspects of developing general and specific tasks and monitoring progress in more detail.

General Tasks

The TC is based on the generation of tasks. Tasks are the instrumental action steps taken by the client and, in some instances, the social worker intended to alter or remediate the target concern and achieve a desired outcome (Coady & Lehmann, 2016). Once you and the client have identified a target problem and possible goals, you are ready to develop general tasks. General tasks are discrete actions to be undertaken by the client. Each general task has specific tasks that direct the incremental actions steps to achieve goals.

Specific Tasks

Specific tasks are derived from general tasks, which are broken down into incremental actionable steps. General tasks can prove to be overwhelming for some clients. Specific tasks direct the actions that the client or you as the social worker attempt between one session and the next.

After agreeing on one or more tasks, the next step is to assist clients in planning and preparing to implement each task. When skillfully executed, these processes enhance client motivation to undertake tasks and substantially increase the likelihood of a successful outcome.

In general, the ongoing in-session review of progress provides immediate feedback of gains as well as alerts you and the client to whether adjustments need to be made. Afterward, you and the client move forward by mutually planning other tasks that facilitate progress, albeit incremental in some instances, toward the final goal. Ultimately, the completion of tasks related to the target concern is an indicator of progress toward goal attainment and the eventual move toward termination. The procedures used for the systematic review of progress made using the task-centered approach include:

1. Once tasks have been identified and agreed upon, devote time in each session to a review of progress.

In this process, both the client and the social worker can document which tasks have been completed and the extent to which the target problem has changed.

2. During the review process, if tasks have not been completed or have not had the intended effect on the target problem, explore possible barriers and obstacles and the reasons for low task performance. When necessary, renegotiate tasks or develop new tasks.

3. In reviewing task accomplishments, it is critical to discuss with the client details about the conditions, actions, or behaviors that facilitated completion of the task. Even when tasks have been only partially completed, it is important to connect the progress made to the client's efforts. In doing so, you are highlighting and reinforcing the client's strengths and sense of competence.

There are a variety of factors that can interfere with a client's ability to accomplish their goals. It is critical that you assess the client's readiness to change, commitment, and ability to carry out tasks. When necessary, it may be important for you to identify and help resolve any barriers and explore possible rewards and incentives to help clients remain motivated to change.

Assess Client Readiness to Engage in an Agreed-Upon Task

A client's readiness to implement a task can be gauged by asking the client to rate their readiness using a scale of 1–10, in which a rating of one represents a lack of readiness, and 10 indicates the client is ready to go (De Jong & Berg, 2012). Should clients indicate their readiness is on the low end of the scale—for example, in the 1–3 range—you should explore the reason for the low rating, as doing so can uncover vital information concerning potential obstacles. Nonverbal behavior on the part of a client also can indicate a level of readiness in the lower range that may signal an obstacle or apprehension about undertaking a task. Because change is difficult, exploring apprehension, discomfort, and uncertainty is especially critical when a client's motivation to carry out a given task is questionable (Brehm & Brehm, 2013; Miller & Rollnick, 2012).

Even when clients have indicated a level of readiness to move ahead, implementing a task can cause a certain amount of tension and anxiety. It is neither realistic nor desirable to expect clients to be comfortable with tasks, despite the fact they were involved in identifying them. To encourage follow-through with tasks, it is important clients perceive that gains of completing a task outweigh the costs (including anxiety and fear) associated with risking a new behavior or dealing with a changed problem or situation. It is advisable to ask clients to identify benefits they may gain by successfully accomplishing the task.

In many instances, the potential gains and benefits of carrying out the task are obvious, and it would be pointless to dwell on this step.

Plan the Details of Carrying Out Tasks

When a task involves both cognitive and behavioral subtasks, it is beneficial to help the client be psychologically prepared before carrying out an overt action. For example, you can coach clients to reflect on past successes or focus on their supportive resources, such as spirituality or faith. By including cognitive (covert behavior) strategies in this step, you are assisting clients to cope with their ambivalence or apprehension regarding implementing actions. Of course, planning behavioral tasks that involve overt actions requires real-life consideration as well, such as transportation, childcare, access to technology, financial resources, and the like.

Because tasks connected to ongoing goals are incremental, it is important you and the client begin with a structured task that is easy and within the individual's capacity to achieve. In the classroom situation, for example, the student's task of raising their hand for five straight days may be difficult to achieve. Alternatively, raising their hand in math class for two out of five days may, with positive feedback from the teacher, increase the likelihood of eventually engaging in the task directed toward the goal of behavioral change.

Analyze and Resolve Barriers and Obstacles

The social worker and the client should deliberately anticipate and subsequently prepare for obstacles that can affect or stall task accomplishment. When tasks are complex, obstacles likewise tend to be complex, and clients may have difficulty identifying obstacles. Tasks that involve changes in patterns of interpersonal relationships tend to be multi-faceted and require developing subtasks as a prerequisite. For example, many intrapersonal tasks require the mastery of certain interpersonal skills. A caveat should be observed: A simple action of making a phone call may prove difficult for a client, depending on their own level of confidence, cognitive capacity, or social ability. Fears and cognitions can be a formidable barrier to accomplishing a task

Clients' capacity to resolve barriers and obstacles varies depending on the nature and the complexity of the task. Some clients overlook or underestimate potential barriers and obstacles, which can result in a delay to take on tasks, needless difficulties, and, in certain cases, outright failure in accomplishing a task. In such instances, explaining that obstacles and barriers are common is helpful. You might take the lead in brainstorming with clients to identify and resolve obstacles that can influence the planned course of action. It is also prudent to inquire about the practical and economic resources needed for completing the tasks (Eamon & Zhang, 2006).

In general, the time and effort invested in overcoming and resolving barriers and obstacles are likely to pay dividends, which result in a higher rate of success in accomplishing tasks. Consider the economy of this process as failure to complete tasks can influence an individual's sense of self-efficacy and can extend the time involved in successful problem solving.

Identify Rewards or Incentives

Given the varied circumstances in which clients may be hesitant to engage in tasks, it may be necessary to identify an immediate reward to support motivation. Rewards and incentives are particularly relevant when a change in behavior or cognition is associated with the choice of pain over pleasure, such as engaging in activities that may be perceived as unattractive (e.g., studying, cleaning house) instead of engaging in self-time. Possible rewards can be identified with the client; however, to be effective, the reward should be realistic. When using an incentive or a reward to motivate, it is important to observe and record incremental change, followed by an immediate reward; otherwise, the client may become discouraged or give up and believe instead they are unable to meet expectations.

Rehearse or Practice Behaviors Involved in Tasks

Certain tasks involve skills people may lack or behaviors with which they have had little or no experience. Part of a social workers' role is to help clients gain experience and mastery in performing skills or behaviors essential to task accomplishment. Specifically, the degree of an individual's positive expectation of their ability to perform is followed by effort expended to meet that expectation, while negative expectations can limit an individual's ability to persist when faced with obstacles or aversive circumstances (Arampatzi et al., 2020). It follows, then, that a major goal in the TC is to enhance a client's sense of self-efficacy to increase their potential for successful task completion. Successful experience, even in simulated situations, encourages a client's belief they can be successful in performing a task.

There are a variety of ways you can rehearse or practice behaviors in tasks. Role play used in an actual session can reduce anxieties and help clients practice new behaviors or coping patterns. Indications for using role play include situations in which a client feels threatened, feels inadequately prepared to face a situation, or is anxious or overwhelmed by the prospects of engaging in each task.

Role Play. In a simulated situation, a client can build on their existing skills, as well as identify potential barriers or obstacles. Modeling behavior through role play, in effect, allows for the vicarious learning of a behavior before having to do so in a real life, potentially difficult situation.

Role play need not be restricted to a session between you and the client. It can include overt behavior such as making a phone call or countering negative self-talk. These defeating feelings and thoughts can then be restructured using more encouraging language. Role play can also be integrated into family or group sessions in which members can model effective and realistic responses or coping for each other in contemplation of engaging in a particular task.

Guided Practice. Closely related to role play, guided practice is another technique to aid task accomplishment. It differs from role play in that it involves you observing the client as they engage in a task related to a target behavior. Afterward, you provide immediate feedback and coach the client as they attempt to gain mastery toward task completion. For example, in a family session, as you observe problematic behaviors or interactions firsthand, you would provide feedback and coach family members so they can master problem solving or conflict resolution skills. Such an on-the-spot intervention enables you to clarify what is occurring as well as coach clients to engage in more productive behavior.

Summarizing the Task Plan and Monitor Progress

Summaries take place at the conclusion of a session. They often consist of a review of the actions or the behaviors a client has agreed to do to accomplish a task. In reviewing task agreements, you and the client confirm you both have a clear understanding of what tasks are to be undertaken, in what sequence, and under what conditions, or whether further discussion or clarification is needed. Confirmation of the plan might proceed with you describing the tasks you or the client will complete:

> **Social worker:** I have agreed to contact the employment information specialist by our meeting next week.
> **Client:** I will make three phone calls to potential employers who have posted job listing online.

Alternatively, the client would be asked to review and summarize their plans:

> **Social worker:** What are your plans for searching for a job by our next session?

Individual clients may find it beneficial for you to provide them with a session-by-session written summary of goals and related tasks. You might also encourage clients to write their own summaries as well. In either case, both you and the client should have copies. In keeping with the ethical obligation of documentation, this information is included in the case record. Documentation is essential to monitoring and evaluating during the duration and termination of the contact.

Failure to Complete Tasks

In actual practice, the process of developing tasks may not be as smooth as you and the client would prefer, even though barriers or obstacles have been anticipated and resolved, and all other possible impediments have been addressed. In the best scenarios, focus and continuity can be derailed for a variety of reasons. Reasons for low task performance are classified into two categories: (1) reasons related to the specific task and (2) reasons related to the target problem.

Reasons Related to Not Completing a Specific Task

Most clients with whom you work want relief from their difficulties and are motivated to act. Nonetheless, their ability to do so can be hampered by their beliefs, unforeseen circumstances, or unanticipated obstacles may influence their ability to complete tasks. When this happens, the obstacles that blocked the task completion should be identified and resolved. There are two reason tasks might not be completed: Factors associated with specific tasks and factors related to the target problem.

Factors associated with specific tasks include:

- *Occurrence of an emergency or crisis.* Should this prove to be the case, it is appropriate for you to empathetically respond to the emotional state of the client. It may also be necessary to focus on the more urgent difficulty and develop a goal or tasks related to the unexpected situation. If possible, an agreement should be reached about the timing for resuming work on tasks that were designated for completion prior to the crisis. If in the course of your work with the client you observe their life appears to reverberate from crisis to crisis, the two of you can discuss whether it would be beneficial to remain focused on the initial tasks and see them through to completion.

- *Lack of skills/support.* In planning tasks, it is important to ensure clients have the necessary skills needed to complete the agreed-upon action. For example, if the task is obtaining a job, it would be prudent to assess whether the client has adequate interviewing skills or knows how to create a resume.

- *Conflicting values and beliefs.* A client may agree to a task but may not fully disclose information about conflicting values or beliefs. For example, a parent who believes children should obey is likely to be hesitant to utilize reward systems and believe instead that parents should not bargain with their children. Being sensitive and respecting different beliefs is important. By listening to the parent, the two of you could renegotiate a task that is consistent with the parent's belief as a solution.

- *Environmental factors.* Support for completing tasks also can be related to family or environmental factors. For example, finding a subsidized apartment may depend on the availability of such housing. These are difficult situations in which a ready-made solution is not apparent, and you and the client need to explore alternatives.

Factors related to target problems include:

- *Conflicting wants/needs.* There may be competing or more pressing concerns. The initial task remains important; however, another issue (either new or existing) demands the client's attention. The situation does not need to be a crisis. It may simply mean even though a client had prioritized a goal and developed a related task, there are other issues competing for their attention. Flexibility is called for in such instances until the competing concern is resolved.

- *Little hope for change.* Despite the fact a client has agreed to undertake a certain task, they may feel that completing the task will have little or no impact on a problem or situation. This is an opportunity for you to help the client by calling attention to their past successes. Crediting clients with past successes is particularly useful to boost confidence when a client's perception of their ability to effect change is uncertain.

Strengths and Limitations of the Task-Centered Model

The task-centered model is the first empirically based social work model of a planned, short-term, problem-solving approach based on the principles and values of the social work profession (Kelly, 2008; Reid & Epstein, 1972). There are several strengths of the task-centered model. The model honors self-determination, strengths, and empowerment by allowing clients to define the problem, develop goals and tasks, and participate in monitoring progress. To increase a client's self-efficacy and opportunity for mastery, obstacles to task completion and goal attainment are identified and resolved. The review of obstacles and barriers is a distinct strength of the approach. Similarly, when tasks are not completed, the reasons for low task performance are reviewed, and new tasks, if indicated, are developed.

Critiques of the central tenets of the model—in particular, time limits and the systematic structure—have led some observers to conclude that a sustained therapeutic relationship with clients is unlikely to evolve (Ramos & Tolson, 2008). Given the utilization and effectiveness of the model with a range of client problems and settings, there is limited evidence to support this claim.

While opinions are mixed about the efficacy of the model with certain populations and in certain situations, the efficacy of the model has been supported by empirical evidence in multiple settings and for a range of voluntary and involuntary client problems (Ramos & Tolson, 2008; Reid, 1992; Tolson et al., 1994). The model's effectiveness also has been demonstrated in worldwide practice settings (Ramos & Garvin, 2003; Ramos & Tolson, 2008; Reid, 1996, 1997, 2000). Key aspects of the model, namely the use of tasks, have become foundational elements of several other intervention approaches (Hoyt, 2000; Ramos & Tolson, 2008).

The Crisis Intervention Model

The crisis intervention approach is growing in popularity, primarily due to an increase in natural disasters such as Hurricane Katrina, the earthquake in Haiti, tsunamis that have hit the Philippines, and terrorism locally (e.g., collapse of the Hard Rock hotel in New Orleans); nationally (e.g., 9/11 and storming of the Capitol a week before President Biden was to assume office); and globally (e.g., the Rwandan genocide or kidnapping of school girls in Nigeria by the Boko Haram, Myer et al., 2013). The current coronavirus (COVID-19) pandemic is another example of a worldwide crisis.

A crisis, as defined by James (2008), is "a perception of an event or situation as an intolerable difficulty that exceeds the resources or coping mechanism of the person" (p. 3). Flannery and Everly (2000) defines a "crisis as a stressful life event that overwhelms an individual's ability to cope effectively in the face of a real or perceived challenge or threat" (p.119). Crisis has the following three critical features:

1. A relatively stable existence prior to the crisis.
2. An individual's primary coping mechanism have not helped them return to homeostasis.
3. The crisis has caused some kind of impairment that is negatively impacting functioning (Flannery & Everly, 2000). Prolonged crisis-related stressors have

the potential to severely affect cognitive, behavioral, emotional, psychological, and physical functioning.

In your work with clients, you have no doubt assisted them to deal with crisis situations. These situations may have ranged from job loss to death, a medical diagnosis, eviction, divorce, domestic violence, child abuse or neglect, crime, relocation, the long-term effects of COVID-19 pandemic or even a natural disaster. It is important to note segments of the population experience cumulative events or circumstances that result in a perpetual state of crisis (Ell, 1995). Consider, for example, the hypervigilance of unauthorized immigrants related to fear of deportation and family disruption, or the very real threats experienced by individuals in the lesbian/gay/bisexual/transgender/queer/questioning (LGBTQ+) community because of hate crimes, brutal beatings, and even murder. Intense anxiety related to threats and potential harm is pervasive in many among many marginalized and oppressed populations. Individuals from these communities face ongoing violence such as negative encounters with the police, poverty-related stressors, and inadequate services or resources, which result in perpetual disequilibrium.

Tenets of the Crisis Intervention Model

According to Flannery and Everly (2000), the basic tenets of the crisis intervention model (CIM) are:

Intervene Quickly

Crises can be physically and emotionally challenging, even hazardous situations or events (Flannery & Everly, 2000). They place individuals in situations where maladaptive coping mechanisms could be employed, which is why it is important to intervene as quickly as possible.

Stability Is Paramount

An important goal in a crisis is to stabilization of the situation. Often, resources and support are critical factors that help create stabilization and help restore order and routine (Flannery & Everly, 2000). Stabilization enables individuals affected by crises to begin to function independent of the people trying to help.

Listen to Understand

Helping to restore and stabilize individuals affected by crises is accomplished by listening to understand what individuals have experienced. You accomplish this task by gathering information about the crisis, listening to individuals tell their story, make space, normalize difficult emotions, and help them understand the impact the crisis has had on their lives.

Problem Solving Is Critical

Social workers working with individuals who have experienced a crisis should help them identify and use all available resources and problem solve any difficulties arising from the crisis that is interfering with functioning.

Restore Independent Functioning

The goal of working with individuals who have experienced a crisis is to help restore their ability to function independently. Helping an individual who has been affected by a crisis assess the problem and identify, develop, and utilize strategies and resources goes a long way toward restoring independent functioning.

Procedures of the Crisis Intervention Model

The crisis intervention model is action oriented, with the central intent of reducing the intensity of a client's emotional, mental, physical, and behavioral reactions to a crisis and restoring client functioning to the precrisis state. Promptness of response, a key aspect of the model, is considered critical to prevent deterioration in functioning. It is during the acute period that people are most likely to be receptive to an intervention. The procedures of the model involve assessing the nature of the crisis, identifying priority concerns, and developing limited goals.

1. Establish a baseline. Where possible, assess and review a client's affective, behavioral, emotional, and psychological functioning to establish a baseline and determine the functioning level prior to and after the crisis (James, 2008).

2. Decide at which level to intervene. Depending on the nature of the crisis and the systems involved, it may be necessary for you to intervene at the micro, mezzo, or macro levels (Gelman & Mirabito, 2005).

3. Information gathering. It is important to gather any information that can be used to ameliorate a crisis (Bolton et al., 2021).

4. Crisis situations inevitably have a subjective element because people's perceptions and coping capacities vary widely. Therefore, a crisis that is severely stressful and overwhelming for one person may be manageable for others. Variations in reaction depend in part on the point at which the social worker has contact with the client.

5. Typically, crisis work is time limited and spans four to eight weeks, although some clients or situations may require prolonged contact. Your contact with a client during the acute crisis period may be daily for a period and may taper off.

6. Social workers must be prepared to work anywhere and under extreme conditions. Meetings with clients can take place onsite, in an office, a shelter, a hospital, a trailer, under a tent, or in their homes.

7. Interventions range from a single-session telephone intervention to comprehensive services with an individual, group, family, or an entire community (Fast, 2003; James & Gilliland, 2001; West et al., 1993).

8. The active, intense, time-limited, focused, and action-oriented nature of the crisis intervention approach is believed to help people return to a level of precrisis functioning (James & Gilliland, 2013; Roberts, 2005; Walsh, 2010).

9. Ultimately, the level of distress, whether the crisis is acute or chronic, and client characteristics (perception of the crisis, ego strengths, and situation-specific resources such as social supports) dictate the time required.

10. The focus of crisis intervention is on the here and now. Hence, no attempt is made to deal with either precrisis personality dysfunction or intrapsychic conflict, although attention to these symptoms may be required.

11. Goals are limited to alleviating distress and assisting clients to regain equilibrium.

Application of the Crisis Intervention Model

To effectively intervene with a variety of crises, there are a series of steps social workers should use to address the crises (Bolton et al., 2021; James, 2008; Myer et al., 2013). These steps guide the application of the approach and are consistent with the eclectic problem-solving approach. While these steps are presented in a linear fashion, crises are not always linear, and social workers must be flexible as to what is needed in any given moment changes rapidly (Myer et al., 2013). It is important to recognize that a client's physical, emotional, and psychological health can shift without notice. Therefore, social workers must follow a client's lead and be present with them in any given moment.

Step 1: Assessment of the Crisis

Depending on the crisis clients can have a variety of reactions. A **crisis reaction** is described as any event or situation that upsets the client's normal psychic balance to the extent their sense of equilibrium is severely diminished (James, 2008; Roberts, 2005). Crisis intervention theory posits people's crisis reactions typically go through several stages, although theorists differ as to the number of stages involved. The stages are similar to the stages of grief. The following description is a synthesis of models and stages identified by various authors (start here Caplan, 1964; James & Gilliland, 2001, 2016; Okun, 2002; Roberts, 2005):

- *Stage 1:* The initial tension is accompanied by shock and perhaps even denial/disbelief of the crisis-provoking event.
- *Stage 2:* Heightened or reduced tension/frustration results from the client's attempts to utilize their usual emergency problem-solving skills. If these skills fail to result in a lessening of tension, the stress level may become heightened.
- *Stage 3:* The client experiences severe tension, feels confused, overwhelmed, helpless, or angry. The length of this phase varies according to the nature of the hazardous event, the strengths and coping capacities of the client, and the degree of responsiveness from social support systems.
- *Stage 4:* Acute depression stems from the reality of the situation hitting them. The more the client can make sense of what happened, the likelihood increases that this increased understanding may result in acute depression. If people have lost loved ones, or the whereabout of loved one is unknown, clients may vacillate between anger, irritation, agitation, and depression, or profound sense of sadness.

In reacting to a crisis, the potential exists for clients to cope in ways that are either adaptive or maladaptive. You should be aware, however, that prolonged stress may exceed a client's coping capacity and usual problem solving to such an extent that they are unable to effectively handle stressors. Achieving equilibrium for some clients may depend on the extent to which their strengths, resilience, and social supports are mobilized. In some instances, the crisis may even evoke a positive change opportunity. Specifically, a client's reaction may be to seek help and succeed, thereby using the opportunity for their benefit (James, 2008). For others, the level of tension can become elevated, in which case the client's coping patterns reach a level of danger. Danger is evident when restoring equilibrium is not immediately possible because the client is unable to function.

Assessment is an ongoing process that is dynamic, fluid, and forever changing. Throughout the course of your work with clients, you also should be assessing the following things:

- The client's current emotional status and level of mobility/immobility

- Alternatives, coping mechanisms, support systems, and other available resources
- The client's level of lethality (specifically whether the client is a danger to self or others)

Finally, assessment of severity often is characterized by the duration of the crises, length of displacement, and repeated trauma, which have an accumulated effect. According to James (2008), there are two distinct crises categories: type 1 and type 2. Type 1 involves a single, distinct crisis experience in which symptoms and signs are manifested; for example, the minor can display fully detailed etched-in memories, misperceptions, cognitive reappraisals, and reasons for the crisis event (James, 2008). The type 1 category seems to fit best with the basic equilibrium crisis intervention approach in which the focus is on restoring the precrisis state. The stages of crisis and the reaction may differ depending on the group. Different groups of people may, for example, need additional help in understanding their reaction to the crisis and in developing problem-solving skills.

Type 2, in contrast, is the result of long-standing, repeated trauma whose cumulative effects result in psyche developing defensive coping strategies, anxiety, depression, or acting-out behavior (James, 2008; Lindsey et al., 2006; Maschi, 2006; Voisin, 2007). For example, residents of New Orleans who experienced Hurricane Katrina and who were displaced went to a variety of places throughout the United States. Whether people left voluntarily or had to be rescued often increased the severity. Additionally, if those people remained in hurricane areas, the chances of them being displaced by another hurricane is high. In October 2020, Hurricanes Laura and Delta hit Lake Charles within the span of a month. As a social worker, your work with someone who has had experienced multiple crises will be different than someone who may be experiencing a crisis for the first time.

Step 2: Make Contact, Establish Rapport, and Provide Support

Introduce yourself to clients. Establish rapport and a connection with clients. The goal is to figure out how you can best support clients. Social supports may include friends, relatives, and, in some cases, institutional programs that care about the client and can provide comfort and compassion (James & Gilliland, 2001).

Step 3: Elicit the Client's Definition of the Problem, Narrow Down, and Triage the Identified Problems

After conducting a thorough assessment, work with clients to identify the problem(s) as they see them. As a social worker in a crisis, you must determine the unique meaning of the crisis and the severity of the situation to the clients. Having clients talk about the meaning and the significance of the crisis provides you with essential information about how clients define their problem, which can be a cathartic process for clients as well.

Begin to triage the problems according to their severity and need for immediate attention. Triaging involves assigning priority levels to determine the best use of resources and the most effective, efficient way of addressing them (Wilkinson, 2020). Triaging is necessary when the need for resources exceeds the available resources.

Figure 13-2 is a triage system developed by the Centers for Disease Control and Prevention (CDC) used with patients suspected of having COVID-19.

When triaging, color coding often is used to distinguish between widespread issues versus more individualized issues. There are different types of triage systems used when dealing with mass causalities or pandemics such as COVID-19. The Simple Triage and Rapid Treatment (START) model is a system that emergency personnel use in natural disasters and mass casualties such as train wrecks. In this instance, they separate injured people into four groups:

- The people who are dead or are beyond help
- The injured who need immediate attention
- The injured whose treatment can be delayed
- Those with minor injuries

Depending on the crisis, there are other ways systems use a triage system. An advanced triage system, as outlined by Bazyar et al. (2019), involves color coding. Figure 13-3 is an example of a color-coded system used in crisis situations. Red is used to describe individuals who will not survive without immediate medical attention. Yellow is for individuals whose condition is stable for the moment and are not in immediate danger of death but still need medical attention. Green is used to represent the walking wounded, which means they are tended to after the more urgent cases are addressed. White is used for individuals with minor injuries that do not require a doctor's care. Black is used for individuals who are deceased or whose injuries are so extensive that existing medical care cannot help.

While some studies have found that advanced triage systems are effective, Bayzar and colleagues (2019) report that:

There are divergent triage systems in the world, but there is no general and universal agreement on how patients and injured people should be triaged. Accordingly, these systems may be designed based on such criteria as vital signs, patient's major problems, or the resources and facilities needed to respond to patients' needs. To date, no triage system has been known as superior, specifically about the patients' clinical outcomes, improvement of the scene management or allocation of the resources compared to other systems. Thus, it is recommended that different countries…design their triage model for emergencies and disasters by their native conditions, resources, and relief forces (p. 482).

Figure 13-2 CDC Triage System

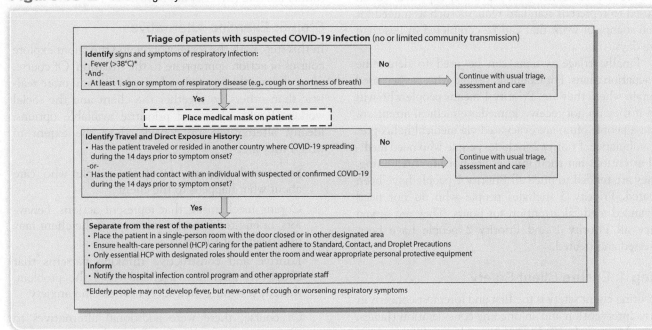

Source: Developed by the Center for Disease Control

Figure 13-3   Triage Color Coding

Advanced Triage System Chart		
Tag Color	**Meaning**	**Description**
Red	Immediate	Needs immediate attention for a critical life-threatening injury or illness; transport first for medical help. Red tags are used to label those who cannot survive without immediate treatment but who have a chance of survival.
Yellow	Observation	Serious injuries needing immediate attention. For those who require observation (and possible later re-triage). Their condition is currently stable and they are not in immediate danger of death. These victims still need hospital care and would be treated immediately under normal circumstances. In some systems, yellow tag patients are transported first because they have a better chance of recovery than red-tagged patients.
Green	Wait	Less serious or minor injuries, nonlife-threatening, delayed transport; will eventually need help but can wait for others. Reserved for the "walking wounded" who will need medical care at some point, after more critical injuries have been treated.
Black	Expectant	Deceased or mortally wounded; Black may not mean the person has already died. It may mean that he or she is beyond help and, therefore, is a lower priority than those who can be helped.
White	Dismiss	No injury or illness (not used in all systems). Also given to those with minor injuries for whom a doctor's care is not required.

Source: Tucci et al. (2017, p. 4)

There also are triage systems used to allocate resources. According to Study Lib (n.d.), red is used to describe severe, widespread problems such as issues that affect public safety, power or network outages, and security exposures. Orange is for problems that impact groups of people such as having to take classroom instruction online and problems that affect loss of essential personnel, applications, or systems. Yellow is for critical issues that affect individuals such as individuals not having viable work, lack of shelter, toiletries and other essential products, and need for access to medication. Blue is used to identify escalated requests such as ongoing issues that still need to be resolved, service delays, and solutions that are needed sooner than previously expected. Green is used to represent standard requests such as a need for food stamps or work that can be completed in less than five days.

Finally, triage systems can be used to determine evacuation plans. For example, people who are deceased remain where they are. Priority 1 means people who will die if they do not receive immediate medical attention. These people often are evacuated via medical helicopter or ambulance. Priority 2 includes people who need medical attention, but their injuries are not life threatening. They are tended to once all Priority 1 people have been treated. Priority 3 includes people who do not need advanced medical attention for hours. They are served once all Priority 1 and Priority 2 people have been assessed and treated.

Step 4: Ensure Client Safety

Ensuring client safety is the first and foremost concern in crisis intervention and an ongoing consideration (James, 2008; Myer et al., 2013). Safety involves deliberate steps taken to minimize the physical and psychological dangers to the client or others. For example, are clients having thoughts of self-harm? If so, this issue would fall into the yellow category. You and the client may need to develop a plan when suicidal or homicidal thoughts arise.

An additional safety concerns might include physical, emotional, or psychological safety. It is important for the social worker to evaluate the extent of a client's adaptive and coping capacities. It is also critical for the social worker to learn about family resources that could be tapped to alleviate distress, as well as options to ensure the client's safety. The goal is to ensure that clients and emergency response/social workers/other personnel are safe (Myer et al., 2013).

Step 5: Examine Alternatives

In this step, both the social worker and the client explore courses of action appropriate to the situation. Of course, some choices they considered were better and more realistic than others, so together the client and the social worker should select and prioritize available options. Ideally, alternatives are considered to the extent to which they are:

- Situational supports, involving people who care about what happens to the client

- Coping mechanisms that represent actions, behaviors, or environmental resources that the client may use to get past the crisis

- Positive and constructive thinking patterns that effectively alter how a client views the problem, thereby lessening their level of stress and anxiety

Of course, there were additional alternatives to consider in stabilizing this crisis. Multiple options can be overwhelming for clients, and the alternatives that you and the client consider should be realistic for the situation (James, 2008).

Step 6: Make Plans

This step is about creating plans to resolve the crisis. This step involves identifying all possible solutions and alternative options to determine the best course of action (Myer et al., 2013). General and specific tasks can vary, of course, according to the nature of the crisis and the unique characteristics of each individual and/or family. In developing and negotiating tasks, the social worker should solicit the client's views on what they believe would help them function at a level of precrisis level. There are times during this step when your interaction with a client may require you to be directive. During this step, you may need to identify and secure additional resources, provide support and encouragement, and assess the viability of the plan to ensure it is realistic given the circumstances. The overall goal of this step is to create a realistic, practical, doable plan that has reasonable success of resolving the crisis (Myer et al., 2013).

Tasks are identified, and task performance is intended to help clients achieve a new state of equilibrium. In crisis situations, the level of incapacity presented by the client may require social workers to have a more active and directive role than they might have in other interventions. Even though you may direct and define tasks, the social worker should encourage the client to participate to the extent that they can do so. Although a client's ability to actively participate and perform tasks may be limited during periods of severe emotional distress, their capacity to do so generally increases as the distress level diminishes.

Step 7: Obtain Commitment

During this step, the social worker is committed to collaboratively engaging in specific, intentional, and positive tasks designed to restore clients to a level of precrisis functioning. It may be helpful for the social worker and the client to develop a list of general and specific tasks that one another will accomplish. The tasks developed should assist clients in regaining a precrisis level of equilibrium.

Step 8: Referral and Follow-up

This step consists of the social worker helping the client connect with the necessary resources and assistance (Myer et al., 2013). While the end goal is to get clients to a point where they can depend on their internal, familial, and community resources, clients need to know that you are there for them and available. Depending on the crisis, clients may need a little more hand holding

from the social worker than normal. This is not a normal circumstance, and it may require social workers to be creative, think outside the box, and respond appropriately.

Anticipatory Guidance

Anticipatory guidance involves assisting clients anticipate future crisis situations and plan coping strategies that prepare them to face future stressors. Similar to identifying obstacles and barriers in the task-centered model, anticipatory guidance involves a discussion of scenarios of potential or future stressors. When using anticipatory guidance, it is important that the social worker does not convey an expectation that people are always able to independently manage future crisis situations. Even though throughout the course of your work together, you have reassured clients of their skills and helped them anticipate future scenarios, you should reaffirm that that you or other professionals are available if clients need future help.

Strengths and Limitations of Crisis Intervention

The crisis intervention equilibrium/disequilibrium model is a structured, time-limited model consisting of a series of steps informed by basic crisis theory. The initial intervention phase has three strategic objectives: (1) relieve the client's emotional distress; (2) complete an assessment of the client's cognitive, behavioral, and emotional functioning; and (3) plan the strategy of intervention, focusing on relevant tasks the client can perform. Strengths of the model are that perceptions of a crisis vary based on associated threats, client cognitions, ego strengths, coping capacity, and problem-solving skills. The model is consistent with generalist practice and utilizes the practice values, knowledge, and skills with which you are already familiar.

The goal of the intervention is to restore the client to a precrisis level of functioning. Ell (1995) questions the assumption of time-limited crisis as well as the notion of homeostasis, specifically whether the goal of restoring clients to a precrisis level of functioning is always possible. For instance, ongoing difficulties in the daily lives of people who are exposed to a chronic and constant state of vulnerability in their environments, such as the COVID-19 pandemic, can mean that the focus on time-limited crisis episodes is neither feasible nor realistic. The efficacy of crisis intervention strategies nevertheless is not entirely diminished by Ell's observations. However, these observations do suggest significant factors that can impact cognitive, affective, and behavioral functioning because of the cumulative effects of ongoing distress for a prolonged period.

Solution-Focused Brief Treatment Model

The solution-focused brief treatment (SFBT) approach has emerged over the past 20 years as a brief therapeutic strategy for working with adults, minors, and families, including clients who are involuntary. It is one of the most popular types of brief therapy (de Shazer et al., 2021). SFBT is a postmodern, constructivist approach that emphasizes identifying solutions rather than resolving problems (De Jong & Berg, 2012; Murray & Murray, 2004).

The approach was developed by Insoo Kim Berg, Steve de Shazer, and some of their colleagues. It assumes that people are constrained by the social construction of their problems. Thus, a goal of the approach is to shift from a problem-oriented perspective to one that is more solution based. Work with clients is facilitated by having them identify and prioritize solutions. Like the task-centered system, the solution-focused approach is based on the premise that change can occur over a brief period.

Tenets of the Solution-Focused Brief Treatment Model

SFBT is based on several tenets that double as guidelines for practice. According to de Shazer et al., (2021), there are eight basic tenets of SFBT as follows:

1. If it ain't broke, don't fix it. The only things you should be focusing on is areas where problems exist. Some schools of therapy believe that there are unconscious reasons that can contribute to present-day problems, and analysis of these reasons could lead to change and possibly prevent problems in the future. However, this is not the focus of SFBT, as a fundamental belief is that analysis of a problem does not necessarily predict a client's ability to problem solve (Corcoran, 2008). A basic premise of SFBT is that there is no need to intervene if no problem exists.

2. Do more of what works! The solution-focused approach draws on people's strengths and capacities, with the intent of empowering them to create solutions. If they are doing things that are helping to resolve the problem, you should be encouraging them to do more of that. Change is believed to occur in a relatively brief time, especially when people are empowered as experts and are encouraged to use their expertise to construct solutions.

3. Stop doing what doesn't work. If clients are doing things that are not working, you should be encouraging them to stop doing what does not work in order to identify potential solutions that could work.

4. Small incremental steps can lead to big changes. As a social worker, you should encourage clients to identify small steps that could lead to resolving the problem. Oftentimes, people are waiting for big solutions, but small steps that lead to resolving the problem also get clients to the same place. Small steps also can help clients stay motivated toward change as they gradually move toward change.

5. Solutions and problems are not necessarily related. Solutions and problems are not necessarily connected. Solutions that could solve the problem may be found in areas of the client's life that have nothing to do with the problem.

6. Solutions should be positive, hopeful, and future focused. The thrust of your work with clients encourages solution talk rather than assessing how problems developed or are perpetuated (de Shazer et al., 2021). The social worker's role is to listen, absorb information that a person provides, and subsequently guide them toward solutions utilizing the change language (De Jong & Berg, 2012). Lee (2003) believed these principles are motivating factors that strengthen the efficacy of the solution-focused approach in cross-cultural practice.

7. There are always exceptions find them. Nothing is ever a problem or true 100% of the time. Look for exceptions and build on those instances as they often hold the key to resolving the problem.

8. The future is not fixed but created. Oriented toward the future rather than the past, the solution-focused treatment approach asserts that clients have a right to determine their desired outcomes. The social worker's role is helping clients understand that outcomes are based on actions. If they want a different outcome, they need to change their behavior.

Solution-Focused Brief Treatment Language and Techniques

SFBT Language

SFBT is unique in many ways. One way it is unique is its focus on language and asking questions in ways that help clients focus on solutions rather than dwell on problems. For example, the way clients are categorized is unique to solution-focused treatment. The model highlights three types of individuals are identified: customers, complainants, and visitors (Corcoran, 2008; De Jong & Berg, 2012; Jordan & Franklin, 2003). **Customers** are individuals who willingly make a commitment to change. Therefore, the series of questions and the tasks to be completed are directed to them. Those individuals who identify a concern but do not see themselves as part of the problem or solution are referred to as complainants. A person who is willing to be minimally or peripherally involved but is not invested in the change effort is designated a visitor. These distinctions allow you to identify where potential clients stand relative to their commitment to change and their ownership of concerns. Distinguishing the various types enables you to focus on the concern and the solution identified by the customer. There may be instances, however, when it is advisable to engage the complainant or visitor, if only to ensure they do not interfere with the customer's change efforts.

SFBT Techniques

SFBT utilizes myriad techniques that are integrated into the process of asking questions.

- *Compliments* provide feedback about a client's efforts and reinforce strengths and successes.
- *Bridging* is also a part of the feedback, clarifying goals, exceptions, or strengths.
- *Amplification* questions encourage clients to elaborate on the "What's different?" question. The question may also be used as a link to a compliment or to link tasks to the miracle question. Used in another way, amplification can inform goals and tasks related to the miracle question.
- *Formula versus predictive.* The tasks that you suggest can be either formula or predictive in nature, and they may be completed during or after a session. For example, a post-session formula task for a couple experiencing relationship conflict would be to imagine how their relationship would be if the miracle occurred. In using a predictive task, you would direct the couple to predict the status of their conflict, for better or for worse, tomorrow (de Shazer, 1988). In essence, the predictive task invites the couple to think about what would be different in their relationship.
- *Looking for previous solutions.* Clients have solved many problems successfully. The focus of your work with clients is to help clients see that they can solve problems, and there were things they did that led to a resolution. In identifying those things, you help clients look for solutions that were used previously to solve the problem.
- *Looking for exceptions.* Exceptions are instances when problems could have occurred, but they did not. It is important to help clients identify times in their lives when something was not true. For example, your client complains that their boss is always

micromanaging them. You would ask your client to describe a time, albeit small, when their boss did not micromanage them. Together, you explore what was different about this instance and use that information to create conditions so this can be true again.

- *Questions as primary communication tool.* Questions are the primary communication tool when using SFBT. The reasons why questions are powerful is because it causes clients to answer and find resolutions to their problems. Traditional therapeutic interventions can be more directive or interpretive. In this approach, rarely do social workers challenge or confront clients. Rather, they ask pointed questions that help the client to see the problem rather than telling the client what the problem is from your perspective.
- *Present and future focused.* The goal is to keep clients focus on solutions, not the problem. Focusing on solutions keeps the client present and future focused.

A series of interview questions used during the phases of the approach are instrumental in the development of solutions (De Jong & Berg, 2012).

Application of the Solution-Focused Approach

Within the solution-focused framework, there are five phases of the helping process: engagement, assessment, goal setting, intervention, and termination. Within each phase, certain types of questions are used to elicit information from clients. These questions are intended to guide clients toward goals and think of solutions. Within each phase, there also are typical interview questions adapted from De Jong and Berg (2012), Lipchik (2002), and de Shazer and Berg (1993) that facilitate a client's capacity to think about the future and to identify solutions. Table 13-3 highlights the different type of solution-focused questions asked in each phase.

Phase 1: Engagement (Description of the Problem)

Clients are invited to give an account of their concern or problem. However, as a practitioner, you refrain from eliciting details about antecedents, severity, or the cause of their concern.

Table 13-3 Types of Solution-Focused Questions

Scaling questions: Phase 1: Engagement
Coping questions: Phase 1: Engagement
Miracle questions: Phase 2: Assessment
Exception questions: Phase 3: Goal Setting

While listening to clients' description of the problem, you are looking for ways in which you can guide them toward a solution.

Scaling questions, in the engagement phase, are to get a sense of the problem, how they are seeing the problem, and how big the client believes the problem is. Scaling questions have a particular structure (e.g., bigger numbers always represent more positive states) and that follow-up questions fit a SF pattern of seeking exceptions. For example:

1. On a scale of 1–10, how much energy would you say that you have today?

2. I don't know, I'd say a four.

3. Let's say that you were able to answer a little bit more, say a six. What would be different for you?

4. I would feel a lightness in my chest. My chest wouldn't feel so heavy.

5. Can you describe a time during the past week when you might have answered a six to my question? Let's talk about what was happening during that time.

If the number on the scale goes up, you should compliment the client and ask for details regarding how they were able to accomplish this. If the number did not change, compliment the client for the number not going down, explore how they kept it from getting worse, and encourage them to continuing doing more of the change. If the client identifies that the problem got worse, coping questions can help. You acknowledge how difficult it is to deal with certain problems and ask them how they are coping with the problem (de Shazer et al., 2021).

Coping questions are intended to highlight and reinforce a client's resources and strengths. For example, how has the client managed the current difficulty, or what resources have they used previously when dealing with the issue? Coping questions credit the client's prior efforts to manage a difficulty and reenergize their strengths and capacities.

Examples of Interview First Session Questions

It is recommended to begin the interview with questions that encourage the client's participation by allowing the client to provide their view of the situation (De Jong & Berg, 2012; de Shazer et al., 2021). Examples include:

- Whose idea was it that you needed to come here?
- Where did the idea of seeking help come from?
- Tell me why you are here?
- Why do you think _____ (pressuring person or mandating authority) suggested we work together?

- How does your view of the situation differ from _____ (pressuring person or mandating authority)?
- What can I do to help?
- What signs indicate to you that others involved in this situation are behaving, thinking, or feeling differently?
- What changes have you noticed between the time you made the appointment and today?
- What would make this a useful session?

Phase 2: Assessment (Developing Well-Formed Goals)

In this stage, your work involves encouraging the client to think about what will be different once the problem no longer exists. This information facilitates the development of a client's goal.

C7

Miracle questions draw the client's attention to what would be different once a desired outcome is achieved (Corcoran, 2008; Lipchik, 2002). Imagine in the middle of the night, a miracle happens, and the problem that prompted you to come here today is solved…. When you wake up tomorrow, what might be the small changes that make you say to yourself, "Wow! The problem is gone?"

Examples of Phase 2 Interview Questions

- How will you know when your problem is solved?
- What will be different when the problem is solved?
- What signs will indicate to you that you don't have to see me any longer?
- What signs will indicate to you that others involved in this situation are behaving, thinking, or feeling differently?

Phase 3: Goal Setting (Exploring Exceptions)

Questions asked of the client in this stage are focused on those times in their life

C8

when the problem was not an issue or was less of a concern. These questions are followed by questions relating to what could happen that would decrease the concern and make exceptions possible.

Exception questions are considered the core of the intervention (Corcoran, 2008). Designed to diminish the problem focus, these questions assist a client to describe life when the current difficulty did not exist (De Jong & Berg, 2012, 2008; Shoham et al., 1995; Trepper et al., 2006). The exception question also advances the client's ability to externalize or separate self from the problem by highlighting strengths and resources (Corcoran, 2008).

Examples of Phase 3 Interview Questions

"What do you want to be different, or "What could be different?" is intended to facilitate the development of a well-formed goal. Have clients explore times when the problem did not exist and reasons why this was the case. Goals sought by the client are framed based on exceptions; specifically, clients are asked about the absence of the problem (the exception), and it is on this basis that the work toward a solution is formed.

Phase 4: Intervention (End-of-Session Feedback)

The aim of this stage is to compliment and reinforce what a client has already done to solve the problem. Feedback is based on the information the client provided about goals and exceptions. Clients are asked what they should do more of to accomplish a goal. The focus of your questions would emphasize signs of what can be and is different.

Example of Phase 4 Interview Questions

- Can you describe what might be different in terms of your behavior, thoughts, or feelings?

- "What signs would indicate to you that others involved in this situation are behaving, thinking, or feeling differently?"

- "What's better?"

Phase 5: Termination (Evaluating Progress)

Monitoring progress is ongoing and specific to evaluating the client's level of satisfaction with reaching a solution. The scaling question facilitates this process. After a client has rated their satisfaction level, you work with them to identify what needs to occur so that the problem is resolved. In later sessions, a central question posed to the client is: "What's better?" When the client's primary concern is resolved in a satisfactory manner, contact with you is terminated.

From Session to Session

- Ask about progress

From one session to the next, you should always ask clients about progress. Examples of progress related questions include:

- What is better, even if the difference is small, since we last met?

- What could the client continue to do more or less of?

The flow and the sequence of the questions can vary depending on the content of the conversation with each client. For example, if a client reports that little or no change has occurred, you would inquire about how they are coping. If indicated, you might ask a scaling question to gauge the level of stress. For instance, you would have the client rate their current level of concern and what would be different or better at the next level. "Would you rate what might be different in terms of your behavior, thoughts, or feelings when you move to the next level?"

- Experiments and homework assignments

End sessions by asking clients to conduct experiments by trying something between sessions. For example, if a parent always complains that their child is disrespectful, you could encourage the parent to look for times when the child is not disrespectful and praise them. Experiments are based on things that clients are doing that are moving them in the right direction. Homework is usually identified and assigned by the client. The client chooses to do more of what they are already doing or try something else they really want to do. Either way, it is beneficial when the homework comes from the client, as it has a greater likelihood of success (de Shazer et al., 2021).

Strengths and Limitations of the Solution-Focused Approach

As the solution-focused approach has matured, a promising body of empirical evidence has shown its efficacy with diverse populations and with the variety of problems presented by clients (Corcoran, 2008; Corcoran & Pillai, 2009; Kim, 2008; Trepper et al., 2006). The solution-focused approach supports the construction of the client's reality and is essential to interactions with diverse groups. In this regard, the expertise of the social worker is minimized, as is the opportunity to rely on basic stereotypes and generalizations. On this basis, well-informed goals are more likely to be relevant to the client. Even so, the assignment of tasks by the social worker would appear to be more directive than collaborative. Aspects of this approach—in particular, the commitment to empowerment and a focus on clients' competence, strengths, and capacities—are values that are consistent with social work's commitment to self-determination.

Particular aspects of the procedures of the solution-focused approach have been criticized. Both critics and proponents have questioned whether the approach is, in fact, collaborative—in particular, the assignment of tasks by the practitioner based on the assumption that assigned tasks help the client to focus on solutions (Lipchik, 1997). To the latter point, research conducted with solution-focused practitioners revealed discrepancies between client experiences and the observations made by therapists related to outcomes (Metcalf et al., 1996). Clients reported that the positive thrust of the approach prevented them from discussing real concerns, and instead, they felt persuaded to explore solutions. Further, they perceived the avoidance of talking about a problem to have limited value (Efran & Schenker, 1993).

Similarly, the limited attention to behaviors instead of feelings ignores the connection between feelings and cognitions (Lipchik, 2002). These critiques, in many respects, ignore the fact that when clients seek help, they have been socialized to talk about and describe problems in great detail in exchange for services. For this reason, it is important that you explain the basic intent of the process and procedures of the solution-focused approach and perhaps give clients time to talk about their concerns.

Some professionals suggest that encouraging solutions, rather than focusing on the problem, results to remedy a situation that may not be fully understood. Nonetheless, the research literature regarding involuntary clients has shown success in using the solution-focused approach with this often neglected and marginalized client group (Berg & Kelly, 2000; Corcoran, 1998).

Practice need not focus exclusively on either problems and deficits or strengths and resources. Rather, an appraisal of each, including risks and protective factors, is important in developing a realistic view of a situation and the systems involved (McMillen et al., 2004). However, we should not assume that clients have within them the solutions to all difficulties. In fact, some clients may lack sufficient cognitive skills and resources or face sociopolitical barriers that affect their ability to achieve their miracle.

Case Management

Case management is a process that enables social workers and clients to collaboratively engage in assessment, planning, identifying, evaluating, and monitoring of individuals and families' comprehensive needs, services, and resources to promote and enhance quality of care, safety, and overall well-being (National Association of Social Workers-NASW, 2013, p. 13). Case management is often referred to in health or institutional settings as care planning, care coordination, or patient-centered care. Case management is viable and often vital to persons in need of comprehensive services.

As a method, case management is a frequently used direct social work approach. This is, in part, because people with unmet needs often are unable to negotiate the complex and often uncoordinated health and human services delivery systems. The underlying philosophy of case management is for individuals and families to reach their maximum potential, all parts of client systems (i.e., level of functioning, support systems, service delivery systems, financial resources) needed to be coordinated to work in unison (NASW, 2013). Case management's primary goal is to identify ways to enhance and optimize functioning through the coordination of services in the most efficient and cost-effective way (NASW, 2013). These goals are accomplished by: (1) addressing the multiple problems that individuals and families experience, (2) improving the quality of services, and (3) conserving public resources (NASW, 2013).

Over time, the momentum for case management has grown, beginning in the 1960s with deinstitutionalization initiatives to relocate and maintain people in their community. To a large extent, the growth of case management has been driven by federal and state-funded programs, the majority of which mandate the coordination and integration of services. Medicaid, for example, requires case management to help beneficiaries gain access to needed medical, social, educational, and other services. In the current human services state and federal reimbursement environment, case management is integral to services in health and mental health settings, long-term care facilities, homeless shelters, schools, adult and juvenile probation situations, and child welfare.

Tenets of Case Management

A critical function of case management is linking individuals or families to a range of services based on their assessed needs. In essence, people can gain access to health, mental health, and social welfare service providers that otherwise might be difficult for them to navigate on their own. The coordination of services by the case manager is intended to reduce duplication, fragmentation, and ultimately the frustration of the client.

Case Management Phases

According to the Case Management Body of Knowledge (2018), there are nine phases of the case management process. Although case management processes may vary with respect to settings and organizational priorities and goals, there is a consensus that case management always includes the following functions or phases. While the phases and the tasks of case management are for the most part self-explanatory, using a case example, a brief explanation is provided.

Case Example

On October 12, 2019, the Hard Rock building in New Orleans, Louisiana, partially collapsed, leaving three people dead. Eighteen people were taken to the hospital, and countless workers, their families, and bystanders were affected (Burke & Samandi, 2019). The City of New Orleans set up brief counseling and case management services to help the workers and the families of workers affected by the collapse.

Phase 1: Intake and Screening

Preliminary to an assessment, intake and screening are an initial step in determining eligibility for services. In this phase, social workers gather critical information related to a particular event or circumstance to identify the extent of the need for services and resources. The social worker's objective during the screening phase is to gather the information needed to support clients.

Jose was injured in the collapse but refuses to go to the hospital because of his undocumented status. The types of information you might gather include:

- Current level of physical, emotional, and cognitive functioning
- Psychosocial network and support system
- Preexisting, prior, and current health condition
- Health insurance coverage
- Socioeconomic and financial status
- Current or past receipt of services
- Risk stratification category or class
- Is there anything else you think it is important for you to know?

Phase 2: Assessment

In this phase, social workers must complete a comprehensive assessment, develop an individualized service plan, and negotiate and coordinate services. Case management begins with an assessed need rather than a service. Using a multidimensional assessment, standardized tools, and checklist, social workers begin collecting the information previously identified. They also begin to assess the client's physical, mental, social, and psychological functioning, which includes strengths and resources. The information gathered and assessed in this stage guides the development of the case plan.

The social worker has three primary objectives in the assessment phase:

1. Identify the most pressing problems and needs that are critical to address.
2. Determine the anticipated time frame and desired outcome
3. Develop a comprehensive plan of care that addresses these problems and needs (Case Management Body of Knowledge-CMBK, 2018).

Returning to our case example:

- Jose's most pressing need was to get him medical attention that would not jeopardize his undocumented status.
- Jose also needed to contact his family to let them know he was fine.
- Jose was worried about how he was going to feed his family now that he was out of work.
- You are worried about Jose's mental health, as his best friend was injured in the collapse. He doesn't know if his friend is dead or alive.
- Jose appears to be in shock, but you are not sure of his mental state once he comes to understand the magnitude of what has happened.

Phase 3: Stratifying Risk

In this phase, the social worker classifies each of the client's needs into one of four risk categories: low, moderate, high, and very high. The goal is to determine the most pressing needs and the appropriate level of intervention. These risk classifications allow the social worker to address the client's needs based on the immediacy, severity, and most critical to client's well-being, health, and safety. Additionally, you also are classifying clients overall in these categories to determine which clients you assist first.

In terms of needs, there may be things on the list that could easily be accomplished and give the client some instant relief (i.e., finding out the status of his friend and contacting his family). If many of the client's needs fall into the very high-risk category, the client may require an intensive amount of time and resources that are beyond your capacity to provide. You may need to partner with someone else to meet very high-risk client's needs.

- Jose most pressing need was to get him medical attention that would not jeopardize his undocumented status. (This need may be high or very high (depending on the extent of the injuries.)
- Jose needed to get a hold of his family to let them know he was fine. (This need may be low or moderate depending on the client's state.)
- Jose was worried about how he was going to feed his family now that he was out of work. (This need is low.)
- You are worried about Jose's mental health, as his best friend was injured in the collapse. He doesn't know if his friend is dead or alive. (This need may be low or moderate depending on the client's state.)
- Jose appears to be in shock, but you are not sure of his mental state once he comes to understand the magnitude of what has happened. (This need is moderate.)

Phase 4: The Planning Phase

In this phase, the social worker and the client develop a case plan which outlines the goals and objectives. The level of risk, goals, and objectives are based, in part, on the client's perception and your determination of needs. For example, client self-determination is important. In Jose's case, he is making decisions in part because of his fear of being undocumented. Depending on the extent of his injuries, he could die. There are a lot of things to consider during the planning phase, and it is critical that clients be involved in the process. Social workers should consider the following:

- Establish specific objectives, care goals (short and long term), and actions (treatments and services) that must be taken to meet clients' needs.
- Risk classification or category for each goal.
- Feedback and perspectives of client's support systems and the client's health-care providers.
- Ensure that specific, measurable, achievable, relevant, time-bound (SMART) goals are action oriented, time specific, and multidisciplinary in nature.
- Ideas that clients can utilize for self-care should be included, if possible.
- Identify and obtain a necessary authorization for clients to receive the necessary services.
- Identify and figure out how to access any resources needed.
- Determine the eligibility criteria of each provider.
- Assess the provider's ability to meet the case management goals.

Once the social worker feels the service plan is reflective of the client's needs and has developed a plan to meet those needs, service agreements are made with the various service providers. Both formal and informal resources and the appropriate service providers are identified. Like the service agreement or contract with clients (refer to Chapter 12), the case management plan specifies the work to be completed.

Phase 5: The Implementing (Case Coordination) Phase

In this phase, social workers focus on ensuring the execution of case management-related services, activities, intervention, and resources are in place and are meeting clients' needs. In the field of social work, this is considered care coordination. The broker role is vital to facilitating interagency coordination and cooperation. In this capacity, you must have a working knowledge of and an effective relationship with a range of service providers, including available informal resources. The broker role specifically connects clients to critical resources.

As a social worker, helping people gain access to available resources may require negotiating with various service providers. Where indicated, advocacy at the systems level may be necessary to ensure clients have access to resources to which they are entitled. In addition to the broker role, in any one case, mediating between a client and various systems may be required.

During this phase, social workers organize, secure, integrate, and modify (as needed) the services, interventions, and resources to ensure that they meet the client's needs and interests. It is also important that key information be shared with other service providers, the client's support system, doctors, mental health professionals, and any other providers that are working with the client. The primary goal of the implementing phase is to review the case management goals and objectives, monitor a client's progress, and adjust as needed.

Phase 6: The Follow-up Phase

In the follow-up phase, the most important tasks are to monitor progress toward the client's goals and whether their needs are being met by service providers. Social workers have three primary tasks in this phase: (1) whether services are provided and attended regularly, (2) review and monitor progress toward stated goals, and (3) the client's overall impression of the services and the extent to which they are satisfied with the services.

In the follow-up phase, social workers observe, review, ascertain, track, reassess a client's goals, health condition, needs, resources, supports, and outcomes. The social worker's primary objective is to periodically review, monitor, and evaluate the client's needs with service provided to determine if the case plan is appropriate and effective, as determined by improvement in their health condition and desired outcomes.

During the follow-up phase, social workers should:

- Gather information from all relevant sources
- Share information with necessary people as determined by the client and their needs
- Document the findings and any changes or adjustments that have been made
- Make minor modifications or identify which tasks have been completed

Phase 7: The Transitioning (Transitional Care) Phase

It is particularly important to be sensitive to changes in a client's needs and adjust or modify the plan as indicated.

Reassessments can be formal or informal and are completed at fixed intervals. The information gathered can also determine the level of change since the initial assessment.

In this phase, social workers are monitoring a client's progress to ensure that they are making progress across the continuum of care depending on their needs, services, resources, and health condition. The social worker also begins to prepare the client and their support system for termination through discharge, completion of services, or time frames based on insurance or organizational requirements. If clients are unable to go home, then the social worker is trying to find alternative care settings or facilities so that when it is time to discharge, clients have places to go. The primary goal of this phase is to ensure clients can safely transition to the next level of care and that clients have what they need to discharge responsibility.

Tasks that social workers complete in this phase include:

- Provide education about plans or services needed post transition.
- Compile a summary of your work together.
- Ensure clients have any needed medical devices and that ongoing services are in place and the next two or three appointments have been scheduled.
- Communicate all necessary information to clients and their support system.
- Brainstorm about possible setbacks or challenges that may arise and how those things will be handled.

Phase 8: Communicating Post-transition Phase

The communicating post-transition phase involves communicating with a client and their support system to check and see how things are going post discharge or transition. As a social worker, you should ask clients about any arranged services where someone was supposed to meet with them regularly and the quality of those interactions, medications, any new or existing issues or concerns, satisfaction with care, self-care, and overall well-being.

During this phase, social workers should:

- Check to see if there are any issues and problems post transition
- Resolve any issues or problems that exist or create a plan to resolve them
- Collaborate with any service providers as needed
- Share any necessary or relevant information with key stakeholders

Phase 9: The Evaluation Phase

In the evaluating phase, social workers review the goals, objectives, treatments, interventions, results, and progress clients have made regarding their case plan. It is also important to review any ongoing needs or long-term services and establish a plan should problems surface. The evaluation phase often leads to termination. In longer-term situations, reassessment and evaluation of outcomes are ongoing.

Case management is an essential role that allows social workers to make unique contributions to the health and well-being of people with complex needs and health conditions (NASW, 2013). Case management is performed by a variety of disciplines such as health related, social work and social services, correctional, work/vocational, veterans, and the legal field. It can be found throughout almost every public, private and nonprofit sector. Its widespread presence conveys the importance of case management across health services, social services, and other sectors (Valentijn et al., 2013).

Strengths and Limitations of Case Management

The utilization of case management has grown over time, in part as a response to federal funding requirements that emphasize improved access to services and the coordination and integration of the services that clients receive. Utilization of this method can also be attributed to goals of the Affordable Care Act—specifically, greater continuity and coordination in care and a reduction of duplication in service delivery systems. Standards and principles of case management developed by the National Association of Social Workers (NASW) and the Case Management Society of America (CMSA) have contributed to the uniformity of case management functions and the role of the case manager across settings.

An assumption of case management is that the resources or service providers that clients need are always available in adequate quality and quantity. Gaps in services exist. In some instances, the service may be available, but the provider may be overwhelmed with demands. Herein lies a challenge for the case manager, particularly in an age in which funding for services are reduced.

Overall, case management is intended to meet the multiple needs of a client in a coordinated, comprehensive manner. The phases and the associated tasks allow for the development of a case plan unique to the client. The greater benefit of case management is the fact that services are identified based on assessed needs, which eliminates clients having to navigate complex helping systems on their own.

Motivational Interviewing

Motivational interviewing (MI) is a collaborative conversation style for strengthening a person's motivation and commitment to change (Miller & Rollnick, 2013, p. 12). MI is commonly used in conjunction with other treatment approaches to strengthen their effects. Motivational interviewing works because it focuses on a client's ambivalence. Think about a time when you were ambivalent about making a change that you and others thought would be good for you to make. This may have involved a health behavior such as exercise or making a shift in your eating habits. It also could involve the use of tobacco, alcohol, or other drugs. With little effort, you probably could have listed reasons why making the change would be a good idea, but there were competing desires that kept you from adopting a new, healthier behavior. You probably had people in your life who could list those reasons too and who may have felt justified in expressing those reasons for you.

Clinical research shows that correcting clients, influencing their opinions through persuasion, and, importantly, advice giving reduce client participation and increase their resistance. They tend of evoke a "yes, but" reaction in which the client focuses not on the benefits of adopting new behavior or of making a change but instead intensifies their focus on why change is hard or on why solving a problem may be hopeless.

Using a motivational interviewing approach, a social worker would refrain from persuading or convincing clients to change their behavior but would instead use communication skills strategically to encourage clients to make their own arguments for change. Motivational interviewing has two basic components: a stylistic component described as the spirit of MI and a technical component that emphasizes the deliberate and strategic use of communication skills. These two components along with MI techniques make up the spirit of MI, which seeks to help clients make decisions in the direction of change by increasing client change talk and decreasing client sustain talk.

MI Spirit—The Style of Motivational Interviewing

The spirt of MI is based on four principles: collaboration, acceptance, compassion, and evocation.

Collaboration/Partnership

Collaboration/partnership consists of the social worker and the client working together to reach their goals (Substance Abuse and Mental Health Services Administration, 2019). Social workers who practice from an MI-informed lens partner with clients regarding their decision-making refrain from using their power over clients or imposing their beliefs or perspectives on clients. Instead, social workers help clients articulate their own reasons for change. A confrontational approach is antithetical to the spirit of MI (SAMHSA, 2019). In order to convey to the client that the social worker is partnering with the client, they must use inclusive language such as, "How do we work together to accomplish your goals?" Collaboration and partnership are intended to encourage an atmosphere that is conducive to change. The social worker shows respect for diversity of thought regarding what constitutes change, how change happens, and that their ideas about change and what is best for the client might be different than the client's ideas. Failing to take a collaborative stance conveys to the client that they are deficient in some way and that the social worker can provide what is missing, which puts the social worker in the solving role as opposed to the client (SAMHSA, 2019).

Acceptance

Acceptance is a belief that people can solve their own problems and that true change rests with the client and whether they choose to change or remain the same. Instead of confronting clients or telling them what to do, MI emphasizes active listening toward greater understanding and acceptance. Within acceptance, there are four key factors (SAMHSA, 2019):

1. Absolute worth, which consists of understanding that we all are doing the best we can to figure out our lives. No matter the circumstances, clients deserve respect, which increases the likelihood that they will be open, honest, and open to receiving help.

2. Autonomy and support, which consists of understanding that responsibility for change is up to the client. Social workers take a long view regarding change and know that clients must be ready and willing to change, and no amount of pressure will get them to change if they are not ready.

3. Affirmation or focusing on the positive. Looking for and acknowledging specific words spoken or actions taken that are congruent with the changes the client wants to make.

4. Accurate empathy or really trying to understand your client, what is happening in their life, what this problem means to them, and their ideas regarding solving them.

Compassion

Compassion is about having empathy, grace, and understanding in our work with clients and working with them in ways that do not judge, shame, find fault, or blame. Compassion is often elicited through understanding the client's point of view and the circumstances that make them who they are. There is a four-step process that can elicit emotions as follows:

1. Recognize your emotions.
2. Recognize the emotions of others.
3. Imagining what it is like to walk in someone else's shoes.
4. Adjust your response accordingly.

Evocation

Evocation means that everything a client needs to change is inside of them, and it is the social worker's job to draw out a client's ideas, beliefs, goals, and desires (SAMHSA, 2019). Through listening, the social worker elicits information from the client that helps them understand their values and reasons why they want to change. The social worker is curious and inquisitive. The social worker gives the client the benefit of the doubt and believes that they want to and are capable of change. The goal is for the client to talk themselves into change as opposed to the social worker giving advice, educating the client, or presenting logical reasons why they should change.

When counselors affirm clients, emphasize their autonomy, strive for collaboration, and ask permission before giving information, they express a positive MI spirit and can be said to be using MI-consistent approaches.

MI and Social Work

Motivational interviewing is based on a humanistic approach to relationships that is highly consistent with the value base of social work. The spirit of MI leads a social worker to use interviewing skills and approaches that empower clients as experts of their own experiences and respects the client's autonomy and self-determination, two bedrock principles of social work. The spirit of motivational interviewing challenges social workers to take stock of their own values and how they are expressed in moment-to-moment encounters with clients. Social work values expressed in the NASW Code of Ethics, along with the orienting perspectives emphasized throughout this text, have a direct effect on the ways we communicate with clients. In addition to the strong and growing evidence base for the effectiveness of MI, motivational interviewing helps social workers focus on how their skills convey social work values. It is to these skills that we turn next.

MI Technical Skills

There are core skills when used that can improve client engagement and reduce conflict between social workers and clients. Chapters 5 and 6 discussed these skills in detail. What distinguishes MI from other approaches to social work is in its contingent application to encourage client change talk and to mute or reduce client sustain talk. Change talk are statements we make that signal our desire and need for change (e.g., "I really want to reduce racial inequality in my organization"), discuss the benefits of change (e.g., "working on racial inequality is the most important thing we can do right now"), our ability to change (e.g., "I am pretty good at labeling microaggressions when they happen"), and strategies that we can undertake to make change (e.g., "one thing I can do is 'call people in' to conversations about microaggressions when they happen). Of course, the strongest change talk are active steps already taken in the direction of change.

The technical skills of motivational interviewing are described in part by the acronym, OARS, which stands for:

- Use of **open**-ended questions
- **Affirmation**
- **Reflective** listening
- **Summarizing**

Use of Open-ended Questions

Open-ended questions invite clients to provide answers that are more likely to elicit details, encourages them to reflect, and requires elaboration. While closed-ended questions typically elicit yes/no answers and often stifle conversation, open-ended questions position clients to do more of the talking and use reflections purposefully to encourage further elaboration of change talk. For example:

> **Social worker:** What makes racial equity the most important contribution you can make to your agency right now?
>
> **Social worker:** What strategies do you use to "call people in" to conversations about racial equity and microaggressions?
>
> **Social worker:** I hear you saying that you are quite observant with people and how they communicate, that you notice when people are being slighted or demeaned.
>
> **Social worker:** Racial equity is important to you.

Affirmation

Affirmations are positive acknowledgements of appreciation and positive regard for clients (Miller & Rollnick, 2013). "By affirming, you are saying, "I see you, what you say matters, and I want to understand what you think and feel" (SAMHSA, 2019, p. 64, as cited in Miller & Rollnick, 2013). Using affirmations increases the likelihood that clients will act and experience positive client outcomes (Romano & Peters, 2016).

According to Miller and Rollnick (2013), Affirmations:

- Focus on a client's strengths, success, abilities, and gains no matter how small.
- Demonstrate you are listening to clients.
- Use "you" statements and when possible keep the focus on the client as opposed to the social worker.
- Require the social worker to look for positive things to highlight and continuously encourage the client toward change.
- Describe versus evaluate. Judgment can cause clients to freeze up and stop sharing with you.
- Account for racial, ethnic, cultural, and other types of difference

Reflective Listening

Reflective listening increases a social worker's ability to express empathy. According to Miller and Rollnick (2013), reflective listening

- Expresses respect and acceptance for who the client is and where they are at any given point in time.
- Can help social workers establish trust.
- Encourages clients to continue exploring their ideas, beliefs, values, and feelings.
- Facilitates a nonjudgmental, collaborative partnership between social workers and clients.
- Allows social workers to convey support without agreeing with everything a client says or does.

According to SAMHSA (2019), there are a variety of reflective listening communication responses:

- Repeating what the client said
- Rephrasing what the client said
- Restate what was said using feeling words
- Interpret meaning based on what the client says
- Acknowledge the desire to change and the difficulty associated with change
- Extreme amplification, which often draws attention to a client's minimization of behavior and the effects

Summarizing

Summarizing focuses on interpreting what the client says in its simplest form. Social workers take the essence of the client's values, beliefs, ideas, and perceptions and gives it back to them (SAMHSA, 2019). Social workers select specific statements and phrases that help them paint a picture for the client so that clients are able to reflect on what they have said. According to Miller and Rollnick (2013), there are different types of summarizations:

- Collecting summary: Connects a series of client statements that are related and tell a story for clients to reflect on.
- Linking summary: Connects a client's statement to what was said previously.
- Transitional summary: Helps the social worker wrap up one part of a session to move on to another.
- Ambivalence summary: Reflect back to clients any ambivalence they may have about sustain talk versus change talk, which provides opportunities for social workers to promote and encourage change talk while minimizing sustain talk (see section that follows on change versus sustain talk).
- Recapitulation summary: Takes conversations from various sessions and connects them. This is especially helpful when clients are moving through the helping process.
- Wrap-up summary: At the end of a session, summarize the session and ask the client whether you accurately reflected what they said. A wrap-up summary allows clients to correct something you have gotten wrong or add more for context. It also can be used to assign homework and forecast or foreshadow your next session and what you want to work on next.

Change Talk Versus Sustain Talk

The goal is to get clients to focus on change through engagement in change talk as opposed to why things may never change, also known as sustain talk. The objective of motivational interviewing is to have clients give reasons for change. When they do, change-related action is more likely. The other side of this is sustain talk. Sustain talk are those statements people make that constitute an argument against taking action to change. These are statements that focus on the challenges of adopting new behaviors (e.g., "I don't want to make conflict"), of pessimism about the possibility of making change (e.g., "this organization is so stuck in White supremacy, I don't think that whatever I can do would matter anyway"), and the desires most of us have to avoid change (e.g., "I just want to put my head down and get through this place").

It is important to recognize that sustain talk is natural and reflects real feelings that people have about adopting new behaviors or changing their circumstances. Thus, while the objective of MI is to increase change talk relative to sustain talk, sensitive social workers adopt a posture of acceptance and curiosity about sustain talk rather than an argumentative posture. Social workers who practice from an MI perspective do not ignore sustain talk. While seeking opportunities to elicit change talk, social workers can respond directly to sustain talk in ways that acknowledge their underlying challenges but soften them. For example:

- **Social worker:** I think I hear you saying that there is a cost to you for engaging in racial equity work.
- **Social worker:** When does it make sense to avoid conflict that comes with racial equity work, and when does it makes sense to jump into it?
- **Social worker:** It really is up to you to decide whether you have the internal resources for racial equity work right now.

The balance of change talk and sustain talk provides clues to ambivalence. Ambivalence is the state of feeling conflicted about making a change. It happens when we know that we want to make a change but can also think of reasons why we don't want to make a change. We want to exercise more but prefer sleep. We want to save money but also desire the temptations of treating others and ourselves. We want to be healthy, but we want to feel the benefits of whatever comes from our unhealthy choices. When clients express ambivalence, when they share change talk and sustain talk at the same time, your task is to adopt a posture of acceptance and curiosity about their sustain talk and actively seek a detailed elaboration of their change talk. This can be done through more complex reflections such as these examples:

- **Social worker:** It sounds like you are the kind of person who prefers to avoid conflict, but on the other hand, you have a way of "calling people" into dialogue. I imagine this can leave people feeling supported.
- **Social worker:** It sounds like you wish you could "put your head down and just get through it," but at the same time, racial equity work seems to be the most important contribution you can make.

MI with Involuntary Clients

As the evidence base for motivational interviewing has grown, its use has expanded to include systems that serve people who are mandated or involuntary. In recent times, MI training for probation officers and child welfare workers has become increasingly common. This growth has occurred because agencies are learning that collaborative approaches are more effective than coercive approaches most of the time.

While it may be counterintuitive that an approach built on acceptance and supporting client autonomy can support successful outcomes with mandated clients, there is good reason for optimism for MI in these settings. One reason is that MI disrupts relational dynamics associated with reactance. You may recall that reactance, or the tendency to resist the loss of freedom, occurs when people perceive that authority figures (social workers) are seeking to restrict or control their choices and when they perceive that authority figures are unfair in their decision-making. MI works in these settings precisely because the elements of MI spirit—acceptance, collaboration, compassion, and evocation—foster client self-determination and support client autonomy. When used with mandated clients, social workers do not deny their authority, nor do they deny the potentially coercive consequences that can follow noncompliance. These should be discussed openly. What MI enables social workers to do is focus on how clients make sense of requirements and make decisions about whether and how they wish to comply. When successful, the focus of client conversations is less about the social worker's authority and more about service mandates and what to do about them.

Ambivalence Regarding Change

Everyone at one time or another feels ambivalent regarding change. This is a normal response, particularly for involuntary clients who often are involved with social services through legal mandates or fear of losing an important relationship. Ambivalence is a fundamental concept of MI. It is important that social workers explore ambivalence with clients, as it can interfere with the change process.

Ambivalence has most often been associated with substance abuse treatment (SAMHSA, 2019). Prochaska et al. (1992) proposed a six-stage process of change (see Table 13-4).

Using the stages of change, social workers can identify where clients are on the continuum associated with change. There are also tips for each stage and how to potentially move clients along the continuum. The model begins with precontemplation, where the person has not considered or understood the behavior to be a problem.

In the motivational interviewing approach, the social worker takes responsibility for fostering a positive atmosphere for change based on accurate empathic understanding, mutual trust, acceptance, and understanding of the world that influenced the client's perspective (Miller & Rollnick, 2013).

Stages of change can be used to create an awareness that clients' behavior is dissonant with their personal goals. Through the use of OARS, social workers can assist the client in deciding whether it makes sense to explore a more manageable change.

Table 13-4   Stages of Change Model

Precontemplation	Client does not believe that they have a problem; is considered unmotivated by others	Raise awareness of concerns held by others: "What does your partner think about the effect of your drinking on your home life?" Stimulate dissonance with risk–benefit analysis: "What are the benefits to you from making your living by selling drugs? What are the costs to you from living by selling drugs?"
Contemplation	Becomes aware of the existence of the problem but is not moved to action. Appears ambivalent—shows awareness, then discounts it	Attempt to tip decisional balance by exploring reasons to change: "As you add it up, what do you think the benefits are in relation to the costs? If you get a legal job, then what?"
Preparation	Recognizes problem; asks what can be done to change. Appears motivated	Strengthen confidence in change as a possibility. Help client plan appropriate course of action
Action	Implements plan of action	Develop plan to implement action. Plan details to make it possible (e.g., transportation, childcare)
Maintenance	Sustains change through consistent application of strategies	Identify strategies to prevent lapses and relapse: "What have been the triggers to expose you to a dangerous situation?"
Relapse	Slips into problematic behavior and may return to precontemplation stage	Attempt to return to contemplation without being stuck or demoralized. Reinforce achievement; treat with respect: "This is a difficult time. You have been at this point before, and you overcame it. What do you think about whether you want to overcome it again?"

Source: Adapted from Kear-Colwell and Pollock (1997) and Prochaska et al. (1992).

Once a client has decided to act, the form of influence can help them decide which action to pursue. For example, after they have decided to deal with a domestic violence problem, the client can be guided toward consideration of alternatives for how to bring about this change. When a goal decision has been made, steps are then made to employ useful actions to reach the goal. When a change has occurred, efforts are aimed at exploring in detail the contingencies and triggers associated with the behavior. Armed with such knowledge, alternatives can be designed and practiced to avoid relapsing into the troubling or offending behavior.

Cognitive Behavioral Therapeutic Approach

Cognitive behavioral therapy (CBT) is a "structured, short-term, present-oriented" approach initially developed for depression (Beck, 1964, as cited in Beck, 2021, p. 3). Over time, it has been used with individuals from a variety of racial and ethnic groups and has been adapted to address myriad problems (Beck, 2021). CBT focuses on understanding a client's maladaptive beliefs and behavioral coping strategies that stem in part from how they think and see the world. These thought patterns often cause individuals to behave in ways that are not useful and often reinforce these beliefs (Beck, 2021). CBT is eclectic in that it pulls from different types of treatments such as dialectical behavior therapy (Linehan, 2018), exposure therapy (Foa & Rothbaum, 1998) and cognitive behavior modification to name a few (Beck, 2021).

CBT is intended to help clients modify their beliefs, faulty thought patterns or perceptions, and destructive verbalizations, thereby leading to changes in behavior. According to Beck (2021), dysfunctional thinking (which influences the client's mood and behavior) is common to all psychological disturbances. When people learn to evaluate their thinking…they experience a decrease in negative emotion and maladaptive behavior (p. 4). The underlying principle of CBT is if social workers can teach people how to interrupt or change these thoughts and find better ways of coping, there can be

C8

significant improvements in an individual's functioning and quality of life.

An assumption of CBT is that people often manifest cognitive distortions, which in turn affects their emotions and actions. Distortions are irrational thoughts derived from negative thoughts and beliefs that lead to unrealistic interpretations of people, events, or circumstances. Although a client may be aware of their thinking, they may still lack the skills needed to alter these negative thought patterns. CBT attempts to alter the client's interpretation of self and their environment. According to cognitive theorists, most social and behavioral problems or dysfunctions are directly related to the misconceptions that people hold about themselves and others (Beck, 2021).

Tenets of Cognitive Behavioral Therapy

The goal of CBT strategies is to increase the client's cognitive and behavioral skills to enhance their functioning. CBT assumes that people construct their own reality. It is within the realm of processing information that people assess and make judgments that fit into their cognitive schemas. According to the American Psychological Association (2017), CBT is based on three primary principles:

1. Psychological problems partially stem from faulty or unhelpful ways of thinking.

2. Psychological problems also stem from learned behavior that has become maladaptive over time.

3. An individual can learn to think and behave differently, thereby improving their symptoms and overall well-being.

The basic tenets of CBT focus on thinking (e.g., changing unhelpful, distorted thinking patterns) and behavior (e.g., maladaptive behavioral patterns). Table 13-5 outlines the steps used in CBT.

- **Thinking** is a primary determinant of behavior and involves statements that people say to or about themselves. This inner dialogue, rather than unconscious forces, is critical to understanding behavior. The ultimate goal of CBT is to help clients recognize when their thinking is distorted and reevaluate their thoughts based on reality. To fully grasp this first tenet, you must clearly differentiate thinking from feeling, as confusing feelings with thoughts tends to create problematic communications. This confusion can be observed in messages such as "I feel our relationship is on the rocks," or "I feel that the teacher does not like me." Here, the use of the word "feel" does not actually identify feelings, but rather, it embodies the client's thoughts or beliefs. Thoughts, per se, are devoid of feelings, although they are often accompanied by and generate feelings or emotions. Feelings consist of emotions, such as sadness, joy, or disappointment.

- **Cognitions** (i.e., thoughts) affect behavior, which is manifested in behavioral responses. Behavioral responses are a function of the cognitive processes of attention, retention, production, and motivation, as well as rewarding or unrewarding consequences (Bandura, 1986). Cognitions that lead to cognitive distortions or faulty thinking can be monitored and changed. There are three levels of cognitions. For lasting change, social workers must help the client address cognitions and beliefs on all three levels (Beck, 2021).

  - Automatic thoughts—most superficial and focus on immediate or initial thoughts (e.g., "I do not feel like doing that.").

  - Intermediate thoughts and beliefs—focus on underlying assumptions that people make (e.g., "If I ask them out, they will say no.").

  - Core beliefs—your thoughts and beliefs about yourself, others, and the world (e.g., "There is no one I can trust."; "The world is not safe.").

- **Behavioral change** involves assisting clients to make constructive change by focusing on their misconceptions and the extent to which they produce or contribute to their problems; helping clients face their fears, which are often based on faulty thinking; and learn to how to manage their behavior in more productive ways. The thrust is that a change in behavior can be accomplished by changing the way a client thinks.

Table 13-5 Steps in CBT

1. Assist clients in accepting that their self-statements, assumptions, and beliefs determine their emotional reactions to life's events. (Tool: explanation and treatment rationale)

2. Assist clients in identifying dysfunctional self-statements, beliefs, and thought patterns that underlie their problem. (Tool: self-monitoring)

3. Assist clients in identifying situations that engender dysfunctional cognitions.

4. Assist clients in replacing dysfunctional cognitions with functional self-statements.

5. Assist clients in identifying rewards and incentives for successful coping efforts.

In identifying distortions and faulty thoughts and behaviors, a basic assumption is that clients can learn new patterns of thinking. You should, of course, temper this assumption by recognizing that other factors influence a client's self-perception and the way the client thinks and processes information. Specifically, cognitions are not necessarily faulty, given the realities of culture, unequal sociopolitical structures, and social interactions in which class, race, gender, and sexual orientation are major contextual life issues. The realities of people's lives and beliefs have a significant impact on thinking and cognitions; therefore, the relationship between cognition, culture, and context should not be minimized or overlooked (Hays, 2009).

Helpful and Unhelpful Thought Patterns

Beck (1967), in separating thinking from cognition, identified automatic thoughts and helpful and unhelpful thought patterns as factors for which CBT is indicated. The processing of information for most of us is automatic, as our minds attempt to navigate and narrate our interactions and environment. Problems occur when thoughts are consistently unhelpful in that they have led to ingrained beliefs and faulty reasoning. While these thought patterns may be irrational, they are very real and make sense to the client. Unhelpful thought patterns often perpetuate negative thinking and reinforce negative emotions.

The most common types of unhelpful thought patterns conceptualized by Beck (1976) have been summarized in the literature (Cormier et al., 2009; Walsh, 2006). Table 13-6 describes beliefs and self-expectations that can lead to unhelpful thought patterns.

Some examples of unhelpful thought patterns are as follows:

- All-or-nothing thinking involves seeing things as all-or-nothing scenarios and, in most instances, seeing the glass as half empty. "I wanted to do well on the exam, and now that I didn't, I will never get into graduate school." "If I don't smoke stuff [dope] with my friends, they won't ever hang with me." "Unless we know the background of these clients, we won't be able to help them." In these statements, you may see the similarities between this thinking and catastrophizing and overgeneralizing.

- Blaming occurs when a client perceives others as the source of negative feelings or emotions and can, therefore, avoid taking responsibility. "I feel so stressed out because a driver cut in front of me on the way home." "Her snippy attitude about going shopping with me put me in a bad mood."

- Catastrophizing is the belief that if a particular event or situation occurs, the results would be unbearable, effectively influencing your sense of self-worth. "I need to study all the time because if I don't get the highest grade possible on the exam, I will lose my financial aid and return home a failure."

- Discounting positives is the tendency to disqualify or minimize the good things that you or others do and instead treat a positive as a negative. "My friends said that I looked great in an outfit from the secondhand store, but really, they were just being nice and feel sorry for me because I don't have money." Similarly, say you are reviewing evaluations after making a presentation and you focus on the following, "Of the 40 people at the presentation, two said that I was boring," instead of focusing on the 38 positive responses.

- Emotional reasoning guides your interpretation based on how you feel rather than on reality. Interpretations and beliefs are facts bolstered by negative emotions, which are assumed to reflect reality. "If I feel stuck [stupid] in social situations, then that's really who I am."

- Inability to disconfirm functions very much like a barricade in that you are unable to accept any information that is inconsistent with your beliefs or negative thoughts. For example, if a relative with whom

Table 13-6 Beliefs and Self-Expectations

Beliefs	Self-Expectations
Beliefs about oneself	I am usually not very good at anything that I do. My accomplishments aren't that significant; anyone could have done it.
Beliefs about others' perceptions and expectations of oneself	My partner dismisses my opinion because I am not very smart. When I compare myself with others, I never quite measure up.
Expectations of oneself	At work, I feel I must perform better than others in my unit. I should be able to do lots of things and perform at a high level.
Expectations of others	My daughter should understand how I feel without my having to tell her. She should want to visit me.

you frequently argue is unwilling to keep your kids because of an appointment, your mental response may be "That's not the real reason; the relative never liked me or my kids," in effect discounting the numerous other occasions on which the relative did care for your children.

- **Judgment focus** leads to a perception of self and others or an assessment of events as good or bad, excellent, or awful rather than describing, accepting, or attempting to understand what is happening or considering alternatives. "I know that when I go to a party people won't talk to me." In some instances, you may establish arbitrary standards by which you measure yourself, only to find that you are unable to perform at this level. "I won't do well in the class no matter how hard I try" is an example of a self-defeating judgment statement, as is "Everyone in the class gets good grades but not me." A judgment in contrast to one that is self-defeating is an assumption that a presentation was good because "a lot of people came."

- **Jumping to conclusions** assumes the negative when there may be limited supporting evidence. Assumptions may also take the form of mind reading and fortune telling based on a prediction of a negative outcome. "If I don't watch the children, she will be upset with me, a risk that I am unwilling to take."

- **Mind reading** assumes that you know what people will think, do, or respond. "There's no point in my asking my daughter to visit me more often. She will just see it as my attempt to get attention or embarrass her. If I bring up the topic, we will end up in an argument; besides, she is busy with her own family."

- **Negative (mental) filtering** results in mentally singling out bad events and ignoring the positives. "As I was standing in the hallway at work, this kid bumped into me, you know, they are all like that. I was so angry. Then he turned around and apologized, but I pretended not to hear him. He should have apologized sooner." In some instances, negative filters are linked to thoughts that are overgeneralized to people or events.

- **Overgeneralizations**, or globalization, involve perceiving isolated events and using them to reach broad conclusions. "Today, when I raised my hand in class, the instructor called on another student. He never calls on me." **Labeling** is another form of overgeneralizing in which a negative label is attached to self or others based on a single incident. "I am not a very good student, so the instructor does not value my opinion." "He is a lousy instructor; otherwise, he would help everyone [me]."

- **Personalizing** assumes that you had a role in or that you are responsible for a negative situation, assuming that the results were in your control. "We were close friends and then she was called to active duty, and we lost contact. I wonder if I did something that caused her to forget about me." Personalizing, when applied to others, is very much like blaming. "She could have written to me while she was away." "The party that I planned in the park was a failure because it rained, and people left early."

- **Regret orientation** is generally focused on the past. "If I had worked harder, I could have gotten a better grade." "I had a chance for a better job if I had been willing to relocate to a different city."

- **"Should" statements** are about self-failure or judgments about others relative to how things should be. "I should be able to take the bus on my own when I work late." "My sister ought to be willing to care for my child when I am working late." Judging statements about others generally result in feelings of resentment and anger. "My sister has a husband, so she doesn't really understand how hard it is for me to manage as a single parent."

- **Unfair comparisons** measure self against others believed to have desirable attributes. "She is prettier than I am." "Everybody in the class is smarter than me." "My college roommate is a CEO already; I'm nothing compared to him." Unfair comparisons can also lead to "I could or should be" or "I shouldn't be" statements when comparing self to others; for example, "My college roommate is a CEO already; I could have a job like that."

- **What ifs** refer to the tendency for people to continually question themselves about the potential for events or the catastrophe that might happen. "I would go to the doctor to examine the mole on my back, but what if I am really sick?" "What if I tell my relative that I can't watch the kids tonight, and they get upset with me and refuses to talk to me ever again?"

According to the American Psychological Association (2017), a primary goal of CBT is to teach clients how to recognize unhelpful thinking, problematic emotions, and maladaptive behaviors that limit an individual's ability to cope and help them learn to change these thoughts and behaviors that can lead to overall well-being. CBT emphasizes a person's current functioning as opposed to what led to their reasons for seeking help. While the history of one's life is important, the focus of your work with clients is helping them move forward and figure out more helpful ways of coping with life's challenges.

CBT sessions are structured. **Guided discovery** is a useful tool to teach clients to respond to unhelpful ways of thinking by asking them questions that help them see and evaluate their cognitions and identify alternative ways of viewing the same situation. The following types of questions can be helpful.

- What evidence do you have that lets you know your thoughts are true or untrue?
- What is another way to think about or an alternate explanation of the same situation?
- What is the worst thing that could happen if this thought is true?
- What is the best thing that could happen if this thought is true?
- How does this thought make you feel?
- How might you feel if you were to change your thinking?
- If a loved one was in the same situation, what would you say to tell them?
- What is a more positive way you could see this same situation?

While the particulars of your work with every client will be different, there are commonalities across clients that serve as the basis of your work (Beck, 2021). Beck Institute has developed 14 principles that help provide structure to your work with clients. This checklist can be used to evaluate your work with clients as well as help you assess your missteps should problems arise. According to Beck (2021):

1. CBT treatment plans are based on an ever-evolving cognitive conceptualization.
2. CBT requires a sound therapeutic relationship.
3. CBT continually monitors client progress.
4. CBT is culturally adapted and tailors treatment to the individual.
5. CBT emphasizes the positive.
6. CBT stresses collaboration and active participation.
7. CBT is aspirational, values based, and goal oriented.
8. CBT initially emphasizes the present.
9. CBT is educative.
10. CBT is time sensitive.
11. CBT sessions are structured.
12. CBT uses guided discovery and teaches clients to respond to their dysfunctional cognitions.
13. CBT includes action plans (therapy homework).
14. CBT uses a variety of techniques to change thinking, mood, and behavior (These principles are found in Beck (2021) *Cognitive behavior therapy: Basics and beyond*, 3rd edition, p. 16 or www.beckinstitute.org/CBTresources.)

CBT is recognized as the gold standard when working with clients (Beck, 2021). CBT can bring about lasting change when you emphasize the following:

- Recognize distorted thinking that leads to problems and how to help people reality test their thoughts to recognize the extent to which they are distorted.
- Understand people's motivations and how these motivations influence their behavior.
- Acknowledge the importance of problem-solving skills and how individuals use them to cope with difficult situations.
- Help people develop confidence in their ability to cope with problems and difficulties in effective ways.
- Work collaboratively with clients to develop a shared understanding of the problem and a treatment strategy.
- Help individuals learn to recognize distorted thinking and find ways to change their thinking, problematic emotions, and behavior.
- Focuses on present problems rather than what has led to current difficulties.

Strengths and Limitations of CBT

CBT is an effective procedure that is intended to address a range of problems related to a client's cognitions and thought patterns. There is research, first published in 1977, demonstrating that CBT is effective in addressing myriad problems including depression, anxiety disorders, alcohol and drug use problems, marital problems, eating disorders and severe mental illness (Beck, 2021). Research studies have shown the procedure to be particularly useful in altering perceptions, distorted beliefs, and thought patterns that result in negative or self-defeating behaviors. As a systematic process and problem-solving procedure, CBT is compatible with crisis intervention, the task-centered system, and solution-focused treatment.

In assisting clients to change, however, social workers must not mistakenly assume that clients will be able to perform new behaviors solely because of changes in their cognitions or beliefs. Clients may lack cognitive and social skills and require instruction and practice before they can effectively perform new behaviors. As noted by Vodde and Gallant (2002), simply changing one's story does not ensure a certain outcome, given the presence of very real external factors. such as oppression or rejection. For example, without an acknowledgment of oppression and racism, diverse clients may perceive CBT as blaming or just another form of social control and ideological domination.

Although cognitive theorists attribute most dysfunctional emotional and behavioral patterns to mistaken beliefs, dysfunctional emotions and beliefs are by no means the only causes. Dysfunctions may be produced by numerous biophysical problems, including brain injury, neurological disorders, thyroid imbalance, blood sugar imbalance, circulatory disorders associated with aging, ingestion of toxic substances, malnutrition, and other forms of chemical imbalance. These possibilities should be considered before undertaking CBT. Nonetheless, CBT can be a useful intervention procedure.

Trauma-Informed Care: An Overview of Concepts, Principles, and Resources

As a trauma-informed practitioner, it is important that you recognize that many of the clients you see in the course of your work have histories of trauma that may or may not be known to you. Consequently, trauma-informed care is a person-centered, strengths-based service delivery approach that recognizes the prevalence of trauma among clients across human services systems, is responsive to the physical, psychological, and emotional impact of trauma, and creates opportunities to rebuild a sense of control and empowerment" in their lives (Hopper et al., 2010, p. 82). A trauma-informed system of care requires a significant shift in an organization's culture, structure, programs, policies, and practices with particular attention paid to safety, connection, and helping client manage emotions that come from managing their daily lives (Bath, 2008).

Tenets of Trauma-Informed Care

Trauma-informed care was created because research has shown that "the development of safety, the promotion of healing relationships, and the teaching of self-management and coping skills" are essential elements of the healing process (Bath, 2008, p. 18). Regardless if you are a therapist, caseworker, or some other kind of social work practitioner, there are key tenets to trauma-informed care that serve as the basis of healing (van der Kolk & Courtois, 2005). With clients who have complex histories of trauma, social workers may need to incorporate a variety of treatment elements into their intervention. Nonetheless, tenets of trauma-informed care have three overarching themes: issues of safety, need for connection, and affect regulation, coping and self-management skills.

Safety

The establishment of trust is the basis of safety.

- Safety is a critical part of people's ability to engage in the change process.
- A lack of safety leads to pervasive mistrust of the world, others, and themselves.
- Healing can only happen when safety is present.
- Establishing safety can take time, but without safety, any intervention is likely to fail.
- Safety includes both physically and emotionally.
- "Consistency, reliability, predictability, availability, honesty, and transparency" are attributes of safe environments (Bath, 2008, p. 19).

Connection

- Validating a part of people's history that often has been dismissed or denied can strengthen and deepen your connection.
- Provide opportunities to plant seeds of hope and demonstrate to clients that they matter.
- Healing can only take place through the context of relationships.
- Therapeutic relationships result in positive change twice as much as the therapeutic techniques used.
- Positive interactions allow people to associate positive emotional responses, which helps them begin to distinguish between harmful and non-harmful people (van der Kolk, 2015).

Emotional Regulation and Coping Skills

- The most pervasive and harmful impact of trauma is the dysregulation of emotions and impulses (Bath, 2008, p. 20).
- Part of your work with individuals who have histories of trauma is to help them learn more helpful ways of managing their emotions and impulses.
- An individual's ability to learn how to regulate their emotions never goes away, even as they age.
- Self-reflection and helping individuals develop empowered versions of stories about their experiences are critical parts of the healing and recovery process (van der Kolk, 2015).

As social workers, it is critical that you understand how prevalent trauma is, the profound impact trauma has on a client's experiences, and recognize that trauma can rupture, even sever connections, causing a range of challenging behaviors. Trauma-informed care is intended to promote healing through creating a sense of safety, creating positive connections, and helping individuals learn how to regulate their emotion in positive, productive ways (Bath, 2008).

Theoretical Framework

Becoming trauma informed is not about simply checking boxes off a checklist or adopting a trauma-specific intervention. Rather, trauma-informed care is an approach which requires practitioners and organizations to use the most current knowledge regarding trauma-related symptoms to make significant shifts in terms of practices, policies, programming, structure, climate, and culture.

Sandra Bloom, Judith Herman, and Bessel van der Kolk are three well known scholars who have developed different models/principles that contribute to healing trauma and should be included in a trauma-informed approach. The Substance Abuse and Mental Health Services Administration (SAMHSA, 2012) also identified six key principles that should be included in a trauma-informed approach when working with clients who have experienced trauma. These six principles are discussed in Chapter 2.

We took facets of each of these approaches and combined them into a comprehensive approach model consisting of six phases to capture the essential components of a trauma-informed intervention strategy. These phases are not mutually exclusive; rather, they are meant as a guide with the full understanding that trauma-informed care is a complex, nonlinear process. Following each phase, we highlight specific actions and skills that we consider to be essential considerations.

Phases of Trauma-Informed Care

Phase 1: Building Trust and Establishing Safety

Given that a violation of trust and safety defines many traumatic experiences (e.g., sexual assault, physical abuse), trauma survivors are often reticent to trust others, including helping professionals, who may want to help them. Think of building trust and establishing safety as ongoing and challenging because, depending on the practice setting, our work with individuals is often time sensitive; the process of building trust and establishing safety can take months or even years (International Society for Traumatic Stress Studies, 2018). Van der Kolk (2015) suggests when trust appears to be stalled, asking the client what is happening and encouraging them to share their thoughts or concerns is important.

In general, building trust can be a balancing act in which the social workers are simultaneously mindful of time restrictions of settings, while also giving the client time to form trust and feel safe, in essence, starting where the client is.

In our work with clients, building trust and safety is essential for the therapeutic relationships to develop and for future therapeutic work. In working with clients who have experienced trauma, it is important to understand that social workers often expect clients to automatically trust them, but that trust needs to be earned and developed over time. Building trust is an evolving, ongoing process. Building trusting can be difficult for involuntary clients because of a deepened sense of vulnerability.

At times, client anger, negativity, or hesitancy to trust may appear to be directed at you, but it is often a reaction to past trauma. Do not let the pressure to move clinical work along (e.g., insurance time limits, long wait list of clients), overshadow the importance of establishing trust and safety. If you rush this phase, you may literally and/or figuratively lose the client. For example, a client may not show up for appointments or may simply show up because they must. In either case, the client is not fully engaged in the work to be done, and as a result, the established trust that the practitioner worked so hard to establish is forfeited.

To endure their trauma and stay safe and alive, many trauma survivors developed a heightened awareness of others' emotions and have an acute ability to read people and situations. Be transparent! Transparency is necessary to build trust and establish safety. Transparent social workers describe their social work interventions, the theories that guide their work, and how they view client change as well as encourage clients to seek clarification regarding the social worker's view of and hypotheses about the presenting problem. A transparent client–social worker relationship is one in which the social worker is open and honest with the client. For example, a parent who is involved with child protection might ask: "Will I lose custody of my children?" Transparency requires social workers to say: "It is possible. My goal is to do everything in my power to prevent that from happening, but I need your help."

Creating an open and collaborative relationship is particularly important for traumatized clients who often feel powerless and out of control. Maintaining trust and safety is an ongoing goal of trauma-informed care.

Phase 2: Collaborative Goal Setting

Traumatic experiences often rob individuals of power, autonomy, and choice. A central goal of trauma-informed social work practice is to empower clients by actively involving them in the helping process/treatment decisions.

Collaborative goal setting involves creating a partnership between the social worker and the client and together establishing treatment goals and a treatment plan. Collaboration is central in social work practice, especially with traumatized clients. Traumatic experiences rob victims of their autonomy and damages self-efficacy; therefore, collaboration can be a reparative and empowering experience for trauma survivors.

The social worker should not act as the omnipotent expert who dictates a treatment plan and the treatment modalities to be used. To the contrary, the social worker should communicate openly and transparently with the client, explaining the course of action they think is best and asking for client input and feedback. The social worker should also share initial impressions and hypotheses about the client's presenting problem and how those impressions and hypotheses inform decisions moving forward. For example, in situations in which intrusive thoughts of trauma are so severe that the client is unable to function in daily life, the social worker might suggest mindfulness relaxation skills such as deep breathing or body scanning exercises, as studies have found that meditation and mindfulness help reduce stress.

Traumatic experiences rob individuals of power, autonomy, and choice, and a central goal of trauma-informed social work practice is to restore these elements in clients. Therefore, clients should be encouraged to evaluate and provide feedback on their treatment goals and plan. In essence, being involved in treatment decisions empowers clients and gives them a sense of autonomy as well as control over their treatment. Collaborative goal setting creates a partnership between the social worker and the client, which serves to strengthen trust and enhance safety and the therapeutic alliance.

Phase 3: Reconciling and Managing Lived Experiences

When a traumatic event occurs, individuals try to identify or reconcile reasons why it happened to them. The result is usually self-blame; clients may feel that if they were different the traumatic experience would have never happened. Clients often make unspoken agreements to never allow themselves to be victimized again. These unspoken agreements often result in emotional, physical, psychological, or relational changes. In order to help clients manage the lived experience of trauma, social workers must understand the possible ways that trauma is manifesting itself emotionally, physically, psychologically, and relationally. Social workers can then help individuals manage and modulate the symptoms and the triggers associated with the trauma. Social workers also must help clients identify the primary ways

that they have coped with trauma and the impact these coping mechanisms are having or have had on their lives. Simultaneously, it is important to address any co-occurring disorders and help clients replace maladaptive ways of coping with healthier ones.

It may be important to explore with clients why they believe the trauma happened to them. This may give you an idea of some of the unspoken agreements they have made to never let it happen again. Further, it is a way to understand the client's trauma narrative and gain insight into parts of their story that may be affecting their lives but remain unconscious. Part of your work should be making that which is unconscious, conscious.

Clients might not realize that some of their symptoms are related to trauma. Psychoeducation (i.e., teaching clients about trauma and its impact) is important in terms of educating clients about the impact of trauma. During this phase, it is important to help the client identify how they have coped with trauma symptoms and identify effective and ineffective coping strategies to support them in replacing ineffective strategies with effective strategies. In this regard, the emphasis on effective strategies can be used to highlight their strengths.

Phase 4: Promoting Empowerment and Leveraging Power

Empowerment is an essential part of the healing process. Empowerment allows clients to understand that sometimes bad things just happen, and they did not do anything to cause it. Empowerment allows clients begin to choose as opposed to being a victim of circumstance. Empowerment helps clients understand that they have power and how to leverage that power in ways that help them reach their desired goals. Empowering clients is one way to help restore some of the power that the trauma stripped away.

You can assist clients to recognize and increase their power by (1) teaching clients to self-soothe or comfort themselves when they begin to feel distressed (Rosenbloom & Williams, 2010); (2) providing an array of choices and letting them decide how they want to act (self-determination); and (3) letting clients know that saying no or remaining silent is also an option. Like building trust and safety, promoting empowerment should be ongoing throughout your work. As a social worker, you should be constantly looking for ways to ensure empowerment is part of the helping process.

Phase 5: Strengthening Resilience

Resilience is the fortitude through which individuals' weather and navigate difficult situations and emerge stronger. This idea of resilience should not be used to blame people or not try to address systemic and structural factors that cause people to be resilient. Social workers must recognize that oppressive systems must also be addressed when doing resilience work. Building upon and strengthening resilience is important so that individuals recognize that they are more than the traumatic experiences. Strengthening resilience involves helping clients to see the positive aspects of their lives and find ways to build on these aspects to get clients where they want to be. Strengthening resilience is about helping clients see there are other ways of being and other ways are possible. First and perhaps foremost, it is important to help the individual recognize they are more than the traumatic event or, in some instances, serial or cumulative traumatic experiences.

This phase consists of helping clients identify factors that build or increase resilience. The process of engaging the individual in a conversation about resilience might begin with helping them identify a pretrauma sense of self and attributes, traits, or strengths that helped them cope. For example, engage the client in a conversation about people in the family, friendship, neighborhood, or religious organization and resources that were helpful in a time of need. This would include connecting with and surrounding themselves with certain people from these groups who can help with the process of healing and recovery. It also involves identifying and/or reestablishing connections and cultural practices that can be leveraged in their healing.

In this stage, social workers should help individuals highlight ways in which they have survived the traumatic experience(s) as well as strategies they can employ to strengthen their coping skills such as relying on friends, attending church, or going to therapy. Essentially, you are helping the client recognize how far that they have come.

Phase 6: Integration, Role Development, Creation of a New Possibilities

Think of this phase as a light at the end of a tunnel in which the client begins to envision a new beginning, reconnects to their sense of power, and assumes new or preexisting roles that move toward new relationships, roles, and coping. Creating new possibilities may not be an entirely linear process. The goal is to help the individual recognize a new sense of self and establish new possibilities and vision for themselves.

In this phase, clients are beginning to dream of new possibilities. It is similar to the brainstorming process. When you are brainstorming, there is no bad idea. The same is true when dreaming of new possibilities. Do not comment on the validity of the dream. Allow clients to shed the former role of victim for a new role. For example, if individuals are always seen as a sex worker no matter what they do, there is no incentive for them to be different. It is the possibility of being seen as a woman, mother, or grandmother that can motivate clients to work through their trauma. Ask the client to envision other roles or activities which facilitate a renewed sense of self and helps the client become active in a community group.

In this phase, especially if the individual feels stuck, it can be useful to develop questions to help them imagine new possibilities. The goal is to help the individual recognize a new sense of self and see ways in which they can begin to reconnect with people, the community, as well as establish new ways of behaving and being. In essence, the creation of new possibilities involves a vision of self as a survivor; hence, the question might be how you see yourself in the future, and what is possible in your relationship to others? In this new role, what do you envision yourself to be?

Recognize that while the creation of new possibilities and the shedding of old identities is exciting, it also has a lot of unknowns, which can be scary. Do not be surprised if a client relapses or reverts to old behaviors. In fact, anticipate it and build it into the process.

From the discussion of the six phases of trauma-informed care, shown in Table 13-7, we highlight tasks to be completed depending on whether the status of the client is voluntarily or involuntary. Involuntary clients differ from voluntary clients with respect to contact with professionals. Unlike those who are willing seek help, involuntary clients are most often individuals who are legally mandated to seek help. In both circumstances, most clients are people of color. (Rooney, 2009). The experience of trauma for clients of color can include the experience of oppression in everyday living. Help-seeking behavior for voluntary and involuntary clients are factors that can make encounters with helping professionals more difficult (Sue et al., 2016).

Trauma-Specific Treatment

It is important to differentiate between trauma-informed care and trauma-specific treatment as these terms are sometimes used interchangeably. Trauma-informed care is a practice framework that impacts organizational culture and practice; adopting a trauma-informed care approach requires training to ensure that clinicians have the skills needed to support trauma survivors (DeCandia et al., 2015). Trauma-specific treatments are clinical interventions that are implemented to address the symptoms of trauma such as posttraumatic stress disorder (PTSD) (DeCandia et al., 2015).

Table 13-7 Application of the Trauma-Informed Care Approach

Tasks Completed in This Phase	All Clients (e.g., Voluntary and Involuntary)	Involuntary Clients
Phase1: Building Trust and Establishing Safety	• Ask why the client has decided to seek help • Review your credentials, history, and how you believe you can help • Review mandated reporting and any other necessary regulations or processes, including clinic rules (e.g., policies regarding canceling or missing appointments) • Obtain signed consents for release of information to any relevant service providers and • Review what client hopes to get out of your work together • Review the safety of client and others involved, which may include a risk assessment	• Ask the client their story and what they believe led to their involvement in services. • Review the identified reasons that led to their involvement. • Review the extent of your power and authority • Explain to clients why you want to talk to other service providers. • If you need to make a referral for additional services, to the greatest extent possible, give the client a choice in providers • Ask if there is anyone that the client believes should be included in the process
Phase 2: Collaborative Goal Setting	• Remain consistent • Follow through on what you tell the client you will do, explain when you are not able to keep your word • Listen more than talk • Review what the client wants to get out of your work together • Collaboratively develop a treatment plan based on the client's stated goals	• While involuntary clients may have less control over their goal setting compared to voluntary clients, strive to make goal setting a collaborative process. The treatment plan must include the goals set by the third party (e.g., lawyers, judge), client should also be encouraged to identify goals. • Work with and include any service providers or stakeholders such as attorneys, judge, service providers, family members as necessary. • Find ways to stagger services, locate those services in conjunction with work, childcare, and other responsibilities clients may have and creating a realistic plan that provides the optimal chance for success.
Phase 3: Reconciling and Managing Lived Experiences	• Explore the primary ways that individuals have coped with trauma and the ways those coping mechanisms have helped and hindered them as well as any negative consequences resulting from the ways they have chosen to cope. • Help individuals modulate their emotions and triggers they have in response to dates, memories, people, and places. • Recognize that individuals may be grieving the loss of relationships, people, status, materials things and making space for the grieving and mourning often associated with trauma to take place.	• Help clients recognize the ways they manage what has happened to them and how maladaptive ways of managing lived experience could hurt their ability to successfully navigate the mandated system. • Assist, encourage, and facilitate the client's participation and completion of services and help them understand that their unwillingness to do so could have an adverse effect.

(Continued)

Table 13-7   Continued

Phase 4: Promoting Empowerment and Leveraging Power	• Look for small and big ways to empower individuals and help them regain control over their lives. • Work with clients to find advantageous ways to advocate for themselves and direct their power in ways that help them reach their desired goals. • Help clients to see the role that they have played in the state of their lives as well as help to put responsibility for trauma and abuse where it belongs.	• Be forthcoming about all information you have about the situation. Be upfront and honest about possible outcomes if clients fail to comply. • Discuss the goals/activities/ services that are negotiable and the ones that are nonnegotiable. • Anticipate that clients may be angry, not trust you, or shut down. When these things arise find ways not to take it personal (i.e., supervision). • Use neutral, nonbiased language when discussing the progress individuals have made or may not have made as well as any recommendations you may have.
Phase 5: Building and Strengthening Resilience	• Explore with clients what has worked or helped in the past. • Explore traditional or cultural practices that can be leveraged throughout the healing process. • Understand the ways that resilience and strength are supported by sociocultural factors such as environment, race, culture, and ethnicity.	• Be mindful of the fact that in restrictive settings (e.g., prison/ residential treatment), particularly when clients are trying new skills, resilience may look different. • Help clients build resilience and strengths in ways that it will not be problematic for them.
Phase 6: Integration, Role Development, Creation of a New Possibilities	• Assist the client in cultivating a new sense of self beyond the trauma experience. • Help clients to explore, restore, and/or establish new relationships that recognize, respect who they want to become. • Review the progress achieved and invite the individual to imagine a new future.	• Be mindful of the fact that cultivation of a renewed sense of self may be difficult for involuntary clients to imagine. Like empowerment, cultivating a sense of self beyond the trauma and as well as the restrictive environment can help the individual to think about the future and act toward developing new roles and behaviors.

There are a variety of evidence-informed practices that are considered trauma-specific treatments. Presently, cognitive behavior treatment (CBT) and trauma-focused CBT (TF-CBT) are the most widely used interventions in treating trauma and are regarded as the most promising (Cohen et al., 2016; Deblinger et al., 2016; Morgan-Mullane, 2018; Pollio & Deblinger, 2017). These trauma-informed treatments include cultural adaptations (Lau, 2006).

There is emerging evidence that eye movement desensitization and reprocessing (EMDR) also is efficacious in treating trauma (Moreno-Alcazar et al., 2017). Additionally, nontraditional forms of healing such as yoga and mindfulness also are being utilized in the treatment of trauma (van der Kolk et al., 2014). *The Body Keeps Score* by van der Kolk (2014) explores practices such as yoga and meditation that have resulted in a significant reduction in PTSD symptomology by individuals who have histories of trauma.

Strengths and Limitations of Trauma-Informed Care

Providing trauma-informed care ensures that best practice is implemented with social work clients. A trauma-informed approach provides clients with the support and the understanding necessary to begin talking about and coping with traumatic experiences. This approach is versatile and can and should be used with all clients, even if they have not yet disclosed a traumatic history. The nonjudgmental, collaborative, and supportive orientation provided by a trauma-informed approach enhances client resilience and confidence, helping clients meet their treatment goals. Further, using trauma-informed care increases the likelihood that clients can move forward.

Although all social workers should be trained in and practice trauma-informed care, not all organizations and systems support this framework. Trauma-informed care is a relatively new approach (Kira et al., 2015). We have included this framework because of the prevalence of trauma in our society. There is a lot of ambiguity around what trauma-informed care is and is not, and as such, outside supervision from a trauma-informed supervisor might be the best we have until this framework is further developed.

Mind–Body Interventions

The use of mind–body interventions has more than doubled among adults in the United States, emerging as a promising approach to health and wellness (National Center for Complementary & Integrative Health, 2016). There are a variety of mind–body interventions that aid in relaxation, improved concentration, and increased movement and flexibility. The most common types of interventions are yoga, mindfulness and meditation, movement therapies such as tai chi and qigong, massage, acupuncture among other types of treatment.

Yoga is a Hindu spiritual discipline that focuses on breathing, meditation, and specific body postures that increase health and relaxation (Gothe et al., 2014). Mindfulness and meditation involve sitting or walking in which individuals are aware of thoughts, feelings, and bodily sensations. Tai chi and qigong also are traditional form of Chinese mind–body movement practices that combine movement, breathing, and a strong focus on training the mind (Richman, 2019). Massage is the rubbing, squeezing, and kneading of body parts with the intent to relieve tightness, tension, and pain. Acupuncture is a type of integrative medicine originating in China consisting of sticking the skin with needles to treat pain and alleviate physical, mental, and emotional ailments. Biofeedback, meditation, guided imagery, and hypnosis are other examples of these types of interventions (Bo et al., 2017). Mind–body interventions are widely used by individuals with a variety of conditions such as fibromyalgia, cancer (Hall et al.,

2018), diabetes, anxiety (Trevino et al., 2020), depression and other types of mood disturbance (Matchim et al., 2011; Musial et al., 2011), stress-related issues (Niles et al., 2018), sexual difficulties, insomnia (Neuendorf et al., 2015), endometriosis (Evans et al., 2019); stroke survivors (Love et al., 2019); neuropsychiatric symptoms (Purohit et al., 2013), schizophrenia, and posttraumatic stress disorder (Cushing & Braun, 2018; Purohit et al., 2013; Sabe et al., 2019).

These types of intervention have been used with various populations such as older adults (Ebner, 2020); menopausal women and breast cancer survivors (Stefanopoulou et al., 2017); and mental health practitioners (Bandealy et al., 2021). According to Richman (2019), mind–body interventions are becoming increasingly popular by the Veterans Administration as standalone treatments as well as used in conjunction with standard treatments for veterans. Yoga and mindfulness have been utilized with individuals in the armed forces (Jha, 2015) as well as individuals who are incarcerated (Onek, 2013) as a way to treat posttraumatic stress disorder, anxiety, and depression.

This alternate form of therapy is intended to improve psychological and physical well-being. Mind–body therapies can disrupt or minimize unhelpful thoughts, behavior, and feelings that often contribute or interfere with peoples' ability to cope with their physical and mental health symptoms. The underlying principles of mind–body interventions are that mind and body are interconnected and can affect overall health. In other words, an individual's mental health can affect their physical health. Further, mind–body interventions enable clients to take an active role in their treatment, increase their ability to cope, and enhance their overall well-being and quality of life (Matchim, et al., 2011; Musial, et al., 2011; Niles et al., 2018).

Example 1: Grounding

Grounding is a tool that can interrupt or help a person manage anxiety, flashbacks associated with trauma, or other types of emotions that are overwhelming (Legg & Caporuscio, 2020). Grounding also can reduce the intensity of a person's feelings by creating a distraction in which they engage their five senses to focus on something else other than what is causing them anxiety or triggering a flashback. Anxiety and flashbacks often take people from present moment and focuses their attention on the past (i.e., what has already happened) or the future (i.e., what might happen). Grounding brings people back to the present moment.

There are several grounding techniques. A popular grounding technique is the 54321. According to Legg and Raypole (2019), the 54321, a technique also known as the five senses, involves the following:

- Name five things you can see in the room with you (e.g., TV, artwork)
- Name four things you can feel (e.g., temperature in the room; chair is uncomfortable)
- Name three things you can hear right now (e.g., your voice, breathing, laughter)
- Name two things you can smell right now (e.g., cologne, someone's lunch)
- Name one good thing about yourself (e.g., I am capable).

There are other types of grounding techniques many of which are sensory related (Legg & Raypole, 2019).

- Imagining smelling chocolate chip cookies, roses.
- Think back to a time when you held an object, such as a baby, seashell, a book in your hands.
- Imagining you are at your favorite concert. What song is playing?

Example 2: Mindfulness

Mindfulness is defined as "the awareness that emerges through paying attention on purpose, in the present moment, and nonjudgmentally to the unfolding of experience moment by moment" (Kabat-Zinn, 2005, p. 125). Decker et al. (2019) used mindfulness with MSW students. At the start of class, a student led the class by choosing a positive affirmation. For example,

- *I am changing the world around me in powerful ways.*

   Procedure: Students were encouraged to close their eyes if they chose, listen closely to the words, and focus their connection on their internal experience as it relates to their clinical work. After the class opened with the entire group engaged in the positive affirmation, students were given the assignment to research a mindfulness technique and prepare themselves to teach it to the class. Each week, a different student would start the class with that affirmation and then lead the class in a mindfulness, meditation, or breathing exercise they selected. This gave students the opportunity to experience group work from the perspective of a member as well as a leader. Success was further encouraged by students having a proscribed activity (the positive affirmation) that was familiar and organized, followed by a structured opportunity to design their own curriculum and leadership/teaching style (Decker et al., 2019, p. 314).

As a result of this mindfulness exercise, MSW students reported they felt more confident and competent to work with clients, their anxiety was reduced, and they gained skills and knowledge regarding how to work with different populations using these techniques and tools (Decker et al., 2019). Additionally, researching techniques and teaching them to other students allowed them to experience and learn how to deal with unanticipated challenges. This applied learning experience taught MSW basic intervention, group work skills, and the importance of self-care, which led to increased confidence and belief in their ability to contribute to the well-being of others in significant, tangible ways (Decker et al., 2019).

Strengths and Limitations of Mind–Body Interventions

Mind–body interventions are increasing in popularity in the United States. They are alternatives to traditional medicine that have shown promise (Nile et al., 2018; Purohit et al., 2013). Clinicians, social workers, physicians, psychiatrists, and other professionals have shown a great deal of interest these alternative treatments as they have very few negative side effects (Richman, 2019). Nonetheless, there is not the same level of evidence regarding all mind–body interventions. Yoga is the most common mind–body therapy that has been studied (Husebo & Husebo, 2017). There is less support for other kinds of mind–body practices in terms of their ability to improve clients' quality of life (Husebo & Husebo, 2017). According to Mayden (2012),

> While some evidence supports mindfulness-based stress reduction, relaxation therapy, cognitive behavioral therapy, hypnosis, biofeedback, music therapy, art therapy, support groups, and aromatherapy as having a place in effective complementary measure for symptom management and improved quality of life, research findings are mixed; additional randomized controlled trials are needed to fully define the optimal use of mind–body therapies (p. 369).

Given the increasing popularity of mind–body interventions, there is a need for more rigorous studies that demonstrates the different types of interventions and the types of ailments they are most effective at treating (Richman, 2019).

Summary

Change strategies are an important part of the helping process as it is the vehicle through which change is possible. In this chapter, we have reviewed several approaches, strategies, and interventions. Some of them are evidenced based, and some rely on practice wisdom of different cultures and customs. We also provided examples of questions that may be used in the selection of an intervention strategy along with factors to be considered in the process, such as evaluating the extent to which an approach has demonstrated its effectiveness, with whom, under what circumstances, and with what types of problems. The theoretical framework and empirical support for each of the approaches were summarized. We have by no means reviewed all strategies and interventions that exist. We merely have identified the strategies and the interventions that we believe will be most useful for new social workers.

Competency Notes

C1 Demonstrate Ethical and Professional Behavior

- Make ethical decisions by applying the standards of the NASW Code of Ethics, relevant laws and regulation, models for ethical decision making, ethical conduct of research, and additional codes of ethics as appropriate to context.

C4 Engage in Practice-Informed Research and Research-Informed Practice

- Apply research findings to inform and improve practice, policy, and programs.

C6 Engage with Individuals, Families, Groups, Organizations, and Communities

- Apply knowledge of human behavior and person-in-environment, and other multidisciplinary theoretical frameworks to engage with clients and constituencies.

C7 Assess Individuals, Families, Groups, Organizations, and Communities

- Demonstrate respect for client self-determination during the assessment process collaborating with clients and constituencies in developing mutually agreed-on goals.
- Apply knowledge of human behavior and person-in-environment and other culturally responsive multidisciplinary theoretical frameworks when assessing clients and constituencies.

C8 Intervene with Individuals, Families, Groups, Organizations, and Communities

- Engage with clients and constituencies to critically choose and implement culturally responsive, evidenced-based interventions to achieve mutually agreed-on practice goals and enhance capacities of clients and constituencies.

C9 Evaluate Practice with Individuals, Families, Groups, Organizations, and Communities

- Select and use appropriate methods for evaluation of outcome.
- Critically analyze outcomes and apply evaluation findings to improve practice effectiveness with individuals, families, groups, organizations, and communities.

Skill Development Exercises

Planning and Implementing Intervention

1. Select the task-centered and solution-focused approach as an intervention and assess the merits of each approach in this case. In what way could you combine aspects of both approaches in this case?

2. A mother who has been sanctioned for failing to comply with the welfare-to-work rule tells you that her caseworker is "out to get her." What additional information or factors would you consider determining how to respond to the client's statement?

3. You are the social worker for a minor in a residential treatment program. How would you determine if the minor is able to give consent for his treatment plan?

4. Review Lipchik's (2002) solution-focused questions and answer the questions based on a current concern that you have. Indicate how you would use scaling, coping, exceptions, and the miracle question.

5. Using the same situation that you have identified, develop a goal using general and specific tasks in the task-centered approach. Indicate how you would measure goal attainment.

6. Choose one of the cognitive distortion statements that you may have used. What strategies would you use to modify your thinking?

7. Review what you have learned about trauma and the principles of trauma-informed care. Reflect on how you might change the way in which you complete an assessment of clients.

Balancing Micro and Macro Social Work Practice: Roles, Theories, and Intervention Strategies

Chapter Overview

Chapter 14 transitions from direct practice assessment and intervention to macro-level intervention strategies. In this chapter, you will become familiar with assessing macro-level problems and utilizing change efforts directed toward systems that benefit individuals as members of groups and communities. Relevant macro-level theories and other factors affecting macro-level practice are discussed. Finally, this chapter concludes with a discussion of the helping process and what it looks like at the macro practice level.

After reading this chapter, you will acquire knowledge that will enable you to:

- Define and understand the scope of macro practice
- Understand the link between micro and macro practice.
- Explore what micro and macro practice have in common.
- Use assessment questions and other available sources of data to guide intervention decisions.
- Evaluate macro practice activities.

The EPAS Competencies in Chapter 14

This chapter provides information that you will need to meet the following practice competencies:

- Competency 1: Demonstrate Ethical and Professional Behavior
- Competency 2: Engage Antiracism, Diversity, Equity, and Inclusion in Practice
- Competency 3: Advance Human Rights and Social, Economic, and Environmental Justice

- Competency 5: Engage in Policy Practice
- Competency 7: Assess Individuals, Families, Groups, Organizations, and Communities
- Competency 8: Intervene with Individuals, Families, Groups, Organizations, and Communities
- Competency 9: Evaluate Practice with Individuals, Families, Groups, Organizations, and Communities

Defining Macro Practice

Mary Richmond and Jane Addams are "the two most influential women in the history of the social work profession" (Franklin, 1986, p. 505). Mary Ellen Richmond is a American social work pioneer. She founded social casework (micro practice) and is considered one of the mothers of professional social work. Mary Richmond is credited with creating the terms "micro" and "macro" social work practice (Richmond, 1922 as cited in Androff & McPherson, 2014). Mary Richmond believed social work should focus on helping individuals and families directly. Jane Addams believed that problems stemmed from social structures, and, therefore, our interventions needed to focus on shifting and changing social structures (Androff & McPherson, 2014). Micro practice takes an individual view, while macro practice takes a broader 30,000-foot view focusing on transforming communities, organizations, institutions, and social structures (Meenaghan et al., 2005).

Macro practice is the overarching and all-encompassing term used to categorize practice that focuses on and facilitates change in organizations, communities, groups, and policy-making levels (Austin et al., 2005; Meenaghan et al., 2005). Brueggemann (2006) summarizes macro social work as the "practice of helping people solve social problems and make social change at the community, organizational, societal and global levels" (p. 7).

Macro social work often is known by different names. Community-centered practice refers to the "planning and organizing of neighborhood and community change based on addressing social problems within the social environment" (Austin et al., 2005, p. 13). Community practice involves empowering individuals to develop, change, and advocate for and engage in socioeconomic and political action to build and sustain communities (Weil, 2005).

Macro-level work broadly focuses on three areas:

- Community organizing
  - Neighborhood and community organizing
  - Socioeconomic and sustainable development
  - Community development
- Organizational assessment and development
  - Social planning
  - Program development
  - Agency/program management
  - Human service management
- Policy development, analysis, social action
  - Coalition building and advocacy work

- Political and social action and social movements intended to bring about progressive change (Austin et al., 2005; Hassan & Wimpfheimer, 2014; Jansson, 2014; Weil et al., 2013).

Macro-Level Practice Skills

Macro-level practice skills consist of:

- Maximizing consumer participation
- Social planning for community change
- Social development
- Program development and evaluation
- Policy analysis
- Management and administration
- Budgeting and grant writing

Macro-Level Social Work Roles

Macro-level social workers assume roles in a variety of capacities:

- Program evaluators
- Researchers
- Community organizers
- Lobbyists
- Legislative aides
- Advocates
- Grant writers
- Policymakers
- Social service administrators such as program directors, supervisors, and executive directors (Ritter et al., 2009)

The underlying rationale of macro social work practice is the belief that seeing the whole picture and intervening can ultimately change and improve people's lives (Burghardt, 2011; Long et al., 2006). In examining the whole picture, social workers can determine the impact of an issue on human behavior (Alexander, 2010; McKinnon, 2008; Saleebey, 2004).

The Link Between Micro and Macro Practice

There is a well-known parable about babies floating downstream. We all have heard some version of this story. This parable does a great job illustrating the link between micro and macro practice. The dilemma that this parable presents has implications for practice and the future of the social work profession.

One day, a group of villagers was working in the fields by a river. Suddenly, someone noticed a baby floating

C5

downstream. A woman rushed out and rescued the baby, brought it to shore, and cared for it. During the next several days, more babies were found floating downstream, and the villagers rescued them, but before long, there was a steady stream of babies floating downstream. Soon, the whole village was involved in the many tasks of rescue work: pulling these poor children out of the stream; ensuring they were properly fed, clothed, and housed; and integrating them into the life of the village. While not all the babies, now very numerous, could be saved, the villagers felt they were doing well to save as many as they did.

Before long, however, the village became exhausted with all this rescue work. Some villagers suggested they go upstream to discover how all these babies were getting into the river in the first place. Had a mysterious illness stricken these poor children? Had the shoreline been made unsafe by an earthquake? Was some hateful person throwing them in deliberately? Was an even more exhausted village upstream abandoning them out of hopelessness?

A huge controversy erupted in the village. One group argued that every possible hand was needed to save the babies, since they barely kept up with the current flow. The other group argued that if they found out how those babies were getting into the water further upstream, they could repair the situation up there to save all the babies and eliminate the need for those costly rescue operations downstream.

"Don't you see," cried some, "if we find out how they're getting in the river, we can stop the problem, and no babies will drown? By going upstream, we can eliminate the cause of the problem! But it's too risky," said the village elders. "It might fail. It's not for us to change the system, and besides, how would we occupy ourselves if we no longer had this to do?" (Mayer, 2008, 1-2).

Micro practice represents the rescue work. Every day, social workers help people in need. They work alongside people to enhance their well-being and ensure their basic needs are met. Macro practice requires social workers to go upstream and determine why so many babies end up in the water and then develop safety nets and other measures to lessen or eliminate babies in the stream. For social workers to create lasting change, it is important to embrace micro and macro practices.

In the United States, the social work profession is commonly divided between micro and macro practice, and students often are forced to choose one or the other (Healy, 2008). However, this dichotomy should not exist (Dooley et al., 2009; Dudziak & Profitt, 2012) because

micro and macro practice are interconnected. However, macro practice is underdeveloped (Shapiro et al., 2013). Secializing in one area of practice does not absolve social workers from needing to understand the other. Social workers must understand how micro and macro practice is interconnected, despite social work having far more interventions and evidence-based practices for micro practice.

Failing to recognize the role of both micro and macro practice severely compromises social workers' ability to advocate for meaningful social justice (Specht & Courtney, 1994). Ensuring students see the connection is why we have included a chapter about macro social work practice in a direct practice textbook (Rothman & Mizrahi, 2014).

The micro-to-macro continuum is a natural extension of helping clients deal with the social problems, conditions, and policies that affect their lives. Understanding this continuum helps practitioners be aware of issues beyond individuals, families, or groups (Hasenfeld & Garrow, 2012; Rothman & Mizrahi, 2014). Connecting micro and macro practices place social workers in an opportune position to connect micro concerns to macro strategies.

Observations of the experiences of individual clients, as illustrated in Figure 14-1, can be the basis of the critical linkage between micro and macro practice. Figure 14-1 illustrates how micro-level observations can inform social workers' understanding of common problems and conditions experienced by individuals, groups, and communities. For example, as a social worker, you work with noncustodial fathers around child support and father involvement. In your work with fathers, you become aware that the law sends fathers to jail who fail to pay child support. As an initial inquiry into the problem, you might ask yourself: To what extent are individual problems pervasive among larger groups? The question provides a snapshot of the whole picture and the information that would inform a macro-level assessment of a problem (Breton, 2006; Burghardt, 2011). In other words, the macro-level assessment uncovers that failing to comply with child support orders primarily affects poor fathers.

Figure 14-1 Linking Micro and Macro Practice

Approximately 76% of fathers who owe past-due child support earn less than $15,000 per year (Hahn et al., 2019). When fathers cannot pay child support, their driver's and professional licenses can be suspended (Hahn et al., 2019). The government can garnish up to 65% of their paycheck. Additionally, fathers often are jailed for their inability to pay child support, which results in them losing jobs that would allow them to contribute financially. It also decreases the likelihood of finding work resulting from criminal records (Hahn et al., 2019; Pate, 2016).

In essence, the question bridges micro and macro practice by moving the focus beyond an individual's problem. Figure 14-1 identifies the ways in which macros and micro practice are interconnected. To further inform the inquiry, assess and document the individual and external factors associated with the problem— for example, substantive socioeconomic conditions that create, perpetuate, and sustain individual client problems (Vodde & Gallant, 2002). In the example, if fathers are poor and trapped in low-wage jobs, they are not intentionally failing to pay child support. They are unable to afford to pay child support. Moreover, suspending driver's and professionals licenses or jailing fathers for their inability to pay is antithetical to the problem these consequences are trying to solve.

Because of the dual, interlocking connection between the public and the private, there are times when a two-prong approach, specifically a combination of micro and macro, is required (Austin et al., 2005; Long et al., 2006).

What Micro and Macro Practice Have in Common

While the differences between micro and macro practice have become more entrenched over the years, several factors transcend both types of practice. Austin et al. (2016) identified a foundation that both micro and macro practices share.

C5

1. Micro and macro practice value advocacy and pursuit of social justice, whether at the individual or systemic levels.

2. Both micro and macro practices evolve and change as new issues arise (e.g., racism related to mass police killings, normalization of same-sex marriages, realities of a living wage) that need to be viewed and understood using social work values.

3. Both micro and macro practitioners are committed to providing high-quality services and socially just, equitable outcomes for individuals, families, groups, communities, and organizations.

4. Both micro and macro practice are vested in promoting and advocating for self-sufficiency and self-determination.

   Both micro and macro practitioners are committed to promoting positive outcomes and increasing accountability to major stakeholders.

Overlapping Skill Sets

In addition to their shared foundation, micro and macro practice have overlapping skill sets (Austin et al., 2016; Hardina & Obel-Jorgensen, 2009). The following are skills that are used in both micro and macro practice:

- Relationship building, which encompasses engagement, creates and establishes trust, and partners with clients and community members
- Assessment of the interplay between the client, the community, and the environment
- Developing, identifying, and monitoring change strategies
- Using self to promote empowerment at the client and community levels
- Using empathy
- Cultural sensitivity and an openness to learn from the community, identifying and building on strengths (Austin et al., 2005)
- Using self-awareness and reflective practice to ensure ethical behaviors, attitudes, and beliefs are being promoted
- Engaging in cultural competence and cultural humility
- Commitment to the process of intervening that includes engagement, problem identification, and assessment
- Facilitating self-determination and client empowerment
- Weighing and evaluating the ethical implications of strategies and outcomes, particularly when related to vulnerable and marginalized communities

Macro-Level Theories

Theories in social science provide ways to understand, explain, and examine a wide range of social problems (e.g.., child abuse, community violence, marital and family problems), the nature of problems, and different ways to affect change.

C7

Table 14-1

The above child support case example highlights how a macro systems issue can cause a micro-level problem. What are some macro-level solutions social workers could engage in to try to address this problem?

There are a variety of macro-level theories, perspectives, and frameworks that inform macro-level change.

Bioecological Systems Theory

Urie Bronfenbrenner (1979) is arguably the most widely cited theorist when describing the bioecological systems theory, formally known as ecological theory. The bioecological systems theory is a tool for understanding individuals, families, organizations, communities, and their surrounding environments. Every individual, family, organization, and community is embedded within interconnected complex systems governed by roles, norms, and rules that influence development within the context of their environment and societal landscape (Darling, 2007; Paquette & Ryan, 2001). To understand individuals, families, organizations, and communities, we must understand the entity and the immediate context and interactions within the larger environment (Paquette & Ryan, 2001).

Systems Theory

Systems theory views families, groups, organizations, and communities as living systems. The underlying rationale of the systems theory is that families, groups, organizations, and communities are greater than their parts. Therefore, when problems occur within these entities, it is essential to look at how various components affect the system. Systems theory shifts the belief that problems and solutions to the problem reside in the individual. Social work practitioners must examine problems through the relationships within these systems to promote change when working with groups and communities. It is essential to focus on the subsystems that interacts with and are influenced by larger systems in the social environment. An important consideration is an extent to which these subsystems are marginalized or have a relationship that promotes and sustains growth and development. For example, do groups and communities have equitable access to resources and have power over the decisions that affect their functioning?

Other Factors Affecting Macro Practice

There are a variety of other factors that affect macro practice. While they do not rise to the level of a theory, they have a profound effect on the overall well-being and experiences of groups of people and communities of color.

Structural Racism

Racism comes in many different forms. Often, when we think of racism, we tend to focus on individual acts committed by white supremacists. Racism is part of the fabric of U.S. society. The U.S. Constitution begins with "we the people." In 1776, "we" only referred to white, land-owning, Anglo-Saxon men. Racism in the United States is systemic and pervasive. According to the Lawrence et al. (2004), structural racism refers to:

> "A system in which public policies, institutional practices, cultural representations, and other norms work in various, often reinforcing ways to perpetuate racial group inequity. It identifies dimensions of our history and culture that have allowed privileges associated with 'whiteness' and disadvantages associated with "color" to endure and adapt over time" (p. 11).

Structural racism is a system that rewards privilege. Black people frequently are on the lower end of the privilege scale. They have the least number of advantages and resources and are more likely to experience the harshest punishments of any group for nonconformity. On the other end of the privilege scale, individuals receive access to opportunities, benefits, and power that historically has been associated with and reserved for whiteness (Lawrence et al., 2004). These privileges are believed to be earned. The predominant belief and narrative is if Black people or other people of color worked hard enough they too could reap the benefits of privilege, which is simply not true for many reasons.

As soon as people of color began to gain access, two things typically happen. The first thing that happens is the rules of the games change. For example, Ivy League institutions use a variety of factors when considering admission decisions, of which race/national origin is one factor. White students have enjoyed access to these institutions based on criteria that elevated predominantly white, affluent applicants. However, some Asian groups of students have cracked the testing and educational codes through stronger SAT scores and higher grades that allowed them to gain access at higher rates relative to their population (Golden, 2017). Consequently, they were taking too many seats from "deserving white students." White students began protesting and suing these institutions, bringing the colleges' admissions practice under scrutiny (Golden, 2017).

Ivy League admission departments began comparing Asian students to one another while white students were still being compared to the whole applicant pool. This amounted to an informal quota system restoring "white affirmative action" practices which gave preference to white applicants, "children of alumni, big nonalumni donors, politicians, and celebrities, as well as recruited athletes in upper-crust sports like golf, sailing, horseback riding, crew and even, at some colleges, polo" (Golden, 2017, para. 4).

Another strategy used to restore status quo is the actual rules are scrutinized. There has been an increase in reverse discrimination cases brought against companies for trying to increase diversity in its leadership positions (Mulvaney, 2020). The U.S. Labor Department scrutinized Microsoft and Wells Fargo, stating that their intent to double their ranks of Black leaders is at odds with Department of Labor practices (Smith, 2020). According to Mulvaney (2020),

"This development could make employers hesitate to take on new diversity measures when faced with the threat of agency enforcement and sanctions, as well as 'reverse' bias lawsuits that can lead to damages...The real result here is that there will be a lot of confusion about reverse discrimination claims, which could have a chilling effect, not because they are violating the law, but because of a large misunderstanding of what companies can do on their own volition to combat racism or sexism in the workplace (para. 3 & 4)."

According to Smith (2020), more than a half of century after the 1964 Civil Rights Act was issued, African American representation in corporate leadership is still woefully low. At Microsoft, Black people hold less than 3% of positions in executive and management job categories as of last year, according to the company's annual report (para. 4). Ashkenas, Park, and Pearce (2017) report that "even after decades of affirmative action, Black and Hispanic students are more underrepresented at the nation's top colleges and universities than they were 35 years ago, according to a New York Times analysis. (para. 1)" What is believed to be unfair advantage is really a level of the playing field because whites have enjoyed unmitigated access to resources once this is threatened reverse discrimination is assumed to be operating.

The structural racism lens highlights the fact that whiteness in terms of its dominance, superiority, and privilege are the norm. Droves of Black students who were rejected to Ivy League colleges did not file lawsuits against these colleges for discrimination. They may have assumed something was wrong or discriminatory about the system, but they accepted the decision and moved on (James, 2016). This is in part because people of color also have been conditioned to believe in their inferiority, but also, they understand the system was not set up to advantage them.

However, the admission lawsuits are just one example of strategies instituted to preserve the gaps between white Americans and Americans of color. According to the Aspen Institute (2016.), "structural racism is not something that a few people or institutions choose to practice. Instead, it has been a feature of the social, economic and political systems in which

we all exist" (para. 1). Structural racism highlights the U.S. historical and cultural context in which institutions are embedded (Lawrence et al., 2004).

Institutional Racism

Institutional racism is one type of structural racism. Institutions maintain structural racism. Institutional racism is defined as:

"The structure, policies, practices, and norms resulting in differential access to society's goods, services, and opportunities by race. Institutionalized racism is normative, sometimes legalized, and often manifests as an inherited disadvantage. It is structural, having been codified in our custom, practice, and law institutions, so there need not be an identifiable perpetrator. Indeed, institutionalized racism is often evident as inaction in the face of need" (Jones, 2002, p. 10).

Most institutions and social structures in the United States were created for and by white men. While many of those institutions currently serve everyone, the experiences within these systems for Black, Indigenous, and People of Color (BIPOC) are entirely different than white people. Institutional policies and practices result in differential, biased outcomes for different racial groups (Lawrence et al., 2004). There is no system or institution in which BIPOC people fare better than white people. Any adverse outcome, BIPOC are always at the bottom or fare the worst. Table 14-2 asks you to identify a system or aspects of a system where BIPOC people fare better than Whites.

Specifically looking at the criminal justice system, differential outcomes are easily detected (Beckett et al., 2006; Carlson, 2020).

"Race bifurcates how different kinds of gun violence are debated and dissected: gun violence associated with boys and men of color is often criminalized as deliberate,

Table 14-2

Name a system where BIPOC people fare better than White people?
- Health
- Education
- Wealth
- Business ownership
- Criminal Justice
- College attendance
- Sports (While BIPOC dominates some sports, the people who primarily profit from those individuals' labor are White.)
- Unemployment
- Wages
- Sports & Entertainment

blameworthy aggression, while gun violence associated with white boys and men is often medicalized as the unfortunate consequence of mental illness" (Carlson, 2020, p. 414). When most people arrested for drugs are African American, it is logical to assume that more African Americans use and sell drugs. When you understand institutional racism, which results in the overpolicing of Black and Brown communities, you understand why a high number of African Americans are arrested for drugs. Lawrence et al. (2004) states,

> "The fact that 46% of the prison population is Black, while Blacks represent only 13% of the overall population, suggests that the criminal justice system must have some institutional features that end up criminalizing Black men more often...There are the pervasive beliefs and narratives that African Americans are lazy, violence-prone, and disinterested in family formation...They add up to a racialized 'frame' or way of looking at the world that allows us, as a nation, to accept the fact that Blacks make up 46% of the prison population as normal rather than as a national emergency" (p. 47).

Interconnectedness of Structural and Institutional Racism

According to Hayes-Greene and Love (2018), structural and institutional racism exists and is currently operating as evidenced by three facts: (1) racial inequity looks the same regardless of the system. No matter what institution or system, BIPOC people fare worse than white people. (2) Socioeconomic status or other factors do not explain racial inequity. For years, a commonly held belief was that racial inequities existed because of poverty not racism. Studies show that even when studies control for socioeconomic status or other factors, BIPOC still fared worse than white people (Centers for Disease Control and Prevention (CDC) 2019; Reardon, 2016). Finally, (3) inequities are caused by systems, regardless of people's culture or behavior. Even if there weren't racist people, systems are structured so that inequities would still exist. Inequities are inherently built into systems.

In the macro sphere, structural and institutional racism are the root causes of many social problems that social workers seek to address. Over the last decade, there have been concerted efforts to eliminate racial disparities across multiple social institutions (e.g., health care, education, criminal justice system). Despite these targeted, intentional efforts, many of the outcomes remain the same.

Racism is called by different names. Many terms have been created to explain the differences and disparate outcomes between groups of people.

- **Racial inequities.** Racial inequity is when two or more racial groups are not standing on approximately equal footing. For example, there are differences between the percentages of each ethnic group in terms of dropout rates, single-family homeownership, access to health care, etc. (Kendi, 2019).

- **Disparity.** "Any differences among populations that are statistically significant and differ from the reference group by at least 10%" (Agency for Healthcare Research and Quality, 2006 as quoted in Hebert et al., 2008, p. 375).

- **Implicit bias.** Refers to the attitudes or the stereotypes that affect our understanding, actions, and decisions in unconscious ways. Implicit biases tend to be negative beliefs or traits that people unknowingly hold about another group of people. Often, these biases are automatic responses acted out unconsciously. For example, white women grabbing their purses when a Black person enters the elevator. In general, the media and society often portray Black people as thieves, thugs, or gang bangers. If this is the only encounters or knowledge that someone has about another group, they are more likely to believe what the media says about another group of people. It is possible for someone to believe in equality and fairness and still implicitly act out biases. The Implicit Association Test (IAT) measures the extent to which individuals have implicit biases concerning race, gender, sexual identity, age, religion, etc. (Staats, 2013).

- **Disproportionality.** The underrepresentation or overrepresentation of a racial or ethnic group compared to its percentage in the total population (Child Welfare Information Gateway, 2016).

- **Achievement gap.** The unequal or inequitable distribution of educational results and benefits. (Glossary of Education Reform, 2013).

- **Learning gap.** Refers to the relative performance of individual students, that is, the disparity between what a student has learned and what they were expected to learn at a particular age or grade level. (Glossary of Education Reform, 2013).

- **Opportunity gap.** The unequal or inequitable distribution of resources and opportunities (Glossary of Education Reform, 2013).

- **Health disparities.** Health disparities are preventable differences in the burden of disease, injury, violence, or opportunities to achieve optimal health that are experienced by socially disadvantaged populations (CDC, 2008).

- **Social determinants of health (SDOH).** SDOH are environmental factors that often impact a myriad of health risks, functioning, and quality-of-life outcomes.

These factors influence socioeconomic and physical conditions that affect how people live, learn, work, and age in society.

Various factors often are attributed to the differences between people who fare well in these systems (white people) and people who do not fare well (BIPOC). Some of these factors include:

- Poverty
- Environmental threats
- Inadequate access
- Individual and behavioral factors
- Educational inequalities
- Lack of physical activity
- Lack of parental involvement
- Safe and affordable housing
- Access to quality education
- Public and personal safety
- Availability of healthy, affordable foods
- Access and affordability of emergency/health services
- Work and living environments that are free of life-threatening toxins

Rarely do we use the words racism, structural racism, or institutional racism to describe the accumulative disadvantage BIPOC experience. Calling structural racism different names serves a couple of purposes. First, it obscures the conversation, when the root cause beneath each term is the same: racism. Second, these terms often are more palatable to white people than structural racism. According to Jones (2002),

> "I have become convinced that it is only by naming racism, asking how racism is operating here? And then mobilizing with others to actually confront the system and dismantle it that we can have any significant or lasting impact on the pervasive 'racial' health disparities that plagued the United States for centuries" (p. 7).

Historical Trauma

Historical trauma is a type of trauma that is experienced over an extended period. The effects are passed down multigenerationally by individuals from different cultural, racial, or ethnic groups. Historical trauma stems from universal events used to annihilate or oppress groups of people by a dominant group (Sotero, 2006). Examples of historical trauma include slavery; the Holocaust; Rwandan genocide; stealing of land, systematic murder, colonization, and forced migration of Indigenous people. A significant hallmark of historical trauma is the mass killing of some people and the looming threat of death to those who manage to survive. Historical trauma can affect people's self-esteem and self-concept (Sotero, 2006) and can lead people to cope with the trauma in maladaptive ways such as substance abuse, violence, aggression, and suicide. Often, the unaddressed grief and trauma related to the event and the subsequent maladaptive coping in the aftermath of the event is passed down to the next generation, resulting in irreversible damage (Maxwell, 2014). There is a myriad of ways that historical trauma is transmitted across generations: biologically, culturally, socially, physically, emotionally, and psychologically (Sotero, 2006).

Historical Trauma and Macro Practice

Historical trauma affects macro practice in several ways. For example, colorism is an important way that historical trauma affects macro-level practice. Colorism is a system of oppression rooted in colonialism (Ortega-Williams et al., 2021). In the United States, this system of oppression began with the transatlantic slave trade. Individuals who looked white or were very light skinned had more access to resources, often were more likely to be able to purchase their freedom, and experienced less violence or less harsh working conditions (Hunter, 2007).

Following slavery, lighter-skinned people had more access to employment, resources, wealth, and other kinds of opportunities, which remains true in our current world. People who have features (skin color, eye color, hair texture, body shape) closely resembling people of European descent fare better in systems than people who more closely resemble people of African descent (Hunter, 2005). These color-based disparities often affect access to housing and health care, sentencing in the criminal justice system, and school discipline (Hamilton et al., 2009; Hannon et al., 2013).

Research suggests that "individuals who present with what is generalized as having more African features encounter discrimination which impacts multiple dimensions of well-being" (Ortega-Williams et al., 2021, p. 296). This is true not only in the United States but also in Southeast Asia, Africa, Europe, and Latinx/Hispanic countries (Ortega-Williams et al., 2021). With respect to any metric of financial, social, emotional, mental, physical well-being, colorism accounts for disparate outcomes (Crutchfield et al., 2017; Hannon et al., 2013; Monroe, 2013; Viglione et al., 2011). For example, Crutchfield et al. (2017) found that darker-skinned individuals are more likely to be killed by the police than lighter-skinned individuals.

Social Justice

Social justice as concept and ideal has been a source of debate within the social work profession (Ross, 2011). As societies change, so do ideas about what it means to be socially just. As a core social work value, the National Association of Social Workers (NASW) stated that social workers should challenge social injustice. The NASW Code of Ethics state that:

> "Social workers pursue social change, particularly with and on behalf of vulnerable and oppressed individuals and groups of people. Social workers' social change efforts are focused primarily on poverty, unemployment, discrimination, and other forms of social injustice. These activities seek to promote sensitivity to and knowledge about oppression and cultural and ethnic diversity. Social workers strive to ensure access to needed information, services, and resources, equality of opportunity, and meaningful participation in decision-making for all people" (p. 12).

While there is no consensus in terms of what constitutes social justice, there appears to be loose agreement that social justice is "principally concerned with social change, access, equality, tolerance, compassion, fairness, and meaningful participation" (Friesen, 2007, p. 145). Social justice and what constitutes social justice are forever changing. For example, a Marxist might believe the socially just remedy to deal with poverty is to eliminate capitalism. At the same time, a capitalist might argue the socially just thing to do is eliminate the barriers that limit access. Which solution is more socially just? According to Ross (2011),

> "Along with broader society, social work has adapted, grown, and changed its ideas of what is right and just ... While people may concur that justice is good, by seeing the definition of injustice, it often becomes clear that justice isn't universally understood to mean the same thing" (p. 19).

When evaluating whether something (action, policy, practice) is socially just, use the below standards as a guide.

Social Justice Differs Depending on the Context

As a social worker, you should be aware of the difference between how the term *social justice* is understood and articulated by the social work profession and how it is understood and communicated by policymakers. Social justice is defined differently depending on public opinion's philosophical and ideological orientation.

Social Justice Is an Ideal Aspiration

Social justice is not socially just unless it ensures access to needed information, services, and resources. An assessment of social justice includes examining the nexus between the problems that people have, the conditions in which they live, and the extent to which social policies remedy or harm individuals, groups, and communities. Using social justice as a framework to assess social problems and conditions contributes to understanding the debilitating effects of inequality and oppression that influence people's ability to reach their potential. Social justice further illuminates how problems are defined, as well as issues of human and civil rights. It raises questions of whether people at the lower stratification level have equal access to resources and opportunities that promote well-being, dignity, and worth or whether stigma and marginal status determine who they are and what they can become.

Who Decides What Is Socially Just?

As a social worker, the assessment information you gather helps you develop a plan of action and potentially build a coalition/alliance that includes the people affected by the problem. If an outcome is to be socially just, the process used to achieve the result also must be socially just. The solution proposed must include the views, opinions, and wishes of the people affected by the problem. Answers also allow a social worker to give voice to the people affected by the problem and frame issues that increase the likelihood that the public becomes invested in the problem, irrespective of their values (Linhorst, 2002).

Macro Practice Is a Vehicle for Social Justice

As a social worker in contact with clients affected by social problems and conditions and by policy decisions, you have access to a wealth of information that can be used to inform policymakers about the realities of clients' lives. Presenting information about a particular problem to the public and to policymakers is a means by which a social worker can lessen the distance between them and those affected by a social problem or a policy and advance social justice. Know your audience, so you can effectively tailor your solution to your audience, and what they care about is a key to making effective change.

Social Justice: Micro Responses and Macro-Level Solutions

Social justice can involve overhauling the system. It also can include removing barriers that make it difficult for people to access services. Social workers need not become revolutionaries to effect change (Breton, 2006). To a large extent, social justice continues to be directed primarily toward individual change (Breton, 2006; Brueggemann, 2006; Long et al., 2006). Over decades, this focus has emphasized personal responsibility at the expense of equality and justice. For the most part, the emphasis pertains to particular segments of the population, mainly the poor and disenfranchised. Furthermore, the funding entities upon which social welfare organizations depend rarely focus on collective social action that promotes system-level change (Breton, 2006). Instead, adherence to the notion of individual change or responsibility tends to emphasize goals and values.

However, justice work demands that we as social workers articulate the consequences of social problems and conditions and evaluate and monitor the impact of policies on those problems or conditions. By acting on behalf of or with client groups and taking an active role in documenting issues, social workers can be instrumental in lessening the distance between policymakers and people while promoting social justice. Social conditions and problems often are beyond the individual's ability to resolve and, as such, often call for a more comprehensive macro-level response (Breton, 2006; Segal, 2010).

The Helping Process

Change at the macro level is often focused on collective, large-scale changes (Burghardt, 2011; Netting et al., 2012). Depending on the problem, different macro social work practices are used to alter conditions, improve environments, and respond to needs found within organizations, groups, or communities. Each phase has distinct goals and tasks related to accomplishing these goals. The helping process assists social work practitioners in effectively engaging and working alongside organizations and communities to assist these entities in reaching their goals and bringing forth change. Just as in micro practice, macro practice follows the same three phases that embody the six steps in the helping process: engagement, assessment, intervention, termination, and evaluation. The three phases are:

- Phase I: Exploration, engagement, assessment, and planning
- Phase II: Implementation and goal attainment
- Phase III: Termination

Using three types of macro level practice (community organizing, organizational change, and policy development), this section walks social work students through the helping process at the macro level.

Types of Macro Social Work Practice

Macro practice refers to community, organizational, and policy-level practice (Council on Social Work Education, 2018). There are different kinds of macro social work practice. This chapter highlights three of the most popular types of macro practice: Community organizing, organizational change, and policy development. Regardless of the types of macro practice, it is essential to consider context, power, ideology, and whose special interests are served and not served by the change (Kingdon, 2011).

Community Organizing

The purpose of community organizing is to create a process by which people who often are overlooked or not allowed to have a say in the decision-making processes to organize around social change to build power and influence and transform the dynamics and the communities' relationship to power to obliterate conditions hurting communities (Racial Equity Tools, n.d.). Like advocacy and social action, community organizing is action oriented on a larger scale and intended to affect social change in which "neighborhood organizations, associations and faith communities join together to address social problems in their community" (Brueggemann, 2006, p. 204). It is an arena in which participants use the power of a coalition to assess and advance their needs, develop and own solutions, and build capacity in partnership with private or governmental organizations (Brueggemann, 2006; Minkler, 2012; Rothman, 2007).

Tasks Related to Community Organizing

1. Develop a shared understanding of the problem
2. Develop a common vision
3. Identify a leadership team
4. Assess the wants and the needs of each stakeholder group
5. Identify and prioritize tasks into short-, medium-, and long-term goals
6. Identify strategies and tactics to promote change
7. Identify the resources needed to implement change
8. Implement the plan
9. Developing ongoing resources
10. Evaluate the results
11. Maintaining accountability and interest
12. Sustaining momentum
13. Expanding the support base

Organizational Change

Organizational change is the process companies, businesses, and nonprofit organizations undergo to change or reorganize significant components (i.e., culture, underlying technologies, infrastructure, internal processes) to increase efficiency, effectiveness, productivity, and impact (Stobierski, 2020). Similarly, organizational change, as conceptualized by Brager and Holloway (1978), can focus on three areas: people-focused change, technological change, or structural change, which may take the form of a new policy, modifications to an existing policy, the development of a program, or the initiation of a project in which the results can be used to inform service delivery.

There are several reasons organizational change happens. The pressure for organizations to change can be external or internal. According to Stobierski (2020), some of the most common reasons for organizational change include:

- Change in leadership
- Reorganization of the team structure
- New technology or industry changes
- Change or major shift in the business model
- Need for more efficiency
- Increase profit margin
- Increase service utilization or effectiveness
- Downsizing or layoffs redistribute workloads

Tasks Related to Organizational Change

1. Define the organizational change, prepare for organizational change, and understand why it is critical
2. Identify and engage those affected by the change
3. Determine what level and type of change is most appropriate
4. Identify the organization's current functioning and root causes of the problems
5. Develop a feedback loop
6. Determine interventions needed to help solve the problem(s)
7. Develop a communication strategy
8. Implement a support structure
9. Measure the change process
10. Ongoing maintenance and monitoring
11. Institutionalization of change

Policy Development

The development of policies includes analysis, development, and changes needed. Policy analysis involves recognizing problems with existing policies or the way things are and identifying policies that could fix or address the problem while keeping in mind the greatest good (Centers for Disease Control and Prevention, 2019c). Policy development is the process used to create and draft new policies or revise existing policies to address problems better (CDC, 2019c). Policy change is the process used to enact the newly created policy and ensure or increase compliance with the policy.

Effective policy changes are built on comprehensive views of the problem where someone can understand and follow the logic behind the changes (Popple & Leighninger, 2015, p. 79). According to Netting et al. (2017), "the planning and policy approach is [a] task-oriented, data-driven approach in which persuasion with the facts prevails" (p. 148). A major mistake social workers make is solely focusing on the heart rationale for why policy is needed. While presenting case studies and showing the real-world impact on people is essential, the explanation must also include cost-benefit analysis, strengths, threats, and opportunities, and bottom-line consequences for failing to make the change.

Tasks Related to Policy Development

1. Identify and define the need for the policy
2. Identify key stakeholders and consult them about developing a strategy
3. Compile and review existing data and resources
4. Determine possible policy options
5. Rank possible policy options to determine the best one
6. Approve final draft of the policy
7. Policy implementation
8. Evaluation of the policy
9. Evaluate results and ongoing monitoring

Phase I: Exploration, Engagement, Assessment, and Planning

Exploration, engagement, assessment, and planning of the helping process lay the groundwork for understanding the problem(s) macrolevel change is trying to address, how to approach and work with the stakeholders affected by those problems, and effective ways of engaging them in the problem-solving process. Phase I involves assessing what steps have already been taken to

C6, 7, 8, and 9

change, resources needed to facilitate change, and different approaches within each type of practice used to solve the problems. Finally, Phase I entails thinking through and planning to implement changes by anticipating potential problems and barriers to change, obtaining the necessary buy-in and feedback from stakeholders, and incorporating their needs in terms of the final changes.

Stage 1: Exploration

Exploration involves awareness that a problem(s) exists. Through exploration, the social worker begins to explore the problems or the areas of concern from each of the major stakeholders' perspectives. Exploration is about identifying the nature and extent of the problem or the condition and what organizations, communities, or entities are trying to accomplish. Exploration of the problem is an essential first step. It is vital to gather the information clarifying the problem(s) and the resulting consequences. Gathering information from clients, particularly their view of the problem or condition, is included in the assessment process. For example, how does a group or community experience the problem, and how do they think things would be different if the problem or the condition did not exist? Both questions are pertinent to empowerment because organizations and communities know what needs to happen to resolve the problem(s).

Community Organizing

From a community organizing perspective, the goal of exploration is to develop a shared understanding of the problem. Depending on the stakeholders, each may have a different understanding of the problem. It is essential to talk to all major stakeholders to understand the problem from their vantage point. A social worker's job is to identify the areas where stakeholders view the problem similarly and use it as your starting point. For example, the People's Institute for Survival and Beyond (PISAB) has been community organizing around racism for over 45 years. PISAB believes in order to dismantle structural and systemic racism, everyone must have a common definition of racism. Imagine how hard it would be to eradicate racism if everyone defined racism differently. If one person thought racism was an individual act against another person, they would be trying to fix problems associated with individual acts of racism, while another person would attempt fixing the problem of how organizations limit access to services. Having a common understanding of the problem allows everyone to work on the same goal to maximize the efforts and the impacts. A shared understanding of the problem is a vital part of problem solving. Once there is a common understanding of the problem, it is crucial to develop a shared vision of the end goal of their collective action.

Organizational Change

From an organizational change perspective, the goal of the exploration stage is to prepare the organization for change. There are various events (e.g., external demands such as diversity, equity, inclusion, internal conflict, complaining customers, losing money, the need for more innovation, high turnover) which signify deeper problems, often making organizations realize changes are needed. The organization must understand why changes are necessary or critical. Sometimes it is clear why changes are needed. Other times, organizations have been doing business a particular way for so long they are not cognizant that changes are needed. However, it is vital to identify and describe the changes required. Organizations must articulate how the changes align with the organization's goals and objectives. Finally, the organization needs to identify how the changes can enhance the organization's performance, financial standing, and service effectiveness.

Policy Development

From a policy development perspective, the goal of the exploration stage is to discover whether there needs to be a policy developed or if changes to an existing policy is sufficient. It is critical to understand the reasons why a policy needs to be created or changed. Depending on the policy, this often is the most politicized part of the process. The policy may affect different stakeholders in different ways. Legislative, regulatory, judicial, or other entities often are crucial to the development, enactment, and enforcement of the policy. Therefore, it is vital to understand the problem from stakeholders' vantage points and what they see as the ideal solution.

For example, the increase in opioid use was a highly politicized problem affecting different stakeholders. In 2019, 70,630 individuals died per year from opioid related overdoses (Hedegaard et al., 2020). Pharmaceutical companies told the medical community that prescribing opioid pain relievers would not lead to addiction. Consequently, doctors prescribed opioids at greater rates, leading to widespread misuse to a highly addictive substance (Doctor et al., 2018). In response to the opioid epidemic, new policies were developed. In the exploration phase, new policies or changes to existing polices may be needed to address problems. For example,

> "There are licenses and limits regarding the class of persons or entities authorized to manufacture, ship, distribute, dispense, and prescribe the approved drugs...The Drug Enforcement Agency has restricted the pool of physicians and other practitioners who are licensed/authorized to prescribe opioids under state and federal law" (National Academies of Sciences, Engineering, and Medicine, 2017, p. 283).

Stage 2: Engagement

During the engagement stage, the social worker should focus on identifying the major stakeholders, building trust and rapport with those stakeholders, if necessary, and developing relationships between stakeholders so mutually agreed upon goals can be determined. The engagement stage is intended to identify major stakeholders, build trust, establish ground rules and norms for your work together, decide how decisions are made, and who is responsible for communicating those decisions. The social worker is actively involved with the stakeholders, listening to the problems from their perspectives, exploring reasons why communities need to organize, examining reasons organizational change and policy development are necessary, and deciding the desired end goals.

During the engagement process, there are two crucial tasks macro practice social workers must do:

1. Identify a suitable spectrum of stakeholders
   - Ministry and government officials
   - Clients
   - Beneficiaries
   - Other donors
   - IFI representatives
   - Relevant program managers/directors/administrators
   - Human resources and IT managers/directors
   - Researchers/teachers/other technical personnel
   - Clients/stakeholders/organizational representatives
   - Support staff
2. Observe the dynamics among stakeholders
   - Nature of meetings with you (who attends, who presides)
   - Levels of participation and involvement of staff
   - Processes for teaching and learning
   - Nature of dealings within the organization
   - How work is conducted; dominant paradigm
   - Attitudes toward monitoring and evaluation

Community Organizing

From a community organizing perspective, the goal of the engagement stage is to identify a core leadership team who can provide inspiration and drive the change (National Education Goals, n.d.) This group of people lays the foundation for a long-term strategy. Social movements come out of a variety of events. Often, the leaders are the closest to the event and those who begin mobilizing people to create change. The most significant mistake people make in this stage is believing they can change systems alone. It is coming together with others who care about the problem and pooling efforts and resources that leads to lasting change.

In this stage, it is crucial to identify a leadership team. Who makes the final decisions? What decisions are each person be responsible for? What decisions need to be made by the collective? In some communities, there are already established leaders. It is essential to determine key stakeholders and coordinate all efforts through this group. The most important qualification to serve on the leadership team is a desire for change, a willingness to put in the time and the energy to push the agenda and gain momentum, and particular expertise to enhance the team's effectiveness. As the team is growing and developing to sustain change, there needs to be broad-based community ownership. Inclusiveness is the goal and a requirement of any effective change effort (NEG, n.d.).

Organizational Change

Once you have an idea of the problem and the things you want to change, it is essential to identify the most affected people at the various levels of the organization (Courtney, 2020). It is important to think through the possible impacts of the change, who may be impacted and in what ways, and how the change might be received. The person leading the change also may need to obtain support from colleagues. If the head of the organization is leading the change, it is still essential to get buy-in from the various levels to minimize any efforts to sabotage the changes. While deans, chairs, executive directors, and chief executive officers have the authority to create change, top-down approaches must include and incorporate individuals affected by the change if changes are to be sustainable (Galpin, 1996).

The type of may be needed whether a top-down or bottom-up approach is most effective (McKibban & Steltenpohl, 2019). According to Sharma and Mukherji (2015):

> "A *strategic change* involves senior management, a consultant, and a small group of employees who take the initial critical decisions for organization-wide change involving technical/analytical aspects and 'soft aspects' for creating momentum. The *grass-root level change* focuses on driving the change deep into the organization by implementing and sustaining change to bring about the desired results." (p. 197)

The scope of the change should determine whether the approach is top-down or bottom-up. Sharma and Mukherji (2015, p. 206) adapted this chart from Sharma (2008) and Galpin (1996). A descriptive phrase serves

Table 14-3 Scope of Change

Scope of Change	Strategic Change (Top Down – Administrator Driven)	Grassroots Change (Bottom-Up – Employee Driven)
Leadership infrastructure	Top management Executive management — a select few at the top	Local management Management and all the employees, "the masses."
Diagnostics	The entire organization	Specific sites, departments, divisions
Comparison points	External benchmarking to internal best practices	Implementation of best practices
Tools	Application of data collection tools to select a few	Application of implementation tools to the masses
Training	Assessment of needs, some design, and delivery	Assessment of needs, extensive design, and delivery
Outcome goals	Recommendations for change and momentum building	Implementation of changes

as title and description. Reprinted from *Management of Permanent Change* (p. 206), by R.R. Sharma & S. Mukherji, 2015, Springer Gabler.

Grassroots Change (Bottom-Up— Employee Driven)

To be an effective organizational change advocate, you must know the benefits and the risks of a proposed change, including assessing the risk to you as a professional. In your benefit–risk analysis, you must document and clarify the need for change. If service delivery is a concern, for example, consider if your proposal will improve the situation (Brager & Holloway, 1978; Netting et al., 2017). In addition, what form should the proposed change take? For example, would you recommend a change in a policy practice or program if service delivery is the target?

What are the expected outcomes of the proposed change? Are other staff also concerned? Who else should be involved? These questions position you to form a coalition to avoid the perception of being seen as inexperienced.

Before initiating a change effort within an organization, it is important to describe and document the issue, including its context. This systems-level goal is consistent with the organization's mission, a proposal to remedy the problem or condition, and the perceived benefits. Frey (1990) has developed a helpful framework to gauge the potential benefit of a change proposal to the organization and minimize potential risk or opposition. The process involves three key groups: (1) administrators, who must approve and allocate resources for the proposal; (2) supervisors and staff, who are responsible for implementing the work involved; and (3) clients, the affected group. Client input is considered essential in determining how the

proposed change offers direct benefits and can effectively alter and enhance the services they receive. By considering the impact of the potential change on each group, benefits can be weighed against any detrimental effects and strategies planned to counter reactions and resistance when the former (i.e., the benefits) clearly and substantially outweigh the latter.

Organizations are systems seeking to maintain equilibrium; therefore, opposition may be encountered to proposals for change. Opposition may arise in response to suggestions that challenge or exceed the organization's capacity due to resource constraints. Likewise, proposals that would significantly change the organization's purpose, mission, and goals may spur resistance. Extending an agency's operating hours may be considered a peripheral change and have little or no effect on organizational goals or mission. In contrast, programmatic changes, which alter a program's objectives, have a greater impact on organizational development.

Policy Development

Concerning policy development, there are three types of stakeholders: Influential, targeted, and content experts. Influential stakeholders are those individuals, communities, groups, or government entities who are affected by the policy and are needed to influence (facilitate or impede) its design and implementation (Food and Agriculture Organization of the United Nations, 2010). Target stakeholders should be included throughout the process when there are targeted questions that need answering. Content experts are those individuals who help draft new policies or change existing policies (Macquarie University, n.d.). Consultation with stakeholders is a vital component of the engagement process that leads to effective policy development (Macquarie University, n.d.).

Stage 3: Assessment

In the assessment stage, macro-practice social workers understand the problem from the organizations and communities' vantage point, strategies they have used to resolve the issues in the past, and what they hope to get out of the community organizing, organizational change, or policy development process. The goal of the assessment stage is to gather as much information as necessary to get a thorough sense of the problem. Assessment is an ongoing process intended to help obtain more precise information about the problem. During the assessment stage, macro social work practitioners should conduct interviews with key stakeholders in the organization and the community to gather the history they believe is relevant and seek guidance on who else should be included in the data collection process.

Community Organizing

From a community organizing perspective, the goal of the assessment stage is to determine the extent of the problem and what each stakeholder group wants and needs to resolve the issue. Assessment includes data collection and gathering information about the current system or systems impacting the problem, how changes were made previously, the challenges associated with the changes, and the people affected by the problem. It also is essential to review the attempts made to solve the problem in the past, any gains and losses connected to the problem, and use of existing efforts, processes, and changes to bolster current efforts to solve the problem.

Organizational Change

In the assessment stage, it is essential to gather information to determine the organization's current functioning and the root causes of the problems. Macro-practice social workers collect data and information to understand and interpret the problem accurately. Surveys, questionnaires, interviews, observations, or reviewing all available data are the primary ways to collect data. Talking with major stakeholders and reviewing data helps social workers identify the root causes of the problems. According to Cummings and Worley (2009), assessments often provide the systematic knowledge needed to develop effective strategies to resolve issues. Correctly assessing the issue is critical to the success of the organizational change.

During the data collection stage, confidentiality, anonymity, a clear purpose, and observer-expectancy bias are important factors that must be decided ahead of time. Social workers must provide informed consent to any participants they speak to know how much and what information will be shared with the leadership. Finally, another critical part of the assessment is ensuring the organization's current function is an anomaly because of an extreme situation or change that, once removed, will return the organization to equilibrium. For example, if a new dean or an executive director is hired, the likelihood of problems or difficulties increases tremendously. Once the organization has had an opportunity to adjust to the change, what once were considered problems may no longer be problems.

During the assessment process, working hypotheses are developed about what are the barriers to change and the root causes of problems (Netting et al., 2017). These are working hypotheses, and as you begin to work toward change, they may need to be tweaked or updated as more information becomes available. Also, it is essential to build support for the changes organizations need to make (Netting et al., 2017). The more people are on board, the less resistance you may experience as changes are made.

Once the various problems are identified, it is crucial to get feedback regarding identified issues to confirm that the data collected and the conclusions made represent the various viewpoints. You have reviewed relevant information up to this point. The biggest challenge is how and from whom to get feedback and at what point. This information is vital to make sure you accurately understand the problems before you start developing interventions.

Policy Development

In terms of policy development, the assessment stage focuses on compiling and reviewing existing data and resources (FAO, 2010). The extent of the data gathering is dependent on the circumstances, resources, and time available for the review. As part of the data collection process, it is essential to review any prior initiatives that were changed or dismantled, shifts in public support, the context of those shifts, and the economic and political realities associated with those changes. During the assessment phase, reviewing existing data and resources includes identifying what worked well and what did not work so well. It is also essential to explore whether goals or targets were met, if incentives or restrictions were counterproductive or conflicted with other goals, and if the conditions under which the policy was developed and implemented were considered (FAO, 2010). Compiling and reviewing existing data helps improve policies by learning from past mistakes and drawing upon lessons could improve policies and the implementation process.

Once the existing data, information, and resources have been reviewed, the next step includes determining possible policy options. Is a new policy needed, or would a change to existing policies better address the problem? Is the problem more with implementation than the policy itself? All these important questions can help determine the best course of action. You must be aware of and identify any barriers affecting policy development. According to the CDC (2019c), when reviewing policy options, you must ask yourself four questions:

1. What populations will be affected by each policy option? By how much and When?
2. What is the context of possible policy options, including political history, environment, and policy debate?
3. What are the cost and benefits associated with each policy option from a budgetary perspective?
4. What are the possible barriers associated with each policy option?

Stage 4: Planning

The purpose of the planning stage is goal development, which incorporates a shared understanding of the problem, provides all major stakeholders the opportunity to give feedback and suggestions in deciding the best approach to take, and explores possible barriers and obstacles. The action plan created should include specific objectives and tasks intended to help organizations and communities accomplish their stated goals, identify who does what, and develop a clear timeline for action.

Community Organizing

Once there is a shared understanding of the issues, it is critical to identify and prioritize goals. There are three types of goals: short-term goals can be accomplished anywhere from six months to a year. Medium goals may take two to five years. Long-term goals can take up to 10 years. These time frames are not set in stone, but it is an excellent way to prioritize goals. You should work on goals simultaneously. When organizing a community around a particular issue, short-term gains (i.e., low-hanging fruit) can build momentum and inspire people to keep pushing towards the desired end goal.

Once goals have been developed, the next step is to identify strategies and tactics enabling community organizers to accomplish their goals, promote change, and help to remove significant institutional barriers to change (NEG, n.d.). Strategies and tactics were initially military terms. **Strategies** are based on long-term goals. A strategy is the overall approach intended to accomplish the goals (Wright, 2021). Dr. Martin Luther King's strategy to achieving racial integration was nonviolence. All strategies stemmed from a nonviolent approach.

Tactics are concrete action steps that are taken to move an agenda forward and achieve a long-term goal (Wright, 2021). The Montgomery bus boycott was a tactic Dr. Martin Luther King used to achieve racial integration. Strategies and tactics are complementary. Both are needed to be successful. The strategies and tactics chosen largely depend on what you are trying to accomplish.

The sequence of tactics should be logical, realistic, methodical, and complementary to the strategy. The decision about which tactic to use depends on the contextual nature and assessment of the target concern and the related goal. In some instances, a particular tactic may be sufficient to achieve the desired outcome. At other times, however, a specific tactic—for example, advocacy to address an issue—may lead to another tactic, such as organizing a group or community in the change effort.

Within the community organizing context, there are different types of resources. Resources can be people, financial, expertise, information, relationships, or anything that helps community organizers accomplish their goals. People followed by financial are among your most valuable resources. In mobilizing community resources, Homan (2008) suggested four steps for eliciting and encouraging people's involvement:

1. Contact people.
2. Give them a reason to join.
3. Ask them to join.
4. Maintain their involvement. (p. 188)

The implementation of the Affordable Care Act (ACA; 2010) and the subsequent open enrollment periods resulted in the need to educate the uninsured about its provisions. Much of this work was accomplished by statewide and nationally coordinated partnerships of community-based advocacy groups, nonprofit organizations, and a range of citizen volunteers. Social workers were involved as educators and navigators, specifically assisting people in selecting an insurance plan suitable to their needs (Andrews et al., 2013). However, the definitive success of informing and educating people depended on volunteers recruited through social media, book clubs, client groups, fraternal and civic groups, and faith and professional communities.

Volunteers held public media events and distributed information in neighborhoods, social services agencies, and community health-care centers. The volunteer recruitment communications appeal, which began with "We need your help," effectively engaged volunteers as active stakeholders in informing the public about provisions in the ACA. Direct requests such as this one have the potential to engage the altruistic instincts and basic values of potential volunteers, many of whom desire equality and dignity for the disenfranchised but are unaware of how to achieve it.

Specific questions may clarify the need for resource development and guide the data to be gathered include:

- What are the resource needs of a particular group?
- How would a group or a community describe its resource needs?
- Are there unmet needs, gaps, or underutilized existing resources?
- How prevalent are the needs across the population and in various subgroups?
- Are there barriers to the utilization of existing resources?

Organizational Change

Once the root causes of the problem(s) present within the organization are understood, you need to determine how to intervene to solve the problem(s). The interventions are a roadmap clearly outlining success and operationalizing the organization's changes, which should be based on the goals you are trying to accomplish (Stobierski, 2020). For example, if an organization is trying to become more equitable, it is essential to define equity and what the organization means when it says equity or equitable. Are they trying to achieve a diverse client base, or are they also exploring ways to create equal opportunities and access for clients of diverse identities? In terms of interventions, an organization may target human resources benchmarks in terms of recruiting new diverse employees. Another intervention may target the training needs of existing employees and incorporate equity into their work product. Deciding how to solve problems within organizations takes time and may require trying different interventions before getting it right. As organizations move toward new ways of being, it is essential to be flexible and adjust interventions as more information becomes available. Nonetheless, asking these questions, assessing facts, and reaching a conclusion based on the information gathered helps you understand the issues involved and use this information to inform the intervention (Kirst-Ashman, 2014).

Who is leading the organizational change and what those leaders are trying to accomplish informs the communication strategy, which focuses on how information and progress is shared with employees? A communication strategy always includes what, who, when, and how: what should be communicated, who should this information be shared with, when should the information be shared, and how should the information be communicated? There may be people such as the executive director or chief executive officer with whom you must have ongoing communication. Other groups of people

may need to know information at different points in time. Communication can make or break organizational change. It is essential to determine how various groups are connected and involved with the organizational change. Any communication strategy should also include a timeline. Ongoing communication with multiple stakeholder groups is an integral part of any organizational change.

Policy Development

Compare and contrast the various options by identifying the pros and cons of each one. Keep in mind cost, benefits, barriers, and context. What might work in one situation or place is not automatically transferable to another location. Rank the options based on the criteria. Compare alternatives to your short-, medium-, and long-term goals. The policy option you ultimately settle on should be feasible, have the potential to impact the problem, and be economically and fiscally viable (CDC, 2019c). There will always be trade-offs, so ensure they are assessed and decide which trade-offs are acceptable and which ones should be rejected because the cost is too high.

Once it has been determined a new policy is needed or changes to existing policies must be made, be sure to obtain approval to proceed before expending energy drafting a policy. Language matters, so it is essential that whoever writes the policy has extensive knowledge of the audience and knows who will implement the policy. Industry language may need to be operationalized or explained. You should remember the problem the policy is intended to solve. Make sure to get feedback and widespread consultation throughout the drafting process. Determine who, how, and when the final draft of the policy will be approved. What stakeholders should be involved? Are there timeframes to keep in mind as the policy is drafted? If the policy is at the legislative level, keep track of when the policy must be submitted and to whom. It also is essential to keep in mind the potential impact the policy or policy changes may have on different populations. Ensure the plan is adequate, everyone's responsibilities are understood, and all outstanding issues or questions have been addressed (Macquarie University, n.d.).

Phase II: Implementation and Goal Attainment

In implementation and goal attainment, the focus is on prioritizing goals, implementing interventions, and maintaining continuity and momentum as change begins to happen. Phase II also involves mobilizing, identifying, and developing ongoing resources to implement strategies, tactics, interventions, or develop policies. Finally, Phase II also entails identifying and addressing barriers to change. Social workers should monitor progress during this phase and identify any challenges, obstacles, or threats to carrying out the action plan. Plans and timelines should be adjusted as needed to incorporate new information or findings or change course if there is limited success to goal attainment.

Stage 1: Implementation

During the implementation stage, the social worker focuses on implementing the strategies and tactics, organizational change, creating new policies, or changing existing ones. The social worker, at this stage, critically evaluates progress. If goals are not being met, it may be necessary to return to the assessment stage to define the problem more clearly.

C8

Community Organizing

Once community organizers have identified the issues impacting the community, identified various groups affected by the problem, and developed goals and objectives based on a strategy and tactics, it is time to implement the plan. It is essential to identify a point person or persons in the implementation stage if any issues arise. It also is vital to monitor logistical considerations such as space, equipment, and transportation (Netting et al., 2017). The final concern during implementation is coordination and communication. Volunteers need to be trained, and transportation, permits, or other legal requirements must be coordinated. A plan needs to be developed to figure out ongoing communication among members, communication and messaging with outside sources, and communication among leaders.

It is critical that community organizers cast a wide net when seeking potential supporters. Resources can be financial, people, and expertise. Assess what resources are needed at any given point in time. Sometimes, financial support is necessary to fund marches/protests or to launch a media campaign. At other times, people who have expertise in building a website are needed. One tactic some community organizations use is to develop a checklist of possible resources needed so when new people get involved, they can reveal which resources they can contribute to the cause. As time goes on, community organizing may require ongoing resources from several sources.

Organizational Change

Creating a support structure within the organization helps with implementation. Depending on the issue, a team of people or an advisory board may need to oversee

the process and provide ongoing support to help the organization stay on track. Adjusting to change can be difficult, mainly if the change is unwelcome. Providing a support structure helps administrators and employees adapt to the changes, provides valuable feedback about the process, and builds the leaders' proficiency in managing and leading change. It also may be necessary to remind administrators and employees of the desired changes and why it is worth the effort. If role changes are required, ensuring employees receive the proper training and support to perform their new role effectively is vital to the implementation process. As part of the implementation process, it may also be necessary to build in feedback loops, conduct town hall meetings, or put the item on the staff meeting agenda. Throughout the implementation process, people need to be able to ask questions and raise any concerns they have as the changes are being implemented. Paying attention to these concerns could save an organization time and money. Depending on their role, some employees may have important vantage points, allowing them to identify potential problems before they become unwieldy.

Policy Development

In terms of policy development, a goal of implementation is monitoring policy as it is being implemented. At the drafting stage, any concerns or potential issues should be identified and addressed. Once the policy is finalized and approved, activities around changing the policy need to cease. At this point, all efforts go into communicating the new policy and any issues related to implementing the policy. As part of the planning stage, an implementation and communication plan should be created. Periodically reviewing plans is a great way to measure results.

Stage 2: Goal Attainment

Continuing to monitor progress to determine when goals are met or whether new goals should be created is the purpose of the goal attainment stage. As part of goal attainment, results should be evaluated continuously to ascertain whether the change effort and the strategies employed are successful. Evaluating results can include collecting quantitative data, qualitative data, or a combination of the two.

C8

Community Organizing

Evaluating results entails monitoring progress, learning from history, and adjusting when needed. For example, marching was an effective tactic in the 1960s to rally around a particular theme. In the 1960s, Dr. Martin Luther King marched for civil rights. In 2017, marches were organized to garner respect for women's rights

(Mazumder, 2017). Research shows organizing marches around a particular issue can have long-lasting political change. Mazumder (2017) identified three key factors successful marches/protests have in common:

1. **Organization.** Community organizers and protesters must be organized and keep adding pressure. The tea party organizers made significant political gains because they remain united and steadfast in their goals by staying involved, applying pressure, and successfully implementing tactics.

2. **Messaging.** Does it resonate with people who may be outside the core group of supporters? According to Mazumder (2017), "the tea party's name and core message of limited government harked back to the founding of the United States and its principle of individual freedom" (para. 19).

3. **Nonviolence.** Organizers must ensure that the march is nonviolent. Research has found that non-violent marches and protests are twice as effective as violent ones (Chenoweth & Stephan, 2011).

Community organizers must continue to monitor goal attainment. While it often takes years to evaluate the effectiveness of actions, it is crucial to continue to assess goal attainment and, if necessary, change tactics. Troubleshooting is a part of goal attainment. When progress slows, is undesirable, or unanticipated results occur, it is important to examine and identify possible reasons why and adjust as needed.

Community organizing requires organizers to be accountable to the communities they serve, particularly when citizens contribute money to the cause. Accountability to stakeholders is important part of sustaining a movement. Additionally, there are a variety of ways to maintain and sustain interest in a cause. Success is the best way to maintain interest because it shows the hard work, time, and energy people are dedicating to a cause is paying off. Another way to sustain interest is ongoing communication and ensuring the messaging continues to get out about progress made (FAO, n.d.). Maintaining interest in a cause is an integral part of ongoing success.

Organizational Change

There should be a formalized structure throughout the change process to measure the impact of the changes (Courtney, 2020). Again, accountability is essential. Accountability could consist of new tasks built into someone's job description or new benchmarks different departments must meet. Organizations put time and money toward the things they value. If the changes organization are trying to make are significant, someone must be held accountable for its success or failure. Sufficient resources (i.e., financial and personnel) need to be set aside to ensure the changes organizations want to make are successful and institutionalized. Institutionalizing change is an important part of ensuring that the changes organizations make last beyond the people who created or implemented the change. Managing the change process may highlight the need for reinforcements and incentives. As organizations move through the process, they should be documenting lessons learned so future changes can go more smoothly or be more impactful.

The biggest obstacles to change are wanting quick fixes and underestimating the impact of resistance, praise, and acknowledgment on the process (Kotter, 1995). Change is hard and often moves much slower than people would like. There are no quick fixes to lasting change. People can derail or usher change. In terms of resistance, you need to constantly monitor people who oppose the change. They may be very vocal in the beginning or may be sabotaging things passive aggressively. It is important to have people throughout the organization that are championing the change so they can help keep an eye on resistance. Additionally, it is important to acknowledge and praise people's efforts throughout the change process. People need to know that the sacrifices, extra time, and energy they are giving to a change effort are noticed and appreciated.

Measures of success used by organizations tend to be reported in aggregated client statistical data; therefore, evaluating the effectiveness of macro-level practice can be challenging. In evaluating the outcome of a program objective, for example, an organization's criterion might be the number of homeless families who received affordable housing. Further analysis might involve examining a change in the status of the families who obtained housing. Here, the evaluation focuses on the overall outcome. According to Kotter (1995), there are eight ways to transform organizational change:

1. Establishing a sense of urgency
2. Forming a powerful guiding coalition
3. Creating a vision
4. Communicating the vision
5. Empowering others to act on the vision
6. Planning for and creating short-term wins
7. Consolidating improvements and producing still more change
8. Institutionalization of new approaches. (p. 61)

Policy Development

Evaluation, irrespective of the method, requires specified goals and concise objectives in measurable terms.

In general, evaluation is an ongoing process for which it is essential to establish indicators at the beginning of the intervention. The process involves continuous, systematic monitoring of the intervention's impact, and this requires the development and the implementation of data management techniques. Systematic analysis of data allows the determination of whether the program activity or intervention is being implemented as planned and whether it is accomplishing the stated program goals (Gardner, 2000; Lewis et al., 2001). Conducting an evaluation requires selecting an appropriate research design, applying techniques of measurement, and analyzing data. The specific details of the various methods are beyond the scope of this book. The requisite knowledge needed to implement the evaluation process is commonly discussed in research courses. However, tracking the impact of a change effort concerning the desired outcomes is essential.

Phase III: Termination

Termination is the last phase of the helping process. During termination, communities and organizations reflect on the accomplishments and progress made. Resources and supports are identified should problems re-emerge. There is no set length of time for any phase or stage, and in some cases, it may be necessary to return to a previous phase or stage, depending on progress or lack thereof. Community members, organizations, and other entities should be at the center of any problem-solving process and offer guidance to support progress and change.

The terminal phase of the helping process involves three major aspects:

1. Assessing when communities' and organizations' goals have been met satisfactorily.
2. Helping communities and organizations develop strategies to maintain change, continue growth, and movement following the termination.
3. Successfully terminating the process.

Macro-level practice often involves goals where growth and changes have no limits. Therefore, deciding when to terminate must be made by the community leaders, leaders of organizations, communities, and individuals affected by a policy change or development.

Community Organizing

To sustain momentum and permanent change, organizations must rely on continuous change models (Abu El-Ella et al., 2015). Sustaining long-term change is primarily based on training, ongoing communication, a reward and recognition system, a clear strategic direction

explicating a continuous process of problem identification, exploration, solution generation, and implementation (Abu El-Ella et al., 2015). From the outset, there is an expectation of continuous improvement as an organizational norm.

As part of creating significant changes in organizations, one principle in Kotter's (1995) eight-step model is "empowering a broad base of people for taking action" (Abu El-Ella et al., 2015, p. 112). Changes in leadership, burnout, and other factors demand the need to expand the support base continuously. Organized movements can last years. Having a variety of people who can step in as needed is essential to keeping a social movement going.

Organizational Change

Social workers have voiced concern over the need to develop strategies that maintain change and continued growth once the formal change has occurred and termination is imminent (Rzepnicki, 1991). These concerns consist in part of organizations returning to their previous level of functioning. Consequently, more attention is now being paid to maintaining change after termination. Follow-up and continued monitoring may be necessary to evaluate results and ensure change becomes institutionalized.

Organizational changes must become institutionalized. When changes are not institutionalized when the people pushing for the changes leave or step down, the likelihood of the organization returning to a previous level of functioning is high. Institutionalizing change consists of formally incorporating (i.e., institutionalizing) it into organizational policies, job descriptions, mission and vision statements, strategic plans, or anything else formalizing the process. Lasting change requires that changes are institutionalized.

Policy Development

Evaluating effective policies consist of reviewing whether the original reasons the policy was created or changed have been met, minimizing risk(s), and deviating between policy and actual practice (Macquarie University, n.d.). Evaluating results and ongoing monitoring of policies and progress should happen for one to two years. Ongoing monitoring and policy reviews should determine if the policy is working as intended, is still necessary, requires changes or amendments based on actual practice, or needs to be adjusted to align with relevant legislative requirements or strategic direction. Review procedures, implementation, and supporting documents, as these things could influence the policy process.

Social Media as a Resource for Macro Practice

In the world of text messaging, email, social media, online tools, and other forms of digital communication, the capacity to reach, engage, and organize a broad spectrum of people about a particular issue is infinite. Social media can be combined with traditional face-to-face contact, such as door knocking. A focused message with direct appeal is essential to recruiting and engaging participants in the change effort. To sharpen the message, consider using social media. However, it is necessary to have clearly defined goals, generate interest, and clarify the intent of the organizing effort.

According to the Black Lives Matter website (n.d.),

"In July 2013, the movement began with the use of the hashtag #BlackLivesMatter on social media after the acquittal of George Zimmerman in the shooting death of Trayvon Martin, an unarmed African American teen 17 months earlier in February 2012. The movement became nationally recognized for street demonstrations following the 2014 deaths of Michael Brown and Eric Garner, two African American males living in Ferguson, Missouri. Since the Ferguson protests, participants in the movement have demonstrated against the deaths of numerous other African Americans by police actions or while in police custody. In 2015, Black Lives Matter activists became involved in the 2016 U.S. presidential election. Alicia Garza, Patrisse Cullors, and Opal Tometi are the originators of the hashtag and call to action. The Black Lives Matter movement expanded the project into a national network of over 30 local chapters between 2014 and 2016. The overall Black Lives Matter movement is a decentralized network of activists with no formal hierarchy" (para. 1–4).

Using the Black Lives Matter movement as a case study, Mundt et al. (2018) found social media builds connections, mobilizes people and resources, aids in coalition building, and amplifies other narratives.

Although the opportunities provided by social media are infinite, this means of communicating presents limitations and challenges. Social media must accompany and be combined with real-world organizing (Mundt et al., 2018). The ease of social media can also derail social movements and launch counterattacks and narratives. There are other challenges and risks associated with the use of social media. For example, particular demographics may not have ready access to this form of communication. Social media may be generational, and its appeal can vary by age. Specifically, it may be easier for young people to access and respond to this form of communication than older people. Other factors should be considered irrespective of age, such as whether individuals or communities can communicate using social media tools. Nonetheless, because these resources provide for connective relationship opportunities between people, their benefit should be evaluated.

Summary

This chapter introduced macrolevel intervention strategies for which the targets of change are communities, organizations, and systems. Current socioeconomic, demographic, and political trends present numerous opportunities for action and intervention at the macro practice level.

Competency Notes

C1 Demonstrate Ethical and Professional Behavior

- Manage personal and professional value conflicts and affective reactions.

C2 Engage Antiracism, Diversity, Equity, and Inclusion in Practice

- Demonstrate anti-racist social work practice at the individual, family, group, organizational, community, research, and policy levels, informed by the theories and voices of those who have been marginalized.

C3 Advance Human Rights and Socioeconomic and Environmental Justice

- Engage in practices that advance social, racial, economic, and environmental justice for equal justice and the dismantling of structural racism and oppression.

C5 **Engage in Policy Practice**

- Assess how social welfare policies affect the delivery of and access to social services.
- Apply critical thinking to analyze, formulate, and advocate for policies that advance human rights and social, racial, economic, and environmental justice.

C7 **Assess Individuals, Families, Groups, Organizations, and Communities**

- Apply knowledge of human behavior and person-in-environment, and other multidisciplinary theoretical frameworks to engage with clients and constituencies.
- Apply knowledge of human behavior and person-in-environment and other culturally responsive multidisciplinary theoretical frameworks when assessing clients and constituencies.

C8 **Intervene with Individuals, Families, Groups, Organizations, and Communities**

- Engage with clients and constituencies to critically choose and implement culturally responsive, evidenced-based interventions to achieve mutually agreed-on practice goals and enhance capacities of clients and constituencies.

C9 **Evaluate Practice with Individuals, Families, Groups, Organizations, and Communities**

- Select and use appropriate methods for evaluation of outcome.
- Critically analyze outcomes and apply evaluation findings to improve practice effectiveness with individuals, families, groups, organizations, and communities.

Chapter
15

Enhancing Family Functioning and Relationships

Chapter Overview

The purpose of this chapter is to introduce you to many of the intervention skills and strategies that social workers commonly employ with families. The chapter is designed to present social work practices across multiple settings and ways in which families are engaged in interventions. Toward that end, the chapter provides an overview of selected skills and intervention strategies that can be employed when social workers seek to teach families new skills or to support families that are experiencing difficult problems related to a variety of concerns, such as psychosocial concerns, communication problems, physical health diagnosis, disability, housing problems, mental health, justice system involvement, and substance abuse, among many others.

The chapter opens with a discussion of engagement strategies, what the family therapy literature often refers to as joining. The chapter proceeds with a discussion of first- and second-order change strategies and examples that are associated with each. This chapter presents intervention skills and

strategies that underlie many of the contemporary evidence-based interventions to which family members can be referred.

In this chapter, you will acquire knowledge that will enable you to:

- Understand intervention and change strategies for family systems

- Assist families in enhancing their interactions by increasing communication skills.

- Assist families in modifying their interactions.

- Assist families in understanding the influence of family roles and modifying them when needed.

- Assist family members in disengaging from conflict.

- Assist families in modifying misconceptions and distorted cognitions that impair their interactions.

- Assist families in modifying family alignments.

The EPAS Competencies in Chapter 15

This chapter will give you the information needed to meet the following practice competencies:

- Competency 2: Engage Antiracism, Diversity, Equity, and Inclusion in Practice

- Competency 6: Engage with Individuals, Families, Groups, Organizations, and Communities

- Competency 8: Intervene with Individuals, Families, Groups, Organizations, and Communities

Family Engagement

In some settings, it makes sense to insist that all family members participate in the helping process. However, the diversity of settings in which social work is practiced, and the diversity of problem areas to which social work interventions are addressed, require social workers to be flexible about who should be present during a family intervention. Moreover, such a rule can itself become a barrier to social work interventions where family members refuse to participate or where their participation is not feasible. Therefore, the decision about who to engage in family interventions should be based in part on a clear understanding of the purpose of the intervention.

What should social workers do when the intervention purpose suggests that certain members of a family actively participate, but for some reason they either refuse or are unable to participate? This can happen when children are encountering problems in school and when school social workers are seeking to enlist a partnership with busy/reluctant parents to resolve school-based problems, or when adult children of parents who reside in nursing homes decline to visit their family member or to participate in critical decisions about end-of-life care. Though it is optimal to engage all caregivers in such situations, the ideal is often simply not feasible. There is no magic formula, but there are options. In many contexts, social workers are forced to accept limited family member engagement. When this happens, it may be important for social workers to inform family members who are present about the limitations of this approach, in the spirit of informed consent. Additionally, the limitation itself can become the topic of problem solving as part of the engagement process. Whether social workers adopt the position that all family members should participate, or that only strategically selected family members should participate, family members who choose not to participate must also be granted the right to self-determination without judgment, blame, or shame. Social workers should consider family member choices about participation as information to consider in an assessment of family system structure. For example, the decision to participate or not can reflect how power dynamics and decision-making authority are wielded in a family, or it could be emblematic of a level of subsystem strength or cohesiveness that either supports or erodes family adaptive capacity. These observations can be tested through a deeper assessment of family system structure.

Social workers may also encounter client systems in which the identified client system insists on the involvement of other family members in the decision-making process. For examples, in families from collectivist cultural backgrounds, clients may prefer the involvement of a variety of family members because of their status and authority and may defer final decisions to them. In this instance, the social worker must avoid imposing a Western framework of individualism and independence. Instead, social workers must honor the client's preference and support family-based decision-making while at the same time providing an informed process that allows the client to explore different avenues before finally choosing whether they would like the involvement of family in the decision-making process.

Joining

Social workers who work with families adopt a distinctive view of client engagement, in which the social worker establishes working relationships with each member of the family as well as with the family as a whole and understands the array of diverse family decision-making processes that exist among different family systems. Family therapists often use the word "joining" to describe this process. The term "joining" implies that, in some respects, the social worker enters a family and becomes part of the family system, and just as individuals within a family have a distinctive relationship with other individual members as well as with the family as a whole, social workers who work with families strive to do the same. In joining the family, the social worker understands, confirms, and supports the family's experiences and needs (Minuchin, 1974).

The spirit of family engagement, or **joining**, requires the social worker to use specific language that encourages family members to think of the family as a collective group. In some cultures, it is typical to refer to oneself as "we" because this implies membership to a group, rather than "I." Social workers who adopt a family perspective tend to use collective language to emphasize the family unit such as, "It seems to me that your family is under a great deal of pressure and that in a way the family is trying to protect itself from [the source of stress]. Is this correct?" or to specific subsystems within the family unit (e.g., "I gather that the parents in this family are worried about the impact of [stress] on the family, and that the kids are trying to be helpful. Does this sound accurate?").

Successful family engagement happens when social workers view the family unit as a collective unit while also establishing working relationships with each member of the family. In viewing the family as a collective unit, the social worker utilizes family systems language that emphasizes boundaries, both around the family as a whole and boundaries that demarcate important family subsystems. To do this, it is recommended that social workers elicit the opinions and

C6

the perspectives of each family member who participates in any meeting or intervention and establish rapport with each member of a family early in an intervention. Indeed, clinical research in family therapy settings suggests that interventions are most successful when all members report strong relationships with their social worker, and interventions are less successful when family members vary widely in the strength of their social worker–client relationships (Friedlander et al., 2018).

When the social worker views the family as a collective, blame for or cause of problems is not placed on one individual family member, even when the family may identify the behaviors of one family members as a reason for the visit. Blame can amplify emotional and behavioral problems in individual family members who shoulder ascribed responsibility for problematic family dynamics. Blame tends to aggravate family conflict and erode family functioning. Thus, blame is inconsistent with the goal of establishing rapport with each family member and the family as a whole. A family systems approach suggests that problematic behaviors of individual family members are seen as influenced by the family systems context in which they are embedded rather than separate from the family's norms or patterns. Using a family systems approach, the entire environment, including all individuals, is involved when a family experiences a problem. The family is treated as a collective, and the primary focus is on the process of communication and problem solving rather than on the content of the problem. For example, the focus would be on how the family communicates with one another during a disagreement, rather than the subject matter about which the family is disagreeing.

Cultural Perspectives on Engagement

The engagement process with families is strongly influenced by culture and cultural differences between social workers and the families they serve. During engagement, social workers must be aware of the potential intrusion of their own bias into the helping process. Different emphases on the quality of family life, nature of relationships, norms, or problem definition may be a function of cultural and class differences between the social worker and the families with whom they are working. Self-awareness about your own positionality and taking a position of cultural humility are ongoing learning processes that are paramount in social work practice with families. Although certain factors may be germane to various cultural or racial/ethnic groups, it is important that you clarify specific content and its relevance to a family's culture, subculture, or ethnic heritage. Social workers must try to distinguish family patterns that are common to a wide

variety of families, culture-specific patterns as well as idiosyncrasies that are unique to a particular family (Goldberg, 2000). Patterns in family interactions vary. Having a strong grasp of this fact essentially minimizes a tendency to formulate generalizations about family dynamics.

Note that culture should not be used as an excuse to minimize or overlook family behavior or relationships that may inhibit basic human rights, as described in the 1948 United Nations Declaration of Human Rights. With these words of caution in mind, we highlight factors that may be considerations when initiating interventions with diverse families.

Differences in Communication Styles

You may find a range of communication styles in which some are more demonstrative in both verbal and nonverbal language such as symmetrical and complimentary communication patterns, longer periods of silence versus continuous back and forth, rules around taking turns versus interrupting, levels of disclosure, among others. Emotions are complex experiences, expressing reactions to past, present, and future events. A person's worldview frames the emotional experience, as does their language. The range of words and language that many of us use daily to describe emotions may, in fact, be unfamiliar to or have a different connotation for diverse groups. It is important that you examine your own communication style and assess how it is informed by your own cultural preferences.

In understanding communication styles and differences, techniques and strategies from postmodern family practice models may be used. For example, the narrative and social constructionist approaches emphasize a more conversational, collaborative approach, allowing for a dialogue that is more meaningful to the client, as well as facilitating communication between the family and the social worker. A narrative approach emphasizes the family as the expert of their own story, with the social worker acting as a facilitator to help highlight areas in a family's story that they would like to change or improve in order to reduce negative impacts on family functioning. A social constructivist approach makes room for alternative ways to understand and construct a family's lived experiences. A social constructivist approach also recognizes the agency of the family by framing experiences as socially constructed through forces such as culture, norms, mores, media, and society. For example, a refugee family's story around war and relocation may be reconstructed to emphasize the hope, strength, and resilience demonstrated by the family during the relocation and resettlement process rather than emphasizing displacement, poverty, and loss of home and country they experienced during their migration. Stories that emphasize hope promote change and growth rather than stories that pathologize families' experiences.

Sue (2006) also draws attention to high- and low-context communications. In low-context cultures, such as the United States, there is a greater emphasis on verbal messages as well as an orientation toward the individual. For example, in low-context communication settings, the provider may think it is acceptable to simply begin a series of questions without explaining the context for the questions to the family. For example, "Does your child require the assistance of an in-home care provider?" may be asked by a social worker who is assessing the family's current level of need; however, the family may understand this question to mean "Do you need an in-home care provider if you don't have one?" The client may answer, "Yes, I need one" because the client may have understood the question as an inquiry about whether a client needs in-home care services. However, this may create a misunderstanding if the social worker is not able to secure a referral to such a service, thus creating confusion about expectations of the service the social worker is providing. When social workers use low-context communication with high-context communicators, the likelihood of miscommunication is high. High-context cultures rely on nonverbal expressions, group identity, longer explanations of context, and a higher reliance on history of interactions between the participants. In high-context communication, the social worker would have to explain the background and the reason for the social worker–client interaction in greater detail due to a lack of history of interaction between the social worker and the client system. In the previous example, the social worker would have to state, "While I'm not in a position to provide you with this service, I must ask this question in order to determine your current ability to meet your child's activities of daily living. Do you currently have an in-home care provider who provides your child with in-home assistance with activities of daily living?" Social workers must continue to develop skills to assess the client's communication style and be able to adjust accordingly. It is also important to keep in mind that clients' individual preferences, the culture of origin, and level of acculturation may influence communication patterns and preferences. It is important not to assume a client's communication style based on their time in the host country or on whether or not they need an interpreter to communicate with you.

Hierarchical Considerations in Communication

It is important to pay careful attention to communication rules and power hierarchies within a family system during the assessment stage. Doing so helps the social worker develop effective interventions that honor the family's traditions, norms, and communication styles while at the same time facilitating the development of new patterns to promote family functioning. First and foremost, it is necessary to observe and ask questions about preferred communication practices when working with families. In some families, hierarchies may be influenced by age or gender where grandparents may be held in greater esteem than adult children and figure prominently in the family's hierarchical arrangement, or the male head of household may be in a role to make most decisions for the household. There are also instances where the eldest sibling or the most industrious sibling makes most decisions for the family.

The social worker must consult with family members about decisions and consider those family members with whom other family members may want to consult. For example, in many families, clients may wish to consult with adult children before making major health-related or financial decisions. Caution is advised when working with immigrant families in which one family member may have greater proficiency in the English language than other members of the family. It is advised that the social worker not rely on the English-speaking family member as to interpret. Asking children to interpret for other family members may cause a disruption in boundaries between subsystems and may result in role conflicts. Using a spouse to interpret for their non-English-speaking spouse may result in omission of information or loss of self-determination and autonomy for the non-English-speaking family member. It is ideal to use a third-party interpreter rather than relying on family members or friends to interpret. In addition, when families come from cultures in which chronological age and familial hierarchy play a significant role, open dialogue between parents and children may not be commonly practiced (Xiong et al., 2018). Also note that what may appear to you to be hierarchically defined roles in the family may instead be complementary. As you join with the family, it is best to ask questions, seek their preferences, and explore their rules with respect to communication, family order and hierarchy.

Authority of the Social Worker

The authority vested in the social worker can vary by culture and race/ethnicity. For some families, the helping practitioner is perceived as a knowledgeable expert who can guide them in the proper course of action, whereas some families may see the social worker as a representative of an oppressive system based on their prior experiences with seeking help. Some families may prefer a more formal approach to working with the social worker, while some may prefer a more informal and egalitarian approach. Asking family members how they would like to be addressed, whether by first name or by formal honorifics, helps the social worker further assess the family's preferred way to relate to the social worker.

A passive response to authority from immigrants, migrants, or refugees, for example, may stem from their social and political status in the United States, a distrust of helpers, and a fear of expressing their true feelings to figures of authority. Eliciting information, for example, through direct questions about the needs and wants of each family member can be problematic if the client does not understand why the question is being asked, or how the information will be used. Also, the informal use of language and expectations of full disclosure may diminish the family's trust. In the case example of Swa Bleh Soe that follows, when the social worker initially used the question, "Do you have friends that you talk to?" to assess the client's social functioning without explaining the context for the question, the client responded "No, I don't have any friends." Perhaps the client did not understand why the social worker needed to know this information, and it was within the client's rights not to disclose this information. However, when the social worker rephrased the question, "Having a social outlet is important, such as friends you can talk to or have shared interests with, so I'd like to ask you about anyone that you might talk to, and if not, we would try to find you ways to create relationships with individuals outside of your family. Tell me about your tattoos. Who did those for you?" the client responded, "My friend did." When the social worker explained the reason for the question, the client was more willing to explore the specific line of questioning.

When the social worker asked the client directly about social relationships without explaining why this was being asked, the client hesitated to disclose this information. However, when the social worker described the context for the question and related the question to an activity in the client's life that he might share with a friend the client was willing to disclose this information. Setting a context for the line of questioning provided transparency, which helped build trust and rapport with the client.

Preventing Alliances

When working with families, it is important that social workers be aware that family members who might identify with the social worker (e.g., race, gender, education level, age, assigned power) may inadvertently try to form an alliance with the social worker based on shared power statuses or worldview. Alliances with one family member based on shared commonalities results in other family members feeling marginalized or excluded from the helping process, resulting in a negative impact on the social worker's ability to provide effective services to the family. During family assessments and interventions, the social worker must give equal time to each family member in order for each family member to feel heard and

Case Example 1: Swa Bleh Soe

Swa Bleh Soe is a 24-year-old Karen immigrant who arrived in the United States in 2011. Karen are an ethnic group from Southeast Asia who began immigrating to the United States in the mid-2000s due to violence in their homeland of Myanmar. In his late teens, he developed muscular dystrophy, which has progressively affected his ability to walk. He is currently fully dependent on his family for his activities of daily living. The family is seeking in-home mental health services and support for activities of daily living for Swa. The social worker is conducting an initial assessment through an interpreter. The social worker is assessing multiple areas of the client's life to determine the client and the family's current level of functioning to develop an intervention plan based on the client's and his family's needs. During this process, the social worker asked the question, "Do you have friends that you talk to?" The cli-

ent responded, "No, I don't have friends." The social worker probed further "Is there anyone that you call on the phone or talk with on social media?" The client responded no. Later in the interview, the social worker stated, "Having a social outlet is important, such as friends you can talk to or have shared interests with, so I'd like to ask you about anyone that you might talk to, and if not, we would try to find you ways to create relationships with individuals outside of your family. Tell me about your tattoo. Who did the tattoo for you?" the client responded, "My friend did." The social worker asked, "Tell me about your friend. How long have you known your friend?" The client stated "He is my friend from high school. He gave me the tattoo a few years ago when we graduated." The social worker asked, "How often do you talk to your friend?" The client stated, "We talk on the phone every day."

included. The utilization of third-party payers often results in billing occurring for only one family member. It is important that the social worker focus their attention equally on all family members regardless on whose insurance policy is being billed. Parents also tend to leverage age and power status to form an alliance with the social worker. The social worker benefits from being transparent with the family and stating they will give each family member equal time and input into the assessment and intervention.

Power and authority are critical elements of the family–social worker relationship, especially for ethnic or racial minorities (Aponte, 1982; D'Arrigo-Patrick et al., 2017). Most diverse families perceive the social worker as acting in their professional role rather than fulfilling a social role; therefore, social workers are viewed as representatives of the majority society. Within this context, the social worker symbolizes the larger society's power, values, and standards. Because of the authority that is assigned to you as a professional, it is important to explicitly recognize families as decision makers and experts on their situations and to ensure that you have their informed consent before proceeding further. Using an anti-oppressive framework, social workers also utilize their power to promote social justice-oriented perspectives in their practice with families.

The Dynamics of Minority Status and Culture in Exploring Reservations

Clients who identify with groups who have historically been disenfranchised may exhibit reservations about seeking help. These are clients and families who, because of their gender identity, immigration status, race or ethnicity, and/or type of family composition, may have experienced discrimination or unjust treatment in the past or who have had family and friends experience such treatment. Due to past experiences, such families may question how information about their personal experiences or information will be used. Families who have experienced discrimination or unjust treatment have good reasons for their apprehensions and anxieties in encounters with helping professionals. This may cause families to delay help seeking until they have escalated to a point of crisis.

Indeed, evidence of continued unjust treatment toward individuals of minoritized identities, as well as beliefs that inhibit help seeking behavior may reinforce their silence. Also, the unspoken rule of keeping family secrets can be more pronounced in some families because of the value placed on privacy or a sense of shame about involving an outsider in family matters. Families may feel more comfortable seeking help when they do not feel the need to defend who they are or their culture and when the social worker takes a

position of cultural humility in which the client is viewed as the expert on their own lives. Utilizing cultural humility and anti-oppressive practice strategies that recognize oppressive forces in a family's life are effective strategies when building trust with families who have experienced discrimination and unjust treatment by mainstream systems. To lessen the family's concerns or reservations about the contact with you, it can be useful for you to affirm the protective function of reluctance, whether in a family member or the family system, as a measure of safety for the family (Detlaff & Fong, 2016).

Orchestrating the Initial Family or Couple Session

The goal of bringing the family together is to identify the problem at hand by eliciting the viewpoints of the various family members. The initial session, whether it occurs in the office, home, or institution is referred to as the social or joining stage (Nichols & Schwartz, 2021). In this stage, a central task is to establish rapport and build an alliance with the family.

In facilitating the social or joining stage, the social worker's tasks are twofold:

C6

1. Ensure that each family member can voice their opinions without interruptions from other family members.

2. Encourage family members to listen so that members feel understood and accepted.

You can further facilitate this stage by adopting an attitude of inquiry and curiosity about the family.

The initial session with families is crucial. The family members' experiences during this session determine in large measure whether they will join with you and contract to work toward specified goals or solutions. Moreover, they may perceive the initial session as a prototype of the helping process. Table 15-1 identifies the objectives to be accomplished that will further lay a solid foundation for future work with the family. All the objectives listed in the table are then discussed, so that you understand their relevance and can use them in both planning for and evaluating initial sessions.

Establish a Personal Relationship with Individual Members and an Alliance with the Family as a Group

In working with couples or families, social workers have a twofold task of establishing a personal relationship with everyone while developing a connectedness

Table 15-1 Orchestrating the Initial Family or Couple Session

1. Establish a personal relationship with individual members and an alliance with the family as a group.
2. Clarify expectations and explore reservations about the helping process, including potential dynamics of minority status and culture.
3. Clarify the roles and the nature of the helping process.
4. Clarify choices about participation in the helping process.
5. Elicit the family's perception of the problem.
6. Identify wants and needs of family members.
7. Define the problem as a family problem.
8. Identify any recent changes experienced by the family.
9. Emphasize individual and family strengths.
10. Establish individual and family goals based on your earlier exploration of wants and needs.

with the family as a unit. To cultivate relationships with family members, you use socializing, a technique that involves brief social chitchat at the beginning of the session to reduce tension. Joining techniques to expedite entry into the family system must respect culture, family form, family rules, and the current level of functioning. You may also find that using the family's language and idioms—for example, "He's messing up in school"—facilitates your connection to the family. You can further connect to the family by conveying your acceptance and by engaging them in identifying their strengths. Conveying acceptance and offering support may be especially critical to vulnerable members of the family.

In the initial session, empathic responding can be particularly useful in establishing rapport with a member who appears to be reserved or reluctant to be involved. For example, when a member does participate spontaneously, your task is to draw them into the session:

> **Social worker:** Tamika, we haven't heard from you about how you felt when you learned you were coming to see a social worker.
>
> **Tamika:** I don't know why I need to see a social worker. I think it will be a waste of time.
>
> **Social worker:** It is not unusual to unsure about the reason for being here. You said you thought that being here would be a waste of time. Would it be helpful if I explained the purpose of the session with you and your family?

The social worker's response included a reflection of Tamika's feelings and empathy as a facilitative skill. Empathic messages show genuine interest that can cause reserved family members to become more active. Conversely, if Tamika's lack of involvement is related to family dynamics rather than to her feelings, you will need to be mindful whether encouraging her to express an opinion has potential risks. In either case, you should endeavor to distribute time and attention somewhat equally among members, to highlight individual strengths, and to intervene when one member dominates the conversation or when the session involves members' communicating blaming, shaming, or put-down messages.

Finally, effectively connecting with families requires understanding, appreciation, and empathy for the sociopolitical and cultural context of the family and for the family's collective strengths and competencies. Often, it is these attributes that have enabled the family to function despite their difficulties.

Clarify Expectations and Explore Reservations about the Helping Process

Family members have varying and often distorted perceptions of the helping process and may have misgivings about participating in sessions (e.g., a waste of time; talking won't help). To identify obstacles to full participation (which is a prerequisite to establishing a viable contract), you should elicit the responses of all family members to open-ended questions like the following:

- What were your concerns about meeting with me?
- What did you hope might happen in our meetings together?
- What were your feelings about what might happen in this meeting today?
- Would you imagine for a moment how you would like things to be different in your family?

Questions of a more specific nature, intended to help family members express their concerns, are illustrated in the following examples:

- Are you concerned that your family might be judged?
- In your community, how do others deal with this problem?
- How do you feel about seeking help from someone outside of your family?
- In what way do you think that I can be of help to your family?

As you explore reservations, concerns, and even hopes from each family member, you can broaden the focus to the family by asking, "I'm wondering if others share the same or similar concerns as...?" As members acknowledge similar feelings, they may begin to realize that, despite their feelings, as a unit they share certain concerns in common. For example, family members might disagree about the functionality of rigid family rules, but they all may have anxieties about less income due to job loss and the financial stability of the family.

In interpreting a family member who is reluctant, unwilling, or inactive in the family session, you should be sensitive to such factors as an individual's personality and cultural norms. Some individuals may prefer to observe processes before they engage or participate. Culture may influence such expressions as feelings, so a family member may be baffled by related questions. Personality or culture aside, certain family members will continue to have strong reservations. You can address their reluctance in the initial session by asking them one of the following questions and addressing their responses:

- What, if anything, would make you feel better about participating?
- Having heard the concerns of other family members, on a scale of 1 to 10, which one would you rate as highest or lowest priority?
- Given your concerns, are you willing to stay for the remainder of the session and decide at the conclusion whether to continue?

The intent of these questions shows willingness on your part to negotiate the terms under which a family member participates and acknowledges their right of choice. If this type of question does not result in a change of heart, you might, for example, ask the member if they are willing to be physically present but emphasize that they are not obligated to talk. This invitation diminishes the pressure on the person to contribute. As a caveat, however, it would be important

to advise the individual that it is expected that they refrain from distracting nonverbal behavior. As a final note on the reluctant family member, be aware that their behavior may be self-protective because they have been identified as the source of the family's problem, especially if the person feels ganged up on by other family members.

Clarify Roles and the Nature of the Helping Process

In exploring misgivings and reservations, you should educate families about the nature of the helping process and clarify both your role and their roles. In educating families about the helping process, your objective is to create an atmosphere and structure in which problem solving can occur. Role clarification is also addressed toward the end of the initial session in which an initial contract is negotiated.

Clarify Choices about Participation in the Helping Process

In the instance of referred contact, you can reiterate that the family is free to decide whether further contact with you can meet their needs and, if so, what to work on, regardless of the concerns of the referring source. If contact is mandated, it is necessary to clarify what you are required to do (e.g., submit a report to the court) and the parameters of required contact. In addition to mandated concerns, you can advise families that they can choose to deal with other problems of concern to them.

Elicit the Family's Perception of the Problem

In initiating discussion of problems, social workers ask questions such as, "Why did you decide to seek help?" (in the case of voluntary contact), "What changes do you want to achieve?" or "How could things be better in the family?" Eliciting the family's view of the problem is equally important in involuntary or referred contacts. In such cases, the mandate or the referral has been summarized, but time and space are provided so that family members can tell their own story—for example, "Your family was required by the juvenile court judge to have contact with our agency because Juan was reported to the school truancy officer. This is the information that I have, but I still need to hear from you why you believe you are here." Juan and his parents both have a point of view, which may be similar or vastly different. As you elicit each person's viewpoint about the problem and its solution, you may, in some instances, hear different accounts. Your task, however, is to move the family toward reaching a consensus about the problem that they can all support.

In sessions with a family or a couple, you will want to be aware of differences in interpretation and the various family roles within the family with respect to issues of gender, power, and boundaries. It is important to pay attention to the language and metaphors used by the family as they describe their concerns and how family members express their views reflects their culture, their realities, and the meaning assigned to the family experience. The family experience also includes exploring spirituality or religion in the life of the family.

Identify Wants and Needs of Family Members

As you engage the family in a discussion of problems, listen for needs that are inherent in their messages, as illustrated in the family session with a foster mother and Twanna, an adolescent parent, in the following case.

Define the Problem as a Family Problem

Using a family system's approach, throughout the family session, emphasize that every member's perspective is important; that family members can do much to support the change efforts of other family members; that all members need to adjust alleviate the family's stress;

Case Example 2: Janet and Twana 1

In the case of Janet and Twanna, Janet is the foster mother of Twanna, a parenting adolescent. Her child is 2 years old. The relationship between Janet and Twanna has generally been good. Janet cares for the child, which allows Twanna to attend school so that she can obtain a high school diploma. Janet called the social worker because she is frustrated, as lately Twanna has returned home after school later than expected. Janet has a strong bond with Twanna's 2-year-old; however, Janet stressed that it was important that Twanna spend time with her child as well. She reported that the situation is affecting the entire relationship between the two of them.

Glenda, the social worker, began the initial session with a summary explanation of their understanding of the contact. They invited Janet, the foster mother who initiated the contact, and Twanna, the adolescent parent, to share their perceptions of the problem. During the initial discussions of needs and wants as expressed by Janet and Twanna, the social worker respected the rights of the foster mother while at the same time created a safe place for the adolescent to express her views. Also, they summarized the situation and empathized with the potential developmental conflict that was occurring with Twanna. That is, even though she is a mother, as an adolescent, her interest in being with friends is developmentally appropriate. In fact,

her main reason for not coming home at the expected time is because she wants to hang out with her friends. Further, she reasoned, "I know that Janet is here, it's not like I am leaving my baby alone."

At the same time, the social worker acknowledged Janet's unspoken need that her caring for the child is not taken for granted. Janet believed that Twanna should bond with the child because she, Janet, will not be there in the future. Attending to the different needs and wants as expressed by Janet and Twanna was a balancing act, as Glenda did not want to convey the perception that the needs of one person had priority and that she only supported that person's position. In summarizing the concerns identified by Janet and Twanna, Glenda asked them to identify what they would like to see changed. In preparation for problem solving, the objective was to pinpoint the conflict and have the two of them explore options that would meet both of their needs. One option considered by Twanna, for example, was "I could call if I am going to be late." By identifying and highlighting common needs, the social worker focused the intervention on the similarities rather than the differences. In this way, Glenda helped Janet and Twanna develop goals and tasks that they could mutually work toward to improve their relationship. The session concluded with the two of them having reached several critical agreements.

Case Example 3: Home for the Holidays 1

Kim, the social worker, is working with a lesbian couple, Jackie and Anna, who came to family treatment in conflict about how open to be about their relationship to their families, especially with the upcoming holiday. Jackie comes from a family in which there is open communication.

She is frustrated with the reticence to deal openly with feelings that is reflected in Anna's family. Near the beginning of the session, Kim states, "Jackie contacted me because the two of you disagree about your holiday plans."

and that the family can do much to increase the quality of relationships and the support that each member receives from others. Despite your efforts to define problems as belonging to the family, you may often encounter a persistent tendency of some members to blame others. In these situations, your tasks are to:

- Monitor your own performance to ensure that you do not collude with family members in labeling others as a problem, thus holding them responsible for the family's difficulties.
- Model the circular orientation to causality of behavior and emphasize that family members reciprocally influence one another in ways that perpetuate patterns of interaction.

In the discussion of wants and needs, you should take care to avoid a potential perception that you support one person's position over that of other family members. When one person is perceived as the source of the family's difficulties, your task is to challenge this linear

thinking by asking others about their role in creating and maintaining the problem.

Unfortunately, this level of generosity is not always present in families, as there is a tendency to blame or label behavior, generally in negative terms. In these instances, you can move to counteract patterns of attributing blame by using the technique of **delabeling**. Rather than focusing on a member's perception of behavior, delabeling emphasizes the reciprocal nature of the problem. Use of the technique can also set the stage for each member to identify positive behaviors that each would like from the other. Consider the following case example in which the social worker poses a series of questions to a mother and son. The two individuals have a history of blaming messages that are counterproductive to their communicating with each other.

In this case, both mother and son were receptive, so the social worker helped them formulate reciprocal tasks that each could work on during the week to minimize the conflict in their relationship. Their reciprocal tasks were

Case Example 4: John and Mrs. G.

John is a young man with mental illness. He has decided to move out of a group home and live independently with his girlfriend of several years. His mother, Mrs. G., is adamant that the move is a stupid decision, and she insists that John is incapable of living independently. Rather than focusing on John, the social worker utilized the following questions to focus on Mrs. G.'s participation in the problematic situation:

- You've said that John doesn't listen to you about your concerns related to his plans. When you discuss your concerns with John, how do you approach him?
- When John says he doesn't want to talk to you about his decision, how do you respond?

- How does John's reluctance to talk to you affect you and your relationship with him?

After posing questions to the mother, the social worker then divided questions between the mother and the son to explore the son's participation in the identified problem by asking the following questions:

- John, how does your mother approach you when she wants to discuss her concerns?
- What is your reaction to her approach?
- What might she do differently that would make you want to talk to her about your plans?

Case Example 5: Janet and Twanna 2

Returning to the case of Janet and Twanna, the patterned interaction between the two consisted of Janet being frustrated because Twanna failed to return home at the agreed-upon time. In turn, Twanna reasoned that Janet was there to care for the child, so the fact that she delayed coming home was not neglectful behavior on her part. Neither had talked about what they really wanted, and their interactions ended up with both being dissatisfied because neither had recognized the ways in which their behaviors contributed to the problem.

Even though Janet attributed their strained relationship to Twanna's behavior, she was careful not to label it. In fact, she said, "I understand that she wants to be with her friends."

intended to change the dynamics of their interaction by changing their individual behavior and, therefore, their responses to each other. For example, the mother would refrain from labeling John's plan as stupid, and John, in turn, agreed to listen to her concerns.

Emphasize Individual and Family Strengths

In work with families, you can highlight family strengths and protective factors on two levels: the strengths of individual members and the strengths of the entire family. At the individual level, you may observe the strengths and the resources of members during the session, drawing them to the attention of the family (e.g., Twanna is a good student). At the family level, you can report on the strengths you have observed in the way members operate as a group (Janet and Twanna have a good relationship). Protective factors and strengths include the presence of a supportive network as well as resources and characteristics of family members that contribute to and sustain the family unit. Examples of strengths-oriented statements follow:

- It is my sense that even though there are problems in your family, you seem to be very loyal to each other.
- Anna, your family's getting together for the holidays seems to connect members to each other.
- Anna and Jackie, your relationship appears to be strong, despite the difficulties that Jackie has experienced with your family.
- Janet, taking care of Twanna's child while she goes to school shows that you are supportive of her goal to obtain a high school diploma.

Family strengths and protective factors may also be utilized to communicate a focus on the future. In particular, the hopes, dreams, talents, or capacities of individual members and the family are means to energize them to resolve

current difficulties. While a goal in the initial session is to move the family toward reaching a consensus on their concerns, it is the strength of the family—rather than the problem itself— that ultimately enables them to resolve their difficulties. By exploring coping patterns with previous difficulties, experiences with positive episodes or past successes, and hopes and dreams for family life, you can activate family strengths and note their resilience in support of their capacity to change (Weick & Saleebey, 1995).

Establish Individual and Family Goals Based on Your Earlier Exploration of Wants and Needs

Goals that flow from this exploration include individual goals, family goals, and goals that pertain to subsystems (Anna and Jackie want to spend the holiday together). You might also help members to identify family goals by exploring answers to the "miracle question" (de Shazer, 1988, p. 5): "Janet and Twanna, imagine that one night while you are asleep, a miracle happens. When you awaken, how will the tension in your relationship have changed?" When asked this question, even the most troubled couples or families can describe a new miracle relationship. This vision and other desired conditions that they identify can then become goal statements, guiding efforts of both the family and the social worker.

Family Interventions

Family interventions are here classified broadly according to two types: first-order and second-order change strategies (Nichols & Schwartz, 2012). The primary distinction between first- and second-order change strategies is that first-order strategies resolve a presenting problem without regard to modifying family system structure, whereas second-order changes involve modification to family

Case Example 6: Home for the Holidays 2

To illustrate, we return to the case Home for the Holidays, in which the focus of the conversation between Anna and Jackie is on family communication styles and family rules. Kim, the social worker, shares their observation about the differences between their families and makes the point that family rules and communication styles influence the interactions in relationships.

To begin to resolve the conflict about these differences, Kim urges Anna and Jackie to consider ways to bring each other into a conversation in such a way that they can work out their differences. By encouraging them to openly discuss family-of-origin rules, they can begin to consider rules that might better serve their relationship needs.

system structures as the primary vehicle for problem solving. Said another way, first-order strategies attempt to solve problems within the current family structure, and second-order strategies attempt to foster changes to family structure itself.

Both first- and second-order change strategies are consistent with a family systems perspective, and both rely on an assessment of family system functioning, as discussed in Chapter 10. For the most part, first-order change strategies treat family system arrangements as resources or barriers to problem solving, and both types of intervention strategies rest on a thorough assessment of family resilience factors that can be leveraged in the support of change.

First-Order Change Strategies

The first-order change strategies reviewed are all directed at helping families overcome challenges that disrupt their equilibrium, helping them to return to a state of homeostasis. They work with resources within families as currently structured to enable them to mitigate family system stress without focusing on such family system topics as boundary maintenance, decision-making power and authority, or implicit family rules. This chapter presents three first-order change strategies: problem solving, skills training, and contingency contracting.

Problem-Solving Approaches

Problem-solving models addressed in Chapter 13 can be extended directly to social work with families with positive effect. For instance, the application of the task-centered model, including the task implementation sequence, can be extended to social work with families with little to no modification. Similarly, solution-focused therapy has a long history of direct application to family interventions (Nichols & Schwartz, 2012). Both models utilize flexible procedures that, from a

process standpoint, vary little whether the target system is an individual, a subset of family members, or all members of a family.

Although the steps or the procedures of problem-solving models may not require modifications when working with families, the case of Janet and Twanna illustrates some of the ways in which family interventions vary from interventions with individuals. First, the case illustrates the importance of engaging family members simultaneously in the intervention process. Thus, social workers using problem-solving approaches with families will seek to obtain the perspectives of multiple family members on matters such as the definition of the problem, goals, exceptions (when using a solution-focused model), and tasks (when using a task-centered model). Often, social workers may need to mediate differences of opinion, all while striving to maintain strong relationships with each individual family member as well as with the family.

Second, although elements of the family system structure are usually not the target of an intervention when using a problem-solving approach as a first-order change strategy, this does not mean that social workers are inattentive to family system structure in their assessment. During the first session with Janet and Twanna, Janet revealed that she was in a dual-role relationship, having the responsibility to assure the baby's care needs and to help Twanna take over the role of primary parent. Role conflict regarding the care of Twanna's baby became central during the second session. In this instance, role conflict represented an important source of conflict and thus a potential barrier to problem solving but also might be a source of strength, as it afforded both Twanna and Janet the knowledge that Twanna's baby would be well cared for. The social worker who adopts a family systems approach may discuss matters of family system structure such as role conflict directly with families during the task implementation sequence, for example, or search for

Case Example 7: Janet and Twanna 3

Twanna, age 17, is a single parenting adolescent. Prior to coming to live with Janet, she had been in placement since the age of eight, with three other foster families. As she grew older, and especially after she became pregnant, she was no longer welcome as a member of the last family. Out-of-wedlock births, especially among adolescents and teens, remain taboo, and the young women are stigmatized. In fact, her previous foster parents were outraged and embarrassed by her pregnancy and requested that she be removed from their home. As Weinberg (2006) notes, young single mothers often represent several marginalized categories: they are young, female, impoverished, racial or ethnic minorities, from lower- or working-class families, and they have had children outside of the institution of marriage. Also, the young women have experienced several failures, from their families, the education system, and in some instances their community. In Twanna's case, she is also vulnerable because of an additional marginal category, that of being a ward of the state. Her biological mother had been judged inadequate; hence, she became a ward, and her child now also has the same status. Until she came to live with Janet in her home, Twanna's support system consisted of a series of child welfare workers.

In working with Twanna, it is important to be aware of the other challenges that she faces, specifically her developmental stage and that of her child. In many respects, her wants and needs and that of her child—related to their developmental journeys—have certain similarities, summarized in these comparisons:

Twanna	Child
Identity and independence	Autonomy
Intimacy	Nurturing
Self-efficacy	Self-esteem
Attachment	Attachment
Relationships	Social interactions

Developmentally, however, they differ, as a young child needs consistency, and the adolescent is in the process of exploration and experimentation. While adolescents search for their identity, separate and apart from their families and through their peers, the young child's sense of self is gained through interactions with their caretaker. In Twanna's case, she is attempting to meet her own needs and those of her child, which, without the support of Janet, could result in role strain and overload. The social worker noted this conflict in her summary statement to Twanna: "What you are saying is that you understand that you are responsible for your child but that you also need to be with your friends."

In the broader scheme of things, changes in the bonds between an adolescent seeking greater autonomy and their adult caretakers may require changes in interactions and communication patterns (Baer, 1999). As a foster parent, Janet makes certain demands that are consistent with her role as a parent, aspects of which include her obligation to ensure the well-being of Twanna and her child. According to Weinberg (2006), interventions with minors who are also parents is a balancing act between being a disciplinarian and an emancipator. It is not uncommon for parents to establish protective boundaries, which may include anxieties about both peers and the neighborhood, and undertake intense monitoring (Jarrett, 1995). For example, Janet wanted to meet Twanna's friends so she could get to know them. This family unit is, however, different from the normative family structure, and the rules of the state that has custody of Twanna and her child set a certain tone for their interactions. For example, as a family unit, their interactions may be primarily with professionals; supportive family networks of kin and friends are not a given. In many respects, Janet and Twanna are attempting to establish functional family rules without the benefit of role models pertinent to their family form and structure.

exceptions to problematic family functioning when using a solution-focused approach.

Third, while problem-solving efforts can appear to be egalitarian processes, this is, in fact, not the case in most families. Power and decision-making authority, both formal and informal, vary across and within subsystems of a family. Social workers need to recognize power hierarchies and make decisions about how to lead the problem-solving process in light of this information. Rarely should a social worker act to negate a formal hierarchy, for example. Instead, interventions with families should reinforce an adaptive utilization of power and authority that maximizes human rights and social justice (McDowell et al., 2012; D'Arrigo-Patrick et al., 2017). At the same time, problem-solving efforts that are conducted without regard to the informal power of individual family members and subsystems may contribute to the failure of a problem-solving effort. Even young children have the power to derail a problem-solving effort through noncooperation and the exercise of personal agency.

Finally, the sociopolitical environment of the family can have important implications for problem-solving interventions as well. For example, in the Janet/Twanna case, Twanna's intersecting identities (teenager/parent/foster child) and the definition of the family (as a foster family) can have important social meaning among her friendship networks as well as for the internal functioning and roles within the family. Social workers should be attentive to the meaning ascribed by family members to sociopolitical factors and to the way in which the sociopolitical environment creates opportunities and barriers for achieving progress in problem-solving efforts (D'Arrigo-Patrick et al., 2017).

Skills Training

Social workers are frequently called upon to teach skills either as a core intervention activity or as an ancillary intervention in support of a larger intervention effort with families. Examples of interventions with skill-training components include parenting skills programs, caregiver support programs, stress reduction, as well as communication skills training. Parenting skills programs teach child-rearing practices to minimize the use of harsh parenting practices and increase the consistency of positive parenting practices such as the use of praise and strategic reinforcement of target behaviors in children (Kaminski et al., 2008). Caregiver support programs, often developed for family members who care for clients suffering from dementia, help caregivers to develop management strategies that meet client emotional and physical needs and de-escalation strategies for helping clients return to a baseline level of emotional functioning after becoming anxious, confused, or upset (Jensen et al., 2015). Mindfulness-based stress reduction skills have been shown to have short- and long-term benefits in emotional, cognitive, and interpersonal functioning (Van Vliet et al., 2017), Communication skills training programs help families maximize their problem-solving and listening skills and decrease criticism and conflict (Hawkins et al., 2008).

For these and other problems, packaged evidence-based intervention programs are available, and their use is recommended whenever possible. In the skill-training

categories presented, large-scale synthesis of published and unpublished outcome research points strongly to the effectiveness of skill training when it is implemented consistently and in accordance with the intervention manuals that are frequently available. At the systems level, implementation of evidence-based skills training can make an important difference for families who are involved in child welfare, juvenile justice, and health care systems.

Often, however, social workers are called upon to teach skills for problems where manualized, evidence-based interventions do not exist. Skill training can be part of larger intervention efforts such as task-centered social work and cognitive behavioral therapy where clients require specific skills in order to complete planned intervention activities. For these instances, research in the field of organizational psychology (Healy & Bourne, 2012), as well as research on skill-training programs in the human service fields, is directly relevant and is suggestive of a set of principles that can be built into any skill-training intervention. These principles are oriented toward skill mastery as well as transferability; that is, they help clients learn the skill and implement the skill under real-world conditions.

The first principle is elementary for social workers: to conduct a careful assessment of clients' potential skill deficits. Care should be taken at this stage because a lack of skill expression does not necessarily indicate a skill deficit. Instead, environmental contingencies could suppress skillful behaviors or reinforce unwanted behaviors. For example, Twanna may know specific soothing behaviors to use when her infant becomes upset or has tantrums, but employing these skills may require specific cues from Janet to act as reminders, or Twanna may need to employ other skills associated with emotion regulation to manage her own agitation. In such a case, an intervention may be needed to modify the environment to make skill expression more likely.

Second, once a skill deficit is ascertained, it is important for the social worker and the client to define the skill as specifically as possible. Often, skills have cognitive as well as behavioral components. Both should be explicated. In conducting this step, it is important to incorporate as much as possible the contingencies and the complications that clients may encounter when they transfer skill training to their day-to-day lives (Healy & Bourne, 2012). Skills training that is divorced from the context in which clients will eventually utilize their new skills can impede skill transferability.

Third, teach skills through presentation and discussion. Often, skills taught by social workers include a series of mental and behavioral steps, so that skill implementation by clients initially requires effortful memory. To facilitate learning, research suggests that clients be engaged in a process of active learning (Healy & Bourne, 2012). Active learning can involve mental rehearsal, linking new knowledge to prior knowledge and experience, and developing their own definitions for key concepts and skill stages. The key is to help clients internalize and reinterpret knowledge, maximizing the depth of mental processing that they engage in on their way to learning.

Fourth, many skill-training programs include role models of successful skill expression. For example, The Incredible Years© program, an evidence-based intervention for the prevention and treatment of disruptive behavior problems in early childhood, utilizes video role modeling (Webster-Stratton, 1984; Webster-Stratton et al., 2014). The videos present vignettes to model implementation of key intervention principles and foster discussion among participants. Of course, video role models are not available, nor required, for most skill-training interventions. The social worker can provide role modeling through role-play exercises in which the social worker demonstrates positive use of skills. Again, it is critical that the role model incorporate the complexity of the target environment in which clients will eventually use the skills.

Finally, clients should be afforded the opportunity for skill practice where direct feedback is possible (Healy & Bourne, 2012). Consideration should be given to the structure of practice, again ensuring that the practice context mirrors the contingencies that clients may face when implementing their skills in the real world. For example, in a meta-analysis of parenting skills programs, among the most important components for parenting outcomes was the opportunity to practice skills under observation with their own children (Kaminski et al., 2008).

Contingency Contracting

Social workers often broker reciprocal agreements among family members. In this kind of quid pro quo or contingency contract, a member agrees to disengage from conflict if the other party agrees to avoid using code words that always prompt a negative response. Code words refer to words used to convey a message indirectly, since stating the message directly would appear aggressive. Individuals are receptive to making changes when other parties agree to make reciprocal changes for two reasons. First, people are more prone to give when they know they are getting something in return. Second, when all parties involved agree to make changes, no single person loses face by appearing to be the sole cause of an interactional problem.

Contracting for reciprocal changes can be a powerful means of inducing change within families. Contingency contracting counters the tendency to wait for others to initiate changes and encourages mutual engagement of family members in the change process. This mutual involvement may spark collaboration in other dimensions of family relationships.

Family members are unlikely to be able to implement reciprocal contracts if they have not moved beyond bickering and blaming one another for their problems. For this reason, we recommend deferring use of this technique (unless clients spontaneously begin to negotiate) until you have assisted family members in listening attentively to one another and changing the tone of their interactions. It is also essential that participants demonstrate a commitment to improving their relationship. If family members view their own or others' changes as emanating primarily from meeting the stipulations of an agreement rather than as a way to improve their relationship, they are likely to devalue the changes. Therefore, you will want to ask family members to explicitly clarify that improving their relationship is the primary factor motivating their willingness to make changes.

The following are examples of reciprocal agreements that could have been utilized with Jackie and Anna (see Case Example: Home for the Holidays) and Janet and Twanna (see Case Example: Janet and Twanna). You may use them as a guide in assisting families to develop their own agreements.

- Jackie agrees to talk with her family if Anna stops pushing and allows her to do so when she is ready.
- Jackie agrees to communicate her feelings if Anna agrees to accept that there are times when Jackie is too tired to talk.
- Janet will refrain from interfering with Twanna's parenting and agrees to help her strengthen her bonds with her child.

In developing reciprocal contracts, it is wise to encourage family members to make their own reciprocal behavioral agreement. By so doing, they become invested in the proposed changes. Moreover, they often generate innovative and constructive ideas based on their knowledge of their family that might not occur to you. To facilitate families in making proposals, you can use a message such as the following: "It's clear that each of you is unhappy with the situation. Perhaps this is a good time for you to develop ideas about what you could do to improve the situation." You could then prompt them to think about reciprocal actions.

As you mutually consider proposals, it is important to explore potential barriers and guard against the tendency to undertake overly ambitious actions. Initial task exchanges in reciprocal agreements should be relatively simple and likely to succeed, especially when intense conflict has marked interactions. When a feasible reciprocal proposal has been agreed upon, you can assist family members to reach a further agreement that specifies the tasks each member will complete prior to the next session. In developing and planning to implement these tasks, follow the steps of the task implementation sequence (outlined in Chapter 13). As you plan task implementation with family members or couples, stress that each person must exercise good faith in carrying out their part of the contract, as illustrated in the following message:

> **Social worker:** You have agreed to make the changes we've discussed in an effort to improve the situation for everyone. To make these changes successful, however, each of you will need to carry out your part—no matter what the other person does. Waiting for the other person to carry out their part first may result in neither of you making a move by the time of our next session. Remember, failure by the other person to honor the contract is no excuse for you to do likewise. If the other person does not keep to the agreement, you can take satisfaction in knowing that you did your part.

Stressing the individual responsibility of all family members to fulfill their respective commitments, as in the preceding message, counters the tendency of clients to justify their inaction in subsequent sessions by asserting, "They didn't carry out their part. I knew this would happen, so I didn't do my part either." If one or more family members have not fulfilled their parts of the agreement, you can focus on obstacles that prevented them from doing so. When the results have been favorable, you can focus on this experience to set the stage for exploring additional ways of achieving further positive interaction.

Second-Order Change Strategies

The second-order change strategies reviewed aim to help families adopt family structural characteristics that are more adaptive than current modes of functioning. While in first-order change strategies social workers help families solve presenting problems as the direct focus of their work together, second-order change strategies consider presenting problems as manifestations of family characteristics and dynamics that we described in Chapter 10 as family structure. Thus, the second-order change strategies presented here solve presenting problems indirectly through changes in family system structure characteristics. These intervention strategies focus on such topics as family rules, boundaries, communication patterns,

and hierarchy. This chapter presents four second-order change strategies: modifying misconceptions and distorted cognitions, modifying communication patterns, modifying family rules, and modifying family alignments and hierarchy.

Modifying Misconceptions and Cognitive Distortions

Cognitive distortions or erroneous beliefs typically lead to dissatisfaction in couple and family relationships. Unrealistic expectations of others and myths are two other forms of misconceptions that contribute to relationship problems. As with rules, unrealistic expectations are not always obvious, so you may have to clarify them by asking family members about their expectations of one another. Myths are like rules in that they govern family operations by shaping beliefs and expectations that can profoundly influence interactions in couple and family relationships.

To diminish misconceptions and dispel myths, bring them out in the open, using empathy to help family members recognize their distorted cognitions (e.g., I can see how you might think that). Misconceptions and myths generally protect people from having to face the reality of their cognitions and perceptions. Therefore, attempts to change them can be perceived as threatening. Seldom are they relinquished without a struggle because introducing an alternative perspective or new information that is contrary to a person's beliefs creates cognitive dissonance. In addition, making essential change entails resolving fears, not the least of which is risking the consequences of learning and implementing new behavior. In these instances, your empathetic response to fears and ambivalence and providing emotional support can be the impetus for people to change (e.g., I can see how it might be difficult to consider that they may have understood that differently).

In this case example, observe that as the social worker addressed the family myth and highlighted the adverse impact of the myths on Gary. This tactic switched the focus from the abstract to the concrete and provided the parents with an opportunity to review and evaluate their beliefs. The social worker then further attempted to invalidate the myth by asking them to apply it to themselves.

You may frequently encounter families who have distorted perceptions of one another that contribute to repetitive dysfunctional interactions. Labeling the behaviors of others is a common source of cognitive and perceptual distortions. Labeling is like wearing a blinder because it places people in a certain frame, thereby limiting their attributes and behaviors to fit the framed image. In effect, the frame effectively obscures other qualities,

Case Example 8: Gary

Consider a family in which an adolescent, age 17, is experiencing extreme tension and anxiety because of parental expectations. During family sessions, it becomes apparent that the parents expect him to be a top student so that he can become a doctor. It is also obvious that the parents embrace the generalized myth "If you try hard enough, you can become anything you want." To reduce the pressure on the son, dispel the myth as it applies to him, and modify the parents' expectations, the social worker meets separately with the parents. The following excerpt is taken from that session:

> **Social worker:** I've been very concerned that Gary has been making an almost superhuman effort to do well in chemistry and physics, but he is not doing well in these subjects. It is my impression that he feels pressured to become a doctor, and that one reason he's so anxious is that he doesn't believe that he can do better despite his best efforts. It's important to him to have you think well of him, but he is falling short even though he continues to drive himself.
>
> **Father:** Poof! Of course, he is working hard. Why shouldn't he? He can become a doctor if he really wants to and

continues to apply himself. You know, I could have been a doctor, but what did I do? I goofed off. I don't want Gary to repeat my mistake. He should recognize that he has opportunities that neither his mother nor I had.

> **Social worker:** I sense your concern and care for Gary. Is it your perception that he is goofing off? I understand that both of you share the belief people can do anything they want. This message has been clear to Gary, and he's blaming himself because he's not making it, no matter how hard he tries.
>
> **Mother:** Don't you think anyone can succeed in anything if they try hard enough?
>
> **Social worker:** Actually, this belief is inconsistent with what I know about differences between people. Each of us has different aptitudes, talents, and learning styles. Some people can handle types of work that require dexterity. Others can visualize spatial relationships. Everyone has certain aptitudes, types of intelligence, and limitations. What's important in deciding a future career is discovering what our own aptitudes are and making choices that match them. I wonder if each of you can identify talents and limitations that you have.

so that in dealing with an individual, a person simply must rely on their preexisting cognitions or perceptions.

Myths that distort individual or family perceptions can extend beyond those that influence internal family dynamics. They can also be linked to discrimination, bigotry, and negative schemas ingrained in societal and institutional perceptions and in attitudes held about certain families. Distortions can be so embedded that for some individuals they do not warrant further critique. Instead, they become the generalized narrative that informs what people believe about others. For example, families of color or immigrant families are often criticized for their children's performance on standardized achievement tests. Conclusions are drawn about youth based on their style of dress or music preferences. Immigrant families are expected to act, dress, and speak in a certain way that is comfortable for mainstream society, and families who are different by virtue of their physical attributes, sexual orientation, language, or customs are mocked, shunned, or threatened. On a macro level, these perceptions and distortions can influence where families choose to live, how they perceive their safety, and with whom their children are allowed to

interact. Social workers must use cultural humility when assessing families and use anti-oppressive strategies when developing interventions in order to accurately reflect the needs and experiences of diverse families.

When you observe myths and distortions about others operating in families, you have a responsibility to address them in the same manner as you would in intervening in other family dynamics because they affect the families toward whom this behavior is directed. They are also a source of stress and strain for those who hold these beliefs, infusing negativity in their interactions. A word of caution is in order, however. In focusing on the impact of labeling, myths, and distorted perceptions, either in intrafamilial or extrafamilial interactions, take care to describe the specific behavior rather than using a label to characterize the behavior.

C2

Modifying Communication Patterns

Communication approaches to families consist of working with families to develop clear communication. The aim is to regulate and modify family communication patterns and alter communication styles to promote positive interactions and family relationships (Jackson & Weakland, 1961; Satir, 1967; Whitaker, 1958). It is believed that the patterns family members use to communicate with one another are often interpreted in various ways and are often punctuated by faulty cognitions and perceptions. What the sender believes is the message is not necessarily what the receiver understands the message to be. A difficult relationship between sender and receiver can also strain or distort the message.

Giving and Receiving Feedback

Positive feedback from significant others (e.g., expressions of caring, approval, encouragement, affection, appreciation, and other forms of positive attention) nourish morale, emotional security, confidence, and the feeling of being valued by others. Thus, increasing positive feedback fosters the well-being of individuals and harmonious family relationships. To enable family members to increase positive feedback, social workers must have skills in the following areas:

- Engaging families in assessing the extent to which they give and receive positive feedback
- Educating families about positive feedback

In the following sections, each of these skills is discussed.

Assessing Positive and Negative Feedback

Destructive communication patterns often result from strained relationships, such that the family system eventually becomes unbalanced. Communication theorists view the family as a functional system that depends on two communication processes: negative and positive feedback. They also believe that all behavior is communication. Thus, they view the social worker's role as one of helping the family change the process of family interactions.

You can help families and individual members to directly explore dimensions of communication by assessing how often and in what manner they convey positive feedback to significant others. Questions you might ask in couple or family sessions to achieve this end include the following:

- How do you send messages that let family members [or your partner] know that you care about them?
- How frequently do you send such messages?
- How often do you give feedback to others concerning their positive actions?

In instances of severe couple or family breakdown, members may acknowledge that they send positive messages infrequently or not at all. In some cases, they may actually have tepid positive feelings, but they usually experience more than they express. Besides exploring how couples or family members convey positive feedback, you can explore their desires to receive increased feedback from one another. Discussing how family members send positive messages, or to what extent they desire increased positive feedback, can open channels for positive communication and improve relationships that have been stuck in a cycle of repetitive arguments, criticisms, blaming, and put-down messages.

Teaching Positive Feedback

To assist families in conveying positive feedback, you can teach them to personalize their messages and guide them in giving positive feedback to others. Timely use of role play as an educational intervention helps family members form positive messages and develop the skills needed to share their experiences in an authentic manner. When negative situations of some intensity have been part of the family's style for an extended period of time, you may also need to help family members learn how to accept and trust positive feedback.

The following are examples of messages that explicitly express a need for positive feedback:

> **Partner:** When we were talking about plans for my mother, I didn't interrupt you. I wish you would notice when I do something different.
> **Adolescent:** I felt discouraged when I showed you my grades yesterday. I really worked hard this term, and the only thing you seemed to notice was the one B. It didn't seem to matter that the rest were As.

In each of these statements, the speaker used "I" to personalize their messages. Each message also clearly indicates what the speaker is seeking from the other person. When messages are less clear, they may lead to a further breakdown in communications. You can intervene in these situations by using the technique of on-the-spot interventions (see On-the-spot Interventions later in this chapter). When using this technique, you coach family members to formulate clear messages that express their feelings and needs, as illustrated in the following exchange. It begins with a message from a child who is seeking positive feedback from their parent, but what they want from the parent is unclear.

> **Zara [to parent]:** I worked really hard at picking up around the house before you came home, but the only thing you noticed was the glass I left near the kitchen sink.
> **Marny [to adolescent]:** Well, let's face it. The glass was there, as you yourself admitted.

Social worker: Marny, Zara was expressing what is important to them in the relationship, and I don't want their point to get lost in an argument. Zara, think for a moment about what you said. What is it you are asking of your mom?

Zara [after pausing]: Do you mean my mom not noticing what I do?

Social worker: In a way, yes. Would you like your mom to let you know you're appreciated for what you have done?

In this scenario, Zara has shared important information—namely, the need to feel valued. People want to receive positive feedback for what they are and what they do. Interactions that continuously focus on negative results may leave an individual feeling discouraged and insecure, and, consequently, relationships suffer. When instructing Zara and Marny about the importance of positive feedback, the social worker used this opportunity to allow them to practice communicating in a different manner:

Social worker: Zara, I'd like you to start over and express that you want positive feedback from your mom. This time, however, send an "I" message so that it is clear what you want from him.

Zara [hesitating]: I hope that I can. Mom, I need you to tell me about the things that I do well and not only about what is wrong.

Initially, clients may feel timid about expressing their feelings clearly. The second part of helping family members to communicate is by assisting them in listening attentively. Asking Marny to repeat what they heard in Zara's message is one way to emphasize listening for content. Because individuals may not always express their needs openly and clearly, family members may need to go beyond just listening. That is, they may need to become attuned to needs expressed in the form of complaints, questions, and the attitudes of others. Tuning in also involves alerting others to pay attention to nonverbal messages and what those messages communicate about feelings.

Because it is difficult for family members to be attuned to the needs inherent in the messages of others, you should take advantage of teachable moments to help them learn this skill, as illustrated in the preceding situation. Specifically, the social worker encouraged Zara to express their need for positive feedback from Marny. Also, when the social worker focused on Zara, she played a facilitative role in prompting them to express themself directly to Marny. The social worker likewise had Marny provide feedback to Zara, thus performing a critical role in facilitating positive interactions between the couple. This is a crucial point. Serving as a catalyst, the social worker helped Marny and Zara learn new communication skills by having them engage in positive interaction, which is an effective mode of learning.

After teaching the use of "I" statements during sessions with families, family members may be ready to work on the ultimate goal—increasing their rates of positive feedback. You can assist them by negotiating tasks that specify providing positive feedback at higher frequencies. Families, of course, must consent to tasks and determine the rate of positive feedback they seek to achieve. Family members can review their baseline information (gathered earlier through monitoring) and can be encouraged to set a daily rate that stretches them beyond their usual level. For example, using the previous example, a parent whose mean baseline daily rate in giving positive feedback to their child is a 1.0 might select an initial task of giving positive feedback twice daily. The parent would then gradually increase the number of positive messages until they reached a self-selected optimal rate of five times daily.

Modifying Family Rules

Family rules govern the range of behavior in the family system and the sequence of interactions or reactions to a particular event. Rules are a means by which the family system maintains its equilibrium. Dysfunctional family rules, however, can severely impair the functioning of family members. Because family rules are often covert, it follows that changes can occur only by bringing them into the open. You can assist family members to consider the effects of rules on family interactions.

It can be useful to have family members make a list of apparent and unspoken rules so that you and they can understand how the family operates. You can prepare families to consider rules by introducing them to the concept, as illustrated in the following message:

Social worker: As we begin to work on problems the family is experiencing, we need to know more about how your family operates. Every family has some rules or understandings about how members are to behave. Sometimes these rules are easy to spot. For example, each person is to clear their own plate after a meal is a rule that all members of a family might be expected to follow. This is an apparent rule because every member of the family could easily tell me what is expected of them at the end of the meal, but the family's behavior is also governed by other rules that are less easy to identify. Even though members follow these rules, they are often unaware that they exist. I'm going to ask you some questions that can help you to understand these two kinds of rules better and to identify some of the ones that operate in your family.

Case Example 9: Sheng and Chao Thao

Consider the social worker's role in the following excerpt from a third session with Sheng, Chao, and their three daughters, in which the social worker assisted the family to identify how hidden rules influence their patterned interactions:

Mai Shoua [age 14]: You took the red jersey again, right out of my closet, and you didn't ask. That's really bogus.

Cynthia [age 15]: You took the phone charger last week, and you still have it. What's up with that?

Chao: In this family, we share, and you girls should know this.

Social worker: This seems to be a family rule. What does this rule mean in this family?

Chao: It means that we have a limited amount of money to spend on extras, so we buy things for the girls to use together, and no one person owns the things we buy. Besides, the girls are expected to share because they are so close in age and like similar things.

Social worker: So, what happens when there is a disagreement about a particular item?

Mai Shoua: I got mad at Cynthia, and I told her so.

Social worker [to Cynthia]: Then what did you do?

Cynthia: I told Mai Shoua she didn't have any right to complain because she wasn't sharing things either.

Social worker: Cynthia and Mai Shoua, the two of you were engaged in blaming messages. Do you see it the same way? [Girls nod.] [To Chao] I wonder if you remember what you did when Cynthia and Mai Shoua were arguing.

Chao: I was trying to get them to stop arguing and yelling at each other and reminding them that they are expected to share.

Social worker [exploring hidden rule]: Is everyone in the family aware of the expectation of sharing? I'd like to begin by asking a few questions to see if you can figure out what the rules are in your family. Are you willing to explore this further?

Social worker [to Jennifer]: You weren't involved in this argument. Do you argue with anyone in the family?

Jennifer [age 12, laughs]: My mother and Mai Shoua, but mainly, I argue with my mother.

Social worker: When you get in an argument with your mother, what happens?

Jennifer: If my dad is home, he tries to stop it. Sometimes he tells my mother to go upstairs, and he'll talk to me.

Social worker [to Sheng]: When your husband stops an argument between the girls, or you and one of the girls, what do you do?

Sheng: Sometimes I let him deal with the problem, with Jennifer, or one of the other girls, but when he gets involved like that, it makes me so furious that sometimes he and I end up in a fight ourselves.

Social worker: We need to do a lot more work to understand what happens in such situations, but for the moment, let's see, Chao, if you can put your finger on the rule.

Chao: I guess I'm always trying to stop everyone from fighting and arguing in the family. I expect the girls to share and get along with each other and not cause their mother grief.

Social worker: It does seem as if you are the family's mediator. I would think that would be a difficult role to play.

Chao: Well, there are no rewards for it, I can tell you that!

Social worker: There's more to the rule. Who lets the father be the mediator?

Sheng: We all do.

Social worker: That's right. It isn't the father's rule; it's the family's rule. It takes the rest of the family to argue and the father to break up the fights.

You can first ask family members to list some apparent rules, coaching them as needed, by asking questions such as, "What are your rules about school–work (or watching television, household chores, friends)"? Once family members have identified some of their common and readily apparent rules, you can then lead them into a discussion of implicit rules. For example, you might ask them to identify family rules about showing anger or positive feelings or to explore decision-making or power (e.g., "Who do people go to in the family when they want something?"). The intent of these questions is not to engage in a lengthy exploration of rules but rather to illustrate how hidden rules can influence family behavior, stressing that certain rules may hamper their interactions.

Many avenues could be explored in this example, but the social worker chose to narrow the focus by helping the family to identify one of its major rules— the expectation to share. They also addressed the rule that specifies the father's role of mediator in disputes. Picture yourself as the social worker in this family situation. After further exploring specific patterned interactions of the family, you can use questions like the following to help them weigh whether they wish to continue relating under the old rules.

To the Father

- How effective are you in stopping the girls and their mother from fighting?
- What are your worst fears about what might occur in the family if you didn't play that role?
- Would you like to free yourself from the role of being the family mediator?

To Other Family Members

- Do you want the father to continue to be the third party in your arguments?
- What are the risks to your relationships if he discontinued playing the role of mediator?
- Do you want to work out your own disputes?

Questions such as these focus the attention of all members on their patterned interactions and encourage them to determine the function of the behavior in the system.

Next, you would have the major task of assisting the Thao family to modify their rules by teaching them new skills for resolving disagreements. Also, you would coach the father in declining the role of mediator and the girls and their mother in requesting that he let them manage their own conflicts.

Modifying Family Alignments and Hierarchy

All families develop patterns of affiliation between members that either enhance or impair opportunities for individual growth or the family's ability to carry out survival functions. The functional structure—that is, the family's invisible or covert set of demands or code of behavior—reflects and regulates family functioning and determines transactional patterns (Minuchin, 1974). In this section, we draw upon structural approach techniques to guide intervention strategies when family functioning is impaired by dysfunctional alignments.

Structural family therapy is intended to strengthen current family relationships, interactions, and transactional patterns. The approach emphasizes the wholeness of the family—that is, its hierarchical organization and the interdependent functioning of subsystems (Goldenberg & Goldenberg, 2004; Minuchin, 1974). Because of its primary focus on improving family relationships, structural therapy

pays attention to subsystems, boundaries, alignments in the family system, and power, using the resources and power inherent in families to effect change. Graphic symbols of the family structure and alignment include lines that show rigid, diffused, or clear boundaries, as well as conflict and coalitions (Nichols & Schwartz, 2012). Using the technique of enactment, family members are encouraged to interact with each other during a family session. This exercise is observed by the social worker, who subsequently intervenes to modify problematic interactions.

Interventions to modify alignments are generally indicated in the following circumstances:

- Bonds are weak between spouses, other individuals who form the parental subsystem, or other family members.
- Enmeshed alliances—that is, rigid or overly restrictive boundaries between members—limit appropriate bonds with other members (or outsiders).
- Two members of a family attempt to cope with dissatisfaction or conflict in their relationship by forming a coalition with a third family member, a phenomenon known as triangulation.
- Family members are disengaged or alienated from one another, tending to go their own ways, with little reliance on each other for emotional support.
- Members of the family have formed alliances with persons outside the immediate family (e.g., friends and relatives) that interfere with performing appropriate family roles or providing appropriate emotional support to other family members.

Structural Mapping

In intervening to modify alignments, structural mapping may be used to delineate family boundaries and highlight and modify interactions and transactional patterns. Structural mapping identifies symptoms that may be exhibited by an individual family member as an expression of difficulties in the family system. The structure of the family is revealed by who talks to whom and in what way—that is, in an unfavorable or favorable position—and how intense the family's transactions are. The goal of the structural approach is to change family structures by altering boundaries and by realigning subsystems to enhance family functioning. Interventions are thus devised to achieve the following goals:

- Develop alliances, cultivate new alliances, or strengthen underdeveloped relationships. For example, a social worker might help a new stepparent and stepchild explore ways to develop a relationship, or the social worker might help a parent who has been in prison strengthen emotional bonds to their children.

- Reinforce an alliance by acting to maintain the alliance or amplify its scope and/or strength. For instance, a social worker might assist a single parent in increasing their ability to operate as an effective executive subsystem (e.g., Twanna).

- Differentiate individuals and subsystems. For example, a social worker might help a parent who gives most of their attention to a newborn infant understand the need for supervision of older children and invest some of their emotional energy in them.

- Increase family interactions in disengaged families to make boundaries more permeable by changing the way in which members relate to one another.

- Help family members accommodate changing circumstances or transitions by decreasing rigid structures or rules that are no longer viable. For example, as a child reaches adolescence, the social worker might help the parents revise their expectations of the child's behavior or modify rules to accommodate this developmental change.

As can be surmised from these examples, structural problems may arise when the family structure is unable to adequately adjust to changing circumstances. Changing circumstances may be the result of external environmental forces, stressful transitions, or dynamics internal to the family system. Before you intervene to restructure the family system, it is important to understand the structural change as unique to the family's situation and make clear the nature of the structural dysfunction. Thus, the family should be involved in determining whether, and in what ways, such changes should take place.

Your first task in this respect is to assist family members in identifying the nature of their alignments. This may be accomplished by asking general questions that stimulate family members to consider their alignments:

- If you had a difficult problem and needed help, whom would you seek out in the family (or extended family/clan)?

- Sometimes members of a family feel closer to some members than to others and may pair up or group together. Which members of your family, if any, group together?

- In most families, members argue to some extent. With whom do you argue? With whom do other members argue?

- Is there one person in the family who is a favorite?

- [To parents] When you make a decision, do you feel that your decision is supported by the other parent? Are other people involved in your decisions?

You can also bring alignments and coalitions to the family's attention as they are manifested in family sessions:

- Mai Shoua, it seems that you're the center of the family. Most of the conversation seems to be directed through you, while other family members, except for Chao, appear to be observers of the discussion.

- Janet, in your description of how you spend your day, it appears that the baby receives a great deal of your attention.

- [To Twanna] When you are upset, who do you talk to about how you feel?

- I noticed that each of you identified the same individual on your map. Can you tell me about this person and their role in your family?

As family members become aware of their alignments, you can assist them in considering whether they wish to become closer to others and identifying obstacles that could prevent this movement from happening. Family alignments may, in fact, involve "complex extended patterns or configurations" (Boyd-Franklin, 1989, p. 124). Members of the various configurations may include clan or tribal members, extended kin, friends, or individuals from the family's religious or spiritual community, such as a minister, shaman, rabbi, monk, medicine person, or priest. Be mindful of the fact that any of these people (or a combination of them) may be involved in family structural arrangements. Consequently, it may be necessary to explore relationships and alignments beyond the immediate family system.

Family Sculpting

Family sculpting is a technique used in experiential family practice models to assist family members in analyzing and observing their alliances and in making decisions concerning possible changes. This technique allows family members to communicate spatial family system relationships in a nonverbal tableau, discern alignments, and recognize the need to realign their relationships. A variation of this technique is to have family members portray historical and current family relationships using the genogram (see Chapter 10).

In family sculpting, family members are instructed to physically arrange other family members in a way that portrays their perceptions of members as well as their own place in the family system. Another aspect of family sculpting involves members expressing themselves by using drawings to disclose their perceptions of each other (Nichols & Schwartz, 2012). For example, instruct the family to draw a picture that shows how they see themselves as a family. After family members have completed their drawings, ask participants to draw family relationships as they would like them to be on the other side of the paper. In a subsequent discussion, ask members in turn to share their drawings of existing family relationships.

The benefit of the expressive exercise is that family members can observe the nature of their alignments and the emotional closeness and distance in their relationships with others. Invite family members to comment on their observations, based on hypothetical responses such as the following, from the Sheng and Chao Thao case in the chapter:

- It looks like Mai Shoua and Cynthia are quite close to each other.
- Jennifer and Cynthia seem to have the least conflict with each other. Jennifer and Mai Shoua are in frequent conflict.

After all family members have an opportunity to make their observations, you can ask them to explain their second drawings, which show how they would like family relationships to be. During this discussion, you can highlight the desired changes, assist individuals to formulate goals that reflect changes they would like to make, and identify exceptional times—for example, when Jennifer and Mai Shoua are not in conflict with each other.

Elements of family sculpting or structural mapping include exercises that can be used with parents to portray family relationships, strengthen parental coalitions, and mark generational boundaries. For example, does one parent triangulate with a child or children or permit children to intrude into the parental subsystem? Does one parent act as a mediator in family conflicts? Does one parent have the final say? Does one child have inordinate power in the family? The hazard associated with these alignments is that children may become adept at playing one parent against the other. In these instances, parental divisiveness is fostered, and in consequence, relationships between the children and the excluded parent are strained. In the case of the parent who expends most of their emotional energy on a newborn, emotional bonds and loyalty between them and their other children and family members may be lacking.

Joined Families

Developing cohesiveness, unity, and more effective alignments is a challenge that often confronts two families who have joined together—for example, in the development of a relationship between a new stepparent and a stepchild. Because these factors are apt to be present in blended, foster, or adoptive families, your attention to alliances and cohesiveness is equally important in such cases, especially when there are biological children in the home.

In blended families, you can assist parents to analyze whether differences or lack of agreement about their parenting styles are factors in parent–child alignments. Strategies for strengthening parental coalitions may include

negotiating united-front agreements in parent–child transactions requiring decision-making and/or disciplinary actions (unless, of course, the other partner is truly hurtful or abusive to the child). Finally, assisting families to realign themselves and forge new alliances is particularly important in instances in which there has been a disruption in the family system. Examples include the reunification of a child who has been placed outside of the home, or when a parent or another key family member has been absent from the family's life for an extended period.

On-the-Spot Interventions

On-the-spot interventions are a potent way of modifying patterns of interaction by intervening immediately when problematic family patterns occur during a meeting with the social worker. On-the-spot interventions are appropriate when:

- A family member sends fuzzy or abrasive messages
- The receiver of a message distorts its meaning
- A receiver of a message fails to respond appropriately to important messages or feelings
- A destructive interaction occurs because of a message

In implementing on-the-spot interventions, you should focus on the destructive effects of the preceding communication, labeling the type of communication so that family members can subsequently identify their own dysfunctional behaviors. In using the intervention, you also need to teach and guide family members in how to engage in more effective ways of communicating.

Teaching and guiding family members toward more effective ways of communication is illustrated in the following example. The social worker intervened in a blind-alley argument, one that cannot be resolved because neither party can be proved right or wrong.

Family Member 1: I distinctly remember telling you to buy some dish detergent when you went to the store.

Family Member 2: You just think that you did, but you didn't. I'd have remembered if you said anything about it.

Family Member 1: No, you just didn't remember. I told you for sure, and you're shifting the blame.

Family Member 2 [with obvious irritation]: Like hell you did! You're the one who forgot to tell me, and I don't appreciate your telling me I forgot.

Social worker: Can we stop for a moment and consider what's happening between you? Each of you has a different recollection of what happened, and there's no way of determining who's right and who's wrong. You are involved in what I call a blind-alley argument because you can't resolve it. You just end up arguing over who's right and feeling resentful because you're convinced the other person is wrong. That doesn't help you solve your problem; it just creates conflict in your relationship. Let's go back and start over. Are you willing to allow me to show you both a more effective way of dealing with this situation?

Alternatively, after describing and intervening in the interaction and guiding the couple to communicate constructively, you might challenge the family members to identify their behavior and to modify it accordingly. For example, interrupt their interactions with a statement like this: "Wait a minute! Think about what you're doing just now and where it's going to lead you if you continue." In modifying patterns, the intermediate objective is for family members to recognize and decrease their counterproductive behavior and substitute newly gained communication skills for the harmful communication style. The goal, of course, is for family members to eliminate the counterproductive processes through concentrated efforts between sessions. The following are some guidelines for making on-the-spot interventions.

Focus on Process Rather Than Content

For you to be infinitely more helpful to family members, you must focus on their interaction processes rather than on the content of their conflicts. Conflicts typically manifest over content issues, but how family members interact in dealing with the focal point of a conflict is far more important. As the blind-alley argument example illustrated, the issue of who is right in a dispute is usually trivial when compared to the destructive effects of the processes. Thus, you should deemphasize the topics of disputes and focus instead on helping family members to listen attentively and respectfully and to own their feelings and their responsibility in creating and maintaining the problem. Ultimately, you want to teach them how to compromise, disengage from competitive interaction, and engage in conflict resolution.

Give Feedback That Is Descriptive and Neutral Rather Than General or Evaluative

As you intervene, it is important that you present feedback in a neutral manner that does not fault family members but rather allows them to pinpoint specific behaviors that produce difficulties. Feedback that evaluates their behavior produces defensiveness; overly general feedback fails to focus on behavior that needs to be changed.

To illustrate, consider a situation in which a partner glares at their spouse and says, "I've had it with going to your parents' house. You spend all the time while we

are there talking with your mother, and I do not feel included or welcomed in the conversation. You can go by yourself in the future." A general and evaluative message would take the following form:

> **Social worker:** "Laura, that message was an example of poor communication. Try again to send a better one."

The following message is neutral and behaviorally specific:

> **Social worker:** "Laura, I noticed that when you just spoke to Lynda, you glared at them and sent a message that focused on what you thought they were doing wrong. I watched Lynda as you spoke and noticed that they frowned and seemed to be angry. I'd like you to get some feedback from Lynda about how your message affected them. Lynda, would you share with Laura what you experienced as they talked?"

In summarizing what occurred, the social worker indicates that Laura's message to Lynda was problematic, but they avoid making an evaluative judgment. By describing specific behavior and eliciting feedback about its impact, the social worker enhances the possibility that Laura will be receptive to examining and modifying their behavior. Note also that this message highlights the interaction of both participants, as specified in the next guideline.

Balance Interventions to Divide Responsibility

When more than one family member is involved in sessions, you must achieve a delicate balance while avoiding the appearance of singling out one person as being the sole cause of interpersonal difficulties. Otherwise, that person may feel that you and other family members are taking sides and blaming. By focusing on all relevant actors, you can distribute responsibility, model fairness, and avoid alienating one person. Although one person may contribute more to problems than others, all members of a system generally contribute to difficulties in some degree. The following example illustrates the technique of balancing in a situation in which the husband and the wife are at odds with each other over caring for their baby and the amount of time the husband spends at work.

In this example, the social worker responded empathically to the feelings of both husband and wife, thereby validating the feelings of each. In so doing, the social worker remained neutral to avoid the appearance of siding with or against either of the participants. The empathic responses also soften the impact of the social worker's messages.

Case Example 10: Validating Feelings

Social worker: Both of you seem to have some feelings and concerns that are legitimate, but for some reason, you seem to be stuck and unable to work things out.

[To wife] You resent your husband when he does not do his part regarding child care. As a result, you feel that you can't

trust him to take care of the children, even though you both agreed that you would return to work part-time.

[To husband] You feel that because you are on a new job, now is not the time to ask for time off for child care.

[To both] I'd like to explore what the two of you can do to make things better for each other.

Redirect Hostile, Blaming Messages

When people are angry, they may express messages that are hostile, blaming, or critical, exacerbating an already difficult situation. Before redirecting messages, you must consider the likely consequences of the ensuing interaction. As you redirect such messages, you should actively intervene to facilitate positive interaction:

- Coach family members to own their feelings: "I am really angry with you for getting this family involved with the police."
- Translate complaints into requests for change: "I wish you would stay in school and stop hanging around with the neighborhood dropouts."
- Clarify positive intentions: "I want you to stay in school because I want your life to be better than mine."

Of course, these messages will be more effective when speakers' nonverbal behaviors are consistent with their verbal message. For example, unless there is a

cultural imperative observed in the family, when family members are speaking, they should face one another and maintain eye contact. You may need to interrupt and direct them as illustrated in the following message:

Social worker: Cassie, please stop for just a moment. You were talking to me, not to Jamal. Will you please start again, but this time talk and look directly at him?

Assisting Families to Disengage from Conflict

One of the most common and harmful types of interaction within families involves arguments that quickly escalate, causing anger and resentment between the participants. Sustained over time, these interactions may eventually involve other family members and subsystems. Often, the family system becomes factionalized, and individual efforts to regain equilibrium may result in further conflict. The content of the conflict is generally

Case Example 11: Janet and Twanna 4

An example of the application of the task-centered model for families can be found in the case of Janet and Twanna. During the first session, the social worker, Glenda, helped Janet and Twanna identify the presenting problem (Twanna does not come home to care for her baby as agreed), to establish a common goal (that Twanna will be home to provide care for her baby), and to identify tasks (to call Janet when Twanna expects to be late, to be home every night to put the baby to bed at 6 p.m., to discuss plans on Sunday evenings, including plans to invite friends over). Further, the social worker asked Janet and Twanna

to rehearse their conversation, and throughout the planning process, she prompted Janet and Twanna to be specific about their plans, including when tasks would be accomplished.

During the second session, completion of the first set of tasks revealed further conflict between Janet and Twanna about proper child-care strategies (whether babies should be pampered with treats) and about Janet's need for advice and help with managing tantrums. In the end, the social worker led Janet and Twanna into a conversation about how to problem solve through these two emergent issues.

secondary to the fact that on a process level each family member is struggling to avoid being one-down, losing face, or yielding power to the other member. To illustrate helping family members in disengaging from conflict, we return to the case of Twanna and Janet. Fortunately, the situation between Janet and Twanna has not reached a crisis point, but if left unresolved, it has the essential ingredients to escalate and affect the prior gains that the two of them have made.

To assist family members in avoiding competitive struggles, you can emphasize that everyone loses in competitive situations or arguments, and negative feelings or emotional estrangement is likely to be a result (e.g., Twanna's withdrawal, slamming the door). It is also vital to stress that safeguarding mutual respect is far more important than winning. The concept of disengaging from conflict simply means that family members avoid escalating arguments by declining to participate further. A graceful way in which people can disengage is by making a comment similar to the following: "Listen, it doesn't really matter who's right. If we argue, we just get mad at each other, and I don't want that to happen." Teaching family members to evaluate their behavior and its effects on others is another strategy: "How do the children react when the two of you are having an argument?" You can further assist family members to avoid conflict between sessions by teaching them to recognize code words that signal the need to disengage or reframe their message. Sentences or questions such as "When you do ...," "How could you think ...," "Did you think ...," "I know that you won't ...," "You never ...," "Don't tell me what to do," and "Why did you ..." are generally powerful prompts, along with labeling, that set the stage for conflict.

Negotiating tasks for disengaging from conflicted interactions between sessions can help family members transfer these skills to their daily lives. Of course, family members may be incapable of intervening to disengage conflict in some instances—for example, in domestic violence situations where there is a threat or the actuality of physical harm. In these situations, you can teach family members, especially children, to call for help as well as to develop a safety plan.

Conflict resolution strategies may vary based on differences in both gender and cultural values. Being aware of these differences can assist you in choosing intervention strategies that recognize how these factors affect the family's behavior. You should explore the family narrative regarding how conflict is managed in the family's particular culture as well as the attached meanings or feelings. By doing so, you can engage members in formulating an effective intervention strategy.

In fact, understanding the family narrative with respect to conflict may yield benefits with all families, irrespective of their culture or ethnicity. Each family has its own style of communicating. In some families, everyone talks simultaneously and makes outrageous statements; other members may remain passive during this display. Perhaps yelling or using swear words is a norm, as are demonstrative hand gestures or belligerent tone of voice, or there has been a history of apparent threats and hostility. Be sensitive to the fact that families do not want to be judged for behaviors. Instead, the goal is to work toward change. Observing the family and inquiring about their patterns of relating to each other and preferences for change enables you to assess family members' communication styles and goals and avoid drawing conclusions about their functional or dysfunctional status.

Summary

This chapter has presented a set of skills that you can utilize to engage and intervene with families across a wide spectrum of social work practice settings. These practice skills will generalize to most of the evidence-based family interventions currently in use today. They will also be useful for settings where social workers engage families in support of interventions with individual clients as well. When joining with families, bear in mind the need to use collective language purposefully to emphasize the relationship you have with the family in addition to the individual members within the family. When selecting interventions, consider the range of first- and second-order change strategies that are most appropriate for the nature of the presenting problem. Your interventions may involve helping families solve problems within the framework of their existing family system structures or helping families to adapt their family system structure toward improved family functioning. Often, you are helping families to do both.

Competency Notes

C2 **Engage Antiracism, Diversity, Equity, and Inclusion in Practice**

- Demonstrate anti-racist social work practice at the individual, family, group, organizational, community, research, and policy levels, informed by the theories and voices of those who have been marginalized.
- Demonstrate cultural humility applying critical reflexivity, self-awareness, and self-regulation to manage the influence of bias, power, privilege, and values in working with clients and constituencies acknowledging them as experts of their own lived experiences.

C6 **Engage with Individuals, Families, Groups, Organizations, and Communities**

- Apply knowledge of human behavior and the social environment, person-in-environment, and other multidisciplinary theoretical frameworks to engage with clients and constituencies.
- Use empathy, reflection, and interpersonal skills to effectively engage diverse clients and constituencies.

C8 **Intervene with Individuals, Families, Groups, Organizations, and Communities**

- Engage with clients and constituencies to critically choose and implement culturally responsive, evidenced-based interventions to achieve mutually agreed-on practice goals and enhance capacities of clients and constituencies.

Skill Development Exercises

Enhancing Family Functioning and Relationships

1. Identify some examples of verbal or nonverbal meta-communication that you have used.

2. Describe how an unspoken rule in your family governs the behavior of family members.

3. List three societal beliefs and reflect upon how these beliefs may affect the families that you work with.

4. Choose several classmates to role play a family situation. Acting as the social worker, facilitate the joining stage in the initial contact session.

5. Using the same family situation, identify the needs and the wants expressed by each family member. What questions would you ask to help members identify their concerns?

6. In a family session in which one member is identified as being the problem, how would you proceed with the family?

Facilitating Social Work Groups

Chapter Overview

Groups are microcosms of the systems in which they are embedded. Classrooms, sports teams, sorority and fraternal organizations, workplaces, committees, self-help groups, and therapeutic groups replicate aspects of larger structures. Racism, patriarchy, power, and hierarchies present themselves in groups. So will the regulation of communications and expression of feelings, avoidance of taboo subjects, efforts at connection, and an array of other articacts of the cultures and systems in which the groups reside. As individuals, employees, and helping professionals, social workers also represent dominant social structures, and they possess power and authority, especially in groups where participation is mandatory. Awareness, humility, and intentionality about the ways this power is perceived and used are core social work skills in all forms of practice, including group interventions.

Chapter 11 described many features of forming groups and offered advice for consciously structuring them while being midful of dynamics such as power, norms, roles-taking, communications, and capacity building. As groups form and meet, social workers must continue this critical awareness and use their skills to foster empowerment, attend to individual and interactional dynamics, and provide direction and focus to the group's

processes at critical moments. This chapter organizes these activities through phases of the group life-cycle, focusing primarily on treatment groups, though many of the concepts apply to the dynamics in task groups as well. Self-help groups experience the same life cycles, but because they are not facilitated by social workers, they are not specifically addressed here.

After reading this chapter, you will be able to:

- Describe the stages through which groups progress and the features of each stage.

- Explain the skills and knowledge needed to effectively intervene at each stage.

- Describe the ways that these concepts reveal themselves in the dialogue of the HEART group.

- Describe common worker errors at different stages of the group process.

- Describe variants on group work such as single-session and technology-mediated groups.

- Explain how concepts of group interventions apply to task groups.

The EPAS Competencies in Chapter 16

This chapter will give you the information needed to meet the following practice competencies:

- Competency 4: Engage in Practice-Informed Research and Research-Informed Practice

- Competency 6: Engage with Individuals, Families, Groups, Organizations, and Communities

- Competency 7: Assess Individuals, Families, Groups, Organizations, and Communities

- Competency 8: Intervene with Individuals, Families, Groups, Organizations, and Communities

Stages of Group Development

In a parallel to the human life cycle, groups also go through natural stages of development, although the pace and the complexity of each stage may vary. Understanding these stages is essential in anticipating and addressing the dynamics that characterize each phase so that the group's objectives can ultimately be met. Social workers have particular responsibility for removing obstacles that threaten to derail the group's development and hinder the success of individual members. In doing so, they must make strategic, informed choices regarding their input and actions across the life span of the group.

Without knowledge of the group's stage of development, facilitators may make errors, such as expecting group members to engage in personal exploration during initial sessions or concluding that they have failed if the group exhibits the discord that is typical of early development. They may also overlook positive behaviors that indicate that the group is approaching a more mature stage of development, or they may fail to intervene at critical periods to assist the group's evolution such as encouraging them to stay on task, to include all members in decision-making, to foster free expression, practice inclusivity, or to adopt many other behaviors that are hallmarks of an experienced group.

The perspectives and planned change process introduced in this text apply to group work, and different models of group development offer various frameworks for organizing your observations about the group's characteristics, themes, and behaviors. All of these models identify progressive steps in group development, although they may organize these steps into four, five, or even six stages. In this chapter, we use the classic model developed by Garland et al. (1965), which delineates five stages:

1. Preaffiliation
2. Power and control
3. Intimacy
4. Differentiation
5. Separation

C6 and 7

After discussing each stage, we present the interventions that are most relevant for each point in group development. As we examine each stage, consider the ways that group composition, context, and structure may affect the ways that the features of each stage manifest themselves. For example, a mandatory group composed of members who differ by age, race, or gender may reflect the ambivalence of the first stage or the conflict of the second in a different way than a voluntary group whose members already have interests or other characteristics in common. Single-session groups and the variations in skills needed are addressed in a subsequent section.

Stage 1. Preaffiliation: Approach and Avoidance Behavior

Stage 1 occurs just as the group is starting, and is thus also referred to as the forming stage (Tuckman, 1963). As anyone who has ever experienced the first day of a new class can attest, the initial stage of group development is characterized by members' exhibiting approach–avoidance behavior. That is, new members may be apprehensive and unlikely to engage in deep or extensive interactions. Reticence is reflected in silence or tentative speech, reluctance to volunteer to answer questions, or hesitancy to engage in group activities. At this stage, participants are wary and uneasy and may be waiting to see what benefits the group will bring to them.

At times during the preaffiliation stage, members may employ proactive behaviors to size up or test other members, to assess the group's limits, to find out how competent the social worker is, and to determine to what extent they will safeguard the rights and well-being of members. Members may also seek common ground with other participants, search for viable roles, and seek approval, acceptance, and respect. Much of the initial communication in the group is directed toward the facilitator, and some members may openly demand that the social worker pursue a directive approach, making decisions regarding group issues and structure and issuing prompt directives to control the behavior of members. The Healthy Eating, Attitudes, Relationships and Thoughts (HEART) group, introduced in Chapter 11, is designed to assist teen girls who are overweight. In this chapter, transcripts from the group are used to illustrate client statements and worker responses that are indicative of various phases of the group process.

Stage 2. Power and Control: A Time of Transition

The first stage of group development merges imperceptibly into the second stage as members, having determined that the group experience is potentially safe and rewarding and worth the preliminary emotional investment, shift their concerns to matters related to autonomy, power, and control. Group members may begin to challenge the facilitator's authority. Thus, this stage is also referred to as the storming stage (Tuckman, 1963). This stage is characterized by transition—that is, members

Case Example 1: Preaffiliation in the HEART Group

Dave: Thank you to everyone for sharing your progress from last week. I would like to do this at the beginning of each session because I think it helps to bring us together and create a space where you feel safe and energized to share and give each other support. I'm wondering if, based on how things went today, anybody has other ideas of how to make this opening ritual go better for them? Does anybody have any ideas about making improvements to what we're doing, or can you tell me how it went for you today?

Amelia: Well, I think that check-in kind of depends on what your mood is. Like, I'm in a kind of okay mood today, so my check-in is more positive, but like, Liz is kinda being bitchy, you know? And so maybe she's really had a bad day or whatever. So, I think to have something that everybody does instead of just a check-in. I don't know. It's just really different for everybody, depending on how you're feeling.

Dave: How you're going to interact in group depends on how you're doing on that day.

Amelia: Yeah

Dave: You know something I heard you say, Amelia, was that you felt that Liz was "bitchy," to use your word, and

I want to check in with Liz to see how she received that, or how she heard that. So, I'm wondering Liz, when Amelia said that, what came to mind?

Liz: It hurts my feelings because I thought people were talking about me all the time anyway, and then I come to this place, where everybody is supposed to be happy, and like me, and you call me bitchy. I think that's bitchy.

Amelia: Sorry.

Dave: Amelia, I think what you were saying was that during her introduction you heard that Liz was having a bad day. How does that sound?

Amelia: Yeah.

Maria: She didn't say you were a bitch, she said bitch-y, like kind of. I don't think she meant it in a mean way.

Liz: Well, that's how I took it, so I think that matters more than what you think you heard.

Dave: And Amelia, I would actually agree with Liz on that point. How someone hears what you're saying matters as much as, or maybe more than, what you meant to say. One of the benefits of participating in group is having experiences like these to learn about how other people perceive you.

---

encounter the ambiguity and the turmoil of change from a nonintimate to an intimate system of relationships.

After dealing with the struggle of whether they belong in the group, members may now become sensitive to their rank in relation to other members. Turning to others like themselves for support and protection, members create subgroups and a hierarchy of statuses. Conflicts between opposing subgroups often occur in this stage, and members may team up to express anger toward the facilitator, other authority figures, or outsiders.

Disenchantment may be expressed through hostility, withdrawal, or reservations about the group's purposes. If not well managed, verbal abuse, attacks, and rejection of lower-status members may occur as well, and isolated members of the group who do not have the protection of a subgroup may stop attending. Attrition in membership may also occur if individuals find outside pursuits more attractive than the conflicted group experience; this depleted membership may put the group's survival in jeopardy.

Stage 3. Intimacy: Developing a Familial Frame of Reference

Having clarified and resolved many of the issues related to personal autonomy, initiative, and power, the group moves from the preintimate power and control stage to that of intimacy. After surviving the tumult of Stage 2, intimacy increases, and group norms become increasingly clear; thus, this stage is also referred to as the norming stage (Tuckman, 1963). In Stage 3, conflicts fade, personal involvement between members intensifies, and members display a growing recognition of the significance of the group experience. In contrast to earlier sessions, they express genuine concern for absent members and may reach out to invite them to return to the group. Members also experience an increase in morale and bonding, a deepening commitment to the group's purpose, and heightened motivation to carry out plans and tasks that support the group's objectives.

Case Example 2: Power and Control in the HEART Group

Maria: You know, Dave, I don't mean to be disrespectful, and I think this is a good discussion, but I just wonder, are we the first group you've done?

Dave: I've done a few others.

Vanessa: With girls?

Dave: A few with girls.

Vanessa: Like our age?

Dave: Some.

Maria: Like, fat?

Dave: Well, I've worked with adults and teenagers with overweight. I'm curious, Amelia, why do you ask?

Maria: Because you're the only skinny person here, and you're the only guy. [group giggles]

Amelia: Mmhmm.

Maria: See, now nobody else dares to say anything.

Liz: Don't you think that maybe if he's skinny, maybe he can teach us some things?

Vanessa: Yeah, but what does he know about what we're going through?

Maria: I mean, he knows boys.

Amelia: He's probably always been thin. He has no idea probably, you probably have no idea, what we've been through.

Dave: I'm hearing you say that you don't believe I can identify with you.

Amelia: Well, you're a boy. You're skinny. I'm a girl, and I'm fat.

Maria: And he's older.

Amelia: Yeah.

Amber: And he's probably always had girlfriends. I've never had a boyfriend.

Amelia: Do you have a girlfriend now?

Dave: I'd rather not answer that question.

Vanessa: Why? We talk about our boyfriends and friends. I mean, we're telling you stuff.

Dave: Actually, I think, you're also telling each other stuff, and the group is about you …

Amelia: And you.

Dave: My role here is to help the group along, and if I take up time with my relationships …

Amelia: So you have one.

Dave: As I said, I'd rather not address it, Amelia, but if I take up time with my business, then it robs the group …

Maria [to Amelia]: I mean, he can't be your boyfriend if he's your worker [taunting].

Dave: No, I can't date anyone in the group.

Amelia: I don't want to date you. Oh my god!

Vanessa: Sure …

Amelia: Don't even, you're so full of yourself! I like girls anyway.

Dave: The other thing I want to say is that I can learn from you and follow your concerns, solutions, and your strategies for dealing with some of the things that you're up against right now. I hope that in my role as facilitator I can help all of you to help yourselves, even though I'm neither overweight nor a girl.

Mutual trust increases as members begin to acknowledge one another's uniqueness, spontaneously disclose feelings and problems, and seek the opinion of the group. To achieve this desired intimacy, however, group participants may suppress reactions that could produce conflict between themselves and others.

During this stage of development, a group character emerges as the group evolves its own culture, style, and values. Clear norms are established based on personal interests, affection, and other positive forces. Roles also take shape as members find ways to contribute to the group and as leadership patterns become firmly settled. The frame of reference for members is a familial one, as members liken their group experience to their experience with their own nuclear families, occasionally referring to other members as siblings or to the facilitator as the parent of the group.

Stage 4. Differentiation: Developing Group Identity and an Internal Frame of Reference

The fourth stage of group development is marked by cohesion and harmony as members come to terms with intimacy and make choices to draw closer to others in the group. A dynamic balance between individual and group needs evolves resulting in a high functioning group. Thus, Stage 4 is also referred to as the performing stage (Tuckman, 1963). Members, who participate in different and complementary ways, experience greater freedom of personal expression and come to feel genuinely accepted and valued as their feelings and ideas are validated by other members of the group. Gradually, the group becomes a mutual aid system in which members spontaneously give emotional support in proportion to the needs of each individual.

In experiencing this newfound freedom and intimacy, members begin to perceive the group experience as unique. Customs and traditional ways of operating emerge, and the group may develop inside jokes or shared sayings or adopt a slogan or insignia that reflects its purpose. The group's energy is channeled into working toward purposes and carrying out tasks that are clearly understood and accepted. New roles—more flexible and functional than those originally envisioned—are developed to support the group's activity, and organizational structures (e.g., officers, dues, attendance expectations, rules) may evolve. Status hierarchies also tend to be less rigid, and members may spontaneously assume leadership roles as the need for a particular expertise or ability arises.

By the time the group reaches the differentiation stage, members have accumulated experience in working through problems and have gained skills in analyzing their own feelings and the feelings of others, communicating their needs and positions effectively, offering support to others, and grasping the complex interrelationships that have developed in the group. Having become conscious about the group's operations, members bring conflict out into the open and identify obstacles that impede their progress. Disagreements are not suppressed or overridden by premature group action. Instead, the group carefully considers the positions of any dissenters and attempts to resolve differences and to achieve consensus among members. New group members may express their amazement at the insight shared by veteran members, who in turn become increasingly convinced of the value of the group experience.

Members may now discuss their group with friends and family, whereas previously membership in the group may have been linked with feelings of embarrassment. Secure in their roles and relationships within the group, members may become interested in meeting with other groups or in bringing in outside culture. In the HEART group, the differentiation stage fostered the safety to talk about painful material and use insights gained from the group.

Stage 5. Separation: Breaking Away

In Stage 5, also called the adjourning phase, members begin to separate, loosening their intense bonds and

---

Case Example 3: Differentiation in the HEART Group

Amber: So, you gonna ask him?

Vanessa: Ask him what?

Maria: Like is he just being a user. Using you.

Vanessa: You know sometimes, I think he was just curious about stuff and that's sometimes why we maybe hooked up, you know? So, maybe he was using me.

Jen: Well, what are you going to do the next time he tries to hook up with you?

Vanessa: Smack him. I mean, not really! But I would say no. I'm not gonna … I don't know, maybe I will, 'cuz it's not all that bad. Awkward! Sorry, Dave. It's not all that bad when it happens.

Maria: I wouldn't know.

Liz: Nah, me neither.

Vanessa: Maybe that's all I'm going to get, I don't know.

Dave: All you're going to get as far as the relationship with him, or …

Vanessa: With him, or others. If all guys think like that, I should maybe just take what's there.

Amber: That's all I've gotten.

Maria: Like guys who only want to be with you in private and not in public?

Vanessa: That's the guy. That's him!

Maria: Well, that sucks!

Vanessa: It does.

Dave: So, does that sound like something that you want to have in your lives?

Maria: I don't think so. I mean, I'm not in the situation, but if a guy's only going to want to be with me when no one else is around, then he doesn't really value me, and he's just using me.

searching for new resources and ties to satisfy their needs. Group members are likely to experience a broad range of feelings about leaving the group. Members may again feel anxiety, this time in relation to moving apart and breaking bonds that have been formed. There may be outbursts of anger against the leader and other members, a reappearance of quarrels that were previously settled, and increased dependence on the facilitator. Denial of the positive meaning of the group may surface.

As we will discuss further in Chapter 19, termination is also a time of evaluation, contemplation of the work achieved, and consolidation of learning. It is a time of finishing unfinished business, getting and giving focused feedback, and savoring the good times and the close relationships gained in the group.[1] Members who have begun to pull back their group investments and put more energy into outside interests speak of their fears, hopes, and concerns about the future and about one another. There is often discussion of how to apply what has been learned in the group to other situations and talk of reunions or follow-up meetings (Toseland & Rivas, 2017).

C8

The Facilitator's Role and Activities

The facilitator's role shifts and changes throughout the stages of group development. As the group gets started, the facilitator initiates and directs group discussion, encourages participation, and begins blending the individual contracts with members into a mutual group contract. In single-session groups, the social worker's role continues in this manner since each session is, in reality, a new group.

C7

Like interventions with families, group work requires the practitioner to attend to multiple sources of data in each meeting. While the content that is shared in group is important, so are the processes observed among members. As with families, facilitators must attend to the messages demonstrated by each individual member and the process of the group as a whole. To do this, the worker reads body language; positioning in the room; who speaks, when, how much, and with what tone; the reactions of other participants when particular members are speaking; and the general tone, mood, or energy of the group. Is the group buoyant? Flat? Angry? Distractible? Is Anthony unusually sullen? Does everyone "tune out" when Jocelyn speaks? Does Juanita seem fidgety and eager to speak but unable to get the group's attention? Does Fareed go on too long?

Once processes are observed, the worker can intervene in different ways depending on how these processes are enhancing achievement of group and individual goals and what phase of work the group is in. For instance, the worker might remark on collective impressions: "Today's group seems to have pretty low energy," or "It seems that you're having an especially hard time getting down to business today," or "I wonder what's happening; I'm hearing a lot of anger." Comments may also reflect observations about individual behavior: "When Jocelyn speaks, the rest of you seem to disengage," or the worker may invite comment or involvement: "Has anyone else noticed that?" "What might be going on with you when that happens?" "Juanita, I notice we haven't heard from you." "Fareed, let's make space to hear from other folks." In more developed groups, the members themselves may observe, comment on, and regulate process. In those cases, the facilitator can comment on those group processes. "I like the way the group helped Jocelyn give her input without getting impatient or checking our phones."

In ongoing groups, as the group moves from Stage 1 to the subsequent stages, the facilitator intentionally steps back from their active role and centers the group members as they supplant some of what the facilitator has been doing. However, because the group has not yet stabilized, the leader's role is variable, and they need to let the process run at its own speed. Sometimes the facilitator might need to move back to a more active role.

The variable role continues in the group during the conflict/disequilibrium stage (Stage 2). When the group enters its maintenance or working phases (Stages 3 and 4), the leader assumes a facilitative role and becomes more peripheral. Inasmuch as the group has achieved full capacity to govern itself, the social worker fulfills a resource role instead of a central role. As the group moves into its separation or termination phase (Stage 5), the facilitator once again returns to a primary role and central location to support the divesting of members, who are launching their own independent journeys. The social worker aids the group in working through any reversion to earlier stages of development to assure the successful ending of the group.

Stage-Specific Interventions

As previously mentioned, a facilitator's focus and activities can be viewed within the framework of the group's stages of development. Thomas and Caplan (1999) suggest a wheel metaphor for the social worker's role. That is, the facilitator takes a particularly active role in getting the wheel spinning, then gradually provides a lighter touch and finally reduces that role as the group gathers its own momentum, while still standing by to help keep the wheel on track.

Single-Session Groups

As described in Chapter 11, single-session groups come together in a particular configuration only once, and each group must negotiate its own purpose and contract (Block, 1985; Ebenstein, 1998). Social workers should have a deep awareness of the issues and themes that concern the population to be served in order to help focus the session on one or two concerns and limit goals to those that are achievable in one session (Ebenstein, 1998; Kossoff, 2003). This knowledge is also important in helping speed up the process whereby the group members develop rapport and sense of commonality in purpose and need (Block, 1985). Because of the condensed time frame, pacing is critical, as sufficient time must be allowed for a real beginning, middle, and end for the group session.

Authors with expertise in single-session groups report that they proceed through the group stages described earlier in this chapter, but they do so in a condensed or concurrent fashion, and it is incumbent on the leaders to structure the group so that the tasks at each phase are met. To do so, leaders use the first five to 10 minutes of a session to facilitate interaction among the members and identify guidelines and feasible goals for the session. Leaders may offer refreshments as members gather, use an innocuous ice breaker such as "What is your favorite ice cream? How many of you are oldest children? Vegetarians? Like to watch football?" Leaders are prepared to share preliminary goals and ground rules, seek input on members' needs, and come to efficient agreement on the ground rules for the group.

To make effective use of the middle phases of group work, leaders should be prepared with various types of content to meet the needs of the particular configuration of individuals at a given session. This content may include educational material (on medications, symptoms, resources, diagnoses, phases of recovery) or activities to foster self-expression and problem solving (Keats & Sabharwal, 2008). Leaders of single-session groups should be especially skilled at exploration and empathy to build trust and cohesion, and at linking to help individual members understand and support each other (Keast, 2012; Kosoff, 2004; Young, 2020). These skills foster self-reflection and sharing among members, both of which are essential for mutual aid (Steinberg, 2004). Facilitators must also be comfortable with flexibly shifting roles and focus based on the composition and needs of any given group. They must balance structure and independence, leaning in and being directive, and leaning back and encouraging the members to take leadership. Leaders must also be attuned to timing and pacing. "Each session needs to be a complete experience and there cannot be any issues that are left unsettled. It is essential that enough time be left to ensure that members leave the space with an integral sense of experience" (Keast, 2012, p. 721).

Time must also be set aside for the closing phase of the group. Many groups utilize structured closing processes or rituals to bring the session to an end. This might involve giving the group a moment to reflect on the meaning of the session, then asking each member to share one insight or something learned in group that he or she might use in the future or identify their needs going forward (Galinsky & Schopler, 1985). Closings could include sharing an inspirational quote, a resource list, or a worksheet to expand on topics from the group. They may also include participant evaluations or posttest questionnaires for research or quality assurance purposes.

Whether the single-session group is analogous to openended/open-member groups or to educational sessions or workshops, some group concepts may be more germane and transferable than others. However, regardless of the type of single-session group, social workers must be attentive not only to the steps in planning but to the structure, dynamics, and worker roles when meetings take place.

Table 16-1 illustrates the evolution of the facilitator's focus as a group advances through the various stages of development. Information contained in the table comes from a variety of sources (Corey et al., 2017; Garland et al., 1965; Yalom & Leszcz, 2020).

Interventions in the Preaffiliation Stage

Chapter 11 describes how pregroup individual interviews serve as an orientation for potential group members.

In initial sessions, social workers can prepare members for the experiences to come by explaining the basics of group process—for example, the stages of development through which the group will pass, ways to create a therapeutic working environment, communications, behaviors and attitudes characteristic of an effective group, and the importance of establishing and adhering to guidelines that lend structure and purpose to the group.

Active listening and other communication skills that foster engagement and trust are prominent here. Empathy, reflection, open questions, and other techniques

Table 16-1 Stages, Dynamics, and Facilitator Focus

Stage	Dynamics	Facilitator Focus
Preaffiliation	• Approach/avoidance Issues of trust, preliminary commitment • Intellectualization of problems • Interaction based on superficial attributes or experiences • Protection of self; low-risk behavior • Milling around • Sizing up of facilitator and other members • Formulation of individual and group goals • Facilitator viewed as responsible for group • Member evaluation as to whether group is safe and meets needs • Fear of self-disclosure, rejection • Uncertainty regarding group purpose • Little commitment to goals or group	• Observe and assess • Clarify group objectives • Establish group guidelines • Encourage development of personal goals • Clarify aspirations and expectations of members • Encourage discussion of fears, ambivalence • Gently invite trust • Give support; allow distance • Facilitate exploration • Provide group structure • Contract for help-seeking, help-giving roles • Facilitate linkages among members • Model careful listening • Focus on resistance • Assure opportunities for participation
Power and control	• Rebellion; power struggles • Political alignments forged to increase power • Issues of status, ranking, and influence • Complaints regarding group structure, process • Challenges to facilitator's roles • Emergence of informal facilitators, factional facilitators • Individual autonomy; everybody for themselves • Dysfunctional group roles • Normative and membership crisis; dropout danger high • Testing of facilitator; other group members • Dependence on facilitator • Group experimentation in managing own affairs • Program breakdown at times; low planning • Feedback highly critical	• Protect physical and psychological safety of individuals • Protect property • Clarify power struggles • Turn issues back to group • Encourage expression and acceptance of differences • Facilitate clear, direct, nonabrasive communication • Examine nonproductive group processes • Examine cognitive distortions • Facilitate member discussion of dissident subgroups • Hold group accountable for decision by consensus • Clarify that conflict, power struggles are normal • Encourage norms consistent with therapeutic group • Consistently acknowledge strengths, accomplishments • Nondefensively deal with challenges to the facilitator • Focus on the here and now
Intimacy	• Intensified personal involvement • Sharing of self, materials • Striving to meet others' needs • Awareness of significance of the group experience • Personality growth and change • Mutual revelation, risk taking • Beginning commitment to decision by consensus • Beginning work on cognitive restructuring • Importance of goals verbalized • Growing ability to govern group independently • Dissipation of emotional turmoil • Member initiation of topics • Constructive feedback	• Assume flexible role as group vacillates • Aid sharper focus on individual goals • Encourage deeper-level exploration, feedback • Encourage acknowledgment, support of differences • Guide work of group • Encourage experimentation with different roles • Encourage use of new skills inside and outside group • Assist members to assume responsibility for change • Give consistent feedback regarding successes • Reduce own activity

(Continued)

Table 16-1 Continued

Differentiation	• Here-and-now focus	• Emphasize achievement of goals, exchange
	• High level of trust, cohesion	of skills
	• Free expression of feelings	• Support group's self-governance
	• Mutual aid	• Promote behaviors that increase cohesion
	• Full acceptance of differences	• Provide balance between support, confrontation
	• Group viewed as unique	• Encourage conversion of insight into action
	• Clarity of group purpose	• Interpret; explore common themes
	• Feelings of security, belonging, "we" spirit	• Universalize themes
	• Differentiated roles	• Encourage deeper-level exploration of problems
	• Group self-directed	• Assure review of goals, task completion
	• Intensive work on cognitions	• Stimulate individual and group growth
	• Goal-oriented behavior	• Support application of new behaviors
	• Work outside of group to achieve personal goals	outside group
	• Members feel empowered	
	• Communication open, spontaneous	
	• Self-confrontation	
Separation	• Review and evaluation	• Prepare for letting go
	• Development of outlets outside group	• Facilitate evaluation and feelings about
	• Stabilizing and generalizing	termination
	• Projecting toward future	• Review individual and group progress
	• Recognition of personal, interpersonal growth	• Redirect energy of individuals away
	• Sadness and anxiety over reality of separation	from group and toward self-process
	• Expression of fears, hopes, and others'	• Enable individuals to disconnect
	anxiety for self	• Encourage resolution of unfinished business
	• Some denial, regression	• Reinforce changes made by individuals
	• Moving apart, distancing	• Administer evaluation instruments
	• Less intense interaction	
	• Plans as to how to continue progress	
	outside group	
	• Talk of reunions, follow-up	

model effective communications, invite sharing, and convey helpful intent. In early sessions, members may be tentative about expressing what they hope to get from the group. They may have fear and apprehension regarding the group experience or worry how they may be perceived by other members, whether they will be pressured to talk, whether they will be misunderstood, whether they will be at risk of verbal attack, and whether they want to go through a change process at all. The facilitator may address and allay these anxieties by acknowledging the presence of mixed feelings or by asking all members to share their thoughts and feelings about coming to the initial group session. Focusing on feelings and reactions normalizes them, highlights commonality among members, and highlights the importance of creating a safe place in which such issues can be expressed openly. It models the intention to invite and welcome difficult or awkward comments, and it can preface suggestions for a group structure that addresses member fears, out

of which may flow the formulation of relevant group guidelines.

In initial sessions, social workers routinely invite ideas for ground rules and the format for sessions. They review basic information regarding the group's purpose and blend individual goals with the group's collective goals, engaging members in a discussion about the ways the group can help each person's initial objectives to be addressed. They may also discss the use of journaling, practice, or **bibliotherapy** readings as they reflect on the themes they are addressing and the insights they have achieved during and between group sessions (Corey, 2006). Session time may be allocated for discussing these insights, thereby reinforcing the value of continuing work between sessions.

Paying attention to the way each session opens and concludes is important for maximizing member productivity and satisfaction. The following procedures in can be helpful

C8

C8

Case Example 4: Norm Setting in the HEART Group

Dave: Amelia, to come back to a point that you mentioned before. There is a guideline that I like, which is to encourage people to participate because a good group is one where everyone contributes, and so I wonder the best way to say that—do the best you can, or …

Maria: Don't talk twice till everybody's talked once?

Dave: Well, I…

Liz: I disagree.

Maria: I'm just putting it out there. I don't know.

Dave: Liz, let's hear why you disagree.

Liz: Sometimes I'm just not in … I just don't want to contribute. I don't feel like talking.

Dave: And it might be too structured, then, Maria, to say to Liz, "We've all talked once and now you have to go." It might make the group unsafe for Liz, for the rule to be so measured out like that.

Maria: So, I don't know what the rule should be.

Amelia: How about we all, like, try our best to actively participate.

Vanessa: But don't call me out.

Jen: And actively participate doesn't necessarily mean talking, just paying attention.

Dave: That's a good point, Jen.

Maria: No sleeping in the group.

Vanessa: Yeah, stay awake.

Amelia: If I'm talking about, like, pouring out my soul, and you're over there, like clearly thinking about something else or doodling or, you know, thinking about whatever, like, it shows on your face. You know what I mean, guys?

Dave: And that's probably covered by one of the rules we already mentioned, which is "Be respectful." So, "no sleeping" Maria, I think comes under "be respectful."

Maria: Okay.

Dave: And, Amelia, I like the idea of encouraging participation—what did you say? Try as hard as we can … Do our best"?

Amelia: Do our best to participate actively.

Dave: How does everybody feel about that? [Agreement]

---

for the facilitator to use when starting a group session (Corey & Corey, 2018):

1. Give members a brief opportunity to say what they want from the upcoming session.

2. Invite members to share their accomplishments since the last session.

3. Elicit feedback regarding the group's last session and give any reflections you have of the session.

To bring meetings to a close, to the facilitators should summarize and integrate the group experience by following these procedures (Corey & Corey, 2018):

1. Ask members what it was like for them to be in the group today.

2. Invite members to identify briefly what they are learning about themselves through their experience in the group. Are they getting what they want? If not, what would they be willing to do to get it?

3. Ask members whether there are any topics, questions, or problems they would like to explore in the next session.

4. Ask members to indicate what they would be willing to do outside of the session to practice new skills.

Incorporating group rituals into the structure of sessions increases the continuity from meeting to meeting. Examples include check-in as a ritual to start each session, structured refreshment breaks, and closing meditations or readings (Subramanian et al., 1995). Routine practice heightens the transfer of insights and new behaviors from the group session into daily life.

Interventions in the Power and Control Stage

In Stage 2 of development, the group enters a period in which its dynamics, tone, and atmosphere are often highly charged, and members often need encouragement and skilled facilitation to address underlying conflicts that threaten the health of the group (Schiller, 1997). In this stage, systemic influences of racism, power, privilege, and discrimination can influence group interactions. Groups may find themselves dealing with divisions among individuals and subgroups, complaints and unrest over group goals, processes, and structure, and challenges to the facilitator. At the same time, the group is trying out its capacity to manage its own affairs. Social workers who demonstrate self-awareness, openness, humility, and trust in process provide assurance and consistency to keep the group intact. Whatever the challenges of the power and control phase, successful groups emerge stronger, with the capacity to cope with individual differences and to manage their own governance. Facilitators can help navigate this phase by the ways that they handle changes, feedback, communication, and norms.

Minimize Changes

During the power and control stage, groups with a closed membership and finite number of sessions are particularly susceptible to inner and outer stressors such as a change of facilitator or location, the addition or loss of members, or a change in the meeting time. Traumatic events such as a runaway, a death, an incidence of physical violence, or acutely disturbing political or natural events at the community or national level may also be significant.

Although such changes or events can be upsetting to a group at any stage of development, they are particularly potent in Stage 2. At this point, members have not yet become deeply comfortable or invested in the group, and changes can shake their trust. In addition, making a significant change without group involvement may disempower and discourage members. Although changes are sometimes unavoidable, they should not be frequent or frivolous, and members' questions, ideas, and reactions should be invited and embraced (Finn, 2021).

Encourage Balanced Feedback

In Stage 2 of group development, facilitators must ensure that feedback is balanced so that encounters among members are not superficial ("We can only focus on the positive") or negative ("Criticism is necessaty to help people get better"). The first experiences in giving feedback to one another are crucial in setting the tone for all that follows in the group. Active listening is a key element in these communications. Social workers "serve as teachers in preparing group members to listen to, question, validate, challenge and respect one another. And they are learners bearing witness to the stories of individual members and the expereicnes of the group as a whole" (Finn, 2021, p. 244)

Along with modeling and encouraging balanced feedback, facilitators reinforce behaviors observed during a session that have helped the group accomplish its tasks. These may include willingness to participate in discussions, answer questions, and risk revealing oneself; showing support to others; taking turns speaking; giving full attention to the task at hand; accepting differing values, beliefs, and opinions; and recognizing significant individual and group breakthroughs. The social worker can

C7

also highlight the absence of unhelpful behaviors that might have occurred earlier (e.g., whispering, fidgeting, introducing tangential topics, dominating, or verbally and physically pestering other members).

In addition, the facilitator uses observation, active listening, reflection, and summarizing to effectively focus the groups' discussion.

> **Rochelle [to Kaj]:** I know you get discouraged sometimes, but I admire the fact you can manage four children by yourself and still work. I don't think I could ever do that in a million years.
> **Kaj:** I don't always manage it. Actually, I don't do near enough for my children.
> **Facilitator:** Kaj, I hear you saying that you feel you are letting your kids down—and we can return to that in a moment—but right now would you reflect on what you just did?
> **Kaj:** I blew off Rochelle's compliment. I didn't feel like I deserved it.
> **Facilitator:** I wonder if others of you have responded in a similar way when someone has told you something positive.

The last response universalizes or broadens the focus to include the experience of other group members. This reinforces commonalities among group members and may lead to a discussion of the difficulties that others might encounter in similar situations and the strategies they have effectivelty employed to work on the shared issue.

Increase Effective Communication

Achieving success during the power and control phase requires modeling effective communication and making moment-by-moment interventions to foster effective group relations. Facilitators aid the acquisition of skills by assuming the role of coach and intervening to shape the display of communications in the group, as illustrated in the following examples:

- *Eliminating negative communications:* "I'd like us to shy away from labeling, judging, sarcasm, and words like 'always' and 'never.' As we discussed in our group contract, try to give self-reports rather than indirect messages that put down or judge another person."

  C8

- *Personalizing messages:* "That was an example of a 'you' message. Could you try again, this time by starting out with the pronoun ' I.' Try to identify your feelings, or what you want or need."

- *Talking in turn:* "Right now, several of you are speaking at the same time. Try to hold to the guideline that we all speak in turn. Your observations are too important to miss."

- *Speaking directly to each other:* "Right now, you're speaking to the group, but I think your message is meant for Rico. If so, then it would be better to talk directly to him."
- *Exploratory questions:* "Switching from closed- to open-ended questions right now could help Luz to tell her story in her own way." (The facilitator explains the difference between these two modes of questioning.)
- *Listening:* "Try to really hear what she's saying. Help her to let out her feelings and to get to the source of the problem."
- *Problem exploration versus problem solving:* "When the group offers advice too quickly, folks can't share their deeper-level feelings or reveal a problem in its entirety. We may need to allow Martin 5 to 10 minutes to share his concerns before the group offers any observations. The timing of advice is critical as we try to help members share and solve problems."
- *Authenticity:* "Could you take a risk and tell the group what you're feeling at this very moment? I can see you choking up, and I think it would be good for the group to know what you're experiencing."
- *Requesting:* "You've just made a complaint about the group. On the flip side of any complaint is a request. Tell the group what would help. Make a request."

Intervening moment by moment to shape the communications of members, as in the instances illustrated here, increases the therapeutic potential of a group.

Influence Constructive Norms

Many group patterns form in the power and control stage. The social worker can intervene then to influence the power structure, the stylistic communications of the group, and the ways in which the group chooses to negotiate and solve problems. Opportunities for these conversations could arise when distracting behavior substantially interferes with the group's task, when one or more members monopolize discussions, or when some members are silent or withdrawn. When these opportunities emerge, the social worker should focus the group's attention on what is occurring by simply describing specific behaviors or the progression of events that have occurred and then requesting group input. The facilitator can then foster discussion and problem solving. Though it may be tempting to take decisive action on their own, ultimately the social worker needs to let the power and responsibility for resolution rest with the group while still assuring psychological and physical safety for everyone (Yalom & Leszcz, 2020).

Interventions should generally focus on the group because the system is affected by the actions of an individual or subset. Some behaviors may be fostered or reinforced by the group as a whole. This approach is illustrated by the following response to a situation in which two members are talking between themselves. Rather than asking the two to pay attention, the facilitator states the following:

> **Social Worker:** I'm concerned about what is happening right now. Several of you don't seem to be tuned in to the group right now. Some of you are whispering. One of you is writing notes. A few of you are involved in the discussion. As individuals, you appear to be at different places with the group, and I'd like to check out what each of you is experiencing right now.

This message focuses on all group members, neutrally describes behavior that is occurring, and encourages the group process. By not imposing a solution on the group, the facilitator assumes a collaborative rather than an authoritarian role and sets the stage for productive group discussion.

Interventions in the Intimacy and Differentiation Stages

Treatment groups in social work share a fundamental premise that change occurs through mutuality, support, and the acquisition of new knowledge and skills. The concepts in Chapter 11 and the interventions suggested in this chapter for the initial group stages create that foundation. During the working parts of the group lifecycle, we may see further differentiation based on the theoretical or clinical underpinning of the particular group or based on the subtype of the group. That is, groups built on a psychoeducational model use these middle phases to emphasize information sharing and skill development. Support groups foster mutual aid by emphasizing connections, problem sharing, and solution-finding. Groups that follow particular theoretical orientations (CBT, DBT, Harm-Reduction, Trauma) will use concepts and curricula that follow those models (Bennett et al., 2013; Finn, 2021).

In Stages 3 (intimacy) and 4 (differentiation) facilitators introduce activities, information, discussion topics, and other strategies to work on individual and commonly held goals for change. Such activities may reduce stress and encourage pleasure and creativity; assist the facilitator in assessment as members are observed while "doing" rather than "saying;" facilitate communication, problem solving, and rapport among members; and help members develop skills and competence in decision making (Northen & Kurland, 2001).

Although art therapy and other expressive techniques generally require specialized training, many group workers incorporate music, movement, theatrical techniques, art, writing, and other experiential tools to help in facilitate expression, regulate emotions, prompt reflection, or enhance connection and skill-building (Tilly & Caye, 2005). Photovoice is an activity that invites participants to represent their social realities through photography, critical reflection, and display or presentation of the results (Finn, 2021; Labbé, et al., 2021; http://photovoice.org). The process uses a series of questions that invite group members to contemplate their own and others' photos, asking, for example, "What do you see here?", How does this relate to our lives?", "Why does this problem or strength exist?" (Finn, 2021).The technique helps deepen members' connections and understanding of common struggles and povides a platform for public education and collective action.

The working phase is a time of intensive focus on achieving members' goals. Much of the group's work during this phase is devoted to carrying out contracts developed in the group's initial sessions. Members may have lost sight of their individual goals, so a major facilitator role involves confirming goals periodically and promoting organized and systematic efforts to work on them. In one HEART group session, when the discussion of fitting in drifted to topics such as college, athletic teams, and peer groups, Dave brought the group back to focus by synthesizing the thread and saying, "I'd like to pose a question to the group. What would be one thing to change about your mindset? What thought could you change that might help you get through high school, or shopping, or gym?"

The social worker has the ongoing responsibility of monitoring the time allocated to each member to work on goals. Toseland and Rivas (2017) suggest that the facilitator help each member to work in turn. If a group spends considerable time aiding one client to achieve their individual goals, the facilitator should generalize the concepts developed in this effort to other members so that everyone benefits. The facilitator should also encourage participants to share relevant personal experiences with the member receiving help, thus establishing a norm for mutual aid. In addition, they should check on the progress of members who did not receive due attention and encourage their participation in the next session.

Finally, the social worker should establish a systematic method of monitoring treatment goals and tasks in sessions. Without attention, monitoring may be haphazard and focus on only those members who are more assertive and highly involved; members who are less assertive or deferential may not receive the same attention; and tasks to be completed between sessions may not receive the proper follow-up.

Interventions in the Termination Stage

Termination is a difficult stage for members who have invested heavily in the group, have experienced intensive support, encouragement, and understanding, and have received effective support for their problems. Social workers must be sensitive to the mixed feelings engendered by termination and carefully intervene to assist the group to come to an effective close. Chapter 19 identifies significant termination issues and change maintenance strategies. Here, we address aspects of the facilitator's role that are specific to planned endings and evaluating group efficacy.

Facilitators may assist group members in completing termination by adopting strategies such as the following:

- As members practice and acquire skills in group, anticipate and apply those to other situations and settings they may encounter after the group ends (Toseland & Rivas, 2017).

- Facilitate members' discussion of how they can respond to possible setbacks in an challenging environment. Build confidence in existing coping skills and abilities to solve problems independently.

- Help members give voice to their reactions at the prospect of the group ending. These can include feeling of success, elation, apprehension, and abandonment.

- Increase review and integration of learning by helping members to put into words what has transpired between themselves and the group from the first to the final session and what they have learned about themselves and others. Solicit information about what members were satisfied and unsatisfied with in the group and ways in which sessions could have had greater impact. Ask members to spontaneously recall moments of conflict and pain as well as moments of closeness, warmth, humor, and joy in the group (Corey & Corey, 1992).

- Facilitate the completion of unfinished business between members. One technique involves an exercise in which each person, in turn, says in a few short phrases, "What I really liked was the way you … (supply a specific behavior exchanged between the persons, such as 'always gave me credit when I could finally say something that was hard for me to say')," and then, "But I wish we … (supplying a specific wish for a behavioral exchange between the two persons that did not occur, such as 'had made more opportunities to talk to each other more directly')" (Henry, 1992, p. 124). Note that this and other closure exercises should not be used to generate new issues but rather to bring resolution to the present situation.

- Encourage members to identify areas for future work once the group concludes. Consider asking participants to formulate their own individual change contracts, which may be referred to once the group ends, and invite each client to share their contract with the group (Corey & Corey, 2018).

- Engage individual members in relating how they have perceived themselves in the group, what the group has meant to them, and how they have grown. Ask the others to give feedback regarding how they have perceived and felt about each person, including measured feedback that helps reinforce the insights gained during the course of the group (e.g., "One of the things I like best about you is …," "One way I see you blocking your strengths is …," or "A few things that I hope you'll remember are …" (Corey, 1990, p. 512).

- Use evaluative measures to determine the effectiveness of the group and the facilitator's interventions. Such measures have the following benefits: (1) they address the social worker's interest in the specific effects of interventions; (2) they help workers improve their facilitation skills; (3) they demonstrate the group's efficacy to agencies or funding sources; (4) they help facilitators assess individual members' and the group's progress in accomplishing agreed-upon objectives; (5) they allow members to express their satisfactions and dissatisfactions with the group; and (6) they help social workers develop knowledge that can be generalized to future groups and other facilitators (Toseland & Rivas, 2017).

C4

Errors in Group Interventions

In addition to attending to recommended interventions across the life of the group and during specific stages of group development, social workers must also take care to avoid errors that inhibit group development and process. Research on damaging experiences in therapeutic groups indicates that group facilitators' actions (e.g., confrontation, monopolizing, criticizing) or inactions (e.g., lack of support, lack of structure) play a primary role in group dropouts (Smokowski et al., 2001). Facilitator mistakes may include (Doel, 2019; Finn, 2021; Thomas & Caplan, 1999):

- Doing one-on-one work in the context of the group. This practice inhibits the mutual aid that is the hallmark of group work.

- Having a rigid agenda or adherence to a curriculum rather than being open to emergent structures, themes, or other forms of member ownership of the group.

- Scapegoating or attacking individual members. This behavior inhibits others' involvement by sending a message that the group is not a safe place.

- Overemphasizing content (dwelling on specific statements or topics) and failing address process (shared themes, underlying issues, nonverbal or meta-communications among members).

- Failing to challenge discrimination or attacking individuals rather than the issue.

- Lecturing the group. This practice disempowers members and inhibits group investment and momentum.

- Failing to address offensive comments or behaviors or colluding with members around bigoted, racist, or sexist statements.

- Not providing sufficient consistency and structure for group sessions.

It may be helpful to think of the preceding list as behaviors that stop the evolution of the group or send it veering off course. In the next HEART group example, Dave demonstrates a common error in group work by focusing on content over process.

Case Example 5: Overemphasizing Content and Lecturing in the HEART Group

Dave: I want us to think about the word "fat" and to think about if that's an appropriate word to use to describe ourselves.

Liz: Not you, you're skinny.

Dave: When I speak to people who have been called fat, or who refer to themselves that way, I use the term "person with overweight." And that's the way I talk about it. None of us are guaranteed to keep the bodies we have. Whether we like them or not, our bodies can always change, so I say people have overweight because it's descriptive of a moment in time rather than an enduring quality that someone possesses.

Amelia: My psychiatrist calls, um, says that I have a disordered relationship with food. [The group laughs.]

Dave: What does that mean?

Amelia: Means I'm fat, I don't know! [more laughter]

Dave: Well, let's look at the words together then. What is disordered?

Amelia: Fat. I don't know, like not right, dysfunctional, not cool.

Maria: Out of order.

Amelia: Out of order. Yes, I'm out of order with food.

Dave: What do you think about that? Do you agree or disagree?

Amelia: I don't know. Whatever. It makes sense to me.

Dave: What about it makes sense?

Amelia: Well, it's kind of a nice way of saying I'm fat.

Dave: When I hear that phrase, it sounds to me as though your psychiatrist is telling you that you're using food for reasons other than nutrition.

Amelia: Yeah, maybe.

Interventions with Task Groups

As described earlier, a significant aspect of professional social work practice is performance in task and work groups. In contrast to treatment groups, task groups are convened to accomplish a purpose, create a product, or develop policies. You are likely to be part of task groups throughout your career, starting with group projects for class, participating in committees, and serving as a leader on a team or an organizer in your practice or personal life. Task group facilitators are usually explicitly chosen and may be selected by the group itself or by an outside entity (voting for president of a professional organization or student government). It should be noted that not all participation in task groups is voluntary. While not synonymous with mandated participation in treatment groups, members may be assigned to task groups as a part of their professional or social roles. For example, a dormitory resident assistant may be expected to participate planning committees for student orientation, case management meetings for residents with substance use infractions, or a task force to address hate crimes on campus. The degree of voluntariness by this member and other participants may affect their investment in the tasks and the ultimate effectiveness of each of the groups to which they are assigned. As you read about task group facilitation, consider how involuntary or semivoluntary membership might affect group processes. For the purpose of discussing interventions with task groups, we use the term "leader" to designate the social worker who is chairing, convening, or facilitating the group, and we focus on groups that are ongoing, such as a committee or governing board.

The stages of group development observed in treatment settings also occur in task groups, though not necessarily in a linear fashion. As groups take on new issues and membership changes, the group may cycle back to revisit earlier stages. Further, the nature of task groups is such that the two middle phases (intimacy and differentiation) may not be distinguishable, and thus may be conceptualized as the working phase of the group.

C6 and 7

Interventions in the Preaffiliation Stage

A crucial part of successfully leading task groups involves getting the group off to a good start: identifying group purpose, helping to build connections among members, and identifying group guidelines. In this and other phases of the group, the leader must be attentive both to group process and group content. Group process refers to how the group is operating. Is there sufficient input and consideration of topics? Are all voices being heard? Is time being used wisely? Group content refers to the issues being discussed as opposed to how they are being discussed. In attending to content, the leader must be sure that the group is addressing relevant issues, that they have proper background information to guide their discussion, and that they are clear on what is being asked of them (to give an opinion, explore options, make a decision, etc.). This is a delicate and challenging balance, as it can be tempting to rush through an agenda item and move on to another issue without assuring that all perspectives have been considered. On the other hand, too much attention to process and viewpoints can lead to analysis paralysis, where one agenda item is discussed endlessly without progress toward action.

In the forming or preaffiliation stage, individuals enter with varying hopes and apprehensions about the group. Leaders can help diminish anxiety by clarifying the purpose of the group, asking members to introduce themselves, and using brainstorming or ice-breaking exercises to facilitate initial member interaction. Identifying the particular skills, experiences, and perspectives that different members bring can help participants become more familiar with each other and more confident sharing their viewpoints. Please note, though, that early development in task groups can be affected by preexisting relationships among group members who already know or have worked with each other in other capacities. Depending on the quality of these past experiences, friction may be carried over into the new group, or friendships may facilitate rapid movement into the work of the group. In either case, it is essential that individuals with existing relationships not form subgroups, as these splinter groups or voting blocs may diminish the comfort and cohesion of all members.

At the preaffiliation stage, leaders solicit member input on how the group should function and begin to develop group guidelines. In ongoing groups, these should be discussed when new members join, and they should be regularly revisited thereafter. As discussed in Chapter 11, topics typically include mutual expectations about attendance, communications, preparation for meetings, homework outside of meetings, confidentiality, and decision-making.

Interventions in the Power and Control Stage

In Stage 2, the power and control or storming phase, task groups often display discord about the issues they will address and the guidelines they will use. The issues may vary from operational concerns ("Why didn't we receive the minutes from the last meeting before today?"

"Why is X on the agenda?") to significant issues that question the group itself ("I don't see why we should be the hiring committee. The CEO will just pick who they want anyway." "It is a waste of time to try to influence legislation this term. We should just focus on our own jobs and services.").

Conflict is to be expected as a sign of the members' investment in the group. Leaders must be prepared for this and respond nondefensively, putting complaints on the table for group discussion and decisions. In this, the process of debate is more important that the content of the issue being debated. All too often, task groups avoid conflict by evading thorny issues, sometimes even tabling an issue despite the availability of enough facts to make a decision. Establishing norms in which differing options are sought and evaluated on their own merits will aid the group in accomplishing its objectives. The leader should attempt to stimulate idea-related conflict while managing and controlling personality-related conflict. Failure to achieve this balance may result in the marginalization of potential contributors and a less complete product. Without such healthy conflict, there is always the danger of groupthink, a condition in which members reach premature and superficial agreements, and alternative views or options are not expressed or taken seriously. Facilitators and members can assist others to express the rationale behind particular opinions, clarifying what information needs to be developed to answer questions raised in the course of the conflict.

Interventions in the Working Phase Stage

Although task groups begin their work from the first time they meet, the middle phase of group process signals the internalization of group guidelines, the emergence of norms, and shared processes for addressing the group's responsibilities. At this stage, we observe shared responsibility for group progress and accepted strategies for preparing for meetings and making decisions.

Task group facilitators model and support the use of effective communication skills, as discussed earlier in this book, regarding communications with clients. These important skills include listening, reframing, probing, seeking concreteness, and summarizing. Leaders contribute to the creation of a productive working atmosphere by conveying that each member has something to contribute and by maintaining civility so that no member—or their idea—is allowed to be marginalized or degraded.

As groups develop procedures for examining and addressing issues, the leader should help them avoid

C6 and 7

responding prematurely—arriving at solutions before the problem is well defined. For example, if a board is discussing budgetary shortfalls, the chair would help the members look at the causes and long-term trends in the budget before focusing on cuts or revenue enhancement strategies. In specifying appropriate problems and goals, the group can employ techniques such as brainstorming and nominal group technique to consider an array of possibilities before selecting a focus. Brainstorming involves generating and expressing a variety of opinions without evaluating them. In the nominal group technique, members first privately list potential problems. The group then takes one potential problem from each member until all are listed. Finally, it evaluates and ranks those potential problems as a group in deciding which should take priority (Toseland & Rivas, 2017).

At this stage, groups also employ strategies for effective decision-making. Some procedures may be prescribed. For example, the charter or bylaws of the group may require certain periods for commentary, use of clearly specified rules on who can vote, and adherence to Robert's Rules of Order. Other groups may determine their own norms, such as decision by consensus or majority rule. A challenge in consensus decision-making is that members may feel compelled or coerced to agree when they do not, creating an aura of unanimity when dissent exists.

Interventions at the Termination Stage

Termination in task groups may occur when individual members leave (unexpectedly or as anticipated at the end of a term of office) or when the group disbands. Evaluation and commencement are often overlooked in task groups, as members may experience relief at the reduction of the demands on their time and their group-related responsibilities, and perhaps satisfaction in successfully achieving their goal. Nevertheless, it is important to evaluate what worked and what did not work well in the group process, acknowledge the contributions of time and effort made by group members, and share gratitude about the roles that facilitated group success.

C8

Summary

This chapter focused on the knowledge and the skills needed to effectively intervene in social work treatment and task groups. As new theories of change and new treatment modalities emerge, they will also be applied to work with groups. Innovations in the ways groups gather and what they do during those sessions lead to novel applications of the group model. Groups can be powerful mechanisms for consciousness raising and mobilization and are well situated to move the focus of change from mirco to macro and from the personal to the political.

In this chapter, we addressed the stages of group development and the common member and group characteristics that arise with each phase, illustrating the roles and skills necessary for an effective group experience. For groups to be successful, facilitators must thoughtfully apply research on effective group practices and flexibly use their role and interventions to suit the needs of the individuals and the group as a whole, from inception to termination.

Competency Notes

C4 Engage in Practice-Informed Research and Research-Informed Practice

• Apply research findings to inform and improve practice, policy, and programs.

C6 Engage with Individuals, Families, Groups, Organizations, and Communities

• Apply knowledge of human behavior and person-in-environment, and other multidisciplinary theoretical frameworks to engage with clients and constituencies.

• Use empathy, reflection, and interpersonal skills to effectively engage diverse clients and constituencies.

C7 Assess Individuals, Families, Groups, Organizations, and Communities

- Apply knowledge of human behavior and person-in-environment and other culturally responsive multidisciplinary theoretical frameworks when assessing clients and constituencies.
- Demonstrate respect for client self-determination during the assessment process collaborating with clients and constituencies in developing mutually agreed-on goals.

C8 Intervene with Individuals, Families, Groups, Organizations, and Communities

- Engage with clients and constituencies to critically choose and implement culturally responsive, evidenced-based interventions to achieve mutually agreed-on practice goals and enhance capacities of clients and constituencies.
- Incorporate culturally responsive methods to negotiate, mediate, and advocate, with and on behalf of clients and constituencies.

Skill Development Exercises

Group Interventions

To assist you in developing group work skills, we have provided a number of exercises with modeled social worker responses. Imagine that you are the facilitator and formulate a response that addresses the member's and group's needs, given the phase and type of group. We have drawn the statements from two types of groups. One is an interdisciplinary task group in a hospital working on policy and practice changes in response to confidentiality laws, undocumented immigrant admissions, indigent patients, and the threat of a pandemic. The other is the HEART therapy group for teen girls with obesity. The five statements contain modeled social worker responses so that you can compare your response with the one provided. (Bear in mind that the modeled response is only one of many possible acceptable responses.)

Client Statements

1. **Task group member** [in fifth meeting, having missed three]: "Well, I think we should reconsider why we need to change the policy at all. After all, we've done it this way for years."

2. **Task group member** [second meeting]: "How are we going to make decisions—majority rule?"

3. **HEART group member** [third meeting]: "You're just here for the paycheck."

4. **HEART group member** [first meeting]: "I'm not sure why I'm even here except to make my mother happy."

5. **Task group member** [first meeting]: It looks like the legal department has this committee membership stacked. Is there any point in meeting if the decisions have already been made?

Modeled Social Worker

Responses

1. "Gene, we talked about the reason we were convened in the first two meetings. I'm wondering why this is coming up at this point?"

2. [To the group] "What do you think are the pros and cons of different decision-making options?"

3. [Inquisitively] "It is true that I'm paid for this work, but it sounds like there really is something more behind your statement."

4. [To the group] "I wonder if some other folks here share that feeling?"

5. It sounds like you have two concerns: who is here and why we are here. I assure you that the decisions have not been made, so the group's input is important and timely. I wonder, though, who is missing? What other perspectives do we need around the table?

Note

1. Reid (1997) has reviewed procedures for evaluating outcomes in groups, including group testimonials, content analysis of audiotapes or videotapes, socio-metric analysis, self-rating instruments, and other subjective measures.

Additive Empathy, Interpretation, and Confrontation

Chapter Overview

Chapter 17 introduces advanced practice problem-solving skills that builds on those discussed in Chapters 5 and 6. As you and the client together move forward toward problem solving, additive empathy and interpretation further support this collaborative effort. By doing so, you are helping clients achieve an understanding of their thoughts and feeling that influence behavior. In addition, clients can become skilled in exploring the behavior of others, as they recognize opportunities for change. Confrontation as a problem-solving skill is meant to further assist clients to gain greater understanding of self. The timing and the ethical use of confrontation are essential considerations that make change possible while supporting a sense of self, dignity, worth, and self-determination. To this end, we discuss the use of confrontation to help clients make informed decisions and have an awareness of the potential consequences of their behavior.

Case examples are featured, each of which are intended to increase your knowledge and inform your use of these advance practice skills and techniques. As you utilize these skills and techniques, we advise that you are mindful of the fact that, in general, human behavior has a purpose, and, therefore, it is not always easy for a client to let go of behaviors and actions they feel have served them in the past. In some instances, some clients may have predetermined decisions or a course of action to be taken. Even so, human agency is an important factor. Specifically, human agency refers to an individual's ability to take purposive action (Bandura, 2006). Additive empathy, interpretation, and confrontation are used in a manner that preserves the collaborative partnership between you and the client.

Throughout this chapter, we integrate the orienting perspectives as critical elements in change conversations. For example, change talk includes recognizing, focusing, and making use of client's strengths. Positionality, your own and that of the client, is also a prominent power dynamic to be considered. As such, we advise you to maintain a responsive sensitivity to the associated dynamics of who you are relative to the client, in particular, the authority vested in you as a professional and that of your affiliated agency. In this regard, some clients may have a negative reaction. With some individuals or client groups, these dynamic forces necessitate extra attention because of the potential influence on collaborative problem solving.

In using the advance practice skills such as additive empathy and confrontation that are discussed in this chapter, you should be aware that doing so may require behavioral adjustments on your part, for example, a nonjudgmental attitude, self-awareness, and self-reflection so that your thoughts and experiences do not intrude and become a disruption to the established problem-solving partnership with the client thus far.

After reading this chapter, you will learn and be able to utilize the following advanced practice skills:

- What additive empathy is and how to utilize it?

- How to construct an interpretation and use interpretation as a tool.

- Engage in ethical confrontation in ways that keep the relationship intact.

The Meaning and Significance of Self-Awareness

Self-awareness refers to an awareness of the various dynamic emotional forces operating in the present for an individual at any given situation. As a social worker, you can help clients become more aware of their needs, emotional states, motives or wants, feelings, and beliefs that contribute to problematic behaviors. Self-awareness can help clients gain a deeper understanding of themselves and be attentive to the effect that certain behaviors and expressions have on other people. For example, certain beliefs or behaviors may be based on a cumulative experience in the context larger social, political, and cultural environment. To this point, members of oppressed, cultural, and disenfranchised groups often see the world differently, resulting from their experiences in the dominant social environment. As such, they may emphasize environmental and societal issues that frame and thus influence an awareness of self, although it may not fit. Furthermore, your recognition that associated behaviors and certain thought patterns can be a means of coping and self- preservation.

In this chapter, sometimes we refer to insight and/ or self-awareness. While they often are used interchangeably, they are different. According to Ryabtseva (2018),

> Insight is an understanding and explanation of our current behaviors, thoughts, feelings, and relationship patterns based on our past experiences . . . But knowing why we do things the way we do, and why we feel the things we feel doesn't give us a choice in the present moment and that brings us to *self-awareness* (para. 2).

The discussion regarding insight and self-awareness is intended to help clients focus on the here and now, which we believe is a critical part of problem solving. We acknowledge, however, that on occasion, a brief excursion into the past may be appropriate, productive, and enlightening. Nonetheless, your primary focus should be to draw attention to or gain insight into current thoughts, feelings, and behaviors and how they relate to the current problem. In other words, an individual can alter the current effects of history but not history itself.

Additive Empathy and Interpretation

As discussed in Chapter 5, empathy is essential for building trust and developing a relational bond with clients that ultimately facilitates growth and change. The essence of empathy is the reflective ability that helps you perceive, understand, experience, and respond to the emotional state of another person without bonding with them. As such, a collaborative working alliance and bond is created and maintained (Sue et al., 2016; Stanley & Sethurnalnigam, 2016, 2016; Barker, 2003, p. 141).[1] Specifically, it is essential for clients to perceive that you understand and respect expressed feelings, cognitions, and emotions. Nonetheless, your worldview or life experiences may differ from that of the client and can inadvertently influence your work with clients. In those instances when you are unsure or lack clarity, humility is important. We advise that you tune in, appreciate, and validate their narrative, specifically that you verify your understanding with the client, which is crucial to maintaining an ongoing productive relationship. In doing so, you create and maintain a supportive environment that fosters a safe place for behavioral change in the context of the here and now.

Fundamental expressions of empathy were discussed in an earlier chapter. The expanded discussion here elaborates on advanced levels. Emotional empathy, specifically at the cognitive level, includes expressed feeling and an understanding that infers or reflects clients' emotions. In addition, cognitive empathy expressed by you translates such feelings into words that ultimately help clients take problem-solving action (Moudatsou et al., 2020; Decety & Jackson, 2004).

Cognitive empathy is consistent with anti-oppressive practice in that cognitive empathy requires continuously checking with the client regarding the expressed or inferred content they have shared. In addition, you are encouraged to pay attention to your perceptions, stereotypes, or images of diverse individuals, including the intersectionality of those identities which may differ from your worldview or experience. Doing so is particularly important in your expression of cognitive empathy. Specifically, cognitive empathetic statements or responses demonstrate to the client that you understand, for example, the stressors and the realties that influence their worldview, position, experiences, behaviors, and feelings. For some, clients, the narrative may include the experience of oppression and marginalized status with an emphasis on the social structure that influences their lives.

Additive empathic responses go beyond what a client has expressed and, therefore, require some degree of inference on your part. These responses are moderately interpretive—that is, they clarify or decode forces operating that result in feelings, cognitions, reactions, and behavioral patterns. Such additive empathic responses lead you to **interpretation** or the identification of patterns, goals, and wishes that clients imply but do not directly express or verbalize (Cormier et al., 2009).

Interpretation is intended to help clients view their problems from a different perspective, thereby creating new possibilities for remedial courses of action. Keep in mind that clients may not be able to hear or accept your interpretation of a situation. It could be that your interpretation is inaccurate or that clients are not ready to face a particular reality. In using this skill, you should be attuned to how the client is receiving the information shared to include **nonverbal cues**. It is also important that you are attentive to the intersectionality of the power, authority, and the privilege vested in your position as a professional. The following is an example of inept, deep interpretation.

Client: My boss is a real tyrant. He never gives anyone credit, except for Fran. She can do no wrong in his eyes. He just seems to have it in for me. Sometimes I would like to punch his lights out.

Social worker: Your boss seems to activate the same feelings you have about your father. You feel he favors Fran, who symbolizes your favored sister. It is your father who you feel was the real tyrant, and you're reliving your resentment toward them. Your boss is merely a symbol of them.

Understandably, in response, the client would be likely to reject and perhaps be offended by this interpretation. The client may question the social worker's ability to help problem solve. Although the social worker may be accurate (the determination of which is purely speculative), the client is struggling with feelings toward their boss. To shift the focus of those feelings toward the father may make the client feel like you are missing the mark or failing to understand their situation with their boss.

The following interpretation, made in response to the same client message, would be less likely to create opposition because it is linked to the recent experience with the client's boss. To be accurate, the interpretation should to the extent possible focus on understanding the client's view and feelings about the workplace situation as illustrated in the following scenario.

Social worker: So, you really resent your boss because he seems impossible to please and shows partiality toward Fran. *[Reciprocal empathy/cognitive empathy.]* Those feelings reminded me of similar ones you expressed during a previous session. You talked about a time when your parents spent a week with you and your sister on vacation. You spoke about how your father seemed to find fault with everything you did but raved about how well your sister did everything. You had previously mentioned he'd always seemed to favor your sister, but nothing you did seemed to please them. I am wondering if it is possible that your feelings might be related to the feelings you're experiencing at work. *[In this response, the social worker is assisting the client toward self-awareness.]*

Client: My boss does not like men like me.

Social worker: As I understand what you are saying, you think that your boss does not like men who look like you. Does your boss act this way with other Black men? I wonder if your feelings might be related to other experiences that you have had?

In the first message, notice that the social worker carefully documented the rationale of the interpretation and offered it tentatively, a technique discussed later in the chapter. Cognitive empathy is demonstrated in the second scenario. Specifically, the social worker attempts to acknowledge and explores the client's experience in relation to his experiences of self and others like them, yet the interpretation is global and shifts the focus from the man's expressed cognition and associated feelings.

Because we discussed, illustrated, and provided exercises related to additive empathy in an earlier chapter, we will not deal with these topics here. Instead, the discussion here focuses on using interpretation and additive empathy to expand clients' self-awareness of: (1) deeper feelings; (2) underlying meanings of feelings, thoughts, and behavior; (3) wants and goals; (4) hidden purposes of behavior; and (5) unrealized strengths and potentialities.

Deeper Feelings

Clients often may have a limited awareness or understanding of some of their emotions. Reactions often involve multiple emotions, but these feelings may be experienced only as dominant or surface feelings. Some clients experience only negative emotions such as anger and may be out of touch with more tender feelings such as hurt and compassion. Additive empathic responses (semantic interpretations) may assist clients in becoming aware of the emotions that lie at the edge of their awareness, thereby enabling them to experience these feelings more sharply and fully, become more aware of their humanness (including the full spectrum of emotions), and integrate these emergent emotions into the totality of an experience.

In these instances, you might use additive empathic responses that are intended to expand clients' awareness of feelings for several purposes, which are identified and illustrated in the following examples.

1. To identify feelings that are only implied or hinted at in verbal messages:

   Client [in sixth session]: I wonder if you feel we're making any progress. [Clients frequently ask questions that represent feelings.]
   Social worker: It sounds as though you're not satisfied with your progress. I wonder if you're feeling discouraged about how our work together is doing?

2. To identify feelings that underlie surface emotions:

   Client: I've just felt so bored in the evenings with so little to do. I text, tweet, go to chat rooms, and play video games, but none of these things seem to help. Life for me is just a bummer!
   Social worker: As I listen to you, my impression is that are feeling a lack of purpose which makes you unhappy. I wonder if you're feeling lonely and wishing you could have in person interactions with others which would help you feel less lonely? To add intensity to feelings clients that may have minimized:

   Thirty-year-old socially isolated woman: It was a little disappointing that Jana [their childhood friend from another state] couldn't come to visit. Because of COVID, their work hours were reduced, and eventually they lost their job. Yesterday, they called to say that they had cancelled the trip, so we scheduled a Zoom session, but for me, it's just not the same as seeing them in person.
   Social worker: I can see that you are disappointed. In fact, even now you seem really down. You had looked forward to their visit and had made plans. Clearly, the visit was important to you and probably to them as well.

3. To clarify the nature of feelings a client vaguely expressed:

   Male client: When Robert told me he didn't want to be with me anymore, I just turned numb. I've been walking around in a daze ever since, telling myself, "This can't be happening."
   Social worker: This change in your relationship has been a great shock to you. You were so unprepared. It hurts so much, and it is hard to admit it's really happening.

4. To identify feelings manifested only nonverbally:

   Client: My sister asked me to tend their kids while she is on vacation, and I will, of course. [Frowns and sighs.]
   Social worker: Your sigh tells me you don't feel good about it. Right now, the message I get from you is that it seems an unfair and an undue burden and that you resent her asking you to care for her kids while she is on vacation.

5. Challenging beliefs stated as facts:

   Adolescent client: My mother will never understand what I have gone through. Her life and experiences are too different from mine.
   Social worker: So, it is your opinion that your mother is unable to understand much about your experience.

Underlying Meanings of Feelings, Thoughts, and Behaviors

Used for this purpose, additive empathy or interpretation helps clients conceptualize and understand feelings, thoughts, and behavior. In consequence, you can assist them to gain an understanding of what motivates them to feel, think, and behave as they do; grasp how their behavior may problems and goals; and ultimately recognize the ongoing influence of those themes and patterns have on feelings, thoughts, and behavior.

As clients recognize similarities, parallels, themes, and associated behavior and experiences, they are gradually expanding their self-awareness in much the same way as single pieces of a puzzle began to fit together. In essence, you are assisting them to form discrete parts that are joined together into a coherent whole. The previous interpretation made to the client who resented the boss for favoring a coworker is an example of this type of additive empathic response and is a propositional interpretation. Empathetic expressions must consider that the boss and the employee come from different worlds but at the same time provide an opportunity to explore the client's experience.

In a more concrete sense, you may utilize this type of interpretation or additive empathy to assist clients in realizing that they experience troublesome feelings in the presence of a certain type of person or in certain circumstances. For example, a client may feel disempowered, disheartened, or inadequate in the presence of people who are critical, in unfamiliar situations, or become extremely anxious in situations where they must perform (e.g., when expected to give a talk or take a test). You may use expressions of additive and cognitive empathy to identify negative perceptual sets and other cognitive patterns that may need to be modified, for example, for those clients who may attend exclusively to trivial indications of their imperfections and completely overlook evidence of competent and successful performance.

Similarly, you may assist a client in recognizing a pattern of anticipating negative outcomes of relatively minor events and dreading or even avoiding events because of their perception is that the outcomes will be absolute disasters. Consider the example of a client who dreaded visiting a lifelong friend who had sustained a severe fall and, as a result, is partially paralyzed. When the social worker explored potential issues that the client feared could occur if they were to visit the friend, they identified the following:

- "What if I cry when I see them?"
- "What if I stare at them?"
- "What if I say the wrong thing?"

Using the skill of an additive empathic in response the client's comments, the social worker asked, "And if you did one of those things, how bad would that be?" The client readily agreed that it would not actually be the anticipated or imagined disaster. The social worker discussed each feared reaction in turn, clarifying that these are understandable feelings, and anyone might react similarly as the client feared. Although such a reaction would be uncomfortable, it would not be a disaster. Hence, the social worker and client jointly concluded that the client had a certain amount of control over how they reacted rather than being totally at the mercy of circumstances.

There are instances in which a client seems to be stuck. When this occurs, it is useful to assist the client in managing feeling and fears. For example, in this situation, the social worker and the client practiced responses using behavioral rehearsal to help the client feel prepared for the visit with the friend instead of being preoccupied with fears of disaster. Behavioral rehearsal can be a useful exercise with clients who seem stuck in a pattern of behavior. Notably, when a client continually voices the "what if" scenario.

The level of additive empathy described in the prior situation can also be used to enhance clients' awareness of perceptual distortions that adversely affect their interpersonal relationships. For example, parents may react or reject children because they perceive certain characteristics in themselves that they dislike. In previous sessions with the parents, explorations disclosed that they identify the same qualities in themselves and, therefore, project behavior pattens onto their children. Place yourself in the position of the social worker. By assisting the parent to recognize their own patterns of behaviors and perceptions, you can help them recognize how self-perceptions, which may be distorted, may influence their perceptions of their children. In doing so, you enable the parents to make discriminations and perceive and accept their children as unique individuals who are different from themselves even though they may share similar traits.

Similar perceptual distortions may occur between couples. These problems may cause spouses to perceive and respond inappropriately to each other because of unresolved and troublesome feelings beyond their awareness that are perhaps based on difficulties experienced in past relationships.

Wants and Goals

Another important use of additive empathy is assisting clients to become aware of implied wants and goals in certain messages that the client may not fully recognize. When overwhelmed by difficulties, some people tend to think in terms of problems and ways to obtain relief. Others, however, may think in terms of an opportunity for growth and change—even though the latter two processes are often implied in the former. When clients become more aware of a movement toward growth that is implied in their messages, they often welcome the prospect and may even become enthusiastic about moving forward. As such, additive empathy has an added advantage of expanding self-awareness and increasing motivation.

Case Example 1

Additive empathy or interpretation can provide a useful role in identifying and exploring patterns of couple behavior. In the case example, "Home for the Holidays," Kim, the social worker listened to the discussions about different communication patterns in clients' Jackie's and Anna's families of origin. She asks Jackie about whether the way the family handled their coming out as a lesbian was symbolic of how other such issues were dealt with in their family. Rather than suggest that they are representative of other such issues, Kim asks a question. Similarly, Kim asks later whether the discussion about the wedding picture and Anna not being included in it is symbolic of challenges they have faced in making decisions or working out problems. Finally, Kim puts their difficulties in the context of becoming a new family: "Often when we are forming new families, new couples, we are torn between the family we come from and the new family we are creating; this plays out in logistical decisions about the holidays."

Additive empathic messages that highlight implied wants and goals often result in the formulation of explicit goals that pave the way to change-oriented actions. Such messages play a critical role in stimulating hope in dispirited clients who feel overwhelmed by problems and, therefore, have been unable to perceive any positive desires for growth manifested in their struggles. This type of message plays a key role both in the first phase of the helping process and in the change-oriented phase as illustrated in the following examples.

> **Client:** I'm so sick of always being imposed upon. Every member in my family takes me for granted. You know: "Good old Marcie. You can always depend on them." I have taken about all of this that I can take.
> **Social worker:** Just thinking about how your family behaves toward you stirs up strong feeling. It seems to me that what you're saying adds up to an urgent desire on your part to be your own person—to feel in charge of yourself and your time instead of always responding to the beck and call of others' requests or demands.
> **Client:** I hadn't thought of it that way, but you are right. That is exactly what I think and want, if I could just be my own person.
> **Social worker:** Maybe that is a goal you'd like to set for yourself. It seems to fit, and accomplishing this goal would release you from the feelings you have described. Perhaps this is a goal that you would like to set for yourself.
> **Client:** Yes, yes! I would like very much to set that goal. Do you really think I could accomplish it?
> **Social worker:** Yes, I do. Now, perhaps we could focus on the steps to accomplish this goal.

In this scenario, additive empathy expressed by the social worker was instrumental in assisting the client to identify feelings and further helped the client begin focusing on their needs and related goals.

Hidden Purposes of Behavior

There are instances in which you may use interpretation to help clients become more fully aware of the basic motivations that underlie specific concerns. There are also times when you may misinterpret clients' motives, and clients themselves may have only a limited awareness of their problematic behaviors.

Prominent among these motives are the following: to protect tenuous self-esteem (e.g., by avoiding situations that involve any risk of failing), to avoid anxiety-producing situations, and to compensate for feelings of their own feelings of impotency or inadequacy. The following are examples of surface behaviors and the hidden purposes that may be served by those behaviors or actions. Example are demonstrated in the following scenarios:

- Underachieving students may exert little effort in school (1) because they can justify failing on the basis of not having really tried (rather than having to face their fears of being inadequate), or (2) because they want to annoy or punish parents who tend to withhold approval and affection when their expectations are not met, or (3) they don't want to be identified with the "smart kids" and be disloyal to certain friends or other relationships.
- Presentation of self with a facade of bravado to hide from self and others underlying fears and feelings of being inadequate.
- Offset or counter physical or emotional pain to counterbalance deep-seated feelings of hurt, guilt, or shame.
- Engage in self-defeating behavior to validate myths that they are destined to be a loser and live their life determined by circumstances beyond their control.

- To protect themselves, some clients may avoid close relationships to others as protection against fears of being dominated or controlled.
- Acting or behaving in aggressively or abrasive manner to avoid risking rejection which serves the purpose of keeping others at a distance.

When using the technique of interpretation, it is essential that you continuously check with the client to ensure that it is based on substantial supporting. Without supporting information, interpretations are mere speculations that a client is unlikely to accept. Be mindful to the fact that such speculations can be influenced by the prominence of your position as the social worker and, in some instances, the requirements or the mandates of the service agency or another entity. In such circumstances, interpretive projections can be inaccurate. Consequently, clients may regard such interpretations as offensive and question your competence. To increase the credibility of an interpretation and to avoid a reaction from the client, it is critical that an interpretation considers such influences as culture and issues related to diversity, including the intersectionality of multiple identities, and worldview experiences. These considerations can assist you in determining the extent to which these influences are relevant to problems presented by clients, as well as consideration of the potential influence on goals or solutions.

The case example illustrates appropriate use of interpretation to expand awareness of the motives underlying a client's behavior.

Challenging Beliefs Stated as Facts

At times, you may encounter clients that have strongly held beliefs that they consider to be facts. Those beliefs may serve a variety of purposes, for instance, to relieve anxiety or to avoid self-doubt, as illustrated in the following case example.

Unrealized Strengths and Potentialities

In some instances, there are clients who may feel unseen or unheard, ignored, or powerless resulting from racism, sexism, and oppression. This is another reason for you to consider your position as a professional with all clients but especially those clients who are members of marginalized or oppressed groups. Another vital reason for utilizing interpretation and additive empathy is to expand clients' awareness of their strengths and undeveloped or underdeveloped potentials. Clients' strengths are demonstrated in a variety of ways, such as status, positionality, and a cultural frame of reference. Therefore. you must be sensitive to these often subtle manifestations by consciously cultivating a positive perceptual set. This objective is critical because clients can be preoccupied with their real or imagined weaknesses. In effect, your acknowledgement of strengths can encourage hope and inspire the necessary courage to take steps toward making a change.

In our work with clients, we always want to find opportunities to recognize their strengths. When a client's stress level is high, it often is useful to begin the discussion by assisting them to identify and recognize strengths. Highlighting strengths can boost self-esteem as well as support the courage to take on tasks that involve making a change, such as an attempt to develop new behaviors. In this process, both the client and you can increase an awareness of the clients' strengths. In an earlier case example, a mother was facing a child welfare investigation because the children were left at home alone. Certainly, part of the assessment must focus on the dangerous circumstances that occurred and

Case Example 2

Glenda, the social worker, is meeting Twanna, an adolescent mother and Janet. The meeting takes place in the foster home. During the meeting, Glenda observes behavioral patterns that are conflicting between a teen parent, Twanna, and her foster parent, Janet. Twanna is coming home late from school, leaving their two-year-old child with the foster mother for extended periods. The foster mother is concerned that Twanna may not be around their child enough to bond with them. Meanwhile, the foster mother is at times pacifying the infant by giving them candy. When Twanna tries to stop this, the child has tantrums. Glenda hears the account of this interaction and suggests that when Twanna refuses to deal with the tantrums, going to their room and putting on their headphones, she may be thinking about Janet. "You made them this way ... you deal with them."

the possible choices or alternatives that were available. Investigations of this type that focus solely on problematic behavior diminish an individual's sense of self and dignity. Consequently, the conversation between you and the client is likely to activate defensive behavior, which although natural may not be productive to problem solving. Instead, clients are more likely to respond positively to explorations for other solutions in instances in which their strengths are recognized and appreciated (De Jong & Miller, 1995; McQuaide & Ehrenreich, 1997). As an example, note that the following case summary begins with strengths, yet the social worker acknowledges and reviews problem in the situation with the mother:

> **Social worker:** You have explained that you did not intend to leave your children alone for an extended period. Your daughter was cooking for their brother when the grease fire broke out, but because of your

guidance as a parent, she knew how to call 911 to get help (strengths perspective). As a result, the fire department came. You and I both wish that this situation had never have happened, but your daughter understood knew what to do in case of an emergency. She was able to prepare a meal, and more importantly, she knew what to do when the fire occurred. This is an example of the many things you have done to prepare your children to manage a problematic situation and to cope. For now, we will identify different arrangements so that your children are not left without adult supervision.

In this case, the social worker engaged in a nonjudgmental, problem-solving approach. In addition, the mother's strengths are acknowledged and paired with identification of the specific concerns. Consequently, the mother and the social worker were able to plan together to eliminate the danger of the current and for future problematic situations.

Case Example 3

Mr. R., age 33, and Mrs. R. entered marital therapy largely at Mrs. R.'s instigation. Mrs. R. complained about a lack of closeness in the relationship and felt rejected because her husband seldom sought affection from her. When she made overtures, he typically pulled back. Mr. R. had revealed in the exploratory interviews that his mother had been and still was extremely dominating and controlling. He felt little warmth toward his mother and saw their no more than was necessary.

The following excerpt from a session with Mr. R. focuses on an event that occurred during the week when the couple went to a movie. Mrs. R. had reached over to hold their husband's hand. He abruptly withdrew it, and Mrs. R. later expressed feelings of hurt and rejection. Their ensuing discussion was unproductive, and their communication became strained. Mr. R. discussed the event that occurred in the theater.

> **Mr. R:** I know Carol was hurt when I didn't hold their hand. I don't know why, but it really turned me off.
> **Social worker:** So, you're wondering why you turn off when she wants some affection. I wonder what was happening inside of you at that moment. What were you thinking and feeling?
> **Mr. R:** Gee, let me think. I guess I was anticipating she would do it, and I just wanted to be left alone to enjoy

the movie. I guess I resented their taking my hand. That doesn't make sense when I think about it. Why should I resent holding hands with the woman I love?
> **Social worker:** Jim, I think you are asking an awfully good question—one that's a key to some of the difficulties in your marriage. May I share an idea with you that might shed some light on why you respond as you do? *[They nod in affirmation.]* You mentioned that you felt resentful when Carol took your hand. Based on the feelings you just expressed, I am wondering if perhaps you feel you're submitting if you respond positively when she takes the initiative and pull back to be sure you're not letting yourself be dominated by her *[the hidden purpose]*. Another reason for suggesting that is that as you were growing up you have said that you felt dominated by your mother and resented her for being that way. Even now, you avoid seeing her any more than you have to. I am wondering if, as a result of your relationship with her, you could have developed a sensitivity to being controlled by a female so that you resent any behavior on Carol's part that even suggests their being in control. *[The latter part of the response provides the rationale for the interpretation.]*

Case Example 4

Marv had been unemployed for several months. However, recently he was accepted to interview for an attractive job. After a week of careful preparation for the interview, Marv shared in his next session: "I don't know why I am doing all this preparation for this job interview. I am not the kind of person they want for this job. I am afraid that I am setting myself up to fail." Following the social work value of self-determination, clients are entitled to their beliefs. However, social workers can help them examine the reasons for their beliefs (George, 2011). The social worker responded to Marv: "When you say you are not the kind of person they are looking for, Marv, what leads you to that conclusion? Did you see something in the job description that you did not see before?" Marv acknowledged that he did not. "Could it be that getting out there and performing in an interview is a little scary right now, that you are out of practice? When you prepared for an important interview in the past, how did you get yourself ready?

Guidelines for Employing Interpretation and Additive Empathy

Considerable finesse is required to effectively use interpretation and additive empathy. The following guidelines can assist you in acquiring this skill.

1. **Use additive empathy sparingly until a sound working relationship has evolved.** Because these responses go somewhat beyond clients' current level of self-awareness, clients may misinterpret the motives of a social worker and respond defensively. Hence, when clients have brief contact with a social worker, such as in discharge planning, they are unlikely to develop the kind of relationship in which additive empathy is appropriate. Conversely, when rapport has been established in the relationship, clients are more likely to be confident of your goodwill and are more receptive and able to tolerate and benefit from additive empathic and interpretative responses.

   The exceptions to this guideline involve messages that identify (1) wants and goals and (2) strengths and potentialities, both of which are also appropriate in the initial phase of the helping process. Caution, however, is advised. You should avoid identifying strengths excessively in the initial phase because some clients may interpret such messages as insincere flattery or as minimizing their distress.

2. **Employ these responses only when clients are engaged in self-exploration or have shown that they are ready to do so.** Individual clients or groups that are not ready to engage in self-exploration are likely to resist your interpretive efforts and may perceive them as unwarranted attempts by you to impose your formulations. Exceptions to this guideline are the same as those cited in the first guideline.

3. **Pitch these responses to the edge of clients' self-awareness and avoid attempting to foster awareness that is remote from clients' current awareness or experiences.** Clients generally are receptive to responses that closely relate to their experiences but resist those that are derived from unfounded speculations. It is not good practice to push clients into rapidly acquiring new insights because many of these deep interpretations can prove to be inaccurate and produce negative effects, including reducing clients' confidence in you, conveying lack of understanding, or engendering resistance. You should not use interpretive responses until the client has enough information to be reasonably confident their responses are accurate. You can then take care to share the supportive information on which the interpretation is based.

4. **Avoid making several additive empathic responses in succession.** Because interpretation responses require time to think through, digest, and assimilate, a series of such responses tends to bewilder and overwhelm clients.

5. **Phrase interpretive responses in tentative terms.** Because these responses involve a certain degree of inference, there is always the possibility that the social worker might be wrong. Tentative phrasing openly acknowledges this possibility and invites clients to agree or disagree (Cormier et al., 2009, p. 132). If you present interpretations in an authoritarian or dogmatic manner, however, clients may not

Case Example 5

In the video "Serving the Squeaky Wheel," the social worker, Ron Rooney, becomes aware of a pattern in many stories from Molly, the client, that concern grievances about being ill served by other social workers and the health system. When she mentions not wanting to be the "greasy wheel" (squeaky wheel), Rooney suggests the possibility that Molly has, in fact, been acting as a squeaky wheel by complaining when she feels underserved, and that pattern of assertiveness is sometimes rewarded by the system and sometimes punished. "You seem to be courageous in fighting battles, and you have learned some skills in assertiveness—and, as you say, that can be a two-edged or three-edged sword. Sometimes your assertiveness gets you what you want, and sometimes your assertiveness causes some people to look at you as the squeaky wheel that has squeaked too much."

feel free to offer candid feedback and may outwardly agree while covertly rejecting interpretations. Tentative phrases include "I wonder if . . .," "Could it be that your feelings may be related to . . .," and "Perhaps you're feeling this way because. . . ." Using additive empathy to explore strengths is, of course, less threatening and can be done with less hesitation. Interpretations must also be consistent with the client's worldview and in consideration of their status.

6. **To determine the accuracy of an interpretive response, carefully note clients' reactions after offering the interpretation.**   `C9`   When responses are on target and clients affirm their validity, continue self-exploration by bringing up additional relevant material or respond emotionally in a manner that matches the moment (e.g., ventilate relevant feelings). When interpretations are inaccurate or premature, clients tend to disconfirm them (verbally or nonverbally), change the subject, withdraw emotionally, argue, become defensive, or simply ignore the interpretation.

7. **If the client responds negatively to an interpretative response,**   `C9`   **acknowledge your probable error, respond empathically to the client's reaction, and continue your discussion of the topic under consideration.** Note that sometimes such interpretations are immediately rejected, but a seed has been planted upon which clients may further reflect.

8. **When providing an interpretation to a client who is culturally different from the social worker, recognize that the client may not readily understand the message the way it was intended.** It has been argued that psychotherapeutic interventions have evolved from the experience of European Americans with a monocultural bias that tends to misunderstand motives and behaviors occurring to persons whose cultural experiences and beliefs are different from the therapist's (Gone, 2015; Jackson, 2015). Indeed, it is best to consider the exchange as a cultural transaction between the client and you, each of which is influenced by their respective cultural identities (Sue et al., 2016; Jackson, 2015).

To assist you in expanding your skill in formulating interpretive and additive empathic responses, exercises and modeled responses appear at the end of this chapter.

Confrontation

Confrontation involves facing clients with some aspect of their thoughts, feelings, or behavior   `C8`   that is contributing to or maintaining their difficulties. Ethical, effective confrontation should be specific and timely and should consider the relationship with the individual as well as the influence of your position. To be productive, confrontation should be utilized in such a way that it helps the client become aware of and examine the consequences of their behavior or actions. For example, "I have observed . . . and it makes me wonder what you are feeling or thinking?"

Ethical, constructive confrontation utilizes such communication skills as clarification, paraphrasing, and empathy. These skills help you communicate, understand, and interpret what a behavior means to the individual. With respect to the latter, it is important that you frame your interpretation as "I" statements, focusing on the behaviors that you have observed. By combining empathy and interpretation, you communicate what you believe the person is thinking or feeling. These statements are followed by descriptions of a specific behavior or concern. These examples are not framed as a demand for change but rather a request for change in collaboration with the individual in a nonthreatening manner.

In this context, several questions are in consideration. When is confrontation appropriate? With whom? And under what conditions? How does human agency figure in confrontations? Is confrontation a skill or a style of practice? In some settings, confrontation becomes a style of practice rather than a selective skill. That is, some professionals believe that some clients are well defended with denial and rationalization, as well as refusing to accept responsibility. In such situations, the belief is that only repeated confrontations would succeed in changing problematic behavioral patterns.

This approach relies exclusively on the professional's interpretation and authority and further lacks the most basic level of empathy as well as respect for human agency, dignity, and worth. Confrontation used in this manner will most likely be met with reactive behavior. Specifically, this approach magnifies the position and power of the professional and, in consequence, diminishes that of the individual. For example, in some settings, the primary focus is to get an individual to take responsibility by owning a behavior rather than blaming others as justification for their actions.

As such, confrontations are believed to be the only way to get the individual to recognize their behavior and accept responsibility for harm. For example, men have claimed that almost every word they [batterers] utter is either victim blaming or justification for their violence. Hence, confronting them in an authoritarian and aggressive style (Miller & Rollnick, 2013) was considered necessary to achieve an admission of guilt—that is, admission that they had a problem and were not in control of their behavior. In this approach, a label was attached to the individual because of behavior, and, therefore, no other exploration is necessary. We stress that ethical confrontation focuses on specific behavior, thoughts, or feeling and does not diminish the whole person.

In short, confrontation is not used to press individuals to give up their own views and accept the interpretation of those in a position of power to confront

and demand behavioral change. Used in this manner, change is prescribed by a professional. It also assumes that disempowered persons—those not motivated and incapable of making their own decisions and controlling their behavior—would then accept and cooperate with the formulation of the problem by the social workers and/or group (Kear-Colwell & Pollock, 1997). If they reacted by showing disagreement and resistance, they were seen as persisting in denial, lacking motivation, and often perceived as demonstrating pathological personality patterns.

Ethical confrontation that supports the dignity and the worth of the client is a specific intervention technique rather than an aggressive power dynamic intended to influence a change in problematic behavior. In using this technique, you should be mindful of the authority-vested position and use it such a manner that contributes to instead of minimizing the opportunity for problem solving. It also is important to understand that confrontation can harm the therapeutic alliance. For example, a client may express racism or homophobia. It is the clinician's responsibility to confront these beliefs. You may need to wait until your relationship is strong enough to handle the confrontation. Nonetheless, you still must address it in some way. You could do everything right and still have a confrontation harm your relationship with clients.

In the middle phase of problem-solving work, ethical confrontation can assist clients achieve awareness of the forces blocking their progress toward growth and goal attainment. At this stage, the technique can enhance their motivation to energize the change effort. There are instances in which confrontation is particularly relevant, for example, when clients are blind to the discrepancies or the inconsistencies in their thoughts, beliefs, emotions, and behaviors, specifically when such thoughts, beliefs, or emotions are the basis of or perpetuate dysfunctional behavior. Of course, self-awareness blind spots are universal. In essence, all humans experience the limitation of an inability to step out of their perceptual fields and look at themselves objectively.

Case Example 6

Note that in the case example "Home for the Holidays," at several points, Kim, the social worker, suggests a tentative interpretation of what one or the other might be feeling and then says, "I don't want to put words into your mouth," giving them an opportunity to correct their interpretation.

As the previous case example with Julie showed, additive empathy and confrontation have much in common. Skillful confrontations incorporate consideration of clients' feelings that underlie obstacles to change. Because fears are often among these feelings, skill in relating with high levels of empathy, including at the cognitive level, is a prerequisite to using confrontation effectively. Indeed, effective confrontation is an extension of empathic communication because the focus on discrepancies and inconsistencies derives from a deep understanding of clients' feelings, experiences, and behavior.

Self-Confrontation

It is important for social workers to possess a range of confrontation skills and not confront clients primarily to vent their own frustration with clients' lack of progress. Social workers would more appropriately consider confrontation to exist along a continuum that ranges from fostering self-confrontation at one extreme to assertive confrontation at the other extreme (Rooney, 2009). That is, clients can often be engaged quickly in self-confrontation by you asking questions, which prompts them to reflect on the relationship between behaviors and values.

Artfully designed, intake forms can serve a similar function, asking potential clients to reflect on concerns and their perceptions of the causes. Such confrontations are subtle and respectful and rarely provoke strong client opposition. As clients gain expanded awareness of themselves and their problems through self-exploration, they tend to recognize and confront discrepancies and inconsistencies themselves. Self-confrontation that supports human agency is generally preferable to social worker-initiated confrontation. In essence, the former is less risky because a client's resistance to professional insights can be an obstacle or cause a reaction, but these factors are diminished when a client is encouraged to engage in self-confrontation.

Clients vary widely in the degree to which they are able or willing to engage in self-confrontation. In addition, human agency is a factor in self-confrontation and includes emotional maturity. For example, reflective persons may be able to self-confront with ease and frequency. In contrast, individuals who are less likely to self-confront tend to be out of touch with their emotions and may also have limited or no awareness of the effects of behavior on others. A potential result is that others are blamed for certain behaviors or difficulties. Such individuals are least likely to engage in self-confrontation.

Inductive questioning can be a form of confrontation that is more active on your part but is conveyed in a respectful manner. For example, you ask questions that lead the client to consider potential discrepancies between thoughts, values, beliefs, and actions. Also, when you ask a question that relates to facts rather than one that requires the client to label themselves, the question is more likely to be effective. For example, asking a client with a chemical dependency problem, "Are you powerless over alcohol?" would require the client to essentially label themselves an alcoholic. On the other hand, "Do you ever have blackouts?" "Do you find it easier to bring up a problem with another person when you have had something to drink?" and "Do you ever find that once you begin drinking you can't easily stop?" are questions that, taken together, raise the possibility that drinking is a problem that might need attention (Citron, 1978). Such questions are less intrusive on an intake assessment form than when presented in sequential interview questions. The latter can cause the client to feel that you are trying to persuade them to immediately acknowledge the risks of their behavior.

Assertive Confrontation

When a danger is imminent, you may not be able to rely on tactful self-confrontation facilitated by inductive questioning. Instead, you may have to engage in more assertive confrontation in which the connection between troubling thoughts, plans, values, and beliefs is stated in declarative form, connecting them explicitly for the client. Such assertive confrontation is a more high-risk technique because clients may interpret the social worker's statements as criticisms, putdowns, or rejections. Paradoxically, the risk of these reactions is greatest among clients who must be confronted most often because they rarely engage in self-confrontation. These individuals tend to have weak self-concepts and are prone to read criticism into messages when none is intended. Ill-timed and poorly executed confrontations may be perceived by clients as verbal assaults and can seriously damage the helping relationships.

Using confrontation requires keen timing and finesse. You must make special efforts to convey your helpful intent and goodwill as you use confrontation as a problem-solving technique. To do otherwise can cause hostility, offend, and alienate clients which disrupts problem solving relationship.

Effective assertive confrontations embody four elements as follows:

1. An expression of a specific concern.
2. A description of the client's purported goal, belief, or commitment.
3. A behavior (or absence of behavior) that is inconsistent with the goal, belief, or commitment.
4. The probable negative outcomes of the discrepant behavior.

The format of a confrontive response may be depicted as follows:

I am concerned because you (believe, (want, are striving to)

_____

(describe desired outcome)

but your _____

(describe discrepant action, behavior, or inaction)

is likely to result in _____

(describe probable negative consequences)

This format is purely illustrative. You may organize these elements in varying ways, and we encourage you to be innovative and develop your own style. For example, you may challenge clients to analyze the effects of behaviors that are incongruous with their purported goals or values, as illustrated in the following excerpt:

> **Social worker [to male on parole]:** Al, I know the last thing you want is to have to return to prison. I want you to stay out, too, and I think you sense that, but I have to level with you. You are starting to hang out with the same bunch you got in trouble with before you went to prison. You are heading in the same direction you were before, and we both know where that leads.

In this confrontation, the social worker begins by referring to the client's purported goal (remaining out of prison) and expresses a like commitment to the goal. The social worker next introduces concern about the client's behavior (hanging out with the same bunch the client got in trouble with before) that is discrepant with that goal. The social worker concludes the confrontation by focusing on the possible negative consequence of the discrepant behavior (getting into trouble and returning to prison).

Notice these same elements in the following examples of confrontive responses:

> **Social worker [to father in family session]:** Mr. D, I would like you to stop for a moment and examine what you're doing. I know you want the children not to be afraid of you and talk with you more openly. Right? [Father agrees.] Okay, let us think about what you just did with Steve. He began to tell you about what he did after the school assembly, and you cut them off and criticized his behavior. Did you notice how he stopped talking and looked down?

> **Social worker [to mother in child welfare system]:** I have a concern I need to share with you. You have expressed your goal of regaining custody of Pete, and we agreed that attending the parents' group was part of

the plan to accomplish that goal. This week is the second time in a row you have missed the meeting because you overslept. I am wondering what missing the parents' group means for your goal of regaining custody of Pete.

Because assertive confrontation runs the risk of putting clients on the defensive or alienating them, expressing concern and helpful intent is a critical element because it reduces the possibility that clients misconstrue the motive behind the confrontation. Tone of voice is also vital in highlighting helpful intent. If the confrontation regarding a specific behavior is conveyed in a warm, concerned tone of voice, the client is much less likely to feel attacked. If the social worker uses a critical tone of voice, any verbal reassurance that criticism was not intended is likely to fall on deaf ears. For example, to the student in the classroom, the social worker crossing arms across the chest might say, "You need to pay attention in class and keep your hands to yourself." People tend to attach more credence to nonverbal aspects of messages than to verbal aspects.

Guidelines for Employing Confrontation

To assist you in employing confrontation effectively, we offer the following guidelines.

1. **When a violation of the law or imminent danger to self or others is involved, a confrontation must occur no matter how early in the working relationship.** Such confrontations may impede the development of the relationship, but the risk of harm to self and others is more important than the immediate effect on the relationship.

2. **Whenever possible, avoid confrontation until an effective working relationship has been established.** This can occur when a client is contemplating action (or inaction) that impedes their own goals but is not an imminent danger to self or others. Employing empathic responsiveness in early contacts conveys understanding, fosters rapport, and enhances confidence in the social worker's perceptiveness and expertise. When a foundation of trust and confidence has been established, clients are more receptive to confrontations and, in some instances, even welcome them.

3. **Use confrontation sparingly.** Confrontation is a potent technique that generally should be employed only when a client's blind spots are not responsive to other, less risky intervention methods. Poorly timed and excessive confrontations can inflict psychological damage on clients (Lieberman et al., 1973).

Another reason to judiciously use confrontation is that some clients may yield to forceful confrontation for counterproductive reasons. Seeking to please social workers (or to avoid displeasing them), they may temporarily modify their behavior, but changing merely to comply with the expectations of a social worker may reinforce the idea that more powerful people can enforce their will on less powerful ones. This is not a model that social workers should want to reinforce with families (Rooney, 2009).

4. **Deliver confrontations in an atmosphere of warmth, caring, and concern.** If social workers employ confrontations in a cold, impersonal, or critical way, clients are likely to feel that they are being attacked. By contrast, if social workers preface confrontations with genuine empathic concern, clients are more likely to perceive the helpfulness intended in the confrontation. In this regard, carrying out a confrontation when the social worker is tired, irritated, angry, disappointed, frustrated, or disillusioned—in a word, when the social worker is emotionally overwrought—is a bad idea. Carrying out a confrontation is about the client's needs, not that of the social workers.

5. **Whenever possible, encourage self-confrontation.** Recall from the previous discussion that self-confrontation has decided advantages over social worker-initiated confrontation. Learning by self-discovery fosters independence and increases the likelihood that clients will act upon their newly gained self-awareness. Social workers can encourage self-confrontation by drawing clients' attention to issues, behaviors, or inconsistencies that they may have overlooked and by encouraging them to analyze the situation further.

For example, the social worker in the following examples may directly intervene in dysfunctional interactions and challenge individuals, couples, families, or groups to identify what they are doing. Responses that encourage self-confrontation in such a context include the following:

- "Let's stop and look at what you just did."
- "What just happened?"

Other inductive question responses that highlight inconsistencies and foster self-confrontation are:

- "I'm having trouble seeing how what you just said (or did) fits with . . ."
- "I can understand how you felt, but how did [describe behavior] make it better for you?"

- "What you're saying seems inconsistent with what you want to achieve. How do you see it?"

Yet another technique is useful when clients overlook the dynamic significance of their own revealing expressions or when their expressed feelings fail to match their reported feelings. This technique involves asking them to repeat a message, listen carefully to themselves, and consider the meaning of the message. Examples of this technique are:

- "I want to be sure you realize the significance of what you just said. Repeat it, but this time listen carefully to yourself, and tell me what it means to you."

- [*To marital partner in conjoint interview*]: "Joan just told you something terribly important, and I'm not sure you really grasped it. Joan, could you repeat it, and I want you to listen very carefully, Bob, and check with Joan as to whether you grasped what she said."

- [*To group member*]: "You just told the group you are feeling better about yourself, but it didn't come through that way. Please say it again but get in touch with your feelings and listen to yourself."

6. **Avoid using confrontation when clients are experiencing extreme emotional strain.** Confrontation tends to mobilize anxiety. When clients are under heavy strain, supportive techniques rather than confrontation are indicated. Clients who are overwhelmed with anxiety or guilt generally are not receptive to confrontation and may not benefit from it. In fact, confrontation may be detrimental, adding to their already excessive tension.

Conversely, confrontation is appropriate for clients who experience minimal inner conflict or anxiety when such conflict or anxiety would be appropriate considering how their problematic behavior is experienced by others. Some persons are self-satisfied and relatively insensitive to the feelings and needs of others (whom they cause to be anxious); such clients often lack the anxiety needed to engender and maintain adequate motivation. Confrontation, when combined with the facilitative conditions, may mobilize the anxiety they need to examine their own behavior and to consider making constructive changes.

7. **Follow confrontation with empathic responsiveness.** Because clients may take offense to even skillful confrontation, it is vital to be sensitive to their reactions. Clients often do not express their

reactions verbally, so you need to be especially attuned to nonverbal cues that suggest hurt, anger, confusion, discomfort, embarrassment, or resentment. If clients manifest these or other unfavorable reactions, it is important to explore their reactions and respond empathically to their feelings. Discussing such reactions provides opportunities for clients to vent their feelings and for social workers to clarify their helpful intent and assist clients to work through negative feelings. If social workers fail to sense negative feelings, or clients withhold expressions of them, the feelings may fester and adversely affect the helping relationship.

8. **Expect clients to respond to confrontation with a certain degree of anxiety.** Confrontation is employed to produce a temporary sense of disequilibrium that is essential to break an impasse. The anxiety or disequilibrium serves a therapeutic purpose in impelling the client to make constructive changes that eliminate the discrepancy that prompted the social worker's confrontation. Empathic responsiveness following confrontation is not aimed at diluting this anxiety but rather seeks to resolve untoward reactions derived from negative interpretations of the social worker's motives for making the confrontation.

9. **Do not expect immediate change after confrontations.** Although awareness paves the way to change, clients rarely succeed in making changes immediately following acquisition of insight. Even when clients fully accept confrontations, corresponding changes ordinarily occur by increments. Known as working through, this change process involves repeatedly reviewing the same conflicts and the client's typical reactions to them, gradually broadening the perspective to encompass increasingly more situations to which the changes are applicable. Pressing for immediate change can inflict psychological damage on clients.

Indications for Assertive Confrontation

As noted previously, confrontation is appropriate in three circumstances: (1) when violations of the law or imminent threats to the welfare and safety of self or others are involved; (2) when discrepancies, inconsistencies, and dysfunctional behaviors (overt or covert) block progress or create difficulties; and (3) when efforts at self-confrontation and inductive questioning have been ineffective in fostering clients' awareness of these behaviors or attempts to make corresponding changes. Discrepancies may reside

in cognitive/perceptual, emotional (affective), or behavioral functions or may involve interactions between these functions. A comprehensive analysis of types of discrepancies and inconsistencies has been presented elsewhere (Hammond et al., 1977, pp. 286–318); therefore, we merely highlight some of the most encountered.

Cognitive/Perceptual Discrepancies

Many clients have behavioral or perceptual difficulties that are a product of inaccurate, erroneous, or incomplete information, and confrontation may assist them in modifying their problematic behaviors. For example, clients may lack accurate information about indicators of alcoholism, normal sexual functioning, or reasonable expectations of children according to stages of development.

Even more common are misconceptions that clients have about themself. The most common of these, in the authors' experience, involve cognitive/perceptual discrepancies, which include interpersonal perceptual distortions, irrational fears, dichotomous or stereotypical thinking, denial of problems, placing responsibility for one's difficulties outside of oneself, failing to discern available alternative solutions to difficulties, and failing to consider consequences of actions. Even people who appear to have it all or are talented and attractive may view themselves as inferior, worthless, inadequate, unattractive, or stupid. Such perceptions are often deeply embedded and do not yield to change without extensive help. Confronting clients about these unhelpful and demeaning views can strengthen and raise their awareness of these thoughts and beliefs and the need to challenge such self-deprecating views.

Affective Discrepancies

Discrepancies in the emotional realm are inextricably linked to cognitive/perceptual processes because emotions are shaped by the cognitive meanings that clients attribute to situations, events, and memories. For example, a client may experience intense anger that emerges from a conclusion that another person has intentionally insulted, slighted, or betrayed them. This conclusion is based on a meaning attribution that may involve a grossly distorted perception of the other person's intentions. In such instances, social workers can assist clients in exploring their feelings, providing relevant detailed information, considering alternative meanings, and realigning emotions with reality.

Affective discrepancies that social workers commonly encounter include denying or minimizing actual feelings, being out of touch with painful emotions, expressing feelings that are contrary to purported feelings (e.g., claiming to love a spouse or child but expressing only critical or otherwise negative feelings), and verbally expressing a feeling that contradicts feelings expressed nonverbally (e.g., "No, I'm not disappointed," said with a quivering voice and tears in the eyes). Gentle confrontations aimed at emotional discrepancies often pave the way to expressing troubling emotions, and many clients appreciate social workers' sensitivity in recognizing their suppressed or unexpressed emotions. If a client appears unprepared to face painful emotions, the social worker should proceed cautiously. Indeed, it may be wise to defer further exploration of those hurtful emotions. Confronting the client vigorously may elicit overwhelming emotions and engender consequent resentment toward the social worker.

Behavioral Discrepancies

Clients may experience many behavioral concerns that create difficulties for themselves and for others. Even though these patterns may be conspicuous to others, clients may remain blind to their patterns or the effects of their behaviors on others. Confrontation may be required to expand their awareness of these patterns and their pernicious effects.

Irresponsible behavior can cause serious interpersonal difficulties for clients as well as problems with broader society. Neglect of children, weak efforts to secure and maintain employment, undependability in fulfilling assignments, failure to maintain property—these and similar behaviors often result in severe financial, legal, and interpersonal entanglements that may culminate in loss of employment; estrangement from others; and loss of property, child custody, self-respect, and even personal freedom.

Irresponsible behavior often pervades the helping process as well, sometimes indicated by clients' tardiness to sessions, unwillingness to acknowledge problems, and failure to keep appointments or pay fees. Effective confrontation with such clients requires using a firm approach. Your expressions of goodwill shows concern about wanting to assist them in avoiding the adverse consequences of not assuming responsibilities. Social workers do a disservice to their clients when they permit them to evade responsibility for their actions or inaction. Social workers must counter a client's tendency to blame others or circumstances for their difficulties by assisting them to recognize that only they can reduce the pressures that beset them.

Other common behavioral discrepancies involve repeated actions that are incongruous with a client's purported goals or values. For example, an adolescent may describe ambitious goals that require extensive training or education yet may make little effort in school, being truant frequently, and otherwise behaving in ways that are entirely inconsistent with their stated goals. Spouses or parents may similarly express goals of improving their marital or family life but persistently behave in abrasive ways that further erode their relationships.

Confrontation can be used to help clients recognize and subsequently give up self-defeating behaviors. In some instances, therapeutic binds (a special form of confrontation) may be used as leverage to motivate clients to discontinue destructive and persistent patterns of behavior such as when an individual threatens to act in a manner that endangers self or others. Even in such situations, the principles of effective and ethical confrontation are to be observed.

Three other common categories of discrepancies or dysfunctional behavior that warrant confrontation are manipulative behavior, dysfunctional communication, and resistance to change. In groups, certain members may attempt to dominate the group, bait group members, play one person against the other, undermine the leader, or engage in other destructive ploys. The price of permitting members to engage in such behaviors may be loss of certain group members, dilution of the group's effectiveness, or premature dissolution of the group. To avert such undesired consequences, the leader may elicit the reactions of other group members to this behavior and assist members to confront manipulators with their destructive tactics. Such confrontations should adhere to the guidelines delineated earlier, and the leader should encourage members to invite offending members to join with them in constructively seeking to accomplish the purposes for which the group was formed.

Because problematic communication frequently interpreted as resistance to change often occurs in individual, conjoint, and group sessions, social workers may encounter abundant opportunities to employ confrontation to good effect. Intervening during or immediately following dysfunctional communication is a powerful means of enabling clients to experience firsthand the negative effects of their dysfunctional behaviors (e.g., interrupting, attacking, claiming, or criticizing). By shifting the focus to the negative reactions of recipients of problematic messages, social workers enable clients to receive direct feedback about how their behavior offends, alienates, or engenders defensiveness in others, thereby producing effects contrary to their purported goals.

Summary

This chapter discussed three vital skills in working through clients' opposition to change and relating openly in the helping relationship: additive empathy, interpretation, and confrontation. If individual clients are left to struggle alone with negative feelings about the helping process or the social worker, their feelings may increase to the point that they resolve them by discontinuing their sessions. If family members or groups are permitted to oppose change by engaging in distracting, irrelevant, or otherwise dysfunctional behaviors, they may likewise lose both confidence in the social worker (for valid reasons) and motivation to continue. For these reasons, social workers must accord the highest priority to being helpful to clients who encounter obstacles or who may be opposed to change.

Competency Notes

C6   Engage with Individuals, Families, Groups, Organizations, and Communities

- Apply knowledge of human behavior and person-in-environment, and other multidisciplinary theoretical frameworks to engage with clients and constituencies.
- Use empathy, reflection, and interpersonal skills to effectively engage diverse clients and constituencies.

C8   Intervene with Individuals, Families, Groups, Organizations, and Communities

- Engage with clients and constituencies to critically choose and implement culturally responsive, evidenced-based interventions to achieve mutually agreed-on practice goals and enhance capacities of clients and constituencies.
- Incorporate culturally responsive methods to negotiate, mediate, and advocate, with and on behalf of clients and constituencies.

C9   Evaluate Practice with Individuals, Families, Groups, Organizations, and Communities

- Select and use appropriate methods for evaluation of outcome.
- Critically analyze outcomes and apply evaluation findings to improve practice effectiveness with individuals, families, groups, organizations, and communities.

Skill Development Exercises

Additive Empathy and Interpretation

To assist you in advancing your skills in responding with interpretation and additive empathy, we provide the following exercises. Read each client statement, determine the type of response required, and formulate a written response that you would employ if you were in an actual session with the client. Keep in mind the guidelines for employing interpretive and additive empathic responses. Compare your responses with the modeled social worker responses provided after the client statements.

Client Statements

C6

1. **White female client** [to African American male social worker]: You seem to be accepting of White people—at least you have been of me, but somehow, I still feel uneasy with you. I guess it is just me. I have not really known many Black people very well.

2. **Married woman, age 28:** I feel I do not have a life of my own. My life is controlled by his work, his hours, and his demands. It is like I don't have an identity of my own.

3. **Prison inmate, age 31** [one week before the date of his scheduled parole, which was canceled the preceding week]: Man, what the hell's going on with me? Here, I have been on good behavior for three years and finally got a parole date. You would think I'd be damned glad to get out of here. So, I get all uptight and get in a brawl in the mess hall. I mean, I really blew it, man. Who knows when they will give me another date?

4. **Male, age 18:** What is the point in talking about going to Trade Tech? I did not make it in high school, and I won't make it there either. You may as well give up on me—I am just a dropout in life.

5. **Widow, age 54:** It was Mother's Day last Sunday, and neither of my kids did so much as send me a card. You would think they could at least acknowledge I'm alive.

6. **Female secretary, age 21:** I do not have any trouble word processing when I'm working alone, but if the boss or anyone else is looking over my shoulder, I make a lot of mistakes and freeze up.

7. **Female, age 26** [in a committed relationship; she is five pounds overweight]: When I make a batch of cookies or a cake on the weekend, Terri [their partner] looks at me with that condemning expression, as though I am not really trying to keep my weight down. I do not think it's fair just because they don't like sweets. I like sweets, but the only time I eat any is on the weekend, and I do not eat much then. I feel I deserve to eat dessert on the weekend at least.

8. **Client with a disability who receives public assistance** [with a back condition caused by a recent industrial accident]: This not being able to work is really getting to me. I see my kids needing things I cannot afford to get them, and I just feel—I don't know—kind of useless. There has got to be a way of making a living.

9. **Male who has been diagnosed with depression, age 53:** Yeah, I know I do all right in my work, but that does not amount to much. Anyone could do that. That is how I feel about everything I've ever done. Nothing is really amounted to anything.

10. **Mother, age 29, who is alleged to have neglected their children:** I do not know. I am just so confused. I look at my kids sometimes, and I want to be a better mother, but after they have been fighting, throwing tantrums, or whining, and I lose my cool, I feel like I'd just like to go somewhere—anywhere—and never come back. The kids deserve a better mother.

11. **Client with mental health diagnosis who is apprehensive about taking a licensing examination:** Sometimes I think I am just not cut out for this. I know I took exams as a student and did okay, but I get really scared when I think of taking a licensing exam. I think that maybe this is too much for me. I am trying to get beyond myself.

Modeled Social Worker Responses for Interpretation and Additive Empathy

1. *[To clarify feelings experienced only vaguely]:* I gather that even though you cannot put your finger on why, you're still a little uncomfortable with me. You have not related closely to that many African Americans, and you're still not altogether sure how much you can trust me.

2. *[Implied wants and goals]:* Sounds like you feel you are just an extension of your husband and that part of you is wanting to find yourself and be a person in your own right.

3. *[Hidden purpose of behavior, underlying feelings]:* So, you're pretty confused about what's happened. Fighting in the mess hall when you did just doesn't make sense to you. You know, Carl, about your getting uptight—I guess I am wondering if you were worried about getting out—worried about whether you could make it outside. I'm wondering if you might have fouled up last week to avoid taking that risk.

4. *[Underlying belief about self]:* Sounds like you feel defeated before you give yourself a chance, like it is hopeless to even try. Jay, that concerns me because when you think that way about yourself, you are defeated—not because you lack ability but because you think of yourself as destined to fail. That belief itself is a big challenge for you.

5. *[Deeper feelings]:* You must have felt terribly hurt and resentful that they did not so much as call you. In fact, you seem to be experiencing those feelings now. It just hurts so much.

6. *[Underlying thoughts and feelings]:* I wonder if, considering your tightening up, you get to feeling scared, as though you're afraid you won't measure up to their expectations.

7. *[Unrealized strengths]:* I'm impressed with what you just said. It strikes me that you are exercising a lot of control by limiting dessert to weekends and using moderation then. In fact, your self-control seems greater than that of most people. You and Terri have a legitimate difference concerning sweets. I wonder if Terri has a concern about sugar. Is that something you have looked into? Sugar can be very addictive, and most of us experience it. Is that something you would want to explore? There are ways to satisfy that craving for sweets that we all have that may not have some of the effects of sugar.

8. *[Unrealized strength and implied want]:* Steve, I can hear the frustration you are feeling, and I want you to know it reflects some real strength on your part. You want to be self-supporting and be able to provide better for your family. Given that desire, we can explore opportunities for learning new skills that won't require physical strength.

9. *[Underlying pattern of thought]:* Kent, I get the feeling that it wouldn't matter what you did. You could set

a world record, and you wouldn't feel it amounted to much. I'm wondering if your difficulty lies more in long-time feelings you've had about yourself that you somehow just don't measure up. I am interested in hearing more about how you've viewed yourself.

10. [*Underlying feelings and implied wants*]: So, your feelings tear you and pull you in different directions. You'd like to be a better mother, and you feel bad when you lose your cool, but sometimes you just feel so overwhelmed and inadequate in coping with the children. Part of you would like to learn to manage the children better, but another part would like to get away from your responsibilities.

11. *Anxiety about exam taking.* Barbara, it sounds as if preparing for the exam has rekindled some old fears about whether you are up to this challenge. Part of you thinks that you have taken other examinations along the way and done alright. Another part of you is fearful that this is too much for you. When these kinds of fears have come to you earlier, such as when you took exams in school, how did you get over them?

Skill Development Exercises

Confrontation

The following exercises involve discrepancies and dysfunctional behavior in all three experiential domains: cognitive/perceptual, emotional, and behavioral. After reading the brief summary of the situation involved and the verbatim exchanges between the client(s) and social worker, identify the type of discrepancy involved and formulate your response (observing the guidelines presented earlier) as though you were the social worker in a real-life situation. Next, compare your response with the modeled social worker response, keeping in mind that the model is only one of many possible appropriate responses. Carefully analyze how your response is similar to or differs from the modeled response and whether you adhered to the guidelines.

Situations and Dialogue

1. You have been working with Mr. Lyon for several weeks, following his referral by the court after being convicted for sexually molesting his teenage daughter. Mr. Lyon has been 15 minutes late for his last two appointments, and today he is 20 minutes late. During his sessions, he has explored and worked on problems only superficially.

   Client: Sorry to be late today. Traffic was sure heavy. You know how that goes.

2. The clients are marital partners whom you have seen conjointly five times. One of their goals is to reduce marital conflict by avoiding getting into arguments that create mutual resentments.

   Mrs. J: This week has been just awful. I have tried to look nice and have his meals on time—like he said he wanted—and I've just felt so discouraged. He got on my back Tuesday and ... [*Husband interrupts.*]

   Mr. J [angrily]: Just a minute. You are only telling half the story. You left out what you did Monday. [*She interrupts.*]
   Mrs. J: Oh, forget it. What is the use? He doesn't care about me. He could not, the way he treats me. [*Mr. J shakes head in disgust.*]

3. The client is a young adult who has a slight mental disability. He was referred by a rehabilitation agency because of social and emotional problems. The client has indicated a strong interest in dating young women and has been vigorously pursuing a clerk (Sue) in a local supermarket. She has registered no interest in them and obviously has attempted to discourage them from further efforts. The following excerpt occurs in the seventh session.

   Client: I went through Sue's check stand this morning. I told them I would like to take her to see a movie.
   Social worker: Oh, and what did she say?
   Client: She said she was too busy. I will wait a couple of weeks and ask her again.

4. Tony, age 16, is a member of a therapy group in a youth correctional institution. In the preceding session, he appeared to gain a sense of power and satisfaction from provoking other members to react angrily and defensively, which disrupted the group process. Tony directs the following message to a group member early in the fourth session.

   Tony: I noticed you trying to talk to Meg at the dance Wednesday. You think you're cool, don't you?

5. The client is a mother, age 26, who keeps feelings inside until they mount out of control, at which time she discharges anger explosively.

Client: I can't believe my neighbor. She sends their kids over to play with Sandra at lunchtime and disappears. It is obvious their kids haven't had lunch, and I end up feeding them, even though she's better off financially than I am.

Social worker: It sounds as if you have some feelings about that. What do you feel when she does that?

Client: Oh, not much, I guess, but I think it is a rotten thing to do.

6. You have been working for several weeks with a family that includes the parents and four children ranging in age from 10 to 17. The mother is a domineering person who acts as spokesperson for the family, and the father is passive and soft-spoken. A teenage daughter, Tina, expresses herself in the following dialogue.

Tina: We always seem to have a hassle when we visit our grandparents. Grandma's so bossy. I don't like going there.

Mother: Tina, that is not true. You have always enjoyed going to their house. You and your grandmother have always been close.

7. Group members in their fifth session have been intently discussing members' social interaction difficulties. One of the members takes the group off on a tangent by describing humorous idiosyncrasies of a person she met while on vacation, and the other group members follow suit by sharing humorous anecdotes about "oddballs" they have encountered.

8. The client is an attractive, personable, and intelligent woman who has been married for three years to a self-centered, critical man. In the fourth session (an individual interview), she tearfully makes the following statements:

Client: I have done everything he's asked of me. I have lost 10 pounds. I support him in his work. I golf with him. I even changed my religion to please him, and he is still not happy with me. There's just something wrong with me.

9. The clients are a married couple in their early 30s. The following excerpt occurs in the initial interview:

Wife: We just seem to fight over the smallest things. When he gets mad, he loses his temper and knocks me around.

Husband: The real problem is that she puts their parents ahead of me. She is the one who needs help, not me. If she would get straightened out, I wouldn't lose my temper. Tell her where her first responsibility is. I have tried, and she won't listen to me.

10. The clients are a family consisting of the parents and two children. Taylor, age 15, has been truant from school and smoking marijuana. Angie, age 16, is a model student and is obviously their parents' favorite. The family was referred by the school when Taylor was expelled for several days. The father, an extraordinarily successful businessman, entered family therapy with obvious reluctance, which has continued to this, the fourth session.

Mother: Things have not been much different this week. Everyone has been busy, and we really haven't seen much of each other.

Father: I think we would better plan to skip the next three weeks. Things have been going well, and I have an audit in process at the office that's going to put me in a time bind.

Modeled Social Worker Responses for Confrontation

1. *[Irresponsible behavior by the client]:* Ted, I am concerned you're late today. This is the third time in a row you have been late, and it shortens the time available to us, but my concerns go beyond that. I know you do not like having to come here and that you'd like to be out from under the court's jurisdiction, but the way you are going about things won't accomplish that. I cannot be helpful to you and can't write a favorable report to the court if you just go through the motions of coming here for help. Apparently, it's uncomfortable for you to come. I'm interested in hearing just what you feel about being here.

   C6

2. *[Discrepancy between purported goal and behavior, as well as dysfunctional communication]:* Let's stop and look at what you are doing right now. I am concerned because each of you wants to feel closer to the other, but what you're both doing just makes each other defensive.

   [To husband]: Mr. J, she was sharing some important feelings with you, and you cut her off.

   [To wife]: And you did the same thing, Mrs. J, when he was talking.

   [To both]: I know you may not agree, but it is important to hear each other out and to try to understand. If you keep interrupting and trying to blame each other, as you've both been doing, you are going to stay at square one, and I don't want that to happen. Let's go back and start over, but this time put yourself in the shoes of the other and try to understand. Check out with the other if you really understood. Then, you can express your own views.

3. *[Dysfunctional, self-defeating behavior]:* Pete, I know how much you think of Sue and how you would like to date her. I am concerned that you keep asking her out, though, because she never accepts and doesn't appear to want to go out with you. My concern is that you are setting yourself up for hurt and disappointment. I would like to see you get a girlfriend, but your chances of getting a date are probably a lot better with persons other than Sue.

4. *[Abrasive, provocative behavior]:* Hold on a minute, guys. I am feeling uncomfortable and concerned right now about what Tony just said. It comes across as a real put-down, and we agreed earlier that one of our rules was to support and help each other. Tony, would you accept some feedback from other members about how you are coming across to the group?

5. *[Discrepancy between expressed and actual feeling]:* I agree, but I am concerned about your saying you don't feel much. I should think you would feel taken advantage of and want to change the situation. Let's see if you can get in touch with your feelings. Picture yourself at home at noon, and your neighbor's kids knock on the door while you are fixing lunch. Can you picture it? What are you feeling in your body and thinking just now?

6. *[Dysfunctional communication, disconfirming Tina's feelings and experiences]:* What did you just do, Mrs. Black? Stop and think for a moment about how you responded to Tina's message. It may help you understand why she does not share more with you. [or] Tina, could you tell your mother what you are feeling right now about what she just said? I would like them to get some feedback that could help them communicate better with you.

7. *[Discrepancy between goals and behavior, getting off topic]:* I am concerned about what the group's doing right now. What do you think is happening?

8. *[Misconception about the self, cognitive/perceptual discrepancy]:* Jan, I am concerned about what you just said because you're putting yourself down and leaving no room to feel good about yourself. You are assuming that you own the problem and that you're deficient in some way. I am not at all sure that's the problem. You are married to a man who seems impossible to please. As we agreed earlier, you have tasks of feeling good about yourself, standing up for yourself, and letting your husband's problem be his problem. As long as your feelings about yourself depend on his approval, you are going to feel down on yourself.

9. *[Manipulative behavior]:* I do not know the two of you well enough to presume to know what's causing your problems.

   [To wife]: When you say, "knock around," what are you referring to?
   [To husband]: If you are expecting me to tell your wife to shape up, you'll be disappointed. My job is to help each of you to see your part in the difficulties and to make appropriate changes so that you resolve such challenges in safe, nonviolent ways. If I did what you asked, I would be doing both of you a gross disservice. Things don't get better that way.

10. *[Discrepancy between behavior and purported goals]:* What you do, of course, is up to you. I am concerned, however, because you all agreed you wanted to relate more closely as family members and give one another more support. To accomplish that means you must work at it steadily, or things aren't likely to change much.

    [To father]: My impression is that you are backing off. I know your business is important, but I guess you must decide whether you're really committed to the goals you set for yourselves.

Note

1. Much of this discussion of empathy is adapted from Gerdes, K., & Segal, E. (2013). Importance of empathy for social work practice: Integrating new science. *Social Work, 16*(1), 141–148.

Managing Barriers to Change

Chapter Overview

This chapter considers potential barriers to change and ways of managing them so that they do not interrupt progress or cause unplanned termination by clients. Obstacles may occur within the client (e.g., interpersonal or intrapersonal dynamics or a mix of both) or be influenced by the client's social or physical environment. We will note how our orienting perspectives relate to these barriers. We also discuss the ways in which social workers' behaviors can either contribute to a resolution of barriers or aggravate them.

After reading this chapter, you will gain skills to:

* Recognize and manage dynamics that can interfere with your relationship with clients and thereby interfere with their progress.

* Understand and manage dynamics when client and worker experience significant differences in culture or race.

* Understand the ways that the perspectives of anti-oppressive practice, cultural humility, and trauma informed practice can help you manage barriers to change.

* Use supportive and facilitative skills to promote change.

* Assess and gauge your behavior with clients and use of self.

The EPAS Competencies in Chapter 18

This chapter provides the information that you will need to meet the following practice competencies:

* Competency 1: Demonstrate Ethical and Professional Behavior

* Competency 2: Engage Antiracism, Diversity, Equity, and Inclusion in Practice

* Competency 6: Engage with Individuals, Families, Groups, Organizations, and Communities

* Competency 7: Assess Individuals, Families, Groups, Organizations, and Communities

* Competency 8: Intervene with Individuals, Families, Groups, Organizations, and Communities

Barriers to Change

Progress toward goal attainment is rarely smooth. There can be rapid spurts of change, plateaus, and relapse periods. Think about how often you have vowed to behave differently only to become involved in a situation in which you revert to old behavioral patterns. The fact that you had a setback does not mean that you are unable or unwilling to change. The same is true for clients. Barriers to change discussed in this chapter are:

• Relational dynamics that occur in the interactions between the client and social worker

• Social worker behaviors

• Dynamics that are challenging when social workers and clients differ in values and/or experience related to culture or ethnic difference

• Attraction toward clients and the ethical and legal implication of this behavior

Relational Dynamics

Relational dynamics include both conscious and unconscious reactions between people. These include both reactions of the social worker to the client and those of the client to the social worker. To maintain positive helping relationships, it is important that you be alert and manage relational dynamics so that they do not become threats.

C1 and 6

The Importance of Reciprocal Positive Feelings

Because of the profound importance of the helping relationship, it is crucial that you be skilled in cultivating an alliance with clients that ensures that the relationship remains intact. Helping relationships that are characterized by reciprocal positive feelings between social workers and clients are conducive to personal growth and successful problem solving. Facilitative conditions, such as high levels of warmth, acceptance, unconditional caring, empathy, authenticity, and sensitivity to differences, promote the development of and sustain positive helping relationships.

Despite best efforts, however, some clients do not respond positively to your offer of a helping relationship. For involuntary clients, distrust and fear can be normal responses. Meanwhile, anyone in a difficult situation may simply feel overwhelmed by the idea of a helping relationship as a partial solution to their presenting concerns. Social workers, too, may have difficulty building a productive alliance with some clients because of their subjective appraisal or bias, such as with clients who have certain personality traits, physical attributes, or a particular presenting concern. For example, consider the following exchange between a social worker and a consultant during a case review session.

In this case, the client and the social worker's relational dynamics prevented problem solving in that neither the social worker nor the client was engaged in this process. First, when we do not like clients for whatever reasons, they are likely to sense our feelings toward them, and, therefore, a psychological connection is unlikely to develop. The nonverbal cues of the social worker communicated a lack of acceptance, warmth, and empathy. Note, for example, the social worker's description of the client as "sitting there like a big lump." What mental image of the mother is conveyed in this statement? Perhaps that she is overweight, passive, lazy, and uncaring about her children? Further, the bias of the social worker appeared to be slanted toward Weinberg's (2006) assertion that

Case Example 1

Social worker [presenting a case]: How can you feel empathy for every client? I have this one client, and when I go to their house, they are just sitting there like a big lump. They don't seem to understand that they may lose their children, even though they say they do not want them to be removed from their care. They tell me that the partner who abused their children is out of their life, but I don't believe them. They tell lies, don't do anything to help themself, and sit there in the midst of a cluttered, filthy apartment watching television. I'm just waiting to catch them in a lie. It's hard for me to feel anything for this client or to help them keep custody of their children.

Consultant: It sounds like you have negative feelings about this client, and they know it! Perhaps they feel, "Why bother to establish a relationship with you?" It is quite possible that they have feelings about your visits in the same way that you dread seeing them.

single mothers are often judged by accepted standards of motherhood behavior, in which case, in the mind of the social worker, this mother was sorely lacking.

Sensing the social worker's reaction to her, the mother may have dreaded the visits. Moreover, the social worker's feelings about the mother set a tone that prevented an exploration of other contributing factors for the mother's behavior and the state of the apartment. For example, the possibility that the mother was depressed was overlooked. Subjective conclusions about clients also affect the way in which the assessment is conducted (for example, accrediting strengths) and decisions that are made with respect to a commitment to change. Clients who are perceived as cooperative and readily accepting the social worker's viewpoint tend to be assessed positively. In contrast, if a client behaves passively, as did the mother in this case, or expresses anger or rejects the social worker's assessment, they are perceived more negatively and are assessed as being less willing to change (Dettlaff & Boyd, 2020).

A second hindering factor in this case was the social worker's concern with whether the client was telling the truth. Understandably, in the helping relationship, truth telling is a reciprocal expectation. Was it necessary for the social worker to determine whether the mother was lying, unless her dishonesty threatened the welfare of her children? Continuing to focus on catching her in a lie distracts the social worker from problem solving, in which case they relinquished their role as a problem solver and instead acted as an investigator. The decisive assessment question is whether this mother could or is willing to (and under what circumstances) take steps to ensure that her children are safe.

Did the social worker come to have greater positive regard for the client? Perhaps not, but after meeting with the consultant, they were able to understand and, therefore, manage reactions to the mother that interfered with a working alliance and effectively stalled professional problem solving. We may not always like clients, but it is essential that we examine the basis of our emotions by examining our bias and behavior. The social worker might acknowledge the reaction they had to the client and take responsibility to learn more about them, looking for points of common ground, exploring their values and strengths. It is normal to have emotional reactions to some clients, but acting on our feelings or judging a client is not the appropriate ethical and professional response.

Steps to Take to Reduce the Risk of Negative Relational Dynamics

You may recall an experience that caused you to react to an individual in a similar

C1

manner. For the social worker in the case consultation scenario, self-awareness might have promoted ethical professional practice. Cournoyer (2016) has also identified preparatory self-reflection, centering, and planning as active steps that you can take to minimize or reduce the risk of relational dynamics that can interfere with establishing a working alliance with a client.

Self-exploration and self-reflection help you clarify your biases, beliefs, values, and stereotypes. This process informs you of how you might judge people and subsequently draw positive or negative conclusions about them. The process helps you manage personal factors, such as your emotional state (e.g., an argument with someone) or physical stressors (e.g., insufficient sleep), either of which can influence your readiness to interact with clients. Self-awareness also includes admitting and assessing your personal thoughts, feelings, and physical sensations, and, if needed, engaging in self-talk. Clearly, as noted earlier, it can be difficult to manage your feelings with some individuals and in some situations. Self-control is the ability to recognize and, therefore, manage your feelings, emotions, and behaviors. Actively taking steps to manage potential reactions before and during a session can prevent you from becoming caught up in dynamics that can sidetrack a relationship. In fact, in preparing to meet with clients, you may find it useful to develop a mental checklist in which you focus on the reason and purpose of the contact and what is to be accomplished, taking into consideration your agenda as well the client's. Included here could be checking yourself for implicit bias, as discussed in Chapters 7 and 8. Could there be something about the client that is not relevant to their situation or concern, but which might trigger an implicit bias?

In your interactions with clients, especially those who may trigger a reaction in you, it is equally important to evaluate your performance relative to the essential elements of the helping relationship, specifically the extent to which you convey warmth, acceptance, and empathy. As you work with clients, it is important that you be attentive to instances that indicate something in the relationship between you and the client is off center. Failure to perceive that something has gone wrong and effectively manage the situation may result in a deadlock in which problem solving becomes stalled. The next section elaborates on the threats to the relationship that result from the social worker's actions or behaviors, those of the client, and a dynamic mix of both.

Under- and Overinvolvement of Social Workers with Clients

Despite your best effort to foster a positive relationship with clients and be attuned to the interference of

Table 18-1 Social Worker's Under- and Overinvolvement with Clients

	Social Worker with Unfavorable Attitude Toward Client	Social Worker with Favorable Attitude Toward Client
Underinvolvement	• Finds it difficult to empathize with the client • Is inattentive to or tunes out the client • Has lapses of memory about important information previously revealed by the client • Is drowsy or preoccupied • Dreads sessions. comes late, or cancels sessions inappropriately • Is off the mark with interpretations • Client perceives feedback as put-downs • Fails to acknowledge client growth • Never thinks about the client outside of sessions	• Withholds empathy inappropriately due to belief in client's strengths • Refrains from interpretation to promote insight • Reflects or reframes excessively without answering • Never considers self-disclosure • Gives advice or assignments that the client feels incapable of carrying out
Overinvolvement	• Has an unreasonable dislike of the client • Is argumentative • Is provocative • Gives excessive advice • Employs inept or poorly timed confrontations • Disapproves of the client's planned course of action inappropriately • Appears to take sides against the client (or subgroup) or actually does so • Dominates discussions or frequently interrupts the client • Uses power with involuntary clients to interfere in lifestyle areas beyond the range of legal mandates • Competes intellectually • Has violent thoughts or dreams about the client	• Is overly emotional or sympathetic • Provides extra time inappropriately • Fantasizes brilliant interpretations • Is unusually sensitive to criticisms • Has sexual thoughts or dreams about the client • Seeks nonprofessional contact with the client

Source: Adapted from Raines (1996).

relational dynamics, there are times when something in the relationship can be off center. Even though you may strive to maintain a balanced attitude, there are situations in which you may be inclined to emphasize one side of the story that is generally favorable or unfavorable to the client. Raines (1996) has described such reactions as **overinvolvement** or **underinvolvement**. Levels of over- or underinvolvement can also be classified according to the social worker's general viewpoint or attitude toward the client, which can be either positive or negative. Table 18-1 presents an adaptation of Raines's schema for classifying involvement.

1. *When the social worker is underinvolved and has a negative attitude toward the* **C2**

client, it can be reflected in their lack of attention or empathy, tuning out, biased or judgmental views, or dismissing or not recalling pertinent information. All social workers have had sessions with clients in which their level of attentiveness was less than desirable. The earlier case consultation scenario is an example of underinvolvement of the social worker because of their negative attitude toward the mother. Such behavior signals that the cause of the behavior must be examined. Hence, part of professional behavior is the capacity for self-observation and correction when indicated. Noting one or more of the patterns highlighted in Table 18-1 is cause for supervision or consultation with peers so that you can develop a plan for rectifying the behavior.

2. *Underinvolvement when there is a positive social worker attitude* can occur when a social worker withholds assistance because of an overly optimistic assessment of an individual client's capacity and need for help. For example, a young client who had made good progress toward their goals was praised by the social worker, yet during a session, the client reported that they often wake up feeling overwhelmed by their responsibilities. In response to the client's complaint, however, the social worker encouraged them to focus on their strengths (e.g., "Look what you have accomplished so far!").

Two relational issues are at risk in this scenario. First, the social worker's level of empathy can be rated as low and as such is a potential barrier. In addition, they ignored the concerns and the feelings expressed by the client. Challenging the client to focus on their strengths hampered the social worker's ability to address what the client had said, a signal that the social worker was underinvolved. Underinvolvement can also take the form of settling on assignments or tasks that the client feels incapable of completing. In these cases, when clients fail, there is a tendency to question their commitment rather than the influence of our own actions. Of course, when faced with the pressure of a large caseload, a social worker may assign a client that they are underinvolved with to a lower level of contact than is warranted. Telesocial work can enhance dangers of underinvolvement if the social worker has difficulty relating to some clients mediated by technology (Fisk et al., 2020; Lombardi et al., in press).

As in negative underinvolvement, positive decisions may happen with certain clients because of positive stereotyping of clients who possess what the social worker perceives to be positive attributes. Patterns of repeated positive underinvolvement, however, call for examination and correction. Again, self-reflection on these patterns and conversations with peers and supervisors can assist you in finding ways to adjust the involvement level. Hence, while focusing on client strengths and having a positive attitude toward clients is generally consistent with social work values, the possibility of positive underinvolvement alerts us to ways that attention to perceived positives can be exaggerated and not completely helpful in all circumstances.

3. *Overinvolvement with a negative social worker attitude* refers to negative attention such that clients may feel punished or in combat with the social worker. Specific patterns such as arguing, acting provocatively, using confrontation inappropriately, using power arbitrarily, and the like can signal negative overinvolvement because of countertransference. This behavior is often observed in high-stress work settings in which social workers have close contact with clients who have been harmed and with individuals who have either harmed those clients or not acted fully to prevent the harm. If the social worker is operating under a legal mandate to provide, for example, services to a parent who has mistreated a child, power and authority could be used appropriately in an ethical manner. Facilitative conditions—for example, empathy, genuineness, and unconditional caring for the client—are equally appropriate. In contrast, in cases of overinvolvement with a negative social worker attitude, the use of power becomes personal and punishing rather than applied in a manner that is appropriate to the circumstance. Negative attitudes can take the form of rigid rules of conduct in educational, residential, and corrections settings, in which clients are stereotyped, and their strengths are ignored. This behavior is contrary to social work values, but as you are perhaps aware, it does occur.

An example of a social worker being overinvolved is illustrated in the following case example.

In case example 2, we see how positive overinvolvement can cause negative interactions between professionals when one is invested in and advocates for a particular outcome. In consequence, other professionals can be perceived as underinvolved, and their actions toward the client are seen as negative or unjust.

Overinvolvement can also lead to conflict between a social worker and members of their team or other professionals that can spill over into these relationships.

If you had been present at the team consultation meeting when the case was presented, how would you respond to the question "Am I too involved in this case?" Perhaps you would credit the social worker for asking the question. Is it clear what help the social worker is seeking? What is the social worker's level of involvement? Are you able to identify the relational dynamics between the social worker and the case manager that have spilled over into the work with the family?

Case Example 2

Social worker [presenting a case]: Police were called to the home in response to a domestic violence incident. The husband was charged with interference in a 911 call because he had thrown the telephone into the pool while the wife was making the call. The court-ordered case plan identified improved communication between the couple and resolution of their domestic violence issues. In the initial session with the couple, they reported that they were attending conflict resolution sessions with their religious leader, and as a result, they were now better able to communicate with each other. They also contended that "we don't have domestic violence issues." The couple's explanation for the incident was that the wife's pregnancy and hormonal changes caused her to experience mood swings that resulted in the conflict that prompted the call to the police. The social worker accepted the explanation but stated in their report that they did have one concern: "Unless encouraged to do so, the wife rarely spoke" during the session with the couple.

Based on the session with the couple, the social worker concluded that no further action was indicated and that the case should be closed. In the termination notes, the social worker noted that the couple "is involved in the community, both are professionals and are happy about the upcoming birth of their baby." Further, "they live in a spacious home, just off the golf course, in an outer-ring suburb." In this situation, the social worker's positive regard for the couple's attributes resulted in them becoming overinvolved with potentially negative consequences. For example, the social worker failed to further assess the meaning of the wife's behavior.

Case Example 3

Social worker [presenting a case]: Am I too personally involved in this case? Some of my colleagues believe that I am, and this is why I am presenting this case. First, there are many topics that I wish to discuss; for example, the county case manager's questioning of my professional boundaries, the boundaries of our agency (here the social worker distributes copies of a dictionary definition of boundaries), and the lack of due process in the county's decisions about the clients. The case manager raised concerns about my boundaries after I submitted the first progress report on the family. In the report, I indicated the family's diligence in addressing the concerns outlined in the county's case plan. They indicated that I had not done a comprehensive report as the report was too positive. Further, they said that I was more involved than necessary with the family. This case manager has done this with other families that receive a positive report from us. The real issue here about boundaries must be dealt with first. If they mean providing the family with resources, listening to them, and advocating on their behalf then, so be it. Who am I to judge on the family's practice of witchcraft, or on parent's attending a witch's ball? I find these people different but interesting, and hey, so are some of us! But I am concerned that my being an advocate for the family may have adverse consequences for them and for our agency. For example, what if the case manager reassigned the case or stopped making referrals to us, in which case my actions would affect all of us.

The following case example illustration of overinvolvement describes a social worker who appears to have little insight into their behavior and its implications for their clients and the goals of the agency. The scenario also emphasizes how overinvolvement may arise because of a combination of positive and negative dynamics.

In this case example, you can observe levels of positive and negative overinvolvement. For example, Marta is passionate about her work, and she has a positive regard for the youth with whom she works. However, her use of self in the situation, particularly her reliance on her own parental and survival

Case Example 4

Marta is a youth worker in a shelter for homeless youth. She is passionate about her work and believes that her relationship with her young clients will help them become independent, productive adults. She sees herself as an advocate for survivors based on her personal experience as a survivor. Her supervisor has raised in supervision that they believe Marta sometimes crosses professional boundaries with her clients. Marta's primary goal is to prepare homeless youth to become independent. Youth gaining independence is a program goal, so her behavior is consistent with the intended program outcome. Another goal of the program, however, is to assist the youth to resolve conflicts with their parents whenever possible and achieve eventual reunification. Marta's work with youth is often in conflict with this goal.

Marta's own youth included many conflicts with her parents. She left home at 17, lived with friends for a period, and eventually became homeless. Her approach and her relationship with the youth in her caseload are generally as a survivor of the streets, encouraging her clients to rely on her for support. Whenever a youth expressed an interest in reconnecting with their parents, Marta often rejected this idea as being unhealthy to the youth's progress. The supervisor considers Marta's work with youth to be generally exemplary except for her negative attitude toward parents. Marta points to the fact that many of her clients have, in fact, become independent. Further, they sometimes seek her out for ongoing support, which she finds frustrating at times, even though the contact is evidence of the importance of her work.

experience, has negative connotations and gets in the way of individual problem solving. Her behavior and lack of self-awareness exemplify a barrier to effective practice because of her own unresolved issues with her parents. In addition, this is a situation in which consulting with her supervisor would be important so that she becomes aware of the origin and influences of her behavior on her work with youth.

The preceding case example illustrated the dynamics of over- and underinvolvement, both positive and negative and in some instances a combination of both. More important, they demonstrated how levels of involvement can obscure professional judgment, the results of which can have an adverse impact on client well-being.

4. *Overinvolvement with a positive social worker attitude can entail excessive preoccupation with a particular client.* The social worker tends to focus on a particular client in such a way that the client dominates the social worker's thoughts and dreams and, in some instances, includes sexual fantasies. In the most extreme cases, positive overinvolvement can lead to more serious consequences—for example, boundary violations such as sexual contact with clients. Because of the seriousness of boundary violations, we discuss this issue later in greater detail.

Burnout, Compassion Fatigue, and Vicarious Trauma

Social work practice is often stressful because of workload demands and issues presented by clients, many of whom have experienced or been exposed to trauma. Constantly attending to the needs of and helping clients can result in burnout, compassion fatigue, or vicarious trauma (Bell et al., 2003; James, 2008; Kanter, 2007).

Leiter, Maslach, and Frame (2014) define burnout as the emotional depletion and loss of motivation that can result from prolonged exposure to chronic emotional and interpersonal stressors on the job. They emphasize that the discomfort experienced and impact on job performance can be related to a mismatch of the person with the job as well as organizational factors with workload (Maslach & Leiter, 2017; Mullen et al., 2017). James (2008) suggests that burnout can be related to identifying closely with clients and a regrettable byproduct of being highly dedicated and idealistic in a challenging environment. In the previous case example, Marta could be a candidate for burnout as she perceives herself as the primary vehicle for ensuring the success of the youth. Burnout occurs over time. Initially, the social worker is often enthusiastic and involved but can move into stagnation, frustration, and apathy. Over a prolonged period, these factors can also result in a crisis state of disequilibrium and chronic indifference (James, 2008, p. 537). Indeed, counselors with high self-awareness have been more prone to counselor burnout (Mullen et al., 2017).

The following describe how over- or underinvolvement with clients can connect with burnout:

- Negative underinvolvement can occur when you feel frustrated because you are unable to solve certain problems, you have a large caseload, and the outcomes of your work are unknown or uncertain (Dettlaff & Boyd, 2020; James, 2008). In working with clients, you may become numb to demands that exceed your mental capacity. Thoughts such as "I have heard this story too many times" or "How can I change anything?" may occur to you, along with a feeling of helplessness.

- Overinvolvement is indicated when you have a strong need to be liked by a client or the urge to save, taking calls or texts at home, feeling responsible for clients' mistakes or relapses, and panicking when carefully detailed plans fail to produce the expected results. During the COVID pandemic, highly responsible social workers who have a tendency toward overinvolvement may have attempted to compensate for lack of in person contact by attempting to provide resources beyond their control. At the administrative level, overinvolvement leading to burnout may take theform of micromanaging or feeling that nothing will get done or done correctly unless you, the social worker, are involved (James, 2008).

- Underinvolvement can occur when a social worker has difficulty in bonding with and enlisting the cooperation of clients from groups who the social worker has little experience with. (Newell & MacNeil, 2010).

- Underinvolved professionals often experience an organization in which the leadership is ineffective. There is a lack of rewards, recognition, or organizational support; decisions are perceived to be unfair or arbitrary; or the environment is unsupportive and the fit organizational and individual beliefs at odds (Leiter et al., 2014). Feeling a lack of control over a prolonged time can lead to apathy and ineffective service delivery to clients.

Compassion fatigue is different from burnout. Burnout is mainly associated with workload demands, uncertainty and stressors, and the urgency and size of caseloads. Compassion fatigue, in contrast, is a constant state of tension and preoccupation with the individual and collective trauma of clients (Thomas, 2013). Social workers who are too deeply drawn into the trauma and emotions of clients and clients' situations are likely to become mentally exhausted (Figley, 1995, 2002). Conversely, the experience of vicarious or secondary trauma is recognized in situations in which knowledge of and exposure to others' trauma and wanting to help increase the susceptibility to indirect or direct trauma for the social worker (Thomas, 2013) Vicarious trauma can also be a factor in burnout. As social workers can be exposed to trauma experienced by their clients, they can experience vicarious trauma (Aparicio et al., 2013). The social worker's response to the client's trauma can be a concern. Sometimes the social worker may distance themselves or blame the client (Michalopoulos & Aparicio, 2012). This form of trauma can occur to social workers who day after day listen to the disturbing narratives of clients in situations of family violence, child sexual abuse, and hospital oncology units. It may also be ignited by past experiences of the social worker— for example, a social worker's own adverse childhood experience—or provoked by the vulnerability of the client (Esaki & Larkin, 2013). Vicarious or secondary trauma has implications for the extent to which social workers become over- or underinvolved with clients. In a study of secondary trauma for family violence professionals, Bell (2003) found that constant "exposure to clients' stories negatively affects cognitions" of social workers and, therefore, their professional judgment. Such constant exposure could result in over- or underinvolvement in the sense of identifying with the client or needing to distance from them.

There is a growing awareness of a need for organizations to recognize and take steps to provide support for staff dealing with vicarious or secondary trauma. Self-care is advanced as an action social workers can take (Bride & Figley, 2007; Kanter, 2007; Lee & Miller, 2013). Lee and Miller (2013), citing the National Association of Social Workers (NASW, 2009b) position on self-care as "a critical foundation for effective social work practice" (p. 98), emphasize the social worker's need for self-care and support in the workplace setting, which effectively counters burnout and secondary trauma. Resources for self-care assessment and strategies include Shannon et al. (2013); Dalphon, (2019).

Assessing Potential Barriers and Intervening in Interactions with Clients

The preceding discussion emphasized social worker behaviors and circumstances that could stimulate a professional

C1 and 6

reaction and thereby influence the helping relationship. The following discussion is focused on barriers in interactions with clients. In the interaction between the social worker and the client, there are times when the relationship can stall because of clients' reactions based on their perceptions of the social worker. Clients may not always initiate a discussion of their negative reactions. The ability to do so may depend on their personality type, their age, cultural differences regarding authority, their status (e.g., voluntary or involuntary), or their sense of power vis-à-vis the social worker's role or that of the organization (e.g., a residential treatment or correctional facility). In view of a real or perceived power differential between the social worker and clients, sharing negative feelings and cognitions can be difficult for some clients and be perceived as risky.

You can reduce the threat that clients experience by being attentive and accepting or by being an advocate. If you are inattentive or insensitive to cues, the associated feelings and cognitions may linger and remain unresolved. To prevent such a development, it is crucial to watch for indicators of negative reactions, which can present, for example, in changing the subject, being silent, frowning, fidgeting, sighing, appearing startled, becoming silent, or clearing the throat. Because you have worked with the client over time, you are apt to be able to observe a change in how they react to you. When you observe a change, it is important to focus the session on the client's here-and-now feelings and cognitions. You should do this tentatively by checking out whether your perception is accurate. If it is accurate, proceed by expressing genuine concern for the client's discomfort and conveying your desire to understand what they are experiencing. Examples of responses that facilitate the discussion of troubling feelings and thoughts follow:

- *To an adolescent:* "I can't read you very well. I am not at all sure what you might be thinking and feeling at this moment. Can you help me understand where you are at?"
- *To a child:* "Are you feeling sad right now? Would it be helpful for you to draw a picture of how you feel, and then you could explain the picture to me?"
- *To an adult client:* "You are quiet right now, looking away from me. I wonder if you have some feelings about my draft progress report to the court that I just shared with you."

Notice that in each of the situations, the verbalizations are specific to the moment that the individual reacted, but they rely on the person to express their own thoughts or feelings.

Eliciting a client's response provides you with an opportunity to correct misunderstandings. Clients may gain self-confidence by realizing that you value them and the relationship enough to be concerned about their thoughts and to rectify your errors of omission or commission.

Sometimes a client may succeed in concealing negative thoughts and feelings, or you may overlook nonverbal cues. The feelings may escalate until it becomes obvious that the client is holding back, being overly formal, or responding defensively. Again, you should give priority to the relationship by shifting focus to what is bothering the client and responding to it. After you have worked through the negative reaction of the client, it is helpful to negotiate a mini contract in which you and the client agree to discuss troublesome feelings and thoughts as they occur. The objective of this contract is to avert the recurrence of a negative reaction in the future. For those clients who may habitually withhold their reactions to the detriment of themselves and others, learning to express negative feelings and thoughts can be a milestone. The following is an example of a message aimed at negotiating an appropriate mini contract:

> **Social worker:** Okay, we have talked about your sense that I was not really hearing and understanding you. Thank you for telling me about how you don't like people to be telling you what you need to do. Because you told me how you felt, you helped me to understand, and you gave me a chance to explain what I really meant last week. For us to work well together, it is important for both of us to put our feelings on the table. Can we agree that we will immediately alert each other to troubling thoughts and feelings that happen between us?

In developing the mini contract, the social worker is conveying to the youth a willingness to be open to and respectful of his reactions. Most of us can recall a situation in which we committed an error in a particular case. Instilled in our memory is the reaction from the client involved and, most important, the steps that were taken to ensure that our behavior did not cause irreparable damage to the helping relationship.

Problematic Social Worker Behavior

Some social workers demonstrate behavior that lacks the values and the basic tenets of a helping relationship—for example, a lack of empathy or being in tune with those seeking their help, a lack of genuine concern, and a lack of appreciation of differences. Their unhelpful behavior may be attributed to anxiety, a lack of skill or experience, dealing with a problem beyond their scope of practice, or an inability to build collaborative relationships with clients. Practices on the part of social workers, such as being abrasive, egotistical, controlling, judgmental, demeaning, patronizing, or rigid can cause an appropriate negative reaction from clients. In these interactions, clients' reactions can become a cycle of escalating conflict. For example, a social worker demeans a client, the client reacts, and so forth. Another disturbing pattern relates to a social worker's attempt to control by exerting their own power which can be expected to escalate a client's reaction. Being late or unprepared for appointments and appearing to be detached or disinterested is troubling behavior. At times, lateness is out of your control, and apologizing is appropriate. Most people react to behavior that they view as disrespectful and unprofessional. In many cases, a social worker would not tolerate similar behaviors in a client.

Incompetent social work behavior can be a serious concern that calls for corrective behavior on the part of the social worker through supervision, skill development, or self-reflection. Social worker behavior in which there is a sustained pattern of repeated errors and insensitive behaviors can cause psychological damage to clients. The social worker's behavior can be the result of their own personal unresolved issues for which they should seek help. Social workers whose behavior harms a client, whether intentionally or unintentionally, may be incapable at this time of providing help to clients because of their own troubles (Haynes et al., 2003).

Many voluntary clients who experience incompetent social work behavior vote with their feet by prematurely terminating their contact. Involuntary clients suffer greater consequences for deciding to terminate early. As a protective precaution, they may evade contact or attempt to be transferred to another social worker. Supervisors should be alert when there are several requests for transfer from the same social worker.

Incompetent social workers harm their clients, their agencies, and the profession. Often, social workers faced with a situation involving a colleague find that deciding what steps to take is easier said than done. Moreover, the privacy of the interaction between a client and a colleague may make it hard to conclude that behavior of a colleague is harmful. It is a challenge to question the behavior or the competence of another social worker. However, individuals who act in a manner that is harmful or demeaning to clients are sometimes open about what they do—for example, telling stories about clients in which their

own status is heightened, giving clients demeaning names as descriptors, breaching confidentiality, and talking down to clients, even when other clients or staff are present. You may also observe or hear a person's constant reactive behavior to the social worker. Unfortunately, when a client reacts, they may be ignored by the agency and other staff, who instead may tend to characterize their behavior as resistant or oppositional. Yet more problematic can be the situation in which such complaining about or ridiculing clients can become a group norm such that group meetings can be caught in a one-upmanship cycle in which social workers seem to compete for the most egregious story. Such behavior may signal individual social worker or group stress and use of an inappropriate method for reducing tension. It can be helpful if group norms are established by supervisors and team members that such social worker behavior is not tolerated or reinforced. Further, the supervisor might have a discussion regarding the circumstances and the environment that is contributing to this negative behavior and explore with the social worker more appropriate ways of coping with the stress.

Both you and your agency have a responsibility to protect clients. By not acting, all involved become a party to a colleague's behavior that assaults the dignity and worth of clients. The primacy of clients' rights is clearly articulated in the NASW Code of Ethics. The Code also speaks directly to your obligation to peers and the employment organization. Reports of problematic behavior should be based on facts, not judgments or bias, and your motive and the outcome you are seeking should be clear. Involving your supervisor and reviewing information with this person or a consultant provide additional safeguards. As a student, it is an expected part of your role for you to ask questions to better understand what you see. To share what you observed with your supervisor can be a step toward dealing with the problematic behavior. Ultimately, a referral to the local NASW state chapter and licensing board or certification authority may become necessary. NASW chapters and regulatory boards have committees that investigate complaints of unethical and unprofessional conduct. Information about misconduct is shared between NASW chapters and state boards of social work. Infractions that constitute egregious harm are routinely reported to the Association of Social Work Boards (ASWB) Public Protection Database (PPD), a system that is intended to protect the public. State social work regulatory boards can access the PPD system to verify the disciplinary background of individuals seeking licensure or renewal (ASWB Member Policy Manual).

Cross-Racial and Cross-Cultural Experience Barriers and Broaching

Clients and social workers may experience adverse reactions when they experience differences in race or culture. The proposed EPAS 2 alerts us to the need to be alert to white supremacy and different experiences with equity and inclusion as factors in interracial encounters (EPAS, 2022, p. 8). Social psychologists have studied how individuals respond when having a cross-racial or cross-cultural interaction (Trawalter et al., 2009). Studies reviewed by these authors consistently shown that interracial interaction often produces stress in the United States. Following the stress model, how a person responds to such a situation is based on their assessment of the situation, how much stress is perceived, and how resources for coping with the interaction are assessed. Optional responses described in Trawalter, Richeson, and Shelton's model include engaging with the interracial partner, freezing or withdrawing, acting in an antagonistic way or acting to avoid the interracial partner. The behavioral response selected is then predicted to level of stress experienced and assessment of coping resources. Too often as a society we have experienced such interactions in the context of police interventions with persons of color, often men. Too often the situation appears to be assessed as highly dangerous, precluding any responses but a decision to employ coercion in a split-second decision.

It is the hope and expectation of authors of this book that you as a social worker will have cross-racial and cross-cultural encounters with clients however you identify your own race or culture. We hope and expect that you can often normalize the encounter such that you reduce your own perception of threat. In addition, we hope and expect that you can increasingly perceive that your own resources are sufficient for the situation, and you choose the option of engaging the client. Such resources might include facility in use of language related to diversity and an emotional sense of safety and comfort in cross-racial or cross-cultural situations. We anticipate that you will gradually become more comfortable in such situations as your experience and skill increases. Those resources might include pursuing cultural humility and anti-oppressive practice principles in which you gather information to diffuse conflict. We expect that you will have scripts or prompts to help you in choosing how to engage.

In Chapter 2, we encountered Isaiah, a 14-year-old African American adolescent boy who had been court ordered to attend an anger management group. He was originally charged with assault of a police officer, a class C violent felony but was eventually adjudicated delinquent for resisting arrest. Isaiah disagreed with the court requirement for anger management classes. From his view, he described an interaction with the police in which he pushed the police officer in support of his little brother who had run up to tell him to come to dinner and had been patted down as the police appeared to be looking for drugs. The social worker engaged with Isaiah, hearing out his account of how the incident occurred and how he perceived the police's role in escalating the interaction. Eventually, they were able to explore options including the pros and cons of complying with the court order for anger management services, including thinking about what if any benefits there might be to such compliance (Rooney & Myrick, 2018).

Trawalter et al. (2009) describe other options for dealing with a cross-cultural interaction including freezing, withdrawing, or acting antagonistically. It is not hard to imagine freezing, becoming less verbal, or attempting to withdraw from the contact if the social worker felt that their resources were inadequate to the task. In fact, antagonism and aggressiveness also would appear to be an understandable if ill-advised way of attempting to have some impact on the situation. Should you assess that you could in fact be in danger from the emotions of a highly agitated client, you should follow guidance in your organization for calling or consulting a supervisor or using a buzzer in some setting.

Employing Broaching Skills

A set of relevant engagement skills has been described for deliberate and intentional efforts by counselors defined as broaching to discuss racial, ethnic, and cultural concerns with clients (Day-Vines et al., 2020). Given demographic changes in the population, such skills are particularly important for social workers to facilitate engagement and avoid inappropriate freezing, withdrawal, and antagonism that is not appropriate. Day-Vines and colleagues developed a continuum of broaching behavior (Day-Vines et al., 2007). Comparable to our discussion of behavioral options in cross-racial situations, Day Vines et al. (2007) describe avoidant counselors as avoiding racial, ethnic, and cultural (REC) concerns by deflecting from those concerns when they emerge and redirecting to more generic topics. For example, should a Black client raise a concern about potential danger from police violence, an avoidant response would be to prematurely redirect the discussion to agreed-upon goals. An isolating social worker response would be to respond in a minimal, perfunctory fashion. Additional skill problems emerge when the social worker lacks the verbal skills or the vocabulary to respond to the client's REC concerns. Integrated congruent counselors make linkages between presenting problems and REC concerns, while infusing counselors broach REC concerns and make linkages to social justice focus on barriers impeding client progress.

An integrated/congruent response might be to ask a client "could you tell me what your experiences has been like as a Latina and the first of your family to graduate from college" (Day-Vines et al., 2020, p. 108).

Broaching opportunities occur in many contexts. At the counseling level, the social worker broaches the idea that discussing REC concerns is permissible in the work together. For example, the social worker might note areas in which they might be like the client demographically and how different (sexual identity, race, culture, parenting status, age) and raise the issue of whether those similarities or differences might be relevant in their work together. Exploring broaching includes reading body language and examining whether differences is relevant to the client or not. The social worker and the client might be similar on many levels but different in others. For example, if the social worker and the client differ in sexual identity, the relevance of that to their work together might be explored.

At the individual level, the social worker would need to avoid seeing the client through only one lens and explore intersectionality and how issues may intersect in multiple aspects of identity such as race, gender, culture, status as a student or immigrant might all be involved. This might be broached by asking about the different communities to which the client is part.

Intra-race-ethnic-culture dimensions relate to how the client might have issues within their REC designation such as differences in values with their parents. Inter-REC dimensions include explorations of experiences with racism and discrimination. In the example shared with Isaiah and his encounter with the police, this might include exploring his assessment of the situation and acknowledging the danger of escalation in cross-racial encounters with the police. Responses should include both support of the individual and advocacy around exploring options such as reducing use of force and increasing access to social and mental health services.

Difficulties in Establishing Trust

Trust in the helping relationship evolves over time. For the most part, most people function at an interpersonal level that enables them to enter into a relationship with you relatively quickly. Others may remain guarded or test you to prove and demonstrate your worthiness. For some, the basis for not readily trusting you or revealing feelings may be related to their experiences or involuntary status. Involuntary clients have not sought a helping relationship and should not be expected to readily trust you. Barriers of social distance and a sense of powerlessness in

their attitude and language might be reflected in addressing you formally or referring to others as "them" or "the system" (G. D. Rooney, 2009). As such, it is important you understand that an individual's mistrust and reactive behavior may not be specific to you. In fact, attempting to persuade clients of your helpful intent is usually counterproductive. Indeed, they may trust your actions over your words. That is, they see trust as a process and product of the relationship that grows over time, reinforced by your helper attributes and action, such as your commitment to them, caring, and respect. These actions are the evidence that you are trustworthy.

Behavior such as showing respect, genuine interest, and caring, along with actions such as reaching out to these clients, can facilitate the perception of you as a trustworthy professional. For example, when they cancel or miss appointments, you can maintain contact by phoning them, making a home visit if your agency permits, or writing a letter. Many involuntary clients urgently need and want help. In some instances, their failure to trust and engage or keep appointments may be caused by a busy life, conflicting commitments to child care and work as well as fear or a pattern of avoidance rather than by a lack of motivation. Assisting such clients to come to terms with their difficulties with engagement can be productive, whereas allowing them to terminate by default can have grave consequences.

Transference Reactions

Unrealistic perceptions of and reactions directed toward you or others are known as the **transference reaction** (Machado et al., 2014; Corey, 2009; Knight, 2006; Nichols & Schwartz, 2006). The transference concept originated in the psychoanalytic approach. Practitioners from other approaches have considered the possibility that current responses from clients might be influenced by past experiences with others. In such reactions, unresolved feelings, wishes, anxieties, and fears that are rooted in past relationships with others could be ignited and applied to you. Transference reactions can be positive or negative. In whatever form, such reactions can affect the development of a productive relationship between you and clients in much the same way that they create difficulties in other interpersonal relatiohips.

Transference reactions tend to stall progress unless they are addressed. On a system-to-individual or system-to-group level, transference can involve responses to authority in any form. Besides preventing a person from making progress in resolving problems, transference reactions in therapeutic relationships can create opportunities for growth. Most studies have been about dynamic psychotherapy and have suggested that positive transference in the form of positive feelings about the client have been associated with more positive outcomes (Machado et al., 2014.) The social work relationship is, in effect, a social microcosm wherein clients' interpersonal behavior and conditioned patterns of perceiving and feeling are manifested. In this context, clients can recreate here-and-now interactions that are similar to those that occur in other relationships. The consequent challenge for the social worker is to assist individuals in recognizing their perceptions. Instead of relying on projections, mental images, or beliefs, the client can eventually develop perceptual sets that help them differentiate between individuals and situations.

Not all negative transference reactions are based on an individual's unconscious unresolved conflicts or distorted perceptions. They can be the result of the social worker's behavior. Historical racial or cultural conflicts can also be the etiology of a negative reactive transference. Specifically, because of the reality of their experience in the larger society, past, present, or current, individuals bring dynamics such as mistrust and emotions and feelings about power into the helping relationship with social workers who are different (Lee, 2014). This type of transference can occur because of the collective psyche of a community. For example, reactions that are subject to racial overtones can happen in interactions with the police, teachers, or other figures of authority, and the experience of oppression can be automatically assigned to you. Broaching skills as described above can assist in exploring this possibility.

Identifying Transference Reactions

Whatever the agency setting and the intervention, you may occasionally encounter transference reactions. To manage transference reactions, you must first be aware of their manifestations. Here are examples of some behaviors symptomatic of transference:

- Transference reactions involving interpersonal trauma are common (Knight, 2006). This includes fear, distrust, and hostile interactions or rages directed toward the social worker, group members, or projections of significant others in response to their grief, frustration, and fears (James, 2008; Knight, 2006).
- Arguing with or baiting the social worker or becoming silent and hostile (Nichols & Schwartz, 2006).
- Questioning the interest of the social worker—in particular, whether they can understand the client's situation without having had a similar experience

(James, 2008). Also, feeling that the social worker does not have a genuine interest because helping clients is their job.

- Misinterpreting a message as a result of feeling put down. Responding defensively, feeling rejected, or expecting criticism or punishment without realistic cause.
- Perceptions that their thoughts and feelings are extreme and questioning whether others, even those with similar experiences, can understand (Knight, 2006).
- Trauma survivors seeing others' behaviors or reactions as signs of betrayal, abandonment, and rejection; assigning others the motivations, thoughts, and feelings of those who caused their trauma (Knight, 2006). It is important to normalize and avoid pathologizing such a reaction. This is often a normal reaction for a trauma survivor. Menakem (2017) describes the process of learning to reprogram the body from harmful traumatic reactions to clean pain, facing what you don't want to face, and moving through the pain.
- Relating to the social worker in a clinging, dependent way or excessively seeking praise and reassurance. Attempting to please the social worker or group members by giving excessive compliments and praise or by ingratiating behavior.
- Attempting to engage the social worker socially, offering personal favors, presenting gifts, or seeking special considerations, and, in some cases, having dreams or fantasies about the social worker.
- Difficulty in discussing problems because the social worker or a group member reminds them of someone else in appearance (Nichols & Schwartz, 2006).

Although such reactions originate in an individual's past, the associated behaviors are manifest in the here and now. In instances in which reactions driven by past experiences are played out in the present, they can be addressed by encouraging clients to engage in a deliberate examination of their current perceptions. Of course, when clients bring up experiences and circumstances from their past, brief historical excursions often facilitate productive emotional catharsis and lead to an understanding of the origins of their patterns of thinking, feeling, and behaving. In working with a client who has experienced ongoing traumatic stressors (physical or sexual abuse, sexual assault, war, injury, or other crisis events), probing and exploring these experiences may be vital to gaining an understanding of and recovery from the detrimental effects of those experiences (Menakem, 2017; Van der Kolk, 1994).

Managing Transference Reactions

When a client's behavior is indicative of a possible transference reaction after any necessary examination of the past, it is important to shift the focus to their here-and-now feelings because such reactions generally cause the client to disengage from the relationship and from productive work, ultimately undermining the helping process. To assist you in managing transference reactions, we offer the following guidelines:

1. Be open to the possibility that the client's reaction is not unrealistic and may be a product of your behavior. If introspection indicates that the client's behavior is realistic, respond authentically by owning responsibility for your behavior.

2. Know that a transference reaction can be triggered by a realistic appraisal of historical and current experiences of racial or cultural individuals, in which feelings of anger, resentment, fear, social distance, and power are aroused. It is important that you acknowledge rather than dismiss, minimize, or attempt to alter the client's perception, even though doing so may be uncomfortable. This is particularly the case in a current environment of heightened sensitivity to the potential for danger because of police violence or fear of being infected by the coronavirus.

3. When a client appears to expect you to respond in an inappropriate manner, as professionals or significant others have in the past, it is important to respond differently, thereby disconfirming those expectations. Responses that contrast sharply with client expectations can result in an experience of temporary disequilibrium. Therefore, it is important that you assist the client to differentiate the experience from past figures or experiences. As a result, the client must deal with you and others as unique and real people rather than perpetuating expectations based on past experiences. Responding differently and authentically can be instrumental when reactions are based on historically oriented racial or cultural conflicts.

4. Assist the client in determining the immediate source of perceptions by exploring how and when the feelings emerged. Carefully explore antecedents and meaning attributions associated with the feelings. Avoid attempting to correct distorted perceptions by immediately revealing your actual feelings. By first exploring how and when problematic feelings emerged, you can help clients expand their awareness of the schematic patterns in which they generalize and make faulty meaning attributions and unwarranted assumptions based on past experience. The aim is to help an individual to recognize feelings that emanate from their conditioned perceptual sets and move toward reality-based feelings and reactions.

5. Examine problematic feelings and assist individuals to explore whether they have experienced similar reactions in other relationships. Through exploration, clients may recognize patterns of distortions that create difficulties in other relationships.

Being aware of and managing transference reactions involves using a range of facilitative and communication skills. For example, it is important to acknowledge and be empathetic to clients' feelings as you attempt to help them recognize their influence in their relationship with you or others. Seeking concreteness by specifically exploring the basis for a client's conclusions assists the client in identifying the source of their perception or feelings and pinpoint when and how these feelings emerged. You can further draw out clients' reactions by using reflection to connect separate but related events to their patterned response in another relationship.

Countertransference Reactions

The counterpart of transference is countertransference. Just as clients can experience unresolved or unconscious thoughts and feelings, so can certain client situations, attributes, or behaviors arouse feelings and unconscious defensive patterns on the part of the social worker. Unmet needs of the social worker, unresolved family conflicts, gender, and parenting roles can be the basis for countertransference reactions. Marta, for example, in one of the overinvolved case examples earlier in the chapter, based her work with youth on her own experience with her family. In addition, fears and anxieties or feelings at an unconscious level about clients who are different may also prompt a reaction in the social worker. In consequence, they may deny or in some instances overestimate or underestimate their reaction to minimize the conflict.

Whatever the source, the social worker's thoughts and feelings interfere with their objectivity, causing an emotional response that effectively blocks productive interactions with a client. For example, a social worker who leads a treatment group reported that he must constantly check their reactions to men in the group when certain topics are discussed: "I say to myself, not this BS again, you know, because I've been there, and I know when they are messing around because I did the same thing when I was in treatment. Sometimes, I want to yell at them, 'Man, I know what you are playing at.' I do a lot of self-talk because if I challenged them, I know that my doing so would change the tone of the group, which would not be at all helpful. My behavior would also be unprofessional, but I admit to you that at times it is hard."

Countertransference in the traditional sense is grounded in psychoanalytic theory in which the social worker's past experiences and conscious and unconscious emotional reactions influence their relationship with a client (Hayes, 2004). A more contemporary view is that the social worker's reactions, real and unreal, to a client can occur no matter the origin and can be based on the social worker's own past or present experiences or client characteristics (James, 2008; Knight, 2006; Nichols & Schwartz, 2006). Proposing a more transactional approach, specifically that of the person-in-the environment, Fauth (2006) maintains that such reactions and behaviors may be related to stressful interpersonal events and the social worker's appraisal as to whether the situation was harmful, was threatening, or taxed their coping resources.

Consistent with Fauth's (2006) transactional stress theory, Knight (2006) and James (2008) assert that countertransference, including vicarious trauma, is a common reaction among professionals who are involved in crisis work and with trauma survivors. Salston and Figley (2004) also point to the consequences of trauma for professionals working with criminal victims. Countertransference in high-stress situations may also signal a stage of burnout. James and Gilliland (2001) note that crisis professionals may experience "reawakened unresolved thoughts and feelings" as a result of working with clients who have had similar experiences (p. 419). Maintaining a professional distance may be difficult, especially when the countertransference reaction is related to the trauma experiences and horror stories of immigrants and refugees (Potocky-Tripodi, 2002). In instances when a social worker experiences compassion fatigue or secondary trauma, there is a tendency to become overinvolved with a client. Neither situation is productive in that either one can severely impair a social worker's ability to work effectively with clients.

Should you find that you are experiencing any one of these behaviors, you should seek supervision or consultation. Also, you should consider whether taking time off can help you refocus and reenergize your professional work.

Countertransference reactions also harm helping relationships by producing distorted perceptions, blind spots, and antitherapeutic emotional reactions or behaviors (Kahn, 1997). Selected reactions that can result in counterproductive dynamics are:

- The social worker lacks the skills to integrate anger or conflict resolution into their coping repertoire or personality. For example, when confronted by a client who is angry, the tendency may be to become

unduly uncomfortable and attempt to divert the expression of such feelings.

- The social worker has unresolved feelings about rejections by significant others and finds it difficult to relate to clients who exhibit similar behavior.
- The social worker fails to resolve resentful feelings toward authority, resulting in, for example, overidentification with a rebellious adolescent.
- The social worker is controlling and overidentifying with clients who have similar problems and is blind to reciprocal behavior between clients—for example, taking sides when working with a couple in marital counseling.
- The social worker has an excessive need to be loved and admired and may behave seductively or strive to impress clients by inappropriate disclosure of personal information. Of course, selective self-disclosure in the form of empathic responsiveness can be beneficial (Goldstein, 1997). Raines (1996) suggests that self-disclosure decisions may be considered within a range of over- and underinvolvement; therefore, personal sharing should be rational and related to the current relationship.

Before discussing how to manage countertransference reactions, it is first important to identify the typical ways in which they can occur. Table 18-2 lists some of the indicators based on the work of Knight (2006) and Etherington (2000). Note the similarities between this table and behaviors of over- and underinvolvement described in Table 18-1. Both sources illustrate behaviors or reactions that prompt you to take immediate appropriate corrective measures. Otherwise, they can contribute to the client's problem and ultimately impair the helping relationship.

Managing Countertransference Reactions

Ordinarily, the first step in resolving countertransference, and often all that is needed, is to engage in introspection. Introspection involves an analytical dialogue with yourself aimed at discovering the sources of your feelings, reactions, cognitions, and behaviors. Examples of questions that facilitate introspection include the following:

- "Why am I feeling uncomfortable with this client? What is going on inside me that I am not able to relate in a professional manner?"
- "How well do I manage my own anxiety, anger, or discomfort with the client or the situation?

Table 18-2 Typical Professional Countertransference Reactions

- Being unduly concerned about or protective of a client, becoming their champion or rescuer
- Having persistent dreams or erotic fantasies about clients
- Dreading or anticipating sessions with clients
- Feeling uncomfortable when discussing certain problems with a client, including those who have anxieties and fears about those who are different
- Hostility directed toward a client or inability to empathize with a client, underestimating the dynamics of differences
- Blaming others exclusively for a client's difficulties
- Feeling bored, being drowsy, or tuning out a client
- Regularly being late or forgetting appointments with certain clients
- Consistently ending sessions early or extending them beyond the designated time
- Trying to impress or being unduly impressed by clients
- Being overly concerned about losing a client
- Arguing with or feeling defensive or hurt by a client's criticisms or actions
- Being overly solicitous and performing tasks that clients can perform
- Probing into a client's sex life
- Liking or disliking certain types of clients (may also be reality based)
- Identifying with the role of an abuser in a trauma situation or feeling responsible for their pain
- Attempting to manage feelings that include minimizing the stories of trauma clients, being disgusted with clients, or acting in a voyeuristic manner

- "Why do I dislike (or feel bored, impatient, or irritated about) this client? Are my feelings rational, or does this client remind me of someone else or my own experience?"
- "What is happening inside of me that I don't face certain problems with this client? Am I afraid of a negative reaction on the client's part?"
- "What purpose was served by arguing with this client? Am I feeling defensive or threatened?"
- "Why did I talk so much or give so much advice? Did I feel a need to give something to the client?"
- "What's happening with me that I'm fantasizing or dreaming about this client?"
- "Why am I constantly taking sides in my work with couples (parents, minors, authority), thereby overlooking one side. Am I over- or underidentifying with certain clients, and if so, why?"
- "Could my own experience, personality, or feelings block my objectivity?"

Managing countertransference reaction requires a social worker's conscious assessment of the dynamics that aroused and subsequently triggered their reaction. As discussed earlier in the social worker–consultation scenario, an assessment would involve preparatory planning, self-reflection and awareness, and centering and focusing on the purpose and content of a session. The self-aware professional understands their own history and manages the consequences of their interactions with individuals in which there is a potential for a reaction (Hayes, 2004).

Introspection and self-assessment, as well as the ability to maintain appropriate boundaries and distance, can assist you in achieving or regaining a realistic perspective on your relationships with clients. Discussion of such topics should also be part of consultation with colleagues and supervisors, in which you expose and explore your feelings and obtain their perspective and advice. Just as clients are sometimes too close to their problems to view them objectively and thus benefit from seeing them from the vantage point of a social worker, you can likewise benefit from the unbiased perspective of an uninvolved colleague, consultant, or supervisor. However, professionals who repeatedly experience countertransference reactions need professional help beyond mere introspection or the input of a colleague. Specifically, ongoing reactions limit their effectiveness and create ethical and relational barriers to effective work with clients.

Realistic Social Worker Reactions

Not all negative feelings toward certain clients are indicative of a negative countertransference reaction to the individual or to situations. Some clients are abrasive, arrogant, obnoxious, act tough, have irritating mannerisms, or are exploitative of and cruel toward others. Even the most accepting social worker may have difficulty developing positive feelings toward such clients. We are, after all, only human; thus, we are not immune from disliking someone or feeling irritated, indifferent, or impatient at times. When faced with this behavior from clients, the inclination is to attach a label to the clients, thereby giving us permission to ignore them. Despite their behavior, however, clients are entitled to service in which their uniqueness, dignity, and worth are respected. In fact, it may be the absence of such respect in their interactions that has caused them to act in such a way that alienates, offends, or irritates others, leaving them isolated and confused about relational difficulties.

When you look beyond the offending behavior or attitude of some clients, you may often discover that beneath their facade are desirable, even admirable qualities and vulnerabilities. A social worker noted in an interview with one of the authors that "during my contact with minors, in particular when race is a factor (the social worker is white), most will affect a negative posture with a big attitude. However, the key is to hang in there and gain their trust. In many instances, trust allows you to access the youth's private world. In asking the simple question "What happened to you?" you may find that they have endured severe emotional and environmental deprivation and, in some cases, physical or sexual abuse or other traumatic experiences that have exceeded their coping ability and capacity to trust. Once you get past the behavior, you often find a fragile kid who has been exposed to a life that you can hardly imagine!" Furthermore, the social worker emphasized that despite the youth's behavior, connecting with them necessitated acceptance and empathy. They also shared that there are days when they are tired of their behavior, and "I tell them so. Oddly enough, most respond to me in a very caring, sometimes humorous way."

Abrasive or aggressive clients may, however, need far more than warmth and acceptance. Such individuals need feedback about how certain aspects of their behavior offend you and others. Feedback can be extremely helpful if it is conveyed sensitively and expressed in the context of goodwill. In providing such feedback, you must be careful to avoid evaluative or blaming comments that tend to elicit defensiveness—for example,

"You boast too much and dominate conversations," or "You don't consider other people's feelings when and say hurtful things." An individual is apt to be far more likely to be receptive to a message that describes a specific behavior. The same is true when a response and the associated feeling are personalized. The following descriptive message embodies ownership of feelings: "When you sneered at me just now, I felt defensive and resentful. You've done that before, and I find myself backing away from you each time. I'm concerned because I suspect that this is how you interact with others." The message is authentic, nonjudgmental, and expresses a genuine concern. Be aware, however, that such a message may be more productive once a sound working relationship has been established. As you point out the specifics of clients' behavior, you can encourage them to risk new behaviors and give them opportunities to learn and practice altering ways of interacting with you and others.

Sexual Attraction toward Clients

Attraction feelings between a social worker and a client can be normal. Romantic or sexual feelings toward clients, however, can be especially hazardous to the helping relationship. Most social workers have at some point in their careers experienced this type of reaction toward a client. A majority of those who responded to a survey believed the attraction to be mutual. Others assumed that the client was unaware of their attraction. When the latter was the case, they believed the attraction did not have any harmful effects on the helping process. By contrast, social workers who believed clients were aware of their attraction understood the detrimental impact on the helping process (Strom-Gottfried, 1999a).

Acting on the attraction has long-lasting grievous consequences for clients. You may have heard about a social worker who justified engaging in sexual activities with clients based on helping them to feel loved or to overcome sexual problems. Such explanations are not justified and are rationalizations for exploiting clients. In other instances, justifications are based on the client's behavior toward the social worker. Intimate involvement with a client, whether emotional or physical, is always unethical.

The consequences of sexual involvement are devastating for social workers as well. When such behaviors are discovered, the offending individuals can be sanctioned, sued for unethical practice, and have their professional license or certification revoked. Ethical standards of conduct established by licensing boards and the NASW Code of Ethics are unequivocal about dual relationships with clients, especially those of a sexual nature. The NASW Code of Ethics states: "The social worker should under no circumstance engage in sexual activities or sexual contact with current clients, whether such contact is consensual or forced" (Section 1.09a).

Managing such attraction appropriately is critical. As Strom-Gottfried notes, "Even a small incidence warrants the attention of the professional, particularly supervisors and educators, to assure that any measures available to reduce the incidence further is fully pursued" (1999a, p. 448). Persistent erotic fantasies about clients who are particularly vulnerable signals an impaired professional, and a more serious remedy is indicated. Effectively managing sexual attraction requires engaging in the corrective measures identified earlier for unrealistic feelings and reactions, namely introspection and consulting with a supervisor. Introspections may also reveal whether you are over- and underinvolved with a client.

You must not allow romantic feelings about a client or those of a client toward you to go unchecked. It is also important that in your interactions with clients you take precautions in the way you dress, communicate, and behave in order to avoid problematic situations.

Motivating Change

Dealing with Reactance

People who do not readily embrace a behavioral change are often considered resistant. The notion of resistance has been used in a fashion that holds clients responsible for their behavior, which, of course, tends to foster resistance and a reactive response. Without further exploration of the reason for resistance, the individual acquires a label that sticks, leading to the conclusion that they are opposed to change. Behaviors such as holding back, disengaging, or in some way subverting or sabotaging change efforts, whether knowingly or not, without open discussion, and any action or attitude that impedes the course of therapeutic work are thought to be general signs of resistance (Meyer, 2001; Nichols & Schwartz, 2006). Substituting the term reactance can allow you to deal with the behavior descriptively rather than judgmentally.

Reactance Theory

Reactance theory provides a more fruitful perspective for considering opposition to change with involuntary clients. Rather than blaming, dismissing, or concluding that an individual is opposed to change, this theory leads you to objectively anticipate the range of responses to be expected when valued freedoms and autonomy are threatened (Miron & Brehm, 2006; First, some individuals may try to regain their freedom directly by attempting to take back what has been threatened (e.g., choice). Second, a frequent response is to restore freedom by implication or to find the loophole in which they engage in superficial compliance while violating the spirit of requirements (e.g., I will sit at my desk, but I won't do any work). Third, threatened behaviors and beliefs are apt to become more valued than ever before. Finally, they may perceive you as the person or the source of the threat, in which case you are faced with hostile or aggressive behavior (Rooney & Myrick, 2018).

Reactance theory also lends itself to proactive strategies designed to reduce this kind of behavior. For example, individuals who perceive global pressure to change their lifestyles are likely to experience reactance. Conversely, they are less likely to react if those pressures are narrowed in scope and the change effort emphasizes behaviors that remain free. Second, reactance is likely to be reduced if the client perceives that they have at least some constrained choices (Rooney & Myrick, 2018). Harping on a partner's unhealthy behavior such as drinking can create reactance and increase drinking. Removing pressure and saying that is up to you can reduce the pressure and sometimes be more effective with the problem drinking (Miron & Brehm, 2006).

Change Strategies

In the helping process, as you encounter behavior that can be characterized as resistant or reactive, it is advisable for you to assess the client's behavior in light of the stages of change model (Prochaska et al., 1992) discussed in Chapter 17.

You may believe that utilizing the stage change strategy shifts the focus away from clients' behavior. Research has shown, however, that a focus on a specific cognition or behavior can be a mediator between actions and change and ultimately increases the frequency of desired behaviors (Nichols & Schwartz, 2006). In addition, how you respond to the individual can create cognitive consonance or dissonance. For example, when a mother says, "This was the one time that I left the kids at home by themselves," your inductive open-ended question might be, "What would others say about leaving the kids at home alone?" or "When the children were home alone this one time, what happened?" In this way, you keep the change dialogue going, maintaining a focus on the specific problematic behavior. In addition to the change model, you may want to critique the appropriateness of the strategies discussed in Chapter 12 with involuntary individuals. Each of the strategies discussed is intended to appeal to the individual's self-interest and their involvement in the process of change. For example, it is possible to explore common ground in which mandated goals can be defined and achieved. With the agreeable mandate strategy, an involuntary client may transition through the stages of change, moving from being involuntary to a level of voluntary status. When individuals feel free to make up their own minds, they are more likely to become engaged. Being able to do so is crucial because pressure often engenders an opposing force of reactance.

Motivational Interviewing and Addressing Barriers to Change

Motivational interviewing (MI), as presented in Chapter 13, contains many principles and techniques related to assisting clients to move forward in the change effort. The approach has a useful reframe when the client encounters an obstacle in pursuing a previously agreed upon task. Rather than considering this oppositional, the social worker reminds themselves that a decision is for the client to make, and the social worker avoids arguing for change. Arguing with clients has a limited effect on their behavior and simply invites opposition.

MI assumes that ambivalence is normal and that ambivalent behavior is not indicative of an individual's incapacity (Miller & Rollnick, 2013. As clients

experience problems, they can become stuck. The role of the social worker is to help them reach their own conclusions through the skillful use of communication skills like listening; open-ended questions intended to elicit information about their views, beliefs, and values; and facilitative skills, such as support, acceptance, and empathy. Acceptance is critical to the relationship in that it contributes to a relational climate in which an individual is free to openly discuss their feelings and misgivings about change without being judged, criticized, or blamed. When motivational interviewing is done well, it is the client's goals rather than those of the social worker that have center stage. By skillfully drawing out the intrinsic motivation, it is the client rather than the social worker who puts forth their own solution. "It is the client who gives voice to concerns, reasons for change, self-efficacy, and intentions to change" (Miller & Rollick, 2012, p. 39).

Positive Connotation

Positive connotation is a technique that is useful in reducing the threat level associated with a client's thoughts and feelings in the face of change. In positive connotation, constructive intentions are attributed to what would otherwise be regarded as a client's undesirable or negative behavior. This allows clients to save face and protect their self-esteem when they risk talking about their feelings or perceptions. The goal of positive connotation is not to condone opposition or to reinforce the client's perceptions. Instead, consistent with the strengths perspective, the objective is to minimize clients' need to defend themselves and to safeguard a sense of self.

Case Example 5

Peter, a social worker, utilized the motivational interviewing approach in meeting with Judy, a client, who had numerous difficulties in completing agreed upon tasks in the past week. Judy had completed drug treatment and was expected to submit regular urine analyses. Responding with empathy, Peter, the social worker, asked her, 'How can I help?" [engaging]. At this point, Judy responded, "Well, I guess I need a bus card" and she explained how having a bus card would help her. A

bus card would make it easier for her to attend her group sessions and leave a urine sample for analysis [focusing]. He supported her self-efficacy, specifically her self-confidence. To assist her in accomplishing the necessary change tasks [evoking], Peter reinforced her ability to do so. In general, a discussion of the content of a client's difficulties can yield cues as to the sources of their difficulties, which otherwise may be thought of as oppositional behavior.

In using this technique, you recognize that the meaning ascribed to the behavior can be viewed in both positive and negative lights, depending on one's vantage point. For example, when a client's behavior or feelings appear to oppose change, thereby becoming an obstacle to progress, you are more than likely to view their behavior as negative. From the perspective of the client, however, the same behavior has a positive intent. For example, a client canceled an appointment. Even though they showed up the following week, during the session, they were mostly silent, barely engaged, and their body language indicated that they were uncomfortable. Exploration of the behavior revealed that they resented the behavior of the social worker, whom they perceived as pressuring them to follow a certain course of action. In the eyes of the social worker, the client's behavior was problematic. Conversely, the client saw the behavior as protecting their right to be self-directed. The usefulness of this technique is that it allows you to explore and understand clients' perceptions and subsequent reactions relative to your behavior as well as theirs.

Redefining Problems as Opportunities for Growth

The technique of redefining problems as growth opportunities is a close relative of positive connotation because it also involves relabeling or reframing. Both clients and social workers tend to view problems negatively. Moreover, clients often view remedial courses of action as necessary evils, dwelling on the threat involved in risking new behaviors. Therefore, it is often helpful to reformulate problems and essential tasks as opportunities for growth. Relabeling or reframing emphasizes the positives—that is, the benefits of change rather than the discomfort, fear, and other costs of modifying one's behavior. At the same time, it is important to not convey an unrealistically positive attitude. A client's fears and threats about the risk of change are very real to them. Thus, being unduly optimistic may simply convey a lack of understanding on your part.

Neither reframing nor relabeling minimizes clients' problems or ignores fears in risking new behaviors. Both do, however, enable clients to view their difficulties in a fuller perspective that embodies positive as well as negative factors. The following are examples of how problem situations might be relabeled as opportunities for growth:

- **Relabeling:** A teenager in a foster home continues to be on the run because the foster parents insist on adhering to a nighttime curfew. The teenager defends this behavior of refusing to return to the home because the foster parents are unreasonable. The social worker acknowledges that returning to the foster home is a challenge; however, doing so deals with the problem head-on and is an opportunity to work out the difficulties with the foster parents rather than avoiding, which has been the youth's pattern.

- **Reframing:** A youth feels embarrassed about taking a battery of vocational tests and attending a vocational–technical school rather than attending college. The social worker acknowledges their discomfort but emphasizes that taking the tests offer an opportunity to learn more about aptitudes and to expand choices in planning their future. In another example of reframing, a client is apprehensive about leaving their abusive spouse. The social worker empathizes but points out that leaving the spouse allows them to have the kind of life that they want for themself and their children.

In some instances, clients fail to make progress toward their goals because of the persistence of pervasive patterns of behavior. Your effort to encourage or offer a different perspective by redefining, reframing, or relabeling can be met with a dismissal of your appraisal. For example, the clients may intellectualize, hold other people or circumstances responsible for their difficulties, or be reluctant to examine or acknowledge their part in creating the situation. Because such patterns of behavior often create an impasse, it is important that you recognize and handle them. Confronting clients with discrepancies between expressed goals and behaviors that prevent accomplishment of those goals is often needed to break an impasse. Because Chapter 17 discussed confrontation at length, the discussion here is limited to a specific type of confrontation: therapeutic binds.

Therapeutic Binds

This technique is used in those instances in which a client stubbornly clings to self-defeating behaviors that perpetuate their difficulties. In such instances, placing the client in a therapeutic bind may be the impetus needed to modify the problematic behaviors. The intent of the technique is to confront clients with their self-defeating behavior in such a way that they must either modify the behavior or own responsibility for choosing to perpetuate the difficulties despite their expressed intentions to the contrary (Goldenberg & Goldenberg, 2004; Nichols & Schwartz, 2006). The only way out of a therapeutic bind, unless one chooses to acknowledge no intention of changing, is to make constructive changes. In this regard, use of the therapeutic bind discrepancy is similar to motivational interviewing.

Following are some examples of situations in which therapeutic binds have been used successfully. Note that the social worker points out the specific inconsistent behavior relative to the client's stated goal:

- Despite efforts to resolve fears of being rejected in relationships with others, a client continued to decline social invitations and made no effort to reach out to others. The social worker asked about the apparent choice to continue their social isolation. "You can either risk being with others or continue as you are, but you said that you wanted your life to be different."

- A supervisor complained to an Employee Assistance Program (EAP) social worker about conflict with other members on his team. In exploring the situation, the supervisor admitted that they consistently made unilateral decisions despite repeated feedback and negative reactions from team members. The social worker asked, "Is it your decision that it is more important for you to be in control rather than to improve your relationships with members of your team?"

- An adolescent persisted in being truant from school, violating family rules, and engaging in antisocial behaviors despite their assertion that they wanted to be independent. The social worker asked them how the things were helping them in becoming more independent.

- In couple counseling, a partner constantly brought up the partner's previous infidelity despite expressing a desire to strengthen their relationship. When this occurred, the other partner's response was to withdraw and disengage from the relationship. Presenting the first partner with the contradiction in their behavior, the social worker stated, "I am unclear about how continuing to bring up your partner's past infidelity helps you in your efforts to preserve your relationship."

In using the therapeutic bind technique, it is vital to observe the guidelines for ethical confrontation, thereby avoiding alienating the client. In this way, being empathic as you ask a reflective question about the apparent contradiction or conclusion can be experienced by the client as a more respectful form of confrontation leading to self-reflection. Be aware, however, that a therapeutic bind is a potent but high-risk technique, and you should use it sparingly. In the best of circumstances, clients can experience an "aha" moment, which permits an opportunity for moving forward. When the technique is used, care should be taken to modify its upsetting effect with empathy, concern, and sensitive exploration of the dynamics behind the self-defeating patterns. Above all, the technique should be used to assist the client and not as a confrontational response to your frustrations about the client's contradictory behavior.

Summary

This chapter described barriers to change with individuals, including relational dynamics that can occur in the social worker–client relationship and racial and cultural barriers. In this chapter, we also described relational reactions that can occur because of your real or imagined perceptions of clients or reactions that may derive from clients' perceptions of you. We emphasized assessing reactions and behaviors that are essential to creating a relational bond and a climate that is conducive to problem solving. Any bond that is created between you and the client in which you have and act on a sexual attraction is unacceptable and unethical and has severe consequences.

Relational reactions, including resistance, are normal manifestations of human behavior and, therefore, may not be indicative of opposition to change. In view of this reality, this chapter discussed at length techniques for recognizing and managing these reactions and increasing the likelihood of change. This chapter also emphasized that barriers to change can be the result of both micro and macro factors—for example, limited resources or environmental influences that are beyond the control of the client and therefore should be explored and addressed. Broaching responses were introduced as promising ways to address racial, culture and ethnic factors in relationships.

Competency Notes

C1 Demonstrate Ethical and Professional Behavior

- Demonstrate professional demeanor in behavior; appearance; and oral, written, and electronic communication.
- Manage personal and professional value conflicts and affective reactions.

C2 Engage Antiracism, Diversity, Equity, and Inclusion in Practice

- Demonstrate cultural humility applying critical reflexivity, self-awareness, and self-regulation to manage the influence of bias, power, privilege, and values in working with clients and constituencies acknowledging them as experts of their own lived experiences.

C6 Engage with Individuals, Families, Groups, Organizations, and Communities

- Apply knowledge of human behavior and the social environment, person-in-environment, and other multidisciplinary theoretical frameworks to engage with clients and constituencies.
- Use empathy, reflection, and interpersonal skills to effectively engage clients and constituencies.

C7 Assess Individuals, Families, Groups, Organizations, and Communities

- Apply knowledge of human behavior and person-in-environment and other culturally responsive multidisciplinary theoretical frameworks when assessing clients and constituencies.

C8 Intervene with Individuals, Families, Groups, Organizations, and Communities

- Engage with clients and constituencies to critically choose and implement culturally responsive, evidenced-based interventions to achieve mutually agreed-on practice goals and enhance capacities of clients and constituencies.

Skill Development Exercises

Managing Relational Dynamics

1. Think about what your thoughts and reactions might be in the following situations. Then assess the nature of your reaction.

   - You are an only child. Your client has four children, and the house seems unclean to you. The oldest child, age 14, complains that their parent rarely pays attention to them.
   - Both of your parents were heavy drinkers, and at times they were difficult. Your client becomes abusive to their partner when they have been drinking.
   - You grew up in a middle-class family. Many of the clients that you work with are low income, and their housing sometimes shows evidence of rodents.
   - A coworker in the residential facility for minors where you work has posted pictures of former residents on their Facebook page, indicating that these clients are friends.

2. Review the case examples in this chapter in which the social worker was over- or underinvolved. As a colleague, what advice would you offer? What are the ethical and legal implications of the social worker's behavior in these cases?

3. After reading the section on barriers what did you learn that could inform your practice with clients who are different?

4. Reflect on an occasion in which you had a strong reaction to a client. How would you handle the situation after reading this chapter?

5. Develop a checklist for yourself, using the barriers to change discussed in this chapter. Use the checklist as a self-assessment tool that you can apply in your work with clients.

6. Consider how you would integrate stages of change in your practice with clients.

Skill Development Exercises

Managing Relational Reactions and Opposition

The following exercises are intended to assist you in expanding your skills in responding appropriately to relational reactions and opposition to change. Study each client statement and determine whether a relational reaction or opposition to change might be involved. Then write the response you would give if you were the social worker. Compare your response with the modeled social worker response provided at the end of the exercises. The modeled response represents one of many possible appropriate responses.

Client Statements

1. Client [has been discussing feelings of rejection and self-doubt after their partner broke up with them. Suddenly, they look down, sigh, then look up]: Say, did I tell you I got promoted at work?

2. Female client, age 23 [to male social worker, age 25]: I've been feeling very close to you these past weeks. I was wondering if you could hold me in your arms for just a moment.

3. Client, age 27 [agitated]: I've been coming to see you for eight weeks, and things haven't changed a bit. I'm beginning to question whether you are able to help me.

4. Adolescent on probation: I think it's crazy to have to come here every week. You don't have to worry about me. I'm not getting into any trouble.

5. Client in welfare-to-work program: Sure, you say you want to help me. All you social workers are just alike. You don't understand the pressure I have to get a good job in the time I have left on welfare. If you really want to help, you would increase the time I have left.

6. Client, age 27 [to male social worker]: I've just never been able to trust men. My old man was an alcoholic, and the only thing you could depend on with him was that he'd be drunk when you needed him most.

7. Male client [to female mental health social worker]: Sometimes I really felt I was cheated in life, you know, with parents who didn't give a damn about what happened to me. I think about you—how warm and caring you are, and—I know it sounds crazy, but I wish I'd had you for a mother. Sometimes I even daydream about it.

8. Client [after an emotional prior session, the client yawns, looks out the window, and comments]: Not much to talk about today. Nothing much has happened this week.

9. Client, age 24 [in fifth session]: I have this thing where people never measure up to my expectations. I know I expect too much, and I always end up feeling let down.

10. Middle-aged minority male [challenging]: I suppose when you see me you see most [minority] males. I want you to know that I'm ambitious and want to do right by my family. I just need a job right now.

Modeled Social Worker Responses

1. "Congratulations! No, you didn't tell me about your promotion, but before you do, I'd like to know more about what you were feeling just a moment ago when you were discussing your breakup with your partner. I was sensing that that you are uncomfortable talking about this. Let's focus on how you feel about this situation."

2. "I'm flattered that you would want me to hold you and pleased you could share those feelings with me. I feel close to you, too, but if I were to become romantically inclined toward you, I'd be letting you down and couldn't be helpful to you. I hope you can understand."

3. "I can see you're anxious to get things worked out, and that's a plus. [Positive connotation] But, you're pretty unhappy with your progress and seem to feel that I am not doing my job. I'd like to better understand your feelings. What do you feel I should be doing differently?" [Exploring feelings and expectations]

4. "You sound pretty angry about having to report to me each week. I can't blame you for that. Still, the judge ordered it, and neither of us really has any choice. How do you suggest that we make the best of the situation?"

5. "I'm sorry you feel I'm not really interested in helping you. I gather you've had some bad experiences with other professionals, and I hope our relationship can be better. I sense your frustration at working under this time pressure and your anxiety about what might occur if you don't succeed in the time

available. I will work with you to make the best use of the time to get a job you can feel good about. Sometimes as we come to the end of the time frame there are some possibilities for an extension, but that can't be guaranteed. I wonder if the best use of our time might be to do the best we can to get the kind of job you want in the time available."

6. "I can understand, then, that you might find it difficult to trust me—wondering if I'm really dependable."

7. [Smiling] "Thank you for the compliment. I gather you've been experiencing my care for you and find yourself longing for the love and care you didn't receive as a child. I can sense your feelings keenly and appreciate your sharing them."

8. "Somehow that doesn't fit with what we talked about last week. You expressed some very deep feelings about yourself and your relationship. I'd like to hear what you've been feeling about what we discussed last time."

9. "I wonder if that's what you're feeling just now in our relationship—that I haven't measured up to your expectations in some way. Could you share with me what you're feeling?"

10. "I appreciate your sharing those feelings with me. I understand how your life experiences would cause you to reach this conclusion about me. Because of this experience, I gather you've wondered how I see you. I won't say to you that I am not like that. I will tell you that I do see you are as responsible person, and that I appreciate this quality in you."

The Termination Phase

19 The Final Phase: Evaluation and Termination

The third and final phase of the helping process encompasses the final evaluation of client progress and the termination of the helping relationship. This final phase is important because the way in which social workers close the helping relationship strongly influences whether clients maintain their progress and continue to grow following termination. Further, many people who receive social work services have previously been subject to difficult endings that involved ambiguity, abandonment, anger, abruptness, or failure. Properly handled, termination may itself be an intervention to model the ways in which relationships are concluded in a constructive and meaningful manner. Social workers must understand how to conclude their work sensitively and skillfully with clients, even if the end of the helping process is unplanned. Finally, the purpose of termination, and the preceding helping relationship, is to leave clients empowered with more social support, safety, material resources, control, and skills than when they started treatment. Therefore, the endings must be conducted in ways that highlight client strengths, accomplishments, and connections. While evaluation and termination are relevant to both micro- and macro-level social work,

Continued

this chapter focuses on evaluation and termination of micro-level services and introduces you to strategies for evaluating case progress in work with individuals, groups, and families. The bulk of the chapter addresses the varieties of planned and unplanned terminations, with the remainder covering ethical considerations, common social worker and client reactions to termination, strategies for maintaining case progress post-termination, and the use of rituals in effectively ending the helping relationship

The Final Phase:
Evaluation and Termination

Chapter Overview

Chapter 19 reviews methods for evaluating client progress, describes various factors that affect the termination process, identifies relevant tasks for both social workers and clients, and discusses skills essential to effectively managing termination.

After reading this chapter, you will be able to:

- Describe how evaluation builds on the assessment measures and goal-setting procedures employed earlier in the helping process.

- Understand the ways that evaluations and endings are affected by assumptions and values.

- Distinguish between outcome, process, and satisfaction forms of evaluation.

- Appreciate the dynamics associated with various forms of planned and unplanned endings.

- Assist clients in solidifying changes made in service.

- Describe common termination reactions and how to address them.

- Describe how to use rituals to achieve closure.

The EPAS Competencies in Chapter 19

This chapter provides the information that you will need to meet the following practice competencies:

- Competency 1: Demonstrate Ethical and Professional Behavior

- Competency 2: Engage Antiracism, Diversity, Equity, and Inclusion in Practice

- Competency 4: Engage in Practice-Informed Research and Research-Informed Practice

- Competency 8: Intervene with Individuals, Families, Groups, Organizations, and Communities

- Competency 9: Evaluate Practice with Individuals, Families, Groups, Organizations, and Communities

Evaluation

Evaluation has assumed ever-increasing significance in direct practice to measure client change and satisfaction, assure worker accountability, monitor the effectiveness of services, and evaluate the impact of the interventions themselves. The conclusion of service is the final point at which goal attainment and other aspects of change can be assessed prior to termination. If you have systematically obtained baseline measures and tracked progress, clients will be prepared for evaluation at termination. You can further enhance their cooperation by again reviewing the rationale and actively involving them in the process. Indeed, social workers should not view themselves as evaluating the client; evaluation is a collaborative process that is done with, not to clients (Finn, 2021). Participatory evaluation is a process where all participants are active in the evaluation process; there is a focus on issues of power, disavowing expert knowledge, and empowering individuals to be the experts of their own lives (Finn, 2021). For example, you can introduce evaluation by making any of the following statements that elicit clients' opinions and feedback:

- "An important part of ending is to assess the results we have achieved and identify what helped you most and least during our work together."
- "As an agency, we're committed to improving the quality of our services.
- Your honest feedback helps us know how we're doing."
- "This questionnaire helps us see how your symptoms have changed since you were admitted."
- "One way we determine success on the case plan is to evaluate how your situation has changed since we began working together."
- "Our agency regularly evaluates the effectiveness of treatment groups. You'll all be sent a survey link each week so that you can give us anonymous feedback about the session."

Several different evaluation methods can be used to determine client progress throughout the helping process and at its conclusion—for example, standardized tests; direct observation; goal attainment; and client self-reports through logs, surveys, and online questionnaires. The power of evaluation is strengthened when multiple sources of information are used. Whatever method is used, evaluations focus on three dimensions of service: (1) outcomes, (2) process, and (3) satisfaction.

Outcomes

Outcome evaluation involves assessing the results achieved against the goals that were formulated during the contracting phase of work. The methods utilized during the assessment and goal-setting phases can, in part, determine which outcomes you measure. As you may recall from Chapter 12, the validity of the evaluation depends on the basis on which the goals were set in the first place. Goals that are imposed on clients, rather than being co-created or client centered, outcomes that meet the needs of the program rather than the individual participants, and measurements that fail to capture the connections between individuals and societal, political, or economic arrangements may be flawed, often to the detriment of vulnerable, marginalized, and involuntary clients. Evaluation based on outcomes must also account for changes in goals over time or partially but satisfactorily met goals (the mother who secures an apartment in a timely manner but who is not able to find one, as hoped, near her child's grandmother). Therefore, outcome-based evaluations must be sensitive to the type of outcome, how it was constructed, and the degree to which it reflects the effects of the helping relationship.

Examples of four frequently measured outcomes are:

1. **Frequency of difficulties**: Assessing the frequency of unwanted behaviors (e.g., being late for work, getting detention, bingeing, overspending, experiencing negative cognitions, forgetting to take medications).
2. **Frequency of target behaviors**: Assessing the frequency of desired behaviors (e.g., exercising, using "I" statements, engaging in safe sex practices, taking family outings).
3. **Severity of problems:** Using self-rated assessment surveys or reports from collateral contacts to evaluate the severity of client-identified problems (e.g., self-esteem scores on rapid assessment instruments, anxiety as measured by a self-anchored rating scale, sleep disturbance as measured by a client's journal, distractibility as measured by observations from a child's classroom teacher and caregivers).
4. **Achievement of goals or tasks**: Acknowledging and assessing the completion of client-set goals (e.g., applying for and getting a job, completing homework, improving parenting and disciplinary practices, maintaining sobriety, developing a safety plan, completing assignments between task group sessions).

Comparing results at the final session with the baseline measures taken prior to work beginning, can help determine the extent of progress and the client's readiness for termination (Epstein & Brown, 2002). For example, single-subject designs (also referred to as single-system research, single-case time series, or $n = 1$ designs), compare the client to themself on baseline scores from earlier administrations.

In addition to comparative measures, you can use interviews or questionnaires to determine clients' views to evaluate their sense of progress against your own observations.

- "To what extent did you learn skills to help your family get along better?"
- "How have your anxiety symptoms changed since you began treatment?"
- "How has your coping changed since you have been in the grief support group?"

The difficulty with these recollections and other forms of self-report are, of course, that they may be highly selective and may be affected by numerous factors, such as the client's desire to please (or punish) the social worker, the client's interest in concluding service, or the hope that problems are resolved and that further services are not necessary. Although it is unwise to challenge clients' perceptions, you can reduce biases by asking them to provide actual examples of recent events (critical incidents) that illustrate their attainment of goals, a decline in difficulties, or an increase in capacities. For example, a social worker leading a group might say: "From what you are saying, it sounds like the group has been helpful to each of you. Can you identify some recent experiences that you handled differently because of your experiences in this group?" This discussion also provides an opportunity for you to reaffirm clients' accomplishments, which in turn heightens clients' confidence and self-efficacy.

The candor of clients' self-reports may be increased through electronic outcome monitoring systems where clients can use cell phones or tablets to provide feedback throughout the therapeutic process (Yalom & Leszcz, 2020). Clients' perceptions of their progress can also be supplemented by other data or sources where feasible. For example, feedback from collateral contacts, such as family members, teachers, other helpers, or fellow clients (in family, group, or residential settings), may provide perspectives on client progress that can be compared with self-reports.

Manualized (guided by a manual) interventions often contain evaluation measures as part of the work. Typically, these instruments would have been used as part of the assessment and treatment or service planning to determine areas of difficulty and strength and establish baseline scores against which progress can be measured. Numerous texts offer standardized scales and information on selecting and administering them in practice to target

outcomes (Bloom et al., 2009; Fischer & Corcoran, 2006a, 2006b; Unrau et al., 2007). Some of these instruments lend themselves to repeated use, enabling social workers and clients to track progress over time.

Process

Another dimension of evaluation involves identifying the aspects of the helping process that were useful or detrimental. Feedback about techniques that enhanced or blocked progress helps you hone certain skills, eliminate others, and use techniques with greater discrimination. Such formative evaluation methods also help organizations determine which elements of their programs were effective in bringing about the desired change or whether the techniques used were consistent with standardized agency protocols and delivered as efficiently as possible (Royse et al., 2006). These evaluations capture the nuances of client–social worker interactions that contribute to treatment effectiveness. A technique that is useful with an assertive client, for example, may produce the opposite effect with someone experiencing depression. Likewise, a family intervention may be effective only if it is carried out in a particular way. A social worker may have attributed a positive outcome to a masterfully executed technique, only to find that the client was helped far more by the practitioner's willingness to reach out and maintain hope when the client had almost given up (McCollum & Beer, 1995).

Clearly, clients' feedback can be used to identify beneficial aspects of the helping process, though self-reports about process are subject to the same biases as self-reports about outcomes previously described. Evaluation instruments can also be used to more precisely measure the aspects of the helping process that were instrumental in achieving change.

With manualized or other evidence-based interventions, fidelity assessments can address how closely the process and the skills used by the program or the individual social worker match the design of the intervention (Substance Abuse and Mental Health Services Administration [SAMHSA], 2003a). These can include qualitative case study reviews in which supervisory meetings, observation of sessions, audit interviews with clinicians, or focus groups with colleagues are used to examine a particular social worker's actions (O'Hare, 2005). Quantitative fidelity measures include statistics on the type, frequency, duration, and pattern of services; chart reviews and other administrative or quality assurance data; the level of congruence with the intervention model; and inventories that capture the degree to which the worker employed particular skills. One such instrument, the Practice Skills Inventory (PSI), documents the number of client contacts, the frequency with which particular skills were used (e.g., "Provided emotional support for my client," "Taught specific skills to deal with a certain problem", O'Hare, 2005, pp. 555–556), and examples of those skills for the case (e.g., "Acknowledged how painful it is to move from home into assisted living," "Role-played ways of meeting other residents").

Published measures are also available for social workers who wish to evaluate outcomes and processes in their work with groups and families. Toseland and Rivas (2017) describe measures that can capture feedback on the therapeutic elements of treatment groups. For example, Yalom's Curative Factors Scale (Stone et al., 1994) might identify the different dimensions of treatment groups and their relative therapeutic effectiveness. You can also construct valid measures of practice effectiveness by combining measures (e.g., records about sessions, client self-reports, observations) to provide an approximate measure of the effectiveness of the intervention processes used.

With children and other clients who lack high written or verbal ability, the use of expressive techniques such as collages or paintings may help social workers gather evaluative content. For example, the client may be asked to draw or display something to illustrate "what I liked best/least about our work together" or "what helped me during my time here." Feedback from caregivers and other observers can be sought on a periodic basis, and their appraisals can be linked to the interventions being used at a given point in time.

Satisfaction

The outcomes achieved and the means used to achieve them are important measures of client progress. Another measure in the increasingly competitive and consumer-conscious practice environment is information about client satisfaction. You may gauge this level of satisfaction in your evaluative discussions with the client. Some settings facilitate the gathering of formal feedback by sending out written evaluation surveys or email electronic prompts at the termination of service or after a specified follow-up period. Some payers, such as managed care companies, also evaluate providers by directly seeking client input.

These instruments address satisfaction with the social worker's service by asking questions such as "Would you refer a friend or family member to us for services in the future?" "Were you and the clinician able to meet your goal?" and "Do you believe you needed additional services that were not provided?" (Corcoran & Vandiver, 1996, p. 57). Satisfaction surveys also evaluate structural or operational issues such as appropriateness of the waiting room, convenience of parking, time elapsed between the client's request for service and first appointment, the worker's promptness in making a home visit, and friendliness of reception staff (Ackley, 1997; Corcoran & Vandiver, 1996). Satisfaction measures may specifically evaluate certain elements of an agency's services or progress on initiatives. For example, they may inquire about the cultural competence of the staff, the openness of the facility to diverse populations, or the turnaround time in responding to client calls and requests.

Hybrid Models

Consistent and relevant evaluation can be difficult to achieve in many service settings. A fourth option incorporates measures of outcome, satisfaction, and progress, and can be administered in two to three minutes. These client-oriented, outcome-informed tools, such as the Partners for Change Outcome Management System (PCOMS; Duncan, 2012), capture feedback through brief questions at the outset and conclusion of each session. The PCOMS has been scientifically validated and is well endorsed for practical utility in a variety of service settings (Duncan, 2012).

The Outcome Rating Scale (ORS) is administered at the beginning of each session. Clients are instructed to indicate with a mark on a line how well they have been doing over the previous week regarding personal well-being, family and social relationships, and overall well-being. On the Session Rating Scale (SRS), at the end of each session, clients mark their responses on a continuum between two statements such as "I did not feel heard, understood, and respected" and "I did feel heard, understood and respected" or "The therapist's approach is not a good fit for me" and "The therapist's approach is a good fit for me." The full instruments are available online, in children's versions, and in more than a dozen languages (Heart and Soul of Change Project, 2015). The findings can be incorporated into the work of the session and can also be tracked over time to measure client progress and encourage retention in services.

The notion of practice evaluation may be conflated with research and thus seems like a cumbersome and irrelevant task, requiring special expertise. Although practice research is important for the development of knowledge, all social workers owe it to themselves, their clients, and funding bodies to assure that services are appropriate and effective. A core competence for social workers involves recognizing the importance of evaluation, selecting proper evaluation measures, critically evaluating findings, and using those findings to improve practice effectiveness (CSWE, 2015). Evaluation holds social workers accountable for supporting clients in making positive changes and allows social workers to reflect upon their work from a social justice perspective (Finn, 2021). A robust array of resources exists to help in this effort, regardless of the setting or population served. Evaluation is also intricately tied to termination, as clients may cease services because of concerns about the quality of care or lack of progress. Evaluations also indicate whether goals are met and thus lead to planned termination or transfer.

Termination

Termination refers to the process of formally ending the individual social worker–client relationship. While termination also comes into play in macro-level social work (e.g., end of community organizing), here we focus on endings in the clinical or direct practice context. It is a feature of practice with all client systems, from individuals and families to support groups, coalitions, and communities, and it occurs regardless of the duration of the helping relationship. Terminations can occur when goals are met, when clients make a transition to other services, when time-limited services are concluded, and when social workers or clients leave the helping relationship. Even if clients are likely to come and go from service over time as their concerns and needs change, it is important to draw closure to each unique episode of care.

The notion of ending is often introduced at the beginning of service, when the social worker discusses the likely duration of care, the number of sessions allotted, or the goals that guide the helping process. In some time-limited treatment models, the fixed length of care is part of informed consent discussions at the outset. For example, the social worker might explain, "We believe that brief treatment is effective and helps both you and me make efficient use of our time together. We'll begin today by getting an idea of the goals you want to work on and the best way to use our time over the next six to eight weeks to achieve those goals."

Whether in short- or long-term individual, group, or family therapy models, successful termination involves preparing clients adequately for separation from the social worker and/or group and accomplishing other tasks that facilitate the transition from being a client to being on one's own. The four primary tasks of termination are:

1. Providing a summary: Evaluating the service provided and the extent to which goals were accomplished

2. Agreeing on timing of termination: Determining when to initiate the end of care

3. Closure and healthy ending: Mutually resolving emotional reactions experienced during the process of ending

4. Reviewing what was learned and planning for the future: Planning to maintain gains achieved and to achieve continued growth

The significance of these tasks and the extent to which they can be successfully accomplished are governed in large measure by the context in which the helping relationship takes place.[2] The intensity of the termination process is affected by factors such as the type of contact (voluntary or involuntary), the size and characteristics of the client system, and the nature of the intervention used. In crisis or single-session services, the focus of termination is narrower—determining the effectiveness of the encounter in meeting the clients' needs and clarifying next steps (tasks, referrals, subsequent contact). In crisis work, this would also include an evaluation of the client's safety and stability before the contact is terminated. In group services or longer-term helping relationships, the separation from important relationships, and regular meetings may be more profound.

Emotional reactions also vary depending on the nature and the length of the helping relationship and the characteristics and past experiences of the individuals involved. That is, involuntary clients and those with more structured or time-limited services may be less likely to experience a sense of loss at termination than people who have engaged in longer and more voluntary relationships with the social worker. For example, termination of a time-limited educational group may be less intense and require less preparation of members than would the ending of an ongoing interpersonal support group or discharge from a residential treatment setting. Terminations from brief crisis intervention, case management, or discharge planning relationships may differ in intensity depending on the nature of the needs met and the length of service. Termination from family sessions may be less difficult than those from individual work because most of the client system will continue to work and be together, albeit without the social worker's involvement. People who have experienced difficult losses in the past or suffered from interpersonal trauma may require more time and sensitivity in bringing the helping relationship to a close. In these cases, termination can be used to create a new experience of loss that is controlled, predictable, and healthy. During the termination process, people with histories of abandonment or trauma may experience the array of emotions that accompany endings in a way that is healing and fulfilling (Many, 2009). Conversely, poorly managed endings can be a harmful recapitulation of past hurts and losses.

Types of Termination

Terminations generally fall into one of two categories: unplanned and planned. Unplanned terminations, or early terminations, occur when clients withdraw (drop out) or are asked to withdraw (kicked out) prematurely from services or when social workers leave helping relationships due to illness, job change, or other circumstances. Sometimes, alienating conditions, poor services, or oppressive rules may prompt a client's withdrawal from service (pushed out). Planned terminations occur when clients' goals are achieved, when transfer or referral is anticipated and necessary, or when service is concluded due to the time-limited nature of the setting (such as hospitals or schools) or the treatment modality used (such as brief treatment or fixed-length groups). Examples of both types of termination, along with their subtypes, are included in Table 19-1 and explained further.

Unplanned Terminations

Unplanned terminations occur when the working relationship is halted suddenly or prematurely. Client-initiated unplanned terminations can be triggered by dropping out of treatment, an adverse event that renders the client unavailable for service, or the client behaving in such a way that services are withdrawn, or they are ejected from the setting. Examples of adverse events include being arrested, running away, dying by suicide or other unexpected or traumatic events. The category of dropouts from service is similarly broad, including clients who have been coerced into seeking services or are unmotivated for other reasons, clients who are dissatisfied with the social worker, clients who feel they have made satisfactory progress and thus are done whether the social worker thinks so or not, and clients who decide to quit for pragmatic reasons such as a lack of funds or the inconvenience of the service setting. A mixed form of unplanned termination can be characterized as a pushout, where the social worker and the client have failed to click and the client's discontinuation

Table 19-1 Termination Subtypes

- Unplanned
    - Dropout, kick out, pushout
    - Client death
    - Worker death, worker incapacitation, worker discharge
- Planned—unsuccessful
- Planned—successful
    - Temporal/structural
    - Goals attained
    - Simultaneous departure
    - Client death

is prompted or reinforced by the practitioner's disinterest, incompetence, or lack of commitment (Hunsley et al., 1999).

Clients of color are at particular risk for unplanned terminations. This may be a result of structural factors that have disproportionate impact (rules about attendance and timeliness; rigidly programmed services that fail to account for individual needs); biases, judgments, and labeling by the service provider; or the inability to engage in dialogue about difficult or painful topics (Meyer & Zane, 2014). Social workers must make space for critical self-reflection when they lose clients to premature and unplanned termination. To break a cycle of pushing people from treatment and then blaming them for dropping out, it is essential to practice with cultural and professional humility, acknowledge histories of mistrust and mistreatment, engage with resistance, and share power.

A common theme of all these client-initiated endings is that they are unanticipated and thus allow little or no opportunity for discussion, processing, or closure, yet the residue of feelings and unfinished business remains. The tasks of termination (reflection on the work together, planning for the future, marking the end of treatment) remain undone, and both parties may experience feelings of abandonment, anger, rejection, failure, relief, and shame.

Unplanned terminations can also be worker initiated—for example, if the social worker dies, becomes incapacitated, or is dismissed. The suddenness and finality of these endings can result in feelings of abandonment, self-blame, and shock. Other practitioner-initiated unplanned endings, such as those due to layoffs or job transfers, may elicit strong reactions from the client but generally allow time for processing and closure. We will discuss managing those feelings and endings in a later section. All unplanned endings require special measures so that the tasks of termination can be approximated to the extent possible.

Managing Unplanned Terminations

Some estimates suggest that 50% of the overall client population drop out of service (Connell et al., 2006) and that this figure may be even higher for certain subgroups. For example, a trauma history (SAMHSA, 2014) and/or being from a racial/ethnic minority status (Kilmer et al., 2019) increase the risk for early termination. Some settings may have their own protocols for dealing with no shows, and a different mechanism may be needed for the client who fails to reappear after a first session (see Meyer, 2001) compared to one who ceases to appear for service midway through the course of treatment.

Ideas In Action

Avoiding Premature Termination

It is important for social workers to understand cases in which the client drops out of service prematurely. A meta-analysis of studies (Swift & Greenberg, 2012) found a weighted average dropout rate of 19.7% among adult voluntary clients. The attrition of one in five clients has significant implications for clients and their loved ones, as well as for wasted resources. It is easy to blame early termination on resistance or another client attribute rather than explore the role that the social worker or the services themselves played in the decision to leave care. By understanding the predictors of early termination, social workers are better able to prevent unnecessary endings. Swift et al. (2013) conceptualize clients' decisions to drop out of care as a cost–benefit analysis wherein the benefits or progress in treatment are weighed against the expense, time, stigma, discomfort, and inconvenience of care. Several interlocking practice strategies may help social workers prevent premature termination (Swift et al., 2012). The recommendations include:

- Educate clients about what to expect regarding the duration and the process of change so that expectations are realistic from the outset of service.

- Explain the roles that each participant plays in the process of care to dispel inaccurate or stereotyped beliefs about counseling. This role induction can be done by video, brochure, or discussion, and should educate the client about what to expect in sessions, how meetings are structured, what the social worker does, and so on.

- Incorporate client preferences about the timing, structure, and form of treatment.

- Instill hope through a focus on strengths, a clear problem formulation and rationale for services, expressions of confidence in the client, and professional compassion, competence, and credibility. Paying attention to pacing and progress, especially early in the helping process, can also encourage hope.

- Foster the therapeutic alliance by creating a safe environment, expressing empathy, and collaborating with the client in setting goals and tasks for service.

- Consistently assess and discuss treatment progress. Does the client's progress deviate from their expectations or from typical change trajectories? Social workers who employ outcome monitoring and feedback systems can get timely input and make changes in service if indicated (Lambert & Shimokawa, 2011).

A common response to unplanned termination by the client is for the social worker to reach out to them by phone, email, or letter. The goals in doing so may be to acknowledge the decision to conclude services, to encourage the client to come in for a closing session, or to achieve the purposes of such a session through the communication itself. For example, one client who was arrested could not receive phone calls or return for services. Nevertheless, the social worker was able to write him a letter in which they summarized the goals he had achieved, conveyed their regard for him, and informed him of the availability of other services during his incarceration and following his release. A similar technique can be used when a social worker must leave abruptly, when a client quits service, or when a client leaves an institution against medical advice. Such endings are not ideal because they do not allow the client the opportunity to express their views or participate in evaluation, but they do help mark the ending and clear the air regarding future services.

When a social worker dies or otherwise becomes incapacitated, it is incumbent upon their colleagues to intervene for the care or transfer of the clients involved. They must also recognize that these clients' needs and reactions may be shaped by the abruptness and nature of the loss, their personal loss histories, and the particular issues for which they were seeking help (Philip, 1994; Philip & Stevens, 1992). Thus, grieving the lost relationship may become a primary task alongside continued work on their treatment goals identified earlier.

Likewise, when a client dies unexpectedly, whether through an accident or a traumatic act such as homicide or suicide, the loss has significant implications for the helping professionals left behind. The social worker would need to document the termination of the helping relationship, alert the agency and other involved parties, and then work to resolve their own grief. Out of respect for the client's continuing right to privacy, the social worker is ethically bound to keep known details about those individuals confidential, even after death. This being the case, the social worker's family members and friends are unable to help address the grief and may not even be aware of the client's death. Therefore, social workers should seek supervisory and collegial support for grieving and processing (Chemtob et al., 1988; Kruger et al., 1979; Strom-Gottfried & Mowbray, 2006).

Unplanned terminations of a member from a group may occur for several reasons. Sometimes, departure is due to the group itself, such as poor fit, discomfort with the leader or other members, or a distressing incident. At other times, members terminate because of transportation difficulties or time conflicts. In any case, the unplanned departure presents challenges for achieving termination-related tasks. Because cohesion is central to the success of a group, the loss of a member can threaten that bond, make members question their own achievements or appropriateness for the group, and make them reluctant to continue building trusting relationships with the remaining group members (Yalom & Leszcz, 2020). The social worker should try to encourage closure in some form, both for the departing member and for the rest of the group. Even if it derails the group's preexisting agenda or timeline, this effort is time well spent because it supports the future health and success of the group process and the individual members.

Planned Terminations with Unsuccessful Outcomes

Sometimes termination occurs in a planned manner, but the endings are not marked by successful achievement of service goals. This may occur when:

- The client is dissatisfied with the helping relationship.
- Progress is stalemated despite vigorous and persistent efforts.
- The social worker is not competent to address the client's needs.
- The client fails to comply with appropriate treatment requirements.

Unlike unplanned terminations, these endings are not accompanied by abrupt disappearance from service and thus afford the social worker and the client a chance to achieve the goals of closure. Groups also occasionally end with unsuccessful results, and members may be frustrated, disappointed, or angry with the leader or with other members (Smokowski et al., 2001).

When the helping process ends unsuccessfully, termination should include discussion of (1) factors that prevented achieving more favorable results and (2) clients' feelings about seeking additional help in the future. This effort requires you to create as safe an atmosphere as possible so that both parties can honestly air concerns

with the intention of both achieving closure and keeping open possibilities for future service. It also requires the ability to hear and share feedback in a nondefensive manner. As a result of this termination conversation, you and a client may come to agreement on the conditions under which you would reconnect and develop a new contract for future services. At this final session, social workers should be prepared to offer referrals to other services if the issue for termination has been a poor fit with the individual practitioner or agency.

Planned Terminations with Successful Outcomes

As noted earlier, planned terminations can take many forms. The nature of the setting, intervention method, or funding source can all impose external pressures to terminate within a specific time period. Other planned endings emerge from the helping relationship itself as clients achieve their goals and move on to independence from the social worker. This step may not signal that the client has completed all their desired goals or tasks (or that they are done in the social worker's eyes) but means only that the client has experienced "at least enough relief so that he no longer wants help at that point" (Reid, 1972, p. 199). Related to this development is what Cummings (1991) calls "brief intermittent therapy throughout the life cycle" (p. 35). That is, individuals who need social work services may come to use them as they do medical and other services—seeking them out in times of need to address acute problems rather than pursuing single episodes of extended treatment. In these termination situations, the social worker and the client may establish contingencies under which they may resume services in the future.

Termination Due to Temporal, Structural, or Financial Limits

In organizations or agencies whose function involves providing service according to fixed time intervals, termination must be planned accordingly. In school settings, for example, services are generally discontinued at the conclusion of an academic year. In hospitals and other institutional settings, the duration of service is determined by the length of hospitalization, confinement, or insurance coverage.

Some service models such as time-limited groups or fixed-length residential programs are clearly designed to pace and conclude services within a specific time frame. For example, some treatment programs are organized such that clients progress from one program (and one set of workers) to another as their needs change. In residential programs or other settings with finite lengths of stay, the course of treatment can involve a relatively predictable process whereby the client progresses through steps or phases leading to termination. Depending on the context of treatment, services may extend from several days to several months. Temporal factors are also central in termination for social work students, who leave a given practicum setting at the completion of an academic year. These can be emotional experiences for social work interns given the intensity of the practicum experience, especially if they are terminating with the entire caseload simultaneously. For clients who have been assigned to a series of social work interns, the endings may be predictable but also aggravating if it is difficult to repeatedly establish trust and continuity of care with a series of time-limited workers-in-training.

Terminations that are prompted by program structure or preexisting time constraints involve certain peculiar factors. First, the ending of a school year or of a training period for students is a predetermined time for termination, which reduces the possibility of clients interpreting time limits as being arbitrarily imposed or a sign of desertion or abandonment. Knowing the termination date well in advance also provides ample time to resolve feelings about separation. Conversely, it also means that in school settings student clients may lose many supports all at one time.

Another factor common to terminations that are determined by time constraints, funding, or agency function rather than by individual factors is that the client's needs may not have been adequately resolved when services end. The predetermined, untimely ending may lead to intense reactions when people lose services and the helping relationship in what feels like midstream (Weiner, 1984). Social workers are, therefore, confronted with the dual tasks of working through feelings associated with untimely separation and referring clients for additional and often scarce services when indicated.

Predetermined endings imposed by the close of a school year or a fixed length of service do not necessarily convey the same expectations of a positive outcome as do time limits that are determined by individual client progress. In other words, to say "I will see you until May because that is sufficient time to achieve your goals" conveys a far more positive expectation than "I will see you until May because that is all the time I have available before leaving the placement." Time-limited treatment can lead to satisfactory outcomes as clients benefit from the focused nature of this work and may develop a fruitful relationship with the social worker even if termination results in referral for other services.

For example, one of the authors of this book worked with a client with serious, long-term mental health problems. During the time allotted for their field placement,

she was able to help the client through a crisis and assist them to build their social supports so that future crises would not inevitably result in rehospitalization. In the termination process, they reviewed the accomplishments made during the year, and the client met their new social worker, who would meet with him on a less intensive basis for support and maintenance of the gains made previously.

Other Determinants of Planned Termination

When terminations are not predetermined by agency setting, client circumstance, or form of service, how do the social worker and client know when to end? When services are effectively goal directed, the termination point may be clear: it occurs when goals are reached, and changes are sustained. When goals are vague or ongoing, however, determining a proper ending point can be more difficult. Theoretically, humans can grow indefinitely, and determining when clients have achieved optimal growth is no simple task. Ordinarily, it is appropriate to introduce the idea of termination when the client has reached the point of diminishing returns—that is, when the gains from sessions taper off to the point of being minor in significance. The social worker may initiate the discussion or clients, through words or actions, may indicate that they are ready to discontinue services. These messages may be subtle. As an example, in group work, a client said that Mondays (the day of the group meeting) was not just like any other day, rather than what she lived for when starting treatment" (Yalom & Leszcz, 2020).

Two other variants on planned termination warrant discussion. **Simultaneous termination** occurs when the client and the social worker leave the service or agency at the same time, as when the end of services aligns with the practitioner's departure from the agency. It offers the advantage of powerful, mutually shared experiences of ending, and it often focuses the time and the attention devoted to termination tasks (Joyce et al., 1996). Simultaneous termination also requires a good deal of self-awareness on the part of the social worker to ensure that their personal reactions to leaving are not projected onto the client. As with other endings involving the social worker's departure from the organization, termination must address the conditions and the resources for the client if they should need future service.

The second type of planned termination occurs when the client dies, but the death is anticipated and planned for. Some settings, such as hospice care, nursing homes, or hospitals, expose social workers and other caregivers to death on a regular basis. The orientation and the supervision offered in such settings must address this crucial aspect of practice, as particular skills are needed to assist individuals in such circumstances and effectively manage professionals' responses. For example, when the helping relationship is expected to end in conjunction with the patient's death, it may involve life review and reminiscences, plans to address end-of-life concerns, and attention to spiritual matters (Arnold, 2002).[4]

Understanding and Responding to Clients' Termination Reactions

Inherent in termination is separation from the social worker (and other clients, in the case of groups, inpatient, or residential settings). Separation typically involves mixed feelings for both the social worker and the client, which vary in intensity according to the degree of success achieved, the strength of the attachment, the type of termination, the cultural orientation of the client, and their previous experiences with separations from significant others (Bembry & Ericson, 1999; Dorfman, 1996). When individuals successfully accomplish their goals, they experience a certain degree of pride and satisfaction as the helping process draws to a close. If they have grown in strength and self-confidence, they view the future optimistically as an opportunity for continued growth.

Most people in individual, family, and group therapy experience positive emotions in termination. The benefits from the gains achieved usually far outweigh the impact of the loss of the helping relationship. Clients may reflect on the experience by saying things like "I was such a wreck when I first came to see you—I'm surprised I didn't scare you away," "You helped me get my thinking straight, so I could see the options I had before me," or "Even if things didn't change that much with my son, it helped me a lot to be in the group and know I'm not alone."

As noted earlier, clients and social workers alike commonly experience a sense of loss during the termination process. Indeed, sadness is a common element of many of the endings that are a part of life itself (even positive ones), such as leaving parents to attend school, advancing from one grade to another, moving to a new community, or changing jobs. The loss in termination may be a deeply moving experience involving the sweet sorrow generally associated with parting from a person whom one has grown to value. Adept social workers help clients give voice to these ambivalent feelings, acknowledging that transitions can be difficult but that successfully handling both good times and difficult ones is a necessary part of growth.

For the social worker, the nature of termination and the comfort with which it occurs appear to be linked to the overall health of the organization in which it takes place and the social worker's level of job satisfaction (Resnick & Dziegielewski, 1996). In work sites where workloads are high, where there is a rapid turnover in cases, or where staff support and effective supervision are lacking, sufficient attention may not be paid to the tasks and emotions that accompany clinical endings. Of course, like other elements of practice, the impact of termination on the social worker is also shaped by their overall well-being, including the ability to maintain a proper balance between their personal and professional lives. This balance is particularly important when the social worker has an illness that might imperil the continuation of services. They must weigh the benefits of honesty and transparency with the risks that self-disclosure about a serious illness might prove distressing to the client and disruptive to the focus of treatment (Farber, 2006).

Because termination can evoke feelings associated with past losses and endings, clients and social workers may respond to it in a variety of ways and in any of these ways to varying degrees, which we discuss here.

C1 and 8

Anger

Clients may experience anger at termination, especially when termination occurs because the social worker leaves the agency. Because the termination is not goal related and occurs with little forewarning, reactions are sometimes similar to those that involve other types of sudden crises. The social worker may need to reach for the feelings evoked by their departure, as clients may have difficulty expressing negative emotions while they are simultaneously experiencing sadness or anxiety about the impending loss. It is important to encourage the verbal expression of emotions and respond empathically to them. It is vital, however, not to empathize to the extent of overidentification, thereby losing the capacity to assist the client with negative feelings and to engage in constructive planning.

When the social worker's departure is caused by circumstances outside their control such as layoffs or firing, it is important that the practitioner not fuel the client's anger to satisfy their own indignation or desire for vindication. Not only is this clinically unhelpful to the client, but it is at odds with the NASW Code of Ethics. The Code of Ethics cautions us not to "exploit clients in disputes with colleagues or engage clients in any inappropriate discussion of conflicts between social workers and their colleagues" (NASW, 2021, 2.04b).

Denial

Clients may contend that they were unaware of the impending termination or time limits on service and behave as if termination is not imminent. They may deny having feelings about the termination or refuse to acknowledge that it affects them. Others may avoid endings by failing to appear for concluding sessions with the social worker (Dorfman, 1996). It is a mistake to interpret this business-as-usual demeanor as an indication that unaffected by the termination or are taking it in stride because the unruffled exterior may represent the calm before the storm.

To assist clients in getting in touch with their emotions, it is helpful to reintroduce the topic of termination and express your desire to assist them in formulating plans to continue working toward their goals after your departure. As you bring up the topic of termination, be sensitive to nonverbal cues to clients' emotional reactions. We also recommend employing empathic communication that conveys understanding of and elicits the hurt, resentment, and rejection experienced when a valued person leaves. The following responses demonstrate this type of communication:

- "I know that being discharged is scary, and that makes you wish you didn't have to leave, but not talking about it won't keep it from happening. I want very much to use the time remaining to reflect on our work together, so you are prepared to carry all that you've achieved here out into the world."

- "You've worked really hard here, and I know a lot of it wasn't easy for you. It's hard for me to believe you now when you shrug your shoulders and say it means nothing. I think it means a lot."

Avoidance

Occasionally, clients may express their anger and hurt over a social worker's leaving by rejecting the social worker before the social worker can reject them. Some people may silently protest by failing to appear for sessions as termination approaches. Others may ignore the social worker or profess that they no longer need them—in effect, employing the strategy that the best defense is a good offense. When clients act in this fashion, it is critical to reach out to them. Otherwise, they may interpret the failure to do so as evidence that the social worker never really cared about them at all. In reaching out, a personal contact by phone, text, email, letter, or home visit is essential because it creates an opportunity for interaction in which the social worker can reaffirm their concern and care and convey empathy and understanding of the client's emotional reaction.

Reporting Recurrence of Old Problems or Generating New Ones

Some people tend to panic as treatment reaches an end, and they experience a return of difficulties that have been under control for some time (Levinson, 1977). To continue the helping relationship, some may introduce new stresses and problems during the terminal sessions and even during the final scheduled session. Clients who normally communicate minimally may suddenly open up, and other clients may reveal confidential information they have previously withheld. Still other people may display more severe reactions by engaging in self-destructive or suicidal acts.

The severity of the client's revelation, regression, or return of symptoms dictates how you respond. It is important to acknowledge the anxiety and the apprehension that accompany termination. Some people may benefit from a preemptive discussion of these issues as termination nears. The social worker might say, "Sometimes people worry that problems will reemerge once services end, but I'm confident about how far you've come. I trust that even if there are setbacks, they won't affect our ending." Some theoretical models suggest that the social worker engage the client in an explicit discussion about what it would take to return to the former level of functioning that necessitated treatment. The underlying idea here is that such a discussion creates significant discomfort and, therefore, paradoxically, inoculates the individual against future setbacks (Walsh, 2007).

On some occasions, it may make sense for you and the client to reconsider a planned ending. Limited extensions by plan (Epstein & Brown, 2002, p. 232) can be made to accomplish agreed-upon tasks if it appears that additional time would enable the client to achieve decisive progress. There may be legitimate reasons for recontracting for additional sessions—for example, identifying key problems only late in the helping process, returning to problems that were identified earlier but had to be set aside in favor of work on more pressing issues, or anticipating transitional events that bear on the client's problems (e.g., getting married, aging out of foster care, regaining custody of a child). In these instances, continuing the working relationship may be warranted, if supported by the agency, especially if the client has achieved substantial progress on other problems during the initial contract period.

Determining whether the emergence of new issues, or the reemergence of old ones, is a ploy to avoid termination or a legitimate cause for developing a new contract can be tricky, but the decision should be based on your sense of the client's progress to date, the degree of dependency, and the significance of the issues being raised (Reid, 1972). Supervisory discussions can help workers look critically at these variables. If you believe that the problem is worthy of intervention but worry that continuing treatment may foster harmful dependence, you might consider referring the client to another clinician or continuing work with the person yourself but in a less intensive format—through groups or through less frequent sessions, for example.

Attempting to Prolong Contact

Sometimes, rather than reveal new or renewed problems, a person may seek continued contact with the social worker more directly by suggesting a social or business relationship following termination. For example, the client may suggest meeting for coffee on occasion or exchanging cards or letters, may try to connect with the worker through online social networking, or may propose joining a training program that puts them in regular contact with the social worker. This phenomenon is also evident when groups decide to continue meeting after the agency's involvement has concluded.

Any security brought by such plans is only fleeting, and the negative effects of continued contact can be serious. Some requests for continued contact would be inappropriate given the profession's ethical proscriptions against dual relationships. Other forms of contact, while not prohibited, may still be unwise in that they may undo the work done in the helping relationship and may undermine the client's confidence in their ability to function without the social worker. Further, continued informal involvement may constrain the client from becoming invested in other rewarding relationships (Bostic et al., 1996).

In the case of groups, it is not usually the social worker's role to discourage the group from continuing to meet, although they should be clear about their own stance and may share the wisdom of experience. For example, at the conclusion of one bereavement group, the group members planned a cookout at one member's home. In response to the invitation to join them, the group leader simply said, "I'll be ending with you after our session next week, but I appreciate your offer to include me." In another group with a particularly fragile and more easily disappointed membership, the social worker said, "I'm glad you feel close enough to one another to try to continue meeting after the group has formally ended. It's been my experience that sometimes it's hard to keep that going outside the group. If that happens to you, I hope you won't be discouraged or take it as a reflection on all you've accomplished in your time together."

This is not to say that planned follow-up phone calls, appointments, and booster sessions are always

inappropriate. To the contrary, such plans are made within the goals of the helping process and have a clear therapeutic purpose rather than being an attempt to evade the inevitability of ending.

Social Workers' Reactions to Termination

Clients are not the only ones who have reactions to termination. Social workers' responses may include guilt (at letting the client down or failing to sufficiently help them), avoidance (delaying announcement of termination to avoid the feelings or reactions evoked), relief (at ending involvement with a difficult or challenging client), sadness (at the end of a positive relationship), anxiety (about the client's future or well-being), and difficulty letting go (because of financial or emotional fulfillment experienced by the clinician (Dorfman, 1996; Joyce et al., 1996; Murphy & Dillon, 2008). In settings where premature terminations are the norm, workers may experience burnout and decreased sensitivity to clients after repeatedly working on cases where closure is not possible and treatment ends before interventions are carried out (Resnick & Dziegielewski, 1996). Self-understanding and good supervision are the essential elements by which even veteran social workers can recognize the reactions involved in terminations. These reactions negatively affect clients, so identifying and managing them is crucial.

Consolidating Gains and Planning Maintenance Strategies

In addition to managing the emotional and behavioral reactions to ending, another task of termination involves summarizing and stabilizing the changes achieved and developing a plan to sustain those changes. A similar aim of group work is to assist members to not only interact successfully within the group context but also transfer their newly developed interpersonal skills to the broad arena of social relationships.

The failure to maintain gains has been attributed to a variety of factors:

1. A natural tendency to revert to habitual response patterns (e.g., use of alcohol or drugs, aggressive or withdrawn behavior, poor communication patterns)

2. Personal and environmental stressors (e.g., family conflicts, financial pressures, personal rejection, loss of job, health problems, deaths of loved ones)

3. Lack of opportunities in the environment for social and leisure activities

4. Absence of positive support systems (peer or family networks may not have changed in the same way the client has)

5. Inadequate social skills

6. Lack of reinforcement for functional behaviors

7. Inadequate preparation for environmental changes

8. Inability to resist peer pressures

9. Return to dysfunctional or destructive environments

10. Inadequately established new behaviors[5]

In planning maintenance strategies, you must anticipate such forces and prepare clients for coping with them. A monitoring phase may be useful for some people. In this phase, the number and the frequency of sessions decrease while support systems are called on to assist the client with new concerns. This technique, in effect, weans the individual from the social worker's support yet allows a transitional period in which they can try out new skills and supports while gradually concluding the helping relationship. The ascendance of electronic communications mechanisms (text messaging, Twitter, email, social networks) has led to an array of promising innovations for aftercare and relapse prevention. These models send reminders about medication or treatment adherence, encouragement and wellness tips, and feedback on symptoms or questions recorded by clients (Aguilera et al., 2010; Shapiro et al., 2009).

When working with individuals and families, you may actively encourage people to consider means for coping with setbacks. One model suggests asking what "would be required of each person to contribute to a resurgence of the problem" and organizing role-plays in which the members engage in old behavioral patterns and describe afterward what thoughts and feelings they experienced in doing so (Walsh, 2007). Similar forms of anticipation and practice may help inoculate clients against future relapses.

Social workers may encourage clients to return for additional help if problems appear to be mounting out of control. Although it is important to express confidence in people's ability to cope independently with their problems, it is equally important to convey your continued interest in them and to invite them to return if they need to do so.

Follow-Up Sessions

Post-termination follow-up sessions are another important technique in ensuring successful termination and change maintenance. These sessions benefit both clients and social workers. Many people continue to progress after termination, and follow-up sessions provide an opportunity for the social worker to acknowledge such gains and encourage them to continue their efforts.

These sessions also provide the social worker with an opportunity to provide brief additional assistance for residual difficulties. Social workers may assess the durability of changes in these sessions—that is, determine whether clients have maintained gains beyond the immediate influence of the helping relationship. Additional benefits of planned follow-up sessions are that they may soften the blow of termination, and they allow opportunities for longitudinal evaluation of practice effectiveness.

By introducing the notion of the follow-up session as an integral part of the helping process, social workers can avoid the risk that clients may later view these sessions as failure, an intrusion into their private lives, or as an attempt to satisfy the social worker's curiosity. When arranging for the follow-up session, social workers should not set a specific date but rather explain that they will contact the client after a designated interval (Wells, 1994). This period of time offers the individual an opportunity to test out and further consolidate the learning and the changes achieved during the formal helping period.

In the follow-up session, the social worker generally relates more informally than during the period of intervention. After observing the appropriate social courtesies, you should guide the discussion to the client's progress and administer postintervention measures when appropriate. The follow-up session also provides an excellent opportunity for further evaluation of your efforts during the period of intervention. In retrospect, what was most helpful? What was least helpful? Further efforts can be made to consolidate gains at this point as well. What was gained from treatment that the client can continue to use in coping with life? Finally, at this point, you can contract for more formalized help if this step appears necessary. Follow-up sessions thus enable social workers to arrange for timely assistance that may arrest deterioration in functioning.

One caution related to follow-up sessions is warranted: They may not allow the client to make a clean break from services. Individuals who had difficulty separating during termination may use follow-up sessions as an excuse to prolong contact with the social worker. This continued attachment is detrimental to the change process and inhibits the person from establishing appropriate attachments with social networks and with other helping professionals. Follow-up should include a clear explanation of and purpose for the contact. Social workers should be alert to this possibility in proposing follow-up sessions and ensure that clients understand the specific purpose and focus of these sessions.

Ending Rituals

In many settings, termination may be concluded by a form of celebration or ritual that symbolically marks the progress made and the relationship's conclusion (Finn, 2021; Murphy & Dillon, 2003). For example, in residential programs and some treatment groups, termination may be acknowledged in graduation or status elevation ceremonies, during which other residents or members comment on the departing member's growth and offer good wishes for the future. Certificates, cards, or memory books (Elbow, 1987) are but a few of the symbolic gifts that terminating clients may receive from staff and/ or fellow clients. In individual and family work, social workers may choose to mark termination with small gifts such as a book, a plant, a framed inspirational quote, a bookmark, or some other token that is representative of the working relationship or the achievements while in service. Groups may conclude by creating a lasting product that is symbolic of the group, such as a collage or mural; in the process of creating this item, participants can reflect on the meaning the group had for them as members (Northen & Kurland, 2001).

The decision to use rituals to mark termination should be based on client preferences, the appropriateness of such actions for the agency or setting, and the meaning that the client may attribute to such actions. Cultural awareness and humility apply to ending rituals as they provide continuing opportunities for the social worker to call upon their knowledge and deepen understanding about the client's culture and values. Giving a personal greeting card may be perceived as a gesture of intimate friendship by some clients; for others, such as a child leaving foster care for a permanent placement, it

Case Example

Horizons is a halfway house for youth whose behavioral problems have resulted in hospitalization or incarceration. The program is intended to help teenagers readjust to community life and establish social supports so that they can return to their homes or move successfully into independent living. Given this focus, the length of stay for any individual resident varies considerably. Some youth encounter difficulties or reoffend; they are then returned to jail or to inpatient settings or simply drop out of sight. These endings can be difficult for staff as they deal with disappointment in the client's failure to make it this time around and perhaps question what they might have done to prevent this outcome. It is also disturbing for other clients as they worry about their own challenges and their ability to successfully move on to the next step.

When residents terminate prematurely from the program, they are asked to attend a community meeting where they can process with the group their experiences in the program and the things they learned that can be of use in the future. Staff and other residents are also invited to share their observations and feelings with the intention of giving supportive and constructive feedback from a caring community—one to which the resident might someday return. When clients quit the program and drop out of sight, such sessions are still held. In these sessions, the residents and the staff who remain process their feelings about the departure and discern lessons they can take away from it.

When residents have met their goals and are ready to move on to a more permanent living situation, staff discuss the plan and the timeline for departure and stay alert to the difficulties that can arise at termination. The staff members make a point of discussing, in groups and individual sessions, the fears that can arise in moving from a comfortable place to the unknown. Sometimes, alumni of the program visit to talk about their experiences and offer advice and encouragement. At this time, goals are reviewed, progress is charted, and the client's views are sought on which aspects of the program facilitated change. Clients and staff work together to anticipate the challenges ahead and put in place the strategies necessary to address them.

During a resident's final days, the Horizons staff and residents create a graduation ceremony, and each resident offers the one who is leaving symbolic gifts to take on the journey. These gifts may consist of inspirational quotes, reminders of inside jokes or shared experiences, and more tangible items, such as towels or pots and pans from the local secondhand store to help get established in the new setting.

Family members, teachers, and workers from other agencies are encouraged to attend the graduation and at the ceremony are asked to support the client in the next steps ahead. These ceremonies are often tearful and moving events, where the emphasis is on achievement and on hope for the future.

may be a source of comfort and continuity. A gift that seems is too lavish or too personal may cause discomfort if the client feels the need to reciprocate in some way. Goodbye parties may reinforce feelings of accomplishment and confidence, or they may obviate the feelings of sadness or ambivalence that must also be addressed as part of closure (Shulman, 1992). Graduation ceremonies may recreate past disappointments and lead to further setbacks if, for example, family members refuse to attend and acknowledge the changes the client has achieved (Jones, 1996).

Throughout the helping relationship, "curiosity is the enemy of assumption" (Isaacson & Isaacson, 2020, p.123). In termination, too, social workers should explore what clients need or want in closing and instead ask how they would like to mark the final session, offering options or examples only if the person seems unsure what to suggest. Useful and meaningful ending rituals are numerous. For example, at the final session of the

"Banana Splits" group for children of families undergoing divorce or separation, participants make and eat banana splits (McGonagle, 1986). A social worker may create a card depicting the gift or wish that they have for the client's continued success; participants in groups may write poems or rewrite lyrics to popular song melodies to mark the ending of a class or group (Walsh, 2007). In trauma-informed practice, visual arts may be used to depict new narratives, such as seeing symptoms. Some clients may ask the social worker to create a diploma or certificate of completion indicating what they have achieved and ask to have a photo taken together (Dorfman, 1996). Events to mark group terminations can facilitate the tasks of termination and model meaningful rituals in a way that clients might not have experienced previously (Jones, 1996). These endings can be linked symbolically to the goals for work and may help motivate other clients strive toward the achievements being celebrated by fellow group or residence members.

Summary

Social workers are aware of the importance of engaging with clients and the skills and attitudes needed to build an effective working relationship. Unfortunately, when this relationship concludes, social workers may not be equally astute about taking the relationship apart. Effective evaluation and termination leave both the practitioner and the client with a shared sense of the

accomplishments achieved in their work together. This process affords the opportunity to model ending a relationship in a way that is not hurtful or damaging to the client. Effective termination equips people with the skills and the knowledge necessary to sustain gains or to seek further help as needed in the future.

Competency Notes

C1 Demonstrate Ethical and Professional Behavior

- Make ethical decisions by applying the standards of the NASW Code of Ethics, relevant laws and regulations, models for ethical decision-making, ethical conduct of research, and additional codes of ethics as appropriate to context.
- Manage personal and professional value conflicts and affective reactions.
- Use supervision and consultation to guide professional judgment and behavior.

C2 Engage Antiracism, Diversity, Equity, and Inclusion in Practice

- Demonstrate anti-racist social work practice at the individual, family, group, organizational, community, research, and policy levels, informed by the theories and voices of those who have been marginalized.

- Demonstrate cultural humility applying critical reflexivity, self-awareness, and self-regulation to manage the influence of bias, power, privilege, and values in working with clients and constituencies acknowledging them as experts of their own lived experiences.

C4 Engage in Practice-Informed Research and Research-Informed Practice

- Identify strategies for use of quantitative and qualitative methods of research to advance the purposes of social work.

C8 Intervene with Individuals, Families, Groups, Organizations, and Communities

- Engage with clients and constituencies to critically choose and implement culturally responsive, evidenced-based interventions to achieve mutually agreed-on practice goals and enhance capacities of clients and constituencies.

C9 Evaluate Practice with Individuals, Families, Groups, Organizations, and Communities

- Select and use appropriate methods for evaluation of outcome.

- Critically analyze outcomes and apply evaluation findings to improve practice effectiveness with individuals, families, groups, organizations, and communities.

Skill Development Exercises

In Evaluation and Termination

Consider a case you have observed in your field work. Reflect on or envision a final session. How would you, as the worker, engage the client(s) in reflecting on the aspects of the helping process that were helpful and unhelpful? Based on your knowledge of evaluation and termination, address the following questions:

1. What goals were reached during the course of the helping relationship?

2. What goals were not achieved?

3. How could you evaluate the efficacy of the helping process beyond asking for the clients' general feedback?

4. What risks does the client face that might lead to a recurrence of problems?

5. What might you, as the social worker do, in the final session to address those risks?

6. What feelings do you and the client(s) have about termination?

Notes

1. For information on the concepts and steps of termination as they apply to macro practice, we suggest an article by Fauri, Harrigan, and Netting (1998).

2. For an excellent source on the considerations and strategies in termination across settings or using various theoretical orientations, see Walsh (2007).

3. See Meyer (2001) for a discussion of the dynamics of no shows and an effective clinical response.

4. For information on services in end-of-life care, see NASW's Standards of Social Work Practice in

Palliative and End of Life Care (www.naswdc.org, 2011).

5. Baker, Piper, McCarthy, Majeskie, and Fiore (2004), Feltenstein (2008), Koob and Le Moal (2008), Matto (2005), Smyth (2005), and others have authored articles and books that describe the neurobiology of relapse, identify various factors that contribute to relapse, discuss beliefs and myths associated with addictions, and delineate models for relapse education and treatment with addicted and impulse-disordered clients.

Bibliography

A

Aboraya, A. (2007). The reliability of psychiatric diagnoses: POINT—Our psychiatric diagnoses are still unreliable. *Psychiatry (Edgmont)*, 4(1), 22–25. https://www.ncbi.nlm.nih.gov/pmc/articles/PMC2922387/

Abramson, M. (1985). The autonomy-paternalism dilemma in social work. *Social Work*, 27, 422–427. doi.org/10.1177/104438948506600701

Abu El-Ella, N., Bessant, J., & Pinkwart, A. (2016). Revisiting the honorable merchant: The reshaped role of trust in open innovation. *Thunderbird International Business Review*, 58(3), 261–275. doi.org/10.1002/tie.21774

ACES Too High. (n.d.) What ACES/PCEs do you have? http://acestoohigh.com/got-your-ace-score/

Ackerman, C. (2017, July 26). *Your ultimate guide on group therapy*. PositivePsychology.com. https://positivepsychology.com/group-therapy/

Ackley, D. C. (1997). *Breaking free of managed care*. Guilford Press.

Adams, R. (2009) Being a critical practitioner, in R. Adams, L. Dominelli and M. Payne (eds) Critical Practice in Social Work, 2nd edn. Basingstoke: Palgrave Macmillan.

Adams, K., Matto, H., & LeCroy, C. (2009). Limitations of evidence-based practice for social work education: Unpacking the complexity. *Journal of Social Work Education*, 45(2), 165–186. doi.org/10.5175/JSWE.2009.200700105

Administration for Children & Families. (n.d.). *Trauma*. U.S. Department of Health and Human Services. https://www.acf.hhs.gov/trauma-toolkit/trauma-concept

Afifi, O., Ford, D., Gershoff, ET., Merrik, TM., Ports, KA., Grogan-Kaylor, A., (2017).Unpacking the impact of adverse childhood experiences on adult mental health. 69, 10–19. doi: 10.1016/j.chiabu.2017.03.016.

Aguilera, A., Garza, M. J., & Munoz, R. F. (2010). Group cognitive-behavioral therapy for depression in Spanish: Culture-sensitive manualized treatment in practice. *Journal of Clinical Psychology*, 66(8), 857–867. doi.org/10.1002/jclp.20706

Ahmed, S. R., Amer, M., M., & Killawi, A. (2017). The ecosystems perspective in social work: Implications for culturally competent practice with American Muslims. *Journal of Religion & Spirituality in Social Work: Social Thought*, 36 (1–2), 1–12. doi.org/10.1080/15426432.2017.1311245

Aisenberg, E. (2008). Evidence-based practice in mental health care to ethnic minority communities: Has its practice fallen short of its evidence? *Social Work*, 53(4), 297–306. doi.org/10.1093/sw/53.4.297

Albert, S. M., Im, A., Brenner, L., Smith, M., & Waxman, R. (2002). Effect of a social work liaison program on family caregivers to people with brain injury. *Journal of Head Trauma Rehabilitation*, 17(2), 175–189. doi.org/10.1097/00001199-200204000-00007

Albritton, T. J, Hall, W. J., & Klein, L. B. (2022). Critical theories for social work practice. In L. Rapp-McCall, K. Corcoran, & A. Roberts (Eds.), *Social workers' desk reference* (4th ed.). Oxford University Press.

Alexander, J. F., Waldron, H. B., Robbins, M. S., & Neeb, A. A. (2013). *Functional family therapy for adolescent behavior problems*. American Psychological Association.

Alexander, R., Jr. (2010). *Human behavior in the social environment: A macro, national, and international perspective*. SAGE.

Al Gharaibeh, F. (2019). Barriers to designing a code of ethics for social workers in the Arab society. In S. M. Marson & R. E. McKinney (Eds.), *Routledge handbook of social work ethics and values* (pp. 83–89). Routledge. doi.org/10.4324/9780429438813-12

Al-Krenawi, A. (1998). Reconciling Western treatment and traditional healing: A social worker walks with the wind. *Reflections: Narratives of Professional Helping*, 4(3), 6–21. https://reflectionsnarrativesofprofessionalhelping.org/index.php/Reflections/article/view/562/409

Al-Krenawi, A. (1999) Social workers' practices in their non-Western home communities: Overcoming conflicts between professional and cultural values. *Families in Society*, 80(5), 488–495. doi.org/10.1606/1044-3894.1478

Alle-Corliss, L., & Alle-Corliss, R. (2009). *Group work: A practical guide to developing groups in agency settings*. John Wiley & Sons.

Allen, S., & Tracy, E. (Eds.). (2009). *Delivering home-based services: A social work perspective*. Columbia University Press. doi.org/10.7312/alle14146

Alley, G. R., & Brown, L. B. (2002). A diabetes problem-solving support group: Issues, process, and preliminary outcomes. *Social Work in Health Care*, 36(1), 1–9. https://doi.org/10.1300/J010v36n01_01

Alvarez, P. (2019, May 16). Administration considers next steps in DNA testing on the border. *CNN*. https://www.cnn.com/2019/05/15/politics/ice-considers-next-steps-in-dna-testing/index.html

American Academy of Child & Adolescent Psychiatry. (2018). *Suicide in children and teens*. https://www.aacap.org/AACAP/Families_and_Youth/Facts_for_Families/FFF-Guide/Teen-Suicide-010.aspx

American Psychiatric Association. (2013a). *Diagnostic and statistical manual of mental disorders* (5th ed.). Author. https://doi.org/10.1176/appi.books.9780890425596

American Psychiatric Association. (2013b). *Highlights of changes from DSM-IV-TR to DSM-5*. https://www.psychiatry.org/psychiatrists/practice/dsm/updates-to-dsm-5

American Psychological Association. (2020a). *Suicide*. https://www.apa.org/topics/suicide

American Psychological Association. (2020b). *Instrumental activities of daily living scale*. https://www.apa.org/pi/about/publications/caregivers/practice-settings/assessment/tools/daily-activities

American Psychological Association. (2017). *What is cognitive behavioral therapy?* https://www.apa.org/ptsd-guideline/patients-and-families/cognitive-behavioral

American Society of Addiction Medicine. (2020). *ASAM criteria*. https://www.asam.org/asam-criteria/about

Anderson, D. (2007). Multicultural group work: A force for developing and healing. *Journal for Specialists in Group Work*, 32(3), 224–244. doi.org/10.1080/01933920701431537

Anderson, D. A., & Worthen, D. (1997). Exploring a fourth dimension: Spirituality as a resource for the couple therapist. *Journal of Marital and Family Therapy*, 23(1), 3–12. doi.org/10.1111/j.1752-0606.1997.tb00227.x

Anderson, K. M., & Mack, R. (2019). Digital storytelling: A narrative method for positive identity development in minority youth. *Social Work with Groups*, 42(1), 43–55. doi.org/10.1080/01609513.2017.1413616

Andrade, J. T. (2009). *Handbook of violence risk assessment and treatment: New approaches for forensic mental health professionals*. Springer.

Andrews, A. B., & Ben-Arieh, A. (1999). Measuring and monitoring children's well-being across the world. *Social Work*, *44*(2), 105–115. doi.org/10.1093/sw/44.2.105

Andrews, C. M., Darnell, J. S., McBride, T. D., & Gehlert, S. (2013). Social work and the implementation of the Affordable Care Act. *Health & Social Work*, *38*(2), 67–71. doi.org/10.1093/hsw/hlt002

Androff, D., & McPherson, J. (2014). Can human rights-based social work practice bridge the micro/macro divide. *Advancing Human Rights in Social Work Education*, 39–56. doi.org/10.4324/9781315885483

Annie E. Casey Foundation (2014). *Race equity and inclusion action guide: Embracing equity: 7 steps to advance and embed race equity and inclusion within your organization*. Baltimore, MD.

Ansara, Y. G., & Hegarty, P. (2014). Methodologies of misgendering: Recommendations for reducing cisgenderism in psychological research. *Feminism & Psychology 24*(2), 259–270. doi.org/10.1177/0959353514526217

Anti-Oppression Resource and Training Alliance. (n.d.). *AORTA*. https://aorta.coop

Anyiwo, N., Palmer, G. J., Garrett, J. M., Starck, J. G., & Hope, E. C. (2020). Racial and political resistance: An examination of the sociopolitical action of racially marginalized youth. *Current Opinion in Psychology*, *35*, 86–91. doi.org/10.1016/j.copsyc.2020.03.005

Aparicio, E., Michalopoulos, L. M., & Unick, G. J. (2013). An examination of the psychometric properties of the vicarious trauma scale in a sample of licensed social workers. *Health & Social Work*, *38*(4), 199–206. doi.org/10.1093/hsw/hlt017

Aponte, H. (1982). The person of the therapist: The cornerstone of therapy. *Family Therapy Networker*, *46*, 19–21.

Applegate, J. S. (1992). The impact of subjective measures on nonbehavioral practice research: Outcome vs. process. *Families in Society*, *73*(2), 100–108. doi.org/10.1177/104438949207300204

Arampatzi, E., Burger, M., Stavropoulos, S., & Tay, L. (2020). The role of positive expectations for resilience to adverse events: Subjective well-being before, during and after the Greek bailout referendum. *Journal of Happiness Studies*, *21*(3), 965–995. doi.org/10.1007/s10902-019-00115-9

Arnold, E. M. (2002). End-of-life counseling and care: Assessment, interventions and clinical issues. In A. R. Roberts & G. J. Greene (Eds.), *Social workers' desk reference* (pp. 452–457). Oxford University Press.

Asakura, K, Strumm, B, Todd, S., & Varghese, R. (2020). What does social justice look like when sitting with clients? A qualitative study of teaching clinical social work practice from a social justice perspective. *Journal of Social Work Education*, *56*(3), 442–455. doi.org/10.1080/10437797.2019.1656588.

Ashkenas, J. Park, H., & Pearce, A. (2017, August 24). Even with affirmative action, Blacks and Hispanics are more underrepresented at top colleges than 35 years ago. *The New York Times*. https://www.nytimes.com/interactive/2017/08/24/us/affirmative-action.html

Aspen Institute Staff (2016, July 11). *11 terms you should know to better understand structural racism*. Aspen Institute. https://www.aspeninstitute.org/blog-posts/structural-racism-definition/

Austin, A., Craig, S. L., & McInroy, L. B. (2016). Toward transgender affirmative social work education. *Journal of Social Work Education*, *52*(3), 297–310. doi.org/10.1080/10437797.2016.1174637

Austin, M. J., Anthony, E. K., Knee, R. T., & Mathias, J. (2016). Revisiting the relationship between micro and macro social work practice. *Families in Society*, *97*(4), 270–277. doi.org/10.1606/1044-3894.2016.97.33

Austin, M. J., Coombs, M., & Barr, B. (2005). Community-centered clinical practice: Is the integration of micro and macro social work practice possible? *Journal of Community Practice*, *13*(4), 9–30. doi.org/10.1300/J125v13n04_02

Averett, P., Crowe, A., & Johnson, T. (2018). Using sketchbooks to facilitate the group process with at-risk youth. *Social Work with Groups*, *41*(1–2), 125–138. doi.org/10.1080/01609513.2016.1273694

Azar, K. M., Aurora, M., Wang, E. J., Muzaffar, A., Pressman, A., & Palaniappan, L. P. (2015). Virtual small groups for weight management: An innovative delivery mechanism for evidence-based lifestyle interventions among obese men. *Translational Behavioral Medicine*, *5*(1), 37–44. doi.org/10.1007/s13142-014-0296-6

B

Baer, J. (1999). Family relationships, parenting behavior, and adolescent deviance in three ethnic groups. *Families in Society*, *80*(3), 279–285. https://doi.org/10.1606/1044-3894.682

Bagci, S. C. (2018). Does everyone benefit equally from self-efficacy beliefs? The moderating role of perceived social support on motivation. *Journal of Early Adolescence*, *38*(2), 204–219. doi.org/10.1177/0272431616665213

Baker, T. B., Piper, M. E., McCarthy, D. E., Majeskie, M. R., & Fiore, M. C. (2004). Addiction motivation reformulated: An affective processing model of negative reinforcement. *Psychological Review*, *111*(1), 33. https://doi.org/10.1037/0033-295X.111.1.33

Bandealy, S. S., Sheth, N. C., Matuella, S. K., Chaikind, J. R., Oliva, I. A., Philip, S. R., ... & Hoge, E. A. (2021). Mind-body interventions for anxiety disorders: A review of the evidence base for mental health practitioners. *Focus*, *19*(2), 173–183. doi.org/10.1176/appi.focus.20200042

Bandura, A. (1986). *Social foundations of thought and action*. Prentice-Hall.

Bandura, A. (1997). *Self-efficacy: The exercise of control*. Freeman.

Bandura, A. (2006). Toward a psychology of human agency. *Perspectives on Psychological Science 1*(2), 164–180. https://doi.org/10.1111/j.1745-6916.2006.00011.x

Banks, S. (2010). Integrity in professional life: Issues of conduct, commitment and capacity. *British Journal of Social Work*, *40*(7), 2168–2184. doi.org/10.1093/bjsw/bcp152

Banks, S., Cai, T., De Jonge, E., Shears, J., Shum, M., Sobočan, A. M., ... & Weinberg, M. (2020). Practising ethically during COVID-19: Social work challenges and responses. *International Social Work*, *63*(5), 569–583. doi.org/10.1177/0020872820949614

Banks, S., & Nohr, K. (2013). *Practising social work ethics around the world: Cases and commentaries*. Routledge.

Barbhuiya, F., & Mazmuder, A. Z. (2020). Transformation of a recreational youth group into community service group during the COVID-19 pandemic. *Social Work with Groups*, *44*(1), 53–59. doi.org/10.1080/01609513.2020.1807774

Barker, R. L. (2003). *The social work dictionary* (5th ed.). NASW Press.

Barnett, J. (2009, December). The role of recording in psychotherapy. *Society for the Advancement of Psychotherapy*. https://societyforpsychotherapy.org/ask-the-ethicist-the-role-of-recording-in-psychotherapy/

Barnhardt, R., & Oscar Kawagley, A. (2005). Indigenous knowledge systems and Alaska Native ways of knowing. *Anthropology & Education Quarterly*, *36*(1), 8–23. doi.org/10.1525/aeq.2005.36.1.008

Barnhill, J. W. (Ed.). (2014). *DSM-5 clinical cases*. American Psychiatric Publishing.

Barrio, C., & Yamada, A. M. (2010). Culturally based intervention development: The case of Latino families dealing with schizophrenia. *Research on Social Work Practice*, *20*(5), 483–492. doi.org/10.1177/1049731510361613

Barsky, A. (2021). New language on self-care and cultural competence/cultural humility takes effect. *The New Social Worker*. https://www.socialworker.com/feature-articles/ethics-articles/special-report-2021-revisions-nasw-code-of-ethics/

Barsky, A. E. (2019). *Ethics and values in social work: An integrated approach for a comprehensive curriculum*. Oxford University Press.

Bateganya, M., Amanyeiwe, U., Roxo, U., & Dong, M. (2015). The impact of support groups for people living with HIV on clinical outcomes: A systematic review of the literature. *Journal of Acquired Immune Deficiency Syndrome*, *68*(3), S368–S374. doi.org/10.1097/qai.0000000000000519

Bath, H. (2008). The three pillars of trauma-informed care. *Reclaiming Children and Youth, 17*(3), 17–21.

Baumann, A. A., Powell, B. J., Kohl, P. L., Tabak, R. G., Penalba, V., Proctor, E. K., ... & Cabassa, L. J. (2015). Cultural adaptation and implementation of evidence-based parent-training: A systematic review and critique of guiding evidence. *Children and Youth Services Review, 53*, 113–120. doi.org/10.1016/j.childyouth.2015.03.025

Bazyar, J., Farrokhi, M., & Khankeh, H. (2019). Triage systems in mass casualty incidents and disasters: a review study with a worldwide approach. *Open Access Macedonian Journal of Medical Sciences, 7*(3), 482–494. doi.org/10.3889/oamjms.2019.119

Beck, A. T. (1967). *Depression: Clinical, experimental, and theoretical aspects.* Harper.

Beck, A. T. (1976). *Cognitive therapy and the emotional disorders.* International Universities Press.

Beck, A. T., Steer, R. A., & Brown, G. K. (1996). *BDI-II, Beck depression inventory: Manual.* Harcourt Brace.

Beck, J. S. (2021). *Cognitive therapy: Basics and beyond.* Guilford Press.

Beckerman, N. L., & Sarracco, M. (2019). The legacy of inherited trauma: Case studies. *Journal of Anxiety and Depression, 2*(1), 1–10. doi.org/10.46527/2582-3264.113

Beckett, K., Nyrop, K., & Pfingst, L. (2006). Race, drugs, and policing: Understanding disparities in drug delivery arrests. *Criminology, 44*(1), 105–137. doi.org/10.1111/j.1745-9125.2006.00044.x

Bee, P. E., Bower, P., Lovell, K., Gilbody, S., Richards, D., Gask, L., & Roach, P. (2008). Psychotherapy mediated by remote communication technologies: A meta-analytic review. *BMC Psychiatry, 8*(1), 1–13. doi.org/10.1186/1471-244x-8-60

Bell, H., Kulkarni, S., & Dalton, L. (2003). Organizational prevention of vicarious trauma. *Families in Society, 84*(4), 463–470. doi.org/10.1606/1044-3894.131

Bell-Tolliver, L., Burgess, R., & Brock, L. J. (2009). African American therapists working with African American families: An exploration of the strengths perspective in treatment. *Journal of Marital & Family Therapy, 35*(3), 293–307. doi.org/10.1111/j.1752-0606.2009.00117.x

Belmont, J. (2016). *150 more group therapy activities & tips.* PESI Publishing & Media.

Bembry, J. X., & Ericson, C. (1999). Therapeutic termination with the early adolescent who has experienced multiple losses. *Child and Adolescent Social Work Journal, 16*(3), 177–189. doi.org/10.1023/A:1022369609530

Bennett, G. G., Foley, P., Levine, E., Whiteley, J., Askew, S., Steinberg, D. M., ... & Puleo, E. (2013). Behavioral treatment for weight gain prevention among black women in primary care practice: A randomized clinical trial. *JAMA Internal Medicine, 173*(19), 1770–1777. doi.org/10.1001/jamainternmed.2013.9263

Berg, I. K., & Kelly, S. (2000). *Building solutions in child protection.* W. W. Norton & Co..

Bergeron, L. R., & Gray, B. (2003). Ethical dilemmas of reporting suspected elder abuse. *Social Work, 48*(1), 96–105. doi.org/10.1093/sw/48.1.96

Berlin, S. B. (2001). *Clinical social work: A cognitive-integrative perspective.* Oxford University Press.

Berliner, L., & Kolko, D. J. (2016). Trauma informed care: A commentary and critique. *Child Maltreatment, 21*(2), 168–172. doi: 10.1177/1077559516643785

Berman-Rossi, T., & Rossi, P. (1990). Confidentiality and informed consent in school social work. *Social Work in Education, 12*(3), 195–207.

Bernal, G., Bonilla, J., & Bellido, C. (1995). Ecological validity and cultural sensitivity for outcome research: Issues for the cultural adaptation and development of psychosocial treatments with Hispanics. *Journal of Abnormal Child Psychology, 23*(1), 67–82. doi.org/10.1007/BF01447045

Biestek, F. (1957). *The casework relationship.* Loyola University Press.

Birkley, E. L., & Eckhardt, C. I. (2015). Anger, hostility, internalizing negative emotions, and intimate partner violence perpetration: A meta-analytic review. *Clinical Psychology Review, 37*, 40–56. doi: 10.1016/j.cpr.2015.01.002

Black Lives Matter. (n.d.). About. https://blacklivesmatter.com/about/

Block, L. R. (1985). On the potentiality and limits of time: The single-session group and the cancer patient. *Social Work with Groups, 8*(2), 81–99. https://www.tandfonline.com/doi/abs/10.1300/J009v08n02_08

Bloom, M., Fischer, J., & Orme, J. G. (2009). *Evaluating practice: Guidelines for the accountable professional* (6th ed.). Allyn & Bacon.

Bo, A., Mao, W., & Lindsey, M. A. (2017). Effects of mind–body interventions on depressive symptoms among older Chinese adults: A systematic review and meta-analysis. *International Journal of Geriatric Psychiatry, 32*(5), 509–521. doi.org/10.1002/gps.4688

Bogo, M., Rawlings, M., Katz, E., & Logie, C. (2014). *Using simulation in assessment and teaching: OSCE Adapted for social work.* CSWE Press.

Bolton, K. W., Hall, J. C., & Lehmann, P. (Eds.). (2021). *Theoretical perspectives for direct social work practice: A generalist-eclectic approach.* Springer Publishing Company.

Borden, W. (2022). Theoretical pluralism and integrative perspective in social work practice. In L. Rapp-McCall, K. Corcoran, & A. Roberts (Eds.), *Social workers' desk reference* (4th ed.). Oxford University Press.

Borum, R., & Verhaagen, D. (2006). *Assessing and managing violence risk in juveniles.* Guilford Press.

Bostic, J. Q., Shadid, L. G., & Blotcky, M. J. (1996). Our time is up: Forced terminations during psychotherapy. *American Journal of Psychotherapy, 50*(3), 347–359. Retrieved from doi.org/10.1176/appi.psychotherapy.1996.50.3.347

Boyd-Franklin, N. (1989). *Black families in therapy: A multisystems approach.* Guilford Press.

Boyd-Franklin, N., & Bry, B. H. (2000). *Reaching out in family therapy: Home-based school and community interventions.* Guilford Press.

Bowers, L. (2014). A model of de-escalation. *Mental Health Practice, 17*(9), 36–37. doi.org/10.7748/mhp.17.9.36.e924

Brager, G., & Holloway, S. (1978). *Changing human service organizations: Politics and practice.* Free Press.

Brehm, S. S., & Brehm, J. W. (2013). *Psychological reactance: A theory of freedom and control.* Academic Press.

Breton, M. (2006). Path dependence and the place of social action in social work. *Social Work with Groups, 29*(4), 25–44. doi.org/10.1300/J009v29n04_03

Brewer, L. P. C., & Cooper, L. A. (2014). Race, discrimination, and cardiovascular disease. *The Virtual Mentor, 16*(6), 270–274. doi.org/10.1001/virtualmentor.2014.16.06.stas2-1406

Bride, B., & Figley, C. (2007). The fatigue compassionate social workers: An introduction to the special issue on compassion fatigue. *Clinical Social Work Journal, 35*(3), 151–153. doi.org/10.1007/s10615-007-0093-5

British Association of Social Workers. (2014). *Code of ethics.* https://www.basw.co.uk/about-basw/code-ethics

Bronfenbrenner, U. (1979). *The ecology of human development: Experiments by nature and design.* Harvard University Press.

Brownstein, Michael, 2015 [2019], "Implicit Bias", in The Stanford Encyclopedia of Philosophy (Fall 2019 edition), Edward N. Zalta (ed.), https://plato.stanford.edu/archives/fall2019/entries/implicit-bias/°.

Bronson, D. E. (2022). Fundamental principles of behavioral social work. In L. Rapp-McCall, K. Corcoran, & A. Roberts (Eds.), *Social workers' desk reference* (4th ed.). Oxford University Press.

Brueggemann, W. G. (2006). *The practice of macro social work* (3rd ed.). Cengage Learning.

Bullmore, E. (2020, January 19). From depression to dementia, inflammation is medicine's new frontier. *The Guardian.* https://www.theguardian.com/commentisfree/2020/jan/19/inflammation-depression-mind-body

Burford, G., & Hudson, J. (Eds.). (2009). *Family group conferencing: New directions in community-centered child and family practice.* Aldine-Transactions.

Burghardt, S. (2011). *Macro practice in social work for the 21st century: Bridging the macro-micro divide.* SAGE.

Burke, M. & Samandi, G. (2019). 2 dead, one missing after Hard Rock Hotel construction site collapses in New Orleans. NBC: US News. https://www.nbcnews.com/news/us-news/large-part-hard-rock-hotel-construction-site-collapses-new-orleans-n1065411

C

Cabral, R. R., & Smith, T. B. (2011). Racial/ethnic matching of clients and therapists in mental health services: A meta-analytic review of preference, perceptions, and outcomes. *Journal of Counseling Psychology, 58*(4), 537. doi.org/10.1037/a0025266

Cabassa, L.J., Baumann, A.A. (2013). A two-way street: bridging implementation science and cultural adaptations of mental health treatments. Implementation Sci, 8 (90). https://doi.org/10.1186/1748-5908-8-90

Cameron, E. L., Fox, J. D., Anderson, M. S., & Cameron, C. A. (2010). Resilient youths use humor to enhance socioemotional functioning during a day in the life. *Journal of Adolescent Research, 25*(5), 716–742. doi.org/10.1177/074355841036659

Cameron, M., & Keenan, E. K. (2010). The common factors model: Implications for transtheoretical clinical social work practice. *Social Work, 55*(1), 63–73. 5 doi.org/10.1093/sw/55.1.63

Cameron, S., & Turtle-Song, I. (2002). Learning to write case notes using the SOAP format. *Journal of Counselling and Development, 80*(3), 286–292. doi.org/10.1002/j.1556-6678.2002.tb00193.x

Campbell Collaboration. (n.d.). *Campbell Collaboration Library of Systematic Reviews.* http:// www.campbellcollaboration.org/library.php

Campbell, J. A. (1988). Client acceptance of single-subject evaluation procedures. In *Social Work Research and Abstracts* (Vol. 24, No. 2, pp. 21–22). Oxford University Press.

Campbell, J. A. (1990). Ability of practitioners to estimate client acceptance of single-subject evaluation procedures. *Social Work, 35*(1), 9–14.

Camper, A., & Felton, E. (2020). *Telemental health: Legal considerations for social workers.* National Association of Social Workers (NASW). https://www.socialworkers.org/About/Legal/HIPAA-Help-For-Social- Workers/Telemental-Health

Canadian Association of Social Workers. (2005). *Code of ethics.* https://www.casw-acts.ca/en/Code-of-Ethics

Caplan, G. (1964). *Principles of preventive psychiatry.* Basic Books.

Caplan, T., & Thomas, H. (1995). Safety and comfort, content and process: Facilitating open group work with men who batter. *Social Work with Groups, 18*(2–3), 33–51.

Caporuscio, J. (2020, March 31). Grounding techniques: Step-by-step guide and methods. *Medical News Today.* https://www.medicalnewstoday.com/articles/grounding-techniques

Carlson, J. (2020). Police warriors and police guardians: race, masculinity, and the construction of gun violence. *Social Problems, 67*(3), 399–417. doi.org/10.1093/socpro/spz020

Carpenter, J. K., Andrews, L. A., Witcraft, S. M., Powers, M. B., Smits, J. A., & Hofmann, S. G. (2018). Cognitive behavioral therapy for anxiety and related disorders: A meta-analysis of randomized placebo-controlled trials. *Depression and Anxiety, 35*(6), 502–514. https://doi.org/10.1002/da.22728

Carrell, S. (2000). *Group exercises for adolescents: A manual for therapists* (2nd ed.). SAGE.

Carter, B., & McGoldrick, M. (Eds.). (1988). *The changing life cycle: A framework for family therapy* (2nd ed.). Gardner Press.

Carter, B., & McGoldrick, M. (Eds.). (2005). *The expanded life cycle. Individual, family and social perspectives* (3rd ed.). Allyn & Bacon.

Case Management Body of Knowledge. (2020). *Introduction to the case management body of knowledge.* https://cmbodyofknowledge.com/content/introduction-case-management-body-knowledge

Case Management Society of America (CMSA). (2010). *Standards of practice for case management.* Author. https://www.abqaurp.org/DOCS/2010%20CM%20standards%20of%20practice.pdf

Center for Community-Based Child Abuse Prevention, & Center for the Study of Social Policy (2011). *Strengthening families and communities: 2011 resource guide.* https://www.childwelfare.gov/pubpdfs/2011guide.pdf

Centers for Disease Control and Prevention (CDC). (2009). *Depression is not a normal part of growing old.* https://www.cdc.gov/aging/depression/index.html

Centers for Disease Control and Prevention (CDC). (2017). *Are you engaged?* https://www.cdc.gov/aging/publications/features/social-engagement-aging.html

Centers for Disease Control and Prevention (CDC). (2018). *HIPAA vs. FERPA infographic 2018.* CDC. Public Health Professionals Gateway. https://www.cdc.gov/phlp/docs/hipaa-ferpa-infographic-508.pdf

Centers for Disease Control and Prevention (CDC). (2019a). *Alcohol and public health.* https://www.cdc.gov/alcohol/fact-sheets/moderate-drinking.htm

Centers for Disease Control and Prevention (CDC). (2019b). *Lesbian, gay, bisexual, and transgender health: LGBT resources.* https://www.cdc.gov/lgbthealth/youth-resources.htm

Centers for Disease Control and Prevention (CDC). (2019c, January 2). *The CDC policy process.* Office of the Associate Director for Policy and Strategy. https://www.cdc.gov/policy/polaris/policyprocess/index.html

Centers for Disease Control and Prevention (CDC). (2019d, December 31). *Preventing adverse childhood experiences.* https://www.cdc.gov/violenceprevention/childabuseandneglect/aces/fastfact.html

Centers for Disease Control and Prevention (CDC). (2020a). *Alcohol and public health.* https://www.cdc.gov/alcohol/faqs.htm

Centers for Disease Control and Prevention (CDC). (2020b). *1991-2019 high school youth risk behavior survey data.* http://yrbs-explorer.services.cdc.gov/

Centers for Disease Control and Prevention (CDC). (2020c). *Preventing adverse childhood experiences.* https://www.cdc.gov/violenceprevention/aces/fastfact.html

Centers for Disease Control and Prevention (CDC), National Center for Health Statistics (NCHS), & Division of Vital Statistics (DVS). (2020, September 24). *Linked birth/infant death records 1995–2016, as compiled from data provided by the 57 vital statistics jurisdictions through the Vital Statistics Cooperative Program,* on CDC WONDER Online Database. https://wonder.cdc.gov/wonder/help/lbd.html

Center for Substance Abuse Treatment. (2005). *Substance abuse treatment: Group therapy treatment improvement protocol.* (Series, No. 41; HHS Publication No. [SMA] 15-3991). Substance Abuse and Mental Health Services Administration. https://store.samhsa.gov/product/TIP-41-Substance-Abuse-Treatment-Group-Therapy/SMA15-3991

Charlet, K., & Heinz, A. (2017). Harm reduction—a systematic review on the effects of alcohol reduction on physical and mental health symptoms. *Addiction Biology, 22*(5), 1119–1159. https://doi.org/10.1111/adb.12414

Chazin, R., Kaplan, S., & Terio, S. (2000). The strengths perspective in brief treatment with culturally diverse clients. *Crisis Intervention, 6*(1), 41–50. https://doi.org/10.1080/10645130008951295

Chemtob, C. M., Hamada, R. S., Bauer, G., Torigoe, R. Y., & Kinney, B. (1988). Patient suicide: Frequency and impact on psychologists. *Professional Psychology Research and Practice, 19*(4), 416. https://doi.org/10.1037/0735-7028.19.4.416

Chen, E. C., Kakkad, D., & Balzano, J. (2008). Multicultural competence and evidence-based practice in group therapy. *Journal of Clinical Psychology, 64*(11), 1261–1278. https://doi.org/10.1002/jclp.20533

Chen, Y., Zhonglin, W., & Ye, M. (2017). Exploring profiles of work regulatory focus: A person-centered approach. *Personality and Individual Differences, 116,* 16–21. https://doi.org/10.1016/j.paid.2017.04.019

Chenoweth, E., Stephan, M. J., & Stephan, M. J. (2011). *Why civil resistance works: The strategic logic of nonviolent conflict.* Columbia University Press.

Cheshire, A. (n.d.). Ethics of genetic testing—a social work perspective. *Social Work Today, 14*(1), 20. https://www.socialworktoday.com/archive/012014p20.shtml

Chiang, M., Reid-Varley, W. B., & Fan, X. (2019). Creative art therapy for mental illness. *Psychiatry Research, 275,* 129–136. https://doi.org/10.1016/j.psychres.2019.03.025

Child Welfare Information Gateway (2016). *Racial disproportionality and disparity in child welfare.* U.S. Department of Health and Human Services, Children's Bureau.

Children's Bureau (HHS), Child Welfare Information Gateway, FRIENDS National Resource Center for Community-Based Child Abuse Prevention, & Center for the Study of Social Policy-Strengthening Families. (2011). Strengthening Families and Communities: 2011 Resource Guide. "https://www.childwelfare.gov/pubs/guide2011/guide.pdf#page=17"www.childwelfare.gov/pubs/guide2011/guide.pdf#page=17.

Chou, Y. C., & Rooney, R. H. (2010). 23. Task-centered practice in Taiwan. In A. E. Fortune, P. McCallion, & K. Briar-Lawson (Eds.), *Social work practice research for the twenty-first century* (pp. 245–250). Columbia University Press.

Chovanec, M. G. (2012). Examining engagement of men in a domestic abuse program from three perspectives: An exploratory multimethod study. *Social Work with Groups, 35*(4), 362–378. https://doi.org/10.1080/01609513.2012.669351

Citron, P. (1978). Group work with alcoholic poly drug-involved adolescents with deviant behavior syndrome. *Social Work with Groups, 1*(1), 39–52.

Clark, A. J., & Butler, C. M. (2020). Empathy: An integral model in clinical social work. *Social Work, 65*(2), 169–177. https://doi.org/10.1300/J009v01n01_05

Cleaveland, C. (2010). "We are not criminals." Social work advocacy and unauthorized migrants. *Social Work, 55*(1), 74–81. http://www.jstor.org/stable/23719839

Clemons, J. W. (2014). Client system assessment tools for social worker practice. North American Association of Christians in Social Work. Presented at the NACSW Convention, Annapolis, MD.

Clifford, D., & Burke, B. (2005). Developing anti-oppression ethics in the new curriculum. *Social Work Education, 24*(6), 677–692. https://doi.org/10.1080/02615470500185101

Coady, N., & Lehmann, P. (Eds.). (2016). *Theoretical perspectives for direct social work practice: A generalist-eclectic approach.* Springer.

Coady, N., & Marziali, E. (1994). The association between global and specific measures of the therapeutic relationship. *Psychotherapy: Theory, Research, Practice, Training, 31*(1), 17. https://doi.org/10.1037/0033-3204.31.1.17

Cohen, J. A., Mannarino, A. P., Murray, L. K. (2011). Trauma-focused CBT for youth who experience ongoing traumas. Child Abuse and Neglect, 35(8), 637–646. https://doi.org/10.1016/j.chiabu.2011.05.002

Cohen, J. A., Mannarino, A. P., Jankowski, M. K., Rosenberg, S., Kodya, S., & Wolford, G. (2016). A randomized implementation study of trauma-focused cognitive behavioral therapy for adjudicated teens in residential treatment facilities. *Child Maltreatment, 21*(2), 156–167. https://doi.org/10.1177/1077559515624775

Collins, C., Landivar, LC., Ruppanner, L, Scarborough, WJ. (2021). COVID-19 and the gender gap in work hours. Gender, Work & Organization, 28 (S1),101–112.

Congress, E. P. (2000). Crisis intervention with diverse families. In A. R. Roberts (Ed.), *Crisis intervention handbook: Assessment, treatment and research* (2nd ed., pp. 430–448). Oxford University Press.

Congress, E. P., & Lynn, M. (1994). Group work programs in public schools: Ethical dilemmas and cultural diversity. *Social Work in Education, 16*(2), 107–114. https://doi.org/10.1093/cs/16.2.107

Conn, V. S., & Ruppar, T. M. (2017). Medication adherence outcomes of 771 intervention trials: Systematic review and meta-analysis. *Preventive Medicine, 99,* 269–276. https://doi.org/10.1016/j.ypmed.2017.03.008

Connell, J., Grant, S., & Mullin, T. (2006). Client initiated termination of therapy at NHS primary care counselling services. Counselling & Psychotherapy Research, 6(1), 60–67.

Connell, C. M., Lang, J. M., Zorba, B., & Stevens, K. (2019). Enhancing capacity for trauma-informed care in child welfare: Impact of a statewide systems change initiative. *American Journal of Community Psychology, 64* (3–4), 467–480. https://doi.org/10.1002/ajcp.12375

Conner, K., & Grote, N. K. (2008). Enhancing the cultural relevance of empirically-supported mental health interventions. *Families in Society, 89*(4), 587–595. https://doi.org/10.1606/1044-3894.3821

Connolly, J. F. (2013). *Stress and coping in university employees: a longitudinal evaluation of stress, personality, coping and psychological distress* (Doctoral dissertation). Queen Margaret University, Edinburgh.

Conrad, D., & Kellar-Guenther, Y. (2006). Compassion fatigue, burnout and compassion satisfaction among Colorado child protection workers. *Child Abuse and Neglect, 30*(10), 1071–1080. https://doi.org/10.1016/j.chiabu.2006.03.009

Contreras, J. M., Banaji, M. R., & Mitchell, J. P. (2013). Multivoxel patterns in fusiform face area differentiate faces by sex and race. *PloS one, 8*(7), e69684. https://doi.org/10.1371/journal.pone.0069684

Cooper, M. (2020, March 15). *Tracking the impact of the coronavirus on the U.S.* https://www.nytimes.com/live/2020/coronavirus-usa

Corcoran, J. (1997). A solution-oriented approach to working with juvenile offenders. *Child and Adolescent Social Work Journal, 14*(4), 227–288. https://doi.org/10.1023/A:1024546425621

Corcoran, J. (1998). Solution-focused practice with middle and high school at-risk youth. *Children and Schools, 20*(4), 232–243. https://doi.org/10.1093/cs/20.4.232

Corcoran, J. (2008). Solution-focused therapy. In N. Coady & P. Lehmann (Eds.), *Theoretical perspectives for direct social work practice: A generalist-eclectic approach* (2nd ed., pp. 429–446). Springer.

Corcoran, J., & Pillai, V. (2009). A review of the research on solution-focused therapy. *British Journal of Social Work, 39*(2), 234–242. https://doi.org/10.1093/bjsw/bcm098

Corcoran, J., & Walsh, J. (2010). *Clinical assessment and diagnosis in social work practice* (2nd ed.). Oxford University Press.

Corcoran, K., & Vandiver, V. (1996). *Maneuvering the maze of managed care: Skills for mental health practitioners.* Free Press.

Corey, G. (1990). *Theory and practice of group counseling.* Brooks/Cole.

Corey, G. (2009). *Theory and practice of counseling and psychotherapy* (8th ed.). Brooks/Cole.

Corey, M. S., & Corey, G. (1992). *Groups: Process and practice* (4th ed.). Brooks/Cole.

Corey, M. S., & Corey, G. (2006). *Groups: Process and practice* (7th ed.). Brooks/Cole.

Corey, M. S., Corey, G., & Corey, C. (2013). *Groups: Process and practice* (9th ed.). Cengage.

Corey, M. S., Corey, G., & Corey, C. (2017). *Groups: Process and practice* (10th ed.). Cengage.

Corey, G., Corey, M. S., Corey, C., & Callanan, P. (2014). *Issues and ethics in the helping professions* (9th ed.). Brooks/Cole.

Corey, MS., Corey, G., Corey, C. (2018). Groups: Process and Practice (10th Edition). Cengage Publishers.

Corey, G., Haynes, R. H., Moulton, P., & Muratori, M. (2014). *Clinical supervision in the helping professions: A practical guide* (2nd ed.). Wiley, American Counseling Association.

Cormier, S., Nurius, P. S., & Osborn, C. J. (2009). *Interviewing and change strategies for helpers: Fundamental skills in cognitive behavioral interventions* (6th ed.). Brooks/Cole.

Corwin, M. (2002). *Brief treatment in clinical social work practice.* Brooks/Cole.

Costa, U. M., Brauchle, G., & Kennedy-Behr, A. (2017). Collaborative goal setting with and for children as part of therapeutic intervention. *Disability and Rehabilitation, 39*(16), 1589–1600. https://doi.org/10.1080/09638288.2016.1202334

Council on Social Work Education (CSWE). (2018). *Specialized practice curricular guide for macro social work practice.* https://www.cswe.org/getattachment/Education-Resources/2015-Curricular-Guides/2015-Macro-Guide-Web-Version.pdf.aspx

Council on Social Work Education (CSWE). (2022). *Educational policy and accreditation standards*. Alexandria, VA: Council on Social Work Education. https://cswe.org/getattachment/Accreditation /Information/2022-EPAS/EPAS-2022-Draft-1-April-2021-(2).pdf.aspx

Council on Social Work Education (CSWE). (n.d.). *International social work degree recognition and evaluation service*. https://www.cswe.org /Accreditation/Other/International-Degree-Review.aspx

Cournoyer, B. (2016). *The social work skills workbook* (8th ed.). Brooks/ Cole, Cengage Learning.

Courtney, S. J. (2020). Why you should reject entrepreneurial leadership. In J. S. Brooks & A. Heffernan (Eds.), *The school leadership survival guide: What to do when things go wrong, how to learn from mistakes and why you should prepare for the worst* (pp. 409–421). Information Age Publishing, Inc.

Creative Social Worker. (2014, April 2). Ending the therapeutic relationship: Creative termination activities. SWHELPER. https:// swhelper./org/2014/04/02ending-therapeutic-relationship-creative -termination-activities/

Crisp, B. R. (2017). *Routledge handbook of religion, spirituality, and social work*. Taylor & Francis.

Crosby, G., & Altman, D. (2011). Integrative cognitive-behavioral group therapy. In J. L. Kleinberg (Ed.), *Wiley-Blackwell handbook of group psychotherapy* (pp. 89–112). John Wiley & Sons, Ltd. https://doi .org/10.1002/9781119950882.ch5

Crosby, S. D. (2016). Trauma-informed approaches to juvenile justice: A critical race perspective. *Juvenile & Family Court Journal, 67*(1), 5–18. https://doi.org/10.1111/jfcj.12052

Crutchfield, J., Fisher, A., & Webb, S. (2017). Colorism in police killings of unarmed African Americans: A retrospective descriptive analysis from 1999–2014. *Western Journal of Black Studies, 41*(3), 1–20.

Cuijpers, P., Veen, S. C. V., Sijbrandij, M., Yoder, W., & Cristea, I. A. (2018). Eye movement desensitization and reprocessing for mental health problems: A systematic review and meta-analysis. *Cognitive Behaviour Therapy, 49*(3), 165–180. https://ssrn.com/abstract=3244037

Cummings, N. A. (1991). Brief intermittent therapy throughout the life cycle. In C. S. E. Austad & W. H. Berman (Eds.), *Psychotherapy in managed health care: The optimal use of time and resources* (pp. 35–45). American Psychological Association.

Cummings, T. G., & Worley, C. G. (2014). *Organization development and change*. Cengage Learning.

Curry-Stevens, A., & Nissen, L. B. (2011). Reclaiming Futures considers an anti-oppressive frame to decrease disparities. *Children and Youth Services Review, 33*, S54–S59. https://doi.org/10.1016 /j.childyouth.2011.06.013

Cushing, R. E., & Braun, K. L. (2018). Mind–body therapy for military veterans with post-traumatic stress disorder: A systematic review. *Journal of Alternative and Complementary Medicine, 24*(2), 106–114. https://doi.org/10.1089/acm.2017.0176

D

10/66 Dementia Research Group (2009). *Helping carers to care: Trainers manual*. Alzheimer's Disease International.

Dalphon, H. (2019). Self-care techniques for social workers: Achieving an ethical harmony between work and well-being. *Journal of Human Behavior in the Social Environment, 29*(1), 85–95. https://doi.org /10.1080/10911359.2018.1481802

Danso, R. (2018). Cultural competence and cultural humility: A critical reflection on key cultural diversity concepts. *Journal of Social Work, 18*(4), 410–430. https://doi.org/10.1080/10911359.2018.1481802

Darling, N. (2007). Ecological systems theory: The person in the center of the circles. *Research in Human Development, 4*(3–4), 203–217. https://doi.org/10.1080/15427600701663023

Darrell, L., & Rich, T. (2017). Faith and field: The ethical inclusion of spirituality and the pedagogy of social work. *Field Educator, 7*(1), 1–11.

D'Arrigo-Patrick,J., Hoff,C., Knudson-Martin,C., Tuttle, A.(2016). Navigating Critical Theory and Postmodernism: Social Justice and Therapist Power in Family Therapy. Family Process, 56(3), 574–588. https://doi.org/10.1111/famp.12236

Datta, A., & Deb, S. (2020). Group work over a digital platform: Understanding middle-class struggle in pandemic. *Social Work with Groups, 44*(1), 34–38. https://doi.org/10.1080/01609513.2020.1796059

Davis, I. P., & Reid, W. J. (1988). Event analysis in clinical practice and process research. *Social Casework, 69*(5), 298–306. https://doi .org/10.1177/104438948806900507

Day-Vines, N. L., Cluxton-Keller, F., Agorsor, C., Gubara, S., & Otabil, N. A. A. (2020). The multidimensional model of broaching behavior. *Journal of Counseling & Development, 98*(1), 107–118. https:// doi.org/10.1002/jcad.12304

Day-Vines, N. L., Wood, S. M., Grothaus, T., Craigen, L., Holman, A., Dotson-Blake, K., & Douglass, M. J. (2007). Broaching the subjects of race, ethnicity, and culture during the counseling process. *Journal of Counseling & Development, 85*(4), 401–409. https://doi .org/10.1002/j.1556-6678.2007.tb00608.x

Dean, M. (2014, May 19). *Group art therapy*. Center for Psyche & the Arts. http://psychearts.org/2014/05/group-art-therapy/

Deblinger, E., Pollio, E., & Dorsey, S. (2016). Applying trauma-focused cognitive–behavioral therapy in group format. *Child Maltreatment, 21*(1), 59–73. https://doi.org/10.1177/1077559515620668

DeCandia, C., & Guarino, K. (2015). Trauma-informed care: An ecological response. *Journal of Child and Youth Care Work, 25*, 7–32. https:// doi.org/10.5195/jcycw.2015.69

Decety, J., & Jackson, P. L. (2004). The functional architecture of human empathy. *Behavioral and Cognitive Neuroscience Reviews, 3*(2), 71–100. https://doi.org/10.1177/1534582304267187

Decker, J. T., Brown, J. L. C., Ashley, W., & Lipscomb, A. E. (2019). Mindfulness, meditation, and breathing exercises: Reduced anxiety for clients and self-care for social work interns. *Social Work with Groups, 42*(4), 308–322. https://doi.org/10.1080/01609513.2019.1 571763

de Shazer, S. and Dolan, Y. (2007) More than Miracles: The State of the Art of Solution-Focused Brief Therapy. Haworth Press, Binghamton.

De Jong, P., & Berg, I. K. (2001). Co-constructing cooperation with mandated clients. *Social Work, 46*(4), 361–374. https://doi.org/10.1093 /sw/46.4.361

De Jong, P., & Berg, I. K. (2002). *Learner's workbook for interviewing for solutions* (2nd ed.). Brooks/Cole.

De Jong, P., & Berg, I. K. (2012). *Interviewing for solutions* (4th ed). Brooks/Cole, Cengage Learning.

De Jong, P., & Miller, S. D. (1995). How to interview for client strengths. *Social Work, 40*(6), 729–736.

Delgadillo, J., & Groom, M. (2017). Using psychoeducation and role induction to improve completion rates in cognitive behavioural therapy. *Behavioural and Cognitive Psychotherapy, 45*(2), 170–184. https://doi.org/10.1017/S1352465816000643

DeLine, C. (2000). *The back door: An experiment or an alternative*. The Back Door.

DeLuca, J. S., O'Connor, L. K., & Yanos, P. T. (2018). Assertive community treatment with people with combined mental illness and criminal justice involvement. In E. Jeglic & C. Calkins (Eds.), *New frontiers in offender treatment* (pp. 227–249). Springer.

Demby, G. (2013). *A battle for fair housing still raging, but mostly forgotten*. http://www.npr.org/sections/codeswitch/2013/12/01/248039354 /a-battle-forfair-housing-still-raging-but-mostly-forgotten

de Shazer, S. (1988). *Clues: Investigating solutions in brief therapy*. Norton.

de Shazer, S., & Berg, I. K. (1993). Constructing solutions. *The Family Therapy Networker, 12*(5), 42–43.

de Shazer, S., Dolan, Y., Korman, H., Trepper, T., McCollum, E., & Berg, I. K. (2021). *More than miracles: The state of the art of solution-focused brief therapy*. Routledge.

Dettlaff, A. J., & Boyd, R. (2020). Racial disproportionality and disparities in the child welfare system: Why do they exist, and what can be done to address them? *Annals of the American Academy of Political and Social Science, 692*(1), 253–274. https://doi.org/10.1177/0002716220980329

Dettlaff, AJ & Fong, R. (2016) Immigrant and Refugee Children and Families Culturally Responsive Practice. Columbia University Press Devore, W., & Schlesinger, E. G. (1999). *Ethnic-sensitive social work practice* (5th ed.). Allyn & Bacon.

Dickson, D. T. (1998). *Confidentiality and privacy in social work.* Free Press.

Dietz, C. (2000). Reshaping clinical practice for the new millennium. *Journal of Social Work Education, 36*(3), 503–520. https://doi.org/10.1080/10437797.2000.10779025

Dishion, T. J., & Tipsord, J. M. (2011). Peer contagion in child and adolescent social and emotional development. *Annual Review of Psychology, 62,* 189–214. https://doi.org/10.1146/annurev.psych.093008.100412

Doctor, J. N., Nguyen, A., Lev, R., Lucas, J., Knight, T., Zhao, H., & Menchine, M. (2018). Opioid prescribing decreases after learning of a patient's fatal overdose. *Science, 361*(6402), 588–590. https://doi.org/10.1126/science.aat4595

Doherty, W. J. (1995). *Soul-searching: When psychotherapy must promote moral responsibility.* Basic Books.

Dominelli, L. (2018). *Anti-racist social work* (4th ed.). Palgrave.

Donovan, K., & Regehr, C. (2010). Elder abuse: Clinical, ethical, and legal considerations in social work practice. *Clinical Social Work Journal, 38*(2), 174–182. https://doi.org/10.1007/s10615-010-0269-2

Dooley, J., Sellers, S., & Gordon-Hempe, C. (2009). Lemons to lemonade: How five challenges in teaching macro practice helped to strengthen our course. *Journal of Teaching in Social Work, 29*(4), 431–448. https://doi.org/10.1080/08841230903249760

Dorfman, R. A. (1996). *Clinical social work: Definition, practice, and vision.* Brunner/Mazel.

Doster, J., & Nesbitt, J. (1979). Psychotherapy and self-disclosure. In G. Chelune & Associates (Eds.), *Self-disclosure: Origins, patterns, and implications of openness in interpersonal relationships* (pp. 177–224). Jossey-Bass.

Drake, R. E., Goldman, H. H., Leff, H. S., Lehman, A. F., Dixon, L., Mueser, K. T., & Torrey, W. C. (2001). Implementing evidence-based practices in routine mental health service settings. *Psychiatric Services, 52*(2), 179–182. https://doi.org/10.1176/appi.ps.52.2.179

Drisko, J. W. (2004). Common factors in psychotherapy outcome: Meta-analytic findings and their implications for practice and research. *Families in Society, 85*(1), 81–90. https://doi.org/10.1606/1044-3894.239

Duan, C., & Hill, C. E. (1996). The current state of empathy research. *Journal of Counseling Psychology, 43*(3), 261–274. https://doi.org/10.1037/0022-0167.43.3.261

Dube, S. R., Anda, R. F., Felitti, V. J., Chapman, D. P., Williamson, D. F., & Giles, W. H. (2001). Childhood abuse, household dysfunction, and the risk of attempted suicide throughout the lifespan: Findings from the adverse childhood experiences study. *Journal of American Medicine, 286*(24), 3089–3096. https://doi.org/10.1001/jama.286.24.3089

Dubowitz, H., & DePanfilis, D. (Eds.) (1999). *Handbook for child protection practice.* SAGE.

Dudley, J. R., Smith, C., & Millison, M. B. (1995). Unfinished business: Assessing the spiritual needs of hospice clients. *American Journal of Hospice and Palliative Care, 12*(2), 30–37. https://doi.org/10.1177/104990919501200209

Dudziak, S., & Profitt, N. J. (2012). Group work and social justice: Designing pedagogy for social change. *Social Work with Groups, 35*(3), 235–252. https://doi.org/10.1080/01609513.2011.624370

Dulcan, M. K. (2009). *Textbook of child adolescent psychiatry.* American Psychiatric Publishing.

Duncan, B. L. (2012). The partners for change outcome management system (PCOMS): The heart and soul of change project. *Canadian Psychology, 53*(2), 93. https://doi.org/10.1037/a0027762

Durlak, J. A., Weissberg, R. P., Dymnicki, A. B., Taylor, R. D., & Schellinger, K. B. (2011). The impact of enhancing students' social and emotional learning: A meta-analysis of school-based universal interventions. *Child Development, 82*(1), 405–432. https://doi.org/10.1111/j.1467-8624.2010.01564.x

Duvall, E. M. (1977). *Marriage and family development* (5th ed.). Lippincott.

E

Eamon, M. K., & Zhang, S.-J. (2006). Do social work students assess and address economic barriers to clients implementing agreed task? *Journal of Social Work Education, 42*(3), 525–542. https://doi.org/10.5175/JSWE.2006.200404131

Ebner, S. A., Meikis, L., Morat, M., Held, S., Morat, T., & Donath, L. (2021). Effects of movement-based mind-body interventions on physical fitness in healthy older adults: a meta-analytical review. *Gerontology, 67*(2), 125–143. https://doi.org/10.1159/000512675

Ebrary. (2021). Forming/preaffiliation. https://ebrary.net/3066/management/formingpreaffiliation

Edgoose, J. Y., Quiogue, M., & Sidhar, K. (2019). How to identify, understand, and unlearn implicit bias in patient care. *Family Practice Management, 26*(4), 29–33.

Edin, K., & Kefalas, M. (2005). *Promises I can keep: Why poor women put motherhood before marriage.* University of California Press.

Efran, J., & Schenker, M. (1993). A potpourri of solutions: How new and different is solution-focused therapy? *Family Therapy Networker, 17*(3), 71–74.

Elbow, M. (1987). The memory books: Facilitating termination with children. *Social Casework, 68*(3), 180–183. https://doi.org/10.1177/104438948706800307

Electris, A. (n.d.). Becoming an effective art therapist in the group format. *Society for the Advancement of Psychotherapy.* https://society.forpsychotherapy.orgbook-review-of-art-based-group-therapy-theory-and-practice/

Ell, K. (1995). Crisis intervention: Research needs. In E. L. Edwards (Ed.), *Encyclopedia of social work* (19th ed., pp. 660–667). NASW Press.

Elliot, D. M., & Briere, J. (1992). Sexual abuse trauma among professional women: Validating the Trauma Symptom Checklist-40 (TSC-40). *Child Abuse & Neglect, 16*(3), 391–398. https://doi.org/10.1016/0145-2134(92)90048-V

Ellis, R. A., & Sowers, K. M. (2001). *Juvenile justice practice: A cross-disciplinary approach to intervention.* Brooks/Cole.

Ellor, J., Netting, E., & Thibault, J. (2021). *Religious and spiritual aspects of human service practice.* University of South Carolina Press.

Encyclopedia of Mental Disorders. (2021). Self-help groups. http://www.minddisorders.com/Py-Z/Self-help-groups.html

Epstein, L. (1992). *Brief treatment and a new look at the task-centered approach* (3rd ed.). Allyn & Bacon.

Epstein, R. S., Simon, R. I., & Kay, G. G. (1992). Assessing boundary violations in psychotherapy: Survey results with the Exploitation Index. *Bulletin of the Menninger Foundation, 56*(2), 150.

Erbacher, T. A., Singer, J., & Poland, S. (2014). *Suicide in schools: A practitioner's guide to multi-level prevention, assessment, intervention, and postvention.* Routledge.

Erez, M. (2013). Cross-cultural issues in goal setting. In E. A. Locke & G. P. Latham (Eds.), *New developments in goal setting and task performance* (pp. 509–519). Routledge.

Esaki, N., & Larkin, H. (2013). Prevalence of adverse childhood experiences (ACE) among child services providers. *Families in Society, 94*(1), 31–37. https://doi.org/10.1606/1044-3894.4257

Etherington, K. (2000). Supervising counselors who work with survivors of childhood sexual abuse. *Counseling Psychology Quarterly, 13*(4), 377–389. https://doi.org/10.1080/713658497

Evans, S., Fernandez, S., Olive, L., Payne, L. A., & Mikocka-Walus, A. (2019). Psychological and mind-body interventions for endometriosis: A systematic review. *Journal of Psychosomatic Research, 124,* 109756. https://doi.org/10.1016/j.jpsychores.2019.109756

Ewing, J. A. (1984). Detecting alcoholism: The CAGE questionnaire. *JAMA, 252*(14), 1905–1907. https://doi.org/10.1001/jama.252.14.1905-1907.

Ezhumalai, S., Muralidhar, D., Dhanasekarapandian, R., & Nikketha, B. S. (2018). Group interventions. *Indian Journal of Psychiatry, 60*(Suppl 4), S514.

F

Farber, B. A. (2006). *Self disclosure in psychotherapy.* Guilford.

Fast, J. D. (2003). After Columbine: How people mourn sudden death. *Social Work, 48*(4), 484–491. https://doi.org/10.1093/sw/48.4.484

Fauth, J., & Hayes, J. A. (2006). Counselors' stress appraisals as predictors of countertransference behavior with male clients. *Journal of Counseling and Development, 84*(4), 430–439. https://doi.org/10.1002/j.1556-6678.2006.tb00427.x

Feigin, R., Cohen, I., & Gilard, M. (1998). The use of single-group sessions in discharge planning. *Social Work in Health Care, 26*(3), 19–38. https://doi.org/10.1300/J010v26n03_02

Feltenstein, M. W., & See, R. E. (2008). The neurocircuitry of addiction: An overview. *British Journal of Pharmacology, 154*(2), 261–274. https://doi.org/10.1038/bjp.2008.51

Felton, E. (2020). Telemental health. *National Association of Social Workers.* https://www.socialworkers.org/LinkClick.aspx?fileticket=evgx77RtVLI%3D&portalid=0

Figley, C. R. (Ed.). (1995). *Compassion fatigue: Dealing with secondary traumatic stress disorder in those who treat the traumatized.* Brunner/Mazel.

Figley, C. R. (2002a). Compassion fatigue: Psychotherapists' chronic lack of self-care. *Journal of Clinical Psychology, 58*(11), 1433–1441. https://doi.org/10.1002/jclp.10090

Figley, C. R. (Ed.). (2002b). *Treating compassion fatigue.* Brunner-Routledge.

Finn, J. L., & Jacobson, M. (2003). Just practice: Steps toward a new social work paradigm. *Journal of Social Work Education, 39*(1), 57–78. https://doi.org/10.1080/10437797.2003.10779119

Finn, J. L. (2021). *Just practice: A social justice approach to social work.* 4th ed. Oxford University Press.

Fischer, J., & Corcoran, K. (2006). *Measures for clinical practice and research: Couples, families, and children, A sourcebook, Vol. 1* (4th ed.). Oxford University Press.

Fischer, J., & Corcoran, K. (2007). *Measures for clinical practice and research: Adults, A sourcebook, Vol. 2* (4th ed.). Oxford University Press.

Fischer, J., Corcoran, K., & Springer, D. W. (2020). *Measures for clinical practice and research.* Oxford University Press.

Fisher, L. (2019). Reading for Reform: The social work of literature in the progressive era. University of Minnesota Press.

Fisher-Borne, M., Cain, J. M., & Martin, S. L. (2015). From mastery to accountability: Cultural humility as an alternative to cultural competence. *Social Work Education, 34*(2), 165–181. https://doi.org/10.1080/02615479.2014.977244

Fisk, M., Livingstone, A., & Pit, S.W. (2020). Telehealth in the context of COVID-19: Changing perspectives in Australia, the United Kingdom, and the United States. *Journal of Medical Internet Research, 22*(6), e19264. https://doi.org/10.2196/19264

FitzGerald, C., & Hurst, S. (2017). Implicit bias in healthcare professionals: A systematic review. *BMC Medical Ethics, 18*(1), 1–18. https://doi.org/10.1186/s12910-017-0179-8

Flannery, R. B., & Everly, G. S. (2000). Crisis intervention: A review. *International Journal of Emergency Mental Health, 2*(2), 119–126.

Flückiger, C., Rubel, J., Del Re, A. C., Horvath, A. O., Wampold, B. E., Crits-Christoph, P., … & Barber, J. P. (2020). The reciprocal relationship between alliance and early treatment symptoms: A two-stage individual participant data meta-analysis. *Journal of Consulting and Clinical Psychology, 88*(9), 829–842. https://doi.org/10.1037/ccp0000594

Foa, E. B., & Rothbaum. B.O. (1998). *Treating the trauma of rape.* Guilford.

Food and Agriculture Organization of the United Nations. (2010). *Developing effective forest policy—a guide.* FAO Forestry. http://www.fao.org/3/i1679e/i1679e00.htm

Food and Drug Administration (FDA). (2018). Finding and learning about side effects (adverse reactions). https://www.fda.gov/drugs//drug-information-consumersfinding-and-learning-about-side-effects-adverse-reactions

Ford, J. D., & Blaustein, M. E. (2013). Systemic self-regulation: A framework for trauma-informed services in residential juvenile justice programs. *Journal of Family Violence, 28*(7), 665–677. https://doi.org/10.1007/s10896-013-9538-5

Ford, J. D., Chapman, J., Connor, D. F., & Cruise, K. R. (2012). Complex trauma and aggression in secure juvenile justice settings. *Criminal Justice and Behavior, 39*(6), 694–724. https://doi.org/10.1177/0093854812436957

Foronda, C., Baptiste, D. L., Reinholdt, M. M., & Ousman, K. (2016). Cultural humility: A concept analysis. *Journal of Transcultural Nursing, 27*(3), 210–217. doi.org/10.1177/1043659615592677

Fortune, A. E. (1985). Treatment groups. In A. E. Fortune (Ed.), *Task-centered practice with families and groups* (pp. 33–44). Springer.

Fortune, A. E., McCallion, P., & Briar-Lawson, K. (Eds.). (2010). *Social work practice research for the twenty-first century.* Columbia University Press.

Fortune, A. E., Pearlingi, B., & Rochelle, C. D. (1992). Reactions to termination of individual treatment. *Social Work, 37*(2), 171–178.

Fortune, C. A., Bourke, P., & Ward, T. (2015). Expertise and child sex offenders. *Aggression and Violent Behavior, 20*, 33–41. doi.org/10.1016/j.avb.2014.12.005

Franklin, D. L. (1986). Mary Richmond and Jane Addams: From moral certainty to rational inquiry in social work practice. *Social Service Review, 60*(4), 504–525. doi.org/10.1086/644396

Franklin, M., Lewis, S., Willis, K., Rogers, A., Venville, A, & Smith, L. (2019). Goals for living with chronic conditions: The relevance of temporalities, dispositions, and resources. *Social Science & Medicine, 233*, 13–20. doi.org/10.1016/j.socscimed.2019.05.031

Fraser, M. W. (2003). Intervention research in social work: A basis for evidence-based practice and practice guidelines. In A. Rosen and E. K. Proctor (Eds.), *Developing practice guidelines for social work intervention: Issues, methods, and research agents* (pp. 17–36). Columbia University Press.

Fraser, M. W. (Ed.). (2004). *Risk and resilience in childhood: An ecological perspective* (2nd ed.). NASW Press.

Frey, G. A. (1990). Framework for promoting organizational change. *Families in Society, 71*(3), 142–147. https://doi.org/10.1177/104438949007100303

Fried, A. E., & Dunn, M. (2012). The Expectancy Challenge Alcohol Literacy Curriculum (ECALC): A single session group intervention to reduce alcohol use. *Psychology of Addictive Behaviors, 26*(3), 615–620. https://doi.org/10.1037/a0027585

Friedlander, M. L., Escudero, V., Welmers-van de Poll, M.,& Heatherington, L. (2018). Alliances in couple and family therapy. In J.C. Norcross & M. J. Lambet (Eds.). *Psychotherapy Relationships that Work: Volume 1* (3rd ed). Pp. 117–166. Oxford University Press.

Friesen, M. (2007). Perceptions of social justice in New Zealand. *Pursuing Social Justice in New Zealand, 14*, 143–158.

Fullerton, C. D., & Ursano, R. J. (2005). Psychological and psychopathological consequences of disasters. In J. J. Lopez-Ibor, G. Christodoulou, M. Maj, N. Sartorius, & A. Okasha (Eds.), *Disaster and mental health* (pp. 25–49). Wiley.

Furman, R. (2009). Ethical considerations of evidence-based practice. *Social Work, 54*(1), 57–59. https://doi.org/10.1093/sw/54.1.82

G

Galinsky, M. J., & Schopler, J. H. (1985). Developmental patterns in open-ended groups. *Social Work with Groups, 12*(2), 99–114. https://doi.org/10.1300/J009v12n02_08

Gallagher, A. (2020). *Slow ethics and the art of care*. Emerald Publishing.

Gallo, J. J. (2005). Activities of daily living and instrumental activities of daily living assessment. In J. J. Gallo, H. R. Bogner, T. Fulmer, & G. Paveza (Eds.), *Handbook of geriatric assessment* (4th ed., 193–240). Jones and Bartlett.

Gallo, J. J., Bogner, H. R., Fulmer, T., & Paveza, J. (Eds.). (2005). *Handbook of geriatric assessment* (4th ed.). Jones and Bartlett.

Gallo, J. J., Fulmer, T., Paveza, G. J., & Reichel, W. (Eds.). (2000). *Handbook of geriatric assessment* (3rd ed.). Aspen.

Galpin, T. J. (1996). *The human side of change: A practical guide to organization redesign*. Jossey-Bass.

Gambrill, E. (1977). *Behavior modification: Handbook of assessment, intervention, and evaluation*. Jossey-Bass.

Gambrill, E. (2007). Views of evidence-based practice: Social workers' code of ethics and accreditation standards as guides for choice. *Journal of Social Work Education, 43*(3), 447–462. https://doi.org/10.5175/JSWE.2007.200600639

Ganna, A., Verweij, K. J., Nivard, M. G., Maier, R., Wedow, R., Busch, A. S., ... & Zietsch, B. P. (2019). Large-scale GWAS reveals insights into the genetic architecture of same-sex sexual behavior. *Science, 365*(6456). doi: 10.1126/science.aat7693

Gardner, F. (2000). Design evaluation: Illuminating social work practice for better outcomes. *Social Work, 45*(2), 176–182. https://doi.org/10.1093/sw/45.2.176

Garland, J., Jones, H., & Kolodny, R. (1965). A model for stages in the development of social work groups. In S. Bernstein (Ed.), *Explorations in group work*. Milford House.

Garner, I. W., & Holland, C. A. (2020). Age-friendliness of living environments from the older person's viewpoint: Development of the age-friendly environment assessment tool. *Age and Aging, 49*(2) 193–198. https://doi.org/10.1093/ageing/afz146

Garthwait, C. (2012). *Dictionary of social work*. University of Montana.

Gartrell, N. K. (1992). Boundaries in lesbian therapy relationships. *Women & Therapy, 12*(3), 29–50. https://doi.org/10.1300/J015V12N03_03

Garvin, C. D., & Galinsky, M. J. (2008). Groups. In T. Mizrahi & L. E. Davis (Eds.), *Encyclopedia of social work*. Oxford University Press.

Gavin, D. R., Ross, H. E., & Skinner, H. A. (1989). Diagnostic validity of the drug abuse screening test in the assessment of DSM-III drug disorders. *British Journal of Addiction, 84*(3), 301–307. https://doi.org/10.1111/j.1360-0443.1989.tb03463.x

Gelkopf, M. (2011). The use of humor in serious mental illness: A review. *Evidence-Based Complementary and Alternative Medicine, 2011*, 1–8. https://doi.org/10.1093/ecam/nep106

Gelman, C. R., & Mirabito, D. M. (2005). Practicing what we teach: Using case studies from 911 to teach crisis intervention from a generalist perspective. *Journal of Social Work Education, 41*(3), 479–494. https://doi.org/10.5175/JSWE.2005.200303116

George, L. (2011). Working in the transference and promoting self-determination: Treating beliefs as opinions rather than certainties. *Psychoanalytic Social Work, 18*(2), 93–106. https://doi.org/10.1080/15228878.2011.611785

Gerdes, K. E., & Segal, E. (2013). Importance of empathy for social work practice: Integrating new science. *Social Work, 56*(2), 141–148. https://doi.org/10.1093/sw/56.2.141

Germain, C. B., & Gitterman, A. (1996). *The life model of social work practice: Advances in theory and practice* (2nd ed.). Columbia University Press.

Gibbs, L. (2002). *Evidence-based practice for the helping professions: A practical guide with integrated multimedia*. Cengage.

Gibson, P. A. (1999). African American grandmothers: New mothers again. *Affilia, 14*(3), 329–343. https://doi.org/10.1177/08861099922093680

Gilbert, N. (1977). The search for professional identity. *Social Work, 22*(5), 401–406.

Gilgun, J. F. (1994). Hand to glove: The grounded theory approach and social work practice research. In L. Sherman & W. J. Reid (Eds.), *Qualitative research in social work* (pp. 115–125). Columbia University Press.

Gilgun, J. F. (2001). CASPARS: New tools for assessing client risks and strengths. *Families in Society, 80*(5), 450–459. https://doi.org/10.1606/1044-3894.1474

Gladding, S. T., & Binkley, E. (2007). Advancing groups: Practical ways leaders can work through some problematic situations. *Professional Counseling Digest*, https://www.counseling.org/resources/library/ACA%20Digests/ACAPCD-11.pdf

Gladstone, R. (2018, June 26). Trump travel ban: How it affects the countries. *New York Times*. https://www.nytimes.com/2018/06/26/world/americas/trump-travel-ban-effects.html

Glisson, C. A., Dulmus, C. N., & Sower, K. M. (2012). *Social work practice with groups, communities, and organizations: Evidence-based assessment and intervention*. John Wiley & Sons.

Glossary of education reform. (2013a, December 19). The achievement gap. https://www.edglossary.org/achievement-gap/

Glossary of education reform. (2013b, August 29). The learning gap. https://www.edglossary.org/learning-gap/

Glossary of education reform. (2013c, September 3). The opportunity gap. https://www.edglossary.org/opportunity-gap/

Gluck, S. (2016). What is a self-help group? Types, examples, benefits. *HealthyPlace*. https://www.healthyplace.com/self-help/self-help-information/what-is-a-self-help-group-types-examples-benefits

Golden, D. (2017, August 9). Who's taking college spots from top Asian Americans? Privileged whites. *ProPublica*. https://www.propublica.org/article/who-is-taking-college-spots-from-top-asian-americans-privileged-whites

Goldenberg, I., & Goldenberg, H. (1991). *Family therapy: An overview* (3rd ed.). Brooks/Cole.

Goldenberg, I., & Goldenberg, H. (2004). *Family therapy: An overview* (6th ed.). Brooks/Cole.

Goldner, V. (1985). Feminism and family therapy. *Family Process, 24*(1), 31–47. https://doi.org/10.1111/j.1545-5300.1985.00031.x

Goldstein, E. G. (1997). To tell or not to tell: The disclosure of events in the therapist's life to the patient. *Clinical Social Work Journal, 25*(1), 41–58. https://doi.org/10.1023/A:1025729826627

Gone, J. (2015). Reconciling evidence-based practice and cultural competence in mental health services: Introduction to a special issue. *Transcultural Psychiatry, 52*(2), 139–149. https://doi.org/10.1177/1363461514568239

Goode, R. W., Kalarchian, M. A., Craighead, L., Conroy, M. B., Gary-Webb, T., Bennett, E., ... & Burke, L. E. (2020). Perceptions and experiences of appetite awareness training among African-American women who binge eat. *Eating and Weight Disorders, 25*(2), 275–281. doi.org/10.1007/s40519-018-0577-z

Goode, R. W., Kalarchian, M. A., Craighead, L., Conroy, M. B., Wallace Jr, J., Eack, S. M., & Burke, L. E. (2018). The feasibility of a binge eating intervention in Black women with obesity. *Eating Behaviors, 29*, 83–90. https://doi.org/10.1016/j.eatbeh.2018.03.005

Goodrich, K. M., & Luke, M. (2015). Group factors and planning issues with the LGBTQI population. In K. M. Goodrich & M. Luke (Eds.), *Group counseling with LGBTQI persons* (pp. 13–26). American Counseling Association.

Gothe, N. P., Kramer, A. F., & McAuley, E. (2014). The effects of an 8-week Hatha yoga intervention on executive function in older adults. *Journals of Gerontology Series A: Biomedical Sciences and Medical Sciences, 69*(9), 1109–1116. https://doi.org/10.1093/gerona/glu095

Grady, M. D., & Strom-Gottfried, K. (2011). No easy answers: Ethical challenges working with sex offenders. *Clinical Social Work Journal, 39*(1), 18–27. https://doi.org/10.1007/s10615-010-0270-9

Grame, C. J., Tortorici, J. S., Healey, B. J., Dillingham, J. H., & Winklebaur, P. (1999). Addressing spiritual and religious issues of clients with a history of psychological trauma. *Bulletin of the Menninger Clinic, 63*(2), 223–239.

Gray, M. (2011). Back to basics: A critique of the strengths perspective in social work. *Families in Society: The Journal of contemporary Human Services*, 91(1), 5–11. https://doi.org/10.1606/1044-3894.4054

Graybeal, C. (2001). Strengths-based social work assessment: Transforming the dominant paradigm. *Families in Society*, 82(3), 233–242. https://doi.org/10.1606/1044-3894.236

Green, D., & McDermott, F. (2010). Social work from inside and between complex systems: Perspectives on person-in-environment for today's social work. *British Journal of Social Work*, 40(8), 2414–2430. doi.org/10.1093/bjsw/bcq056

Green, R. G., Kiernan-Stern, M., & Baskind, F. R. (2005). White social workers' attitudes about people of color. *Journal of Ethnic and Cultural Diversity in Social Work*, 14(1–2), 47–68. https://doi.org/10.1300/J051v14n01_03

Greenwald, A. G., & Lai, C. K. (2020). Implicit social cognition. *Annual Review of Psychology*, 71, 419–445. https://doi.org/10.1146/annurev-psych-010419-050837

Grondin, F., & Lomanowska, A. M. (2019). Empathy in computer-mediated interactions: A conceptual framework for research and clinical practice. *Clinical Psychology Science and Practice*, 26(4), e12298. doi.org/10.1111/cpsp.12298

Grote, N. K., Zuckoff, A., Swartz, H., Bledsoe, S. E., & Geibel, S. (2007). Engaging women who are depressed and economically disadvantaged in mental health treatment. *Social Work*, 52(4), 295–308. https://doi.org/10.1093/sw/52.4.295

Guadalupe, K. L., & Lum, D. (2005). *Multidimensional contextual practice: Diversity and transcendence*. Brooks/Cole.

H

Haas, A. P., & Drescher, J. (2014). Impact of sexual orientation and gender identity on suicide risk: Implications for assessment and treatment. *Psychiatric Times*, 31(12), 24–25. https://www.psychiatrictimes.com/view/impact-sexual-orientation-and-gender-identity-suicide-risk-implications-assessment-and-treatment

Hackney, H., & Cormier, S. (2005). *The professional counselor: A professional guide to helping* (5th ed.). Pearson.

Hahn, H., Kuehn, D., Hassani, H., & Edin, K. (2019). *Relief from government-owed child support debt and its effects on parents and children*. Urban Institute. https://www.urban.org/research/publication/relief-government-owed-child-support-debt-and-its-effects-parents-and-children/view/full_report

Hall, D. L., Luberto, C. M., Philpotts, L. L., Song, R., Park, E. R., & Yeh, G. Y. (2018). Mind-body interventions for fear of cancer recurrence: A systematic review and meta-analysis. *Psycho-oncology*, 27(11), 2546–2558. https://doi.org/10.1002/pon.4757

Hall, J. A., Carswell, C., Walsh, E., Huber, D. L., & Jampoler, J. S. (2002). Iowa case management: Innovative social casework. *Social Work*, 47(2), 132–141. https://doi.org/10.1093/sw/47.2.132

Hall, W. J., Chapman, M. V., Lee, K. M., Merino, Y. M., Thomas, T. W., Payne, B. K., ... & Coyne-Beasley, T. (2015). Implicit racial/ethnic bias among health care professionals and its influence on health care outcomes: A systematic review. *American Journal of Public Health*, 105(12), e60–e76. doi:10.2105/AJPH.2015.302903

Hallett, N., & Dickens, G. L. (2017). De-escalation of aggressive behavior in healthcare settings: A concept analysis. *International Journal of Nursing Studies*, 75, 10–20. https://doi.org/10.1016/j.ijnurstu.2017.07.003

Hamilton, D., Goldsmith, A. H., & Darity Jr, W. (2009). Shedding "light" on marriage: The influence of skin shade on marriage for black females. *Journal of Economic Behavior & Organization*, 72(1), 30–50. doi.org/10.1016/j.jebo.2009.05.024

Hammond, D., Hepworth, D., & Smith, V. (1977). *Improving therapeutic communication*. Jossey-Bass.

Hannon, L., DeFina, R., & Bruch, S. (2013). The relationship between skin tone and school suspension for African Americans. *Race and Social Problems*, 5(4), 281–295. doi.org/10.1007/s12552-013-9104-z

Hanson, J. (2005). Should your lips be zipped? How therapist self-disclosure and non-disclosure affects clients. *Counseling and Psychotherapy Research*, 5(2), 96–104. https://doi.org/10.1080/17441690500226658

Hanson, R. F., & Lang, J. (2016). A critical look at trauma-informed care among agencies and systems serving maltreated youth and their families. *Child Maltreatment*, 21(2), 95–100. doi: 10.1177/1077559516635274

Hardina, D., & Obel-Jorgensen, R. (2009). Increasing social action competency: A framework for supervision. *Journal of Policy Practice*, 8(2), 89–109. doi.org/10.1080/15588740902740074

Harkin, B., Webb, T. L., Chang, B. P., Prestwich, A., Conner, M., Kellar, I., ... & Sheeran, P. (2016). Does monitoring goal progress promote goal attainment? A meta-analysis of the experimental evidence. *Psychological Bulletin*, 142(2), 198.

Haroz, E. E., Ritchey, M., Bass, J. K., Kohrt, B. A., Augustinavicius, J., Michalopoulos, L., ... & Bolton, P. (2017). How is depression experienced around the world? A systematic review of qualitative literature. *Social Science & Medicine*, 183, 151–162. doi.org/10.1016/j.socscimed.2016.12.030

Harpine, E. C. (2011). Group cohesion: The therapeutic factor in groups. In E. C. Harpine (Ed.), *Group-centered prevention programs for at-risk students* (pp. 117–140). Springer.

Harrigan, M. P., Fauri, D. P., & Netting, F. E. (1998). Termination: Extending the concept for macro social work practice. *Journal of Sociology and Social Welfare*, 25(4), 61–80.

Harris, M., & Fallot, R. D. (2001). Envisioning a trauma-informed service system: A vital paradigm shift. *New Directions for Mental Health Services*, 2001(89), 3–22. https://doi.org/10.1002/yd.23320018903

Hartford, M. (1971). *Groups in social work*. Columbia University Press.

Hartman, A. (1994). Diagrammatic assessment of family relationships. In B. R. Compton & B. Galaway (Eds.), *Social work processes* (5th ed., pp. 153–165). Brooks/Cole.

Hartman, A., & Laird, I. (1983). *Family-centered social work practice*. Free Press.

Hassan, A., & Wimpfheimer, S. (2014). *Human services management competencies: A guide for public managers*. Network for Social Work Management.

Hasenfeld, Y., & Garrow, E. E. (2012). Nonprofit service organizations, social rights, and advocacy in a neoliberal welfare state. *Social Service Review*, 86(2), 295–322. doi.org/10.1086/666391

Hawkins, A. J., Blanchard, V. L., Baldwin, S. A., & Fawcett, E. B. (2008). Does marriage and relationship education work? A meta-analytic study. *Journal of Consulting and Clinical Psychology*, 76(5), 723–734. https://doi.org/10.1037/a0012584

Hayes, S. C. (2004). Acceptance and commitment therapy, relational frame theory, and the third wave of behavioral and cognitive therapies. *Behavior Therapy*, 35(4), 639–665. https://doi.org/10.1016/S0005-7894(04)80013-3

Haynes, R., Corey, G., & Moulton, P. (2003). *Clinical supervision in the helping professions: A practical guide*. Brooks/Cole.

Hays, P. A. (2009). Integrating culturally competent based practice and evidence-based practice in cognitive behavioral therapy. *Professional Psychology Research and Practice and Multicultural Therapy*, 40(4), 354. https://doi.org/10.1037/a0016250

Love, B. & Hayes-Greene, D. (2018). The ground water approach: Building a practical understanding of structural racism. Racial Equity Institute, Retrieved from https://www.racialequityinstitute.com/groundwaterapproach

Healy, A. F., & Bourne, Jr., L. E. (Eds.). (2012). *Training cognition: Optimizing efficiency, durability, and generalizability*. Psychology Press. https://doi.org/10.4324/9780203816783

Healy, K. (2005). *Social work theories in context: Creating frameworks for practice*. Palgrave Macmillan.

Healy, L. M. (2008). Exploring the history of social work as a human rights profession. *International Social Work*, 51(6), 735–748. doi.org/10.1177/0020872808095247

Healy, L. M. (2013). International social work: Overview. In *Encyclopedia of social work*. Oxford Reference. doi: 10.1093/acrefore/9780199975839.013.561

Hebert, P. L., Sisk, J. E., & Howell, E. A. (2008). When does a difference become a disparity? Conceptualizing racial and ethnic disparities in health. *Health Affairs*, *27*(2), 374–382. doi.org/10.1377/hlthaff.27.2.374

Heck, N. C. (2016). Group psychotherapy with transgender and gender nonconforming adults: Evidence-based practice applications. *Psychiatric Clinics of North America*, *40*(1), 157–175. doi.org/10.1016/j.psc.2016.10.010

Hedegaard, H., Miniño, A. M., & Warner, M. (2020). Drug overdose deaths in the United States, 1999–2018. *NCHS Data Brief no 356*. Hyattsville, MD: National Center for Health Statistics. https://www.cdc.gov/nchs/data/databriefs/db356-h.pdf

Heisel, M. J., & Flett, G. L. (2006). The development and initial validation of the Geriatric Suicide Ideation Scale. *American Journal of Geriatric Psychiatry*, *14*(9), 742–751. https://doi.org/10.1097/01.JGP.0000218699.27899.f9

Heisel, M. J., Flett, G. L., Duberstein, P. R., & Lyness, J. M. (2005). Does the geriatric depression scale (GDS) distinguish between older adults with high versus low levels of suicidal ideation? *American Journal of Geriatric Psychiatry*, *13*(10), 876–883. https://doi.org/10.1097/00019442-200510000-00007

Hennen, A. (2014). *Stages of group development*. University of Minnesota. https://actonalz.org/sites/default/files/images/Stages%20of%20Group%20Development%20-%2010-21-14%20Extension%20Presentation.pdf

Henry, S. (1992). *Group skills in social work: A four dimensional approach* (2nd ed.). Brooks/Cole.

Herring, S. J., Cruice, J. F., Bennett, G. G., Darden, N., Wallen, J. J., Rose, M. Z., ... & Foster, G. D. (2017). Intervening during and after pregnancy to prevent weight retention among African American women. *Preventive Medicine Reports*, *7*, 119–123. doi.org/10.1016/j.pmedr.2017.05.015

Hersen, M., & Thomas, I. (Eds.). (2007). *Handbook of clinical interviewing with children*. SAGE.

Herschell, A., D., Kolko, D. J., Baumann, B. I., & Davis, A. C. (2010). The role of therapist training in the implementation of psychosocial treatments: A review and critique with recommendations. *Clinical Psychology Review*, *30*(4), 448–466. https://doi.org/10.1016/j.cpr.2010.02.005

HIPAA Medical Privacy Rule. (2003). https://www.socialworkers.org/about/legal/hipaa-help

Hoagwood, K. E., Kelleher, K., Murray, L. K., & Jensen, P. S. (2006). Implementation of evidence-based practices for children in four countries: A project of the World Psychiatric Association. *Brazilian Journal of Psychiatry*, *28*, 59–66. https://doi.org/10.1590/S1516-44462006000100012

Holbrook, T. L. (1995). Finding subjugated knowledge: Personal document research. *Social Work*, *40*(6), 746–750.

Holosko, M. (2015). Neoliberalism, globalization, and social welfare. In K. Corcoran & A. Roberts (Eds.) *Social workers' desk reference* (3rd ed., pp. 941–950). Oxford.

Homan, M. S. (2008). *Promoting community change: Making it happen in the real world* (4th ed.). Brooks/Cole.

Hook, J. N., Davis, D., Owen, J., & DeBlaere, C. (2017). *Cultural humility: Engaging diverse identities in therapy*. American Psychological Association.

Hopper, E. K., Bassuk, E. L., & Olivet, J. (2010). Shelter from the storm: Trauma-informed care in homelessness services settings. *Open Health Services and Policy Journal*, *3*(1). 80–100. https://www.homelesshub.ca/sites/default/files/cenfdthy.pdf

Horton, S. (2006). The double burden on safety net providers: Placing health disparities in the context of the privatization of health care in the US. *Social Science & Medicine*, *63*(10), 2702–2714. doi:10.1016/j.socscimed.2006.07.003

Horvath, A. O., & Bedi, R. P. (2002). The alliance. In J. C. Norcross (Ed.), *Psychotherapy relationships that work: Therapist contributions and responsiveness to patients*. Oxford.

Houston-Vega, M. K., Nuehring, E. M., & Daguio, E. R. (1997). *Prudent practice: A guide for managing malpractice risk*. NASW Press.

Howes, R. (2012, May 11). Swearing in therapy: When bad language is good. Psychology Today. https://www.psychologytoday.com/us/blog/in-therapy/201205/swearing-in-therapy

Hoyt, M. F. (2000). *Some stories are better than others: Doing what works in brief therapy and managed care*. Brunner/Mazel.

Hubble, M. A., Duncan, B. L., & Miller, S. D. (1999). *The heart and soul of change: What works in therapy?* American Psychological Association.

Human Rights Watch (2019). *World Report 2019: Our annual review of human rights around the globe*. https://www.hrw.org/sites/default/files/world_report_download/hrw_world_report_2019.pdf

Hummer, V. L., Dollard, N., Robst, J., & Armstrong, M. I. (2010). Innovations in implementation of trauma-informed care practices in youth residential treatment: A curriculum for organizational change. *Child Welfare*, *89*(2), 79–95.

Hunsley, J., Aubrey, T., Verstervelt, C. M., & Vito, D. (1999). Comparing therapist and client perspectives on reasons for psychotherapy termination. *Psychotherapy: Theory, Research, Practice, Training*, *36*(4), 380. https://doi.org/10.1037/h0087802

Hunter, M. (2007). The persistent problem of colorism: Skin tone, status, and inequality. *Sociology Compass*, *1*(1), 237–254. doi.org/10.1111/j.1751-9020.2007.00006.x

Hurster, T. (2017). Ethically informed group practice. In C. Haen, & S. Aronson (Eds.), *Handbook of child and adolescent group therapy: A practitioner's reference* (pp. 66–80). Routledge.

Husebø, A. M. L., & Husebø, T. L. (2017). Quality of life and breast cancer: How can mind–body exercise therapies help? An overview study. *Sports*, *5*(4), 79–92. https://doi.org/10.3390/sports5040079

I

International Federation of Social Workers (IFSW). (2018). *Global social work statement of ethical principles*. https://www.ifsw.org/global-social-work-statement-of-ethical-principles/

International Federation of Social Workers (IFSW). (2019). *New definition of social work*. Berne, Switzerland: International Federation of Social Workers.

International Society for Traumatic Stress Studies (ISTSS) (2018). *ISTSS PTSD prevention and treatment guidelines: Methodology and recommendations*. https://istss.org/clinical-resources/treating-trauma/new-istss-prevention-and-treatment-guidelines

Irvine, A., Drew, P., Bower, P., Brooks, H., Gellatly, J., Armitage, C. J., ... & Bee, P. (2020). Are there interactional differences between telephone and face-to-face psychological therapy? A systematic review of comparative studies. *Journal of Affective Disorders*, *265*, 120–131. https://doi.org/10.1016/j.jad.2020.01.057

Isaacson M. (2014). Clarifying concepts: cultural humility or competency. J Prof Nurs. 30(3), 251–258. https://doi.org/10.1016/j.profnurs.2013.09.011. PMID: 24939335.

Ivanoff, A. M., Blythe, B. J., & Tripodi, T. (1994). *Involuntary clients in social work practice: A research-based approach*. Aldine de Gruyter.

Isaacson, L., & Isaacson, K. (2020). Children. In H. C. Edwards, D. MacDonald, S. Whitney, & P. M. Riviera (Eds.), A practice beyond cultural humility: How clinicians can work more effectively in a diverse world (pp. 120–127). Routledge.

J

Jackson, D. D., & Weakland, J. H. (1961). Conjoint family therapy: Some considerations on theory, technique, and results. *Psychiatry*, *24*(Suppl 2), 3–45. https://doi.org/10.1080/00332747.1961.11023261

Jackson, V. (2015). Practitioner characteristics and organizational contexts as essential elements in the evidence-based practice versus cultural competence debate. *Transcultural Psychiatry*, *52*(2), 150–173. https://doi.org/10.1177/1363461515571625

James, K. (2013, April). To (all) the white girls who didn't get into the college of their dreams. *Racialicious*. https://www.reddit.com/r/Foodforthought/comments/1c3bex/to_all_the_white_girls_who_didnt_get_into_the/

James, R. K. (2008). *Crisis intervention strategies* (6th ed.). Brooks/Cole.

James, R. K., & Gilliland, B. E. (2001). *Crisis intervention strategies* (4th ed.). Brooks/Cole.

James, R. K., & Gilliland, B. E. (2005). *Crisis intervention strategies* (5th ed.). Brooks/Cole.

James, R. K., & Gilliland, B. E. (2016). *Crisis intervention strategies* (8th ed.). Cengage Learning.

Jansson, B. S. (2014). *Becoming an effective policy advocate: From policy practice to social justice* (7th ed.). Brooks/Cole.

Japan Social Workers Federation. (2005). *Code of ethics.* http://jfsw.org/code-of-ethics/

Jarrett, R. L. (1995). Growing up poor: The family experience of socially mobile youth in low-income African American neighborhoods. *Journal of Adolescent Research, 10*(1), 111–135. https://doi.org/10.1177/0743554895101007

Jennings, H. (1950). *Leadership and isolation.* Longmans Green.

Jensen, M., Agbata, I. N., Canavan, M., & McCarthy, G. (2015). Effectiveness of educational interventions for informal caregivers of individuals with dementia residing in the community: Systematic review and meta-analysis of randomized controlled trials. *International Journal of Geriatric Psychiatry, 30*(2), 130–143. https://doi.org/10.1002/gps.4208

Jessop, D. (1998). Caribbean norms vs. European ethics. *Sunday Observer* (Jamaica), *13*.

Jha, A. (2015). Minds "at attention": Mindfulness training curbs attentional lapses in military cohorts. https://doi.org/10.1371/journal.pone.0116889

Jones, C. P. (2002). Confronting institutionalized racism. *Phylon 50*(1/2), 7–22. https://doi.org/10.2307/4149999

Jones, D. M. (1996). Termination from drug treatment: Dangers and opportunities for clients of the graduation ceremony. *Social Work with Groups, 19*(3–4), 105–115. https://doi.org/10.1300/J009v19n03_09

Jordan, C, & Franklin, C (2020). Clinical assessment for social workers: Quantitative and qualitative methods (5th ed.). Oxford University Press.

Jordan, C., & Hickerson, J. (2003). Children and adolescents. In C. Jordan & C. Franklin (Eds.), *Clinical assessment for social workers: Quantitative and qualitative methods* (2nd ed., pp. 179–213). Lyceum Books.

Joyce, A. S., Duncan, S. C., Duncan, A., Kipnes, D., & Piper, W. E. (1996). Limiting time-unlimited group therapy. *International Journal of Group Psychotherapy, 46*(6), 61–79. https://doi.org/10.1080/00207284.1996.11491484

K

Kabat-Zinn, J. (2005). Bringing mindfulness to medicine: an interview with Jon Kabat-Zinn, PhD. Interview by Karolyn Gazella. *Advances in Mind-Body Medicine, 21*(2), 22–27.

Kagle, J. D. (1994). Should systematic assessment, monitoring and evaluation tools be used as empowerment aids for clients? Rejoinder to Dr. Jayaratne. In W. W. Hudson & P. S. Nurius (Eds.), *Controversial issues in social work research* (pp. 88–92). Allyn & Bacon.

Kagle, J. D., & Kopels, S. (2008). *Social work records* (3rd ed.). Waveland Press.

Kahn, M. (1997). *Between therapist and client: The new relationship.* W. H. Freeman.

Kahn, K. B., & Martin, K. D. (2016). Policing and race: disparate treatment, perceptions, and policy responses. *Social Issues and Policy Review, 10*(1), 82–121. https://doi.org/10.1111/sipr.12019

Kaminski, J. W., Valle, L. A., Filene, J. H., & Boyle, C. L. (2008). A meta-analytic review of components associated with parent training effectiveness. *Journal of Abnormal Child Psychology, 36*(4), 567–589. https://doi.org/10.1007/s10802-007-9201-9

Kansas University Research and Training Center on Independent Living (2020). Guidelines: How to write about people with disabilities (9th ed.). Lawrence, KS.

Kanter, J. (2007). Compassion fatigue and secondary trauma: A second look. *Clinical Social Work Journal, 35*(4), 289–293. https://doi.org/10.1007/s10615-007-0125-1

Karvinen-Niinikoski, S. (2016). Social work supervision: Contributing to innovative knowledge production and open expertise. In M. Baldwin (Ed.) *Social work, Critical Reflection and the Learning Organization* (pp. 33–50). Routledge. https://doi.org/10.4324/9781315609690-8

Katiuzhinsky, A., & Okech, D. (2014). Human rights, cultural practices, and state policies: Implications for global social work practice and policy. *International Journal of Social Welfare, 23*(1), 80–88. https://doi.org/10.1111/ijsw.12002

Katz, S., Ford, A. B., Moskowitz, R. W., Jackson, B. A., & Jaffe, M. W. (1963). Studies of illness in the aged: The index of ADL: A standardized measure of biological and psychosocial function. *Journal of the American Medical Association, 185*(12), 914–919. https://doi.org/10.1001/jama.1963.03060120024016

Kazdin, A. E. (2008). *Parent management training: Treatment for oppositional, aggressive, and antisocial behavior in children and adolescents.* Oxford University Press.

Kealy, D., Ogrodniczuk, J. S., Piper, W. E., & Sierra-Hernandez, C. A. (2016). When it is not a good fit: Clinical errors in patient selection and group composition in group psychotherapy. *Psychotherapy, 53*(3), 308. https://doi.org/10.1037/pst0000069

Kear-Colwell, J., & Pollock, P. (1997). Motivation or confrontation: Which approach to the child sex offender? *Criminal Justice and Behavior, 24*(1), 20–33. https://doi.org/10.1177/0093854897024001002

Keast, K. (2012). A toolkit for single-session groups in acute care settings. *Social Work in Health Care, 51*(8), 710–724. https://doi.org/10.1080/00981389.2012.699024

Keats, P. A., & Sabharwal, V. V. (2008). Time-limited service alternatives: Using therapeutic enactment in open group therapy. *Journal for Specialists in Group Work, 33*(4), 297–316. https://doi.org/10.1080/01933920802424357

Kelly, M. S. (2008). Task-centered practice. In T. Mizrahi & L. Davis (Eds.), *Encyclopedia of social work* (20th ed., pp. 197–199). NASW Press-Oxford University Press.

Kendi, I. X. (2019). *How to be an antiracist.* One World.

Kernis, M. H., & Goldman, B. M. (2006). A multicomponent conceptualization of authenticity: Theory and research. *Advances in Experimental Social Psychology, 38*, 283–357. https://doi.org/10.1016/S0065-2601(06)38006-9

Kessler, D., Lewis, G., Kaur, S., Wiles, N., King, M., Weich, S., ... & Peters, T. J. (2009). Therapist-delivered internet psychotherapy for depression in primary care: A randomised controlled trial. *The Lancet, 374*(9690), 628–634. https://doi.org/10.1016/S0140-6736(09)61257-5

Kettenbach, G. (2003). *Writing SOAP notes: With patient/client management formats* (3rd ed.). Davis.

Keum, B. T., Miller, M. J., & Inkelas, K. K. (2018). Testing the factor structure and measurement invariance of the PHQ-9 across racially diverse US college students. *Psychological Assessment, 30*(8), 1096. https://doi.org/10.1037/pas0000550

Kilmer, E. D., Villarreal, C., Janis, B. M., Callahan, J. L., Ruggero, C. J., Kilmer, J. N., ... & Cox, R. J. (2019). Differential early termination is tied to client race/ethnicity status. *Practice Innovations, 4*(2), 88–98. https://doi.org/10.1037/pri0000085

Kilpatrick, A. C., & Holland, T. P. (2006). *Working with families. An integrative model by level of need* (4th ed.). Allyn & Bacon.

Kim, J. S. (2008). Examining the effectiveness of solution-focused brief therapy: A meta-analysis. *Research on Social Work Practice, 18*(2), 107–116. https://doi.org/10.1177/1049731507307807

Kim, H., & Rose, K. M. (2014). Concept analysis of family homeostasis. J Adv Nurs, *70*(11), 2450–2468. https://doi.org/10.1111/jan.12496

Kim, J. S., & Bolton, K. W. (2017). Strengths perspective. In Cynthia Franklin (Ed.), Encyclopedia of Social Work, On-line. Oxford University Press.

Kingdon, J. W. (2011). *Agendas, alternatives and public policies* (2nd ed.). Longman.

Kira, I. A., Ashby, J. S., Omidy, A. Z., & Lewandowski, L. (2015). Current, continuous, and cumulative trauma-focused cognitive behavior therapy: A new model for trauma counseling. Journal of Mental Health Counseling, 37(4), 323–340. https://doi.org/10.17744/mehc.37.4.04

Kirst-Ashman, K. K. (2014). *Human behavior in the macro social environment: An empowerment approach to understanding communities, organizations and groups.* Brooks/Cole.

Kleinman, A., & Benson, P. (2006). Anthropology in the clinic: The problem of cultural competency and how to fix it. *PloS Medicine,* 3(10), e294. https://doi.org/10.1371/journal.pmed.0030294

Knight, C. (2006). Groups for individuals with traumatic histories: Practice considerations for social workers. *Social Work,* 51(1), 20–30. https://doi.org/10.1093/sw/51.1.20

Knight, J. R., Sherritt, L., Shrier, L. A., Harris, S. K., & Chang, G. (2002). Validity of the CRAFFT substance abuse screening test among adolescent clinic patients. *Archives of Pediatrics and Adolescent Medicine,* 156(6), 607–614. https://doi.org/10.1001/archpedi.156.6.607

Koksvik, J. M., Linaker, O. M., Gråwe, R. W., Bjørngaard, J. H., and Lara-Cabrera, M. L. (2018). The effects of a pretreatment educational group programme on mental health treatment outcomes: A randomized controlled trial. *BMC Health Services Research,* 18(1), 1–10. https://doi.org/10.1186/s12913-018-3466-2

Kolivoski, K. M., Weaver, A., & Constance-Huggins, M. (2014). Critical race theory: Opportunities for application in social work practice and policy. *Families in Society,* 95(4), 269–276. https://doi.org/10.1606/1044-3894.2014.95.36

Kondrat, M. E. (2008). Person-in-environment. In T. Mizrahi & L. E. Davis (Eds.), *Encyclopedia of social work* (20th ed., Vol. 3, pp. 347–354). http://social work.oxfordre.com/view/10.1093/acrefore/9780199975839.001.0001/acrefore-9780199975839-e-285

Konrad, S. C. (2019). *Child and family practice: a relational perspective.* Oxford University Press.

Koob, G. F., & Le Moal, M. (2008). Addiction and the brain antireward system. *Annual Review of Psychology,* 59(1), 29–53. https://doi.org/10.1146/annurev.psych.59.103006.093548

Koob, J. J. (2003). Solution-focused family interventions. In A. C. Kilpatrick & T. P. Holland, *Working with families: An integrative model by level of need* (3rd ed., pp. 131–150). Allyn & Bacon.

Kosoff, S. (2004) Single session groups: Applications and areas of expertise. *Social Work with Groups,* 26(1), 29–45. https://doi.org/10.1300/J009v26n01_03

Kotter, J. P. (1995). Leading change: Why transformation efforts fail. *Harvard Business Review,* 86, 97–103. https://studydaddy.com/attachment/82895/6m6z2lk2vp.pdf

Krähenbühl, S., & Blades, M. (2006). The effect of interviewing techniques on young children's responses to questions. *Child Care Health and Development,* 32(3), 321–333. https://doi.org/10.1111/j.1365-2214.2006.00608.x

Kress, V., & Marie, M. (2019, October 2). Counseling termination and new beginnings. *Counseling Today.* https://ct.counseling.org/2019/10/counseling-termination-and-new-beginnings/

Kretzmann, J. P., & McKnight, J. L. (1993). *Building communities from the inside out: A path toward finding and mobilizing a community's assets.* Institute for Policy Research.

Kroenke, K., Spitzer, R. L., & Williams, J. B. (2001). The PHQ-9: Validity of a brief depression severity measure. *Journal of General Internal Medicine,* 16(9), 606–613. https://doi.org/10.1046/j.1525-1497.2001.016009606.x

Kruger, L., Moore, D., Schmidt, P., & Wiens, R. (1979). Group work with abusive parents. *Social Work,* 24(4), 337–338.

Kurland, R., & Salmon, R. (2006). Purpose: A misunderstood and misused keystone of group work practice. *Social Work with Groups,* 29(2–3), 105–120. https://doi.org/10.1300/J009v29n02_08

Kurman, J., Liem, G. A., Ivancovsky, T., Morio, H., & Lee, J. (2015). Regulatory focus as an explanatory variable for cross-cultural differences in achievement-related behavior. *Journal of Cross-Cultural Psychology,* 46(2), 171–190. https://doi.org/10.1177/0022022114558090

L

Labbé, D., Mahmood, A., Routhier, F., Prescott, M., Lacroix, E., Miller, W. C., & Mortenson, B. W. (2021). Using photovoice to increase social inclusion of people with disabilities: Reflections on the benefits and challenges. Journal of Community Psychology, 49, 44–57. https://doi.org/10.1002/jcop.22354

Ladhani, S., & Sitter, K. C. (2020). The revival of anti-racism: Considerations for social work education. *Critical Social Work,* 21(1), 54–65. https://doi.org/10.22329/csw.v21i1.6227

Laing, R. (1965). Mystification, confusion and conflict. In I. Boszormenyi-Nagy & J. Framo (Eds.), *Intensive family therapy: Theoretical and practical aspects.* Harper & Row.

Laird, J. (1993). Family-centered practice: Cultural and constructionist reflections. *Journal of Teaching in Social Work,* 8(1–2), 77–109. https://doi.org/10.1300/J067v08n01_05

Lamb, M., & Brown, D. (2006). Conversational apprentices: Helping children become competent informants about their own experiences. *British Journal of Developmental Psychology,* 24(1), 215–234. https://doi.org/10.1348/026151005X57657

Lambert, M. J., & Ogles, B. M. (2009). Using clinical significance in psychotherapy outcome research: The need for a common procedure and validity data. *Psychotherapy Research,* 19(4–5), 493–501. https://doi.org/10.1080/10503300902849483

Lambert, M. J., & Shimokawa, K. (2011). Collecting client feedback. In J. C. Norcross (Ed.), *Psychotherapy relationships that work* (2nd ed., pp. 203–223). Oxford University Press. https://doi.org/10.1093/acprof:oso/9780199737208.003.0010

Larsen, J. (1980). Accelerating group development and productivity: An effective leader approach. *Social Work with Groups,* 3(2), 25–39. https://doi.org/10.1300/J009v03n02_03

Lau, A. S. (2006). Making the case for selective and directed evidence culturally addressed evidence-based-treatment: Examples from parent training. *Clinical Psychology,* 13(4), 295–310. https://doi.org/10.1111/j.1468-2850.2006.00042.x

Lawrence, K., Sutton, S., Kubisch, A., Susi, G., & Fulbright-Anderson, K. (2004). *Structural racism and community building.* Aspen Institute Roundtable on Community Change.

Lazarus, A. A. (1994). How certain boundaries and ethics diminish therapeutic effectiveness. *Ethics and Behavior,* 4(3), 255–261. https://doi.org/10.1207/s15327019eb0403_10

Leahy, R. H., & Holland, S. J. (2000). *Treatment plans and interventions for depression and anxiety disorders.* Guilford Press. https://doi.org/10.1891/0889-8391.14.4.409

Lee, E. (2014). A therapist's self disclosure and its impact on the therapy process in cross-cultural encounters: Disclosure of personal self, professional self, and/or cultural self? *Families in Society,* 95(1), 15–23. https://doi.org/10.1606/1044-3894.2014.95.3

Lee, J. J., & Miller, S. E. (2013). A self-care framework for social workers: Building a strong foundation for practice. *Families in Society,* 94(2), 96–103. https://doi.org/10.1606/1044-3894.4289

Lee, M. (2014). *Clinician's guide to research methods in family therapy: Foundations of evidence-based practice.* Guilford Press.

Lee, M. Y. (2003). A solution-focused approach to cross-cultural clinical social work practice: Utilizing cultural strengths. *Families in Society,* 84(3), 385–395. https://doi.org/10.1606/1044-3894.118

Legg, T. J. & Raypole, C. (2019, June 26). How cognitive behavioral therapy can rewire your thoughts. https://www.healthline.com/health/cognitive-behavioral-therapy

Leiter, M. P., Maslach, C., & Frame, K. (2014). Burnout. In *Encyclopedia of Clinical Psychology,* 1–7. https://doi.org/10.1002/9781118625392.wbecp142

Levack, W, M., Weatherall, M., Hay-Smith, E. J., Dean, S. G., McPherson, K., & Siegert, R. J. (2015). Goal setting and strategies to enhance goal pursuit for adults with acquired disability participating in rehabilitation. *Cochrane Database of Systematic Reviews,* (7). Levi, D. (2007). *Group dynamics for teams* (2nd ed.). SAGE.

Levinson, H. (1977). Termination of psychotherapy: Some salient issues. *Social Casework, 58*(8), 480–489. https://doi.org/10.1177/104438947705800805

Levy, A. J., & Frank, M. G. (2011). Clinical practice with children. In J. Brandell (Ed.), *Theory and practice in clinical social work* (2nd ed., pp. 101–121). SAGE.

Lewey, J. H., Smith, C. L., Burcham, B., Saunders, N. L., Elfallal, D., & O'Toole, S. K. (2018). Comparing the effectiveness of EMDR and TF-CBT for children and adolescents: A meta-analysis. *Journal of Child & Adolescent Trauma, 11*(4), 457–472. https://doi.org/10.1007/s40653-018-0212-1

Lewis, J. A., Lewis, M. D., Packard, T., & Souflee, F. (2001). *Management of human service programs* (3rd ed.). Brooks/Cole.

Lieberman, M., Yalom, I., & Miles, M. (1973). *Encounter groups: First facts*. Basic Books.

Lietz, C. A. (2006). Uncovering stories of family resilience: A mixed methods study of resilient families: Part 1. *Families in Society, 87*(4), 575–582. https://doi.org/10.1606/1044-3894.3573

Lietz, C. A. (2007). Uncovering stories of family resilience: A mixed methods study of resilient families: Part 2. *Families in Society, 88*(1), 147–155. https://doi.org/10.1606/1044-3894.3602

Lind, K. (2020). Mutual aid during a pandemic: A group work class example. *Social Work with Groups, 43*(4), 347–350. https://doi.org/10.1080/01609513.2020.1790230

Lindberg, N. M., Stevens, V. J., Vega-López, S., Kauffman, T. L., Calderón, M. R., & Cervantes, M. A. (2012). A weight-loss intervention program designed for Mexican-American women: Cultural adaptations and results. *Journal of Immigrant and Minority Health, 14*(6), 1030–1039. https://doi.org/10.1007/s10903-012-9616-4

Lindsey, M. A., Korr, W. S., Broitman, M., Bone, L., Green, A., & Leaf, P. J. (2006). Help-seeking behaviors and depression among African American adolescent boys. *Social Work, 51*(1), 49–58. https://doi.org/10.1093/sw/51.1.49

Linehan, M. M. (2018). *Cognitive-behavioral treatment of borderline personality disorder*. Guilford Publications.

Linhorst, D. M. (2002). Federalism and social justice: Implications for social work. *Social Work, 47*(3), 201–208. https://doi.org/10.1093/sw/47.3.201

Linker, M. (2015). *Intellectual empathy: Critical thinking for social justice*. University of Michigan Press. https://doi.org/10.3998/mpub.5914478

Linzer, N. (1999). *Resolving ethical dilemmas in social work practice*. Allyn & Bacon.

Lipchik, E. (1997). My story about solution-focused brief therapist/client relationships. *Journal of Systemic Therapies, 16*(2), 159–172. https://doi.org/10.1521/jsyt.1997.16.2.159

Lipchik, E. (2002). *Beyond technique in solution-focused therapy: Working with emotions and the therapeutic relationship*. Guilford Press. https://doi.org/10.1521/jsyt.1997.16.2.159

Living Well. (2017). Foundations: Group facilitation, knowledge, skills, preparation, tips, and challenges. *Living Well*. https://learn.livingwell.org.au/mod/page/view.php?id=188

Lochman, J. E., Dishion, T. J., Boxmeyer, C. L., Powell, N. P., & Qu, L. (2017). Variation in response to evidence-based group preventive intervention for disruptive behavior problems: A view from 938 coping power sessions. *Journal of Abnormal Child Psychology, 45*(7), 1271–1284. https://doi.org/10.1007/s10802-016-0252-7

Locke, E. A., & Latham, G. P. (2006). New directions in goal-setting theory. *Current Directions in Psychological Science, 15*(5), 265–268. https://doi.org/10.1111/j.1467-8721.2006.00449.x

Loewenstein, D. A., Amigo, E., Duara, R., Guterman, A., Hurwitz, D., Berkowitz, N., ... & Eisdorfer, C. (1989). A new scale for the assessment of functional status in Alzheimer's disease and related disorders. *Journal of Gerontology, 44*(4), 114–121. https://doi.org/10.1093/geronj/44.4.P114

Long, D. L., Tice, C. J., & Morrison, J. D. (2006). *Macro social work practice: A strengths perspective*. Brooks/Cole.

Lopez, R. A. (2005). Use of alternative folk medicine by Mexican American women. *Journal of Immigrant Health, 7*(1), 23–31. https://doi.org/10.1007/s10903-005-1387-8

Lotz, J. E. (2013). Focused Brief Group Therapy Treatment Manual [Doctoral dissertation, Wright State University]. OhioLINK Electronic Theses and Dissertations Center. http://rave.ohiolink.edu/etdc/view?acc_num=wsupsych1349319908

Lovell, E., Hutchison, B., Cabulagan, K. A., McMullin, J., & Child, C. (2015). Homelessness and the high performance cycle: A new lens for studying exit strategies. Journal of Social Service Research, *41*(4), 508–529. https://doi.org/10.1080/01488376.2015.1049397

Love, M. F., Sharrief, A., Chaoul, A., Savitz, S., & Sanner Beauchamp, J. E. (2019). Mind-body interventions, psychological stressors, and quality of life in stroke survivors: A systematic review. Stroke, 50(2), 434–440. https://doi.org/10.1161/STROKEAHA.118.021150

Lukas, S. (1993). *Where to start and what to ask: An assessment handbook*. Norton.

Luke, M., & Hackney, H. (2007). Group coleaderhip: A critical review. *Counselor Education and Supervision, 46*(4), 280–293. doi.org/10.1002/j.1556-6978.2007.tb00032.x

Lum, D. (2007). *Culturally competent practice: A framework for understanding diverse groups and justice issues*. Brooks/Cole.

Lustick, H., Norton, C., Lopez, S. R., & Greene-Rooks, J. H. (2020). Restorative practices for empowerment: A social work lens. Children & Schools, 42(2), 89–97. doi.org/10.1093/cs/cdaa006

M

Machado, D. D. B., Coelho, F. M. D. C., Giacomelli, A. D., Donassolo, M. A. L., Abitante, M. S., Dall'Agnol, T., & Eizirik, C. L. (2014). Systematic review of studies about countertransference in adult psychotherapy. *Trends in Psychiatry and Psychotherapy, 36*, 173–185.

Macquarie University (n.d.). Policy tool kit. https://policies.mq.edu.au/download.php?associated=1&id=473

Maddux, J. E. (Ed.). (2013). *Self-efficacy, adaptation, and adjustment: Theory, research, and application*. Springer-Verlag.

Maguire-Jack, K., Lanier, P., & Lombardi, B. (2020). Investigating racial differences in clusters of adverse childhood experiences. *American Journal of Orthopsychiatry, 90*(1), 106–114. https://doi.org/10.1037/ort0000405

Mailick, M. D., & Vigilante, F. W. (1997). The family assessment wheel: A social constructionist perspective. *Families in Society, 78*(4), 361–369. https://doi.org/10.1606/1044-3894.794

Makhubela, M. S. (2016). Measurement invariance of the Beck Depression Inventory-Second Edition across race with South African university students. *South African Journal of Psychology, 46*(4), 449–461. https://doi.org/10.1177/0081246316645045

Malekoff, A. (2006). Strengths-based group work with children and adolescents. In C. D. Garvin, L. M. Gutierrez, & M. J. Galinsky (Eds.), *Handbook of social work with groups* (pp. 227–244). Guilford Press.

Mänttäri-van der Kuip, M. (2019). Conceptualising work-related moral suffering: Exploring and refining the concept of moral distress in the context of social work. *British Journal of Social Work, 50*(3), 741–757. https://doi.org/10.1093/bjsw/bcz034

Many, M. M. (2009). Termination as a therapeutic intervention when treating children who have experienced multiple losses. *Infant Mental Health Journal, 30*(1), 23–39. https://doi.org/10.1002/imhj.20201

Margolin, J. (1999). Breaking the Silence: Group Therapy for Childhood Sexual Abuse, A Practitioner's Manual (1st ed.). Routledge. https://doi.org/10.4324/9781315809915

Markland, C., Ryan, R. M., Tobin, V. J., & Rollnick, R. (2005). Motivational interviewing and self-determination theory. *Journal of Social and Clinical Psychology, 24*(6), 811–831. https://doi.org/10.1521/jscp.2005.24.6.811

Markman, A. (2014, August). Creating shared memories. *Psychology Today*. https://www.psychologytoday.com/us/blog/ulterior-motives/201408/creating-shared-memories

Marsh, J. C. (2002). Learning from clients. *Social Work, 47*(4), 341–342. https://doi.org/10.1093/sw/47.4.341

Marsh, P., & Doel, M. (2005). *The task-centered book*. Routledge. https://doi.org/10.4324/9780203339732

Marson, S. M., & McKinney, R. E. (Eds.). (2019). *Routledge handbook of social work ethics and values*. Routledge. https://doi.org/10.4324/9780429438813

Maschi, R., & Leibowitz, G. S. (Eds.). (2018). *Forensic social work: Psychological and legal issues across diverse populations and settings*. Springer. https://doi.org/10.1891/9780826120670

Maschi, T. (2006). Unraveling the link between trauma and male delinquency: The cumulative versus differential risk perspective. *Social Work, 51*(1), 59–70. https://doi.org/10.1093/sw/51.1.59

Maschi, T., Bradley, C., & Ward, K. (Eds.). (2009). *Forensic social work: Psychosocial and legal issues in diverse practice settings*. Springer.

Maslach, C., & Leiter, M. P. (2017). New insights into burnout and health care: Strategies for improving civility and alleviating burnout. *Medical Teacher, 39*(2), 160–163. https://doi.org/10.1080/0142159X.2016.1248918

Mason, M. (2009). Rogers redux: Relevance and outcomes of motivational interviewing across behavioral problems. *Journal of Counseling & Development, 87*(3), 357–362. https://doi.org/10.1002/j.1556-6678.2009.tb00117.x

Matchim, Y., Armer, J. M., & Stewart, B. R. (2011). Effects of mindfulness-based stress reduction (MBSR) on health among breast cancer survivors. *Western Journal of Nursing Research, 33*(8), 996–1016. https://doi.org/10.1177/0193945910385363

Mattaini, M. (2008). Ecosystems theory. In B. A. Thyer (Ed.). *Comprehensive handbook of social work and social welfare: Vol. 2. Human behavior in the social environment* (pp. 355–377). Wiley. https://doi.org/10.1002/9780470373705.chsw002015

Matto, H. C. (2005). A bio-behavioral model of addiction treatment: Applying dual representation theory to craving management and relapse prevention. *Substance Use & Misuse, 40*(4), 529–541. https://doi.org/10.1081/JA-200030707

Mattsson, T. (2014). Intersectionality as a useful tool: Anti-oppressive social work and critical reflection. *Affilia, 29*(1), 8–17. https://doi.org/10.1177/0886109913510659

Maxwell, K. (2014). Historicizing historical trauma theory: Troubling the trans-generational transmission paradigm. *Transcultural Psychiatry, 51*(3), 407–435. https://doi.org/10.1177/1363461514531317

Mayden, K. D. (2012). Mind-body therapies: Evidence and implications in advanced oncology practice. *Journal of the Advanced Practitioner in Oncology, 3*(6), 357. https://doi.org/10.6004/jadpro.2012.3.6.2

Mayer, S. E. (2008). Saving the babies: Looking for upstream solutions. *Effective Communities LLC*. https://effectivecommunities.com/wp-content/uploads/2017/09/ECP_SavingBabies.pdf

Mayo Clinic. (2007, January 12). *Elder abuse: Signs to look for, action to take*. http://www .mayoclinic.com/health/elder-abuse/HA00041

Mayo Clinic. (2018). *Teen depression*. https://www.mayoclinic.org/diseases-conditions/teen-depression/symptoms-causes/syc-20350985

Mayo Clinic. (2019). *Teen suicide: What parents need to know*. https://www.mayoclinic.org/healthy-lifestyle/tween-and-teen-health/in-depth/teen-suicide

Mazumder, S. (2018). The persistent effect of US civil rights protests on political attitudes. *American Journal of Political Science, 62*(4), 922–935. https://doi.org/10.1111/ajps.12384

McCollum, E. E., & Beer, J. (1995). The view from the other chair. *Family Therapy Networker, 19*(2), 59–62.

McDowell, T., Libal, K., & Brown, A. L. (2012). Human rights in the practice of family therapy: Domestic violence, a case in point. *Journal of Feminist Family Therapy, 24*(1), 1–23. https://doi.org/10.1080/08952833.2012.629129

McGoldrick, M., Gerson, R., & Petry, S. (2008). *Genograms: Assessment and intervention* (3rd ed.). Norton.

McGonagle, E. (1986). *Banana splits: A peer support group for children of transitional families*. Author.

McGovern, J. (2015). Living better with dementia: Strengths based social work practice and dementia care. *Social Work in Health Care, 54*(5), 408–421. https://doi.org/10.1080/00981389.2015.1029661

McKibban, A. R., & Steltenpohl, C. N. (2019). Community organizing, partnerships, and coalitions. *Introduction to Community Psychology*. https://press.rebus.community/introductiontocommunitypsychology/chapter/community-organizing-partnerships-and-coalitions/

McKinnon, J. (2008). Exploring the nexus between social work and the environment. *Australian Social Work, 61*(3), 256–268. https://doi.org/10.1080/03124070802178275

McMillen, J. C., Morris, L., & Sherraden, M. (2004). Ending social work's grudge match: Problems versus strengths. *Families in Society, 85*(3), 317–325. https://doi.org/10.1177/104438940408500309

McQuaide, S. (1999). Using psychodynamic, cognitive-behavioral and solution-focused questioning to construct a new narrative. *Clinical Social Work, 27*(4), 339–353. https://doi.org/10.1023/A:1022818112744

McQuaide, S., & Ehrenreich, J. H. (1997). Assessing client strengths. *Families in Society, 78*(2), 201–212. https://doi.org/10.1606/1044-3894.759

Menakem, R. (2017). My grandmother's hands: Racialized trauma and the pathway to mending our hearts and bodies. Central Recovery Press.

Meenaghan, T. M., Gibbons, W. E., & McNutt, J. G. (2005). *Generalist practice in larger settings: Knowledge and skills concepts*. Lyceum Books.

Merrick, M. T., Ports, K. A., Ford, D. C., Afifi, T. O., Gershoff, E. T., & Grogan-Kaylor, A. (2017). Unpacking the impact of adverse childhood experiences on adult mental health. Child Abuse & Neglect, 69, 10–19. https://doi.org/10.1016/j.chiabu.2017.03.016

Mental Health Association of New Jersey. (n.d.). *New Jersey self-help clearinghouse*. https://www.njgroups.org/

Mersky, J. P., Topitzes, J., & Britz, L. (2019). Promoting evidence-based, trauma-informed social work practice. *Journal of Social Work Education, 55*(4), 645–657. https://doi.org/10.1080/10437797.2019.1627261

Metcalf, L., Thomas, R., Duncan, B., Miller, S., & Hubble, M. (1996). What works in solution-focused brief therapy: A qualitative analysis of client and therapist's perceptions. In S. Miller, M. Hubble, & B. Duncan (Eds.), *Handbook of solution-focused brief therapy*. Jossey-Bass.

Meyer, O. L., & Zane, N. (2014). The influence of race and ethnicity in clients' experiences of mental health treatment. *Journal of Community Psychology, 41*(7), 884–901. https://doi.org/10.1002/jcop.21580

Meyer, W. S. (2001). Why they don't come back: A clinical perspective on the no-show client. *Clinical Social Work, 29*(4), 325–339. https://doi.org/10.1023/A:1012211112553

Michalopoulos, L. M., & Aparicio, E. (2012). Vicarious trauma in social workers: The role of trauma history, social support, and years of experience. *Journal of Aggression, Maltreatment & Trauma, 21*(6), 646–664. https://doi.org/10.1080/10926771.2012.689422

Migration Policy Institute. (2018, October 1). *International migration statistics*. https://www.migrationpolicy.org/programs/data-hub/international-migration-statistics

Miller, A., Hess, J. M., Bybee, D., & Goodkind, J. R. (2018). Understanding the mental health consequences of family separation for refugees: Implications for policy and practice. *American Journal of Orthopsychiatry, 88*(1), 26–37. https://doi.org/10.1037/ort0000272

Miller, S. D., Hubble, M. A., Chow, D. L., & Seidel, J. A. (2013). The outcome of psychotherapy: Yesterday, today, and tomorrow. *Psychotherapy, 50*(1), 88–97. https://doi.org/10.1037/a0031097

Miller, W. I. (2000). *The mystery of courage*. Harvard University Press.

Miller, W. R., & Rollnick, S. (2013). *Motivational interviewing: Helping people change* (3rd ed.). Guilford Press.

Miller, W. R., & Sovereign, R. G. (1989). The check-up: A model for early intervention in addictive behaviors. In T. Løberg, W. R. Miller, P. E. Nathan, & G. A. Marlatt (Eds.), *Addictive behaviors: Prevention and early intervention* (pp. 219–231). Swets and Zeitlinger.

Minuchin, S. (1974). *Families and family therapy*. Harvard University Press.

Miron, A. M., & Brehm, J. W. (2006). Reactance theory—40 years later. *Zeitschrift für Sozialpsychologie, 37*(1), 9–18. https://doi.org/10.1024/0044-3514.37.1.9

Monroe, C. R. (2013). Colorizing educational research: African American life and schooling as an exemplar. *Educational Researcher, 42*(1), 9–19. https://doi.org/10.3102/0013189X12469998

Montross, C. (2014). *Falling into the fire*. Penguin Books.

Moon, B. L. (2016). *Art-based group therapy: Theory and practice* (2nd ed.). Charles C. Thomas.

Moreno, J. K. (2007). Scapegoating in group psychotherapy. *International Journal of Group Psychotherapy, 57*(1), 93–104. https://doi.org/10.1521/ijgp.2007.57.1.93

Moreno-Alcázar, A., Radua, J., Landín-Romero, R., Blanco, L., Madre, M., Reinares, M., ... & Amann, B. L. (2017). Eye movement desensitization and reprocessing therapy versus supportive therapy in affective relapse prevention in bipolar patients with a history of trauma: Study protocol for a randomized controlled trial. *Trials, 18*(1), 1–10. https://doi.org/10.1186/s13063-017-1910-y

Morgaine, K., & Capous-Desyllas, M. (2015). *Anti-oppressive social work practice: Putting theory into action*. SAGE Publications.

Morgan, A. (2000). *What is narrative therapy?* Dulwich Centre.

Morgan-Mullane, A. (2018). Trauma focused cognitive behavioral therapy with children of incarcerated parents. *Clinical Social Work Journal, 46*(3), 200–209. https://doi.org/10.1007/s10615-017-0642-5

Morrison, J. (2016). *The first interview* (4th ed). Guilford Press.

Morton, S., & Hohman, M. (2016). "That's the weight of knowing": Practitioner skills and impact when delivering psychoeducational group work for women who have experienced IPV. *Social Work with Groups, 39*(4), 277–291. https://doi.org/10.1080/01609513.2015.1052915

Moudatsou, M., Stavropoulou, A., Philalithis. A., & Koukouli, S. (2020). The role of empathy in health and social care profession. *Healthcare, 8*(1) 26. https://doi.org/10.3390/healthcare8010026

Moyers, T. B., Martin, T., Manuel, J. K., & Miller, W. R. (2003). *The motivational interviewing treatment integrity (MITI) code, Version 2.0.* http://casaa.unm.edu/download/miti.pdf

Mulder, T. M., Kuiper, K. C., van der Put, C. E., Stams, G. J. J., & Assink, M. (2018). Risk factors for child neglect: A meta-analytic review. *Child Abuse & Neglect, 77*, 198–210. https://doi.org/10.1016/j.chiabu.2018.01.006

Mullen, P. R., Morris, C., & Lord, M. (2017). The experience of ethical dilemmas, burnout, and stress among practicing counselors. *Counseling & Values, 62*(1), 37–56. https://doi.org/10.1002/cvj.12048

Mulvaney, E. (2020, October 8). Diversity fueled "reverse" bias claims put employers in quandary. *Bloomberg Law.* https://news.bloomberglaw.com/daily-labor-reportdiversity-fueled-reverse-bias-claims-put-employers-in-quandary

Mundt, M., Ross, K., & Burnett, C. M. (2018). Scaling social movements through social media: The case of Black Lives Matter. *Social Media+ Society, 4*(4). https://doi.org/10.1177/2056305118807911

Muñoz, R.F. , Le, H-N, Ippen, C.G., Diaz, M.A., Urizar, G.G., Soto, J., Mendelson, T., Delucchi, K., Lieberman, A.F. (2007). Prevention of Postpartum Depression in Low-Income Women: Development of the Mamás y Bebés/Mothers and Babies Course, Cognitive and Behavioral Practice, (14)1, pp. 70–83. https://doi.org/10.1016/j.cbpra.2006.04.021.

Murdach, A. D. (1996). Beneficence re-examined: Protective intervention in mental health. *Social Work, 41*(1), 26–32. https://doi.org/10.1093/sw/41.1.26

Murphy, B. C., & Dillon, C. (2003). *Interviewing in action: Relationship, process, and change* (2nd ed.). Brooks/Cole.

Murphy, B. C., & Dillon, C. (2008). *Interviewing in action in a multicultural world* (3rd ed.). Brooks/Cole.

Murphy, B. C., & Dillon, C. (2010). *Interviewing in action in a multicultural world* (4th ed.). Brooks/Cole.

Murphy, B. C., & Dillon, C. (2015). *Interviewing in action in a multicultural world*. Cengage Learning.

Murphy, C. M., & Baxter, V. A. (1997). Motivating batterers to change in the treatment context. *Journal of Interpersonal Violence, 12*(4), 607–619. https://doi.org/10.1177/088626097012004009

Murray, C. E., & Murray Jr, T. L. (2004). Solution-focused premarital counseling: Helping couples build a vision for their marriage. *Journal of Marital and Family Therapy, 30*(3), 349–358. https://doi.org/10.1111/j.1752-0606.2004.tb01245.x

Musial, F., Büssing, A., Heusser, P., Choi, K. E., & Ostermann, T. (2011). Mindfulness-based stress reduction for integrative cancer care–a summary of evidence. *Complementary Medicine Research, 18*(4), 192–202. https://doi.org/10.1159/000330714

Myer, R., Lewis, J., & James, R. (2013). The introduction of a task model for crisis intervention. *Journal of Mental Health Counseling, 35*(2), 95–107. https://doi.org/10.17744/mehc.35.2.nh322x3547475154

N

National Academies of Sciences, Engineering, and Medicine. 2017. *Pain management and the opioid epidemic: Balancing societal and individual benefits and risks of prescription opioid use.* The National Academies Press. https://doi.org/10.17226/24781

National Alliance on Mental Illness. (2020). *Black/African American.* https://www.nami.org/Your-Journey/Identity-and-Cultural-Dimensions/Black-African-American

National Association of Social Workers (NASW). (2006). *Immigration policy toolkit.* NASW Press. https://www.socialworkers.org/LinkClick.aspx?fileticket=5y6LlGaBFRw%3D&portalid=0

National Association of Social Workers (NASW). (2009a). Cultural and linguistic competence in the social work profession. In *Social work speaks: National Association of Social Workers policy statements, 2009–2012* (8th ed., pp. 70–76). NASW Press. https://cdn.ymaws.com/www.naswnyc.org/resource/resmgr/imported/Cultural%20and%20Linguistic%20Competence%20in%20the%20SW%20Profession.pdf

National Association of Social Workers (NASW). (2009b). Professional self-care and social work. In *Social work speaks: National Association of Social Worker policy statements, 2009–2012* (8th ed., pp. 268–272). NASW Press.

National Association of Social Workers (NASW), & Association of Social Work Boards (ASWB). (2013). *Best practice standards for social work supervision.* National Association of Social Workers.

National Association of Social Workers (NASW). (2015). *Standards and indicators for cultural competence in social work practice.* National Association of Social Workers. https://www.socialserviceworkforce.org/system/files/resource/files/Standards%20and%20Indicators%20for%20Cultural%20Competence%20in%20Social%20Work%20Practice.pdf

National Association of Social Workers (NASW) (2017a). *Technology in social work practice.* National Association of Social Workers. https://www.socialworkers.org/includes/newIncludes/homepage/PRA-BRO-33617.TechStandards_FINAL_POSTING.pdf

National Association of Social Workers (NASW). (2017b). *NASW code of ethics.* https://www.socialworkers.org/About/Ethics/Code-of-Ethics/Code-of-Ethics-English

National Association of Social Workers (NASW). (2021). *Code of ethics.* NASW Press. https://www.socialworkers.org/About/Ethics/Code-of-Ethics/Code-of-Ethics-English

National Association of Social Work Foundation. (n.d.). *International resources.* https://www.naswfoundation.org/Our-Work/International/International-Resources

National Association of Social Workers Massachusetts Chapter (NASWMA). (n.d.). *Online therapy and the clinical social worker.* https://www.naswma.org/page/351/Online-Therapy-and-the-Clinical-Social-Worker.htm

National Education Goals (n.d.) *Community organizing guide.* https://govinfo.library.unt.edu/negp/reports/orguide.pdf

National Institute of Mental Health. (2019). *What is psychosis?* https://www.nimh.nih.gov/health/topics/schizophrenia/raise/what-is-psychosis.shtml

National Institute of Mental Health. (2020). *Suicide*. https://www.nimh
.nih.gov/health/statistics/suicide.shtml

Naughton, J. (2019, January 20). "The goal is to automate us":
Welcome to the age of surveillance capitalism. *The Guardian*, *20*, 19. https://www.sfu.ca/~palys/Zuboff-2019-The%20
goal%20is%20to%20automate%20us%27-Welcome%20to%20
the%20age%20of%20surveillance%20capitalism.pdf_

Netting, F. E., Kettner, P. M., McMurtry, S. L., & Thomas, M. L. (2012).
Social work macro practice (5th ed.). Pearson. https://doi.org/10.1093
/acrefore/9780199975839.013.230

Netting, E. F., Kettner, P. M., McMurtry, S. L., & Thomas, M. L. (2017).
Social work macro practice (6th ed.). Pearson.

Neuendorf, R., Wahbeh, H., Chamine, I., Yu, J., Hutchison, K.,
& Oken, B. S. (2015). The effects of mind-body interventions
on sleep quality: A systematic review. *Evidence-Based
Complementary and Alternative Medicine*, *2015*, 1–17. https://
doi.org/10.1155/2015/902708

Newell, J. M., & MacNeil, G. A. (2010). Professional burnout, vicarious
trauma, secondary traumatic stress, and compassion fatigue. *Best
Practices in Mental Health*, *6*(2), 57–68.

Nichols, M. P. (2012). *Family therapy: Concepts and methods* (10th ed.). Pearson.

Nichols, M. P., & Schwartz, R. C. (2006). *Family therapy: Concepts and
methods* (7th ed.). Allyn & Bacon.

Niles, B. L., Mori, D. L., Polizzi, C., Pless Kaiser, A., Weinstein, E. S.,
Gershkovich, M., & Wang, C. (2018). A systematic review of
randomized trials of mind-body interventions for PTSD. *Journal of
Clinical Psychology*, *74*(9), 1485–1508. https://doi.org/10.1002
/jclp.22634

Norrick, N., & Spitz, A. (2008). Humor as a resource for mitigating conflict in interaction. *Journal of Pragmatics*, *40*(10), 1661–1686. https://
doi.org/10.1016/j.pragma.2007.12.001

Northen, H., & Kurland, R. (2001). The use of activity. In H. Northen
(Ed.), *Social work with groups* (3rd ed., pp. 258–287). Columbia
University Press.

O

Office for Civil Rights. (2008, May 7). *Summary of the HIPAA Privacy
Rule*. HHS.gov. https://www.hhs.gov/hipaa/for-professionals/privacy
/laws-regulations/index.html

O'Hanlon, W. (1996, January/February). Case commentary. *Family
Therapy Networker*, pp. 84–85.

O'Hare, T. (2009). *Essential skills of social work practice: Assessment, intervention and evaluation*. Lyceum Books.

O'Hare, T. (2020). *Evidence-based practices for social workers: An interdisciplinary approach*. (*3rd ed*). Oxford University Press.

Okun, B. F. (2002). *Effective helping: Interviewing and counseling techniques*.
Brooks/Cole.

O'Nell, T. D. O. (1996). *Disciplined hearts: History, identity, and depression
in an American Indian community*. University of California Press.

Onek, D. (2013). Search inside yourself: Integrating mindfulness into the
criminal justice
system. *Life of the Law*. https://www.lifeofthelaw.org/2013/10
/integrating-mindfulness-into-the-criminal-justice-system/

O'Quin, K. E., Semalulu, T., & Orom, H. (2015). Elder and caregiver solutions to improve medication adherence. *Health Education Research*,
30(2), 323–335. https://doi.org/10.1093/her/cyv009

Ortega-Williams, A., Crutchfield, J., & Hall, J. C. (2021). The colorist-
historical trauma framework: Implications for culturally responsive
practice with African Americans. *Journal of Social Work*, *21*(3),
294–309. https://doi.org/10.1177/1468017319890083

Oulanova, O., & Moodley, R. (2017). Lessons from clinical practice:
Some of the ways in which Canadian mental health professionals practice integration. In S. L. Stewart, R. Moodley, & A. Hyatt
(Eds.). *Indigenous cultures and mental health counselling: Four directions
for integration with counselling psychology*. Routledge.

Owen, J., Tao, K. W., Drinane, J. M., Hook, J., Davis, D. E., & Kune, N.
F. (2016). Client perceptions of therapists' multicultural orientation:
Cultural (missed) opportunities and cultural humility. *Professional
Psychology: Research and Practice*, *47*(1), 30–37. https://doi
.org/10.1037/pro0000046

Oyserman, D., Lewis Jr, N. A., Yan, V. X., Fisher, O., O'Donnell, S. C.,
& Horowitz, E. (2017). An identity-based motivation framework for
self-regulation. *Psychological Inquiry*, *28*(2–3), 139–147. https://doi.or
g/10.1080/1047840X.2017.1337406

P

Padgett, D. K. (Ed.). (2004). *The qualitative research experience*. Brooks
/Cole.

Padilla, Y. C., Shapiro, E. R., Fernandez-Castro, M. D., & Faulkner, M.
(2008). Our nation's immigrants in peril: An urgent call to social
workers. *Social Work*, *53*(1), 5–8. https://doi.org/10.1093/sw/53.1.5

Palmer, E. J. (2016). Moral reasoning assessment. In: R. J. Levesque (Ed.)
Encyclopedia of adolescence. Springer. https://doi
.org/10.1007/978-3-319-32132-5_10-2

Papero, D. V. (1990). *Bowen Family Systems Theory*. Allyn and Bacon.

Papouli, E. (2019). Moral courage and moral distress in social work
education and practice. In S. M. Marson & R. E. McKinney (Eds.),
Routledge handbook of social work ethics and values (pp. 223–232).
Routledge. https://doi.org/10.4324/9780429438813-29

Paquette, D., & Ryan, J. (2001). Bronfenbrenner's ecological systems
theory. https://www.dropoutprevention.org/wp-content/up-
loads/2015/07/paquetteryanwebquest_20091110.pdf

Park, Y. (2019). *Facilitating injustice: The complicity of social workers
in the forced removal and incarceration of Japanese Americans,
1941–1946*. Oxford University Press. https://doi.org/10.1093
/oso/9780199765058.001.0001

Pate, D. J. (2016). The color of debt: An examination of social
networks, sanctions, and child support enforcement policy. *Race
and Social Problems*, *8*(1), 116–135. https://doi.org/10.1007
/s12552-016-9167-8

Payne, B. K., Vuletich, H. A., & Brown-Iannuzzi, J. L. (2019). Historical
roots of implicit bias in slavery. *Proceedings of the National Academy
of Sciences*, *116*(24), 11693–11698. https://doi.org/10.1073
/pnas.1818816116

Perron, B. E., Taylor, H. O., Glass, J. E., & Margerum-Leys, J. (2010). Information and communication technologies in social work. *Advances
in Social Work*, *11*(2), 67–81. https://doi.org/10.18060/241

Peterson, A. L., Goodie, J. L., & Andrasik, F. (2015). Introduction to
biopsychosocial assessment in clinical health psychology. In F.
Andrasik, J. L. Goodie, & A. L. Peterson (Eds.), *Biopsychosocial assessment in clinical health psychology* (pp. 3–8). Guilford Press.

Peterson, T. J. & Fuller, K. (2021). Eclectic therapy: How it works, types,
and what to expect. Retrieved from https://www.choosingtherapy
.com/eclectic-therapy/

Pew Research Center. (2020). *Internet/broadband fact sheet*. https://www
./pewresearch.org/internet/fact-sheetinternet-broadband
/#who-has-home-broadband

Philip, C. E. (1994). Letting go: Problems with termination when a
therapist is seriously ill or dying. *Smith College Studies in Social Work*,
64(2), 169–179. https://doi.org/10.1080/00377319409517407

Philip, C. E., & Stevens, E. V. (1992). Countertransference issues for the
consultant when a colleague is critically ill (or dying). *Clinical Social
Work Journal*, *20*(4), 411–419. https://doi.org/10.1007/BF00756403

Pokorny, A. D., Miller, B. A., & Kaplan, H. B. (1972). The brief MAST:
A shortened version of the Michigan Alcoholism Screening Test.
American Journal of Psychiatry, *129*(3), 342–345. https://doi
.org/10.1176/ajp.129.3.342

Pollack, S. (2013). An imprisoning gaze: Practices of gendered, racialized
and epistemic violence. *International Review of Victimology*, *19*(1),
103–114. https://doi.org/10.1177/0269758012447219

Pollio, D. E. (1995). Use of humor in crisis intervention. *Families in Society*, 76(6), 376–384. https://doi.org/10.1177/104438949507600606

Pollio, E., & Deblinger, E. (2017). Trauma-focused cognitive behavioural therapy for young children: Clinical considerations. *European Journal of Psychotraumatology*, 8(Suppl7), 1433929. https://doi.org/10.1080/20008198.2018.1433929

Poortvliet, P. M., Anseel, F., & Theuwis, F. (2015). Mastery-approach and mastery-avoidance goals and their relation with exhaustion and engagement at work: The roles of emotional and instrumental support. *Work & Stress*, 29(2), 150–170. https://doi.org/10.1080/02678373.2015.1031856

Pope, K. S., Sonne, J. L., & Greene, B. (1993). *What therapists don't talk about and why: Understanding taboos that hurt us and our clients.* American Psychological Association.

Popple, P. R., & Leighninger, L. (2015). *The policy-based profession: An introduction to social welfare policy analysis for social workers* (6th ed.). Pearson Education, Inc.

Potocky, M., & Naseh, M. (2019). *Best practices for social work with refugees and immigrants* (2nd ed). Columbia University Press. https://doi.org/10.7312/poto18138

Potocky-Tripodi, M. (2002). *Best practices for social work with refugees and immigrants.* Columbia University Press.

Potocky-Tripodi, M. (2003). Refugee economic adaptation: Theory, evidence and implications for policy and practice. *Journal of Social Service Research*, 30(1), 63–91. https://doi.org/10.1300/J079v30n01_04

Prochaska, J. O., & DiClemente, C. C. (1982). Transtheoretical therapy: Toward a more integrative model of change. *Psychotherapy: Theory, Research, and Practice*, 19(3), 276–288. https://doi.org/10.1037/h0088437

Project Implicit. (2011). *Take a test.* https://implicit.harvard.edu/implicit/takeatest.html

Pulla, V. (2017). Strengths-based approach in social work: A distinct ethical advantage. *International Journal of Innovation, Creativity and Change*, 3(2), 97–114.

Purohit, M. P., Wells, R. E., Zafonte, R., Davis, R. B., Yeh, G. Y., & Phillips, R. S. (2013). Neuropsychiatric symptoms and the use of mind-body therapies. *Journal of Clinical Psychiatry*, 74(6), e520–526. https://doi.org/10.4088/JCP.12m08246

R

Racial Equity Tools (n.d.). Community organizing. https://www.racialequitytools.org/resources/act/strategies/community-organizing

Racine, N., Hartwick, C., Collin-Vezina, D., & Madigan, S. (2020). Telemental health for child trauma treatment during and post-COVID-19: Limitations and considerations. *Child Abuse & Neglect*, 110, 104698. https://doi.org/10.1016/j.chiabu.2020.104698

Ragg, D., Okagbue-Reaves, J., & Piers, J. (2007, October 28). *Shaping student interactive habits: A critical function of practice education.* Presentation at Council of Social Work Education Annual Program Meeting #74a.

Ragg, D. M. (2011). *Developing practice competencies: A foundation for generalist practice.* John Wiley & Sons.

Raines, J. C. (1996). Self-disclosure in clinical social work. *Clinical Social Work Journal*, 24(4), 357–375. https://doi.org/10.1007/BF02190743

Ramos, B. M., & Garvin, C. (2003). Task-centered treatment with culturally diverse populations, In E. R. Tolson, W. J. Reid, & C. D. Garvin (Eds.), *Generalist practice: A task-centered approach* (2nd ed., pp. 441–463). Columbia University Press.

Ramos, B. M., & Tolson, E. R. (2008). The task-centered model. In N. Coady & P. Lehmann (Eds.), *Theoretical perspectives for direct social work practice. A generalist-eclectic approach* (2nd ed., pp. 275–295). Springer.

Ramsundarsingh, S., & Shier, M. L. (2017). Anti-oppressive organizational dynamics in the social services: A literature review. *British Journal of Social Work*, 47(8), 2308–2327. https://doi.org/10.1093/bjsw/bcw174

Rapp, C. A. (1998). *The strengths model: Case management with people suffering from severe and persistent mental illness.* Oxford University Press.

Rapp, C. A. (2002). A strengths approach to case management with clients with severe mental disability. In A. R. Roberts & G. J. Greene (Eds.), *Social workers' desk reference* (pp. 486–491). Oxford University Press.

Rapp, C. A., & Goscha, R. J. (2006). *The strengths model: Case management with people with psychiatric disabilities* (2nd ed.). Oxford University Press.

Rathbone-McCuan, E. (2008). Elder abuse. In T. Mizrahi & L. E. Davis (Eds.), *Encyclopedia of social work.* National Association of Social Workers and Oxford University Press.

Reamer, F., & Reamer, F. G. (2018). *Social work values and ethics.* Columbia University Press. https://doi.org/10.7312/ream18828

Reamer, F. G. (1994). *Social work malpractice and liability: Strategies for prevention.* Columbia University Press.

Reamer, F. G. (1995). Malpractice claims against social workers: First facts. *Social Work*, 40(5), 595–601.

Reamer, F. G. (1998). *Ethical standards in social work.* NASW Press.

Reamer, F. G. (1999). *Social work values and ethics* (2nd ed.). Columbia University Press.

Reamer, F. G. (2006). *Social work values and ethics* (3rd ed.). Columbia University Press.

Reamer, F. G. (2013). The digital and electronic revolution in social work: Rethinking the meaning of ethical practice. *Ethics and Social Welfare*, 7(1), 2–19. https://doi.org/10.1080/17496535.2012.738694

Reamer, F. G. (2019a). Boundary issues and dual relationships in social work. In S. M. Marson & R. E. McKinney (Eds.), *Routledge handbook of social work ethics and values* (pp. 157–164). Routledge. https://doi.org/10.4324/9780429438813-21

Reamer, F. G. (2019b). Ethical theories and social work practice. In S. M. Marson & R. E. McKinney (Eds.), *Routledge handbook of social work ethics and values* (pp. 15–21). Routledge. https://doi.org/10.4324/9780429438813-3

Reardon, S. F. (2016). School district socioeconomic status, race, and academic achievement. *Stanford Center for Educational Policy Analysis.* https://cepa.stanford.edu/sites/default/files/reardon%20district%20ses%20and%20achievement%20discussion%20draft%20april2016.pdf

Reese, D. J., Ahern, R. E., Nair, S., O'Faire, J. D., & Warren, C. (1999). Hospice access and use by African Americans: Addressing cultural and institutional barriers through participatory action research. *Social Work*, 44(6), 549–559. https://doi.org/10.1093/sw/44.6.549

Reich, D., Shapiro, I., Cho, C., & Kogan, R. (2017). Block-granting low-income programs leads to large funding declines over time, history shows. *Center on Budget and Policy Priorities.* https://www.cbpp.org/research/federal-budget/block-granting-low-income-programs-leads-to-large-funding-declines-over-time

Reid, W. J. (1975). A test of the task-centered approach. *Social Work*, 20(1), 3–9.

Reid, W. J. (1996). *Task-centered social work.* In F. J. Turner (Ed.), *Social work treatment: Interlocking theoretical approaches* (4th ed., pp. 617–640). Free Press.

Reid, W. J. (1997). Research on task-centered practice. *Social Work*, 21(3), 131–137. https://doi.org/10.1093/swr/21.3.132

Reid, W. J. (2000). *The task planner.* Columbia University Press. https://doi.org/10.7312/reid10646

Reid, W. J., Abramson, J. S., & Wasko, N. (1992). *Task strategies.* Columbia University Press.

Reid, W. J., & Epstein, L. (Eds.) (1972). *Task-centered casework.* Columbia University Press.

Reid, W. J., & Fortune, A. E. (2002). The task-centered model. In A. R. Roberts & G. J. Greene (Eds.), *Social workers' desk reference* (pp. 101–104). Oxford University Press.

Reid, W., & Hanrahan, P. (1982). Recent evaluations of social work: Grounds for optimism. *Social Work*, 27(4), 328–340. https://doi.org/10.1093/sw/27.4.328

Reid, W., & Shyne, A. (1969). *Brief and extended casework*. Columbia University Press.

Reisch, M. (2019). Social work under Trump: Experiences from the USA. In J. Fischer & K. Dunn (Eds.), *Stifled progress–international perspectives on social work and social policy in the era of right-wing populism* (pp. 147–166). Verlag Barbara Budrich. https://doi.org/10.2307/j.ctvfrxr60.13

Resnick, C., & Dziegielewski, S. F. (1996). The relationship between therapeutic termination and job satisfaction among medical social workers. *Social Work in Health Care, 23*(3), 17–33. https://doi.org/10.1300/J010v23n03_02

Richardson, V. E., & Barusch, A. S. (2006). *Gerontological practice for the twenty-first century: A social work perspective*. Columbia University Press.

Richman, M. (2019). Review study points to most effective mind-body therapies for PTSD. U.S. Department of Veterans Affairs. https://www.research.va.gov/currents/0119-Mind-body-therapies-for-PTSD.cfm

Richmond, M. (1922). *What is social casework?* Russell Sage Foundation

Richmond, M. E. (1899). *Friendly visiting among the poor: A handbook for charity workers*. Macmillan.

Richmond, M. E. (1917). *Social diagnosis*. Russell Sage Foundation.

Risica, P. M., Nelson, T., Kumanyika, S. K., Camacho Orona, K., Bove, G., Odoms-Young, A. M., & Gans, K. M. (2021). Emotional eating predicts weight regain among Black women in the SisterTalk intervention. *Obesity, 29*(1), 79–85. https://doi.org/10.1002/oby.23045

Ritter, B., & Dozier, C. D. (2000). Effects of court-ordered substance abuse treatment on child protective services cases. *Social Work, 45*(2), 131–140. https://doi.org/10.1093/sw/45.2.131

Ritter, J. A., Vakalahi, H. F. O., & Kiernan-Stern, M. (2009). *101 careers in social work*. Springer Publishing Company.

Riva, M. T., & Smith, R. D. (2017). Termination in group therapy: The neglected stage. In D. Viers (Ed.), *The group therapist's notebook* (2nd ed., pp. 245–253). Routledge. doi.org/10.4324/9781315457055-29

Roberts, A. R. (2005). *Crisis intervention handbook: Assessment, treatment, and research* (3rd ed.). Oxford University Press.

Roberts, A. R., & J. J. Green (Eds.) (2002). *Social workers' desk reference*. Oxford University Press.

Roberts, D. (2002). Shattered bonds: The color of child welfare. *Basic Books*. https://doi.org/10.1016/S0190-7409(02)00238-4

Rogers, C. R. (1957). The necessary and sufficient conditions of therapeutic personality change. *Journal of Consulting Psychology, 21*(2), 95. https://doi.org/10.1037/h0045357

Romano, M., & Peters, L. (2016). Understanding the process of motivational interviewing: A review of the relational and technical hypotheses. Psychotherapy Research, 26(2), 220–240. https://doi.org/10.1080/10503307.2014.954154

Rooney, R. H. (Ed.). (2009). *Strategies for work with involuntary clients* (2nd ed.). Columbia University Press.

Rooney, R. H. (2010). The task-centered approach in the United States. In A. Fortune, P. McCallion, & K. Briar-Lawson (Eds.). *Social work practice research for the twenty-first century* (pp. 195–202). Columbia University Press.

Rooney, R. H., & de Jong, M. (2012). From focusing on deficits to appreciative inquiry: work with teen parents uncovering promising practices. In T. Rzepnicki, S. McCracken, & H. Briggs (Eds.), *Task centered social work to evidence based and integrative practice* (pp. 200–218). Lyceum.

Rooney, R. H., & Myrick, R. G. (2018). *Strategies for work with involuntary clients*. Columbia University Press. https://doi.org/10.7312/roon18266

Rosenbloom, D., & Williams, M. B. (2010). *Life after trauma* (2nd ed.). Guilford Press.

Rosenzweig, J. M., & Sundborg, S. A. (2022). The neurobiology of toxic stress: Implications for social work. In L. Rapp-McCall, K. Corcoran, & A. Roberts (Eds.), *Social workers' desk reference* (4th ed.) (p. 292). Oxford University Press.

Ross, D. E. (2000). A method for developing a biopsychosocial formulation. *Journal of Child and Family Studies, 9*(1), 1. https://doi.org/10.1023/A:1009435613679

Ross, L. (2011). Sustaining youth participation in a long-term tobacco control initiative: consideration of a social justice perspective. *Youth & Society, 43*(2), 681–704. https://doi.org/10.1177/0044118X10366672

Rothman, J. (2007). Multi modes of intervention at the macro level. *Journal of Community Practice, 15*(4), 11–40. https://doi.org/10.1300/J125v15n04_02

Rothman, J., & Mizrahi, T. (2014). Balancing micro and macro practice: A challenge for social work. *Social Work, 59*(1), 91–93. https://doi.org/10.1093/sw/swt067

Royse, D., Thyer, B. A., Padgett, D. K., & Logan, T. K. (2006). *Program evaluation: An introduction* (4th ed.). Brooks/Cole.

Ruffolo M, Nitzberg L, & Schoof K. (2011). Single session family psychoeducational workshops for bipolar disorder and depression. Psychiatric Services. 62(3), 323. https://doi.org/10.1176/ps.62.3.pss6203_0323

Ryabtseva, E. (2018, May 14). The difference between insight and awareness. myTherapyNYC. https://mytherapynyc.com/difference-insight-and-awareness/

Ryan, C. (2018). Computer and internet use in the United States: 2016. *American Community Survey Report*. https://www.census.gov/content/dam/Census/library/publications/2018/acs/ACS-39.pdf

Rybak, C., & Decker-Fitts, A. (2009). Understanding Native American healing practices. *Counselling Psychology Quarterly, 22*(3), 333–342. https://doi.org/10.1080/09515070903270900

Rzepnicki, T. L. (1991). Enhancing the durability of intervention gains: A challenge for the 1990s. *Social Service Review, 65*(1), 92–111. https://doi.org/10.1086/603818

S

Sabe, M., Sentissi, O., & Kaiser, S. (2019). Meditation-based mind-body therapies for negative symptoms of schizophrenia: Systematic review of randomized controlled trials and meta-analysis. *Schizophrenia Research, 212*, 15–25. https://doi.org/10.1016/j.schres.2019.07.030

Sackett, D. L., Rosenberg, W. M., Gray, J. M., Haynes, R. B., & Richardson, W. S. (1996). Evidence based medicine. *British Medical Journal, 313*(7050), 170. https://doi.org/10.1136/bmj.313.7050.170c

Sacks, V., & Murphey, D. (2018). The prevalence of adverse childhood experiences, nationally, by state, and by race or ethnicity. *Childhood Trends*. https://www.childtrends.org/publications/prevalence-adverse-childhood-experiences-nationally-state-race-ethnicity

Sadock, B. J., Sadock, V. A., & Ruiz, P. (2022). *Kaplan and Sadock's synopsis of psychiatry* (12th ed.). Wolters Kluwer.

Safran, J. D., & Muran, J. C. (2000). Resolving therapeutic alliance ruptures: Diversity and integration. *Journal of Clinical Psychology, 56*(2), 233–243. https://doi.org/10.1002/(SICI)1097-4679(200002)56:2<233::AID-JCLP9>3.0.CO;2-3

Saguil, A., & Phelps, K. (2012). The spiritual assessment. *American Family Physician, 86*(6), 546–550.

Salazar, M. D. C. (2018). Interrogating teacher evaluation: Unveiling whiteness as the normative center and moving the margins. *Journal of Teacher Education, 69*(5), 463–476. https://doi.org/10.1177/0022487118764347

Saleebey, D. (1996). The strengths perspective in social work practice: Extensions and cautions. *Social Work, 41*(3), 296–305.

Saleebey, D. (2002). The strengths perspective in social work practice (3rd ed.). Allyn & Bacon

Saleebey, D. (Ed.). (1997). *The strengths perspective in social work practice* (2nd ed.). Allyn & Bacon.

Saleebey, D. (2004). The power of place: Another look at the environment. *Families in Society, 85*(1), 7–16. https://doi.org/10.1606/1044-3894.254

Saleebey, D. (2006). A Paradigm Shift in Developmental Perspectives?. *Handbook of community-based clinical practice*, 46–62. https://doi.org/10.1093/acprof:oso/9780195159226.003.0004

Saleebey, D. (2013). *The strengths perspective in social work practice* (6th ed.). Pearson.

Salston, M., & Figley, C. R. (2004). Secondary traumatic stress effects of working with survivors of criminal victimization. *Journal of Traumatic Stress*, 16(2), 167–174. https://doi.org/10.1023/A:1022899207206

Sanger, J. B., & Sage, M. (2015). Technology and social work practice micro, mezzo, and macro applications. In K. Corcoran & A. Roberts (Eds.), *Social workers' desk reference* (3rd ed., pp. 176–188). Oxford University Press.

Sarkisian, N., & Gerstel, N. (2004). Kin support among Blacks and Whites: Race and family organization. *American Sociological Review*, 69(6), 812–836. https://doi.org/10.1177/000312240406900604

Satir, V. (1967). *Conjoint family therapy*. Science & Behavior Books.

Saulnier, C. F. (2002). Deciding who to see: Lesbians discuss their preferences in health and mental health care providers. *Social Work*, 47(4), 355–365. https://doi.org/10.1093/sw/47.4.355

Schiller, L. Y. (1997). Rethinking stages of development in women's groups: Implications for practice. *Social Work with Groups*, 20(3), 3–19. https://doi.org/10.1300/J009v20n03_02

Schnelle, J., Brandstatter, V., & Knöpfel, A. (2010). The adoption of approach versus avoidance goals: The role of goal-relevant resources. *Motivation and Emotion*, 34(3), 215–229. https://doi.org/10.1007/s11031-010-9173-x

Schopler, J. H., & Galinsky, M. J. (2005). Meeting practice needs: Conceptualizing the open-ended group. *Social Work with Groups*, 28(3–4), 49–68. https://doi.org/10.1300/J009v28n03_05

Schwalbe, C. S. (2012). Toward an integrated theory of probation. *Criminal Justice and Behavior*, 39(2), 185–201. https://doi.org/10.1177/0093854811430185

Schwalbe, C. S., Oh, H. Y., & Zweben, A. (2014). Sustaining motivational interviewing: A meta-analysis of training studies. *Addiction*, 109(8), 1287–1294. https://doi.org/10.1111/add.12558

Schwalbe, C. S. J., & Koetzle, D. (2020). Condition comprehension predicts compliance for adolescents under probation supervision. *Psychology, Public Policy, and Law*, 26(3), 286–296. https://doi.org/10.1037/law0000235

Schwartz, G. (1989). Confidentiality revisited. *Social Work*, 34(3), 223–226. https://doi.org/10.1093/sw/34.3.223

Schwartz, S. H. (2012). An overview of the Schwartz theory of basic values. Online readings in Psychology and Culture, 2(1), 2307-0919. https://doi.org/10.9707/2307-0919.1116

Segal, E. A. (2010). *Social welfare policy and social programs: A values perspective*. Brooks/Cole.

Seijts, G., H., & Latham, G. P. (2000). The construct of goal commitment: Measurement and relationships with task performance. In R. D. Goffin & E. Helmes (Eds.), Problems and solutions in human assessment: Honoring Douglas N. Jackson at seventy. Kluwer.

Selzer, M. L. (1971). The Michigan Alcoholism Screening Test: The quest for a new diagnostic instrument. *American Journal of Psychiatry*, 127(12), 1653–1658. https://doi.org/10.1176/ajp.127.12.1653

Shamai, M. (2003). Therapeutic effects of qualitative research: Reconstructing the experience of treatment as a byproduct of qualitative evaluation. *Social Service Review*, 77(3), 454–467. https://doi.org/10.1086/375789

Shannon, P. J., Simmelink McCleary, J., Becher, E. H., Hyojin, I., & Crook-Lyons, R. (2013). Developing Self-Care Practices in a Trauma Treatment Course. Journal of social work education. 50. 10.1080/10437797.2014.917932

Shapiro, J. R., Bauer, S., Andrews, E., Pisetsky, E., Bulik-Sullivan, B., Hamer, R. M., & Bulik, C. M. (2009). Mobile therapy: Use of text-messaging in the treatment of bulimia nervosa. *International Journal of Eating Disorders*, 43(6), 513–519. https://doi.org/10.1002/eat.20744

Shapiro, V. B., Oesterle, S., Abbott, R. D., Arthur, M. W., & Hawkins, J. D. (2013). Measuring dimensions of coalition functioning for effective and participatory community practice. *Social Work Research*, 37(4), 349–359. https://doi.org/10.1093/swr/svt028 Sharma, R. R. (2006). *Change management: Concepts and applications*. Tata McGraw-Hill.

Sharma, R. Change management: Concept & applications. New Delhi: McGraw-Hill Co.

Sharma, R. R., & Mukherji, S. (2015). Organizational transformation for sustainable development: A case study. In H. Albach, H. Meffert, A. Pinkwart, & R. Reichwald (Eds.), *Management of permanent change* (pp. 195–216). Springer Gabler.

Sherwood, D. A. (1998). Spiritual assessment as a normal part of social work practice: Power to help and power to harm. *Social Work and Christianity*, 25(2), 80–100.

Shoham, V., Rohrbaugh, M., & Patterson, J. (1995). Problem and solution-focused couples therapies: The MRI and Milwaukee models. In N. S. Jacobson & A. S. Gurman (Eds.), *Clinical handbook for couple therapy* (pp. 142–163). Guilford Press.

Shulman, L. (1992). *The skills of helping individuals and groups* (3rd ed.). Peacock.

Shulman, L. (2009). *The skills of helping individuals, families, groups, and communities* (6th ed.). Brooks/Cole.

Siegal, H. A., Rapp, R. C., Kelliher, C. W., Fisher, J., Wagner, J. H., & Cole, P. A. (1995). The strengths perspective of case management: A promising inpatient substance abuse treatment enhancement. Journal of Psychoactive Drugs, 27, 67–72. https://doi.org/10.1080/02791072.1995.10471674

Silvawe, G. W. (1995). The need for a new social work perspective in an African setting: The case of social casework in Zambia. *British Journal of Social Work*, 25(1), 71–84.

Simmons, C. A., & Rycraft, J. R. (2010). Ethical challenges of military social workers serving in a combat zone. *Social Work*, 55(1), 9–18. https://doi.org/10.1093/sw/55.1.9

Simonds, V. W., & Christopher, S. (2013). Adapting Western research methods to indigenous ways of knowing. *American Journal of Public Health*, 103(12), 2185–2192. https://doi.org/10.2105/AJPH.2012.301157

Singer, G. H. S., Biegel, D. E., & Conway, P. (Eds.). (2012). *Family support and family caregiving across disabilities*. Routledge/Taylor & Francis Group.

Singh, A. A., & Salazar, C. F. (2014). Using groups to facilitate social justice change: Addressing issues of privilege and oppression. In J. DeLucia-Waack, C. Kalodner, & M. Riva (Eds.), *Handbook of group counseling & psychotherapy* (pp. 288–302). SAGE. https://doi.org/10.4135/9781544308555.n23

Skeem, J. L., Louden, J. E., Polsachek, D., & Camp, J. (2007). Assessing relationship quality in mandated community treatment: Blending care with control. *Psychological Assessment*, 19(4), 397–410. https://doi.org/10.1037/1040-3590.19.4.397

Sluzki, C. E. (2008). Migration and the disruption of the social network. In M. McGoldrick & K. V. Hardy (Eds.), *Re-visioning family therapy* (2nd ed., 39–47). Guilford Press.

Smith, B. D., & Marsh, J. C. (2002). Client-service matching in substance abuse treatment for women with children. *Journal of Substance Abuse Treatment*, 22(3), 161–168. https://doi.org/10.1016/S0740-5472(02)00229-5

Smith, L. H. (2017). 'Blaming-the-poor': Strengths and development discourses which obfuscate neo-liberal and individualist ideologies. *International Social Work*, 60(2), 336–350. https://doi.org/10.1177/0020872815594218

Smith, P. (2020, October 7). Trump breaks tradition with Microsoft-Wells Fargo race inquiry. *Bloomberg Law*. https://www.bloomberg.com//news/articles/2020-10-07trump-race-inquiry-into-microsoft-wells-fargo-at-odds-with-norm

Smokowski, P. R., & Bacallao, M. (2011). *Becoming bicultural: Risk, resilience, and Latino youth*. New York University Press. https://doi.org/10.18574/nyu/9780814740897.001.0001

Smokowski, P. R., Rose, S. D., & Bacallao, M. L. (2001). Damaging therapeutic groups: How vulnerable consumers become group casualties. *Small Group Research, 32*(2), 223–251. https://doi.org/10.1177/104649640103200205

Smyth, N. J., & Wiechelt, S. A. (2005). Drug use, self-efficacy, and coping skills among people with concurrent substance abuse and personality disorders: Implications for relapse prevention. *Journal of Social Work Practice in the Addictions, 5*(4), 63–79. https://doi.org/10.1300/J160v05n04_05

Snyderman, D., & Rovner, B. W. (2009). Mental status examination in primary care: A review. *American Family Physician, 80*(8), 809–814.

Social workers and psychotherapist-patient privilege: Jaffee v. Redmond *revisited.* (2005). https://www.socialworkers.org/LinkClick.aspx?fileticket=OMPKbIxBUeg%3d&portalid=0

Sodano, S. M., Guyker, W. M., DeLucia-Waack, J. L., Cosgrove, H. E., Altabef, D. L., & Amos, B. S. (2014). Measures of group process, dynamics, climate, behavior, and outcome: A review. In J. DeLucia-Waack, C. Kalodner, & M. Riva (Eds.), *Handbook of group counseling & psychotherapy* (pp. 159–177). SAGE. doi.org/10.4135/9781544308555.n13 https://doi.org/10.4135/9781544308555.n13

Soler, M. (2005). No turning back: Promising approaches to reducing racial and ethnic disparities affecting youth of color in the justice system. *Building Blocks for Youth Initiative.* https://docplayer.net/95413-No-turning-back-promising-approaches-to-reducing-racial-and-ethnic-disparities-affecting-youth-of-color-in-the-justice-system.html

Sommers-Flanagan, R. (2007). Ethical considerations in crisis and humanitarian interventions. *Ethics and Behavior, 17*(12), 187–202. https://doi.org/10.1080/10508420701378123

Sotero, M. (2006). A conceptual model of historical trauma: Implications for public health practice and research. *Journal of Health Disparities Research and Practice, 1*(1), 93–108.

Soto, A., Smith, T. B., Griner, D., Domenech Rodriguez, M., & Bernal, G. (2018). Cultural adaptations and therapist multicultural competence: Two meta-analytic reviews. *Journal of Clinical Psychology, 74*(11), 1907–1923. https://doi.org/10.1002/jclp.22679

Sousa, L., Ribeiro, C., & Rodrigues, S. (2006). Intervention with multiproblem poor clients: Toward a strengths-focused perspective. *Journal of Social Work Practice, 20*(2), 189–204. https://doi.org/10.1080/02650530600776913

Specht, H., & Courtney, M. E. (1994). *Unfaithful angels: How social work abandoned its mission.* Free Press.

Spiel, K., Haimson, O. L., & Lottridge, D. (2019). How to do better on surveys: A guide for HCI researchers. *Interactions, 26*(4), 62–65. https://doi.org/10.1145/3338283

Spielfogel, J. E., & McMillen, J. C. (2017). Current use of de-escalation strategies: Similarities and differences in de-escalation across professions. *Social Work in Mental Health, 15*(3), 232–248. https://doi.org/10.1080/15332985.2016.1212774

Sprenkle, D. H., & Blow A. J. (2004). Common factors and our sacred models. *Journal of Marital and Family Therapy, 30*(2), 113–129. doi.org/10.1111/j.1752-0606.2004.tb01228.x https://doi.org/10.1111/j.1752-0606.2004.tb01228.x

Staats, C. (2013). State of the Science: Implicit Bias Review... Kirwan Institute for the Study of Race and Ethnicity, The Ohio State University.

Staats, C., Capatosto, K., Wright, R. A., & Jackson, V. W. (2016). *State of the science: Implicit bias review.* The Kirwan Institute. http://www.kirwaninstitute.osu.edu/implicit-bias-training/resources/2017-implicit-bias-review.pdf

Stanley, S., & Sethuramalingam V. (2016). Empathy in psychosocial interventions: A theoretical perspective. *International Journal of Psychosocial Rehabilitation, 20*(1), 6–11.

Stark, C. (2018). The neoliberal ideology, its contradictions, the consequences and challenges for social work. *Annual of Social Work, 25*(1), 39–63. https://doi.org/10.3935/ljsr.v25i1.196

Starnino, V. R., Gomi, S., & Canda, E. R. (2014). Spiritual strengths assessment in mental health practice. *British Journal of Social Work, 44*(4), 849–867. https://doi.org/10.1093/bjsw/bcs179

Staudt, M., Howardw, M. O., & Drake, B. (2001). The operationalization, implementation, and effectiveness of the strengths perspective: A review of empirical studies. *Journal of Social Service Research, 27*(3), 1–21. https://doi.org/10.1300/J079v27n03_01

Stefanopoulou, E., & Grunfeld, E. A. (2017). Mind–body interventions for vasomotor symptoms in healthy menopausal women and breast cancer survivors. A systematic review. *Journal of Psychosomatic Obstetrics & Gynecology, 38*(3), 210–225. https://doi.org/10.1080/0167482X.2016.1235147

Steinberg, D. M. (2004). *The mutual aid approach to working with groups: Helping people help one another* (6th ed.). Haworth Press.

Steinberg, L. (2008). A social neuroscience perspective on adolescent risk-taking. *Developmental Review, 28*(1), 78–106. https://doi.org/10.1016/j.dr.2007.08.002

Stewart, L., Usher, A., & Allenby, K. (2009). *A review of optimal group size and modularisation or continuous entry format for program delivery.* Research Report R-215. Ottawa: Correctional Service Canada. https://www.csc-scc.gc.ca/research/005008-0215-01-eng.shtml

Stobierski, T. (2020, January 21). *Organizational change management: What it is and why it's important.* Harvard Business School Online. https://online.hbs.edu/blog/post/organizational-change-management

Stone, M. H., Lewis, C. M., & Beck, A. P. (1994). The structure of Yalom's curative factors scale. *International Journal of Group Psychotherapy, 44*(2), 239–245. https://doi.org/10.1080/00207284.1994.11490745

Strom, K. J. (2022). Navigating complex boundary challenges. In L. Rapp-McCall, K. Corcoran, & A. Roberts (Eds.), *Social workers' desk reference* (4th ed.). Oxford University Press.

Strom, R. E., & Savage, M. W. (2014). Assessing the relationships between perceived support from close others, goal commitment, and persistence decisions at the college level. *Journal of College Student Development, 55*(6), 531–547. https://doi.org/10.1353/csd.2014.0064

Strom-Gottfried, K. J. (1998). Informed consent meets managed care. *Health and Social Work, 23*(1), 25–33. https://doi.org/10.1093/hsw/23.1.25

Strom-Gottfried, K. J. (1999). Professional boundaries: An analysis of violations by social workers. *Families in Society, 80*(5), 439–448. https://doi.org/10.1606/1044-3894.1473

Strom-Gottfried, K. J. (2005). Ethical practice in rural environments. In L. Ginsberg (Ed.), *Social work in rural communities* (4th ed., pp. 141–155). Council on Social Work Education.

Strom-Gottfried, K. J. (2007). *Straight talk about professional ethics.* Lyceum Books.

Strom-Gottfried, K. J. (2008). The ethics of practice with minors: High stakes, hard choices. *Lyceum Books.*

Strom-Gottfried, K. J. (2009). Ethical issues and guidelines. In S. Allen & E. Tracy (Eds.), *Delivering home-based services: A social work perspective* (pp. 14–33). Columbia University Press. https://doi.org/10.7312/alle14146-002

Strom-Gottfried, K. J. (2015). *Straight talk, about professional ethics* (2nd ed.). Lyceum Books.

Strom-Gottfried, K. J. (2019). Ethical action in challenging times. In S. M. Marson & R. E. McKinney (Eds.), *Routledge handbook of social work ethics and values* (pp. 65–72). Routledge. https://doi.org/10.4324/9780429438813-10

Strom-Gottfried, K. J., & Mowbray, N. D. (2006). Who heals the helper? Facilitating the social worker's grief. *Families in Society, 87*(1), 9–15. https://doi.org/10.1606/1044-3894.3479

Substance Abuse and Mental Health Services Administration (SAMHSA). (2003a). *Family psychoeducation fidelity scale.* https://store.samhsa.gov/sites/default/files/d7/priv/evaluatingyourprogram-fp_0.pdf

Substance Abuse and Mental Health Services Administration (SAMHSA). (2003b). *Assertive community treatment: Monitoring client outcomes.* https://store.samhsa.gov/sites/default/files/d7/priv/theevidence_1.pdf

Substance Abuse and Mental Health Services Administration (SAMHSA). (2020). *Substance use disorder treatment for persons with co-occurring disorders.* Treatment Improvement Protocol (TIP) Series No. 42. SAMHSA Publication No. PEP20-02-01-004. Substance Abuse and Mental Health Services Administration. https://store.samhsa.gov/sites/default/files/SAMHSA_Digital_Download/PEP20-02-01-004_Final_508.pdf

Substance Abuse Mental Health Administration (SAMHSA). (2012). *National Center for Trauma-Informed Care (NCTIC).* https://ncsacw.samhsa.gov/userfiles/files/SAMHSA_Trauma.pdf

Substance Abuse and Mental Health Services Administration. (2014a). *Improving cultural competence.* Treatment Improvement Protocol (TIP) Series No. 59. HHS Publication No. (SMA) 14-4849. Rockville, MD: Substance Abuse and Mental Health Services Administration. https://store.samhsa.gov/sites/default/files/d7/priv/sma14-4849.pdf

Substance Abuse and Mental Health Services Administration (SAMSHA). (2014b). *Results from the 2013 National Survey on Drug Use and Health: Summary of national findings.* NSDUH Series H-48, HHS Publication No. (SMA) 14-4863. Author. https://www.samhsa.gov/data/sites/default/files/NSDUHresultsPDFWHTML2013/Web/NSDUHresults2013.pdf

Substance Abuse and Mental Health Services Administration (SAMSHA). (2014c). *Trauma-informed care in behavioral services. TIP 57.* U.S. Department of Health and Human Services. https://store.samhsa.gov/sites/default/files/d7/priv/sma15-4912.pdf

Substance Abuse and Mental Health Services Administration (SAMSHA). (2015). *Substance abuse treatment: Group therapy.* SAMHSA Publications and Digital Products. https://store.samhsa.gov/sites/default/files/d7/priv/sma15-4024.pdf

Substance Abuse and Mental Health Services Administration. (2019). *Enhancing motivation for change in substance use disorder treatment.* Treatment Improvement Protocol (TIP) Series No. 35. SAMHSA Publication No. PEP19-02-01-003. Substance Abuse and Mental Health Services Administration. https://store.samhsa.gov/sites/default/files/d7/priv/tip35_final_508_compliant_-_02252020_0.pdf

Sudeall, L., & Richardson, R. (2019). Unfamiliar justice: Indigent criminal defendants' experiences with civil legal needs. *UC Davis Law Review, 52*(4), 2105–2164.

Sue, D. W. (2006). *Multicultural social work practice.* John Wiley & Sons.

Sue, D. W., Capodilupo, C. M., Torino, G. C., Bucceri, J. M., Holder, A., Nadal, K. L., & Esquilin, M. (2007). Racial microaggressions in everyday life: Implications for clinical practice. *American Psychologist, 62*(4), 271–284. https://doi.org/10.1037/0003-066X.62.4.271

Sue, D. W., Rasheed, M. N., & Rasheed, J. M. (2016). *Multicultural social work practice: A competency-based approach to diversity and social justice* (2nd ed.). John Wiley & Sons.

Sundel, M., & Sundel, S. S. (2017). *Behavior change in the human services: Behavioral and cognitive principles and applications* (6th ed.). Sage Publications. https://doi.org/10.4135/9781506352671

Swift, J. K., & Greenberg, R. P. (2012). Premature discontinuation in adult psychotherapy: A meta-analysis. *Journal of Consulting and Clinical Psychology, 80*(4), 547–559. https://doi.org/10.1037/a0028226

Swift, J. K., Greenberg, R. P., Whipple, J. L., & Kominiak, N. (2012). Practice recommendations for reducing premature termination in therapy. *Professional Psychology: Research and Practice, 43*(4), 379–387. https://doi.org/10.1037/a0028291

Swift, J. K., Tompkins, K. A., & Parkin, S. R. (2017). Understanding the client's perspective of helpful and hindering events in psychotherapy sessions: A micro-process approach. *Journal of clinical psychology, 73*(11), 1543–1555. https://doi.org/10.1002/jclp.22531

Szapocznik, J., & Hervis, O. E. (2020). Brief strategic family therapy. American Psychological Association. https://doi.org/10.1037/0000169-000

Szubiak, N. (2017). Behavioral health brief: Medication-assisted treatment needs social work support. *Social Work Today, 17*(5), 6. https://www.socialworktoday.com/archive/SO17p6.shtml

T

Taylor, R. J., Chatters, L. M., Woodward, A. T., & Brown, E. (2013). Racial and ethnic differences in extended family, friendship, fictive kin, and congregational informal support networks. *Family Relations, 62*(4), 609–624. https://doi.org/10.1111/fare.12030

Theodos, K., & Sittig, S. (2021). Health information privacy laws in the digital age: HIPAA doesn't apply. *Perspectives in Health Information Management, 18*(Winter). https://www.ncbi.nlm.nih.gov/pmc/articles/PMC7883355/

Thibault, J. M., Ellor, J. W., & Netting, F. E. (1991). A conceptual framework for assessing the spiritual functioning and fulfillment of older adults in long-term care settings. *Journal of Religious Gerontology, 7*(4), 29–46. https://doi.org/10.1300/J078V07N04_03

Thomas, H., & Caplan, T. (1999). Spinning the group process wheel: Effective facilitation techniques for motivating involuntary clients. *Social Work with Groups, 21*(4), 3–21. https://doi.org/10.1300/J009v21n04_02

Thomas, J. (2013). Association of personal distress with burnout, compassion fatigue, and compassion satisfaction among clinical social workers. *Journal of Social Service Research, 39*(3), 365–379. https://doi.org/10.1080/01488376.2013.771596

Thomas, M., & Strom-Gottfried, K. J. (2011). *The best of boards: Sound governance and leadership for nonprofit organizations.* AICPA.

Tilly, N. & Caye, J. (2005). Using writing and poetry to achieve focus and depth in a group of women parenting sexually abused children. Social Work With Groups, 27(2-3): 129–142. http://dx.doi.org/10.1300/J009v27n02_09

Thyer, B. A. (2001). Single case designs. In B. A. Thyer (Ed.), *Handbook of social work research methods* (pp. 239–235). SAGE. https://doi.org/10.4135/9781412986182

Thyer, B. A. (2002). Principles of evidence-based practice and treatment development. In A. R. Roberts & G. J. Greene (Eds.), *Social workers' desk reference* (pp. 739–742). Oxford University Press.

Tohn, S. L., & Oshlag, J. A. (1996). Solution-focused therapy with mandated clients: Cooperating with the uncooperative. In S. D. Miller, M. A. Hubble, & B. L. Duncan (Eds.), *Handbook of solution-focused brief therapy* (pp. 152–183). Jossey-Bass.

Tolson, E. R., Reid, W. J., & Garvin, C. D. (1994). *Generalist practice: A task-centered approach.* Columbia University Press.

Toseland, R. W., & Rivas, R. F. (2017). *Introduction to group work practice* (8th ed.). Pearson.

Tourigny, M., & Hébert, M. (2007). Comparison of open versus closed group interventions for sexually abused adolescent girls. *Violence and Victims, 22*(3), 334–349. https://doi.org/10.1891/088667007780842775

Tracy, K., & Wallace, S. P. (2016). Benefits of peer support groups in the treatment of addiction. Substance abuse and rehabilitation, 7, 143–154. https://doi.org/10.2147/SAR.S81535

Tracy, E. M., & Whittaker, J. K. (1990). The social network map: Assessing social support in clinical practice. *Families in Society, 71*(8), 461–470. https://doi.org/10.1177/104438949007100802

Trawalter, S., Richeson, J. A., & Shelton, J. N. (2009). Predicting behavior during interracial interactions: A stress and coping approach. *Personality and Social Psychology Review, 13*(4), 243–268. https://doi.org/10.1177/1088868309345850

Trepper, T. S., Dolan, Y., McCollum, E. E., & Nelson, T. (2006). Steve De Shazer and the future of solution focused therapy. *Journal of Marital and Family Therapy, 32*(2), 133–139. https://doi.org/10.1111/j.1752-0606.2006.tb01595.x

Trevino, K. M., Raghunathan, N., Latte-Naor, S., Polubriaginof, F. C., Jensen, C., Atkinson, T. M., ... & Mao, J. J. (2021). Rapid deployment of virtual mind-body interventions during the COVID-19 outbreak: Feasibility, acceptability, and implications for future care. *Supportive Care in Cancer, 29*(2), 543–546. https://doi.org/10.1007/s00520-020-05740-2

Trotter, C. (2006). *Working with involuntary clients: A guide to practice* (2nd ed.). SAGE.

Trotter, C. (2013). Reducing recidivism through probation supervision: What we know and don't know from four decades of research. *Federal Probation, 77*, 43–88.

Trotter, C. (2015). *Working with involuntary clients: A guide to practice.* London, UK: Routledge. https://doi.org/10.4324/9781315880587

Truax, C. B., & Carkhuff, R. R. (1967). *Toward effective counseling and psychotherapy: Training and practice.* Aldine-Atherton.

Tucci, V., Ahmed, S. M., Hoyer Jr, D. R., Greene, S., & Moukaddam, N. (2017). Stabilizing intentional overdoses in freestanding emergency departments: A good idea. Journal of General and Emergency Medicine, 5, 2.

Tuckman, B. (1965). Developmental sequence in small groups. *Psychological Bulletin, 63*(6), 384.https://doi.org/10.1037/h0022100

Turner, H. (2011). Concepts for effective facilitation of open groups. *Social Work with Groups, 34*(3–4), 246–256. https://doi.org/10.1080/01609513.2011.558822

Turner, S. G., & Maschi, T. M. (2015). Feminist and empowerment theory and social work practice. *Journal of Social Work Practice, 29*(2), 151–162. https://doi.org/10.1080/02650533.2014.941282

Tyler, T. R. (2006). *Why people obey the law.* Yale University Press. https://doi.org/10.1515/9781400828609

U

Unrau, Y. A., Gabor, P. A., & Grinnell, R. M. (2007). Evaluation in social work: The art and science of practice. Oxford University Press.

U.S. Department of Health and Human Services. (2003). *Office for Civil Rights: HIPAA.* https://www.hhs.gov/hipaa/for-individuals/guidance-materials-for-consumers/index.html

U.S. Department of Health and Human Services. (2006). *Agency for Healthcare Research and Quality: 2005 National Healthcare Disparities Report.* Publication #06-0017, Agency for Healthcare Research and Quality. https://www.ahrq.gov/research/findings/nhqrdr/nhqdr19/index.html

V

Valentijn, P. P., Schepman, S. M., Opheij, W., & Bruijnzeels, M. A. (2013). Understanding integrated care: A comprehensive conceptual framework based on the integrative functions of primary care. *International Journal of Integrated Care, 13*, 1–12. https://doi.org/10.5334/ijic.886

Van der Kolk, B. A. (1994). The body keeps the score: Memory and the evolving psychobiology of posttraumatic stress. *Harvard Review of Psychiatry, 1*(5), 253–265. https://doi.org/10.3109/10673229409017088

Van der Kolk, B. A. (2015). *The body keeps the score: Brain, mind, and body in the healing of trauma.* Penguin Books.

Van der Kolk, B. A., & Courtois, C. A. (2005). Editorial comments: Complex developmental trauma, *Journal of Traumatic Stress, 18*(5), 385–388. https://doi.org/10.1002/jts.20046

Van Vliet, K. J., Foskett, A. J., Williams, J. L, Singhal, A., Dolcos, F., & Vohra, S. (2017). Impact of a mindfulness-based stress reduction program from the perspective of adolescents with serious mental health concerns. Child and Adolescent Mental Health, 22(1), 16–22.

Van Wormer, K., & Boes, M. (1997). Humor in the emergency room: A social work perspective. *Health and Social Work, 22*(2), 87–92. https://doi.org/10.1093/hsw/22.2.87

Veltman, A., & La Rose, T. (2016). Anti-oppressive approach to assessment. In A. Hategan, J. A. Bourgeois, & C. H. Hirsch (Eds.) *On-call geriatric psychiatry* (pp. 55–62). Springer International Publishing. https://doi.org/10.1007/978-3-319-30346-8_5

Vera, E. M., & Speight, S. L. (2003). Multicultural competencies, social justice, and counseling psychology: Expanding our roles. *The Counseling Psychologist, 31*(3), 253–272. https://doi.org/10.1177/0011000003031003001

Viglione, J., Hannon, L., & DeFina, R. (2011). The impact of light skin on prison time for black female offenders. *Social Science Journal, 48*(1), 250–258. https://doi.org/10.1016/j.soscij.2010.08.003

Vodde, R., & Gallant, J. P. (2002). Bridging the gap between micro and macro practice: Larger scale change and a unified model of narrative-deconstructive practice. *Journal of Social Work Education, 38*(3), 439–458. https://doi.org/10.1080/10437797.2002.10779109

Voisin, D. R. (2007). The effects of family and community violence exposure among youth. Recommendations for practice and policy. *Journal of Social Work Education, 43*(1), 51–64. https://doi.org/10.5175/JSWE.2007.200400473

Vroland-Nordstrand, K., Eliasson, A. C., Jacobsson, J., Johansson, U., & Krumlinde-Sundholm, L. (2015). Can children identify and achieve goals for intervention? A randomized trial comparing two goal-setting approaches. *Developmental Medicine & Child Neurology, 58*(6), 589–596. https://doi.org/10.1111/dmcn.12925

W

Wahler, E. A. (2012). Identifying and challenging social work students' biases. *Social Work Education, 31*(8), 1058–1070. https://doi.org/10.1080/02615479.2011.616585

Wakefield, J. C. (1996). Does social work need the ecosystems perspective? Part 1. Is the perspective clinically useful? *Social Service Review, 70*(1), 1–32. https://doi.org/10.1086/604163

Walitzer, K. S., Dermen, K. H., & Connors, G. J. (1999). Strategies for preparing clients for treatment: A review. *Behavior Modification, 23*(1), 129–151. https://doi.org/10.1177/0145445599231006

Wall, S. (2008). A critique of evidence-based practice in nursing: Challenging the assumptions. *Social Theory & Health, 6*(1), 37–53. https://doi.org/10.1057/palgrave.sth.8700113

Waller, D. (2014). *Group interactive art therapy: Its use in training and treatment.* Routledge. https://doi.org/10.4324/9781315744285

Walsh, F. (2016). Strengthening family resilience. Guildford Press.

Walsh, J. (2006). *Theories for direct social work practice.* Brooks/Cole.

Walsh, J. (2007). *Endings in clinical practice: Effective closure in diverse settings* (2nd ed.). Lyceum Books.

Walsh, J. (2010). *Theory for direct social work practice* (2nd ed.). Wadsworth Cengage Learning.

Wampold, B. E., Flückiger, C., Del Re, A. C., Yulish, N. E., Frost, N. D., Pace, B. T., ... & Hilsenroth, M. J. (2017). In pursuit of truth: A critical examination of meta-analyses of cognitive behavior therapy. *Psychotherapy Research, 27*(1), 14–32. https://doi.org/10.1080/10503307.2016.1249433

Watts, L., & Hodgson, D. (2019). *Social justice theory and practice for social work: Critical and philosophical perspectives.* Springer. https://doi.org/10.1007/978-981-13-3621-8

Wayne, J., & Gitterman, A. (2003). Offensive behavior in groups: Challenges and opportunities. *Social Work with Groups, 26*(2), 23–34. https://doi.org/10.1300/J009v26n02_03

Weathers, F. W., Litz, B. T., Keane, T. M., Palmieri, P. A., Marx, B. P., & Schnurr, P. P. (2013). *The PTSD checklist for DSM-5 (PCL-5).* https://www.ptsd.va.gov/professional/assessment/adult-sr/ptsd-checklist.asp

Webster-Stratton, C. H. (1984). Randomized trial of two parent-training programs for families with conduct-disordered children. *Journal of Consulting and Clinical Psychology, 52*(4), 666–678. https://doi.org/10.1037/0022-006X.52.4.666

Webster-Stratton, C. H., Reid, M. J., & Marsenich, L. (2014). Improving therapist fidelity during implementation of evidence-based practices: Incredible Years program. *Psychiatric Services, 65*(6), 789–795. https://doi.org/10.1176/appi.ps.201200177

Weick, A., & Saleebey, D. (1995). Supporting family strengths: Orienting policy and practice in the 21st century. *Families in Society, 76*(3), 141–149. https://doi.org/10.1177/104438949507600302

Weil, M. O. (2005). Introduction: Contexts and challenges for the 21st century. In M. O. Weil (Ed.). *The handbook of community practice* (pp. 3–33). SAGE.

Weil, M. O., Gamble, D. N., & Ohmer, M. L. (2013). Evolution, models, and the changing context of community practice. In M. O. Weil, M. Reisch, & M. L. Ohmer (Eds.), *The handbook of community practice* (pp. 167–193). SAGE. https://doi.org/10.4135/9781412976640

Weinberg, M. (2006). Pregnant with possibility: The paradoxes of "help" as anti-oppression and discipline with a young single mother. *Families in Society, 87*(2), 161–169. https://doi.org/10.1606/1044-3894.3509

Weiner, M. F. (1984). *Techniques of group psychotherapy.* American Psychiatric Press.

Weiss, C. H. (1998). *Evaluation: Methods for studying programs and policies* (2nd ed.). Prentice-Hall.

Wells, S. (2008). Child abuse and neglect. In T. Mizrahi & L. E. Davis (Eds.), *Encyclopedia of social work* (20th ed). Oxford University Press. https://www.oxfordreference.com/view/10.1093/acref/9780195306613.001.0001/acref-9780195306613-e-47?print

Wendt, D. C., & Gone, J. P. (2018). Complexities with group therapy facilitation in substance use disorder specialty treatment settings. *Journal of Substance Abuse Treatment, 88,* 9–17. https://doi.org/10.1016/j.jsat.2018.02.002

West, L., Mercer, S. O., & Altheimer, E. (1993). Operation Desert Storm: The response of a social work outreach team. *Social Work in Health Care, 19*(2), 81–98. https://doi.org/10.1300/J010v19n02_04

Whitaker, C. (1958). Psychotherapy with couples. *American Journal of Psychotherapy, 12*(1), 18–23. https://doi.org/10.1176/appi.psychotherapy.1958.12.1.18

Wickham, R. E., Reed, D. E., & Williamson, R. E. (2015). Establishing the psychometric properties of the self and perceived-partner authenticity in relationship scale-short form (AIRS-SF): Measurement invariance, reliability, and incremental validity. *Personality and Individual Differences, 77,* 62–67. https://doi.org/10.1016/j.paid.2014.12.049

Wiger, D. E. (2009). *The clinical documentation sourcebook: The complete paperwork resource for your mental health practice* (4th ed.). John Wiley & Sons.

Wilkinson, D. (2020). ICU triage in an impending crisis: uncertainty, preemption and preparation. *Journal of Medical Ethics, 46*(5), 287–288. https://doi.org/10.1136/medethics-2020-106226

Williams, B., Perillo, S., & Brown, T. (2015). What are the factors of organisational culture in health care settings that act as barriers to the implementation of evidence-based practice? A scoping review. *Nurse Education Today, 35*(2), e34–e41. https://doi.org/10.1016/j.nedt.2014.11.012

Williams, L. F. (1990). The challenge of education to social work: The case for minority children. *Social Work, 35*(3), 236–242.

Wilson, S. (2008). *Research is ceremony: Indigenous research methods.* Fernwood.

Wodarski, J. S., Holosko, M. J., & Feit, M. D. (Eds.). (2015). *Evidence-informed assessment and practice in child welfare.* Springer. https://doi.org/10.1007/978-3-319-12045-4

Wolgien, C. S., & Coady, N. F. (1997). Good therapists' beliefs about the development of their helping ability: The wounded healer paradigm revisited. *The Clinical Supervisor, 15*(2), 19–35. https://doi.org/10.1300/J001v15n02_02

Wong, D. F. (2007). Crucial individuals in the help-seeking pathway of Chinese caregivers of relatives in early psychosis in Hong Kong. *Social Work, 52*(2), 127–135. https://doi.org/10.1093/sw/52.2.127

Wood, S. A. (2007). The analysis of an innovative HIV-positive women's support group. *Social Work with Groups, 30*(3), 9–28. https://doi.org/10.1300/J009v30n03_02

Woodbury, M. G., & Kuhnke, J. L. (2014). Evidence-based practice vs. evidence-informed practice: What's the difference. *Wound Care Canada, 12*(1), 18–21.

Woodward, A. T., Bullard, K. M., Taylor, R. J., Chatters, L. M., Baser, R. E., Perron, B. E., & Jackson, J. S. (2009). Complementary and alternative medicine for mental disorders among African Americans, black Caribbeans, and whites. *Psychiatric Services, 60*(10), 1342–1349. https://doi.org/10.1176/ps.2009.60.10.1342

World Health Organization (WHO). (2020). *Classifications.* https://www.who.int/classifications/icd/en/

Wright, T. (2021, April 11). Strategy vs. tactics: What's the difference? *Cascade.* https://www.cascade.app/blog/strategy-vs-tactics

Wylie, M. S. (1990). Brief therapy on the couch. *Family Therapy Networker, 14*(2), 26–34.

X

Xiong, E. T., Dauphin, B. & Weisfeld, C. (2018). The influence of Hmong Americans' acculturation and cultural identity on attitudes toward seeking professional mental health care and services in comparison to traditional health beliefs and practices. Hmong Studies Journal, 19(2).

Y

Yale University. (2019). HIPAA guidance on photos, video, and audio recording in clinical areas. https://hipaa.yale.edu/sites/default/files/files/Guidance%20Audio%20Visual%20Recording_.pdf

Yalom, I. D., & Leszcz, M. (2020). *The theory and practice of group psychotherapy* (6th ed.). Basic Books.

Yan, M. C. (2008). Exploring cultural tensions in cross-cultural social work practice. *Social Work, 53*(4), 317–327. https://doi.org/10.1093/sw/53.4.317

Yeh, M., McCabe, K., Hurlburt, M., Hough, R., Hazen, A., Culver, S., ... & Landsverk, J. (2002). Referral sources, diagnoses, and service types of youth in public outpatient mental health care: A focus on ethnic minorities. *Journal of Behavioral Health Services & Research, 29*(1), 45–60. https://doi.org/10.1007/BF02287831

Yip, K. S. (2006). Self-reflection in reflective practice: A note of caution. British Journal of Work, 36(5), 777–788.

Young, I. M. (2004). Five faces of oppression. In L. Heldke & P. O'Connor (Eds.), *Oppression, privilege, and resistance* (pp. 37–63). McGraw Hill.

Z

Zerden, L. D. S., Guan, T., Lombardi, B. M., Sharma, A., & Garcia-Rico, Y. (2020). Psychosocial interventions in office-based opioid treatment: A systematic review. *Journal of the Society for Social Work and Research, 11*(1), 103–131. https://doi.org/10.1086/708369

Zuckerman, E. L. (2008). *The paper office: The tools to make your psychotherapy practice work ethically, legally, and profitably: Forms, guidelines, and resources* (4th ed.). Guilford Press.

Author Index

Subject Index